Desire and Its Interpretation

Jacques Lacan

Desire and Its Interpretation

The Seminar of Jacques Lacan
Book VI

Edited by Jacques-Alain Miller

Translated by Bruce Fink

polity

First published in French as *Le Séminaire de Jacques Lacan. Livre VI. Le désir et son interprétation (1958–1959)* © Éditions de La Martinière et Le Champ Freudien, 2013

This English edition © Polity Press, 2019

Polity Press
65 Bridge Street
Cambridge CB2 1UR, UK

Polity Press
101 Station Landing
Suite 300
Medford, MA 02155, USA

ISBN-13: 978-1-5095-0027-7

A catalogue record for this book is available from the British Library.

Typeset in 10.5 on 12 pt Times NR MT by
Servis Filmsetting Ltd, Stockport, Cheshire
Printed and bound in the UK by TJ International Limited

The publisher has used its best endeavours to ensure that the URLs for external websites referred to in this book are correct and active at the time of going to press. However, the publisher has no responsibility for the websites and can make no guarantee that a site will remain live or that the content is or will remain appropriate.

Every effort has been made to trace all copyright holders, but if any have been overlooked the publisher will be pleased to include any necessary credits in any subsequent reprint or edition.

For further information on Polity, visit our website: politybooks.com

Contents

Abbreviations   vii
Bibliographical Note   viii
Figures, Tables, and Illustrations   ix

INTRODUCTION

I   Constructing the Graph   3
II   Further Explanation   25

ON DESIRE IN DREAMS

III   The Dream about the Dead Father: "He did not know he was dead"   43
IV   Little Anna's Dream   60
V   The Dream about the Dead Father: "As he wished"   78
VI   Introducing the Object of Desire   95
VII   Desire's Phallic Mediation   111

A DREAM ANALYZED BY ELLA SHARPE

VIII   The Little Cough as a Message   133
IX   The Fantasy about the Barking Dog   152
X   The Image of the Inside-Out Glove   171
XI   Sacrificing the Taboo Queen   191
XII   The Laughter of the Immortal Gods   210

SEVEN CLASSES ON *HAMLET*

XIII   Impossible Action   233
XIV   The Desire Trap   249
XV   The Mother's Desire   269

XVI   There is No Other of the Other   291
XVII   Ophelia, the Object   306
XVIII   Mourning and Desire   323
XIX   Phallophanies   339

THE DIALECTIC OF DESIRE

XX   The Fundamental Fantasy   357
XXI   In the Form of a Cut   374
XXII   Cut and Fantasy   391
XXIII   The Function of the Subjective Slit in Perverse
        Fantasies   407
XXIV   The Dialectic of Desire in Neurosis   422
XXV   The Either/Or Concerning the Object   436
XXVI   The Function of Splitting in Perversion   453

CONCLUSION AND OVERTURE

XXVII   Toward Sublimation   471

APPENDIX

Marginalia on the Seminar on Desire,
    by Jacques-Alain Miller   489

Index   519

Abbreviations

Écrits   *Écrits: The First Complete Edition in English*, by Lacan
GW   *Gesammelte Werke*, by Sigmund Freud (Frankfurt am Main: S. Fischer Verlag)
IJP   *International Journal of Psychoanalysis*
PQ   *Psychoanalytic Quarterly*
PUF   Presses Universitaires de France
RFP   *Revue Française de Psychanalyse*
SE   *Standard Edition of the Complete Psychological Works of Sigmund Freud*

Words followed by an asterisk (*) are found in English in the original.

Bibliographical Note

All quotations from Shakespeare's *Hamlet* are from The Complete Pelican Shakespeare: *William Shakespeare: The Complete Works* (New York: Viking Press, 1969). Exact quotes from Shakespeare's and other authors' texts are placed in double quote marks, whereas Lacan's paraphrases or extrapolations of their texts are placed in single quote marks.

All references here to Lacan's *Écrits* (Paris: Seuil, 1966) are to the pagination of *Écrits: The First Complete Edition in English* (New York & London: W. W. Norton & Co., 2006). When I refer to Lacan's Seminars, I provide the pagination of the English editions, when they exist; when they do not, I give the page number(s) in the French editions. All the extant Seminars except the present one were published in French by Éditions du Seuil in Paris. Seminars that have yet to be published in French are indicated by volume number and date of class.

References to Freud's work here are always to *The Standard Edition of the Complete Psychological Works of Sigmund Freud* (24 volumes) published in London by Hogarth Press, abbreviated here as SE, followed by the volume number and page(s).

All text in square brackets has been added by the translator.

Figures, Tables, and Illustrations

Figure 1.1	The first level [*étage*]	12
Figure 1.2	The second level	14
Figure 1.3	The second level completed by "*Che vuoi?*"	15
Figure 1.4	The third stage [*étape*]	18
Figure 2.1	The simultaneity of the four trajectories	27
Figure 2.2	The homology between the two relationships	36
Figure 5.1	Interpretation between statement and enunciation	89
Figure 5.2	Distribution of the four elements between the two characters in the dream	91
Figure 7.1	New distribution of the statement and enunciation	114
Figure 7.2	The L schema	117
Figure 7.3	The inverted bouquet illusion	127
Figure 7.4	Rotation of the plane mirror	127
Figure 8.1	Simplified graph	133
Figure 9.1	It is a message	158
Figure 9.2	The first loop of associations	168
Figure 13.1	The "He knew" in *Hamlet*	243
Figure 15.1	The interrogative hook	283
Figure 15.2	The unconscious signifying chain	283
Figure 15.3	The line of desire	284
Figure 15.4	The unconscious circuit of desire	285
Figure 25.1	The bad internal object	445
Table 19.1	Table of lacking objects	348
Table 20.1	Synchronic schema of the dialectic of desire	370
Table A1	The process of logical generation	509
Illustration plate 1	*Ophelia*, Sir John Everett Millais	
Illustration plate 2	*Melancholia*, Albrecht Dürer	

Book VI

Desire and Its Interpretation

1958–1959

INTRODUCTION

I

CONSTRUCTING THE GRAPH

Reintroducing the word "desire"
Poets and philosophers
The three schemas
A defense against distress
Darwin and the Devil's shudder

This year we are going to talk about desire and its interpretation.

A psychoanalysis is a therapeutic process, as people are wont to say. Let us say that it is a treatment, a psychical treatment.

This treatment concerns different levels of the psyche, first and foremost what I will call marginal or residual phenomena, such as dreams, slips of the tongue, and witticisms. These were the first scientific objects of psychoanalytic experience and the ones I emphasized last year.

Examining the curative aspect of this treatment, we find that it also concerns symptoms, broadly speaking, insofar as they manifest themselves in subjects in the guise of inhibitions. The latter form symptoms and are sustained by symptoms.

Lastly, it is a treatment that modifies structures – namely, those that are known as neuroses or neuropsychoses – which Freud at first characterized as "neuropsychoses of defense."

In what way does psychoanalysis intervene so as to deal at various levels with these different phenomenal realities? It intervenes insofar as they involve desire.

The phenomena that I called residual or marginal were initially apprehended by Freud, in the symptoms that we see described from one end of his work to the other, under the heading of desire and as significant as regards desire.

Similarly, anxiety [*angoisse*], inasmuch as we consider it to be key to the determination of symptoms, arises only insofar as some activity that enters into the play of symptoms becomes eroticized – or, to put it better, is taken up in the mechanism of desire.

Finally, what does the very term "defense" mean when it is used regarding the neuropsychoses? What is there a defense against, if it is not desire itself?

To conclude this introduction, it will suffice to indicate that libido, a notion that lies at the heart of psychoanalytic theory, is nothing but the psychical energy of desire.

I previously indicated in passing – recall my metaphor of the factory – that in order for the notion of energy to hold up, certain conjunctions of the symbolic with the real are necessary. I cannot, however, go into this specific point right now.

Analytic theory is thus thoroughly based on the notion of libido – that is, on the energy of desire.

1

Yet, as we have been seeing for some time now, analytic theory is moving ever further in a different direction.

Those who champion this new orientation very consciously indicate its originality, at least those among them who are most conscious of what they are doing. Fairbairn, who is the most typical representative of this trend, has written on several occasions – because he never stops writing – and, specifically, in a collection entitled *Psychoanalytic Studies of the Personality*, that modern psychoanalytic theory has changed its axis somewhat compared to the one Freud initially gave it, inasmuch as it no longer considers libido to be "pleasure-seeking"* but, rather, to be "object-seeking."*

I have frequently discussed this trend, which views libido as correlated with an object that is supposed to be in some sense predestined for it. I have already shown you its impact on psychoanalytic theory and technique in a thousand ways. I believe that I have managed on several occasions to designate the deviations from analytic practice that this trend entails, several of which might well be characterized as dangerous.

In order for us to broach the problem we will be focusing on this year, I wish to point out the importance of simply reintroducing the word "desire" into our vocabulary, a word that is manifestly veiled in all of current psychoanalytic experience. By reintroducing it, we produce a feeling, not of revitalization, but of disorientation. I mean that, if instead of speaking about "libido" or the "genital object," we speak about "genital *desire*," it may seem harder to take for granted that the development of this desire automatically implies the possibility of opening oneself up to love, or the possibility of a total actualization of love. The latter seems to have become a doctrinal tenet in a certain perspective regarding the maturing of libido over time.

This trend regarding the maturing of libido is all the more surprising in that it has arisen at the heart of a doctrine that was the first to not simply highlight but even to account for what Freud classified under the heading of debasement in our love lives. Freud argued that, whereas desire seems in fact to bring with it a certain quantum of love, it is very often a love that leads to conflict within oneself, a love that is not owned, a love that refuses to be owned.

On the other hand, the simple fact that we reintroduce the word "desire" – instead of currently used terms like "affectivity" and "positive" or "negative feeling" that stem from what I would call a disgraceful approach to the forces at work in the analytic relationship, especially regarding transference – creates a split that will in and of itself, it seems to me, have an enlightening effect.

Indeed, if – instead of considering transference to be constituted by affects or positive or negative feelings, given everything those terms bring with them that is vague and veiled – we name what is experienced here with the single term "desire," and speak of sexual desire and aggressive desire with respect to the analyst, it will become immediately visible that these desires do not constitute the whole of transference. It will become clear that transference must be defined by something other than more or less confused references to the notion of affect, whether positive or negative.

The final benefit of pronouncing the word "desire" and of using it in its fullest sense is that we will ask ourselves, "What is desire?"

This is not a question that we will be able to answer simply. Were 14 I not bound here by what I might call an urgent rendezvous with the needs of psychoanalytic practice, I would allow myself an investigation into the meaning of the word "desire" in the work of those who are the most qualified to highlight its usage – namely, poets and philosophers. But I will not do so.

We will see how the word "desire" is used, transmitted, and functions in poetry later, assuming we take our investigation far enough. If it is true, as all of my work this year will show you, that desire's position is profoundly marked by, moored to, and riveted to a certain linguistic function – that is, to a certain relationship between the subject and the signifier [or: system of signifiers, *le signifiant*] – psychoanalytic experience will take us far enough in this exploration (at least I hope it will) for there to be ample time to take advantage of the specifically poetic evocation of this term. This will also allow us, in the end, to better understand the relations between the nature of poetic creation and desire.

I will simply comment that the difficulties characteristic of the game of hide-and-go-seek that lies at the basis of what our experience reveals to us can already be seen in the fact, for example, that poetry clearly bridles, as it were, at the depiction of desire's object. In this respect, figurative poetry – the kind that I would say virtually paints beauty's "roses and lilies" – always expresses desire with a singular coldness. Curiously enough, the opposite is true in the type of poetry that is dubbed metaphysical. This is owing to the law that, strictly speaking, rules the evocation of desire. For those among you who read English, I will refer here only to the most eminent of the metaphysical poets of English literature, John Donne, inviting you to read a famous poem like "The Ecstasy," for example, in order to observe how impressively the question of the structure of our relation to desire is raised in it.

The very title of Donne's poem indicates the beginnings of the direction taken by the poetic approach to desire, on the lyrical level at least, when desire itself is targeted. To be sure, when the poet's play girds itself with dramatic action, it goes much further in rendering desire present to mind. For the time being, I will leave this dimension to one side. But I am mentioning it already because we broached it last year – it is the dimension of comedy. We will have to come back to it later.

Let us not dwell on poets any longer here. I mentioned them only as a preliminary pointer, and in order to indicate that we will return to them later, more or less sporadically. I would like to dwell for a moment, instead, on a position espoused by certain philosophers, for it is quite exemplary, I believe, as regards where the problem lies for us.

I have taken the trouble to write the following terms on the blackboard for you: "pleasure-seeking"* and "object-seeking."* Speculative thinkers and moralists have always broached the problem in just such terms. I am referring to theoretical morality, the morality that is enunciated in the form of precepts and rules and in the operations of philosophers – above all, those referred to as ethicists.

I have already pointed out to you the basis of all morality that one could call "physicalistic," in the sense in which, in medieval philosophy, people talked about the physical theory of love as opposed to the ecstatic theory of love. Up to a certain point, we could say that every theory of morality that has hitherto been expressed in the philosophical tradition has, in short, taken as its basis what one might call the hedonistic tradition. The latter involves establishing a sort of equivalence between two terms, pleasure and the object, in the sense in which the object is the libido's natural object insofar as

15

it is a boon [*bienfait*]. Once one adopts this criterion, pleasure must be admitted into the ranks of the goods [*biens*] sought by the subject and even into the ranks of the Sovereign Good, even if one refuses oneself pleasure.

Once we enter into Scholastic debates, the hedonistic ethical tradition no longer surprises us and we no longer perceive its paradoxes. Yet, in the end, what could be more contrary to what I shall call the experience of practical reason than the supposed convergence of pleasure with the good?

If we look at it closely – if we look, for example, at how things are expressed in Aristotle's work – what do we see being developed? In Aristotle's work it is very clear, things are very pure: pleasure and the good can only be equated in what I will call the master's ethics. This flattering ideal awards itself the term "temperance," as opposed to "intemperance," suggesting as it does the subject's mastery over his own habits. Yet the inconsistency of this theory is quite striking.

16

If you reread the famous passages [in Aristotle's *Ethics*, Book 7] concerning the use of pleasures, you will see that everything that enters into this moralizing perspective has to do with the register of mastery, with a master's morality, and with that over which the master can achieve mastery [*discipliner*]. He can achieve mastery over many things, primarily his behavior when it comes to his habits – in other words, when it comes to the handling and use of his ego. But as concerns desire, things are quite different.

Aristotle – who was quite lucid about and conscious of what results from this practical and theoretical conceptualization of ethics – himself recognizes that desires (*epithumia*) go beyond a certain limit, which is precisely that of mastery and the ego, and that they very quickly enter the realm of what he calls "brutishness" or "beastiality." Desires are exiled from the field proper to man, assuming man identifies with the master's reality. Brutishness is, in this case, akin to perversion. Aristotle has, moreover, in this regard a singularly modern conception that might be translated by saying that the master cannot be judged on this score. This is almost tantamount to saying, in our vocabulary, that he cannot be recognized as responsible [for his desires]. These texts are worth recalling to mind and will enlighten you if you reread them.

In the camp opposing this particular philosophical tradition, there is someone whom I should like to name. He is, in my view, the precursor of something that I believe to be new, that we must consider to be new in, let us say, the progress or meaning of a certain relationship of man to himself, which is that of psychoanalysis such as Freud developed it. This someone is Spinoza.

It is, after all, in his work that we read, at least with a rather exceptional stress, a formulation like the following: "Desire is the very essence of man." So as not to separate the beginning of his formulation from what follows, I will add: "inasmuch as it is understood to be based on one of his inclinations, understood as determined and dominated by one of his inclinations to do something."

We could already spell out in detail what in this formulation remains unrevealed, as it were. I say "unrevealed" because, of course, one cannot translate Spinoza using Freud. But I am mentioning it here as a quite singular bit of evidence. I no doubt have a greater fondness for Spinoza's work than others do, owing to the fact that I spent a lot of time reading Spinoza a very long time ago. Yet I do not believe that this is the reason why, in rereading his work on the basis of my own experience, it seems to me that someone who is involved in Freudian practice can feel quite at home reading texts like *De Servitute Humana*, written by someone for whom all of human reality is structured and organized on the basis of the attributes of divine substance. But let us leave this introductory remark aside as well for the time being, with the understanding that we will return to it.

I would like to give you a far more accessible example, with which I will conclude my philosophical references to our topic. I selected it at the most accessible level, or even the most common you can find. Open the dictionary by the late, charming Lalande, his *Vocabulaire technique et critique de la philosophie* ["Technical and Critical Dictionary of Philosophy" (Paris: PUF, 1960)]. Attempts to establish such dictionaries are extremely perilous and yet simultaneously fruitful, language being crucial to every problem we examine. You can be sure that in putting together a dictionary, you will come up with something suggestive. Here we find the following: "Desire: *Begehren, Begehrung.*" It is worth recalling what desire means in German philosophy; it is:

A spontaneous and conscious need tending [*tendance*] toward a known or imagined end. Desire is thus based on need, of which it is a special and more complex case. It opposes the will (or willing in general) insofar as the will also presupposes: (1) at least temporary coordination of the needs; (2) opposition between the subject and the object; (3) consciousness of its own effectiveness; and (4) an idea of the means by which the wished-for end can be realized.

These reminders are extremely useful, except for the fact that, in an article designed to define desire, there are but two lines to situate it in relationship to the needs, while the rest is related to the will. This is what the discourse on desire in this dictionary comes down to, except that the following is added to it: "Lastly, according to certain philosophers, there is a specific kind of fiat in the will that is irreducible to the needs and that constitutes freedom." There is an air of irony in that last line, which is quite striking on the part of this philosophical author.

18

In a footnote, Lalande adds, "Desire is the need to procure oneself an emotion that has already been experienced or imagined; it is the natural will to have a certain pleasure." He follows this with quotes from the work of Rauh and Revault d'Allonnes, the term "natural will" being of interest as a reference. To which Lalande personally adds the following:

> This definition strikes me as a bit too narrow in that it does not adequately take into account the fact that certain needs precede their corresponding emotions. Desire essentially seems to me to be the desire for an act or a state, without a [mental] representation of the affective character of this end being necessary in every case.

I think he is referring to the representation of pleasure or of something else. Whatever the case may be, it certainly does not fail to raise the question of what is at stake, whether it is the representation of pleasure or pleasure itself. I certainly do not believe that it is a simple task to home in on the signification of desire by means of such a dictionary, all the more so in that one cannot say that the way was paved for this task by the tradition to which the author refers.

Is desire a psychological reality that rebels against all organization? Would we manage, in the final analysis, to broach the reality of desire by subtracting the characteristics indicated [by Lalande], insofar as they are those of the will? We would then have the contrary: we would have a non-coordination of the needs, even if only temporary; and the opposition between the subject and the object would truly disappear. Similarly, we would be faced with a need lacking in consciousness of its own effectiveness, and without an idea of the words by which it would realize the desired end. In short, we would find ourselves in a field in which psychoanalysis has contributed more precise formulations.

In effect, within these negative determinations, psychoanalysis very precisely traces out different levels: the drive, inasmuch as it is the non-coordination of the needs, even if only temporary; and fantasy, inasmuch as it introduces an essential link [*articulation*] or, more precisely, an altogether blatant type of link within the vague determination that we designate as the non-opposition between the subject and the object. It will be our goal this year to try to define what fantasy is, perhaps even a bit more precisely than the psychoanalytic tradition has hitherto been able to.

As for what remains of Lalande's definition, which implies idealism and pragmatism, I will retain but one thing for the time being – namely, how difficult it seems to be to situate and analyze desire with reference to objects alone.

I am going to stop here, in order to turn more specifically to the terms with which I believe I can lay out the problem of our experience for you this year: the terms "desire" and its "interpretation."

2

The internal or connecting link between desire and its interpretation in psychoanalytic experience has a feature that habit alone stops us from seeing – namely, the degree to which the interpretation of desire is already, in and of itself, subjective [or: concerns the subject, *subjective*], being linked just as internally to the very manifestation of desire.

You are aware of the vantage point from which we, I won't say are starting out, but are making headway. We have been working together for quite some time. We have been trying to conceptualize the outlines of our experience for five years already. These outlines are converging this year on a problem – which may be where all these points, some of which are quite far flung, converge – a problem that I am trying to pave a way to broach for you.

Since we have marched side by side these last five years, I can immediately posit that psychoanalysis essentially shows us what I will call the taking up [*prise*] of man in the constituent [*constituant*] of the signifying chain. This taking up is undoubtedly linked to the existence of human beings, but it is not coextensive with it. Humans speak, and in order to speak they must enter into language and into a pre-existing discourse. The law of subjectivity that psychoanalysis forcefully brings out – namely, the fundamental dependence of subjectivity on language – is so essential that all of psychology literally hinges on it.

I will say that, at the very least, there is a form of psychology that is utterly subject to language, the psychology that we can define as the sum total of studies concerning what I might call sensory experience [*sensibilité*], in the broadest sense, insofar as that experience functions so as to maintain totality or homeostasis. What is involved are, in short, an organism's sensory functions. Here everything is included: not only all of the experimental data of psychophysics, but also everything that can be contributed, most broadly speaking, by employing the notion of form in grasping the means by which constancy is maintained in an organism. An entire field of psychology is inscribed therein; it is sustained by the experience that is characteristic of it and it gives rise to research that continues to be carried out.

Nevertheless, the subjectivity in question – insofar as man is caught up in language, whether he likes it or not, and insofar as he is caught up in it far beyond his knowledge of it – is not immanent in sensory experience, if we understand the latter in terms of the stimulus–response pair. This is because the stimulus is given [by a researcher] as a function of a code that imposes its own order on need [that of the subject involved in the experiment], which must express itself in that code.

From an experimental perspective, one can at least try to account for the workings of the stimulus–response cycle in terms of signs. One can say that a stimulus is a sign given by the external environment that requires an organism to respond or defend itself, and that the organism in turn gives a sign. If you tickle the soles of a frog's feet, the frog responds with a certain muscular relaxation. But when it comes to subjectivity that is caught up in language, it is not a sign that is given, but rather a signifier.

Keep in mind the following, which appears to be simple: in the theory of communication, people talk about the sign as something that addresses someone and concerns a third thing that the sign represents. Quite recently again, we have been told that three is the minimum number of terms. Without even bothering to include a sender, they claim that, apart from someone who hears, we need but a sign, which signifies the third thing that the sign simply represents.

Now, as regards signifiers, this construction is false because a signifier does not concern a third thing that it supposedly represents but concerns another signifier that it is not.

I would like to show you, not the genesis, but rather the construction of the three schemas I just put up on the blackboard [Figures 1.1, 1.2, and 1.3]. Now don't go thinking that we are talking about "stages" [*étapes*] here, even if we do occasionally find something like stages that are in fact gone through by the subject. The subject must come to occupy his place therein, but don't think of these schemas as typical stages of development; what is at stake is rather a generation, or a logical anteriority of each schema with respect to the one that follows it.

What does capital D represent? D represents the signifying chain. This basic, fundamental structure subjects every manifestation of language to the condition of being regulated by a succession – in

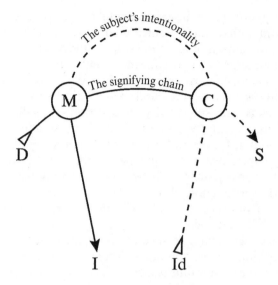

Figure 1.1: The first level (*étage*)

other words, by diachrony, that is, by something that unfolds over time. S stands for "signifier."

I will leave to one side the temporal properties that are involved; we will perhaps be led to return to them later. Let us say that the fullness of the fabric [*étoffe*] of temporality, as they say, is not at all involved here. Things boil down to the notion of succession here and to what it may already imply as regards the notion of scansion, but we are not there yet.

Our concern is with the subject's involvement [or: embeddedness, *implication*] in the signifier. It can only be established on the basis of a discrete or differential element.

Given what I just pointed out – namely, that a signifier is defined and takes on its value and meaning on the basis of its relationship to another signifier in a system of signifying oppositions – the signifying chain develops in a dimension that implies a certain synchrony of signifiers: a signifying battery.

We can raise a question: "What is the smallest possible battery?" I've tried to answer this little question. It seems to me that four is the smallest possible battery. Can one construct a language with four signifiers? I do not believe that it is unthinkable. Trying to figure out if it is possible will not lead you too far away from your experience, but let us leave that to one side. It is clear that, given the current state of affairs, we are far from being reduced to only four.

The following is of the essence: that which is indicated by the dotted line intersects the line that represents the signifying chain twice, first on the right and then on the left [*d'avant en arrière*].

The first intersection [the one on the right] takes place at the synchronic level, that of the simultaneous existence of signifiers. Point C is what I call the point at which the dotted line intersects the code. In other words, we have here the play of the signifier, something akin to a chatterbox. The child addresses a subject whom he knows to be a speaking subject, whom he has seen speaking, and who has talked his ear off since the beginning of his awakening to the light of day. Very early on, the subject must learn that, in order for his needs to be satisfied, their manifestations have to stoop to get through this doorway or narrow passageway.

M, the second point of intersection, is the one where the message is produced. It is always through the retroactive play of a series of signifiers that signification is, in fact, affirmed and becomes precise. It is only afterward that the message takes form, on the basis of the signifier or code that precedes it. Conversely, the message, as it is being formulated, constantly gets ahead of the code, placing a bet on the future [*tire une traite*].

I have already told you what results from the intentional process that runs from the id to capital I.

23

What is at its origin presents itself in the form of the blossoming of need, or of "disposition" [or: predisposition, *tendance*], as psychologists say. This is represented in my schema at the level of the id. Here there is no return pathway that closes the circle, for the id is caught up in language, but it does not know what it is; it is not reflected on the basis of this innocent approach to language in which the subject initially turns himself into discourse.

The fact that the subject has relations with other speaking subjects results in the following, even when this is only just barely apprehended by him: what I have called the first or primal identification, I, occurs at the end of the intentional chain.

This is the first realization of an ideal about which one cannot even say at this point in the schema that it involves an ego-ideal, but simply that the subject receives the first stamp [*seing*] or *signum* of its relationship with the Other here.

3

Now for the second stage of the schema.

It can be thought to overlap in a sense with a certain stage of development, assuming that we do not view these stages as discontinuous. There are clear discontinuities in development, but they are not found in the stages of this schema. These discontinuities can be found, as Freud observes somewhere, at the level of the judgment of attribution in relation to simple naming. That is not what I am talking about now, although I will turn to it later.

The first part of this schema represents the infant (*infans*) level of discourse, for it is perhaps not even necessary that the child begin to speak before the mark or seal placed on need by demand begins to work, as his alternating cries show. The second part implies that the child, even if he does not yet know how to speak coherently [*tenir un discours*], already knows how to speak, for this starts quite early on.

24

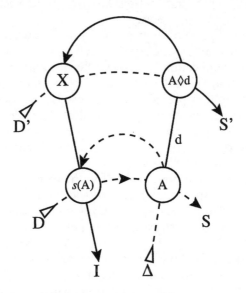

Figure 1.2: The second level

When I say that he knows how to speak, I mean that, at the second level of the schema, there is something that goes beyond being in the grip of language. There is a relationship here with the Other, strictly speaking, inasmuch as there is an appeal to the Other as presence, presence against a background of absence. This is the moment of the *fort-da* that so impressed Freud in 1915, as we can determine, when he had been called in to see one of his grandsons, the one who would later go on to become a psychoanalyst. I am speaking of the child whom he observed.

At the first level, what the chain of discourse articulates as existing beyond the subject imposes its form on the subject, whether he likes it or not. We have here, as it were, an innocent apprehension by the subject of linguistic form. But beyond this articulation and beyond this apprehension, something else occurs, which is based on his experience of language – namely, the subject's apprehension of the Other as such. This takes us to the second level of the schema.

The Other involved is the one who can respond to the subject, answer his call. We see this Other to whom he fundamentally asks a question in *The Devil in Love* by Jacques Cazotte; it is the bellowing of the terrifying form that represents the appearance of the superego, in response to he who invoked it in a Neapolitan cave; the response is *"Che vuoi?"* or "What do you want?" The subject asks the Other what he wants. The question is asked from the place where the subject first encounters desire, desire being initially the Other's desire.

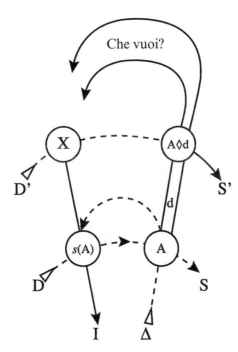

Figure 1.3: The second level completed by *"Che vuoi?"*

This experience of the Other's desire is essential because it allows the subject to realize something that is beyond linguistic articulation, around which the following revolves: it is the Other who does or does not enunciate certain signifiers. Up until then, the battery of signifiers, among which a choice could be made, was there, but only in itself. Now, experience shows that this choice is commutative, inasmuch as it is within the Other's power to make it such that one or another of the signifiers be there.

26   This entails that two new principles be introduced, at this level of experience. They are added to what was initially a pure and simple principle of succession implying the principle of choice.

The first new principle is that of substitution. The following point is essential: what I call the "bar" between the signifier and the signified is established for the subject on the basis of commutativity. That is to say, there is coexistence or simultaneity, which is marked at the same time by a certain impenetrability, between the signifier and the signified. I mean that the difference or distance between the signifier and the signified is maintained.

$$\frac{S}{s}$$

Curiously enough, group theory, as we learn about it in the abstract study of sets, shows us the absolutely essential link between all commutativity and the very possibility of using what I am calling the "bar," a sign that is used to represent fractions. This is a tangential remark that I shall set aside for the time being.

From the moment at which the structure of the signifying chain makes us call on the Other [a réalisé l'appel de l'Autre] – in other words, at which the process of enunciation is distinguished from the formulation of the enunciated and is superimposed on it – the taking up of the subject in the articulation of speech, a taking up that was initially innocent, becomes unconscious. Similarly, the commutativity of the signifier becomes an essential dimension for the production of the signified. This means that the very substitution of one signifier for another signifier comes to lie at the origin of the multiplication of significations that characterize the enriching of the human world in an effective way – that is, in a way that reverberates in the subject's consciousness.

A second new principle can also be seen: the principle of similarity. A certain dimension, the metonymic dimension, begins to operate as a function of the fact that, within the signifying chain, one signifying term may resemble another. It is essentially in this dimension that the characteristic and fundamental effects of what we might call poetic discourse – that is, the effects of poetry – are produced. I will show you this in what follows.

27   What happens at this second stage [étape] will thus allow us to situate the appearance of what constitutes the signified of the Other, $s(A)$ – as opposed to the signifier given by the Other, $S(A)$ – in the very place where the message was in the first schema. The latter [$S(A)$] is produced along the dotted chain line, since it is a chain that is only partially articulated, merely

implicit, and represents the subject solely insofar as he underpins speech.

As I told you, the second stage [*étape*] is produced by the experience of the Other as an Other who has a desire. From the very first moment of its appearance, at its very origin, desire, *d*, is manifested in the interval or gap that separates the pure and simple linguistic articulation of speech from what marks the fact that the subject actualizes something of himself in it, something that has no scope or meaning except with respect to the production of speech, and that is his being – what language calls "being."

A horizon of being is situated for the subject between, on the one hand, the manifestations of his demand [*demande*] and what these manifestations have made him become and, on the other hand, the demand [*exigence*] to be recognized by the Other, which we might, in this case, call the demand [*exigence*] to be loved. We want to know if he can reach that horizon or not.

The experience of desire is situated in this interval or gap. It is first apprehended as being experience of the Other's desire, and it is within this experience that the subject has to situate his own desire. His own desire cannot be situated anywhere other than in this space.

4

This [Figure 1.4] represents the third stage [*étape*], form, or phase of the schema.

Here is what constitutes it. Finding himself in the primitive presence of the Other's desire as obscure and opaque, the subject has no recourse, he is *hilflos*. *Hilflosigkeit*, to use Freud's term, is known in French as the subject's "distress." It is the foundation of what, in psychoanalysis, has been explored, experienced, and qualified as "trauma."

What Freud taught us, at the end of the journey that allowed him to finally situate the experience of anxiety in its true place, is that anxiety has nothing to do with the in some sense diffuse, or so it seems to me, nature of what people call the existential experience of anxiety.

In philosophy, people have gone so far as to say that anxiety confronts us with nothingness. Such formulations are assuredly justifiable from a certain vantage point. Nevertheless, you should be aware that, on this topic, Freud teaches us something that is positive and clearly formulated. He views anxiety as something that is thoroughly situated in a theory of communication, when he says that anxiety is a signal. Assuming that desire must be produced in the

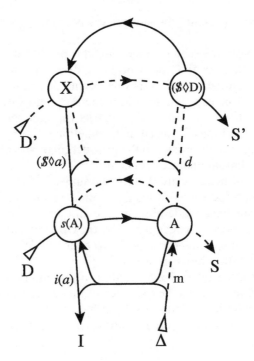

Figure 1.4: The third stage [*étape*]

very same place where distress originates and is experienced, anxiety is not produced at the level of desire.

We will carry out a detailed, line-by-line study of Freud's work entitled *Inhibitions, Symptoms, and Anxiety*. As it is our first class of the year, I can only sketch out for you today a few major points that we will come back to, specifically the following: Freud tells us that anxiety is produced as a signal in the ego, on the basis of *Hilflosigkeit*, which anxiety is called upon to remedy insofar as it is a signal. I realize that I am going too quickly and that this would warrant an entire Seminar; but I will not be able to talk to you about anything if I do not begin by tracing out the pathway that we must follow.

Specular experience – that is, the experience of one's relationship to the other's image insofar as it is at the core of the ego's *Urbild* – comes in at this third stage. We thus find here anew what I laid out at the end of my first Seminar concerning the relationship between the ideal ego and the ego-ideal. I am not simply alluding here to what I said and propounded about specular relations – namely, the subject's confrontation with his own image in the mirror – but to the O–O' schema: the one where we find the concave mirror, which allows us to conceptualize the function of a real image that is itself reflected, and that cannot be seen as reflected except from a certain position – namely, a symbolic position which is that of the ego-ideal.

We shall use all of this in a context that will give it a very different resonance, insofar as we shall be led to reconceptualize it in the context of the kind of symbolic action that I am showing you to be essential.

If the imaginary element – namely, the relationship between the ego, m [for moi], and the other, $i(a)$ – thus comes in at the third stage of the schema, it is inasmuch as it allows the subject to deal with his distress in his relationship with the Other's desire.

How does he deal with it? With something he borrows from the game of mastery that the child, at a specific age, learned to handle with reference to his semblable as such. We are talking here about the experience of the semblable in the sense in which he is a gaze, the other who gazes at you, and who brings into play a certain number of imaginary relations, first and foremost, the relations of bearing [*prestance*], and also those of submission and defeat. The subject proceeds by means of this.

In other words, just as we must not say that the soul thinks, but, like Aristotle, that man thinks *with* his soul, we must say that the subject defends himself with his ego. This is what psychoanalytic practice shows us.

The subject defends against his distress; and with the means given to him by his imaginary experience of his relationship with the other, he constructs something with the other that, unlike specular experience, is flexible. In effect, what the subject reflects are not simply games of bearing, and not simply his appearance to the other in [the form of] prestige and feigning; it is himself as a speaking subject. This is why fantasy is what I am designating to you here as the exit or reference point by which desire learns to situate itself.

I formulate fantasy for you with the following symbols: ($\$\lozenge a$). The subject is barred here because he is a speaking subject, one who relates to the other as a gaze – that is, to the imaginary other. Whenever you come up against something that is a fantasy, strictly speaking, you will see that it can be articulated in these primary terms, qua relationship between the speaking subject and the imaginary other. This is what defines fantasy. The function of fantasy is to provide the subject's desire with its proper level of correction or situation. This is why human desire is fixed, attached, and coapted, not to an object, but always essentially to a fantasy.

This is a fact of experience. Although it managed to remain

30

mysterious for a long time, let us not forget that it is nevertheless an experiential fact that psychoanalysis made common knowledge.

It is only thanks to psychoanalysis that this ceased being an anomaly – something opaque, something like a deviation, corruption, or perversion of desire.

It is on the basis of psychoanalysis that all of this – which can at times be called corruption, perversion, deviation, or even delusion – was conceptualized and articulated in a dialectic that, as I have just shown you, can reconcile the imaginary with the symbolic.

5

I realize full well that I am not leading you along an easy path in our first class of the year. But if I did not begin by laying out our main terms immediately, if I confined myself to proceeding slowly, step-by-step, in order to suggest to you the need for such and such a term, what could I accomplish?

If I did not immediately provide you with what I call the graph [of desire], I would have to provide you with it little by little as I did last year, and this would make it all the more obscure. This is why I decided to begin with it directly. Which is not to say that, by doing so, I have made your task easier.

To ease your task, I would now like to give you a little illustration, taken from the simplest level, since what is involved are the relations between the subject and the signifier. The least one can expect, and the first thing one can expect, from a schema is to see what purpose it can serve with respect to commutation.

I recalled an anecdote I had once read in Darwin's book, *The Expression of the Emotions in Man and Animals*, which, I must say, amused me quite a bit. Darwin recounts that at a soirée he heard a man named Sydney Smith, who was, I assume, a high-society Englishman of Darwin's time, come out quite placidly with the following sentence: "I hear that dear old Lady Cork has been overlooked."*

Etymologically speaking, "to be overlooked"* means that one has not been noticed, that one has been neglected or forgotten – by an overseer, for example. Literally, someone's eye passed over you. The verb "to overlook"* is commonly used in English, but there is no corresponding expression in French. This is why languages are so useful and so harmful at the same time; they allow you to avoid making an effort, to avoid carrying out in French the substitution of signifiers thanks to which we might manage to target a certain signified; for we would have to change the entire context in order to obtain the same effect.

Darwin marvels at the fact that the quip was perfectly clear to everyone present. In fact, no one there had the slightest doubt that it meant that the Devil had overlooked the dear old lady and had forgotten to carry her off to the tomb, which seems to have been at that time, in the minds of his audience, her natural place, even the place they wished she would occupy. Darwin raises a question about this but leaves the question unanswered. "What did Sydney Smith do in order to have this effect?" he asks himself more or less, and opines, "I truly can't say."

We should appreciate the fact that he highlights, in an especially significant and exemplary way, that he experienced his own limits in broaching this question. Since Darwin had broached the problem of the emotions in a certain way, he could have said that the expression of the emotions was nevertheless involved here because the subject did not manifest any emotion – because he said it "placidly"* – but that would perhaps have been taking things a bit far. In any case, Darwin does not say that. He was truly astonished by the fact he relates, and we must take him literally, because, as always when we study a case, we must not reduce it by rendering it vague. Everyone understood that the guy was talking about the Devil, Darwin says, whereas the Devil was nowhere to be found in what he said. And this is what is interesting: the fact that Darwin tells us that the Devil's shudder was felt by all those assembled there.

Let us now try to understand this a bit. I will not dwell on Darwin's intellectual limitations – we will inevitably come to them, but not right away. What is clear is that there is, right from the outset, something along the lines of knowledge here, and this is what is striking. There is no need to posit the principle of metaphorical effects – that is, the substitution of one signifier for another – nor to require Darwin to have had some inkling of it, to immediately realize that the effect of Smith's statement stemmed first and foremost from the fact that he did not say what was expected.

A sentence that begins with "Lady Cork" should usually end with "ill."* [We would usually expect to hear something like,] "I hear she is not well." It seems, in fact, that everyone was expecting news concerning the old lady's health, for, when people talk about old ladies, it is always their health that is foremost in their minds at the outset. A substitution thus took place here: the expected news was replaced by something else, which was, in certain ways, irreverent. Smith did not say that she was on death's doorstep, nor did he say that she was quite well; he said that she had been forgotten.

What then came into play to produce this metaphorical effect? If the word "overlooked"* had been expected, there would have been no such effect. It is inasmuch as it was not expected, but was

32

33

rather put in the place of another signifier, that a new signified was produced. It was neither along the lines of what was expected, nor of what was unexpected. This unexpected thing was not characterized as unexpected, but it was something original that had to be created in the minds of all of those present in accordance with their own ways of thinking. In any case, a new signified arose from something that made it such that, for example, Sydney Smith came across in his circle as a witty man – in other words, as someone who did not express himself in clichés.

But why the Devil? It will help us a great deal to look at our little schema. If we create schemas, it is in order to use them. We could arrive at the same result without it, but the schema guides us and shows us what is really [*réel*] happening. What is rendered present here is, strictly speaking, a fantasy.

And by what mechanisms? It is here that the schema allows us to go further than the naive notion, I would say, that things are designed to express something that wants to be communicated, an emotion, as they say, as if emotions did not pose in and of themselves plenty of other problems – namely, what they are, assuming they do not already need to be communicated.

Our speaker was perfectly placid, we are told. In other words, he presented himself in some sense in a pure state, the presence of his speech being a pure metonymic effect, I mean his speech qua speech in the continuity of speech. And in this continuity he conjured up the following: the presence of death insofar as a subject can or cannot escape it.

Stated differently, he conjured up the presence of something that is closely tied to the coming into the world of the signifier itself. In effect, if there is a dimension in which death (or the fact that there is no longer any death) can be both directly conjured up and at the same time veiled (but is, in any case, incarnated), in which death can become immanent in an act, it is certainly that of signifying articulation.

It is clear that this subject who spoke so easily of death did not wish Lady Cork especially well. But, on the other hand, the perfect placidity with which he spoke of her implies that, in this regard, he had dominated his desire, insofar as his desire could express itself as in *Volpone* where we find the lovely formulation, "Die, and stink"! Sydney Smith did not say that; he simply and serenely articulated that the fate that awaits each of us in turn had been forgotten for a moment. But this was not the Devil, if I may put it thus, it was death, and it would come one day or another. Simultaneously, this character presented himself as someone who was not afraid of comparing himself with the lady about whom he was speaking, not afraid to place himself at the same level, subject to the same flaw, and thus to the same final equalization by the absolute master [i.e., death] that he rendered present to mind here.

In other words, in his full command of the language, he revealed himself as having a sort of familiarity with what is veiled in language. This suggests something on which I want to end class today, which was missing in everything I said in my discussion of the three stages, and it will complete the mainspring of what I wanted to formulate for you.

In the first schema, we have the innocent image of the subject. He is unconscious of course, but it is an unconsciousness that is just waiting to be [or: is itching to be, *ne demande qu'à*] transformed into knowledge. Let us not forget that the Latin term *scire* is present in "unconsciousness" [*inconscience*], and that even in French *avoir conscience* [to be aware] implies the notion of knowledge.

In the next two stages, we have, as I told you, a far more conscious use of knowledge; the subject knows how to speak and he speaks; this is what he does when he calls on the Other. It is nevertheless here that we find the originality of the field that Freud discovered, which he calls the unconscious.

There is, in fact, something in this Other that always places the subject at a certain distance from his being, and which makes it such that he can never join up with that being, can never reach it except in "the metonymy of being" in the subject that is known as desire. Why is that? Because at the level at which the subject is himself caught up in speech, and thereby in a relationship with the Other as the locus of speech, there is a signifier that is always missing. Why? Because it is the signifier that is specifically assigned to the relationship between the subject and the signifier [or: signifying system, *le signifiant*]. This signifier has a name; it is the phallus.

Desire is the metonymy of being in the subject; the phallus is the metonymy of the subject in being. We will come back to this. The phallus is the signifying element that is subtracted from the chain of speech, insofar as speech is involved in any and every relationship with the Other. This is the ultimate principle which is such that the subject, inasmuch as he is caught up in speech, falls under the sway of what has been conceptualized under the heading of the "castration complex," with all its clinical consequences.

35

What is suggested by any type of usage – I would not say pure, but perhaps rather impure – of "the tribe's words"? Every type of metaphorical inauguration, assuming it is audacious, defies what language always veils. What it always veils is, in the final analysis, death. This always tends to bring out the enigmatic figure of the missing signifier: the phallus. It is the phallus that appears here, and as always, in a diabolical form, as it is called – ear, skin, even the phallus itself.

The phenomenon is inscribed here, of course, in the tradition of English wit, which, although restrained, nevertheless dissimulates a violent desire. But metaphorical usage suffices, in and of itself, to make the image of the subject, insofar as he is marked by his relation to the special signifier known as prohibition, appear in the imaginary – that is, in the other who is there as a spectator: little *a*.

In this case, Sidney Smith violated a prohibition, for one simply does not speak of old ladies in this manner. He revealed what lies beyond the prohibitions that constitute the law of language. Wishing to speak as placidly as possible, he nevertheless made the Devil appear. So much so that dear old Darwin wondered, 'How the *devil* did he do that?'

I will leave it at that for today.

Next time, we will once again take up a dream found in Freud's work, and we will try to apply our analytic methods to it. This will simultaneously allow us to situate different modes of interpretation.

November 12, 1958

FURTHER EXPLANATION

Two levels and four processes
Continuity and fragmentation
The two *I*'s
What does "I desire you" mean?
From the first to the second topography

I will first lay out the limits of what I would like to do in class today.

I will thus enunciate what I mean to show you by taking up the example of the interpretation of a dream, as well as the use of what we have, for some time now, been conventionally calling the graph [of desire].

As I do not wish to discuss things in a way that goes over your heads, if I dare express myself thus, I would like it if a certain communication, as they say, could be established through this discussion. I did not fail to receive echoes of the difficulties that some of you, even many of you, had last time when faced with the repositioning of this graph, even though the graph is far from being new to all of you.

We constructed this graph together last year, and perfected it progressively. You watched it come together to answer the needs of a certain formulation centered around what I called "unconscious formations." The fact that its usage is not yet unequivocal to you, as some have remarked, is not surprising, since a part of what I shall have to explain this year about desire will show you its utility and will simultaneously teach you how to use it.

Our first order of business is thus to understand it. This is precisely what seems to have been difficult for some here, to different degrees, perhaps less than they let on. I would like you to note that the term "understanding" [*compréhension*] – I assure you that I am not being ironic here – is problematic. If there are among you some who always understand, in every situation and at all times, I congratulate and envy them. Even after twenty-five years of practice, that is not the case for me.

The term "understanding" truly shows us the dangers it brings with it. In all understanding there is a danger of illusion, to such a degree that the point is not so much to understand what I am doing as to know what I am doing. They are not always the same thing. They cannot be confused, and you will see that there are internal reasons for not confusing them. You can, in certain cases, know what you are doing and where you are at, without always understanding what is at stake, at least not immediately.

To pique your interest, I will say that I think I can today, if I have enough time, begin to show you how this graph, and this graph alone, I believe – or something analogous, for we must not become too attached to how it is clothed – can eminently help you distinguish three things that you all too frequently confuse to the point of slipping carelessly from one to the other: the repressed, desire, and the unconscious, to simply take up the way Freud defines them.

The graph is designed to help us map things. Before applying it, let me reconstruct it step by step so that, at least, what is represented by what I call the two levels will no longer be in doubt.

The difficulty for many of you has to do with the fact that these two levels do not correspond to anything that is usually presented to you as what I might call the architecture of the upper and lower functions: the functions of synthesis and of automatisms. It is precisely because you do not find these architectonics therein that the two levels confuse you. I am therefore going to try to reformulate them for you.

It seems that what is especially difficult to some of you is the second level [*étage*] of the construction, which is not necessarily a second stage [*étape*] – "level" being abstractly defined because, as this graph is a discourse, one cannot say everything at the same time.

I will thus take things up anew.

39   **1**

What is my goal in constructing this graph? To show the relations between the speaking subject and the signifier, relations that are essential to us insofar as we are psychoanalysts.

In the final analysis, the question around which these two levels are divided is the same for the speaking subject as it is for us. This is a good sign. I was just saying, "Do we know what we are doing?" Does the subject himself know what he is doing when he speaks? This means, "Can he, in fact, signify his own signifying action to himself?" It is around this very question that the two levels can be differentiated.

As this seems to have escaped some of you, I will tell you immediately that we must view the two levels as functioning at the same time in even the slightest speech act. And you will see what I mean by "speech act" [*acte de parole*] and how far I take this term.

What I will tell you is something that I had the opportunity to formulate for one of you to whom I gave a bit of additional explanation after the last class. I am mentioning this because my interlocutor indicated that it included something he had not perceived at the time.

Namely, how to think about the processes that occur in the subject insofar as the signifier is involved in his activity. The processes in question begin simultaneously at four different points: Δ, A, D, and X. These points are, respectively – and you will see what underpins my exposé today – the subject's intention, the subject qua speaking I, the act of demanding, and X, which we will give a certain name later and which I will leave unspecified for the time being.

The processes are thus simultaneous in the four trajectories, D→S, Δ→I, A→*s*(A), and the trajectory of the upper line [D'→S'

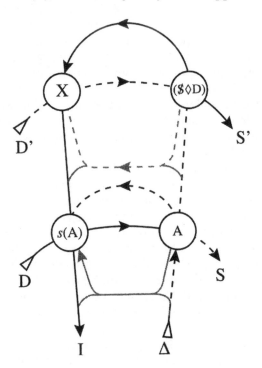

Figure 2.1: The simultaneity of the four trajectories

or possibly ($◊D)→X]. I believe that this should now be sufficiently clear.

If these two levels exist, it is because the subject does something that is related to the signifier's predominant action or structure.

40   Let us begin by detailing what happens at the lower level. Here the subject receives, or is submitted to, this structure. This is especially apparent and illustrated – not uniquely, but especially – in the context of demand.

Pay close attention to what I am saying here, for it is not in the least bit improvised. Those who are taking notes have the right idea. The fact that it is especially illustrated [in the context of demand] is such that it is especially comprehensible, but at the same time it can be such that you do not see it in all its generality, which leads to a certain amount of incomprehension. You should get it into your heads right away that it is dangerous to think you understand.

At the lower level of the graph we find a line that represents the intentionality of the subject, the intentionality of what we assume the subject to be. The subject in question has not yet become a speaking subject; he is the subject about whom people speak. I would even say that he is the one people have always spoken about up until now, for I do not believe that anyone has ever truly and

41   clearly made the distinction that I am trying to make here between the subject and the speaking subject. To put it in a nutshell, [the former] is the subject of knowledge, a subject who is correlated with the object and around whom the eternal question of idealism revolves, he himself being an ideal subject.

This subject has always been problematic in some way, since after all, as people have remarked and as his name indicates, he is merely supposed [to exist]. This is not true of the subject who speaks, for he forces us to take notice of him.

In the context of demand, what is involved is the first state – a state without form, so to speak – of our subject, of he whose conditions of existence we are trying to spell out by means of the graph. Here the subject is no more than the subject of need. He expresses need in his demand. This is my precise point of departure.

It follows that the subject's need is profoundly modified by the fact of having to be expressed in demand, passing thus through the defiles of the signifier. Without going any further into this point, because I assume we all agree on it, I simply want to point out what happens owing to the exchange that occurs between the unconstituted, primitive position of the subject of need and the structural conditions that are imposed by the signifier.

You see in the schema that the line of demand, D→S, is continuous [it is a solid, not a dotted, line] until it arrives at A, whereas beyond A it is fragmented. Inversely, the part of the line that precedes $s(A)$, the line that represents the subject's intentionality here [running from Δ to A to $s(A)$], is fragmented, and it only becomes continuous afterward – that is, in the segment $s(A)\rightarrow I$. Let us even provisionally say – for I will have to emphasize this later on – that it is continuous in that segment insofar as we do not have to take into account the line $A\rightarrow m\rightarrow i(a)\rightarrow s(A)$ [see Figure 1.4].

Why is this so? I will tell you why briefly, because I must not talk endlessly about the graph, and because we will have occasion to return to it.

Let us begin by investigating what is represented by the continuity of the line $D\rightarrow S$ up to point A.

Capital A is, as you know, the locus of the code, the locus in which the treasure trove of language in its synchrony resides, I mean the sum total of the taxiematic elements without which beings who are subject to the conditions of language have no means by which to communicate. The continuity of the line $D\rightarrow S$ up to point A represents the synchrony of the systematic organization of language. Synchronically, it [A] is posited as a system or set in which each element has its own value insofar as it is distinct from the other elements of the system – that is, from the other signifiers. This is the mainspring of everything I say about communication. What is always forgotten in theories of communication is that what is communicated is not the sign of something else; it is simply the sign of what [or: of the fact that, *de ce que*], in its place, another signifier is not.

It is on the basis of the solidarity of this synchronic system, insofar as it resides in the locus of the code, that the discourse of demand takes on its solidity prior to arriving at the code. Stated otherwise, we see in diachrony – in other words, in the unfolding of this discourse – what is known as the minimum duration necessary for the satisfaction of the slightest goal (even what is known as "magical satisfaction") – namely, the time it takes to speak [*le temps de parler*].

Since the discourse of demand is composed of signifiers, the line that represents it *should* appear here in the fragmented form in which we see it subsist – namely, in the form of a succession of discrete elements, which are thus separated by intervals. If it is nevertheless continuous here, it is owing to the synchronic solidarity of the code from which the succession of elements is borrowed. Continuity expresses the solidity of diachronic assertion, in the constitution of what is called the time it takes to formulate something, the time it takes for demand to be articulated. This is why, prior to or shy of the code, the line of demand is presented here as continuous.

42

Why, then, is the line that represents the subject's intentionality fragmented here? [Lacan is presumably pointing to the dotted line running from Δ to A to s(A).]

Let us note that the context of demand, in and of itself, simplifies the supposed diversity of the subject – in other words, the moments and variations of this point [Δ], which presents itself as essentially shifting [*mouvant*]. The problem of the continuity of the subject has, as you know, been apparent to psychologists for a long time. How can a being, who is essentially given over to what one might call fluctuations [*intermittences*] – not merely those of the heart, as some have said, but of many other things – establish himself and assert himself as an ego? This is the problem at hand. Now, putting a need into play in demand is already something that assuredly simplifies the subject with respect to the more or less chaotic and random interferences of the different needs among themselves.

If, nevertheless, the first part of the line Δ→I, namely, the part up until s(A), appears in a fragmented form, it is because it represents the retroactive effect of the form of discourse's discrete elements on this shifting [*mouvance*]; the latter is both continuous and discontinuous, and assuredly confused, and we must assume it to be that of the primitive manifestation of needs [or: of (pre)disposition, *de la tendance*]. Discursivity is retroactively imposed on need, which is thereby subjected to its form. This is why the line appears in a fragmented form shy, not of the code, but of the message.

What happens beyond the message [s(A)]? I have underscored it at other times, so I can cover it quickly here. It is the following: the subject identifies with the Other to whom his demand is addressed [*l'Autre de la demande*], insofar as this Other is omnipotent. I do not think that I need to go back over the topic of omnipotence, which is sometimes attributed by psychoanalysts to thought and sometimes to speech. The fact remains that we see here, as I have often pointed out, how wrongheaded it is to attribute omnipotence to the subject; we can see here the depreciative stance that psychologists get into the habit of adopting, inasmuch as they are always more or less pedantic, in the original sense of the term. For the omnipotence in question here is that of the Other, insofar as the Other quite simply has the sum total of signifiers at his disposal.

To show you that by articulating things in this way we are not moving away from concrete experience, I will expressly point them out in development, and more precisely in language acquisition, which lies at the heart of mother–child relations.

Capital I – at which the segment that begins from s(A), the signified of A, arrives – is what primary identification is based on. Edward Glover conceptualized this as the first nucleus of the formation of the ego. This process leads to the nucleus of identification because the mother is not simply the person who offers the breast [*sein*]; she is also the one who gives the seal [*seing*] of signifying articulation. This is not due simply to the fact that she speaks to her child, for it is quite clear that she speaks to him well before she can assume that he understands what she is saying, just as he understands some of what she is saying long before she thinks he does. In effect, before properly linguistic exchange occurs, all sorts of games – hiding games, for example, that so quickly make children smile or laugh – already involve symbolic action, strictly speaking.

While playing these games, what a mother reveals to her child is the function of symbols qua revealing. In making something disappear and reappear – his own face, for example, by covering and then uncovering the child's face – she reveals the revealing function to him. It is already a function raised to the second power.

It is here that the first identifications occur with what people call the mother as omnipotent.

As you can see, this has a very different scope than the pure and simple satisfaction of need.

Let us turn now to the second level of the graph, my presentation of which last time seems to have created a bit of difficulty for some of you.

44

2

At the second level of the graph, the subject is something other than a subject who passes through the defiles of signifying articulation. It is the subject who begins to speak – that is, the subject qua *I*.

I must, nevertheless, stop before providing a specific formulation in order to add an essential proviso. After all, I would not be dwelling on this *I*, for it is not our concern today, if I had not alluded, in previous work, to the *I* in "I am thinking, therefore I am." This is merely a parenthetical remark.

All the difficulties that have arisen regarding the *I* have concerned this "I am thinking, therefore I am." But this is said to be pointless, because the *I* was unjustifiably introduced into what is after all merely a *cogitatum* – that is, an "it [*ça*] is thinking." Why then would I be *I* in that?

I believe that all the difficulties that have been pointed out here stem from a failure to distinguish between two subjects in the way that I first formulated the distinction between them. In the experience that philosophy invites us to consider, people refer, more or less wrongly, to the fact that the subject is faced with an object, an

45

imaginary object, consequently; it should come as no surprise that
the *I* turns out to be but one object among others. If, on the contrary, we take up the question at the level of the subject defined as
speaking, it takes on a totally different import, as phenomenology
shows us and as I will simply indicate now. For those who would
like to read something about the *I* of the *cogito*, let me remind you
that there is an article I have already mentioned by Sartre in the
journal *Recherches philosophiques*.

The *I* involved in the *cogito* is not simply the *I* that is articulated in
discourse, the *I* insofar as it is pronounced in discourse, and that linguists have, at least for some time now, been calling a "shifter." The
I of the *cogito* is a semanteme whose only articulable use depends
on the code, I mean that it purely and simply depends on the lexi-
cally articulable code. On the other hand, the shifter *I*, as the most
basic experience shows, is related to nothing that can be defined as
a function of other elements of the code, thus to a semanteme, but
is simply defined as a function of the messaging act. It designates he
who underpins the message – namely, someone who varies from one
moment to the next.

That's all there is to it. But let us note that the upshot is that
the shifter *I* is essentially distinct from what one might call the
true subject of the act of speaking as such, as I will show you quite
quickly. It is even what gives the simplest *I* discourse the appearance
of indirect discourse. I mean that this *I* could rather easily be followed in discourse itself with a parenthesis: "I (who am speaking)"
or "I (am saying that . . .)."

This is made quite clear, as others before me have noted, by the
fact that a discourse that formulates "I am saying that . . .," and
adds, "and I am repeating," is not saying something devoid of value
with the second clause, for it is distinguishing between the two *I*'s
that are in question: "the one who said that . . .," and the one who
endorses what the latter said. If you need other examples to grasp
this, I would propose the difference between the *I* in "I love you"
and the one in "I am here."

Owing to the structure that I am evoking, the *I* in question is especially tangible where it is fully hidden, that is, in forms of discourse
that realize what I will call the vocative function – namely, the forms
whose signifying structure brings out the fact that the addressee is
absolutely not *I*. It is the *I* of "Rise and walk" [Luke 5:23].

This same fundamental *I* can be found in any imperative vocative
form and in a certain number of other forms, too, that I will provisionally place under the heading of vocative. It is, if you will, the vocative
I about which I spoke to you already in my Seminar on Schreber
[Seminar III]. I am not sure I was able to bring it out fully at that time.

There is also an *I* that underlies the sentence "You are the one who will follow me" [*Tu es celui qui me suivras*] which I emphasized in that Seminar. It is inscribed, with the whole problem of a certain future tense, in vocatives, strictly speaking, vocatives of vocation. For those who were not here at that time, let me recall the difference we find in French – it is a subtlety that not every language allows us to bring out – between *Tu es celui qui me suivras* and *Tu es celui qui me suivra* without an *s* [both mean "You are the one who will follow me"]. In this case, the difference in the performative power of the "you" is in fact an actual difference of the *I* insofar as it is involved in this act of speaking. We see clearly here that the subject always receives his own message in an inverted form – namely, that it is the *I* that must own itself here via the form it gives to the "you."

This discourse – in other words, the discourse that is formulated at the second level – is a discourse with which we have always been familiar. Every discourse is the Other's discourse, even when it is the subject who speaks it. In this regard, the distinction between the two levels is merely arbitrary.

Nevertheless, what we find at the second level is fundamentally a call for being [*un appel de l'être*], which is made with more or less force. It always more or less contains a "So be it!" ["*Soit!*"], and we have here yet another of the marvelous homophonic equivocations for which French allows. In other words, it contains a "*Fiat*" which is the source and root of what, in need, comes to be inscribed for speaking beings in the register of wanting [*vouloir*]. Or, stated otherwise, it is the root of the *I* insofar as the latter splits into the two terms that we are examining here: the one in the imperative "Rise and walk" and the other in the erection by the subject of his own *I*.

You can now see at what level the question that I articulated last time in the form "*Che vuoi?*" is situated. "*Che vuoi?*" is, as it were, the Other's response to the subject's act of speaking. This question responds – indeed, I would say that questions always respond. This response prior to the question responds to the question – that is, to the redoubtable question mark whose very form in my schema articulates the act of speaking. 47

The act of speaking goes much further than the speech of the subject alone, since his whole life is taken up in acts of speaking. His life as such – namely, all his actions – are symbolic actions if only because they are recorded, because they are subject to recording, and because they are often actions designed to be taken note of. Like everything that happens before the examining magistrate, everything the subject does can be held against him. All his actions are imposed upon him in a language context, and his very gestures are never anything but gestures chosen in a pre-established ritual, namely in a linguistic articulation. To the question, "Does he know what he is doing?" Freud answers "No." This is exactly what is expressed by the second level of my graph. The latter takes on its value only on the basis of the Other's question, "*Che vuoi?*": "What do you want?"

Prior to the moment at which the question is asked, we are mired in ignorance and stupidity. I am trying to show here that didacticism does not necessarily involve stupidity. I obviously cannot demonstrate this on the basis of those of you who are present here.

With regard to this question and in the responses given to it, the second level of the schema spells out where the following intersect anew: the true discourse offered up by the subject, on the one hand, and what is manifested in the guise of wanting [*vouloir*] in the articulation of speech, on the other hand. Where are these intersections located? Therein lies the whole mystery of the symbol that seems opaque to some of you.

The discourse that presents itself at this level as a call for being is not what it seems to be, as Freud tells us. This is what the second level of the graph tries to show us. I can only be surprised if you did not immediately recognize this.

What did Freud actually say? What do we, insofar as we are psychoanalysts, do every day? We bring out the fact that at the level of speech acts, the code is given, not by primitive demand, but by a certain relationship between the subject and this demand, insofar as the subject remains marked by manifestations [*avatars*] of this demand. We call these the oral, anal, and other forms of unconscious articulation.

The first point of intersection [($\lozenge$D)] thus does not seem to me to raise many objections. We take quite simply as a premise that the second level, the code of discourse, which is being's true discourse, corresponds to the formula ($\lozenge$D) – the subject, qua marked by the signifier, in the presence of his demand as providing the material [for it].

What can we say now regarding the message the subject receives?

I have alluded to this message several times; I have given it several forms, all of which are more or less slippery, and this is no accident, for the whole aim of analysis is to figure out what it is. For the time being, at this point in my discourse, I can still leave it in a problematic state and symbolize it with a presumed signifier. It is a purely hypothetical form, an x. It is one of the Other's signifiers, of course, since it is at the level of the Other that the question is raised; it is the signifier of an Other who is missing a part – namely, who is missing the problematic element in the question about this message.

Let me summarize. The subject's situation at the level of the unconscious, such as Freud articulates it – and it is not me but rather Freud who says this – is that he does not know with what he is speaking. We must thus reveal to him the properly signifying elements of his discourse. Nor does he know the message that really comes back to him at the level of being's discourse [*du discours de l'être*] – let us say "truly," if you prefer, but I will not take back "really."

In other words, the subject does not know the message that comes back to him from the response to his demand in the field of what he wants. But you already know the answer, the true response. There can only be one. Namely, the signifier, and nothing but it, that is especially designed to designate the relations between the subject and the signifier [or: signifying system as a whole, *le signifiant*]. This signifier is the phallus, and I have already told you why.

I ask those who are hearing this for the first time to accept it provisionally. This is not the point; the point is that the subject cannot have the answer [*réponse*], because the only answer is the signifier that designates his relations with the signifier. The subject annihilates himself and disappears to the degree that he articulates this answer. This is what makes it such that the only thing he can sense about it is a threat directly targeting the phallus – namely, castration, or the notion of the lack of the phallus, which is what the termination of analysis revolves around in both sexes, as Freud formulated it and as I am pointing out. But my goal is not to repeat such elementary truths.

I know that it gets on some people's nerves that I have been juggling being and having a little too much for a while, but they will get over it. For it does not mean that along the way we cannot harvest something precious, a clinical harvest – a harvest that can even allow people who follow my work to present themselves with all the characteristics of what I would call medical charlatanism.

What we must do now is situate what desire means.

As I have said, the second level of the graph, like the lower level, involves a synchronic treasure trove or battery of unconscious signifiers for each subject, and a message in which the response to "*Che vuoi?*" is announced. As you may have noticed, the latter is announced dangerously. I will mention this, too, in passing – just to evoke in you colorful memories of what makes the story of Abelard and Heloise the most beautiful love story.

What does desire mean? Where is it situated? In the complete form of the graph you have a dotted line that runs from the code, at the second level, to its message via two elements: *d*, which signifies the place where the subject descends [or: gets off or dismounts, *descend*], and $ across from little *a*, which signifies fantasy [see Figure 1.4].

This has a homologous layout to the line that, starting from A, includes the ego in discourse – the *m* on the schema, let us call it the "filled-out" person – and the image of the other, *i(a)*. Symbolization of the specular relationship [between *m* and *i(a)*] is, as I told you, fundamental to the establishing of the ego.

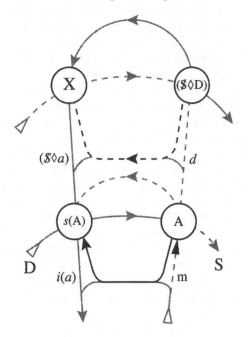

Figure 2.2: The homology between the two relationships

The homological relationship between the two levels warrants fuller discussion. I will not provide it today, not because I do not have time, for I am inclined to take my time to tell you what I have to tell you, but because I prefer to approach things in an indirect manner.

This is what seems to me to be most likely to get you to grasp its scope.

3

You undoubtedly can now guess at the riches that stem from the fact that an imaginary relationship is inscribed in the field of the determinant gap between the two discourses, an imaginary relationship that homologically reproduces the relationship with the other involved in the game of bearing [between *m* and *i(a)*].

You may have some inkling of it, but it is altogether insufficient   51
to have such an inkling. Before articulating it fully, I would simply
like to get you to dwell for a moment on what is implied by the term
that is situated or planted in this economy: "desire."

As you know, Freud introduced this term at the very beginning
of psychoanalysis. He introduced it regarding dreams in the form
of *Wunsch*. *Wunsch* is not, in and of itself, desire; it is a formulated
or articulated desire – in other words, it is rightfully laid out on this
line. What I would like you to ponder momentarily is the distinction
between *Wunsch* and what deserves to be called "desire" in what I
am introducing and establishing this year.

You have undoubtedly read *The Interpretation of Dreams* and we
are going to begin to talk about it now. Just as last year we began by
talking about *Jokes and their Relation to the Unconscious*, this year
we will begin by talking about dreams.

You must have noticed right from the outset, and all the way to
the end of *The Interpretation of Dreams*, that you do not find desire
in it in the form in which, I would say, you constantly deal with it in
your analytic experience – namely, in the form in which it gives you a
hard time owing to its excesses, deviations, and (why not say it after
all?) all-too-frequent failings. I am referring to sexual desire, the
desire that plays tricks. We should nevertheless note that, for some
time now, a quite remarkable placing of sexual desire in the shadows
has been occurring in the entire analytic field. You should thus note
the difference [between Freud's work and others']. Assuming that
you read *The Interpretation of Dreams* carefully, in other words, that
you do not continue to think about your own little problems while
your eyes scan its pages, you perceive that it is very difficult to grasp
the desire that we are supposed to find everywhere in every dream.

Recall the "inaugural dream," that of Irma's injection, about
which we have already spoken a number of times, about which I
have written a little and will write more, and about which we could
talk inordinately. What exactly does it mean? This remains very
unclear.

In the desire in the dream, Freud wants to make Irma give in; he
wants her to no longer, as he tells us, stubbornly reject his interpretations. What does he want? Does he want to undress her? Does he
want to get her to talk? Does he want to discredit his colleagues?   52
Does he want to force his own anxiety out of hiding to so great an
extent as to see it projected onto Irma's throat? Or does he want to
calm his anxiety regarding the harm he did to Irma? But this harm
is, it seems, irremediable, as is clearly articulated in the dream. Is
this what is at stake, to prove that no crime was committed? This
would not stop us from saying that, since no crime was committed,

everything will be fine, since everything has been repaired; and, moreover, all of this is due to the fact that certain people take incredible liberties, that someone else is responsible, and so on and so forth. We could go exceedingly far with all of that.

Let me point out, moreover, that Freud himself energetically underscores in a footnote in *The Interpretation of Dreams*, added in the seventh edition, that he never said that the desire at work in a dream is always a sexual desire. He did not say the opposite of that either, but in any case he did not say that; he writes this to respond to those who reproached him for it.

But let us not be fooled by this. Sexuality is always involved in dreams to some degree. But it is involved in some sense tangentially or in some roundabout way. We want to discover why, but to discover why I want to dwell for a moment on obvious things we know from the usage and employment of language.

What does it mean when a man says to someone – to a man or to a woman, we have to choose, for if it is a man, that will perhaps entail a number of contextual references – what does it mean when a man says to a woman, "I desire you"? Does it mean, as the moralizing optimism with which you see me doing battle from time to time in psychoanalytic theory would have it, "I am ready to grant your being as many, if not more rights than my own; I am willing to provide for all your needs and think about your satisfaction? Lord, thy will be done before my own"? It suffices to mention this to make you smile, as I see people doing around the room. Moreover, when one chooses the right words, no one is fooled by the aim of a term like this one [i.e., "desire"], as genital as that aim may be.

Another possible statement is the following; let us say, to use the crudest, most direct terms, "I want to sleep with you, I want to fuck you." It is much truer, we must admit. But is it as true as all that? It is true in a certain context, a social context, I would say. After all, given the extreme difficulty we have following through on the formulation "I desire you," we can perhaps find nothing better to prove it.

Believe me, it perhaps suffices that such speech not be linked to the incommensurable quandaries and dish-breaking brought on by statements that *have* a meaning, and that it be pronounced only *in petto* [in private] for us to immediately grasp that, if "I desire you" has a meaning, it is a meaning that is much more difficult to formulate. "I desire you," articulated in one's own mind, so to speak, concerning an object, has more or less the meaning "You are beautiful," around which all those enigmatic images, whose flow is known in my book as desire, collect and condense. In other words, "I desire you because you are the object of my desire." Stated differently, "You are the common denominator of my desires."

God only knows – if I can bring God into the picture, and why not? – what desire stirs up in one. It is something that in reality mobilizes and orients something quite different in one's personality than that toward which, conventionally speaking, one's precise goal seems to be oriented. To refer to an infinitely less poetic experience perhaps, but it seems that one need not be an analyst to mention it, we cannot misrecognize how quickly and front and center the structure of fantasy emerges in connection with the slightest distortion of the personality, as they say, or of images.

The subject's involvement in desire always brings out this structure, and it is rightfully predominant. To tell someone, "I desire you," is to tell him, "I include you in my fundamental fantasy." But experience does not always show us this, except in the case of those nice, instructive little perverts, little and big.

Since I have decided this year not to go beyond a certain time limit during which I ask you to listen to me here, and I still hope to hold myself to that, I will leave it there, at a point that falls far short of where I thought I would stop today, and put an end to your travails for the time being.

I will conclude by designating the key or decisive point in fantasy where desire must be interpreted, assuming the term "desire" has a different meaning than that of the wish in a dream.

This point is located here on the graph. You might say that it is part of the dotted circle that traces out a type of little tail at the second level. I would simply like to say, in order to whet your appetite a bit, that elements spin around this dotted circuit. It is constructed in this way because, once it is fueled [or: powered up, *alimenté*] by the beginning, it goes around inside indefinitely. What are these elements? They are the ones that have been repressed. In other words, it is the locus of the unconscious as such, as located on the graph. This and this alone is what Freud spoke about up until 1915, when he wrote two articles that are entitled "The Unconscious" and "Repression."

I will pick it up there the next time, to tell you to what extent Freud articulated the very substance of what I am trying to convey to you regarding the signifier. What Freud himself clearly and unambiguously formulated is that the only thing that can be repressed are signifying elements. This is found in Freud's work. The only thing missing there is the word "signifier." I will show you, by re-examining the article on the unconscious, that only signifiers can be repressed.

On the graph you see the two systems that are juxtaposed.

The dotted system, as I have said, is the locus of the unconscious, the one where the repressed goes around and around until it makes

54

itself felt – in other words, until some part of the message at the level of being's discourse [*discours de l'être*] upsets the message at the level of demand, which is the whole problem of psychoanalytic symptoms.

There is another dotted system. It is the one that paves the way for what I call the little landing – namely, the discovery of manifestations [*l'avatar*]. While we were already having so much trouble getting used to the first system [the first topography: conscious, preconscious, and unconscious], Freud made the fatal kind deed [*bienfait*] of taking the next step himself before his death by proffering the second topography [id, ego, and superego], which is the little landing I mentioned. He discovered the register of the other system.

In other words, Freud asked himself what happens at the level of the prediscursive subject as a function of the fact that the subject who speaks does not know what he is doing when he speaks – that is, as a function of the unconscious that Freud truly discovered. Let us say, if you will, to schematize things, that Freud sought to figure out at what level the ego is constituted with regard to the original place from which it speaks, and at what moment it is constituted with respect to an aim which is that of the endpoint of the process at I.

Freud also discovered a primitive discourse there, which is both purely imposed and marked by a fundamental arbitrariness, which continues to speak. It is the superego.

Nevertheless, he also left something undone. He left us something to discover and articulate, which completes his second topography and which allows us to resituate it in and restore it to the whole of his discovery. It is the fundamentally metaphorical function of language.

November 19, 1958

ON DESIRE IN DREAMS

THE DREAM ABOUT THE DEAD FATHER: "HE DID NOT KNOW HE WAS DEAD"

Taking being literally
From associationism to psychoanalysis
Affects and signifiers
Elision = metaphor
The instance of the half-dead

I will begin by keeping my promises.

Last time I mentioned an article by Sartre that is entitled "The Transcendence of the Ego: Outline of a Phenomenological Description." You can find it on pages 85–123 of volume 6 of the *Recherches philosophiques* [1936–37], an excellent journal that the war put an end to, as did the death of its publisher, Boivin. As for Freud's remark [also mentioned last time], it is found on page 397 [SE V] of his *Interpretation of Dreams*:

The assertion that all dreams require a sexual interpretation, against which critics rage so incessantly, occurs nowhere in my *Interpretation of Dreams*. It is not to be found in any of the numerous editions of this book and is in obvious contradiction to other views expressed in it.

Many of you attended the clinical paper presented last night on the topic of obsessives by one of our comrades, who is an excellent psychoanalyst. You heard him speak about desire and demand. We are trying to highlight the difference in structure between desire and demand here because the distinction between them is not simply theoretical, but is linked to the crux of our practice and applies directly to clinical work, bringing it alive and rendering it, I would say, understandable.

I would almost say that, if you sense that there is something inadequate here, it is a sign of the fact that we have explored this

distinction too exclusively at the level of understanding. The level of
understanding is far from exhausting the mainsprings of structure
that we are trying to penetrate, because it is on structure that we
are attempting to have an impact. The distinction between demand
and desire immediately clarifies demand. But it truly locates human
desire in its place – in other words, at its strictly enigmatic point.

The relationship between the subject and the signifier is key to
all of this. What characterizes demand is not simply that it is a
relationship between one subject and another subject; it is that this
relationship is constituted by language as an intermediary – that is,
by the signifier.

As promised, we will turn now to the topic of what desire is
insofar as it is the bedrock of dreams. It is not easy to know what
the desire that is the motor force of a dream is. At the very least you
realize that it is twofold.

First of all, it initially aims at safeguarding sleep – Freud articulates this in the most explicit of terms – that is to say, at safeguarding
the state in which reality is suspended for the subject. Secondly, it
[*désir*] is a death wish [*désir de mort*]. It is a death wish by way of
contrast [*d'autre part*], and at the same time it is a death wish in a
perfectly compatible way, inasmuch as it is often by means of this
second desire that the first is satisfied, the death wish being that by
which the wishing subject [*sujet de la* Wunsch] is satisfied.

I would like to place this subject in brackets of some sort. We do
not know what the subject is and yet we would like to know who the
wishing subject in the dream is. When certain people say that he is
the ego, they are mistaken – Freud assuredly asserts the opposite.
And if we say that he is the unconscious, we are not saying anything.
Thus when I say that the wishing subject is satisfied, I am bracketing
the subject. The only thing Freud tells us is that there is a wish that
is satisfied.

Satisfied by what? I would say that "it is satisfied by being." You
should understand this in the sense of "by [coming into] being, it is
satisfied." That is all we can say, for dreams do not bring with them
any other satisfaction than satisfaction at the level of wishes – in
other words, a verbal satisfaction, so to speak. The wish in a dream
makes do with appearances. The character of this satisfaction is
thus reflected in language, in this "satisfied by being" as I expressed
myself a moment ago, in which the ambiguity of the word "being"
shows through.

61   Being is there, it slips in everywhere, and it also takes on the grammatical form of referring to being, "satisfied being" [*l'être satisfait*].
Can this be broached from the perspective of substance? There is
nothing substantial in being other than the word itself, "it is satisfied

by being." We can only broach being by taking it literally. In the final analysis, wishes are satisfied by something like being. All in all, it is only in dreams, at least at the level of being, that wishes can be satisfied.

Here I would like to provide a short preamble, as I often do, and take a look back in order to open your eyes to something that comprises no less than the whole history of psychological speculation.

1

As you know, modern psychology began with formulations involving psychological atomism.

You are all aware that we are no longer at that point, that we have abandoned associationism, as it is called, and that we have made considerable progress since we began taking into consideration the demand for totality, the unity of the field, intentionality, and other forces.

Yet the question is hardly settled, precisely because of Freudian psychoanalysis. People fail to see how this settling of accounts, which is not really one, actually played out. I mean that people completely overlook the essence, and simultaneously the persistence, of what was supposedly eliminated.

It is true that associationism, which belongs to the tradition of the British psychological school, initially involves a thorough misunderstanding, as it were.

The problem is that of the field of the real and of our psychological apprehension of it. What we in fact need to explain is not only that there are men who think, but that there are men who move around in the world while apprehending the field of objects in a more or less suitable way. Now, where does this field of objects get its fragmented, structured character from? From the signifying chain, quite simply. Associationism does nothing, in fact, but immediately provide the field of the real with the fragmented and structured character of the signifying chain.

Once this is realized, people naturally perceive that something has gone awry. They tell themselves that there must originally, as it were, be relations with the real that are less structured by the signifying chain, without even realizing that it is the signifier that is at work. People thus go off in search of cases in which our apprehension of the world seems to be more primitive, on the basis of a proportionalist notion of things. They look to animal psychology, they mention all the visual ways in which animals manage to structure their world, and they make this into the foundation of human apprehension of

62

the real. They thereby challenge the well-known elements of associationism for being based on a first and false conception of this apprehension of the real, they proceed to eliminate those elements, and they bury the whole thing in a sort of field theory in which the real appears to be animated by the vector of a primordial desire.

They then imagine that they have solved the problem, whereas, in fact, they have done nothing at all. They have described something else, another psychology, one that seeks to grasp the degree to which the subject's sensorimotor field is coapted to its *Umwelt* – that is, to its surroundings. Nevertheless, the elements of associationism live on perfectly well despite the establishment of this new psychology. Associationism is not in the least eliminated; the field that is targeted by psychology has simply been displaced.

The proof of this is found in the psychoanalytic field where all the principles of associationism reign supreme. Nothing thus far has managed to gloss over the fact that when we analysts began exploring the field of the unconscious, we did so on the basis of something that in theory is called "free association," and we continue to do so every day. Even though the term is approximate and inexact, the aim of free association remains valid for designating analytic discourse.

Consider the earliest experiments with word association. Even if they no longer have any therapeutic or practical value to us, they still orient us in our exploration of the field of the unconscious. This alone suffices to show us that we operate in a field in which words or signifiers reign supreme.

What is associationism – and thus what comes after it related to the same experiential ground – based on? On the observation that elements, atoms, or ideas – as people say, no doubt approximately and insufficiently, but not for no reason – are coordinated at a certain level in a subject's mind. And what did the first experimental explorations of the phenomenon show? That it is conditioned by what people called relations of contiguity. Examine the texts to see what they talk about and what examples they are based on, and you will clearly see that this continuity is nothing but the discursive combination on which the effect that I call metonymy is based.

There is contiguity between two things that occur to us, inasmuch as they are evoked in memory at the level of the laws of association. A life event was experienced in a context that we can, overall, call a random context. One part of the event being evoked, the other part comes to mind. An association based on contiguity is thereby constituted, which is nothing other than an encounter. What does this mean? It means in short that the contiguity disintegrates [*elle se brise*], and that its elements are taken up in one and the same narrative text. If we speak here of contiguity, it is inasmuch as the event evoked in memory is a narrated event, inasmuch as a narrative forms the text thereof.

There is, by way of contrast, the kind of contiguity that we see in an experiment involving word association, for example. One word brings another with it. I [the experimenter] say the word "cherry" and the subject mentions the word "table." It is a relationship based on contiguity because on such and such a day there were cherries on the table.

A relationship based on similarity is different from a relationship based on contiguity, but it is also a relationship between signifiers inasmuch as similarity involves the passage from one term [to another] owing to a similarity of being. There is a similarity between them insofar as, the one and the other being different, some existing subject [or: extant subject, *sujet d'être*] makes them similar. I am not going to enter into the entire dialectic of the same and the other, with everything that it brings with it that is difficult and infinitely richer than a first glance allows us to suspect. Those who are interested in it can read Plato's *Parmenides*. They will see that they can spend quite a lot of time on it before exhausting the topic.

64

What I am simply saying here, and what I am trying to get you to sense, is that there are other usages than metonymic usages. If I speak of lips as being like cherries, I make a metaphorical use of the word "cherry." Someone says the word "lip" and it brings to my mind the word "cherry" – why are they linked? Because they are both red? Because they both have the same shape, analogically? Because they are similar owing to some attribute? No, not just that. Regardless of what is involved, we are immediately, and this is palpable, faced with an altogether substantial effect that is known as a metaphorical effect. When I speak of cherries with regard to lips in a word-association experiment, there is no ambiguity whatsoever – we are at the level of metaphor in the most substantial sense of the term. And at the most formal level, a metaphorical effect always comes down to an effect of substitution [of one term for another] in the signifying chain, as I have shown you.

If cherries come to mind here, it is inasmuch as they can be inscribed in a context, whether structural or not, in which lips figure. To which you could object that cherries might come to mind in relation to lips owing to the function of contiguity, it being possible that cherries disappear between the lips, or that a woman presented me with cherries while holding them with her lips. This is of course possible. It can happen. But what sort of contiguity is involved, if not the contiguity of the narrative I mentioned earlier?

From the vantage point of the real, we must not allow ourselves to be deluded by the event in which this contiguity was integrated, which was such that a cherry was in fact momentarily in contact with the lips. What is important here is not that a cherry touch the lips but that it be swallowed. It is not that it be held with the lips, it is that it be offered to us via an erotic gesture. If we stop the cherry for an instant while it is in contact with the lips, it is as a function of a snapshot [flash*] that is provided by the narrative. What momentarily suspends the cherry between the lips is a sentence and words.

Inversely, it is because the dimension of narrative that can freeze the frame [flash*] exists that the image created by the suspension of the narrative in effect becomes, in this case, something that stimulates desire. It is the involvement of language in the act that sets the tone here. It is after the fact that language introduces into the act a stimulation or stimulating element that is related to the stopping of the narrative. This suspension, which at times comes to fuel the act itself, takes on the value of fantasy, which gives a specific meander [détour] of the act an erotic signification.

This, I believe, suffices to show you that the instance of the signifier is at the crux of the very structuring of a certain psychological field. It is not the totality of the field. It is a part of it, assuming that we conventionally call "psychology" a discipline constituted on the basis of what I will call an intentional or appetitive unitary theory. The fact remains that the presence of the signifier, as Freud never ceases to remind us, is articulated in an infinitely more insistent, powerful, and effective way in analytic experience.

We have an odd tendency to forget this. People would like psychoanalysis to go in the same direction as psychology did. They accept the unconscious only in the realm of a clinical force field. In this perspective, psychoanalysis is a type of well or drilling path, as it were, that runs parallel to the general development of psychology, which has supposedly given us access to elemental forces, to a field of depths reduced to the life functions, whereas what we see at the surface is thought to be the field of the conscious and the preconscious.

This is a mistake.

And it is precisely in this context that what we say takes on its value.

2

Did some of you follow my advice and reread the two articles by Freud that came out in 1915?

If you consult, for example, his article on the unconscious

[*Unbewusste*], the part that is most relevant to our topic, you will observe that what is at work [in the unconscious] is nothing other than signifying elements. When I speak here about the signifier, those who understand absolutely nothing unremittingly repeat that I am espousing an intellectualist theory, to which they naturally oppose affective life and dynamics. I am far from contesting the existence of the latter, since it is precisely in order to explain them clearly that I am mentioning Freud's article on the *Unbewusste*. We will thus turn to a consideration of unconscious feelings, inasmuch as Freud mentions them.

66

In the third part of his article, Freud explains very clearly that the only thing that can, strictly speaking, be repressed is what he calls the *Vorstellungsrepräsentanz*. The German here means "representative of the representation." Of what? Of drive impulses, which he calls *Triebregungen* here, which we can even refer to more exactly as the units [*unité*] of drive motion.

Freud's text leaves absolutely no ambiguity on this score: we cannot consider the *Triebregungen* to be unconscious, nor can we consider them to be conscious. What does this mean? It means that what we call *Triebregung* must be taken as an objective concept. It is an objective unit because we look at it and it is neither conscious nor unconscious; it simply is what it is – namely, an isolated fragment of reality that we conceptualize as having its own active impact.

It is thus, in my view, all the more remarkable that what represents the *Triebregung* – namely, the "representative of (the) representation," this is the exact value of the German term, and it is the sole representative of the drive (*Trieb*) – is said by Freud to belong to the unconscious. Now, the latter implies the exact term that I wrote on the board earlier with a question mark next to it – namely, an unconscious subject.

You, of course, can already see *not* where I am heading with this, but where we will necessarily wind up. Whereas Freud, at his time, was at the stage at which things could be said in the form of scientific discourse, you must clearly sense that this *Vorstellungsrepräsentanz* is strictly equivalent to the notion of the signifier, to the term "signifier."

I am merely announcing this to you, even if its demonstration strikes me as already quite advanced; if not, what was the point of everything I said to you earlier today? I will, naturally, demonstrate it to you more thoroughly, ever more thoroughly. The signifier is precisely what is at work here.

Freud, on the other hand, articulates in the most unmistakable way that none of what we connote with the terms sensation, feeling, and affect, which he lumps together, can be called unconscious

except when we express ourselves sloppily. Depending on the
67 context, such sloppiness, like all sloppiness, may or may not have
disadvantages; but when it comes to theory he categorically denies
such things any and all possibility of unconscious impact. This is
expressed and repeated by Freud in a manner that can leave no
doubt or ambiguity.

When we talk [sloppily] about an affect as being unconscious,
we are implying that the affect is perceived but misrecognized.
Misrecognized in what regard? In what it is connected with, but that
does not make it unconscious, for it has nevertheless been perceived.
It has simply, as Freud tells us, become connected to a different
representation, one that is not repressed. Stated otherwise, the affect
had to adapt to the context found in the preconscious; this allows
the affect to be taken by consciousness – which in this case is not
very exacting – to be a manifestation of this preconscious context.
This is articulated by Freud, and not just once, but a hundred times;
he reiterated it when discussing all kinds of different topics.

It is precisely here that we come upon the enigma of what is
known as the transformation of affect; affect turns out to be incredibly plastic. Moreover, all psychoanalytic writers are struck by this
as soon as they take up the topic of affect – in other words, every
time their eyes alight on it, I mean insofar as they dare broach the
topic. For, what is altogether striking is that someone like me, who
apparently is developing an intellectualist form of psychoanalysis,
is going to spend a whole year talking about it, whereas you can
count on the fingers of one hand the small number of articles that
have been devoted to the topic of affect in psychoanalysis – even
though analysts talk about it constantly when they present a case,
for naturally they always resort to affect.

To the best of my knowledge, there is but one worthwhile article
on the topic of affect, an article by Glover, which is often mentioned in texts by Marjorie Brierley. Glover endeavors to take a
step forward regarding the discovery of the notion of affect, Freud's
discussions of the topic leaving a little something to be desired.
Glover's article is, moreover, appalling, as is the whole of Brierley's
book, which is devoted to what she calls *Trends in Psycho-Analysis*.
It is a rather fine illustration of all the truly absurd places in which
psychoanalysis is currently sticking its nose – morality, personol-
ogy, and other eminently practical perspectives around which our
era's blah blah blah loves to spin its wheels.

68 To return to the things that concern us, namely to serious things,
what do we read in Freud's work? We read that, as regards affect,
the problem is to figure out what becomes of it when it is disconnected from the repressed representation and no longer depends on

anything but the substitute representation to which it has managed to get connected. A possibility that is characteristic of it – that of being annexed by another representation – corresponds to this being "disconnected"; it is in this respect that affect presents itself in analytic experience as something problematic.

We see this, for example, in the hysteric's lived experience. Psychoanalysis began with this and this is where Freud set out from when he began to formulate analytic truths. We see affects arising in the ordinary, comprehensible, communicable text of hysterics' everyday lives, and the affects that are there – and that appear to be integrated into the whole text of their lives except to those with a more exacting gaze – are nevertheless the transformation of something else.

This something else is worth dwelling on, for it is not another affect which would supposedly be in the unconscious. Freud rules that out absolutely. It is absolutely nothing of the kind. There is absolutely nothing which is really in the unconscious at that moment. What is transformed is the purely quantitative factor of the drive. The "something else" is the quantitative factor in a transformed guise.

The point then is to figure out how such transformations are possible – namely, for example, how an affect which is in the depths, an affect about which we might conclude that it corresponds to such and such in the unconscious text, can present itself in another guise in the preconscious context.

What does Freud tell us? A first citation: "The whole difference arises from the fact that ideas [*Vorstellungen*] are cathexes – basically of memory-traces – whilst affects and emotions correspond to processes of discharge, the final manifestations of which are perceived as feelings" [SE XIV, p. 178]. This is the rule of affect formation.

As I told you, affect refers to a quantitative factor. By that Freud means that it is not simply changeable and mobile, but that it is subjected to the variable constituted by this factor. He articulates this precisely by saying that the vicissitude of an affect may be threefold: "Either the affect remains, wholly or in part, as it is; or it is transformed into a qualitatively different quota of affect, above all into anxiety" – this is what he writes in 1915, and we see here the outlines of the position he articulates in 1926 in *Inhibitions, Symptoms, and Anxiety* in the context of the second topography – "or it is suppressed, i.e., it is prevented from developing at all" [SE XIV, p. 178].

"In comparison with unconscious ideas," Freud writes, "there is the important difference that unconscious ideas continue to exist after repression as actual structures in the system *Ucs.*, whereas all

69

that corresponds in that system to unconscious affects is a potential beginning which is prevented from developing" [SE XIV, p. 178].

I could not avoid providing this preamble before beginning to raise questions here about the interpretation of the desire in dreams.

I announced that I would borrow for this purpose a dream taken from Freud's work, since he is, after all, the best guide for us if we want to be sure of what he means when he talks about the desire in a dream.

3

I will borrow a dream from the article entitled "Formulations on the Two Principles of Mental Functioning," published in 1911 just before the case of Schreber.

I have chosen to extract a dream and Freud's analysis of it from this particular text because in it Freud articulates in a simple, exemplary, significant, and unambiguous way how he intends to handle *Vorstellungsrepräsentanzen*, inasmuch as in this article the formulation of unconscious desire is examined.

The upshot of the whole of Freud's work as regards the relations between the *Vorstellungsrepräsentanzen* and the primary process – insofar as they are under the sway of the first principle, known as the pleasure principle – leaves no room for doubt. There is no other way to conceptualize the opposition between the pleasure principle and the reality principle if it is not to realize that what we are told about the emergence of hallucinations by which the primary process – that is, desire at the level of the primary process – finds its satisfaction concerns not simply an image but a signifier.

70   It is, moreover, surprising that people did not discover this in other realms, I mean on the basis of clinical work. If people never realized this in other realms, it is because the notion of the signifier had not yet been developed at the moment of the great blossoming of classical psychiatry. For in what form do hallucinations usually present themselves in the lion's share of clinical experience? What are the major forms that are the most problematic and insistent in which hallucinations arise for us? They are those of verbal hallucinations, or verbally structured hallucinations, when there is an intrusion or inmixing into the field of reality, not of an image or fantasy, not of something that a simple perceptual process would prop up, but a signifier. If a hallucination poses its own specific problems to us, it is because it involves signifiers, not images, things, or perceptions, not those "false perceptions of reality," as people put it. In Freud's work, this is unmistakable.

At the end of the article, Freud mentions a dream to illustrate what he calls a *neurotische Währung*, a "neurotic currency" [*valorisation*, which also means "valuation"], insofar as the primary process irrupts into it. *Währung* is a term we should keep in mind, as it is not very common in German. It is related to the verb *währen* [to last], which is a durative form of the verb *wahren* [to look after, keep, safeguard, or protect]. While it means duration, it is most commonly used in the sense of value or valuation.

The dream in question was dreamt by a subject who was mourning the loss of his father whom he had, Freud tells us, nursed throughout the long painful illness that led to his death. Here is the dream:

His father was alive once more and was talking with him in his usual way. But he felt it exceedingly painful that his father had really died, only without knowing it. [SE XII, p. 225]

It is a short dream. And it is one that the patient had repeatedly in the months following his father's passing. It is a dream that, as always, Freud brings us in the form of a transcript, for what is essential in Freudian analysis is always based on the narrative of the dream as it is initially articulated. How does Freud broach it?

It is out of the question, of course – if only because of the distinction Freud always made between the manifest content and the latent content – that Freud ever thought a dream could be immediately brought into connection with what, in psychoanalysis, people have no compunction about calling "wishful thinking,"* a term that has no equivalent in French. By pronouncing it, I would almost like to force it to make a sound like that of an alarm bell. The use of such a term should, all by itself, put analysts on their guard or even on the defensive, and persuade them that they have set off down the wrong path.

Freud does not even for an instant entertain this "wishful thinking." He does not say that, if the subject dreams about his father it is simply because he needs to see him and that to see him gives him pleasure. That is not at all sufficient, for the simple reason that this dream does not seem to bring any satisfaction whatsoever with it. Its painful character is quite clearly indicated, and this should allow us to avoid jumping to such inane conclusions. Nevertheless, if I am bringing this up here, it is in order to indicate the possibility of doing so, even though in the end I do not believe that any analyst could go that far when it comes to a dream. And it is precisely because we cannot go that far when it comes to dreams that psychoanalysts are no longer interested in dreams.

71

How does Freud broach things? We will stick to the level of his text:

> The only way of understanding this apparently nonsensical dream is by adding "as the dreamer wished" or "in consequence of his wish" after the words "that his father had really died," and by further adding "that he [the dreamer] wished it" to the last words. The dream-thought then runs: it was a painful memory for him that he had been obliged to wish for his father's death (as a release) while [his father] was still alive, and how terrible it would have been if his father had had any suspicion of it! [SE XII, p. 225]

This leads us to give its full weight to the way in which Freud approaches the dream: via the signifier. What Freud inserts into the text, and what he lays out for us as allowing us to understand the dream, as delivering up the meaning of the text, are clausulae. I will try to articulate what they are at the linguistic level.

Please pay attention to what I am saying here. I am not saying that this is the interpretation. It may in fact be the interpretation, but I am not yet saying so. I am freezing the frame here at a moment at which a certain signifier is designated as being produced by the fact that it is missing. It is by resituating it in the context of the dream that we can immediately accede to what we are given to understand to be the meaning of the dream.

We find ourselves faced with a typical case here, a case in which one's self-reproach concerning a loved one leads back to the infantile signification of a death wish. The term transference, *Übertragung*, is used here by Freud in the way he first used it in *The Interpretation of Dreams* to designate the carryover of an early situation – of an early death wish, in this instance – into a current situation. A wish that is analogical, homologous, parallel, or in any way similar is introduced in order to revive the archaic wish in question.

Freud thus approaches the problem via the signifier. It is on that basis that we can try to elaborate what interpretation means. But let us begin by settling a score with the type of interpretation we set aside, which refers to "wishful thinking."* One remark will suffice here.

This English term cannot be translated by *pensée désireuse* or *pensée désirante* for a very simple reason. It has a meaning, of course, but people use it in analysis in a context in which that meaning is not valid. Whenever you encounter the term, in order to put the pertinence of its usage to the test, you need but make the following distinction. It must not signify "take one's desires for realities," as people say nowadays [in French] – that is the meaning

72

of thought insofar as it slip slides and gives way – but rather "take one's dream for reality." This in and of itself makes it altogether inapplicable to the interpretation of dreams, to this type of comprehension of dreams. In the case of dreams, it simply means that we dream because we dream. An interpretation at this level is in no wise applicable at any moment to dreams.

We must thus turn to the procedure known as the addition of signifiers.

If we follow Freud here, this procedure assumes that there had been a prior subtraction of a signifier – "subtraction" is the exact meaning of the term that Freud uses to designate the operation of repression in its pure form, in its *unterdrückt* effect, I would say. It is here that we find ourselves brought up short by something that appears to be an objection and an obstacle.

If we had not decided in advance to find everything in Freud's work wonderful – in other words, if we had not decided in advance to believe we believe, as Prévert puts it – we would stop to consider the following: that the pure and simple restoring of the two clausulae, "*nach seinem Wunsch*" and "*daß er [der Träumer] es wünschte*" – that is, that the son wished for his father's death – provides nothing, strictly speaking, as regards what Freud himself designates as the final goal of interpretation, namely, the reconstruction of the unconscious desire in the dream.

What are we actually formulating with these additions? Nothing but what the subject already knew perfectly well. During his father's extremely painful illness, the subject indeed wished for his father's death as a solution and end to his torments. Naturally, he did everything possible to hide this desire or wish from his father, but it was totally accessible to the son in this context, in his recent life experience. We need not even speak about it being preconscious in this regard – it was a conscious memory that was part and parcel of the continuous text of his consciousness.

It is thus the dream that subtracts from its text an element that is not at all hidden from the subject's conscious mind. And it is thus the phenomenon of subtraction that takes on a positive value here, as it were. I mean that this is the problem of repression. What is repressed here is indubitably a *Vorstellungsrepräsentanz*, one that is even quite typical.

If something deserves to be termed a *Vorstellungsrepräsentanz*, it is certainly something that is, in and of itself, I would say, a form that is devoid of meaning. Taken all by itself, isolated [from its context], "as he wished" means nothing. It means "in consequence of the wish mentioned earlier." The meaning depends on the sentence that came before it.

This is the direction in which I would like to lead you in order to get you to grasp the irreducible character of what is at stake in any and every conception based on an imaginary elaboration – or even on an abstraction of object-like data – whereas what is actually involved is the signifier and the originality of the field that is established by the signifier's action in the psyche, lived experience, and the human subject. What we have here are signifying forms that hang together only insofar as they are linked with other signifiers.

74 I am well aware that I am raising points here that would require far more discussion.

Psychologists from what is known as the Marburg School, which involved a small group of people working in a closed circle, conducted all sorts of experiments, with a great deal of perseverance, regarding a kind of intuition that they called thought without images. The point was, without using images, to think up kinds of forms that were nothing but signifying forms without any context, *in statu nascendi*. Moreover, the problems that are raised here for us by the notion of *Vorstellung* warrant that we recall that Freud attended the course given by Brentano for two years, we having unambiguous evidence thereof. It would be necessary to examine Brentano's *Psychologie* and his conception of *Vorstellung* in order to grasp the exact weight this term could have had in Freud's mind and not simply in my interpretation.

What is the problem we encounter? It is that of the relationship that exists between repression, on the one hand, insofar as it applies, as Freud tells us, to something like *Vorstellungen*, and the appearance, on the other hand, of a new meaning owing to something which, to our way of thinking, at the point where we are making headway, is different from repression – namely, the elision of the two clausulae in the context of the preconscious. Is this elision the same thing as repression? Is it the precise counterpart or contrary of repression?

We must first explain this elision at the most formal level. What effect does it have? It is clear that it has a meaning effect. I am saying "elision" and not "allusion," for it is not a "figuration," to use everyday language. Far from alluding to something that preceded it – namely, the relations between the father and the son – the dream introduces something that sounds absurd and has an entirely original range of signification at the manifest level. What is involved is a *figura verborum*, a figure of words [or trope], to employ a term that is a counterpart to the first one. The elision creates a signified effect. In this regard it is equivalent to the substitution of a blank or zero for the missing terms – but a zero is not nothing. In short, the effect involved can be qualified as a metaphorical effect.

The dream is a metaphor. In this metaphor, something new emerges that is a meaning or signified. The latter is undoubtedly enigmatic, but it is certainly not something that we have no need to take into account. It is, I would say, one of the most essential forms of human experience, since it is this very image which, for centuries, forced people, at one moment or another of mourning in the course of their existence, onto the most hidden of pathways that led them to consult necromancers.

What necromancers summoned up in the magic circle were what are called shades [or spirits, *ombres*], and what took place was no different than what takes place in this dream. A shade is a being who is there without us knowing how he exists, and before whom one can literally say nothing. This being speaks, of course, but that is not important, for, up to a certain point, what he says is also what he does not say, and the dream does not even tell us what it is. His speech only takes on its value owing to the fact that the person who summoned this loved one from the nether regions can literally say nothing to him regarding his innermost truth.

This confrontation, structured scene, or scenario invites us to wonder what it is. What is its import? Does it have the fundamental, structured, and structuring value of what I am trying to lay out for you this year by the name of fantasy? Is it a fantasy? Are there a certain number of characteristics that can be required in order for us to recognize the characteristics of fantasy in such a scenario?

Unfortunately, we cannot begin to answer these questions until next time. But rest assured that we will answer them very precisely. Our answers will allow us to glimpse the way in which it is in fact a fantasy and in what regard it is a dream fantasy [*un fantasme de rêve*].

Let me make a first point right away. In the precise sense that we can give the word "fantasy," a dream fantasy takes very specific forms, and it does not have the same import as that of a waking fantasy, whether it be unconscious or not. We will see in this regard how we must conceptualize the function of fantasy.

A second point: we will see on this basis where what Freud called the mechanisms of the dream-work [*élaboration*] are situated – namely, in the relationship between the repressed, which is assumed to be prior, and the signifiers about which I showed you to what degree Freud pinpoints them and how he articulates the impact of their absence in terms of pure signifying relations, by which I mean relations that exist between signifiers.

We will try to situate the signifiers of the narrative – first, "he is dead," second, "he did not know it," and third, "as the dreamer wished" [see SE V, pp. 430–1] – and put them to work along the trajectories of the chains that I call the "chain of the subject" and the "signifying chain," respectively, such as they are posited, repeated, and insistently presented to you in the form of our graph of desire.

You will see what this graph can do for us, and that there is no possible functioning of discourse except on the basis of structures in which the topological position of elements and of their relations are inscribed. You will also see that the notion of these structures alone allows us to give meaning to the analysis of this dream. In other words, up to a certain point, we can say that the two clausulae in question are truly the content of the repressed – namely, the *Real verdrängt*, as Freud puts it, what is really repressed.

But that is not enough. We must also distinguish how and why the dream uses these elements. They are undoubtedly repressed, but at the level of the dream they are not repressed. Whereas the earlier immediately lived experience brought them into play as such, in the dream, far from being repressed, they are elided as clausulae. Why? In order to produce what sort of effect? It is not easy to say. In short, it is a signification that is produced, there is no doubt about that; but we will shall see that the elision of the same wish can have effects that are altogether different in different structures.

To pique and stimulate your curiosity a bit, I would simply like to observe that there is perhaps a relationship between the elision of the clausula "as he wished," and what we see in other contexts, which are not dream contexts – in psychosis, for example, where we sometimes observe a misrecognition of death, misrecognition by the subject of his own death. At the formal level, it suffices that the words "he did not know it" or "he wanted to know nothing about it" be linked otherwise with "he is dead" for the one to lead to the other, unless we immediately distinguish the clinical con-texts, as *Verwerfung* [foreclosure] is distinguished from *Verneinung* [negation].

77 In psychosis this articulation can lead to feelings of being invaded or penetrated, or to fertile moments in which the subject thinks that he in fact has across from him something far closer still to a dream image than we might expect – namely, someone who is dead. The subject lives with a dead man, but a dead man who quite simply does not know that he is dead.

Perhaps we can go so far as to recognize a similar phenomenon in normal life, the kind we experience every day. Perhaps it happens to us more often than we think to have in our presence someone who appears to behave satisfactorily, socially speaking, but who – in terms of his being of interest to us, in terms of what allows us to get along with a human being – is truly dead, and has been for some time, dead and mummified, who is just waiting for the pendulum to swing – for I know not what, for [the last straw that reveals he is mere] semblance – to be reduced to the sort of dust that must spell his demise. I know more than one of them. Now that I have brought this to your attention, look around among those you know.

Being half-dead is perhaps far more prevalent than we think in relations between subjects. Isn't it true that the part of every living being that is half-dead does not leave us a perfectly clear conscience? Perhaps a large part of our behavior with our fellow men sets off in us an incidental reaction that is always present and essential, which is denoted by the precautions we must take in order not to comment to the half-dead that where he is, where he is in the process of talking to us, he is half-prey to death.

Perhaps this is something that we must take into account, whose importance we must weigh, when we take it upon ourselves to listen to the speech, revelations, and free discourse of people undergoing analysis. Undertaking something so audacious with analysands cannot fail to have an impact upon ourselves, which is precisely what we defend against most strongly. [We defend against] what there is in us that is most fictitious and most repeated – namely, what is half-dead in us, too.

At the point at which we have arrived at the end of today's class, I have raised more questions than I have answered.

If this dream teaches us something about the relations between the subject and desire, it is because it has a value that should not surprise us given its protagonists – namely, a father, a son, death incarnate, and, as you will see, a relationship to desire.

It is thus no accident that I chose this example and that we will have to explore it further next time.

November 26, 1958

IV

LITTLE ANNA'S DREAM

Hallucination, between pleasure and reality
The topology of signifiers
The palimpsest of repressions
The *I* of the statement and the *I* of enunciation
Repression, from the unsaid to not-knowing

I left you last time in the midst of discussing a dream, a dream that at least superficially seems simple. I announced that, with regard to this dream, we would strive to articulate the strict meaning we give here to the following terms: the desire in the dream and interpretation. We will return to those. I also think that this dream is quite valuable, theoretically speaking.

I have once again been rereading *The Interpretation of Dreams*, having told you that this was the first text we would be examining this year on desire and its interpretation.

I must admit that, up until a certain point, I allowed myself to reproach people in the analytic community for being unfamiliar with its twists and turns – which is indisputable – yet my reproach, like every reproach, has another facet, which is that of an excuse. For in fact, it does not suffice to have read this book hundreds of times in order to remember its contents. This is a phenomenon that we encounter quite often, but that has been brought home to me especially clearly the last few days. Everyone knows how easily we forget everything that has to do with the unconscious.

For example, it is quite obvious to what degree people forget funny stories and stories that are considered to be witty. This highly significant fact cannot be explained even one iota outside of a Freudian perspective. Let us say that you are meeting with some friends. Someone makes a joke, not even recounting a funny story, but making a pun at the beginning of the get-together or at the end of the lunch, and by the time the coffee comes at the end of the meal you ask yourself, "What was that incredibly funny thing the person sitting to my right said earlier?" And you cannot for the life of you recall it. This is an almost sure sign of the fact that witticisms arise from the unconscious.

When we read or reread *The Interpretation of Dreams*, we have the impression that it is what I would call a magical book, if the word did not lend itself, in our vocabulary, to so much ambiguity and even error, which is quite unfortunate. We stroll through *The Interpretation of Dreams* as if we were truly in the book of the unconscious, which is why we have so much trouble holding onto what is so well articulated in it. We have here a phenomenon that is worth noting.

To that we have to add the almost insane distortion introduced by the French translation. The more closely I examine it, the more I find truly inexcusable the crude inaccuracies it contains. Some of you ask me for explanations and I immediately refer back to the text. There is, for example, in Chapter VI, devoted to the dreamwork, a section entitled "Considerations of Representability," the first page of which in the French translation is more than just a web of inaccuracies – it has nothing whatsoever to do with the German text, and it confuses everything and puzzles us. I will not develop this point any further, but obviously none of this makes it especially easy for readers of the French to get a handle on *The Interpretation of Dreams*.

We began to decipher the dream we took up last time in a way that may not have seemed very straightforward to you, but which was nevertheless intelligible, at least I hope it was. To clearly see what is at stake, we will articulate it using the graph of desire.

If a dream interests us, it is in the sense in which it interests Freud – that is, in the sense in which it fulfills [*réalisation*] desire. Desire is at work in the dream here insofar as the dream is its fulfillment. How are we going to be able to articulate it? I will first bring up another dream, one I already mentioned before [see Seminar V, Chapter XII], and whose exemplary value you will see. It is not terribly well known – one has to go looking for it.

At the beginning of Chapter 3, whose title is "A Dream Is the Fulfillment of a Wish," we find dreams whose existence I am sure none of you are unaware of, children's dreams, and they are presented to us by Freud as what I will call an early stage of desire in dreams.

The dream I will discuss was already included in the first edition of the *Traumdeutung* [*The Interpretation of Dreams*]. Freud mentions it at the moment at which he begins to spell out the nature of dreams for his contemporaries. The fact that the *Traumdeutung* takes the

81

form of an expository text explains many things to us, especially
the fact that things are brought out first in a sweeping sort of way,
giving us a first approximation of things, only to be unpacked later.
When we do not look very closely at this passage, we content
ourselves with what Freud says about the direct, undistorted (that
is, without *Entstellung*, distortion) character of children's dreams,
whereas dreams usually appear to us in a profoundly modified guise
as regards their deepest thought content. In children, it is all supposedly quite simple – desire purportedly goes straight, and as directly
as possible, to what the subject desires. Freud gives us several examples of this. The first is worth recalling, because it truly illustrates his
point. Here it is:

> My youngest daughter [Anna Freud] who was at that time
> nineteen months old, had a fit of vomiting one fine morning
> and was forced to fast. During the night that followed this day
> of fasting, we heard her call out in her dream *"Anna F.eud,*
> *Er(d)beer, Hochbeer, Eier(s)peis, Papp!"*

Er(d)beer is a child's way of pronouncing strawberries, *Hochbeer*
also means strawberries, *Eier(s)peis* corresponds more or less to
the word "custard," and *Papp* means porridge. Freud tells us the
following:

> She thus used her name to express taking possession, and the
> enumeration of all the prestigious dishes, or those that seemed
> to her such, [to express] food worth desiring.

The appearance of strawberries in the dream (in the form of two
varieties, *Erdbeer* and *Hochbeer* – I did not manage to precisely
pin down *Hochbeer*, but Freud's commentary suggests that they
correspond to two varieties of strawberries) was a demonstration
or protest against the health police in the house, and was rooted
in the circumstance clearly registered by Anna that the day before
the nurse had attributed her illness to having eaten too many
strawberries. Because of the nurse's unwanted and annoying recom-
mendation, Anna immediately took revenge on her in her dream.
Leaving aside the dream that Freud's nephew Hermann had,
which raises other problems, I would point to a passage that is not
found in the first edition, because it was added later after discussions
of the Viennese school, the minutes of which we have. Ferenczi corroborated Freud's views by reminding people of the proverb, "Pigs
dream of acorns and geese dream of corn." Freud then brought up
the proverb, "What do geese dream of? Maize," that he undoubtedly

did not borrow so much from the German context, I think, given the specific form of the last word. Lastly, there was the Jewish proverb, "What do chickens dream of? They dream of millet."

Let us dwell upon this for a moment.

I will begin with a brief tangential remark.

1

Regarding Granoff's paper last night, I mentioned an essential problem, which is that of the difference between the directive of pleasure and that of desire.

Let us return for a moment to the directive of pleasure and let me spell it out once and for all as quickly as possible.

It is obviously related to questions people ask me or that arise about the function I attribute to *Vorstellung* in what Freud calls the primary process.

To put it concisely, as this is but a parenthetical remark, when we investigate the function of *Vorstellungen* in the pleasure principle we realize that Freud gives it short shrift. To put it in a nutshell, we could say that he needs an element with which to construct what he perceives intuitively and that he finds this element in *Vorstellungen*.

It is characteristic of brilliant intuition to come up with something that had absolutely never been perceived hitherto. This is the conception of the primary process as distinct and separate from the secondary process. We do not perceive how original this is; we think that what Freud is saying is comparable to what we thought before, whereas it is utterly and completely different. The composition or synthesis of these two principles is highly original.

The primary process signifies the presence of desire, but not of just any old desire. It signifies the presence of the desire that presents itself as the most fragmented. As for the perceptual element, it is what Freud uses to explain and get us to grasp what is at stake.

When the primary process alone is active, what happens? It leads to hallucination. Recall the first schemas Freud gives us on this score. Hallucination is produced by a process of regression that he calls "topographical." The different schemas Freud drew of what motivates and structures the primary process all have in common the fact that they are grounded in the trajectory of the reflex arc, with its two pathways – the afferent pathway, the afference of something known as sensory "stimuli," and the efferent pathway, the efference of something that is known as "motor activity" [SE V, p. 537].

In this perspective perception is conceptualized, in a way I would call terribly debatable, as something that accumulates somewhere on the side of the senses owing to a flood of excitations and stimuli from the outside world, and it is situated at the origin of action. All kinds of other things are assumed to happen afterward. Namely, it is here that Freud inserts a whole series of superimposed layers that run from the unconscious to the preconscious and so on, to arrive at something that may or may not lead to motor activity.

Whenever Freud speaks to us about what happens in the primary process, look closely at what is involved: a regressive movement. When excitation's advance toward motor activity is, for some reason, blocked, something like regression always occurs. It is here that something appears, a *Vorstellung*, which turns out to give the excitation in question a satisfaction that is, strictly speaking hallucinatory.

This is what is new in what Freud introduced.

The schemas he uses are provided for their functional value, I mean in order to establish, as Freud explicitly says, a series or sequence, which should be considered to be temporal rather than spatial, as he points out [SE V, p. 537]. To Freud, the hallucinatory phenomenon is of interest, I would say, owing to its insertion in a circuit. In short, what Freud describes to us as being the result of the primary process is the fact that something in the circuit gets turned on.

I will not provide a metaphor here. I will merely indicate, in substance, what is highlighted by the explanation Freud draws from the phenomenon and the translation he gives of it, by referring here to the functioning of a circuit with a homeostatic goal, running through a series of relays in which the electrical activity is always implicitly measurable by reflexometry. Under certain conditions, the fact that something happens at the level of one of the relays takes on, in and of itself, the value of a terminal effect, identical to what we see occur in any kind of measuring device when, in a series of lights, one of them goes on. What is important is not so much what appears – namely, light – but what it indicates by way of a certain tension (which is produced, moreover, owing to a resistance) and state of the whole circuit at a given point in time.

Let us begin by underscoring the fact that an hallucination does not in any wise correspond to a need, to use that word, for naturally no need is satisfied by an hallucinatory satisfaction. Need, in order to be satisfied, requires the intervention of the secondary process – and even of secondary processes, for there is a wide variety of them – and these processes exact realities, as their name indicates. They are under the sway of the reality principle.

If there are secondary processes that occur, they only occur because there were primary processes. This is a truism, but the following remark is no less obvious, which is that the division between the two principles makes instinct unthinkable, however it may be conceptualized. Instinct evaporates.

Consider what all research regarding instinct – especially the most modern, elaborate, and intelligent – is moving toward. It aims to explain how a structure that is not purely preformed (we are no longer at that stage, we no longer view instinct like Fabre did, to us instinct is a structure that engenders and maintains its own sequential chain) lays down pathways in the real that lead a living being toward objects that have not yet been tested by that being.

85

This is the problem of instinct. We are told that there is an appetitive stage and then a searching stage. The animal puts itself in a certain state involving motor activity that leads to movement in all sorts of directions. We arrive next at a stage of specialized triggering. Even if this specialized triggering gives rise to a behavior that leads him astray – in other words, even if he grabs onto a few colorful bits of string, as it were – the fact remains that he detected these bits in the real.

What I would like to indicate to you here is that an hallucinated behavior can be radically distinguished from a self-guided behavior based on a regressive cathexis, as it were, which is translated by the lighting up of a light along the conducting circuits. This luminous phenomenon can, at most, illuminate an already tested object. But if the object just so happens to already be there, it does not in any way show us the way to it – and still less, of course, if it shows the very same object when the object is not there, which is what actually happens in hallucinatory phenomena. At best, the subject can inaugurate on that basis the mechanism of searching, and this is what happens in the secondary process.

In short, according to Freud the secondary process takes the place of instinctual behavior. But, on the other hand, it is absolutely different from it, since, owing to the existence of the primary process, the secondary process presents itself as behavior that tests whether something is an hallucinatory reality or an experience (*Erfahrung*) that is at first organized like the effect of a light on a circuit. The secondary process accounts for judging behavior – "judgment" being a word that is proffered by Freud when he explains things at this level.

It should be clear that I am not endorsing all of this. I am extracting the meaning of what Freud articulates in order to transmit it to you.

In the final analysis, human reality is constructed, according to Freud, against a backdrop of prior hallucination, which is the universe of pleasure in its illusory essence. The whole process is out in the open. I am not saying that it betrays itself – not even!

What term does Freud constantly use when he needs to explain the succession of impressions into which the process of the psychical apparatus breaks down, and specifically in the *Traumdeutung*? The term is *niederschreiben*. We encounter this term every time he postulates, in this text and in all the others too, a succession of levels, piled on top of each other, on which elements come to be written – *niederschreiben* does not mean to be stamped, it means to be inscribed – and registered, which Freud formulates differently at different moments in his thinking. In a first layer, what is at stake, for example, are relations of simultaneity, which will later be organized in other layers.

This is how the schema breaks down into a succession of inscriptions, of *Niederschriften* – a word that we cannot actually translate – that are superimposed on each other. Everything that happened at the outset – that is, prior to arriving at another form of articulation which is that of the preconscious – namely, everything that is strictly speaking in the unconscious, can only be conceptualized in a sort of typographical space. We find here a true topology of signifiers. This conclusion is inescapable when we follow Freud's articulation exactly.

In letter 52 to Fliess, we see that Freud is necessarily led to assume at the outset a kind of ideal, that cannot be taken to be a simple *Wahrnehmung*, a taking of truth [*prise de vrai*]. If we literally translate this topology of signifiers, we arrive at a *begreifen* [grasping or comprehending] of reality, a term Freud uses all the time.

How, according to Freud, do we manage to get a handhold on reality? Not at all through a selective triage, nor by anything that resembles what every theory of instinct presents as the first approximate behavior that directs an organism along the pathways of successful instinctual behavior. What is involved is, instead, a veritable, recurring critique of the signifiers that are evoked in the primary process. This critique, like all critique, does not of course eliminate what came before it, and which it concerns, but rather complicates it. It complicates it by connoting it as what? As indices of reality that are themselves part of the signifying order.

What I am articulating here as being what Freud conceptualizes and presents to us as the primary process emphasizes the function of the signifier, but there is absolutely no way to escape this emphasis. If you peruse any of the texts he wrote at the different stages of his work, you will see that he repeated this every time he broached the problem, from its introduction in the *Traumdeutung* right up until what he formulated about it later when he proposed a second way of laying out his topography, starting in *Beyond the Pleasure Principle* and *Group Psychology and the Analysis of the Ego.*

What happens now to representations [*Vorstellungen*]?

Allow me to provide an image for a moment by playing with the etymology, as I did for [*wahrnehmung*, interpreting it as the kind of] taking of truth that would lead a sort of ideal subject to the real, which would lead him to alternatives by which he would create the real through his propositions [*induit le réel dans ses propositions*] – breaking the word *Vorstellungen* down as follows: *Vor-stellungen.*

Vorstellungen have a signifying organization. If we wanted to speak in Pavlovian terms, we would say that they are not part, at the outset, of a first system of significations connected to need, but are part of a second system of significations. They resemble the lighting up of a light in a slot machine when the ball has fallen in the right hole. The right hole, as Freud also says, means the same hole in which the ball fell before. The primary process does not seek a new object but rather an object to be found anew, and it does so by means of a *Vorstellung* that is evoked anew because it was the *Vorstellung* that corresponded to a first facilitation [*frayage*, corresponding to Freud's *Bahnung*]. The lighting up of the light pays a bonus. That's the pleasure principle.

Except that in order for this bonus to be paid, there has to be a certain reserve of coins in the machine. In this case, the reserve is reserved for the second system – that is, for the secondary processes. In other words, the switching on of the light is a satisfaction only within the machine's overall workings, insofar as the machine is that of a gambler from the moment at which he begins to gamble.

That said, let us return to Anna's dream.

2

Anna's dream is presented by Freud as a dream that manifests desire in the naked state.

It seems quite impossible to me, in the revelation of this nakedness, to avoid or elide the very mechanism by which this nakedness is revealed. In other words, the mode of revelation of this nakedness cannot be separated from the nakedness itself.

I have the impression that this so-called naked dream is known to us only by hearsay. When I say that, it does not at all mean what certain people have claimed I have said, that in short, we never know what someone has dreamt except by what he tells us of it, such that everything related to a dream should be bracketed owing to the fact of his having related it. While it is certainly not insignificant that Freud grants so much importance to the *Niederschrift* that constitutes the dream's residue, it is clear that this *Niederschrift* is related to an experience that the subject tells us about.

Freud is light years from sanctioning for so much as an instant the obvious objection that a spoken narrative is one thing, whereas a lived experience is something else. On the contrary, he rejects it energetically and he even expressly grounds his entire analysis in the narrative, going so far as to advise us to use a sort of *Niederschrift* technique, based on how the dream is *set down in writing*. This clearly shows what he thinks, at bottom, about lived experience – namely, that such experience gains from being broached via the signifier. If experience is articulated, it is not its own doing, of course, for it is already structured as a series of *Niederschriften*.

We have here a kind of palimpsest writing, as it were, assuming we could imagine a palimpsest on which the different superimposed texts were related to each other, even if we did not know how. But if we tried to determine how, we would see that the relationship between them was far more to be sought out in the shape of the letters than in the meaning of the text. I am thus not in the process of saying that.

What I am saying in this case is that what we know of Anna's dream is strictly speaking what we know at the very moment at which it occurs as an articulated dream. Stated otherwise, the degree of certainty we have about this dream is linked to the fact that we would also be far more certain about what pigs and geese dream about if they themselves told us their dreams. But in this earliest example, we have more. The exemplary value of the dream overheard by Freud is that it was spoken out loud while Anna was sleeping, and this leaves no room for ambiguity whatsoever concerning the presence of the signifier in its actual text.

It is impossible to cast the slightest doubt on the dream by pointing to the supposedly added character of the information that comes to us about it through speech. We know that Anna Freud is dreaming because she pronounces the words, *"Anna F.eud, Er(d)beer, Hochbeer, Eier(s)peis, Papp!"* We know nothing about the dream images in this case, but they find in these words a symbolic "affix" [*affixe*], if I may borrow a term from the theory of complex numbers, an affix in which we in some sense see the signifier present itself in a flocculated state – in other words, in a series of names.

These names constitute a sequence whose choice of elements is not random. In effect, as Freud tells us, what is involved here is precisely everything that she was prohibited, inter-dicted, from having, everything which, when she asked for it, she was told "No, you can't have any!" This common denominator brings unity to the diversity of terms, even if we cannot but observe conversely that this diversity reinforces the unity and even designates it. In short, this series juxtaposes this unity to the electiveness of need satisfaction.

People attribute a desire to pigs and to geese. Well, you need but reflect on the effect it would have if, instead of saying, as in the proverb, that pigs dream of *kukuruz*, maize, we set out to enumerate everything that pigs presumably dream of. You would see that this would have a rather different effect. And even if we wanted to claim that only an insufficient education of the glottis stops pigs and geese from making this known to us – and even if we argued that we could make up for this by perceiving in both species the equivalent, so to speak, of linguistic articulation in certain tremblings of their mandibles – the fact remains that it would hardly be likely that these animals would include their own names, as Anna Freud does, in the sequence. 90

Let us even assume that our pig is named Toto and our goose is named Bel-Azor. If something like this were to occur, it would turn out that they would mention their names in a language which obviously – no more nor less obviously, moreover, than in human beings, but in human beings we see this less clearly – has nothing whatsoever to do with the satisfaction of their needs, since they would go by these names in the farmyard – in other words, in a context that corresponds to the needs of men, not to their own needs.

As I said earlier, we want to dwell first of all on the fact that Anna Freud articulates words. The mechanism of motor activity is thus not absent from this dream, since it is thanks to motor activity that the dream comes to our attention. But secondly, we want to dwell on the fact that the signifying structuring of the dream sequence places a message at the top (or beginning), as you can see illustrated if you know how people communicate using the complicated machines that are those of our modern era. For example, when one places a telephone call from the head to the tail of an airplane, or from one phone booth to another, one announces oneself, one announces who it is that is speaking. Anna Freud, at nineteen months of age, in her dream, announces herself; she says, "Anna Freud," and then she provides a series. I would almost say that after having heard her speak her dream aloud, one expects but one thing, which is that she say at the end, "Over and out!"

This introduces us to what I call the topology of repression – the clearest, the most formal as well, and the most articulated.

At the moments at which Freud speaks, at least twice in the *Traumdeutung*, about the *anderer Schauplatz* ["other stage (or scene)"; see SE IV, p. 48, and SE V, p. 536] – a term that had struck him when he read Fechner's work, so much so that we get the impression that it was a kind of lightning bolt, illumination, or revelation to him – he always highlights the fact that it is not another neurological locus. I would say that this other locus must be sought out in the structure of the signifier itself.

What I am trying to show you with this graph is the very structure of the signifying system. As soon as the subject enters into it, with the minimal hypotheses required by the fact that the subject enters into the play of the signifier – namely, that the signifier is given and that the subject is defined as nothing more than what is going to enter into the signifying system – things necessarily become organized accordingly, and all sorts of consequences flow therefrom. This necessity is based on the fact that there is a topology that we must conceptualize; it suffices to conceptualize it as constituted by two superimposed chains.

How do things present themselves in Anna Freud's dream? They present themselves in a problematic and ambiguous way which, up to a certain point, legitimates the distinction Freud makes between a child's dream and an adult's dream.

Where is the chain of names that is found in Anna Freud's dream situated? On the upper or the lower chain?

You may have noticed that, in the upper part of the graph, the chain is represented as a dotted line – this emphasizes the element of discontinuity in the signifier – whereas the lower chain is represented as a continuous line [see, for example, Figure 2.1]. I told you, moreover, that both chains are involved in every process.

At the level at which we are posing the question, what does the lower chain mean? It is the level of demand, and – inasmuch as I told you that the subject qua speaking takes on solidity there that is borrowed from the synchronic solidarity of the signifier – it is quite obviously related to the unity of a sentence. This is what got people talking, and in a way that spilled a lot of ink, about the function of holophrasis, of a sentence qua whole. There is no doubt that holophrasis exists.

Holophrasis has a name: interjection. To illustrate the function of the lower chain at the level of demand, it is "[Give us] bread!" or "Help!" These interjections reside in the dimension of universal discourse. I am not speaking for the time being about children's discourse. This form of sentence exists; I would even say that in certain cases it takes on a value that is quite pressing and exacting. Need, which must undoubtedly pass through the defiles of the signifier qua need, is expressed here in a way that is certainly deformed but at least monolithic, with the proviso that it is the subject himself who constitutes the monolith in question at this level.

What happens on the upper line is something else altogether. What one can say about it is not easy to say, but for good reason – it is because what happens on the upper line is the basis for what happens on the lower line.   92

Even in something that is presented to us as being as primitive as Anna's dream, something indicates to us that the subject is not simply constituted in the sentence and by the sentence; whereas, when an individual, crowd, or mob cries "[Give us] bread!" the whole weight of the message bears upon the sender. The latter is the dominant element and this cry suffices, all by itself, in the forms that I just mentioned, to constitute this sender as a subject who is truly unique, even if he has a hundred or a thousand mouths. He need not announce himself – the sentence announces him adequately.

By way of contrast, when a human subject operates with language, he counts himself, and that is even his initial position. I am not sure if you remember a certain test Binet came up with, designed to shed light on difficulties subjects have going beyond a certain stage, which I personally find far more suggestive than the stages mentioned by Piaget. I will not tell you what stage it is because I do not want to go into detail here, but it seems to be distinctive and consists in the fact that the subject realizes that there is something fishy in the sentence, "I have three brothers, Paul, Ernest, and me."

This [kind of construction] seems quite natural to the child up until a rather advanced age, and for the best reason imaginable, because it truly captures the human subject's involvement in the act of speech – he counts himself therein, he names himself therein. It is thus the most natural and the most coordinated form of expression, so to speak. It is simply that the child has not yet found the correct formulation, "There are three brothers in my family: Paul, Ernest, and me." But we should certainly not feel obliged to reproach him for this, given the ambiguities of the function of being and having. It is clear that a step must be taken in order for a distinction to be made between the *I* qua subject of the statement [*l'énoncé*] and the *I* qua subject of enunciation [or: enunciating subject], for that is what is involved here.

When we take the next step, we say that what is articulated on the lower line is the process of the statement [*le procès de l'énoncé*]. In the dream we talked about last time, what is stated is that "He is dead."

Let me observe in passing that everything that is novel about the dimension that speech introduces into the world is already implied in this statement. "He is dead" means absolutely nothing in any perspective other than that of speaking. "He is dead" means "He no longer exists." One need not say it since he is already no longer   93 there. In order for us to say "He is dead," he must have been a being who was underpinned by speech.

We do not expect anyone to realize that, of course; but we do expect people to realize that the act of enunciating the statement "He is dead" commonly requires that we have at our disposal in discourse itself all sorts of landmarks [*repères*] that are distinguished from landmarks derived from the statement of the process [*l'énoncé du procès*]. If what I am saying here were not obvious, all of grammar would evaporate.

For the time being, I am simply getting you to note the need to use the future perfect, inasmuch as there are two temporal landmarks. One of them concerns the act that will be involved – for example, in the statement "At such and such a time, I will have become her husband"; this is the landmark of the *I* that will be transformed by marriage. Nevertheless, since you express it in the future perfect tense, there is a second temporal landmark: the current point from which you are speaking, which situates [*repère*] you as the *I* in the act of enunciation. There are thus two subjects – that is, two *I*s.

The stage that the child must reach in Binet's test – namely, the distinction between these two *I*s – seems to me to have literally nothing to do with the well-known reduction to reciprocity that Piaget makes into the pivotal point of the child's ability to use personal pronouns. But let us leave this aside for the time being.

3

We have thus begun to grasp these two [horizontal] lines as representing what is related to the enunciation process, on the one hand, and what is related to the process of the statement, on the other.

There are two lines, but that is not because each one represents a specific function. We encounter a twofold structure whenever language functions are involved.

Let us say, moreover, not only that there are two of them, but that they will always have opposite structures, the one being discontinuous while the other is continuous, and conversely.

Where is Anna Freud's articulation situated?

94   I am not developing this topology in order to simply give you the answer. I mean, I am not going to declare right from the outset "it is here or there" because it suits me or even because I might see a bit more than you do, since I am the one who constructed this thing and I know where I am going with it. If I have formulated this question, it is because the question arises of what this articulation represents,

which is the guise in which the reality of Anna Freud's dream presents itself to us.

This child was quite capable of perceiving the meaning of what her nurse said. Whether true or false, Freud implies this. Freud assumes it to be true, and rightly so, of course, because a nineteen-month-old child very clearly understands when her nurse is about to make life difficult for her.

What she enunciates in her dream is articulated in a form that I called flocculated. Signifiers follow one another in a certain order, but this order takes the form of a piling up. These signifiers are superimposed on each other, as it were, in the form of a column. They replace each other, like so many metaphors for each other. What we need to bring out here is the reality of the satisfaction qua interdicted.

We will not go any further with Anna Freud's dream. Since the topology of repression is involved in it, we will take the next step now by asking ourselves how what we are beginning to articulate allows us to clarify what is at stake in an adult's dream. What is the true difference between the form taken by the child's desire in Anna Freud's dream and the form taken by an adult's dream? The latter is assuredly more complicated since it is going to give us far more trouble, at least as regards its interpretation.

What Freud says on this score is in no way ambiguous – it suffices to read what he says. The function of what intervenes is akin to censorship. Censorship operates exactly as I illustrated it in the course of my previous Seminars. I am not sure if you recall the well-known story we liked so much, that of the typist caught up in the Irish revolution who said, "If the King of England were an idiot, then all would be permitted." I gave you a different explanation of it, based on what we find in Freud's work regarding punishment dreams. Specifically, we assumed the existence of a law stipulating that "Whoever shall say that the King of England is an idiot will have his head cut off," and I proposed we imagine that the next night I dream that I have my head cut off.   95

There are still simpler forms that Freud also articulates. Since for some time now people have managed to get me to read the Tintin comic books, I will borrow an example from him. In a Tintinesque vein, I can evade the censorship in another manner: I can articulate out loud, "Whoever says that General Tapioca is no better than General Alcazar will have to deal with me." If I articulate something like that, it is clear that neither General Tapioca's supporters nor General Alcazar's supporters will be satisfied, and, what is more surprising still, those who support both of them will be the least satisfied.

Freud explains this very precisely: what is said places us before a highly peculiar difficulty which, at the same time, opens up very specific possibilities. Here is what is quite simply at stake.

What a child has to deal with is an interdiction, a no-saying [or: saying no, *dit que non*] – shaped by some principle of censorship and by the entire process of education – in other words, he has to deal with an operation on the signifier that makes it into something unspeakable. Yet the signifier is spoken, which assumes that the subject realizes that the no-saying remains said even if it is not executed. The upshot is that "doing but not saying" is distinct from "obeying and not doing."

Stated otherwise, the truth of desire is in and of itself an offense against the authority of the law. Thus the possible outcome of this new drama is to censure the truth of desire. But, censorship, however it operates, is not something that can be sustained with the stroke of a pen, because it is the enunciation process that is targeted.

To stop a statement from being enunciated, some pre-knowledge of the process of the statement is necessary. All discourse that is designed to banish this statement from the enunciation process is thus going to find itself more or less seriously at odds with its goal. The matrix of this impossibility is presented in the upper line of our graph – and it will provide us with plenty of other matrices. The fact that a subject articulates his demand means that he is caught up in a discourse in which he himself cannot help but be constructed as an agent of enunciation, and this is why he cannot give up this statement, because he would thereby efface himself as a subject who knows what is at stake.

The relationship between these two lines that represent the enunciation process and the statement process is quite simple: it is the whole of grammar. If you like, I can tell you where and how, in what terms and in which tables, this has been articulated within the framework of a rational grammar. But for the time being, what we are dealing with is the following: Repression, when it arises, is essentially linked to something that appears to be absolutely necessary – namely, that the subject be effaced and disappear at the level of the enunciation process.

How and by what empirical pathways does the subject accede to this possibility? It is altogether impossible even to articulate it if we do not grasp the nature of the enunciation process.

As I have said, all speech begins from the intersection that I situate at point A on the graph. In other words, all speech [or every word, *toute parole*], insofar as the subject is implicated in it, is the Other's discourse [*discours de l'Autre*]. It is for this exact reason that children initially believe that all of their thoughts are known to others.

As opposed to the definition given by psychologists, thought is not a first sketch of action. Thought is first and foremost something that is part and parcel of the dimension of the unsaid [*non-dit*] that I have just introduced by way of the distinction between the enunciation process and the statement process. But, of course, in order for something unsaid to be unsaid, one must speak. In order for the unsaid to subsist, it must be spoken at the level of the enunciation process – that is, qua the Other's discourse. This is why children do not doubt for a single instant that those who represent for them the locus in which this discourse resides – that is, their parents – know their thoughts.

This is, in any case, their first impression. It persists as long as something new has not been introduced, which we have not yet articulated here, concerning the relation between the upper line and the lower line – namely, what, apart from grammar, keeps them at a certain distance from each other.

I have no need to tell you how grammar keeps us at a distance in sentences like "I do not know if he is dead," "He is not dead as far as I know," "I have not heard he was dead," and "I am afraid he is dead" [*C'est la crainte qu'il fût mort*]. All of these subtle taxemes,   97
which run the gamut from the subjunctive to a *ne* that Le Bidois calls, in a way that is truly incredible for a philologist who writes for the *Le Monde* newspaper, "the expletive *ne*" – all of this is designed to show us that a whole part of grammar, the essential part, the taxemes, are designed to maintain a necessary distance between the two lines.

Next time, I will situate the articulations at stake here on these two lines. For a subject who has not yet learned these subtle forms [of expression], the distinction between the two lines comes well before. Certain conditions are required to reach this goal, which form the basis of the investigation that I am engaging in today. I would simply say that whenever the distinction between the two lines is based on the difference of tense [*temps*], which is not simply a temporal landmark, but a tension-related landmark, you can see the relationship that exists between this and the topology of desire.

This is where we are at. For a while, children are, in short, entirely caught up in the play of these two lines. What does it take here to bring about repression?

I hesitate to do something which, after all, I would not want to appear as it in fact is – making concessions. This involves appealing to notions of development. I would say that in the empirical process at the level at which repression occurs, an intervention, accident, or

impact of an empirical kind is certainly necessary – but the necessity
with which this empirical impact reverberates, the necessity that this
empirical impact precipitates in its form, is of another nature.

Whatever the case may be, at a certain moment a child perceives
that the adults who were supposed to know all his thoughts actually
don't. This assumes that he not take the step, at least not immediately, of entering into the fundamental possibility of what I will
briefly and rapidly designate as the so-called mental form of hallucination. In the latter, we see the primitive structure of what I will call
the backdrop of the enunciation process – parallel to the ongoing
statement of existence – which is known as the echo of actions, the
echo of explicit thoughts.

98

The fact remains that if a *Verwerfung* [foreclosure] has not
occurred, the child perceives at a certain moment that the adult
who supposedly knows all his thoughts doesn't in the slightest. The
adult actually does not know – whether in a dream "He knows he
is dead" or "He does not know he is dead." Next time, we shall see
the exemplary signification of this relationship in this case. We need
not for the time being link these two terms, knowledge and death,
for the reason that we have not yet gone far enough in formulating
what will be targeted by repression.

What is the fundamental possibility of what can but be the goal of
this repression, assuming it is successful?

It is not simply that it assigns the sign "no" to the unsaid, which
says that the unsaid is not said, all the while leaving it said. If the
unsaid involved in repression is truly such a thing, there is no doubt
that the kind of negation that is at work here is so primordial that
Freud situates *Verneinung* [negation] – which nevertheless appears
to be one of the most elaborate forms of repression in the subject,
since we find it in subjects with a high psychological efflorescence –
right after the earliest *Bejahung* [affirmation]. You will observe that
it is thus true that he proceeds, as I am doing for the time being, by
means of a possibility – and even by means of a deduction – that is
logical, rather than pointing to its genesis at a specific moment in
time [*génétique*].

The earliest negation is what I am in the process of talking to you
about regarding the unsaid. The next step is "He does not know," by
means of which the Other, who is the locus of my speech, becomes
the dwelling place of my thoughts; and by means of which the subject's *Unbewusste* [unconscious] can be established, into which the
content of repression will enter.

Do not ask me to go any further or any more quickly here than
I am already going. Although I tell you that the subject proceeds
by following the example of this Other in order for the repression

process [*processus du refoulé*] to be inaugurated in him, I never said that it was an easy example to follow. Moreover, I have already indicated that there is more than one mode of negation, since I mentioned in this regard *Verwerfung* [foreclosure] and I also mentioned *Verneinung* [negation] again. I will rearticulate the latter next time.

Verdrängung, repression, cannot be such an easy operation to bring about, since what it involves in essence is that the subject be effaced. As regards repression, it easily comes to the child's attention that the others, the adults, know nothing. Naturally, a subject who comes into existence does not know that, if the adults know nothing, it is, as we all know, because they have had all kinds of experiences involving repression. A subject knows nothing of this, and it is not an easy task for him to imitate them. For a subject to hide himself qua subject requires a form of sleight of hand that is rather trickier than many others I am led to present to you here.

There are three ways in which the subject can perform this trick: through *Verwerfung* [foreclosure], *Verneinung* [negation], and *Verdrängung* [repression].

Verdrängung involves the following: in order to mark what must be made to disappear as unsaid, in a way that is at least possible if not durable, the subject operates by the pathway of the signifier; he operates on the signifier. This is why, regarding the dream about the dead father that I mentioned last time – around which we continue to dance here even if I did not actually get back to it in today's class – Freud articulates that repression bears essentially on the elision of two clausulae, namely, "*nach seinem Wunsch*" and "*daß er* [*der Träumer*] *es wünschte.*"

At its origin or root, repression, as it is presented in Freud's work, cannot be articulated otherwise than as bearing on the signifier.

We did not take a major step today, but we nevertheless took an additional step.

This step will allow us to see what sort of signifiers the operation of repression comes to bear on, for not all signifiers can be equally damaged, repressed, or rendered fragile.

It is of essential importance that we were already able to see that repression bears on what I called two clausulae, for this will put us in a good position to designate what is at stake, strictly speaking, when we talk, first, about the desire in a dream, and then about desire *tout court*.

December 3, 1958

V

THE DREAM ABOUT THE DEAD FATHER: "AS HE WISHED"

The foreclusive and the discordant
The subject's vacillation when faced with the object of desire
"To be a beautiful blonde and popular, too . . ."
The dream laid out on the graph
Death, pain, castration, and necessity

At the point at which I left you last time, you could already see that I was tending to broach our topic, desire and its interpretation, by means of a certain ordination of signifying structure.

I showed you that what is enunciated in the signifier involves an internal split [*duplicité*] between the process of the statement and the process of the act of enunciation.

I emphasized the difference between the *I* of the statement and the *I* of enunciation. The former is involved in every statement insofar as, like any other [subject], it is the subject of a stated process, for example, which is moreover not the only mode of statement. The latter is involved in any and every enunciation, but especially when it announces itself as the *I* of enunciation.

The way in which this *I* announces itself is not unimportant. In little Anna Freud's dream, it announces itself by naming itself at the beginning of the dream's message. I indicated to you that something ambiguous remained there – is this *I*, qua *I* of enunciation, authenticated at that moment, or not? I am hinting that it is not yet authenticated, which is what accounts for the distinction Freud makes between the desire in a child's dream and the desire in an adult's dream.

In children, something has not yet been completed, precipitated by the structure, or distinguished in the structure. I showed you the reflection and trace of this something, an undoubtedly late trace, in a psychological test. Although the clearly defined conditions of the experiment do not allow us to judge in advance what the situation is for the subject at his core, it appears that the difficulty distinguishing between the *I* of enunciation and the *I* of the statement lasts a long time, going so far as to manifest itself in a form of fumbling that occurs during a test that chance and psychological flair made Binet point out, "I have three brothers, Paul, Ernest, and me," where we see that the subject does not yet know how to "uncount" himself.

The trace that I pointed out is an index – there are others too – of the element that is essential to the subject, which is constituted by the difference between the *I* of enunciation and the *I* of the statement. As I told you, we are not taking things up by way of deduction, but by a pathway about which I cannot say that it is empirical, since it was already traced out and constructed by Freud.

Freud tells us that the desire in an adult's dream is a borrowed desire, which is the mark of repression, a repression he characterizes at this level as [an instance of] censorship. What does he emphasize when he takes up the mechanism of censorship? He emphasizes the impossibilities of this censorship, and it is in this sense that he shows us what censorship is. I was trying to get you to dwell for a moment on this point by showing you the type of contradiction in terms implicit in anything that is unsaid at the level of enunciation, I mean the self-contradictory nature of a formulation like, "I am not saying that . . ."

Last time, I tried to convey this to you in various funny forms: "Anyone who says such and such about so and so whose speech must be respected, who must not be offended, will have to deal with me!" What does this mean, if not that in taking this obviously ironic stand, I find myself proffering exactly what one must not say?

Freud himself often highlighted how frequently dreams adopt this path – namely, that what they articulate as not being supposed to be said is [*est*] precisely what they have to say, and is that by which what is effectively said in the dreams transits.

As this formulation "I am not saying that . . ." brings us to something that is connected with the signifier's deepest structure, I would like to dwell on it further before taking an additional step.

1

It is no accident that Freud makes *Verneinung* [negation], in the article he devotes to it, into the mainspring and the very root of the most primitive phase in which the subject is constituted as such, and is specifically constituted as unconscious.

A question thus begins to arise for us regarding the relation between *Verneinung* and the earliest *Bejahung* [affirmation] – that is to say, between *Verneinung* and a signifier's access to the dimension of questions, for that is what a *Bejahung* is.

What is inscribed at the earliest [*plus primitif*] level? Is it, for example, the coupled terms "good" and "bad"? You are aware of the role this couple, which is clearly very early, has played in certain psychoanalytic approaches. To choose one or another of such primitive terms, or to refuse to do so, is already to opt for an entire orientation of one's analytic thinking.

I am dwelling on the function of the *ne* [not] in the formulation "I am not saying . . . [*Je ne dis pas* . . .]" because I believe that it is the essential articulation. By saying that one is not saying something, one says it. This makes clear, through a sort of *reductio ad absurdum*, what I have already pointed out to you as the most radical property, as it were, of the signifier.

If you recall, I already tried to direct you down the pathway of an exemplary image that showed the relationship between the signifier and a certain type of index or sign that I called a trace, that the signifier itself already bears, which is the mark of some sort of flip side of the stamp of the real.

I spoke to you about Robinson Crusoe and the trace of Friday's footstep [Seminar III, p. 167]. Is that trace already a signifier? I told you that the signifier begins not with a trace, but with the fact that one effaces the trace. Nevertheless, an effaced trace does not a signifier make. What inaugurates the signifier is the fact that it is posited as capable of being effaced. Stated otherwise, Robinson Crusoe effaces the trace of Friday's footstep, but what does he put in its place? If he wishes to remember where Friday's foot was, at the very least he makes a cross at that spot – in other words, a bar [or: line, *barre*] and another bar on top of that one. This is what specifies the signifier.

104   The signifier presents itself both as being able to be effaced and as being able, in the very operation of effacement, to subsist as such. I mean that the signifier presents itself as already endowed with the properties characteristic of the unsaid. With my bar, I cancel out the signifier, but I also perpetuate it indefinitely, inaugurating the dimension of the signifier as such. To make a cross is to do something that, strictly speaking, does not exist in any form of mapping available to animals.

We must not believe that nonspeaking beings, such as animals, map nothing, but they do not intentionally leave traces of traces with something that is said [*avec le dit*]. When we have time, we will turn to the mores of the hippopotamus, and we will see what he deliberately leaves on his tracks for his fellow creatures. What man leaves behind him is a signifier, a cross, a bar qua barred.

One bar is covered over by another bar, indicating that it is, as such, effaced. The function of the no of the no [or the no's no, *non du non*], insofar as it is a signifier that cancels itself out, in and of itself warrants a very long discussion. Logicians, who are always overly psychological in bent, have, strangely enough, left aside the earliest facet of negation in the formulations and classifications of it that they have provided.

You may or may not know what the different modes of negation are. I do not intend, after all, to tell you everything that can be articulated about this concept as regards what distinguishes the meaning of negation from privation, and so on. We must rely on the phenomenon of speaking, linguistic experience, to find what is earlier than all of that and more important to us. I will focus on that alone.

I cannot avoid turning here, at least momentarily, to research that has an experiential value – namely, the research that was done by Édouard Pichon, who was, as you know, one of our elder psychoanalysts, and who died at the beginning of the war from a serious heart condition. Pichon perceived something regarding negation and he made a distinction of which you should at least have a little glimpse, notion, or idea.

It was in his capacity as a logician that he made this distinction, but he manifestly wanted to be a psychologist and he wrote that what he was doing was exploring the realm that runs *Des Mots à la pensée*, from words to thought – like so many others, he was quite capable of deluding himself. Luckily for us, what is weakest in his work is the claim that he is working upward from words to thought. But he turned out to be an admirable observer of linguistic usage. I mean that he had a feeling for the stuff of language which was such that he taught us a great deal more about words than about thought.

He dwelled especially on the use of negation in French, and in this realm he could not avoid making a discovery that he formulated with the distinction between the "foreclusive" and the "discordant." I will immediately give you some examples of this.

Let us consider a sentence like, *Il n'y a personne ici* [No one is here, or There is no one here]. This is foreclusive – it is ruled out for the time being that there is anyone here. Regarding this, Pichon pointed out that whenever you are dealing with a pure and simple foreclosure, French always employs two terms: a *ne*, and secondly something that is represented here by the word *personne*, but that can be represented by other words like *pas* and *rien*, as in *Je n'ai pas où loger* ["I have no place to stay"] and *Je n'ai rien à vous dire* ["I have nothing to say to you"].

Moreover, he observed that there is a very large number of uses of *ne*, and they are the most indicative – they are, as usual, those that

105

pose the most paradoxical problems – in which it appears all alone. A *ne* all alone is never, or almost never, used to indicate pure and simple negation, which is the kind of negation that in German is incarnated in the word *nicht* and in English in the word *not*. By itself, *ne*, when it is left to its own devices, expresses what Pichon called discordance. Now this discordance is situated precisely in between the enunciation process and the statement process.

I am going to discuss the example on which Pichon dwelled the most, for it is especially illustrative. It is the use of *ne* that people who understand nothing – in other words, people who want to understand – call the "expletive *ne*." I mentioned this last time, when I referred to an article in *Le Monde* that had struck me as slightly scandalous as regards this so-called expletive *ne*.

This *ne*, which is altogether essential to the use of the French language, is the one that is found in sentences like *Je crains qu'il ne vienne*. Everyone knows that it means *Je crains qu'il vienne* [I am afraid he is coming] and not *Je crains qu'il ne vienne pas* [I am afraid he is not coming], but in French this is how you say it. In other words, at this point in its linguistic usage, French grasps the *ne* somewhere at the level of its wandering, as it were, as it descends from the enunciation process to the statement process.

At the level of enunciation, negation concerns the very articulation of the signifier, the pure and simple signifier said to be in action [or: at work, *en acte*]. It is the negation in *Je ne dis pas que* . . . – for example, *Je ne dis pas que je suis ta femme* [I am not saying that I am your wife]. At the level of the statement, it becomes the following negation: *Je ne suis pas ta femme* [I am not your wife].

We are obviously not here to explore the genesis of language, but something related to it is implied in psychoanalytic practice. Freud's articulation of negation implies, in any case, that negation descends from enunciation to the statement. Why should we be astonished by this? For, after all, every negation in statements involves a certain paradox, since it posits something in order to posit it at the same time as nonexistent – well, at least in a certain number of cases.

The level at which discordances are introduced is situated somewhere between enunciation and statement. Since some aspect of my fear precedes the fact that he is coming, since I am hoping he will not come, can I do otherwise than articulate *Je crains qu'il ne vienne*? In passing, this grabs ahold, as it were, of the discordant *ne* that is distinguished from the foreclusive *ne* in the realm of negation.

You will tell me, "This phenomenon is peculiar to the French language alone. You yourself said so earlier when you mentioned the term *nicht* in German and the term *not* in English." Quite so. But that is not what is important.

In English, for example, we find traces in the articulation of the linguistic system of something analogous. I cannot bring this out here, as I am not here to give you a class on linguistics, but keep in mind that, in English, negation cannot be applied purely and simply to the verb that designates the process in statements. You do not say "I eat not,"* but rather "I do not eat."* In other words, for everything involving negation, statements are led to borrow a form that is based on the use of an auxiliary [verb], the auxiliary being typically what introduces the dimension of the subject into a statement, as in "I don't eat,"* "I won't eat,"* or "I won't go."*

In French, *Je n'irai pas* [I won't go] merely expresses the fact that the subject will not go, whereas "I won't go"* implies a resolution on the subject's part not to go.

The fact that in English all pure and simple negation brings out something like an auxiliary dimension is the trace of something that links negation to the earliest position of enunciation in an essential manner.

Thus at the outset, the subject is constituted in the process of distinguishing between the *I* of enunciation and the *I* of the statement. In our last class, I began to articulate what comes next, the second time or stage.

That is what we will turn to now.

2

In order to show you by what route the subject enters into a dialectic involving the Other [*la dialectique de l'Autre*], insofar as this dialectic is imposed on him by the very structure of the difference between enunciation and statement, I have led you by a path that is not the only one possible, but that I deliberately made an empirical one – in other words, I have introduced the subject's real history into it.

The next step in this history is, as I told you, the dimension of "knowing nothing about it."

The subject puts it to the test against the backdrop of the idea that the Other knows all about his thoughts, since at the outset his thoughts are, by their very nature and structure, this Other's discourse. The discovery that the Other knows nothing about his thoughts, which is factually true, inaugurates the pathway by which the subject develops the opposite requirement that lies within the unsaid. From there, he will have to find the difficult path by which he must implement the unsaid in his being, going so far as to become the sort of being with which we deal – namely, a subject who has the dimension of the unconscious.

The essential step that psychoanalysis has us take in the experience of humanity is that – after many centuries in which philosophy has, I would say, entered obstinately and ever further into a discourse in which the subject is merely the correlate of the object in the knowledge relationship, where he is what is presupposed by the knowledge of objects, where he is a sort of strange subject about which I said somewhere, I do not recall where, he could fill up philosophers' weekends, because the rest of the week (namely, during the workweek) everyone can naturally neglect altogether this subject who is in some sense but the shadow and underside [*doublure*] of objects – we analysts realized that something about this subject had been overlooked, namely, the fact that he speaks.

This is the case only from the moment at which we can no longer overlook him – that is, from the moment at which his domain as a subject who speaks stands on its own two feet, as it were, whether the subject is there or not. But what completely changes the nature of his relations to the object is the crucial thing known as desire.

It is in the field of desire that we try to articulate the relations between the subject and the object. These are relations involving desire, for it is in the field of desire that psychoanalytic experience teaches us that the subject must be articulated. The relationship between the subject and the object is not based on need; it is a complex relationship that I am trying to elucidate for you.

I will begin by quickly indicating that, inasmuch as the relationship between the subject and the object is situated in the field of desire, the object cannot be the correlate of, or something that merely corresponds to, one of the subject's needs. The object is something that props the subject up at the precise moment at which the subject has to face, as it were, his existence. The object is something that props him up in his existence in the most radical sense – namely, in the sense in which he exists in language. Otherwise stated, the object is something that is outside of him and whose true linguistic nature he can grasp only at the very moment at which he, as a subject, must be effaced, vanish, or disappear behind a signifier. At that moment, which is a moment of panic, so to speak, the subject must grab hold of something, and he grabs hold of the object qua object of desire.

Someone whom I will not name immediately today, in order not to create confusion, someone who is quite contemporary but is now dead, wrote somewhere: "To ascertain exactly what the miser whose treasure was stolen lost: thus we should learn much." This is exactly what we must learn, I mean learn for ourselves and teach to others.

Psychoanalysis is the first locus or dimension in which one can ascertain this. Of course, in order to get you to grasp what I mean, I will have to find another example, a more noble example, because the miser is ridiculous – in other words, far too close to the unconscious for you to be able to bear it.

If I were to articulate it to you in the same terms that I used in speaking of existence earlier, in two minutes you would take me for an existentialist, which is not what I want. I will take an example from the film by Jean Renoir entitled *La Règle du jeu* [*The Rules of the Game*].

In this film there is a character played by Marcel Dalio, who is an old man – the kind we see in everyday life, in certain social circles, and we must not believe that he is limited to this particular social circle – who collects objects and especially music boxes. If you still remember the film, recall the moment at which, in front of quite a few people, Dalio comes across his latest find: an especially beautiful music box. At that moment the character is literally in a position which is one we can or rather must call shame [*pudeur*] – he turns red, effaces himself, disappears, and is very ill at ease. What he has shown, he has shown – but how could the onlookers understand that we are faced here with the precise point of oscillation that manifests itself to the highest degree in the subject's passion for the object he collects, which is one of the forms of the object of desire?

Is what the subject shows none other than the major point, the most intimate point of himself? No, for what is propped up by this object is precisely what the subject cannot reveal even to himself. It is something that is at the cusp of the greatest secret. It is in this direction that we must seek to figure out what the treasure chest is for the miser. Another step is certainly required here for us to move from the level of the collector to that of the miser. This is why misers can only be presented in comedic registers.

But this has already introduced us to what is at stake when the subject finds he has begun, starting at a certain moment, to articulate his wish insofar as it is secret. How does he express his wish here? This expression varies according to different languages, and according to the forms that are characteristic of each language to which I alluded last time. Different modes and registers have been invented, which all strike different chords. Do not always lend credence to what grammarians say on this score – the subjunctive is not as subjunctive as it seems, and other verbal modes can express the type of wish in question here just as well.

I looked around for something that could illustrate this for you and, I do not know why, a little poem came back to me from the recesses of my memory, which I had some trouble reconstructing, and even resituating.

Être une belle fille
blonde et populaire
qui mette de la joie dans l'air
et lorsqu'elle sourit
donne de l'appétit
aux ouvriers
de Saint-Denis.

[To be a beautiful blonde
and popular, too,
who brings joy to all
and when she smiles
makes the workers
in Saint-Denis horny.]

This was written by a contemporary of ours, a discrete poetess. She happens to be petite and black, and undoubtedly expresses, in her nostalgia for making the workers in Saint-Denis horny, something that can be rather strongly tied to some stray moment of her ideological reveries. But we cannot say that such is her usual occupation.

I would like to get you to dwell on this phenomenon, this poetic phenomenon, for a moment, because we find here first of all something that is quite important as concerns temporal structure.

We have here what is perhaps the pure form, I am not saying of a wish [*voeu*], but of what is wished for [*souhaité*] – that is to say, of what in a wish is enunciated as wished for. As you see, what is wished for presents itself here in the infinitive tense, and the primitive subject seems to be elided here. But this does not mean anything – in reality she is not in the least bit elided. By entering into the structure in order to map the position of what is articulated here, we see that this articulation is situated before the subject and determines her retroactively. We are not talking here either about a pure and simple aspiration or a regret, but rather about an articulation that is positioned before the subject as retroactively determining her to be a certain type of being.

111   This doesn't mean much. The fact remains that what is wished for is articulated in this way. We have here something that we have reason to remember when we seek to give meaning to the sentence with which *The Interpretation of Dreams* ends: "Indestructible desire models the present on the image of the past." We immediately chalk

up what this sentence, whose purring we hear, says to repetition or ex post facto action; but is this so very clear if we examine it closely? If indestructible desire models the present on the image of the past, it is perhaps because, like the proverbial carrot held out in front of the donkey, it is always in front of the subject and always retroactively produces the same effects.

Once we have indicated the structural characteristics of this statement, we are simultaneously confronted with its ambiguity. After all, the gratuitous characteristic, as it were, of this enunciation does not fail to have certain consequences, which nothing stops us from exploring. Hence the following remark.

Having gone back to the text [of the poem], I saw that it was entitled, as if by chance, *Voeux secrets* [Secret wishes]. This is thus what I retrieved from my memory when, some twenty-five or thirty years after reading it, I was looking for something that would bring us to the secret of wishes. This secret wish is poetically expressed – that is, it is, of course, communicated. And this is the whole problem – how to communicate to others something that has been constituted as a secret? Answer: through some sort of lie.

In fact, to us, and we are a bit cleverer than others are, this can in the final analysis be translated by saying, *"True as it is* that I am a beautiful blonde and popular, too, I desire to bring joy to all and make the workers in Saint-Denis horny." Now, it is not clear or self-evident that every being, no matter how generous or poetic or a poetess, has such a strong desire to bring joy to all. After all, why bring joy to all? Why if not in fantasy and in order to demonstrate to what degree the object of fantasy is metonymic? Joy therefore circulates here like a metonymy.

As for the workers in Saint-Denis, they take a lot. Let them divide it up among themselves. In any case, there are enough of them that we would not know which one of them to turn to.

In this digression, I have introduced the structure of wishes to you by the pathway of poetry. We can now enter into it by the pathway of serious things – I mean by locating the actual role that is played   112
in it by desire.

3

We have seen, as we should have expected, that desire has to find its place somewhere on the graph between, on the one hand, the point from which we began when we said that the subject is alienated there [A], inasmuch as he must enter into the defiles of the signifier – in other words, essentially the alienation of the appeal [to the Other], that related to need – and, on the other hand, the beyond in which the dimension of the unsaid is introduced as essential.

The dream that I selected, the one involving the dead father, will allow us to show how and where desire is articulated.

This dream is assuredly among the most problematic, insofar as it is a dream in which a dead man appears. The appearance of dead people in dreams is far from having revealed its secret to us, even if Freud talked a good deal about it already – see page 433 of the German edition [SE V, p. 431]. Throughout his analysis of dreams in the *Traumdeutung*, Freud never stopped emphasizing the profound ambivalence of feelings we have about those we love and respect, this having been his first take on the psychology of the unconscious. He broached this topic anew regarding the dream about the dead father, which I selected in order to begin to try to spell out for you the function of desire in dreams.

I remarked last time that we always forget what is in the *Traumdeutung*. Having decided for various reasons to reread the first edition of it, I realized that I had forgotten that this dream was only added in 1930. More precisely, it was first added as a footnote shortly after its publication in the *Sammlung kleiner Schriften zur Neurosenlehre*, 1913, volume 3, page 271 of the second edition, and it was moved into the text in the 1930 edition. Since then it has thus been in the main body of the *Traumdeutung*.

I will indicate once again how this dream goes. The dreamer sees his father appear before him, a father whom he has just lost after a long, drawn-out, and tormenting illness. The dreamer sees his father in front of him and is "penetrated," as Freud tells us, with profound pain at the thought that his father is dead and "did not know it." Freud emphasizes the absurd resonance of this formulation and he tells us that it can be understood if we add that the father was dead "as he [i.e., the son] wished." In short, "he did not know" that it was "as he wished" that "he was dead."

These are the elements that I must thus situate on the different levels of the graph. We will try to verify this in detail at the experiential level.

I will place "he did not know" on the lower line, insofar as it is essentially related to the dimension of the constitution of the subject. It is, in effect, on the basis of a useless "he did not know" that the subject must situate himself, and it is precisely here that he must constitute himself as not knowing, for it is the only exit offered to him in order for what is not said to actually take on the import of the unsaid.

"He did not know" is situated at the level of the statement, but it is clear that no statement of this type can be made, if it is not

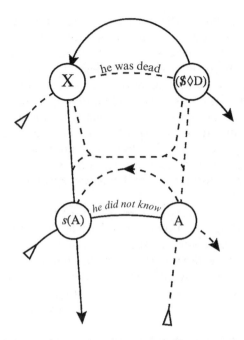

Figure 5.1: Interpretation between statement and enunciation

propped up by an underlying enunciation. Indeed, "he was dead" means absolutely nothing to a being who does not speak. We have proof thereof. I would go even further – this is continually shown by the immediate indifference that most animals manifest to the remains or cadavers of their fellow beings once they are cadavers.

An animal can, no doubt, be attached to the deceased. People talk about dogs being so attached. But it should be pointed out that dogs are exceptions in the sense that, although they do not have an unconscious, they have a superego. Stated otherwise, [to be attached to a dead being] it is necessary that something come into play that allows for the emergence of something along the lines of signifying articulation. But let us leave that aside.

"He was dead" already assumes that the subject has entered into something like existence. Existence here is nothing other than the fact that a subject, from the moment at which he is posited in the signifier, can no longer destroy himself; he enters into this intolerable sequence that immediately unfolds for him in the imaginary, and which is such that he can no longer conceive of himself except as forever re-emerging in existence.

This is not a philosophical construction. I have been able to observe it in those whom we call patients. It was, I remember, one of the turning points of the inner experience of a female patient of mine when, in a certain dream – which did not arrive at just any old moment in her analysis, naturally – she alighted upon something that was apprehended and experienced in a dream, which was nothing other than a sort of pure feeling of existence. It was the sense of existing, as it were, in an indefinite way. And from the heart of this existence a new existence continually re-emerged for her – for her innermost intuition, so to speak – a new existence that extended as far as the eye could see. Existence was apprehended and felt by her to be something that, by its very nature, is extinguished only to re-emerge forever further on, and this was accompanied in her by intolerable pain.

This is quite close to what the content of the dream [about the dead father] brings us. For the person who has the dream is the dreamer. It is always good to keep this in mind when we talk about the characters in a dream. Here, as the dream is that of a son, the question of what we call identification arises especially easily. We have no need for dialectic to think that there is some identificatory relationship between the subject and his own dreamlike fancies [*fantaisies de rêve*].

What do we see here? We have a dreamer, in pain of the most profound kind, standing before his father. And we have a father who does not know he is dead, or more precisely – for we must consider the verb tense in which the subject apprehends and communicates it to us – *il ne savait pas* ["he did not know"].

I am emphasizing this point without being able to emphasize it maximally for the time being. The rule that guides me here is to proscribe half-baked formulations and to always strive not to give you approximations. But as, on the other hand, I cannot give precise formulations from the outset, this leads me at times to be less than clear, and in any case naturally leaves certain doors open.

As for dreams, it is important that we remember the way in which they are communicated to us. It is always by a statement. A dreamer recounts what to us? Another statement, but it is not at all adequate to say that. He presents this other statement to us as an enunciation.

Indeed, if a dreamer tells us a dream, it is for an entirely different reason than for the statement he recounts to us. It is in order for us to seek its key or meaning – that is to say, in order for us to figure out what it means. From this vantage point, the fact that "he did not know" – which is inscribed on the graph at the first level of the split – is said in the imperfect tense takes on great importance.

For those who are interested in the relationship between a dream and the speech by which we become cognizant of it, let us continue and see how things break down.

What do we find on the side of what is presented in the dream as the subject? We find an affect: pain. Pain related to what? To the fact "that [his father] was dead." What corresponds to this pain on the father's side is "he did not know." He did not know what? The same thing, "that he was dead." By way of a complement, I would add "as he wished."

THE SUBJECT'S SIDE	THE FATHER'S SIDE
pain	he did not know
(owing to the fact) that he was dead	that he was dead

as he wished

Figure 5.2: Distribution of the four elements between the two characters in the dream

When Freud tells us that the meaning, and implicitly the inter-   116
pretation, of the dream is found in "as he wished," it all seems quite simple. Yet I have indicated that it is not quite so simple. But what does this mean? If we are at the level of the signifier, as Freud formally indicates – not just in this passage, but also in the one about repression that I asked you to reread – you must immediately see that we can make more than one use of "as he wished."

Where does "he was dead as [the dreamer] wished" take us? It seems to me that some of you at least can recall the point to which I once led you in discussing the story of Oedipus.

Recall that, after having exhausted in every form the pathway of desire, insofar as it is not known to the subject, and suffering the effect of punishment – for what crime? for no other crime than that of having existed in this desire – Oedipus finds himself led to a point where he can proffer no other exclamation than *me phúnai*, "Never to have been born," where existence, having arrived at the extinction of his desire, ends up. Well, the pain that the dreamer feels in the dream – let us not forget that he is someone about whom we know nothing other than the immediately prior fact that he witnessed his father's demise in the course of a long illness – is close, in experience, to the pain of existence when nothing any longer inhabits it other than existence itself, and that everything, when suffering is excessive, tends to abolish a term that cannot be uprooted: the desire to live.

If the pain of existing after desire had dried up was experienced by someone, it was no doubt by he who was far from being a stranger to the dreamer – namely, his father. But what is certain, in any case, is that the dreamer knew about this pain. We will never know if he who felt this pain in the real knew or did not know the meaning of the pain, but what *is* clear is that the dreamer does not know what he is taking on, which is the pain itself. He does not know it in the dream, of course – nor, quite surely, outside of the dream – before interpretation leads us there.

117   The proof thereof is that in the dream he can only articulate this pain in a way that, in his relation to the other, is both faithful and cynical, and takes an absurd form. What does this form correspond to? If we turn back to the short section in the *Traumdeutung* that discusses absurd dreams [SE V, pp. 426–45], we see that the impression of absurdity, which is often linked in dreams to a sort of contradiction that is linked to the structure of the unconscious itself, can lead to something laughable, but that in certain cases absurdity is introduced to express a particularly violent repudiation of the designated meaning. Freud says this quite specifically regarding this dream, and it confirms what I was trying to articulate for you here even before having reread the passage.

What does "he did not know" mean? It assuredly means that the dreamer can see that his father did not know the dreamer's wish – his wish that his father die in order to be done with his suffering. In other words, at this level, the dreamer is cognizant of his own wish. He can see – or not see, it all depends on what point he is at in his analysis – that, in the past, he himself had wished his father would die, although not for the sake of his father, but of the son, his rival.

But there is something that he cannot see at all at the point he is at, which is that he has taken on his father's pain without knowing it. He cannot see, moreover, that it is absolutely necessary for him to keep situating ignorance across from him [i.e., outside of himself] – in the father as a character in the dream, that is, in the object, in the form "he did not know" – in order not to know that it would have been better to have never been born. If there is nothing at the end of existence but the pain of existing, it would be so much better to take that pain as though it were the other's [*l'assumer comme celle de l'autre*] – as though it were that of the other who is there, and who continues to speak, just like I, the dreamer, continue to speak.

That would be far preferable than to see the final mystery revealed, which is the most secret content of this wish. What is it in the final analysis? We have no element of it in the dream itself, we know it only through our knowledge of analytic experience. Its secret content is the wish for the father's castration – in other words, the wish par excellence which, at the moment of the father's death, is reflected back onto the son because it is his turn to be castrated. This he must not see at any cost.

118   Although I am not, for the time being, in the process of detailing the terms and stages by which to lay out the interpretation [of

this dream], it is easy to show on the graph that a first interpretation can immediately be made at the lower level, at the level of the continuous line on which are inscribed the dreamer's words "he did not know." This would be a remark of the type: "In your dream, your father has no pain, since, as you wished, he did not know you had enunciated this wish." This would be all fine and well, but on condition that the analyst already include in this remark something problematic that would be such as to make emerge from the unconscious what had up until then been repressed and discontinuous at the upper level – namely, that "[his father had been] dead" already for a long time "as he wished," as in his Oedipal wish.

However, the point now is to give its full import to what, as we saw earlier, goes well beyond this wish.

In effect, the wish to castrate the father, which is reflected back on the dreamer, has an import that goes beyond any and all justifiable desire. This wish here is but the mask of what is most profound in the structure of desire as it is revealed in the dream – namely, the structuring, signifying necessity that prohibits the dreamer from escaping from the concatenation of existence insofar as it is determined by the nature of the signifier. This necessary sequence is not expressed by "his wish"; it is expressed by nothing other than the essence of *selon* [as, in *selon son voeu*, as he wished].

In the end, *Verdrängung* rests entirely on the problematic of the subject's effacement, which is, in this case, his saving grace, at this final point where the subject is doomed to a final ignorance. This is the meaning I tried to convey to you at the very end of our last class. The mainspring of *Verdrängung* is not the repression of something full that is discovered, seen, and understood, but rather the elision of a pure and simple signifier, that being *nach* or *selon* – the elision of what serves as the signature of the agreement or discordance, the agreement or discord between enunciation and the signifier, the relationship between what lies in the statement and what lies in the necessities of enunciation. Everything revolves around the elision of a clausula – that is, of a pure and simple signifier.

In the final analysis, what is manifested in the desire in the dream is the following: "he did not know." What does that thus mean, in the absence of any other signification that we have within our grasp?

We will see it when we take up the dream of someone we know better, namely Freud. Next time we will take up a dream that is quite close to this one in the *Traumdeutung* – the dream in which Freud sees his father again in the guise of Garibaldi [SE V, pp. 427–9, 447–8, 478]. We will go further with that one, and we will see what Freud's desire truly is. Those who reproach me for not making enough of anal eroticism will be repaid in spades.

119

For the time being, let us stick to the dream about the dead father.

This schematic dream figures the dreamer's confrontation with death. But the shade who is summoned up by the dream makes his mortal meaning fall away. What, indeed, does the appearance of a dead man mean, if not that the dreamer is not dead, because he can suffer in the dead man's stead?

But that is not all. Behind this suffering there lies a lure, the only one the subject can still hold onto at this crucial moment. And what is it? It is the lure of his rival, the lure of killing the father, the lure of imaginary fixation.

We will pick it up there next time, for I believe that, with what I have said today, I have sufficiently paved the way for the elucidation of the constant formula of fantasy in the unconscious: barred S, lozenge, little a ($\$ \Diamond a$).

The subject, insofar as he is barred, canceled out, and abolished by the action of the signifier, finds his prop in the other who, for the speaking subject, is what defines the object as such. We will try to identify this other, who is the prevalent object of human eroticism.

In fact, we will identify him very quickly. Those who attended the first year of this Seminar heard me talk about this for a whole term. This other is the image of one's own body, in the broad sense we shall give it.

In this case, it is here – in this human fantasy, which is the subject's fantasy and which is no longer anything but a shade – that the subject maintains his existence, maintains the veil that is such that he can continue to be a subject who speaks.

December 10, 1958

VI

INTRODUCING THE OBJECT OF DESIRE

The three levels of interpretation
The algorithm ($◊a) guides us
From castration to aphanisis
From use to exchange
From hippos to women

Last time, I mentioned Jacques Damourette and Edouard Pichon's *Des Mots à la pensée: Essai de grammaire de la langue française*. The details about foreclosure and discordance that I mentioned can be found in two different places in the second volume, where we find a whole, condensed entry on negation. There, in particular, you will see that the foreclusive is incarnated in French by such odd words as *pas* and *point*, as well as by *personne, rien, goutte*, and *mie*, that bear in themselves the sign of their origin in traces. In effect, they are all words that designate traces. It is here that the symbolic act of foreclosure or rejection is found in French, the word *ne* remaining reserved for the discordance that negation more originally is.

Last time I tried to show you that, at its origin, in its linguistic root, negation is something that emigrates from enunciation toward the statement.

I showed you in what respect this could be represented on the little graph that we use here, by situating the elements of the dream "he did not know he was dead" on it.

It was around the phrase "as he wished" that we designated the point of desire's real impact, inasmuch as the dream both bears and marks it.

To continue to break new ground, we must ask ourselves in what way and why such action is possible on the part of desire in dreams.

122

1

I indicated at the end of the last class by what path I intend to investigate the function of desire, as it is articulated in Freud's work, namely at the level of unconscious desire – that is, on the basis of the formula ($\lozenge a$) to which we are led by everything we have demonstrated regarding the structure of the dream about the dead father.

What does the dream consist of? It shows us the confrontation between the subject and an other, a small other in this case.

In the dream, the father seems to be alive again, and he turns out to be related to the subject in ways whose ambiguities we began to investigate. It is the father who makes it such that the subject takes upon himself what I called the pain of existing. It is the father whose soul the subject witnessed to be in agony. It is the father whose death he wished for – insofar as nothing is more intolerable than existence reduced to itself, existence beyond anything that can sustain it, existence sustained despite the abolition of desire.

I indicated what we could glimpse here by way of a distribution of intra-subjective functions, as it were. The subject takes responsibility for the other's pain, all the while rejecting onto the other what he does not know – namely, the subject's own ignorance. His desire is, in effect, to stay ignorant. This is the precise desire in the dream.

The desire for death takes on its full meaning here. It is the desire not to awaken – not to awaken to the message, the most secret message that is borne by the dream itself, which is that the subject, through his father's death, is now confronted with death, having been protected from it hitherto by the father's presence. "Confronted with death" – what does that mean? Confronted with an x that is linked to the father's function, that is present here in the pain of existing, and that is the pivotal point around which what Freud discovered in the Oedipus complex revolves – namely, the signification of castration.

Such is the function of castration.

What does "to take castration upon oneself" [*assumer la castration*] signify? Does one ever truly assume [one's own] castration? What is this sort of point on which the last waves of "Analysis Terminable and Interminable," as Freud calls it, crash? And up to what point is the analyst not simply within his rights, but in a position to be able to interpret it in this dream and regarding this dream?

At the end of what I said last time about the dream, I raised, without answering it, a question regarding the three ways in which the analyst can bring the subject's "as he wished" into the interpretation.

There is, first of all, the way that proceeds according to [*selon*] the subject's speech, according to what he wanted, which he recalls perfectly well, it having not been forgotten by him in the least. "He did not know, as he wished." The phrase "as he wished" is inserted here at the level of the statement line.

Re-established afterward at the level of the upper line – that is, at the level of the enunciation that is hidden in unconscious memory – it restores the traces of the Oedipus complex, which are those of the child's desire for the father's death: "He was dead, as he wished."

Recall here what Freud tells us about the child's desire, which is, when any dream forms, the capitalist, the latter finding his entrepreneur in a current desire. The current desire, which is far from always being unconscious, is the one that is expressed in the dream, and it is strictly speaking the desire in the dream. In this case, once the phrase "as he wished" is restored to the level of the child's desire, isn't it clear that the latter finds itself in a position to go in the direction of the desire in the dream?

What is, in effect, the desire in this dream? It is indisputably – at this crucial moment in the subject's life, the disappearance of his father – to interpose the image of the object [$i(a)$], in order to make it into the prop of a perpetual ignorance veiling desire. In short, "he did not know" buttresses what was up until then desire's alibi. It maintains and perpetuates the very function of prohibition that the father conveyed. The latter is what gives desire here its enigmatic and even abyssal form. It separates the subject from his desire; it gives the subject shelter from or a defense, in the final analysis, against this desire; it gives him a moral excuse not to confront it.

This was very clearly glimpsed by Ernest Jones, whose extraordinary insights about certain points of this psychical dynamic I will have the opportunity to show you today.

Lastly, can't we say that there is some intermediate stage of the interpretation of the dream to which the pure and simple interpretation of Oedipal desire is connected, like: "You wished for your father's death at such and such a time and for such and such a reason"? You will recognize the nature of this third stage once I have designated it as "identification with the aggressor." Identification with the aggressor lies somewhere in one's childhood. Haven't you recognized that, being one of the typical forms of defense, it is essential, and that it emerges at the very place where "as he wished" is elided?

124

The meaning of "as" [*selon*] is undoubtedly essential if we are to reach a full interpretation of the dream.

The fact remains that the conditions and opportunities that allow the analyst to reach it will depend on the stage of the treatment and on the context of the response that the subject gives – by what means? By his dreams – since we know that the dreams dreamt by a subject in analysis are responses to the analyst, at least to what the analyst has become in the transference – but essentially, I would say, by the logical position of terms.

The fact remains, above all, that we can wonder if, to the question "What is the wish in 'as he wished'?" we do not always risk giving some precipitated or premature response, and thus giving the subject an opportunity to avoid what is at stake – namely, the dead end in which he is placed by the fundamental structure that turns the object of any desire into the prop of an essential metonymy.

As such, in effect, the object of human desire presents itself in a vanishing form, about which we can perhaps glimpse that castration turns out to be what we might call the final temperament.

In order to investigate more precisely what human desire means and signifies, we are thus led to broach the question from the other end, an end that is not given in dreams – namely, to take up the question via our algorithm, in which the barred S is confronted with and placed across from little a, the object.

2

I introduced the algorithm ($\lozenge a$) last time. Why not put it to the test of the phenomenology of desire, as the latter presents itself to us as analysts? If we allow ourselves to be guided by this algorithm, it will lead us to investigate together our shared experience.

Let us try to see in what form the desire that is in us – that has been there since Freud, that lies at the heart of analysis, and that curiously enough has not been investigated as it should have been heretofore – presents itself in the subject.

The subject is not obligatorily nor always a neurotic subject. But if he is, it is no reason to assume that our research concerning desire does not have to take his structure into account, for that structure reveals a more general structure. The neurotic indubitably finds himself situated somewhere along the continuum of an experience that, to our way of thinking, is universal. All of Freud's theories are constructed upon this foundation.

Before examining some of the ways in which the dialectic of the relations between the subject and his desire have already been broached – that is, before coming to Jones's thought, which I mentioned earlier – I want to discuss something I came across quite recently in my clinical practice, which seems rather well designed to introduce what I am seeking to illustrate.

The patient in question was impotent. It is not bad to start with impotence in order to begin to investigate what desire is. We are sure, in any case, to be talking about human beings.

He was a young man who, of course, like many of those who are impotent, was not at all impotent. He had made love quite normally in the course of his existence, and had had a few liaisons. He was married and it was with his wife that things were not working anymore. This is not to be chalked up to impotence. The term does not seem appropriate given that the problem concerned the precise object with whom relations were for him the most desirable, for he loved his wife.

Now, here is more or less what, after a certain amount of analytic work, emerged from the subject's remarks. It was absolutely not the case that he had no passion [*élan*] for her, but if he allowed himself to be guided by it on any particular night, would he be able to sustain it? This was the particular point he was at in his analysis.

Things had gone very far in the conflict ignited by the difficulty he had been having. Did he have the right to impose on his wife some new test, some new addition to his attempts and failures? In short, was this desire – whose possibility of fulfillment was far from zero, as one could sense in every regard – legitimate?

I cannot take my discussion of this particular case any further here, and give you the whole case history, if only because it is an ongoing analysis, and for many other reasons as well. This is one of the disadvantages we always encounter when we allude to ongoing analyses. I will thus borrow from other analyses a term that is altogether decisive in certain developments, which sometimes lead to detours, or even what we call perversions, which are of a much greater structural importance than what, so to speak, nakedly played itself out in this case of impotence.

Does he have a big enough phallus? In certain cases, the question emerges in the subject's lived experience and comes to the light of day in analysis. It may serve a decisive function, and, as in other places, reveal a structure: the point at which the subject raises the question. From certain angles or directions, this question can in and of itself lead the subject to try out a whole series of solutions, which – being superimposed, forming a series, and being added to each other – can lead him quite far from the field of a normal execution of what he has everything he needs to execute.

This "big enough phallus," or more exactly this phallus that is essential to the subject, thus turns out to be foreclosed at a certain moment of his experience. This is something that we encounter in a thousand different forms, which naturally are not always apparent or manifest, but which are latent. But it is precisely in the case in

126

which this moment or stage of the subject's experience is exposed for all the world to see [*à ciel ouvert*] that, as La Palice would say, we can see and put our finger on it, and also give it its full import.

At the moment of the subject's life at which he encounters the sign of desire, which is often situated at the moment of the awakening of puberty, we see him more than once confronted, as it were, with something that is similar to what I mentioned earlier – is his desire legitimated or sanctioned by something else? We can take up what appears here already in a flash, in the phenomenology in which the subject expresses it, in the following form – does he have at his disposal an absolute weapon? If he does not, he will find himself drawn into a series of identifications, alibis, and games of hide and seek that may take him very far afield.

For the aforementioned reasons, I cannot go into the dichotomies that are at work here. This is not too important, for the essence of what I want to indicate does not lie there. The point is to get you to grasp where desire finds the origin of its peripeteia.

The subject always alienates his desire in a sign, promise, or anticipation, something that brings a possible loss with it as such. Because of this possible loss, desire turns out to be linked to the dialectic of a lack. It is subsumed by a stage [*temps*] which, as such, is not there – no more than a sign is desire – a stage which, in part, is yet to come. In other words, desire must confront the fear that it will not stay the same over time and that, qua *artifex*, it perishes, if I may put it thus.

Of course, the desire that man feels and senses as an *artifex* can perish only with regard to the artifice of his own speaking. It is in the dimension of speaking that this fear develops and stabilizes. And it is here that we encounter a term that is so surprising and that has so curiously been left behind by psychoanalysis, the one that Jones makes into the mainstay of his reflections or meditations on castration – namely, "aphanisis."

In the as-it-were modern practice of analysis, whose norms reorient the analyst's relation to the patient in an entirely different direction, the phenomenology of castration is ever more veiled, as we see in recent publications. On the other hand, at the stage [in the history] of psychoanalysis at which Jones found himself, different tasks forced themselves on him; he was confronted with the need to give Freud's thought a certain interpretation, exegesis, apology, and explanation concerning what is involved in the castration complex, in particular. It was there that he found a way to get his point across – a ruse, if you will – that consists in saying that people are afraid of being deprived of their own desire.

The word "aphanisis" means disappearance. As you will see

in Jones's text, what is at stake is the disappearance of desire. Aphanisis served him as a sensible introduction to a problematic that gave the dear man a lot of worries, of which he never managed to rid himself – that of the relations between women and the phallus.   128

From the outset, he used the term to give men and women's relations to their desire the same common denominator. This was tantamount to a dead end, for it completely neglected what Freud discovered – namely, that these relations are fundamentally different owing to the asymmetry in the different sexes with regard to the phallus as a signifier. I believe that I have conveyed this to you adequately enough that, for the time being, we can take this for granted, at least provisionally.

Moreover, this use of "aphanisis," whether it was at the root of Jones's invention or whether it only arose from its consequences, marked a sort of inflection point that, in short, deflected its author from the true question, which is, "What does the possibility of aphanisis signify in the structure of the subject?" Doesn't it oblige us to [postulate] a structuring of the human subject as such, precisely insofar as he is a subject for whom existence is supposable and pre-supposed beyond desire, a subject who exists and subsists outside of his desire?

The question is not whether or not we must objectively take into account desire in its most radical form – namely, the desire to live or the "life instinct," as we say. What psychoanalysis shows us is entirely different – it is that the desire to live is, as such, subjectively put into play in the subject's lived experience. This does not merely mean that human experience is sustained by desire – this we naturally suspect to be true – but that the human subject takes desire into account and counts on it.

When the dear old and well-known *élan vital* [vital impulse] – that charming incarnation of human desire in nature that truly warrants the term anthropomorphism, and with which we try to make nature, about which we do not understand much, hang together – is at stake, the human subject sees it before him and is afraid that it will fail him.

What is at stake here is, all the same, something other than reflections of the unconscious. In and of itself, this suggests that we would do well to have a few structural requirements here. I mean that the subject/object relationship, which is conceived of as immanent, as it were, in the pure dimension of knowledge, nevertheless raises problems for us that are a bit more complicated once desire comes into the picture, as Freudian practice proves to us.   129

Since we began with impotence, we can turn now to the other term. Human beings sometimes manage to satisfy their desire, sometimes managing to anticipate it being satisfied. But when they are within range of satisfying it, I mean when they are not struck with impotence, it also sometimes happens that they become afraid of satisfying it – whereas, on this score, someone who is impotent fears neither potency nor impotence. The very remarkable cases in which the subject is afraid of the satisfaction of his own desire occur more often than they should. This is because the satisfaction would then make him dependent on the other who is going to satisfy him.

This is an everyday occurrence, phenomenologically speaking. It happens all the time in human experience. There is no need for us to refer to the great dramas that have taken on the role of exemplary illustrations of this problematic in order for us to observe how someone's life story unfolds. The subject spends his time avoiding each and every opportunity to encounter what has always been his most powerful desire in life. For the dependence on the other that he is afraid of, which I just mentioned, is there too.

In fact, dependence on the other is the form in which what the subject fears is presented in fantasy, and it makes him deviate from the path of satisfying his desire.

The fear in question may not concern what one might simply call the other's caprice [or whim]. I am not sure you realize that the word "caprice" has little to do with the usual etymology, that found in the Larousse dictionary, which relates it to goats [chèvre]. The French have in fact borrowed it from Italian, in which capriccio means frisson [thrill, chill, or shiver]. It is the very same word that is so cherished by Freud, sich sträuben, which signifies se hérisser [i.e., to bridle, prickle, stand up straight, or be rubbed the wrong way], and which is, as you know, throughout his work one of the metaphorical forms in which he incarnates in the most tangible way possible how resistance manifests itself. He uses it in every context, when speaking about his wife, when speaking about Irma, and when speaking in general about subjects who resist.

What the subject is afraid of when he thinks about the other is not essentially becoming dependent on his caprice [or whim], but the fact that the other will mark this caprice with a sign [c'est que l'autre ne marque ce caprice de signe]. This is what is veiled. There is no adequate sign of the subject's goodwill if not the totality of the signs by which he subsists. In truth, there is no other sign of the subject than the sign of his abolishment as a subject, the sign that is written $.

This shows you, in short, that, as regards his desire, man is not true, since – however little or much courage he puts into it – the situation radically escapes him. When he finds himself in the presence of object a, the subject vanishes. What I wanted to convey to you on this score last time was called, by someone who spoke with me afterward, "an umbilication of the subject at the level of his will," an image that I quite willingly accept inasmuch as it is strictly in line with what Freud designates when he speaks about dreams.

A dream's navel is the point of final convergence of all the signifiers in which the dreamer is caught up, to such an extent that Freud calls it the "unknown" [SE V, p. 525]. He himself did not realize what was at stake in this *Unbekannt* [unknown], which is a very strange term to flow from his pen and concerns the radical difference of the unconscious that he discovered. As I have tried to show you, the Freudian unconscious is not constituted and instituted as unconscious in the simple dimension of the subject's innocence with respect to the signifier that organizes and articulates in his stead, for we find in the subject's relation to the signifier an essential impasse. I just reformulated this by telling you that there is no other sign of the subject than the sign of his abolition as a subject.

As you might well suspect, things do not remain at this stage. After all, if there were nothing but an impasse here, it would not take us very far, as they say. The characteristic of impasses is that they are fruitful, and this impasse is of interest to us only owing to the ramifications that we see it develop, which are precisely those where desire comes in.

Let us try to perceive this sort of aphanisis at the moment in your analysis at which it must appear in a flash. However, it is not merely an experience, there are mental modes in which you are led to conceptualize it.

Regarding the Oedipus complex, people tell you that there is a moment at which the subject flees [*se dérobe*]. It is the so-called moment of the inverted Oedipus in which the [male] subject glimpses a solution to the Oedipal conflict in the possibility of purely and simply attracting the love of the strongest party – namely, the father. If he then flees from this love, it is, we are told, because his narcissism is threatened, for to receive the father's love implies castration for him.

131

People tell you this as if it were self-evident, because when they cannot resolve a problem, they naturally consider it to be comprehensible, and this is what usually makes it such that it is nevertheless not as clear as all that. This is certainly the case here.

This solution is indeed possible, all the more possible in that it is, at least in part, the path that is usually followed, the one that leads to the introjection of the father in the form of the ego-ideal. In any case, that is what it looks like. But, if the so-called inverted Oedipus is involved in the normal solution, this moment was nevertheless perceived and especially brought out in the problematic of homosexuality in which the subject feels his father's love to be essentially threatening. We qualify this threat as a castration threat, not having a more suitable term at our disposal.

But this term is not all that unsuitable, after all. Psychoanalytic terms have, in the end, fortunately retained enough meaning and fullness, enough dense, heavy, and concrete character, to continue to guide us.

People sense that there is some narcissism involved here, narcissism being involved at this particular turning point in the Oedipus complex. This is confirmed by later pathways of the dialectic that lead the subject into the path of homosexuality. These later pathways are, as you know, far more complex than the pure and simple, summary requirement that the object have a phallus, even if this requirement is fundamentally hidden therein.

But that is not where I would like to head now. I will simply note that, at the outset of the problematic of the signifier, the subject, in order to deal with the suspension of desire, has more than one trick up his sleeve, as it were.

These tricks naturally bear first and foremost on the manipulation of the object, the manipulation of a in the formula.

132

3

The taking up of the object in the dialectic of the subject's relations with the signifier must be placed at the core of the relationship to the phallus that I have tried to articulate for you over the past few years.

The relationship to the phallus is seen all the time and everywhere. Need I recall to mind the moment in little Hans's life when, at the age of two, he asked about every object, "Does it have a widdler, a *Wiwimacher*, or not?" It suffices to observe children to see this essential function operating right out in the open in all its forms.

Freud remarks in passing that the question raised by Hans constitutes a mode of interpretation of the phallic form, which defines a sort of analysis. This position, of course, merely translates the presence of the phallus in the dialectic, without informing us in any way either about the nature of the process or about its stability, or even about its goal, which I tried to show you at the time [in Seminar IV]. What I simply want to indicate is that we constantly find evidence that we are not going astray here, and that the terms involved are truly the following: the subject, owing in this case to his disappearance, faced with an object, which sometimes turns out to be the essential signifier around which the fate of the entire relationship between the subject and object is played out.

I will begin by rapidly mentioning in what sense, in the most general sense, the object, I mean little *a* in our algorithm, impacts what one might call the instinctual specificity of need.

When the signifier's interposition makes a relationship between the subject and the object impossible – in other words, when the subject cannot maintain himself in the presence of the object – we know what happens: his object undergoes a sort of volatilization that in our concrete practice we call the possibility of displacement. This does not simply mean that the human subject, like all animal subjects, sees his desire displace from one object to another, but that displacement itself is what allows the fragile equilibrium of his desire to be maintained.

In the final analysis, what does displacement involve? What it involves is, I will say, the thwarting of satisfaction while nevertheless preserving an object of desire. But, on the other hand, it is still, as it were, a way of metonymically symbolizing satisfaction.

We are heading straight for the dialectic of the treasure chest and the miser, which is far from being the most complicated, even if people barely perceive what is at stake. Which is, namely, that in this case, a certain retention of the object – as we say, bringing in an anal metaphor – is the necessary condition for desire to subsist. But this is only to the degree to which the retained object, which props up desire, not itself be the object of any jouissance.

Legal terminology bears traces of this. When we say in French that we give someone the *jouissance* [usufruct] of a piece of property, what do we mean? We mean precisely that it is altogether humanly conceivable to possess property that one does not enjoy but that someone else enjoys [or benefits from, *jouisse*]. Here the object reveals its function as desire's collateral [*gage*], so to speak, not to say desire's hostage.

We can, if you will, try to connect this up with animal psychology. As regards ethology, I myself am inclined to believe what one of our colleagues said that was most exemplary and most colorful. I realized this while reading a monograph that the publisher Plon just brought out entitled *L'Ordre des choses* [*The Order of Things*]. I did not want to tell you the title because reading the book would distract you from our work here; but fortunately it is a short book, and it is by Jacques Brosse, someone who was completely unknown up until now.

The book is a sort of brief natural history – that is how I interpret it – fitting for our times. I mean by this that the book reminds us of what we find so subtle and charming when we read Buffon's work, and can never find in any contemporary scientific publication. But what stops us from giving ourselves over to this kind of exercise,

133

even if we know much more about the behavior of animals and ethology than Buffon did? What we find in specialized journals is unreadable. What is said in this short monograph is expressed, as you will see, in a style that I must say is verily and truly remarkable. Read, above all, the middle section, which is called "parallel lives" and which discusses the lives of tarantulas and ants.

I thought of this short book because its author has something in common with me, which is that the question of mammals is resolved for him. Apart from man, who is an essentially problematic mammal – it suffices to consider the role that breasts [*mammes*] play in our imagination – there is but one truly serious mammal, which is the *'potamus*. Everyone agrees here, at least those who have some slight degree of sensitivity. T. S. Eliot, whose metaphysical ideas are awful, but who is nevertheless a great poet, immediately symbolized the militant Church as a hippopotamus – we will come back to that.

What does the hippopotamus do? People highlight the difficulties of his existence. They are great, so it seems, and one of the essential things he does is guard his grazing ground [*pacage*] – because he must nevertheless have a reserve of resources – with his excrement. This is an essential point: he maps his territory, as it is called, by delimiting it with a series of relays or points designed to adequately indicate to all those whom this concerns – namely, his fellow creatures – that this is his turf. As you see, we find a first sketch of symbolic activity in animals. In mammals, it is a specifically excremental symbolism.

Whereas the hippopotamus thus turns out to guard his grazing ground with his excrement, man does not guard his grazing ground with shit; it is his shit that he keeps as collateral for the essential grazing ground, the grazing ground that remains to be determined. This is the dialectic of what people call anal symbolism, which was one of the hitherto absolutely unsuspected dimensions that Freud revealed to us – a new revelation of the *Noces chymiques*, if I may put it thus, of man with his object.

In truth, the progress made by man depends on language alone – this singular intermediary – and we do not know where it comes from. It seriously complicates our relationship with objects – in other words, it leads us to have a problematic relationship with objects.

This is, in short, the same question that Marx raises, without resolving it, in his polemic with Proudhon – namely, how is it that human objects shift from having use value to having exchange value? I simply wanted to indicate to you why this happens and give at least a brief sketch of an explanation.

You must read a piece by Marx called *The Misery of Philosophy:*

134

A Response to Proudhon's "Philosophy of Misery" (1948). The pages **135**
in which he ridicules Proudhon for having decreed that the shift
from use value to exchange value occurred by a sort of pure decree
among those who were cooperating – and we would have to figure
out why they began cooperating and with the help of what – are
rather salubrious. The way in which Marx excoriates Proudhon for
a full twenty or thirty pages, without counting the rest of the book,
provides good intellectual training.

This is thus what happens regarding objects and the meaning of
their volatilization. To value an object is also to devalue it, I mean
to rip it away from the field of pure and simple need. This is, after
all, merely a reminder of the essential phenomenology, the phenomenology of property [or commodities, *bien*], strictly speaking – and
in every sense of the word *bien*, imagine that! But let us leave that
merely sketched out for the time being.

Let us simply say that when the object involved is another person,
or other people [*l'autrui*], and especially a sexual partner, a certain
number of consequences ensue, of course, which are all the more
palpable since we were talking earlier about the social dimension.
What is at stake here is assuredly at the very root of the social con-
tract. We must, in effect, take into account the elementary structures
of kinship in which the female partner is, as Lévi-Strauss demonstrated, an object of exchange, and in a way that is not lacking in
latency or repercussions.

This exchange is not self-evident. Indeed, as an object of exchange
women are, as it were, a very bad deal for those who carry out the
operation, since all of this brings about a real mobilization, as it
were, known as the offering [*prestation*] of the phallus, the contrac-
tual renting out of its services. Here we situate ourselves naturally
in the perspective of social utilitarianism, which, as you know, presents several disadvantages. This was my precise point of departure
earlier.

Once women are included in this dialectic, namely as socialized
objects, they undergo a transformation that is truly disturbing. It is
amusing to see how Freud, in the innocence of his youth, spoke of it.
See pages 192–3 of the first volume of Jones's biography of Freud.

In a letter to his fiancée, Freud indicates what purpose a woman, a **136**
good woman, serves. He does so in connection with the topic of the
emancipation of women in John Stuart Mill's work, which, as you
know, Freud translated for a while, at the insistence of Gomperz.
This is quite priceless when you think that his passion for his fiancée
was, at the time, at its height.

The letter ends with the fact that a woman must stay in her place
and render all the services that are expected of her – this at a time

at which Freud was willingly making himself the possible mentor of his wife – and which are no different from the famous *Kinder, Küche, Kirche* [children, kitchen, and church]. I must read you a passage here based on the English, since Jones's biography has never been published in another language: "Law and custom have much to give women that has been withheld from them, but the position of women will surely be what it is: in youth an adored darling and in mature years a loved wife." We have here something that is not devoid of interest to us, for it shows us both from what experience Freud began and the path he had to travel.

Faced with this problematic position, another solution is possible for the subject. And it is no accident that we have broached the question from the angle of the social dialectic, for this other solution, as we also know from Freud's work, is identification. Identification with what? Identification with the father.

Why identification with the father? Because, as I already indicated, the father is in some way perceived as someone who has succeeded in really overcoming the impasse in the conjugal link, because he is supposed to have really castrated the mother. I say "supposed to have" [*censé*] because, naturally, it is merely supposed.

We have here the problematic of the father. If I am emphasizing it again today, it is perhaps because of what was said at our scientific meeting last night regarding the father's imaginary function, his lordliness [*seigneurialité*] in certain spheres of culture.

The figure of the father does not fail to present all sorts of possibilities for slippage. In effect, we must see that the solution that is prepared here, as it were – namely, identification with the father – stems directly from the fact that the father is already a *type*, in the strict sense of the term. There is no doubt but that this type is subject to temporal variations, but this does not bother us because we cannot conceive of it otherwise than in relation to an imaginary function. It is thanks to the subject's identification with the father ideal, which denies the reality of the subject's relationship with his father, that we can perhaps say that, on average, wedding nights turn out alright, and in the final analysis are a success – even if a truly rigorous statistical study of them has never been done.

Whatever the case may be, to us, identification with the father, which is obviously linked not only to factual data but also to imaginary data, resolves nothing when it comes to the problematic of desire – neither for us nor, of course, for our patients, and perhaps on this point we are no different from them.

Identification with the father's image is but a specific case of what we must now broach as being the most general solution of the subject/object relationship, the most general solution of the confrontation between the barred subject and object a, the object as a – namely, the introduction of the imaginary function in its most general form, otherwise stated, the dimension of narcissism.

It is narcissism that offers the subject a prop, solution, or solution pathway to the problem of desire. Human eros gets caught up in a relationship with a certain image that is none other than that of one's own body. Here an exchange or reversal occurs by which I am going to try to articulate for you the confrontation between $ and little a.

As it is already a quarter to two, and as I was unable to take things any further today, we will begin anew on this point when we meet on January 7th after the Christmas vacation.

We will finally have the opportunity to specify little a in its essence, function, and essential nature.

I have already indicated at length in prior Seminars that any and every human object is fundamentally marked by a narcissistic structure, by a profound relationship with narcissistic eros. In the most general structure of fantasy, this human object normally ends up receiving the lion's share of the subject's *Angst* – that is, neither more nor less than his affect in the presence of desire, this fear, this feeling of imminence that I mentioned earlier, it being what essentially thwarts the subject when he is on the verge of realizing his desire. The whole nature of fantasy is to transfer this fear to the object.

In studying anew a certain number of fantasies whose dialectic we have hitherto developed, we will see that the subject's affect in the presence of his desire is transferred onto the object qua narcissistic. A single fundamental fantasy, "a child is being beaten," will suffice – because it was one of the first that was discovered – to bring out the most essential features of this transfer.

What then becomes of the subject? How is he structured? Why is he structured as an ego and as an ego-ideal? We can only glimpse this in its absolutely rigorous structural necessity as the return or echo of the affect that the subject delegated to the object, a.

We have never yet truly spoken about a, in the sense that I have not yet shown you that it must necessarily be posited not qua a but qua image of a, image of the other, which is one and the same thing as the ego. I designate this image with a capital I, for *Idéal du moi* (ego-ideal), insofar as it is itself the heir of the subject's first relationship, not with his own desire, but with his mother's desire. This ideal thus takes the place of what it felt like to the subject to be a child who was wanted.

Following this necessary development, capital I comes to be inscribed in a certain trace. A transformation of the algorithm is necessary here, that I can already put on the blackboard as a sort of preannouncement. The I is inscribed in a certain relationship to the other, *a*, inasmuch as the latter is affected by the subject himself, inasmuch as the latter is affected by his desire.

$$\frac{i(a)}{\not S} \quad \Diamond \quad \frac{a}{I}$$

Formula of the ego-ideal

We will see this next time.

December 17, 1958

VII

DESIRE'S PHALLIC
MEDIATION

The symptom in the RIS knot
The imaginary interposition of the dead father
The signifying privilege of the imaginary phallus
The subject's primary masochism
Love and desire in men and women

Our practice confronts us with the need to make an essential distinction between two functions. There is in the subject what we must call desire. And yet this desire's constitution, manifestation, and contradictions – which, in the course of treatments, come out clearly between the subject's discourse and his behavior – oblige us to distinguish it from the function of demand.

If there is something that psychoanalysis has brought out – not only in its original Freudian form but also in the contradictions that have arisen subsequently – it is certainly the role played by demand and its problematic character.

The development of psychoanalysis since Freud's time has, in effect, granted ever greater importance and emphasis to what, going by various names, converges in the final analysis on the general notion of dependency neurosis. This is where the theoretical slippages, not to mention failures in terms of practice, of a certain conception of the results [*réduction*] that must be obtained by therapeutic treatment converge. What is hidden or veiled behind the notion of dependency neurosis is the fundamental fact of demand, whose effects impress, compress, and oppress the subject.

Have we adopted the right attitude toward this function, which we reveal to be formative in the genesis of the subject? Have we adopted, I mean, an attitude that allows for the elucidation of symptoms as well as for their alleviation?

Symptoms do not result from the mere subtraction or suspension that is known as frustration, nor are they merely a sort of

140   deformation of the subject – however it might be envisioned – owing
to something that is supposedly doled out as a function of a certain
relationship to the real. For an imaginary frustration is, as I have
said, always related to something real. Between what we in fact discover in psychoanalysis as the aftermath, consequences, and effects
of frustration, on the one hand – and even its long-lasting effects, for
it makes an impression on us – and symptoms, on the other hand,
there is something known as desire that is characterized by an infinitely more complex dialectic.

Now, what I have tried to demonstrate is that desire does not result
from a few impressions left by the real, but rather that it cannot be
grasped or understood except in the tightest knot by which the real,
the imaginary, and its symbolic meaning are tied together for man.
This is why the relationship between desire and fantasy is inscribed
on the graph in the field that lies midway between the two structural
lines of any and every signifying enunciation [d→($◊a)].

If what constitutes a symptom – namely, let us say, a metaphorical phenomenon, that is, interference by a repressed signifier with a
patent signifier – is truly based on desire, we would be barking up
the wrong tree altogether were we not to seek to situate, organize,
and structure the place of this desire.

We have begun to do so this year, by taking up a dream that I
have already discussed at length.

1

It turns out that Freud highlighted this odd dream, the one in
which the dead father appears, on two different occasions. After
having given it an especially useful place in his 1911 article on
the two principles of mental functioning [SE XII, pp. 225–6], the
pleasure principle and the reality principle, he integrated it into the
Traumdeutung.

I have tried to situate the elements of this dream on what we
might call the graph of the inscription of the elementary biological
subject – that is, the subject characterized by need – in the defiles of
demand. This graph includes a chain or articulation that is fundamentally twofold, which corresponds to a structural distinction. I
showed you how we must view it.

Namely, we must see that demand is never purely and simply a
141   demand for something, since behind every precise demand, every
demand for satisfaction, there is, owing to language, the symbolization of the Other, the Other as presence and absence, the Other
who may be a subject who provides the gift of love. What he gives is

beyond anything he can give. What he gives, he gives by his presence and by his presence alone. What he gives is precisely that nothing which amounts to everything in the determination of presence versus absence.

I have articulated this dream by didactically shifting onto the twofold nature of signs something that allows us to grasp, in the dream's structure, the relationship that is established by the fantasized production whose structure Freud attempted to elucidate throughout his life, and first of all, masterfully, in the *Traumdeutung*.

The son, who is in mourning for a father whom he undoubtedly loved and whom he watched over until the very end of his death throes, makes his father reappear under conditions that the dream articulates with exemplary simplicity. The father appears as he was when alive, he speaks, and before him the son remains dumb, oppressed, and gripped by pain – pain, he says, that stems from the thought "that his father was dead and did not know it." We must complete this, as Freud tells us, "that he was dead as he [the dreamer] wished. He did not know" what? That it was "as he wished."

This is the whole dream. If we try to go further into its construction and examine its structure more closely, we note that the subject is confronted with a certain image under very specific conditions. I would say that a distribution or dividing up is established between this image and what the subject assumes responsibility for in his dream, which will show us the essence of the phenomenon.

I have already tried to home in, so to speak, on the structure of this dream by distributing the dream's characteristic signifying themes on what we might call a signifying ladder.

"He did not know," which I have situated on the upper line of the graph, is an essentially subjective reference, for it concerns nothing factual as such. It concerns the deepest dimension of the subject, going to the core of his structure, and we know that this structure is ambiguous here. "He did not know" is attributable not only to the person to whom it is attributed by the dreamer – in a paradoxical, absurd, and contradictory way that even resonates nonsensically, since we are, after all, talking about someone who is dead – but it is also present in the structure of the dreamer inasmuch as he too shares in this ignorance, and this is essential.

142

How does the subject position himself in the suspension, as it were, of the dream narrative? He views himself as knowing what the other does not know. The upshot is that the other's subjective position is that he is found wanting [*d'être en défaut*], so to speak.

The statement that he is dead obviously cannot affect him. But a symbolic expression like *être mort* ["to be dead" or "dead being"]

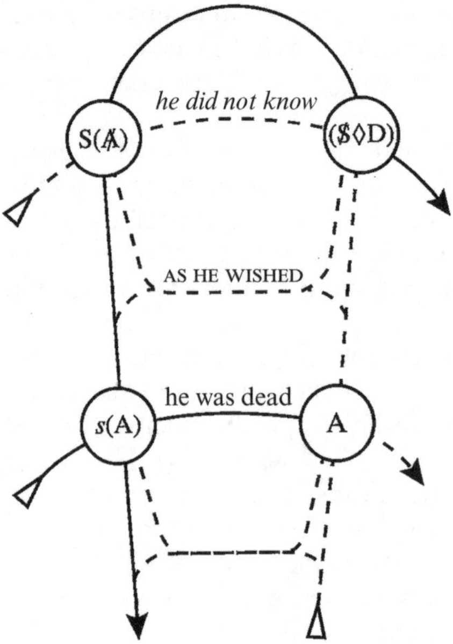

Figure 7.1: New distribution of the statement and enunciation

harbors within itself a paradox, for it makes the very person that it concerns subsist, preserving him in being, whereas there is no being here who can be dead. There can be no symbolic assertion of someone being dead [*de l'être mort*] that does not immortalize him, in a certain manner. This is clearly what is at work in the dream about the dead father.

The fact remains that the position of this being who is found wanting, that this subjective minus value [*moins-value*], does not aim at the fact that he is dead but that he is the one who does not know it. This is how the subject [i.e., the dreamer] is situated in relation to the other. Not only does the other not know that he is dead but I would say that, in the end, he must not be told this. Such protecting of the other is always found more or less at the root of any and all communication between beings, where the question of what one can and what one cannot make known to the other always arises. This is something whose impact you should always weigh carefully whenever you are engaged in analytic discourse.

We talked last night about those who cannot speak, those who encounter obstacles to expressing themselves. What was at issue was the resistance of discourse itself, strictly speaking. It is essential that we mention this dimension if we are to relate the dream about the dead father to another dream, one that I will borrow from a page near the end of *Trotsky's Diary in Exile*. It is a dream he had shortly after the end of his stay in France, I believe.

It is an especially poignant dream. Trotsky had it at a moment when, perhaps for the very first time, he began to notice the first signs of the diminishing of his life force that had been so inexhaustible. In his dream he sees his companion Lenin, and Lenin conveys to him that Trotsky is perhaps no longer at the height of his powers, as his old companion had always known him to be. But faced with this old companion, who emerges so significantly at a critical moment in his own vitality, what Trotsky thinks, in a way whose value derives from the ambiguity we always encounter in dialogue, is that he should spare Lenin's feelings. And wishing to remind him of a time related to the precise moment at which Lenin's own forces failed him, Trotsky says to him, in order to designate to him the moment at which he died, "the moment at which you were very, very ill . . ." – as if some precise formulation of what was involved would, by its mere utterance, have blown away the shade in the dream with which Trotsky himself was grappling, at the same turning point in *his* existence.

Well, if in the distribution between the two figures who confront each other in the dream about the dead father, ignorance is imputed to the other, how can we fail to see that there is also, conversely, the subject's own ignorance? For the dreamer does not know, not simply the signification of his dream – namely, everything that underlies it and that Freud brings out, that is, his unconscious history, his old wishes for his father's death – but, further still, the nature of the pain that he (the dreamer) feels. In seeking its origin, we have realized that it was the pain that he had felt and glimpsed while witnessing his father's last moments on earth. But it is also the pain of existence as such, at the limit at which this existence subsists in a state where we no longer apprehend anything but its inextinguishable character and the fundamental pain that accompanies it when all desire disappears from it, when all desire has vanished from one's existence.   144

This is the exact pain that the subject takes on, but he explains it absurdly since he explains it solely by the other's ignorance. In the final analysis, if we look very closely, this ignorance is no more a reason for his pain than the affect that emerges in an hysterical fit is explained by the context from which it seems to arise, the affect being in fact related to some other context.

It is precisely by taking this pain on himself that the subject blinds himself to what has taken place in his immediate proximity – that is, to the fact that his father's death throes and disappearance have actually threatened him, the son. He experienced these things, and in the dream he distances himself from them by recalling his father's image to mind. This image separates him from the sort of abyss or vertigo that opens up before him whenever he is confronted with the final term of his existence, and attaches him to something that calms men down – namely, desire. What he needs to interpose between himself and unbearable existence is, in this case, a desire.

He does not cite just any old prop for his desire, just any old desire, but the closest and most urgent one, the best one, the desire that had long dominated him, the one he had subdued but that he must now bring back to life imaginarily for a while.

In the power struggle that lies at the core of his rivalry with his father, it is the dreamer who finally wins out. If he triumphs, it is because the other does not know, whereas he does. Here we see the flimsy footbridge [*passerelle*] thanks to which the subject does not feel directly invaded – or swallowed up by the gaping hole that opens up before him – when he is directly confronted with the anxiety that death provokes.

To put this more crudely, we know that the death of one's father is always experienced as the disappearance of a sort of shield, of the interposition or substitution that the father was with respect to the absolute master, death.

145 We thus begin to see a sort of prefiguration of something; we see something being sketched out. What is it, if not the formula that I am trying to present, which is what props desire up – the fundamental formula of the essential intra-subjective relationship within which all desire, as such, must be inscribed: ($\lozenge a$)?

2

In this simplest form possible, the formula ($\lozenge a$) expresses the same relationship as the one that interposes itself in the partially unconscious discourse coming from the Other with a capital *O* [*grand Autre*] and going toward the subject, in the quadrilateral schema that you already know, the one known as the L schema.

The imaginary tension *a–a'* between the ego and the other – that we could call, in certain regards, the tension between little *a* and the *image of a* – generally structures the relationship between the subject and the object, whereas the formula ($\lozenge a$) specifically expresses the absence of the subject that is characteristic of the impact of desire on the relationship between the subject and the imaginary functions.

Indeed, desire as such raises for man the question of his subjective elision, $, with regard to any and every possible object.

To the degree to which the subject is inscribed in the dimension of speech as a plaintiff [or: petitioner, *demandeur*], he approaches

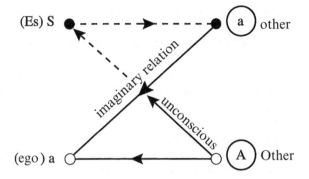

Figure 7.2: The L schema

the most elaborate and evolved object that certain analysts more or
less deftly conceptualize as the object of "oblativity." This notion is   146
problematic, as I have often indicated. I, too, try to conceptualize
what is involved here and endeavor to formulate it more rigorously.

Inasmuch as a subject, qua desire – that is, in the fullness of a
human destiny which is that of a speaking subject – approaches this
object, he finds himself caught in a sort of impasse. He cannot reach
this object qua object except by finding himself, as a subject of speech,
effaced in a kind of elision that leaves him in the darkness brought
on by trauma, and in what is, strictly speaking, beyond anxiety itself.
Or else he finds that he must take the place of the object, substitute
himself for it, and subsume himself under a certain signifier.

Which one? The phallus. For the time being, I am simply stating
this. I am not justifying it; our whole discussion will justify it. All
of psychoanalytic experience attests to it. It is owing to this that, in
every instance of assuming a fully developed [mûre] position, the one
we refer to as genital, something occurs which has an impact at the
imaginary level – it is called castration.

It is from this perspective alone that one can understand the
problematic of the phallic phase that raised truly infinite questions
and contradictions from which analysts have found it impossible to
extricate themselves. The dialogue between Freud and Jones on this
topic is, I would say, singularly moving. It suffices to see the impasse
that Jones ends up in when he revolts against the conception – which
is too simple for his taste – that Freud offers of the phallic function,
as the one and only term around which all concrete and historical
development of sexuality in men and women revolves. Jones highlights instead what he refers to as the functions of defense linked to
the image of the phallus.

Freud and Jones end up saying the same thing, but they come at it from different angles. If they assuredly cannot agree, it is because they do not have at their disposal the central notion according to which the phallus must, in this case, be conceptualized as subtracted, as it were, from the imaginary community, as isolated when confronted with the variety and multiplicity of other images that come to take on bodily functions. Its function is privileged, it constituting the signifier of the subject.

147   Let us look at this still more closely, and distinguish the level of the call [appel] from that of the wish [voeu].

The level of the call is first, immediate, apparent, and spontaneous. When we call out, "Help!" or "Give us bread!" – each of which is, in the end, a cry – the subject is identical to his need for an instant, and in the most total way possible. A call must, nevertheless, be articulated at the interrogative [quésitif] level of demand. It is articulated in the experience between child and mother, and in everything he puts in her place – namely, the whole society that speaks her [or: his, sa] language.

On the other hand, the articulation of the votive [votif] level is at one remove. It is the dimension in which the subject, throughout his life, must find himself anew – that is to say, must find what got away from him because it was outside and beyond all that is filtered out by language qua form. As it develops, such filtration rejects and represses ever more thoroughly that part of the subject's need that tended to be expressed at first. What we do in analysis is attempt to go beyond what was filtered out, shaped, and transformed by the subject's speech.

We could say that everything that must be articulated at the interrogative level resides in the Other, here at A [on the lower level of the graph], as a predetermined code that completely pre-exists the subject's experience, it being offered up to the play of language – that is, to the first signifying battery the subject experiences, assuming he learns to speak.

What do we do in analysis, what do we encounter, and what do we recognize when we say that the subject is at the oral stage or at the anal stage, etc.? We must first of all express it in a full-fledged form, which assumes that we do not forget the complete element – namely, that what is always involved is the subject qua marked by speech and in a certain relation to his demand. Next, we must see that an interpretation by which we convey to the subject the structuring of his demand, does not simply consist in getting him to recognize the oral, anal, or other character [caractère] of the demand in question, but, literally, to confront him with this characteristic [caractère]. What we interpret is not simply a characteristic that is immanent in the subject's demand; we confront the subject with the structure of his demand as such.

It is precisely at this point that the emphasis of our interpretation must shift, oscillate, and vacillate. If we know how to emphasize it in a certain way, we teach the subject to recognize at the upper level of the graph – which is the votive level, the level of what he wishes for, the level of his wishes insofar as they are unconscious – the signifying props that are hidden and unconscious in his demand. Interpretation must stay entirely within this register. In short, we do nothing but teach the subject, as it were, to speak and to recognize himself as a subject in what corresponds to D [on the graph; see Figure 2.2], yet without giving him answers.

148

On the other hand, to reveal this unconscious vocabulary to the subject without confronting him with his demand comes down to producing a collapse in the function of the subject as such; it comes down to asking him to efface himself and disappear. This is clearly what happens in a type of psychoanalytic practice in which the analysis of the unconscious is reduced to teaching the patient a vocabulary. What disappears and escapes, what turns out to be progressively eliminated, is the requirement that the subject manifest himself – beyond all of that – in his being. Constantly bringing him back to the level of demand – which is known in a certain form of technique as "analyzing the resistances" – ends up purely and simply eliminating his desire.

It is simple and easy to see that the two levels of the graph include the vector of a retroactive response. In the subject's relation to the Other, this vector goes backward toward the subject in order to confirm the meaning of his demand for him, and at times to identify him with his own demand. Similarly, at the level at which the subject seeks to recognize himself in what is beyond this demand, there is a place for a response, which is schematized by the abbreviation S($\cancel{A}$), which is the signifier of barred A. This is a reminder that the Other too is marked by the signifier, that he too is in a certain way abolished in discourse.

This serves no other function than to indicate a theoretical point, and we shall see the form it must take. Let us simply say that this form is essentially the recognition of what is castrated in any living being who attempts to approach this living being when the latter is approached through language. Of course, it is not at this level that we can instantly give an answer, but we must target, respect, and explore it.

In order to do so, we can use what the subject already expresses beyond the answer's locus – namely, the imaginary situation in which he places, maintains, and suspends himself in a position that, in certain ways, assuredly includes the artifices of defense. This is what leads to the ambiguity of so many manifestations of desire,

149

of perverse desire, for example. This is the most essential point at
which the subject's being attempts to express and assert itself.

This is all the more important to consider, as it is precisely here,
in this very locus, that we expect what we so blithely call optimal
genital development to occur, and the fully developed [*achevé*]
object to appear. Thanks to which we should note that everything
that constitutes the relations between men and women, as Jones
expresses himself biblically somewhere, remains marked by structural difficulties that stem from the fact that man is a speaking
subject and that express the relationship between $ and *a*. Why are
there such difficulties?

Up to a certain point in development, the vocabulary and code of
demand can pass through a certain number of relations that involve
a detachable object – namely, to limit ourselves to two, nourishment
in oral relations and excrement in anal relations. Nevertheless, when
genital relations are at stake, it is quite clear that it is only through
a type of borrowing or continuation of the subject's signifying fragmentation in relations involving demand that something can appear
to us – and indeed appears to us, but in a morbid way, including all
its symptomatic forms of impact – namely, the phallus. And this
is true for a good, simple reason, which is that the phallus is not a
detachable object and that it only becomes one by shifting to the
status of a signifier.

What is involved in optimal genital development is based on the
following, that nothing that presents itself in the subject as related
to the fulfillment of his desire can, to put it as clearly as possible, be
demanded [or: asked for, *se demander*]. The essence of neurosis, the
essence of what we deal with when we work with those characterized by neurotic structure, consists very precisely in the fact that
what cannot be demanded in this realm – that is to say, everything
having to do with desire – is nevertheless inscribed and formulated
in the register of demand. This neurotic phenomenon appears, more
or less sporadically, in the development of all subjects characterized
by neurotic structure.

While rereading Jones's work recently, I re-examined every-
150   thing he wrote about the phallic phase. What he contributes that
stems from his most perceptive and direct experience is always very
interesting.

> I could relate cases of a number of male patients whose failure
> to achieve manhood – in relation to either men or women – was
> strictly to be correlated with their attitude of needing first to
> acquire something from women, something which of course
> they never actually could acquire. [p. 461]

"Why?" asks Jones, and when he asks why in his article and in this context, it is a genuine question. He does not know why, but he underscores it as a point on the horizon, an opening, a perspective, and a point where he no longer has any guide.

Why should imperfect access to the nipple give a boy the sense of imperfect possession of his own penis? I am quite convinced that the two things are intimately related, although the logical connection between them is certainly not obvious. [p. 461]

At least, not to him.

Even the most superficial phenomenology allows us to see at every moment the necessary preconditions for a subject to be able to fully put his desire into action. We can reconstruct them in detail right up to the point of finding what I would call the labyrinthine pathways into which his desire skids. Here we see what constitutes an essential fact – namely, the position he took up in the structural relation between desire and demand.

This is why people say, for example, that the continued existence of the incestuous position in the unconscious has variously ravaging consequences on the manifestations and fulfillment of the subject's desire. If this proposition has any meaning, it is only inasmuch as this so-called incestuous position, which is supposedly preserved somewhere in the unconscious, is a position characterized by demand. When Jones says that the subject must, at a given moment, choose between his incestuous object and his sexual organ [*sexe*], and that if he wants to preserve the one he must give up the other, I would say that what he has to choose between at such an early moment is between his demand and his desire.

151

After these general indications, I am now going to start down a path that is designed to show you the actual structuring of desire at the imaginary level, and what it has in common with imaginary elements that are inflected and taken up in the necessary play of the signifying game, inasmuch as this game is commanded by the twofold structure of the votive and the interrogative.

3

Let us consider the most banal or common fantasy, the one Freud paid special attention to: "A child is being beaten" [SE XVII, pp. 179–204].

Let us re-examine it from the perspective I am developing in order to see in what respect fantasy is desire's necessary prop.

Freud encountered the *Schlagephantasie* [beating fantasy], in his own era, in a certain number of predominantly female subjects. When the first phase of the fantasy is remembered, whether in fantasies or in the subject's memories, it is described, Freud tells us, by the following sentence: *Der Vater schlägt das Kind* [The father is beating the child]. Freud underscores the fact that, in this case, the child who is being beaten is, in relation to the subject, in a position that is expressed by the more complete sentence: "The father is beating the child that I hate."

Freud thus brings us from the initial point to the very heart of being, where the most intense degree of love and hate is situated. In effect, the other child is represented here as being subjected, by the father's violence and whim [*caprice*], to a maximal fall from grace [*déchéance*] or symbolic devaluing, as being absolutely frustrated and deprived of love. Hatred targets him in his very being, targeting in him what is demanded beyond all demand – namely, love. The so-called narcissistic injury done to the hated child is utter and complete here.

The child's subjective fall from grace, which is linked for him to his first encounter with corporal punishment, leaves various traces depending on the modalities of its repetition. In the times in which we live, children are mostly spared such punishment. Nevertheless, as everyone can observe, if it happens that a child who has never been beaten is, late in the game, the object of physical chastisement, however justified it may be, this experience has prostrating consequences for him, at least momentarily, that one cannot imagine in advance.

Be that as it may, assuming we agree that the earliest stage of the beating fantasy is as Freud presents it to us, "Profound transformations [take] place between this first phase and the next" [SE XVII, p. 185]. Freud describes the second phase as follows:

> The person beating remains the same (that is, the father); but the child who is beaten has been changed into another one and is now invariably the child producing the fantasy. The fantasy is accompanied by a high degree of pleasure, and has now acquired a significant content, with the origin of which we shall be concerned later. Now, therefore, the wording runs: "I am being beaten by my father." [p. 185]

But Freud adds the following:

> This second phase is the most important and the most momentous of all. But we may say of it in a certain sense that it has

never had [any] real existence. It is never remembered, it has never succeeded in becoming conscious. It is a construction of analysis, but it is no less a necessity on that account. [p. 185]

My sense is that no one gives enough weight to the consequences of Freud's assertion here. In the final analysis, we never encounter the most significant phase. Nevertheless, it has to exist since it leads to a third phase.

Now, the formulation of the second phase is of great interest to us. It is tantamount, in effect, to the formulation of primary masochism. The latter comes in at the precise moment at which the subject gets closest to realizing himself as a subject in the signifying dialectic.

Freud rightly says that something essential happens between the first and the second phase: the subject sees the other being cast down from his dignity as an elevated subject, as a little rival. The opening that ensues makes him perceive that his whole being, qua existing being, resides in the very possibility of subjective cancellation. It is in coming as close as possible to being abolished that he weighs the dimension in which he subsists as a being who is subject to will, a being who can formulate a wish.

We must seek out the phenomenology of masochism in masochistic literature, whether we like it or not, and whether it is pornographic or not. What is the essence of the masochist's fantasy, in the end, whether we look at a classic novel or a recent novel brought out by a semi-clandestine publisher? The subject imagines a series of experiences that go in a direction whose flank, border, or limit is based essentially on the fact that he is purely and simply treated like a thing, like something that, at its most extreme, is negotiated, sold, mistreated, and removed from any and every votive possibility of viewing himself as autonomous. He is treated like a dog, I would say, and not just any old dog – a dog that is mistreated and especially like a dog who has already been mistreated.

This is the turning or pivotal point of the second phase that we can only assume to exist. It is also the transformational base starting from which the subject will seek to enter into the final phase, in order to find therein the swivel or balance [or: tipping] point of his position – namely, $. For once he has entered into the dialectic of speech, assuming he enters into it, he must formulate himself as a subject somewhere.

Nevertheless, in the end, the neurotic subject is like Picasso. Picasso once came out with the following truly sovereign formulation: "I do not seek, I find." In effect, there is a certain type of person who seeks, and another type that finds. Believe me, neurotics

153

– namely, everything man's struggle with speech spontaneously produces in subjects – find.

I would point out in this connection that *trouver* [to find] comes
from the Latin word *tropus* [trope]. This refers quite explicitly to
what I always talk about, the difficulties of rhetoric. It is curious
that in the Romance languages the word that designates the fact of
finding is borrowed from the language of rhetoric, whereas in the
Germanic languages it is a different root that serves this purpose.

Let us stop for a moment at this third phase at which the subject
thus gains his balance. It is immediately known to us, but perhaps
154   worth dwelling on nevertheless. What do we see right off the bat in
the fantasy *On bat un enfant* ["A child is being beaten"]?

Who is doing the beating? It is *On* [the impersonal pronoun One].
When Freud would insistently ask his patient who was doing the
beating, this person or that, there was nothing doing, he remained
evasive. It was only after a certain amount of interpretive work that
the subject could refind a certain paternal figure or image in his
fantasy, insofar as the latter served as a prop for his desire when
masturbating. But at the outset, the subject of the sentence was completely neutralized: it was *On*.

As for who is beaten, it is not difficult to grasp. It is multiple –
many children, boys when the fantasizer is a girl. But there is no
necessary connection between the sex of the child who fantasizes
and the sex of the image fantasized about.

The greatest variations and uncertainties center, too, on the position of the child whose fantasy it is. We know that, up to a certain
point, the child – in some way, whether it is *a* or *a'*, *i(a)* or *a* – is
involved in this fantasy since he is the one who has it. But the child
does not situate himself anywhere in a precise, unequivocal manner;
his position swivels indefinitely.

I would now like to highlight something that is closely related to
what I earlier called the distribution of the intra-subjective elements
of the dream. Where is affect emphasized? In the dream about the
dead father, this affect is pain and it targets the dreaming subject.
Similarly, in the fantasy "a child is being beaten," which is indisputably a sadistic fantasy – and, moreover, in virtually all sadistic
fantasies that we can observe, taken in their broadest extension
– affect targets the fantasized image of the partner, not so much
insofar as he is beaten but insofar as he is going to be beaten or does
not know how he will be beaten.

I will come back to this extraordinary element when we talk about
the phenomenology of anxiety. But I am already pointing out to you
a nuanced distinction found in Freud's text, and which no one naturally has ever brought out regarding anxiety. We must not confuse

the pure and simple loss of the subject in the darkness of subjective indetermination with something that is completely different from it: the fact that the subject becomes alert or erect, as it were, when faced with danger.

In *Inhibitions, Symptoms, and Anxiety*, Freud introduces a still   155
more astonishing phenomenological distinction that is so subtle that it is not easy to translate into French. It is the distinction between *abwarten*, which I will endeavor to translate by *subir* [to undergo], *n'en pouvoir mais* [to be unable to do anything about it], or *tendre le dos* [brace oneself], and *erwarten*, which is *s'attendre à* [to expect]. The affect that is emphasized and attached to the other or partner – attached to he who is across from one, little *a* – is situated in this register or range in the sadist's fantasy.

Where, in the final analysis, is this subject – this subject who, in this case, is prey to something that he does not have [and that he would have to have] in order to know where he is? It would be easy to say that he is between the two [the beater and the beaten]. I would go further still – I would say that he is so truly between the two that he plays, in an exemplary manner, the role of the instrument with which the one hits the other. The subject is identical here to the instrument.

Indeed, the instrument is very frequently the essential personage in the imaginary structure of desire that we are trying to formulate here. We are always flabbergasted to see this, and we always have the best of reasons to be astonished by this, unless we do not want to see it. What is most paradoxical and the biggest warning for us is, in short, that the subject abolishes himself behind this signifier, which is altogether unveiled here in its nature as a signifier, insofar as he recognizes his essential being in it, if it is true that we can say with Spinoza that this essential being is his desire.

It is, in effect, to this same crossroads that we are led whenever a sexual problematic is brought up. The crux of the sexual problematic in women is the phallic phase. We began with this two years ago and Jones returns to it constantly in order to dispute and develop it. Jones's text manifests the kind of working over of a topic that we see in the course of a psychoanalysis.

The central focus of the phallic phase in girls is the relationship between hatred for the mother and desire for the phallus. It is on this very point that Freud bases the requirement [or: demand, *exigence*] that everyone have a phallus, a requirement that plays a role in the resolution of the Oedipus complex in boys, and a role in the entry into the Oedipus complex for girls. This requirement has a truly fundamental, generative [or: developmental, *génétique*] character.

The link between hatred for the mother and desire for the phallus

is the strict meaning of *Penisneid* [penis envy]. Jones rightly underscores the ambiguities encountered every time we use this term. If
156   the desire to have a penis is inscribed in a rivalry with another, it
presents itself in an ambiguous guise that clearly shows us that its
meaning must be sought out beyond this. "Desire for the phallus"
means desire mediated by the phallus. The mediating phallus plays
an essential role in the mediation of desire.

This leads me to formulate the problem in terms that already
introduce what I will later have to develop in my analysis of the
construction of fantasy. We will have to figure out how to situate the
place of the phallus as a signifier in imaginary experience. The latter,
as we know, is profoundly structured by narcissistic forms that
govern the relations between the subject and his semblable – that is
to say, between the speaking subject, $, and little *a*, the other that
the subject bears within himself.

Today, we have identified it with *a*. This means that the imaginary
other is what the subject has inside himself as a "drive" – I put it in
quotes, for what we have here is a drive that is not yet developed,
a drive before it is taken up in the signifying dialectic, a drive in its
primitive nature where it represents one or another manifestation
of the subject's need. Nevertheless, if the subject, through the intermediary of specular reflection, must situate his needs in the image
of the other, we see on the horizon what I initially referred to as
the first identification with the Other in the radical sense – namely,
identification with the Other's insignias. This is, in other words, the
signifier capital I over little *a*.

$$\frac{I}{a}$$

I am going to put on the board a schema that will be recognized
by those who were here for the first year of my Seminar, when we
spoke about narcissism. It is the schema of the parabolic mirror
thanks to which we can make the image of a hidden flower appear
in a vase sitting on a tray, whether it is lit from below or on the tray;
owing to the property of spherical rays, this image is projected as
a real image. This means that it momentarily produces the illusion
that the flower is in the vase.

157   To conjure up this image in space, we must have a little screen over
here [Lacan points to a part of the schema]. This might seem mysterious, but it is not. In effect, the illusion – namely the sight of this
real image in the air – can only be perceived within a certain spatial
field which is precisely determined by the diameter of the spherical
mirror and mapped out in relation to the center of the mirror. The

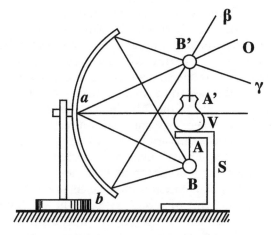

Figure 7.3: The inverted bouquet illusion

upshot being that, if the mirror is narrow, in order to see the image one must place oneself in a field where the rays reflected from the mirror cross anew its center, which assumes a certain lighting up [or: blossoming, *épanouissement*] of the spatial zone.

What was important in my little explanation back then was the following: if someone wanted to see this fantasized image get produced somewhere in space – inside the vase, or a little to the side of it, it makes no difference – where there is already a real object, and if this observer is situated at S_1, he could rotate the plane mirror in order to occupy the symmetrical and virtual position S_2, which is

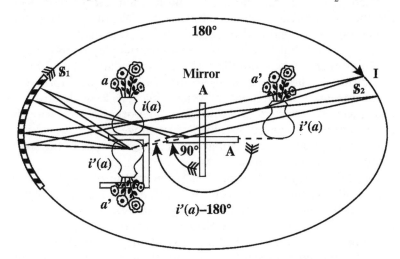

Figure 7.4: Rotation of the plane mirror

inside the cone of visibility of the image, and he would see the image of the flower in the plane mirror at the symmetrical point.

158   In other words, the ray of light that is reflected toward the observer is strictly symmetrical to what occurs on the other side, insofar as this observer has virtually come to occupy the place from which he will see the vase in the plane mirror – which he can expect since he is there – and, on the other hand, the real image which is produced in a place where he cannot see it directly.

This optical device is thus apt for representing the relationship or interplay between the subject's imaginary elements and his symbolic identificatory elements. I do not think that the way in which it does so betrays the psychoanalytic tradition, since, in the *Traumdeutung*, Freud offers up a schema of successive lenses in which the progressive passage from the unconscious to the preconscious is refracted. He was thus looking for analogous references in optics, as he says precisely [SE V, pp. 536, 611].

This is but a metaphor, one that represents the specular pathway by which the subject tries in fantasy to return to his place in the symbolic. Consequently, the $ is something other than an eye. The spherical mirror, which helps him return to his place in the symbolic, represents capital A here – it is a symbolic mirror. It is not the mirror in front of which the small child plays. What we have here is in fact a certain reflection that is constructed with the help of words,

159   in the course of the first learning of language, and thanks to which the subject learns to situate at the right distance the insignias with which he identifies.

These symbolic insignias correspond to what, on the other side, are the first imaginary ego identifications. We thus already find something preformed and open to symbolic fragmentation at the imaginary level, but which only enters into the play of fragmentation inasmuch as the symbolic exists and opens up its field to him. It is inside this field that, owing to the symbolic, a transformation of the imaginary relation occurs which is such, as I am already indicating to you, that there will always be, in erotic relations with the other, however advanced or fully developed we assume them to be, a reduction point that you can grasp as extrapolations of the erotic blueprint [*épure*] between subjects.

What is the transformation that is undergone by the first, fundamentally specular relationship between *a* and *a'* or *i(a)*, which regulates the relations between the subject and the other? The imaginary set of fragmented bodily elements must be distributed across the puppet with which we deal in the symbolic, inasmuch as we are puppets and our partners are too. But these puppets are missing something: the phallus.

The phallus is busy elsewhere, in the signifying function. When faced with the other, the subject identifies with the phallus, but he fragments qua himself when he is in the presence of the phallus. To spell this out as clearly as possible, I will ask you to dwell on what happens in relationships between men and women, even the most loving.

In men, desire is found outside the love relationship. The fully developed form of this relationship assumes, in effect, that the subject gives what he does not have, which is the very definition of love. On the other hand, the ideal form of desire, as it were, is realized in him inasmuch as he finds anew the complement of his being in a woman, insofar as she symbolizes the phallus.

In love, man truly becomes a slave of [s'aliéné à] the object of his desire, a slave to the phallus. But in the erotic act this same phallus nevertheless reduces the woman to being an imaginary object. This is why we find in men a splitting of the object [of love from that of desire], even at the very heart of the deepest, most intimate love relationships. I have often emphasized this when I have criticized the so-called genital relationship.

When we turn, on the other hand, to women's relationships to men, which people like to believe are more monogamous, we see that they present the same ambiguity – except that women find the real phallus in men. They are thus in a position to in fact obtain from such relationships a jouissance that satisfies their desire.

But, to the degree to which their desire is satisfied at the level of the real, their love, not their desire, concerns beings who are beyond the encounter with desire – namely, men insofar as they are deprived of the phallus, men insofar as, by their nature as fully developed beings, speaking beings, are castrated.

January 7, 1959

160

A DREAM ANALYZED
BY ELLA SHARPE

VIII

THE LITTLE COUGH
AS A MESSAGE

The enigma of enunciation
The subject's being lies in fantasy
The positional affects of being
Text and context of the dream
The brilliant Ella Sharpe

Since we spoke about desire quite a lot in the last few classes, we are now going to begin to broach the topic of interpretation. The graph of desire will serve us here, in the following form:

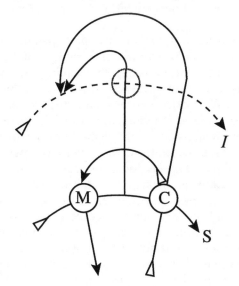

Figure 8.1: Simplified graph

I will talk today about the interpretation of a dream that I will take as an example. I would like to introduce it by making a few remarks about what results from the indications Freud gives us on the topic of the interpretation of dreams.

164

1

In Chapter 6 of the *Traumdeutung*, Freud discusses the subject's mental impressions at the moment at which he recounts a dream.

We find that he has the impression that there is something missing in his narrative, which he has forgotten, or something that is ambiguous, doubtful, or uncertain. He underscores this uncertainty, doubtfulness, or ambiguity by saying things like, "It's not clear," "It was either this or that," "I don't remember now," or "I can no longer say." He even calls into question the degree of reality of what he saw in the dream – whether the fact that something was asserted in it with such realism that he took notice of it or that the dream struck him, on the contrary, as absurd. All of this, Freud tells us, in every case, must be taken to enunciate what he calls one of the "latent dream-thoughts."

In short, everything regarding the dream-text that is said by the subject as an aside – as if in the form of annotations accompanying a musical score to provide accents of tonality, like *allegro, crescendo*, or *decrescendo* – is part and parcel of the dream-text. This is truly fundamental.

I believe that for most of you, whom I assume to be already familiar with the *Traumdeutung* and the technique of dream interpretation, this is not new. I am thus merely recalling it to mind, for I do not have time here to go into the specific examples of this that we find in Freud's work. We see there, for instance, how the feeling of doubt the subject experiences at the moment at which he recounts a dream is integrated by Freud as one of the elements of the dream – indeed, as an element without which the dream cannot be interpreted.

Many of Freud's disciples took this rule of thumb regarding dream interpretation as an article of faith, without looking any further, lending credence, in some sense, to the unconscious. We, on the other hand, cannot simply accept it as it is. We do not take Freud's approach to interpretation as our point of departure without raising questions about what it implies.

Freud tells us that when your memory of a dream begins to fade, or on the contrary is called into question or stressed, this is not due solely to the unconscious tension that is at work there, but is connected to the latent dream-thoughts themselves. What does this imply? What we have agreed to call the graph of desire allows us to indicate and articulate it more clearly and surely.

165

What do we do when we communicate a dream, whether it be in or outside of analysis? What, among all the possible enunciations, specifies the enunciation of a dream? Statements [*énoncés*] have, in effect, a certain structure with respect to the subject, and people did not wait for psychoanalysis to formulate it.

Among a discourse's event-related statements – I mean the statements that report events – we can legitimately distinguish, with regard to the signifying register, statements that we can group under the general heading of indirect speech [*discours indirect*]. These are statements that relate the enunciations of other subjects – that is, the signifying articulations of other people. Many things are introduced thereby, including statements involving hearsay: "I was told . . .," "So-and-so said . . .," and "Someone told me that this is what happened. . . ." Indirect speech is the most fundamental, or one of the most fundamental, forms of everyday speech [*discours universel*], for most of the things that we report stem from what we have gleaned from others.

Let us say that, generally speaking, a statement involves the reporting of a pure, simple, factual statement that we take as our own, on the one hand, and the dimension of enunciation that is latent, that is not necessarily made clear, but that becomes so as soon as we report someone else's statement, on the other hand. But we can also relate one of our own statements: we can say that we said such and such, that we bore witness to something to someone, and we can even enunciate that a statement we made [at a certain time and place] was completely false – in other words, we can admit that we lied.

One of these possibilities will hold our attention for a moment. What do we do when we enunciate a dream? We do something that is not entirely unique, at least not in the way I am going to define it now.

How did people view dreams before we psychoanalysts weighed in on the age-old debate? People objected to Freud that dreams have no signification and that they are simply the product of unfocused [*décomposition*] mental activity. This so-called scientific position was, as it turned out, maintained for only a short time in history, whereas Freud underscored the fact that he was merely aligning himself with the longer-standing tradition. It is already quite important to know, as I just indicated, that the longer-standing tradition never failed to wonder about the signification of dreams.

166

In other words, as soon as a subject recounts his dream to someone else, the very form of enunciation in which he states the dream involves a question mark that is not just any old question mark, for it assumes that behind the dream there is something of which the dream is the signifier. We can write this, in our way of formalizing things, as follows: $E(e)$. It involves the enunciation $[E]$ of a statement $[e$ for *énoncé*$]$ that is itself marked by enunciation – in other words, that is itself assumed to take on a value which, naturally, is not factual or event-related.

In order to remain in the purely descriptive dimension, we must add a supplemental point here.

A small child who begins to tell you his dreams, says, "Last night, I had a dream." His spontaneous attitude is the same as the traditional attitude, but it is highly ambiguous here. If we observe closely, it is as if, at some moment, it had been revealed to the child that he had the possibility to express such things. And it goes so far that quite frequently one cannot truly know, at the age at which the child begins to tell you such matters in confidence, whether what he tells you is truly what he dreamt or something he brings you because he knows that people dream and that people can recount their dreams.

As we observe when we have contact with children, their dreams often seem to verge on fabrication. But if children have and tell dreams in such ways, it is with the lowercase e, marked by enunciation. There is something beyond the statement with which they play a game with you, making you wonder or become fascinated.

In short, every type of statement that recounts a dream, whether it be in or outside of analysis, corresponds to the formula $E(e)$. This formula is not specific to dreams alone. I would say that it is the general formula of enigmas.

What then is signified by what Freud means? Let us look at it on our little graph, which in this case takes the form you see on the blackboard [Figure 8.1]. How are we going to project the different elements of this formalization onto it? We can do so in several different ways.

This graph is of interest to us because it is structural. It is a structure that allows us to map the relationship between the subject and the signifier. In effect, from the very moment at which the subject is caught up in the signifier – and it is essential that he be caught up in it, for that is what defines him, the subject being the relationship between the individual and the signifier, between the individual and the signifier's structure – a network is necessarily imposed that forever remains fundamental. Let us thus try to see here how we can distribute the various functions involved in the enunciation of a dream on the graph.

A dream, which is a spontaneous creation, presents itself at first glance as being relatively total or monolithic – it is, I would say, a total statement. In French we say, "*J'ai fait un rêve*" [literally: "I made a dream," instead of "I had a dream" as in English], and we distinguish the dream from the one that followed it, which was not the same. A dream has the character of a discourse. At the moment at which we have/make a dream, nothing reveals the fragmentation or decomposition of the signifier in it. We have all sorts of retroactive indications that the fragmentation is there, having an impact on the function of all discourse, but at the moment at which the subject generates a discourse, and inasmuch as he cleaves to it, the choice he makes at each moment among signifiers remains in abeyance and unnoticed – otherwise it would be far more arduous for him to communicate it.

Insofar as it is given to us as a whole, a dream is the statement or signifying chain that is produced at the lower level of the graph, and that presents itself in the usual form of language, a form that is all the more global since it is closed. Nevertheless, the subject must make his report, must produce an enunciation about this statement; he must situate himself in relation to it, and stress certain portions of it to you in accordance with the greater or lesser degree of conviction he has about them. All of that, which accompanies the dream and which, in some sense, comments on it from a position for which the subject assumes more or less responsibility, is inscribed at the level of discourse for the Other, which is also the discourse in which the subject assumes responsibility for his dream.

In other words, when he tells you his dream, the subject himself is already present within the statement. And it is in the discourse in which the subject assumes responsibility for the dream vis-à-vis the person to whom he tells it that, as we see, he stresses certain things and downplays others, expressing his greater or lesser assumption of responsibility for the narrative. He says, "It seemed to me, it appeared to me, that this was what happened at that moment." "At that moment, it was as if the person in the dream were at the same time someone else or turned into someone else."

These are what I am calling "stresses" [*accents*]; they are the different modes of enunciation according to which the subject assumes more or less responsibility for the lived experience of his dream, of this psychical event. These modes are situated on our graph on the line of the *I* of enunciation, a line that is fragmented and discontinuous. The graph indicates to you that this fragmentation is a feature of what is articulated at the level of enunciation, insofar as it involves the signifier.

I placed at the lower level the retroactive effect of the code [C] on the message [M], which, at every moment, gives meaning to a

168

sentence. Let us note that phrasal units come in different sizes. At the end of a long lecture [*discours*], at the end of one of my classes here, for example, or at the end of one of my year-long Seminars, there is something that retroactively closes [*boucle*] the meaning of what I enunciated to you previously. But, up to a certain point, a similar loop [*boucle*] forms after each of the parts of my lecture, after each of the paragraphs.

We might want to know what the smallest unit is in which we find the effect that I call a "signification effect" – which must, in order to deserve its name, be a new creation, something made of language that goes beyond the usual ways of using the signifier. The smallest unit is obviously a sentence.

Let us ask now how this unit presents itself when a dream is reported to us. It is altogether clear here that what the subject does or does not assume responsibility for, believes or does not believe, or calls into question is not necessarily the whole of what he tells us. The subject's enunciative grip [*prise*] may be of a smaller scope: he may take responsibility for or challenge but one single sentence or even just fragments of a sentence.

In other words, the retroactive loop introduces the possibility of a much smaller degree of fragmentation at the upper level than at the lower level.

169   This remark puts us on the scent of what Freud implies when he says that when the dreamer stresses the fact that he does or does not assume responsibility [for certain details], it is connected to the latent dream-thoughts.

Which tells us that this stress is situated at the level of enunciation, inasmuch as it is there that the importance of the signifier implied by free association is highlighted.

2

The signifying chain has two facets.

The first is the unity of a sentence's meaning, its phrasal significa-tion or monolithic nature – in short, its "holophrastic" character. More accurately put, a sentence can be taken to have a meaning that is unique, to be something that forms a [single] signifier, even if it is transitory, but which stands on its own two feet, as it were, for as long as it exists.

The other facet of the signifier is what we call "free association." The latter is such that, for each of the elements of a sentence – no matter how minutely we break it down, stopping only when we reach its phonetic elements – something can intervene that makes one of its signifiers disappear and puts another signifier in its place. Therein lies the essential property of the signifier.

This is related to the aspect of the subject's will [*vouloir*] that is indicated by the retroactive loop. Without the subject knowing it, in a way of which he is unconscious and which is beyond his intention, his speech is at every moment affected by some parenthetical clause [*incidente*] that intervenes in the choice of elements in the signifying chain. We see the effects of this emerge at the surface, for example in the form of a phonemic slip of the tongue – this is the most elementary form. The simple change of a syllable in a word suffices to show that another signifying chain is present and active there, this second signifying chain having interrupted the first one in order to implant another meaning in it.

At the level of the assuming of responsibility for the statement by the subject, which is apparently the most developed level, the interpretive rule proposed by Freud implies that the *I* is posited as conscious. Nevertheless, we shall not say that the statement is produced by this *I*, since the enigma here remains complete: whose statement is it that we talk about at the level of enunciation? The subject does not come down on any one side; but if he says "I dreamt," it is with a characteristic connotation and stress that shows that he who has dreamt nevertheless presents himself to the subject as problematic. 170

Who is the subject of enunciation contained in the statement in question? Thus far, we are still at the stage of wondering about this. This subject was long considered to be a god, before becoming, more or less with Aristotle, the "himself" of the subject.

As for what lies beyond the subject – that is to say, the Freudian unconscious – the question of its alterity is no less perennial. An entire oscillation or vacillation is produced around it. What the subject then takes up from this beyond is of the same fragmenting nature and has the same value as a signifying element, as what is produced in the spontaneous phenomenon of substitution or malfunctioning of the signifier, which is what Freud shows us to be the normal pathway for deciphering the meaning of a dream.

In other words, the fragmentation that occurs at the level of enunciation, insofar as the latter implies assumption of responsibility for the dream by the subject, is situated for Freud at the same level and is of the same nature as the pathway of the dream's interpretation – namely, the maximal breaking down [*décomposition*] or spelling out of signifying elements. This spelling out highlights the dream's possibilities, which appear only inasmuch as the signifying chain is intersected by all the other chains that can cross it and interweave with it, at each of its elements and at each of the gaps that it leaves.

When does interpretation most nearly approach what Freud considers to be unconscious? When, in the subject's discourse, we make the current signification vacillate in order to allow the signifiers that are involved in the enunciation to become detached from each other. This is true of dreams in a still more exemplary fashion than of any other sort of discourse.

What are we on the trail of in psychoanalysis? What are we analysts seeking? We are looking for something essential that happened in the subject that keeps certain signifiers repressed. Well, this unconscious lies precisely in the gaps where the signifier is involved. The signifier also puts us on a path toward the subject's desire.

171 Desire is the *x* in the subject that is caught up in the signifying network, in the links in the signifying system, that is subjected to the filtering and sifting of the signifier. Our goal is to reveal and restore it in his discourse. How can we do so? What does it imply that we can do so?

According to Freudian theory and practice, as I have told you, the status of desire is to be excluded and enigmatic. With respect to the subject, it is essentially tied to the existence of repressed signifiers as such, and restoring desire involves the return of these signifiers. But this is not to say that restoring these signifiers purely and simply enunciates desire.

What is articulated in repressed signifiers, which is always a demand, is one thing; desire – inasmuch as desire is that by which the subject situates himself, owing to the existence of discourse, with respect to this demand – is another. It is not so much a matter of what he demands but of what he is as a function of this demand.

To the degree to which his demand is repressed or masked, the subject's being is expressed in a closed way in his desire's fantasy. There would be no question of the subject's being if there were no demand or discourse. It is fundamentally language that introduces the dimension of being for the subject and at the same time robs him of it.

The restoring of the meaning of the fantasy – that is, of something that is imaginary – is inscribed on the graph [see Figure 2.2] between the two lines: between the statement of the subject's intention, on the one hand, and the enunciation in which the subject reads his intention in a profoundly decomposed, fragmented, and refracted form through spoken language [*langue*], on the other. Fantasy – in which the subject usually suspends his relationship to being – is always enigmatic, more enigmatic than anything else. And what does the subject want? That we interpret it.

To interpret desire is to restore something to which the subject cannot gain access by himself – namely, the affect that designates his being and that is located at the level of the desire that is truly his. I am referring here to the precise desire that intervenes in one or another of his life events – whether masochistic desire, suicidal desire, or even selfless [*oblatif*] desire. What must happen is that something that occurred in a way that was closed off to the subject take on anew its meaning in relation to the masked discourse that is involved in this desire, take on anew its meaning in relation to being, confronting the subject with being.

This true meaning is, for example, meaning that is defined by what I would call "positional affects related to being." These are the affects that we refer to with essential terms – "love," "hate," and "ignorance" – but there are many others as well which we should catalogue and examine.

What people refer to as affect is not something that is purely and simply opaque and closed off, not something that is somehow beyond discourse or a nucleus of lived experience that comes to us out of the blue. Affect is something that is always and very precisely connoted by a certain stance the subject adopts with respect to being. I mean, with respect to being insofar as what is proposed to him is, in its fundamental dimension, symbolic. But it also happens that, on the contrary, affect constitutes, within the symbolic, an eruption of the real that is highly disturbing.

It is hard not to see that a fundamental affect like anger is nothing but the following: the real that intervenes at the very moment at which we have woven a fine symbolic web, where everything is going well, order, law, our merit, and our pleasure [*bon vouloir*]. We realize suddenly that the square pegs do not fit into the round holes. That is the origin of anger as an affect. All is well on the bridge formed by the ships on the Bosphorus, but a tempest blows in that whips up the sea. All anger involves whipping up the waters.

Affect can also be related to the intrusion of desire itself. This intrusion gives rise to a form of affect to which we will return.

But when it comes to a whole category of fundamental affects at least, affect is essentially the connotation that is characteristic of a stance adopted by a subject – a stance that involves, among other possible stances, putting himself into play or putting himself to work in relation to the necessary lines that are imposed on him by his envelopment in the signifier.

3

Let us now turn to an example.

I have selected this example from someone posterior to Freud. It allows us to clearly articulate what we mean in psychoanalysis by the desire in a dream. And in order to proceed in a way that leaves no room for an overly arbitrary choice, I selected Chapter 5 of the book entitled *Dream Analysis* by Ella Sharpe, in which she proceeds to analyze a single, simple dream, one whose analysis she takes as far as possible, as far as is possible for her, that is.

In the preceding chapters, she discusses a certain number of perspectives, laws, and mechanisms, examining, for example, the impact of dreams in psychoanalytic practice, and – going further still – the problems posed by the analysis of dreams or of what happens in the dreams of people who are in analysis. But Chapter 5 is the crux of the book, for in it she provides a singularly exemplary dream. She uses it to bring in and illustrate everything she has to say regarding the way in which analytic practice shows us that we must in fact be guided when we analyze dreams.

What this practitioner contributes that is new – in other words, that is not already included in Freud's *Traumdeutung* – is essentially the idea that a dream is not simply something that turns out to be significant, but that it plays a role in the ongoing analytic dialogue, which is not the same at one moment in the analysis as it is at another. In short, dreams accompany analytic discourse in an active, determined way that clarifies and extends the work accomplished. Briefly stated, dreams are dreamt not only for the analysis but often for the analyst, and they bear a message within the analysis.

Ella Sharpe, like a number of other authors, should be credited for not shying away from dream analysis, whereas certain analysts believe they have no need to concern themselves with dreams – I drew this to your attention in the talk I gave at Royaumont on the direction of the treatment – because they believe they involve some sort of intellectual activity.

The status of thought with regard to dreams is no inconsiderable question. It is all a matter of how we stress it. If dreams present themselves as the subject matter of discourse or discursive elaboration, this fact is in itself important as regards the nature of the unconscious. The unconscious is not located in some sort of psychical pouch [*besace*] in which it is found in some unconstituted state, but is rather located in the latencies of discourse. Is it shy of or is it immanent in what the subject formulates, with respect to his discourse or his enunciation? That is another question. The fact remains that it is legitimate to take dreams as they have always been taken – that is, as "the royal road to the unconscious" [SE V, p. 608].

To come now to the dream that Sharpe presents us, I will begin by reading it to you, before showing you the problems that it poses. I will highlight a brief warning she provides about the topic, and will, in fact, highlight the whole chapter. Our coordinates apply, as you will see, better than any others, to what she enunciates, while allowing us to better orient ourselves in it.

The patient in question arrives at his session one day – I will mention various circumstances that help us contextualize the dream later, for he only recalls them after having certain very important associations [– and eventually proffers the following]:

> I do not know why I should now think of my dream last night. It was a tremendous dream. It went on for ages and ages. It would take me the rest of the hour to relate it all. But don't worry; I shall not bore you with it all for the simple reason that I cannot recall it. But it was an exciting dream, full of incident, full of interest. I woke hot and perspiring. It must have been the longest dream I ever had. [p. 132]

He says that he does not remember the infinity or flood of elements in the dream he had, but brings up a rather short scene instead.

"*I dreamt I was taking a journey with my wife around the world.* . . ." There is a subtle nuance here that is perhaps not sufficiently emphasized. The order in which the circumstantial complements appear is worth noting, for it is not, it seems to me, the normal order in French, which would be: "I was taking a journey around the world with my wife." I do not believe that I am mistaken in saying that the patient's wording might be striking even to an English ear.

> *I dreamt I was taking a journey with my wife around the world, and we arrived in Czechoslovakia where all kinds of things were happening. I met a woman on a road, a road that now reminds me of the road I described to you in the two other dreams lately in which I was having sexual play with a woman in front of another woman.* [p. 132]

Here, Sharpe switches from italics to Roman type to indicate that the patient is making a tangential remark about the dream.   175

> So it happened in this dream. [Then back to the dream itself in italics, interspersed with associations in Roman type:] *This time my wife was there while the sexual event occurred. The woman I met was very passionate looking* and I am reminded of a woman I saw in a restaurant yesterday. She was dark and had very full lips, very red and passionate looking . . .

The patient thus describes them both as passionate looking.

... and it was obvious that had I given her any encouragement she would have responded. She must have stimulated the dream, I expect. In the dream the *woman wanted intercourse with me and she took the initiative which as you know is a course which helps me a great deal.* If the woman will do this I am greatly helped. In the dream *the woman actually lay on top of me; that has only just come to my mind. She was evidently intending to put my penis in her body. I could tell that by the manoeuvers she was making. I disagreed with this, but she was so disappointed I thought that I would masturbate her.*

Here again the patient editorializes: "It sounds quite wrong to use that verb transitively. One can say 'I masturbated' and that is correct, but it is all wrong to use the word transitively" [pp. 132–3].

In effect, the English verb "masturbate" does not take on the reflexive form as in French. The English "I masturbate" means "*Je me masturbe*" in French [the latter is a reflexive construction]. The analyst immediately picks up on this remark. The patient then adds a few confirmatory remarks, beginning to associate to his own masturbatory activities. He goes further into things later, too.

So there we have the statement of the dream. It gives you an inkling of why it will be of interest to us here.

I am, I must say, adopting a thoroughly arbitrary mode of exposition here, and I could just as easily approach things differently. Don't think that the pathway by which I am proceeding here is one that I am recommending you follow systematically when you interpret dreams. I am doing so here simply in order to provide a quick sketch of what we are trying to see and demonstrate.

In the dream about the dead father, I was able to designate – following Freud, and in such a way that you could see my approach was not devoid of artifice – the signifiers "as he wished," "he" referring here to the son. Similarly, we shall see in the dream reported by Sharpe's patient with what signifier the fantasy in the dream [*fantasme du rêve*] culminates. This fantasy is expressed in the following words: "I disagreed with this, but she was so disappointed I thought that I would masturbate her." The subject immediately remarks that it is altogether incorrect to use the verb "to masturbate" transitively. The entire analysis of the dream will show us that the true meaning of what is at stake here can be found by re-establishing the intransitivity of the verb.

She is "so disappointed" by what? The whole text of the dream indicates it well enough: she is disappointed by the fact that our subject is barely participating, even though, according to what he says, everything in the scene in the dream is designed to incite him to

176

do so, such that he would normally be greatly aided by the position she assumes. This is no doubt what is at work here, and I will say that the second part of the sentence ["I thought that I would masturbate her"] presents itself as having an understandable content, a feature that closely corresponds to what Freud articulates as being one of the characteristics of dream formation – namely, secondary revision.

Nevertheless, the subject himself observes that this is not as straightforward as it seems because his use of the verb does not sound quite right. It suffices for us to follow the rule of thumb given by Freud to realize that this observation puts us on the trail of the dream-thought. And therein lies the desire.

In effect, the subject tells us that one would usually say, 'I thought she could masturbate,' which is the normal form in which the wish would present itself: 'She can just go ahead and masturbate if she isn't happy!' The subject indicates rather energetically that masturbation is an activity that is not transitive, in the sense that it is not carried out by one subject on another, but rather intransitive, which means in this case something done by the subject to himself, since "I masturbated" means "*Je me suis masturbé.*" It is important not to come down on any particular side here; we must simply note that the first indication given by the subject immediately goes in the direction of rectifying a signifying articulation.

We are now going to turn to an earlier part of the chapter – prior to the narrative of the dream, before the arrival center stage of this scene, and before the account of this particular session – where we find a short preamble by the author regarding the patient's psychical constellation. What she puts into her premises are found anew in her results. And we will find reasons to critique these results.   177

Let us turn immediately to what will allow us to move forward here. Ella Sharpe comments that the patient is obviously very bright. We will get a better and better sense of his behavior as we focus in on things.

He is a man of a certain age who is married and works as a lawyer. What she tells us is worth being highlighted word for word. "When the time came for him to practise at the bar he developed severe phobias. Put briefly this" – this is all she tells us about the mechanism of his phobia, but we lend credence to what she says because she is one of the best analysts, one of the most intuitive and penetrating who ever lived – "meant that he dare not work successfully but that he must stop working in reality because he would be only too successful" [p. 127]. The comment the analyst makes here – that it was not that he had an affinity to failure, but rather that he stopped short, as it were, when the immediate possibility of throwing his ample gifts into relief presented itself – is worth keeping in mind. You will see how we shall make use of it in what follows.

Let us leave aside what the analyst tells us right from the outset about how this might connect up with his father – we will return to it later. We simply need to know that his father died when the patient was three years old and that he had said nothing about him in his analysis for a very long time other than that he "is dead" [p. 126]. This rightly draws the analyst's attention. She hears – and it seems hardly possible to dispute this – that he does not wish to recall that his father ever lived. When he recalls that his father was alive, it is, she tells us, an altogether "startling"* event for him that frightens him [p. 126].

The subject's stance in the analysis is immediately taken to imply that the death wish he had toward his father is the mainspring both of this forgetting of his living father and of any and every articulation of his desire, inasmuch as the dream reveals it. Nevertheless, nothing indicates to us in any way that this aggressive intention is at the origin of a fear of reprisal. An attentive study of the dream will allow us to show this in detail.

What else does the analyst tell us about this patient? She tells us that that day, like other days, she did not hear him arrive at her office, and on this score she provides a short paragraph that is truly brilliant on the topic of the patient's nonverbal presentation. Her description corresponds to the recent trendy practice of noting in patients all the little behavioral details that an attentive analyst knows how to detect. She tells us that she can never hear this one arrive.

The reader grasps from the context that people reach her office by climbing a flight of stairs. She can easily detect a patient of hers who climbs the stairs two at a time, because he makes an "extra thud"* [p. 129]. The English term here has no equivalent in French, designating as it does a flat, dull sound, the sound that might be made by a foot on a stair covered with carpet, a sound that gets a bit louder when one goes up the stairs two at a time. "Another [patient] hurries and I detect the hustle. . . ." The whole paragraph runs on in this vein and is quite delectable, literarily speaking. It is nevertheless but a tangent, for what is important is what this particular patient does.

The patient is perfectly polite, a bit uptight, and always does things in the exact same way:

He never varies. He always gets on the couch one way. He always gives a conventional greeting with the same smile, a pleasant smile, not forced or manifestly covering hostile impulses. There is never anything as revealing as that would be. [p. 130]

The analyst's sensibility keeps her well oriented here: "There is no sign of hurry, nothing haphazard, no clothes awry; no marks of a quick toilet; no hair out of place. [. . .] He lies down and makes himself easy" [p. 130].

And he never immediately mentions any sort of upsetting event, for example, that his maid did something that made him late for his session – if she did, it will only be mentioned after quite a while, at the end of the session or even at the next session. "He talks the whole hour, clearly, fluently, in good diction, without hesitation and with many pauses. He speaks in a distinct and even voice for it expresses thinking and never feeling" [p. 130].

As for what should be made of the distinction between thought and feeling, we will all naturally agree [that it is spurious]. What is important here is obviously to know what is signified by the specific mode of communication adopted by the subject. We see here a sort   179
of sterilization of the text of the session that makes the analyst wish that something more deeply felt would come out. Nevertheless, the fact that the subject expresses himself in this way must naturally have a meaning. Any analyst would think that the patient must be afraid of something. The absence of feelings, as the analyst puts it, does not necessarily imply that there is absolutely nothing to include under the heading of feeling.

I spoke earlier about affect as concerning and revealing the subject's relation to being. We must wonder what, in this case, can be communicated by the pathway of affect. It is all the more germane to wonder about this as the session that day opens with a communication regarding affect.

The discordance that exists between the analyst's silence when faced with something she had already noted a few days earlier, and the surprise she experiences, as she herself notes, the day the patient begins talking about it to her of his own accord, clearly shows what additional step must be taken with respect to the analyst's ordinary stance in order to gauge what is at stake in this particular case. For what begins to open up here, is going to open up more and more, as we shall see, right up until the analyst's final interpretation and its astonishing effect. What is truly astonishing is not the simple fact that this interpretation was made, but that it is classified by Sharpe as a satisfying and even exemplary interpretation owing to its fruitful nature.

What happens? In this context, which is characterized by the subject's perfect politeness – he keeps his nose completely clean – something has been happening for the last few days. He has been arriving at his analyst's door, and just before entering he has been going "Uh, hum!" That is even saying too much, for it is, as Sharpe tells us, the "discreetest of coughs" [p. 130].

Ella Sharpe was a brilliant woman, as every aspect of her style indicates. She was some sort of elementary school teacher before becoming an analyst, which is very fine training for being able to see deeply into people's psychology. She was certainly a very talented woman. She hears this "little cough" as though it were the arrival of the dove at Noah's Ark. The cough announces that, hidden somewhere, there is a place where feelings live. Oh, she tells herself, I would never speak to him about that, because if I did he would tuck it all away again.

This is the classic analytic stance in such cases. The rule is to never make comments to a patient about his physical comportment at a certain stage of his analysis, when it is important to simply observe it. I mean, his way of coughing, lying down, buttoning or unbuttoning his jacket, everything that his ingrained motor bearing says about him – inasmuch as this attitude can take on the value of a signal and inasmuch as all of that goes right to the quick of his narcissism.

Yet, this rule in no wise applies to something like this little cough. Here we see the symbolic power and dimension insofar as it extends to everything in the vocal register. Regardless of the fact that a cough may give the impression of being a purely somatic event, it is situated in the same dimension as sounds like "Uh, huh" and "Yes . . ." that certain analysts sometimes make, quite authoritatively, and that clearly have the effect of encouraging the patient to say more.

The best proof of this is that, to the analyst's great surprise, the cough is the first thing the patient speaks to her about that day. In his "customary even and deliberate voice," he tells her:

I have been considering that little cough that I give just before I enter the room. The last few days I have coughed I have become aware of it, I don't know whether you have. To-day when the maid called me to come upstairs I made up my mind I would not cough. To my annoyance, however, I realized I had coughed just as I had finished. It is most annoying to do a thing like that, most annoying that something goes on in you or by you that you cannot control, or do not control. One would think some purpose is served by it, but what possible purpose can be served by a little cough of that description it is hard to think. [p. 131]

The analyst advances with snakelike stealth, and asks, well, "What purpose could be served" by it?

He replies, "Well, it is the kind of thing that one would do if one were going into a room where two lovers were together." He recounts that he once did something like that when he was a child before entering a room where his brother was with his girlfriend – he coughed just before entering because he thought they were perhaps kissing and that it would be better if they stopped before he came in, for they would then feel less embarrassed than if he surprised them.

The analyst then asks, "And why cough before coming in here?" He replies:

> That is absurd, because naturally I should not be asked to come up if someone were here [. . .]. There is no need for a cough at all that I can see. It has, however, reminded me of a phantasy I had of being in a room where I ought not to be, and thinking someone might think I was there, and then I thought to prevent anyone from coming in and finding me there I would bark like a dog. That would disguise my presence. The "someone" would then say, "Oh, it's only a dog in there." [pp. 131–2]

"A dog?" the analyst cautiously inquires. The patient continues:

> That reminds me of a dog rubbing himself against my leg, really masturbating himself. I'm ashamed to tell you because I did not stop him. I let him go on and someone might have come in. [p. 132]

Then he coughs lightly and recounts the dream I mentioned earlier.

We will come back to this in detail next time, but can't we already note that the dream comes to his mind right after the coughing episode? In all probability, the little cough is a message. Sharpe herself suspects as much, moreover, since she brings it into the analysis of the dream and even places it in the spotlight. The little cough is a message, but we want to know about what.

Secondly, we can observe that it is a message twice over [or: to the second power, *au second degré*], insofar as the patient speaks about it explicitly and not unconsciously, and it is by this very pathway that he introduces the dream. Were he simply to say, "I coughed," it would already be a message, but he does not simply say that he coughed, he says, 'I coughed, and that means something.' And immediately afterward, he begins telling stories that are singularly

181

182   suggestive. The cough obviously means 'I am here. If you're doing something fun but that you would rather not have somebody else see, it's time to cut it short.'

But we will fail to see what is at stake in this cough if we do not take into account the narrative that is provided at the same time. He tells us that he thought of dissimulating his presence in a room – his presence *as such*, I would say – by doing the very thing that would obviously attract attention, namely, barking. This presents itself with all the trappings of fantasy.

First of all, it is the subject himself who presents this as a fantasy, one he had in his childhood. Moreover, nothing shows better than this fantasy in what way the subject fills out his empty form – namely, that he must adorn himself [or: invest or protect himself, *se parer*] with a signifier, that he finds himself adorned by the effect of the signifier. Indeed, we find anew here all the characteristics of the use made by children of what present themselves as natural signifiers, when they use them as attributes to signify something – a dog, for example, which children sometimes call a bowwow. But here, where the subject is included in a fantasized activity, he attributes the bowwow to himself.

In this fantasy, in short – a fantasy that is altogether unrealizable [*inapplicable*] – if he signals his presence it is insofar as he makes himself into something other than what he is. He is supposed to manifest himself as other than he is; he makes himself absent; he even banishes himself from the realm of speech, making himself into an animal, literally naturalizing himself. No one will go check to see if he is there because he will have presented and articulated himself in the most elementary signifier [barking]. They will not think "There's nothing there," but literally that "There is no one there [*Il y a personne*]." This is truly what the subject announces to us in his fantasy: Inasmuch as I am in the presence of the Other, I am no one. This is Odysseus' response, "*οὖτις*" [meaning nobody or no one] when asked his name by the Cyclops.

These are no more than the subject's associations to his dream. We will have to take the analysis further in order to see in what sense and how the subject is no one [*personne*]. There is of course something correlated to this on the side of the other who must be warned and who turns out to be, in this case as in the dream, a woman. His relation to women in general certainly plays a role in the situation.

183   To articulate the something that the subject is not, and that he cannot be, will direct us, as you shall see, toward the most fundamental of symbols involved in the subject's identification.

If the subject absolutely wants, and everything points to this, his female partner to masturbate, to take care of herself, it is assuredly so that she will not take care of him. Why doesn't he want her to take care of him? In what way doesn't he want it?

The usual time granted to us for this class does not allow us to articulate it today, so we shall put it off till next time.

January 14, 1959

IX

THE FANTASY ABOUT THE BARKING DOG

The cough, a signifier of the Other
Analyzing the fantasy without understanding it
Dogs go meow, cats go bowwow
Darwin and the duck's quack
Masturbating dog = ego-ideal

When we ended last time, we were in the middle of analyzing a dream that Ella Sharpe calls "single" – that is, singular or unique. She devotes an entire chapter to it; it is a chapter on which the whole earlier part of her book converges, and she [then goes on to] add to it in various ways.

Her book, which is made up of lectures given to analysts-in-training and based on some thirty years of wide-ranging psychoanalytic experience, is original in that it is explicitly devoted to the analysis of dreams, which is why it is important to us.

This extremely interesting dream was the main topic of one session she had with a patient. Her discussion of it – along with the connections she establishes, not merely among the dream associations and her interpretations, but also among all the messages of the session taken as a whole – demonstrates that she has considerable sensitivity regarding the direction and meaning of the analysis.

She interprets the dream line by line, as one should. As we shall see in detail, she interprets it as though it were a desire linked to her patient's wish for omnipotence. Whether this is justified or not, you should already realize that, if this dream can be of interest to us, it is with respect to the angle by which I tried to show you what is ambiguous and misleading in the one-sided notion according to which – in the wish for omnipotence, this wish for the possibility or perspective of potency that one might call the neurotic wish – it is always the subject's omnipotence that is at issue.

For it is quite obvious that the omnipotence at issue is the omnipotence of discourse. This does not imply in the least that the subject feels himself to be the mainstay or guardian of discourse. If what he is dealing with is the omnipotence of discourse, it is via the Other that he proffers it.   186

This is especially forgotten in the way Ella Sharpe orients her interpretation of the dream.

1

I will begin by indicating to you what we will see at the end, because we will probably not manage to finish our discussion of the dream in today's class. Such an elaborate piece of work brings up a host of things – and a still greater host of things when we realize that, in the final analysis, almost nothing has been said on the topic [of dreams], even though we operate in this realm every day.

Ella Sharpe thus argues with her patient about his wish for omnipotence, and as she puts it, his aggressive omnipotence [p. 145].

To begin with, this patient, about whom she absolutely does not give us all the background information, has in his profession – he is a lawyer – major difficulties whose neurotic character is so obvious that she goes into them in detail. Indeed, she indicates that it is not so much that he is afraid of failure but rather of success, of having too much success. It is by modulating the very definition of his symptom that she highlights a split and introduces into the analysis a nuance that warrants our attention owing to its obviously subtle nature.

She mentions that the patient has other difficulties as well that go beyond his professional activities, extending to the whole of his relations with other people. They manifest themselves especially in games – in tennis, for instance. The sorts of difficulties he has concern, for example, the fact that he has a hard time doing what is necessary to win a game or a set – namely, to corner his adversary at one end of the tennis court and, as people often do, hit the ball to the opposite end of the court where his opponent cannot reach it. The highlighting of such symptoms by the analyst is quite helpful in confirming that the patient suffers from a problem manifesting his potency, or more accurately stated, his power.

This leads her to intervene in a certain way, which elicits in the patient a certain number of reactions in which she clearly rejoices,   187
in a word. This is the crowning moment at which she indicates where his desire lies, and it is truly in the sense in which we define desire here. One might almost say that she aims at desire in its relation to demand – as you will see, this is truly what she does.

The problem is that she interprets this desire as if it were an aggressive conflict, situating it at the level of an imaginary conflict. She thinks essentially and primarily in terms of dyadic relations. I will show you what justifies her in broaching things in this way, but I want to immediately raise the question here whether the appropriateness of this type of interpretation is truly legitimated by the two reactions with which she justifies it.

The first reaction comes three days after the session in which the patient related to her the lovely dream we discussed, which was a crucial moment in the analysis and one in which she delivered the first sketch of her dyadic-type interpretation that his aggressiveness was grounded in a [feared] repercussion or transference of his wish for omnipotence. The patient tells her what resulted from this – for the first time in ages, since childhood, he wet his bed! This is striking and astonishing in an adult patient. We will come back to this in detail in order to indicate the problem that is raised by it.

The second reaction occurs in the course of the week that followed the session in which he recounted the dream, on the occasion of a game of tennis that he lost. He happened to have one of those difficulties well known to tennis players who have the opportunity to glimpse the way they put their abilities to work, who are sometimes unable to garner the reward for their obvious superiority, for they are unable to manifest it. One of his usual partners teased him regarding the lost game, with a sensitivity to his unconscious impasses that in the end constitute the fabric of this game, and that are reflected in the skirmishing dialogue between the players, joking and teasing each other about which one got the upper hand. At that point, the patient became so furious he grabbed his opponent by the neck and cornered him in the back of the court, ordering him to never tease him like that again [pp. 147–8].

I am not saying that the general direction of and order in which Ella Sharpe made her interpretations have no foundation whatsoever. We shall see that she employed elements that ring true on the basis of the minutest dissection of the material. But she also has preconceived ideas. The latter are, after all, often founded – for an error is never generated except through a lack of truth – but they are grounded in another register that she knows neither how to articulate nor how to handle, even if she provides us with the necessary elements, which is what makes this case study precious to us.

The point on which her interpretation bears is at a lower degree of complexity, since she situates everything at the level of imaginary rivalry and power struggles. Yet if we carefully sift the material included in her text, we will see – and in a striking manner, I believe – what she leaves out. What is at work in the session she analyzes,

188

and the dream that lies center-stage in that session, manifests itself with so much coherence that it incites us to see if we cannot center things better with the help of the categories that I have been proposing for a long time, and whose map I have tried to give you in the form of the topological schema, the graph, that we use.

Let me remind you that in the dream the patient takes a journey with his wife around the world. He arrives in Czechoslovakia, "where all kinds of things were happening" [p. 132]. He underscores the fact that there were plenty of things that took place before that moment in the dream, but that he has forgotten them, such that the dream does not take very long to recount.

He meets a woman on a road, and the road reminds him of another road he has dreamt about, which he already described to his analyst in two recent dreams. On this road, there had been "sexual play with a woman," and this had occurred "in front of another woman" [p. 132]. The same thing happens in this dream, as he tells us in a digression.

This time my wife was there while the sexual event occurred. The woman I met was very passionate looking and I am reminded of a woman I saw in a restaurant yesterday. She was dark and had very full lips, very red and passionate looking, and it was obvious that had I given her any encouragement she would have responded. She must have stimulated the dream, I expect. In the dream the *woman wanted intercourse with me and she took the initiative which as you know is a course which helps me a great deal.* If the woman will do this I am greatly helped. In the dream the *woman actually lay on top of me; that has only just come to my mind. She was evidently intending to put my penis in her body. I could tell that by the manoeuvers she was making. I disagreed with this, but she was so disappointed I thought that I would masturbate her.* [pp. 132–3]

189

Immediately thereafter comes the remark that only makes sense in English: "It sounds quite wrong to use that verb transitively. One can say 'I masturbated' and that is correct" [p. 133]. We shall see in what follows in the text another example that clearly shows that when you employ "to masturbate" in English, in French it means "*se masturber.*" The originally reflexive nature of the verb is so strong that the patient makes on this score what is, strictly speaking, a philological remark, and it is obviously no accident that he does so at that very moment.

As I said last time, if we proceed as we did in the previous dream, we can complete this sentence by restoring the avoided signifiers, as follows: "she was so disappointed" to not have my penis, or to not have a penis, that I thought 'she should masturbate,' and not "I would masturbate her." She can just go ahead and masturbate! You will see in what follows what allows us to complete things in this way.

After that, we have a series of associations and a dialogue between the analyst and the patient. They do not go very far, but nevertheless give us quite enough food for thought. As there are almost three pages of them in all, I will pick up on them later so as not to tire you.

Ella Sharpe wrote this chapter for pedagogical purposes. Finding herself in a didactic role, she summarizes what we read in the session and establishes a catalogue of what the patient brought her, in order to show to those she is teaching exactly what the material is from which she makes a choice in order to ground both the interpretation that she has in mind and her selection of a part of the interpretation to convey to the patient. She emphasizes the fact that the two are far from coinciding, since what should be said to the patient is probably not all of what there is to say about the patient. In what the patient brought her, there are things that are worth saying and others that should not be said.

190

The first thing he brought up was the cough, the little cough that the patient gave that day before entering the consulting room, and that she had already heard him give at the same moment for the past few days.

Given the way the patient behaves, which is so contained and uptight, so obviously indicative of defense – Sharpe senses this very clearly and she is far from reducing it to a defense like "defense against his own feelings" – she sees in this cough a manifestation, that she considers spontaneous, of a more immediate presence than his attitude in which everything is reflected upon and in which nothing is reflected. This "little cough," as the patient calls it, might have given no pause for thought to others, whereas for her, however miniscule it may be, it is literally like an olive branch. In this cough she hears the announcement that some sort of drop in the level of the floodwaters has begun. Thus it is as if she says to herself, "Let's respect that," and refrains from pointing it out to him.

Then the unexpected happens: the patient himself begins talking at great length about the little cough. I discussed this with you last time, and we will return to it and to the way in which Ella Sharpe understands it – and to the way in which we should, in my view, understand it.

In this crucial session, the patient does not bring up the dream he had right away. He begins by recounting the series of associations that came to him after having noticed the cough he was giving before entering the consulting room, whereas he had always climbed the flight of stairs so discreetly that the analyst did not hear him. He had resolved not to cough again this time, but a cough came out all the same. It bothers him a lot that there is something in him that he cannot control, and he wonders what it might mean.

We are now going to return to what he says by following the way in which Ella Sharpe registers it in her own perspective. She establishes a catalogue of what she calls the "ideas concerning the purpose of a cough" [p. 136].

First of all, this cough brings with it "thoughts of lovers being together." What did the patient say? After having spoken about his cough and wondered what purpose it might have served, he said the following:

> Well, it is the kind of thing that one would do if one were going into a room where two lovers were together. If one were approaching such a place one might cough a little discreetly and so let them know they were going to be disturbed. I have done that myself when, for example, I was a lad of fifteen and my brother was with his girl in the drawing-room I would cough before I went in so that if they were embracing they could stop before I got in. They would not then feel as embarrassed as if I had caught them doing it. [p. 131]

191

It is not insignificant to underscore in this regard that the cough is a message. The patient indicated this, and we suspect as much anyway because everything that followed corroborated it. Let me immediately comment on this.

Even if this seems a bit persnickety, consider nevertheless that the order of the remarks that I am going to make now will show you that starting from here, everything else follows – namely, what I called the drop in level that characterizes Sharpe's interpretation. Given the way she analyzes things, she does not grasp, or at least does not highlight, what it is important to bring out. Which is that the subject did not simply cough but that he in some sense came to tell the analyst – to her great surprise, even she mentions this – that it was a message. She leaves this out.

We need but look at the catalogue she establishes of her total number of kills [or: of hits, *tableau de chasse*] – we are not yet at the stage of examining what she chooses to put in that catalogue, which depends on what she at first recognized – to observe that she takes note of the cough, but that she elides the fact, which she herself nevertheless underscores, that the subject wonders what its purpose is, what it announces. Yet this is the important point regarding this

message-bearing cough, assuming it is a message: the subject literally begins by saying that the cough is a message; he marks it as a
message. Moreover, in the dimension in which he announces that it
is a message, he wonders what the purpose of the message is.

What happens in analysis, according to the definition and articulation that we are trying to give of it? An analysis is first and
foremost a discourse. We cannot forget its structural framework.
Our requirement that this discourse be dissected [*désarticuler*] does
not proceed from any particular persnicketiness, but merely reflects
our interest in analyzing it, strictly speaking.

We are going to see what its importance is. Up to a certain point,
192   we can already begin to get our bearings thanks to our graph. When
the patient wonders what his cough is about, it is a question raised
to the second power [*au second degré*] regarding the event. He raises
this question using the Other as his starting point [*à partir de l'Autre*;
see Figure 9.1], since it is insofar as he is in analysis that he raises
the question.

I would say that, in this case, the patient shows himself to be
further advanced than Sharpe imagines he is, as is witnessed by
her surprise. This reminds us of how parents are always behind the
curve regarding what their children do and do not understand. Here
the analyst is behind the curve, for the patient had long since figured
out that it was important to wonder about symptoms that arose in
connection with the analysis, and that the slightest hitch gave rise to
a question.

In short, the question regarding the cough as a message is clearly
presented in the form of a question mark in the upper part of the
graph [Figure 9.1]. In order to allow you to locate the point we are
at, I am also including the lower part of the graph, which I defined
in another context by telling you that it was the level of the Other's
discourse.

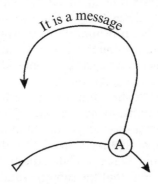

Figure 9.1: It is a message

It is quite clear here that the subject has entered into analytic discourse and that he literally raises a question concerning the Other that is in him – namely, his unconscious. This level of articulation is insistently present in every subject inasmuch as he asks himself, "But what does this Other want?"

This is not an innocent statement that is supposedly made within the analysis. There is absolutely no doubt but that this question is enunciated at a level that is distinguished from the first verbal level, that of innocent statements, and that it clearly indicates the locus where we situate what must in the end be the shibboleth of analysis – namely, the signifier of the Other [or: the Other's signifier, *le signifiant de l'Autre*]. This signifier is precisely what is hidden from the neurotic, inasmuch as he does not know its impact and he wonders about it. In this case, he recognizes it but he is far from having an answer. Hence the question, "What is this signifier of the Other doing in me?"

Let us say, in short, in terms that are suitable here at the beginning of my exposé, that the subject is, and for good reason, far from being able to recognize that the Other is castrated, but no further than he is from being able to recognize that he himself is. For the time being, from this position of innocence or educated ignorance [*ignorance docte*], which is constituted by the fact of being in analysis, he simply wonders what this signifier is insofar as it signifies something in his unconscious which is the signifier of the Other.

This is what is elided in Sharpe's way of proceeding.

She enumerates his "ideas concerning the purpose of a cough" – this is her way of approaching things. Naturally, they are ideas concerning the cough, but they already give us a great deal more than a simple linear chain of ideas.

Something is already sketched out, which is mapped, here in particular [Lacan is undoubtedly pointing to part of the graph], on our graph.

2

Sharpe tells us that the cough first brings with it "thoughts of lovers being together" [p. 136].

I read you what the patient said, and in my view it can in no wise be summarized in that way.

If we listen to him, he imagines someone who arrives as a third party, interrupting lovers who are together. He arrives as a third party, but not in just any old way, since he orchestrates things so as not to arrive as a third party in an overly embarrassing way.

In other words, it is very important, right from the outset, to point out that if there are three people involved, the being together [of the two lovers] involves variations over time, coherent variations – namely, they are together as long as the third party is outside. Once the third party has entered, they are no longer together – that is plain to see.

It should be clear to you that if it took us a week of meditation to get to the bottom of what the patient tells us – as it is going to take us two classes to cover the material this dream brings with it and its interpretation – the analysis of it might appear to be something insurmountable, especially because things could only expand still further and we would be quickly overwhelmed. But in reality, this is not a valid objection at all, for the very good reason that, to a certain extent, what is essential is in the schema that has already been traced out. That is to say that, when the third party is outside, the two are together; when the third party is inside, the two are no longer together.

I am not saying that everything we are going to see regarding the dream is already contained in this, for that would be a bit simplistic. But we are going to see the following develop, extend and, in short, become involute like a leitmotif that is indefinitely reproduced and enriched at every point of the fabric, eventually constituting the entire texture of the whole. You will see what that texture is.

Which idea does Sharpe highlight next? The "rejection of a sexual phantasy concerning the analyst" [p. 136]. Does that account for what the patient brings up?

Immediately after he explains to her what purpose the cough might serve if there are lovers in the room, the analyst asks him the following question: "And why cough before coming in here?" He replies,

> That is absurd, because naturally I should not be asked to come up if someone were here, and I do not think of you in that way at all. There is no need for a cough at all that I can see. It has, however, reminded me of a phantasy I had of being in a room where I ought not to be . . . [pp. 131–2]

This is what Sharpe summarizes by saying that we have here the "rejection of a sexual phantasy concerning the analyst." Is this sound?

It seems to me that we are not dealing with an absolute rejection here, but rather with an admission; it is a roundabout admission, naturally, but an admission nonetheless owing to the associations that follow it. One cannot say that the subject is in a position of pure and simple negation, that he is purely and simply rejecting the analyst's proposal, which seems like it could serve, on the contrary, as a model interpretation in being so opportune, since it leads to everything that follows. A sexual fantasy associated with the patient's entrance into the analyst's office, where she is supposed to be alone, is clearly what is at issue, and you will see quickly enough that it does not take a genius to shed light on it.

The third element the patient's associations bring us is, according to Sharpe, a fantasy: the "phantasy of being where he ought not to be, and barking like a dog to put people off the scent" [p. 136]. "To put off the scent" is a metaphorical expression, and there is always a reason why one metaphor is used instead of another; yet there is no trace of the word "scent" in what the patient tells us. We have no means of knowing whether it is repressed or not. I am saying this because scent is what certain analysts joyfully look forward to. Let us confine our attention here to what the patient tells us about the dream.

In response to the analyst's question, he says: "It has, however, reminded me of a phantasy I had of being in a room where I ought not to be" – this conforms to what the analyst surmises* – "and thinking someone might think . . ." [p. 131].

The structure here is twofold, as it refers to the subjectivity of another person: 'I think that someone might think. . . .' This is what I will emphasize, for is absolutely rampant [in this patient's discourse], it is what is constantly at work here, and it is here alone that we can focus in on his desire. This is also what is constantly left out of Sharpe's account, and of the way in which she accounts for the different impacts of need [*incidences tendancielles*].

The patient proffers the following: I had a fantasy in which I was "thinking someone might think I was there, and then I thought to prevent anyone from coming in and finding me there I would bark like a dog. That would disguise my presence. The 'someone' would then say, 'Oh, it's only a dog in there'" [p. 131].

The patient clearly indicates that this fantasy dates back to late childhood or early adolescence. Despite the not very coherent, paradoxical, and even absurd nature of the fantasy, Sharpe nevertheless perceives its full value, and includes it in her catalogue of important ideas. She thus summarizes it in the terms I mentioned: "Phantasy of being where he ought not to be, and barking like a dog to put people off the scent" [p. 136].

This is correct, except that, if he imagines being where he ought not be, the goal of the fantasy – its meaning or obvious content – is to show that he is not where he is. This is the flip side. It is very important because, as we shall see, it characterizes and is the very structure of every subjective assertion made by the patient.

To cut to the chase, as the analyst does, and tell him that he wanted, at some point, to kill his fellow man, and that what he fears here are repercussions and reprisals, is assuredly to take a stand, and under conditions in which your chances of being wrong and of succeeding at the same time – in other words, your chances of in effect getting him to subjectively adopt or subjectify what you are cutting to the chase about – are particularly obvious. This is what makes Sharpe's text interesting.

In any case, this interpretation brings out his structure insofar as it manifests itself here, and already appears in the fantasy – namely, that he is not where he is. We are going to see both the meaning this interpretation may have and a completely different interpretation to which this could perhaps lead.

Whatever the case may be, he does not employ just any old means to make himself not be where he is; he sets about barking like a dog. To do so in a room where one ought not to be is certainly not the best way of going unnoticed. From the vantage point of reality, it is only too clear that this fantasy is untenable.

The only value of this sentence [describing the fantasy] is to get us to observe that we are not in the realm of the comprehensible but of imaginary structure. When we hear things like that during sessions, we believe we understand, but this is a retroactive effect – the patient seems to understand and that is good enough for us. Being understandable is, as I have already told you, a characteristic of any and every affect, of the whole margin, accompaniment, or fringes of inner discourse – and, especially, such as we can reconstruct it when we have the feeling that it is not as continuous as we think. Continuity is an effect that is primarily obtained by means of affect. It is a law: the less affects have an explainable cause [*sont motivés*], the more understandable they appear to be to the subject.

197   But there is no reason for us to follow his lead here. This is why the remark I made, as obvious as it may seem, nevertheless has its import. What we need to analyze is the fantasy, and without understanding it – in other words, by finding within it the structure it reveals.

Now what does this fantasy mean here? Earlier, it was important for us to see that the subject told us that his cough was a message. Similarly, it is important to perceive that this fantasy truly makes no sense, owing to its totally impossible efficacy, and that by barking, the subject simply says, "It's [only] a dog."

Here, too, he makes himself into something other than what he is [*il se fait autre*], but that is not the point. He does not wonder here what the signifier of the Other in him is – he has a fantasy.

Nevertheless, when such fantasies are brought up in analysis, we should perceive what precious material we have been given.

He makes himself into something other than what he is with the help of what? A signifier, precisely. Barking is the signifier here of what he is not. He is not a dog, but thanks to this signifier, in the fantasy, he obtains the desired result: he is other than what he is.

3

Although we have not exhausted everything that came out solely in association with the cough – for there is yet a fourth element that we will examine later today – I am going to turn to a different topic: the function of the signifier in fantasy.

We are going to set this dream aside in order to come back to a small, elementary, clinical observation that I alluded to at the end of a recent scientific paper, which I mentioned I would bring to you here.

It must be said that, given how abundant psychoanalytic material is, what should be taught is so incommensurate with what is taught – in other words, with what gets repeated over and over – that some days I truly feel ridiculously crushed by the task I have undertaken.

In the case of Ella Sharpe's patient, it is clear that he considers himself to be sufficiently hidden by his fantasized barking. Consider his words: "It's [only] a dog" [p. 132]. I would like to draw your attention here to a point that concerns child psychology.

198

We would like to understand children, so we try to construct a psychology about them that is referred to in French as "genetic" [*génétique*, referred to in English as "developmental"]; it consists in wondering how the dear little ones, who are so dumb, begin to acquire their ideas. We wonder how children proceed. We say that their world is initially autoerotic, and that objects only come into view later. I hope that you all have enough experience with children, thank God – if not directly, at least via patients who tell you stories about their children – to see that no one is more interested in objects and in the reflections of objects than very young children.

But let us leave that to one side, for the point, for the time being, is to perceive how the signifier begins to operate for children. I say that we can see it operate in children, at the source or origin of its grasp on the world that is offered to them; this world is above all a world of language, a world in which people speak to them, which obviously requires a rather astounding adjustment [or: confrontation or alignment, *affrontement*] on their part. How does the signifier enter into their world?

I have already alluded to the following fact that people can take note of, on the condition that they have an attentive ear rather than trying to confirm at any cost the preconceived notions with which they begin to broach children.

A friend of mine recently made the following comment to me: having decided to look after his child himself, a child to whom he devotes a lot of time, he had only ever spoken to his child about the family dog by calling it "the dog." He did not fail to be a bit surprised at the fact that the child, who had clearly figured out what was designated by the adult's initial name for the animal, began to call it a "bowwow."

"Bowwow," which the child used solely to designate the dog, is the feature that was first chosen by the child among the dog's myriad characteristics. And why should we be surprised by this? The child obviously is not going to begin by listing his dog's qualities. Well before being able to handle any sort of attribute, he begins to bring into play what he can say about it – namely, that by which the animal presents itself as itself producing a sign, which is not a signifier.

199   Let us note that language is served here by a boon offered to it by something that is rather isolated in what manifests itself – namely, the animal's presence – in order to furnish material, something that is already laryngeal. The child takes this material as what? As something that replaces "the dog," a term that he has already clearly heard and understood, to such an extent that, when one says "dog," he can just as easily direct his gaze at the dog as at a picture of the dog. To replace "dog" by "bowwow" is to create a first metaphor, and it is here that predication first begins to operate. Nothing is closer to the true genesis of language.

People have noticed that, in primitive forms of language, metaphors are what play the role of adjectives. This is confirmed in this child, except that we do not find ourselves faced here with some mysterious primitive operation of the mind, but rather with a structural necessity of language, a necessity which is such that in order for something to be generated in the realm of the signified, one signifier must be substituted for another.

You will ask, "Why assert that it is the substitution of 'bowwow' for 'dog' that is essential? How do you know that?"

I will answer first by a common enough observation that was recounted to me not long ago by people who speak to me at times, in a way which, although it is not directly clarified by the investigative maps I provide, is oriented by my teaching. From the moment a child has learned to call a dog "bowwow," he will call a slew of other things "bowwow" that have absolutely nothing to do with dogs.

This immediately shows you that what we are talking about here is the transformation of a sign [the dog's barking] into a signifier, and the power of the signifier being put to the test. It is put to the test of all sorts of substitutions and thus it is of little importance whether it is substituted for other signifiers or for real things.

The culminating point of this process is the decisive moment that I highlighted at the end of the aforementioned scientific paper, in which the child declares with the greatest authority and insistence that "dogs go meow" and "cats go bowwow." This is an absolutely decisive culmination, for it is at this moment that primitive metaphor – which is purely and simply constituted by means of signifying substitution – engenders the category of qualifiers [or: attribution, *qualification*].

Pay close attention here. We can, in this case, formalize the step or progress that is being made here.

I would say that a monolinear chain is at first established, which says "dogs" = "bowwow." Next, the child superimposes and combines one chain with another; he makes one chain, "dogs go bowwow," intersect another chain, "cats go meow." In short, by substituting "meow" for "bowwow," he creates the possibility of a division of each of the chains into two parts, one of which will provisionally be fixed in place and the other of which will no less provisionally be mobile. One part of the chain will remain, and the part that can be exchanged will revolve around it.

In other words, the signified S' of cats is associated with S, "bowwow," which is the signifier of dogs [i.e., which signifies dogs]. This presupposes that below – and to begin with, there is no below – the child links "meow," the signifier of cats, with the signified of "bowwow," that is, dogs.

$$\frac{S' \,.\, S}{S \,.\, S'}$$

Crossing and exchange

The importance that the child gives to this exercise is quite obvious and it is demonstrated by the following fact: if the parents are so tactless as to intervene and to correct, reprimand, or berate him for proffering such nonsense, the child reacts very emotionally – in short, he cries. For he knows perfectly well what he is doing, unlike the adults who think that he is uttering stupidities. He is constructing a metaphor.

According to the formulation that I have given of it, a metaphor, from the vantage point of the graph, consists essentially of the

200

following: something at the level of the upper line is displaced or elided with respect to something that in the lower line, that of the signified, is also displaced. The enunciation "dogs go bowwow" is a simple imitative connection with respect to reality. From the moment the game begins, from the moment "dogs go bowwow" and "bowwow," which is elided, sinks into the what lies below the enunciation concerning the dog, the latter becomes a true signifying enunciation.

201   Whether the dog is indicated or named makes no difference. But when a quality is attributed to him, it is literally not on the same line; it is on that of quality as such, where there are those who go "bowwow" and those who go "meow," and there are also all of those who make other sounds, all of which are implied in the vertical schema [of paradigmatic relations]. Here the dimension of adjectives begins to be born from metaphor.

As you know, such things have been glimpsed for quite some time – Darwin discussed them long ago. But, having no linguistic theory at his disposal, such things remained very problematic to him. But it is such a general, essential, and functionally dominant phenomenon in child development that Darwin, even though he was mostly inclined to provide naturalistic explanations, did not fail to be struck by the following fact.

He found it quite funny that a child, who was already astute enough to detach the "quack" from the duck that made it, applied this "quack" to a whole series of objects whose generic nature is sufficiently indicated by the fact that, if I recall correctly, wine and a sou were included among the objects.

I am not too sure what the term "sou" designated, if it was a "penny"* or something else; I did not verify what it meant at Darwin's time, but in any case it was a coin. Darwin, floundering around for an explanation, observed that the coin had the image of an eagle in one corner, thanks to which one could explain that the quack was unified and tied in general to volatiles. The wine obviously still posed a problem, but perhaps we could simply assume that there is some relationship between wine and, let us say, liquids, insofar as ducks paddle around in them.

Nevertheless, even if we would like to believe that it is its liquid nature that allows the child to apply the duck's quack to wine, and that he applies it to the coin because an image as ambiguous as that of an eagle with its wings spread on the coin can be, by a child, assimilated to his apperception of ducks, the fact remains that we observe once again that what is at stake is far more marked and shot through and through with the signifying element than it is associated with the contiguity of perception. In any case, it is in the

register of the signifying chain that we can grasp what grounds the   202
child's apprehension of the world as a world structured by speech.

It is not that he is seeking the meaning or essence of birds, fluid, or coins. It is that he literally finds them through the use of nonsense. If we had time, we would raise questions regarding what nonsense is technically – I mean, "nonsense"* as it is understood in English.

Nonsense is a [literary] genre. The English language has two eminent examples of nonsense: Edward Lear, the author of books of nonsense that he defined as such, and Lewis Carroll, whose *Alice's Adventures in Wonderland* I think you all know, at the very least.

If I had an introductory book to recommend to anyone who was going to become a child psychiatrist or psychoanalyst, I must say that, rather than any of the books by Jean Piaget, I would recommend beginning by reading a book which I have the best reasons to think, given what we know about the author, is based on profound experience of children's mental play – namely, *Alice's Adventures in Wonderland.*

There he would grasp the value, impact, and dimension of nonsensical play as such. Today I can do no more here than mention this.

I brought all of this up as a kind of parenthesis regarding the comment made by Sharpe's patient, "It's only a dog."

We shall return to him now in concluding today's class.

4

"It's only a dog" must be interpreted in a signifying manner.

Some facet of the fantasy is sketched out here.

Indeed, you will find anew here what I proposed as the formula of fantasy – namely, that the subject appears elided in it. It is not him, inasmuch as there is another there, an imaginary other, little *a*. This is a first indication, which will allow you to see that there is a fantasy as such in this scene, and which will assure you of the validity of our mapping of the fantasy.

Let me turn to the fourth association that Ella Sharpe lists in her catalogue of ideas. "Dog again brought memory of masturbating a   203
dog" [p. 136].

As we have seen, the verb "to masturbate" in fact has a naturally intransitive use. We have here a dog that is masturbating, given that the patient recounted this memory right after talking about the scene involving "It's only a dog": "That reminds me of a dog rubbing himself against my leg, really masturbating himself. I'm ashamed to tell you because I did not stop him. I let him go on and someone might have come in" [p. 132].

The "memory of masturbating a dog" in Sharpe's list takes on the connotation of an element that should be placed at the end of the chain [of associations]. Is that something that should completely satisfy us here? I don't believe so. This element allows us, in effect, to go a bit further into what is at stake in the message that brings the dream in its wake.

Nothing is clearer in this case than the line that is followed by the patient's associations. Where is it? It is in the subject's enunciation. This first loop of associations is drawn on the graph [Figure 9.2] with a dotted line.

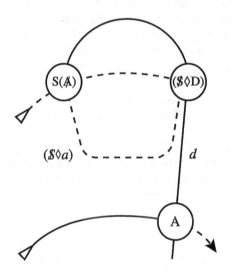

Figure 9.2: The first loop of associations

As in ordinary and normal speech, the signifying elements of this dotted chain pass through the two landmarks of the message and the code. But at the upper level where we are, the message and the code are of a different nature than they are at the lower level, where the Other, A, merely designates the partner who speaks the same language as the subject.

The upper line of associations arrives at the point S(Ⱥ), the signifier of the Other which is in me. That is the question. What the subject begins to spill out regarding this does no less than pass through the point (Ş◊a) – we will return to this – and then through d, the level at which the question of his desire is located.

204

What does the patient do by giving a little cough at the very moment he enters a place where there is something he knows nothing about? "Sexual phantasy concerning analyst," says Sharpe [p. 136], but what fantasy is it? What is shown by the associations that follow is his own fantasy – namely, that if he were in the place of the other person, he would think first of all about not being there, or more precisely, about being taken for something other than himself.

So what do we arrive at now? We arrive at something that actually happened. A scene is suddenly revealed here. It is related by the patient. What happened?

The dog, insofar as it is [the patient] himself, was not there. Now we have a dog, and this time he is no longer fantasized but real. This time, it is an other who is no longer a signifier at all, but who is an image, a companion in the room, and a companion who is all the more obviously close to him, likened to him, as it is against his own leg that the dog masturbates.

How can we schematize what happened at that moment? We know that the other – in this case, the animal qua real – had a relationship with the subject, because the latter took the time to tell us about it beforehand. The subject could be this animal in his imagination, on the condition of taking on the signifier "barking." This other who was present masturbated. He showed the patient something – he showed him, very precisely, how to masturbate.

Was the situation then over with? No. As the patient himself tells us, there was the possibility that someone else might come in. And then, how shameful! The situation would no longer be tenable. The subject would literally die [*disparaîtrait*] of shame if someone witnessed what was happening.

In other words, this is what is articulated here: 'Show me what I must do, on the condition that the other – insofar as he is the Other with a capital *O*, the third party – not be there. I watch the other that I am, this dog, on the condition that the Other not come in, otherwise I would die of shame. But on the contrary, this other that I am – namely, this dog – I view him as the ego-ideal, as doing what I do not do' – as an ideal of "potency," as Sharpe puts it later.

Assuredly this must not be taken in the sense in which she understands it, because this has nothing to do with words. It is inasmuch as the dog is not a speaking animal that he can be the model and ideal image here, and that the subject can see in him what he wants to see – namely, that he be shown what he must do and what he can do, as long as he cannot be seen by the Other, the one who might enter and who speaks.

Otherwise stated, it is insofar as I have not yet entered my analyst's office that I can imagine her, Ella Sharpe, the poor, dear

205

woman, showing me how to masturbate. And I cough in order to
warn her that she must get back into her normal position.

We have here an oscillation [or: game, *jeu*] between two figures of
the other – the one who does not speak and that we imagine, and the
one to whom we are going to speak, but who is asked to ensure that
the confrontation not occur too quickly, that the subject not start to
disappear [*disparaître*].

It is in this oscillation that we find the pivotal point where the
patient suddenly remembers the dream he had.

We will come back to the dream next time, and we shall see that
it runs quite counter to the patient's fantasy that was created in the
waking state, whose main lines we homed in on today.

January 21, 1959

X

THE IMAGE OF THE INSIDE-OUT GLOVE

The link between fantasies and dreams
Behind the door lies an enigma
The Queen of Sweden and the Lady from China
The narcissistic relationship to the penis
Separating the male and female principles

We already make use of the notion of desire, practically speaking, in our analytic work.

What am I trying to do here? I am trying to show you that, in the use we make of it, we unwittingly presuppose a number of coordinates that are always the same, coordinates that I am attempting to situate.

It is worth recognizing them, for when we fail to do so, our thinking always slips a bit to one side or the other, and gets caught up in ill-defined relationships. This can put us at a disadvantage when it comes to interpretation.

Today I am going to continue to analyze the dream that I chose from Ella Sharpe's work owing to the fact that it is exceptionally well elucidated. And we shall see things from two different perspectives.

On the one hand, what is most acute, astute, and remarkable in what she says – in her account of the session in which this dream is analyzed and of the two following sessions – fits so well into the categories that I am trying to teach you how to use, that these categories allow us to give their full value to the elements she assembles. Nevertheless, on the other hand, in failing to perceive the originality of these elements, she minimizes their import, in a sense, taking their color and relief down a notch. She mixes them up and reduces them to more rudimentary and simplistic notions, which stop her from getting as much out of what she has in the palm of her hand as she might otherwise.

In order to help you firmly fix in your mind something that should
continue to get a bit better and more precisely sketched out, I will
begin by turning to the graph again for a moment.

I think you are beginning to glimpse what the two different levels
of the graph mean.

What, in short, does this trajectory [Lacan is pointing at a part of
the graph] – which loops back on itself, and which is that of analytic
enunciation insofar as it is liberated, I would say, by the rule of free
association – tend to do? It brings out, as far as possible, what is
included in every discourse – namely, a signifying chain insofar as
it breaks down into what we are all familiar with: interpretable elements. These interpretable elements, insofar as they are pinpointed,
appear precisely to the degree to which the subject tries to recover
[*se reconquérir*] what he originally was, tries to be beyond what
demand has frozen or imprisoned in him when it comes to his needs.

In effect, in the expression of his needs, the subject finds himself
initially caught in and poured into [the mold of] necessities that are
characteristic of demand, and that are based on the following: the
form of demand is already altered and alienated by the fact that we
are obliged to think in (the form of) language, and that demand
must already be inscribed in the Other as a register and in the
Other's code. What need is at its core cannot be the same as it is at
its point of arrival where it can only be reconquered, or conquered
beyond demand, in a linguistic guise, in the form of the subject who
speaks.

It is at this level that the initial gap or distance arises between
the subject and need. The subject of need [or: the subject as need, *le
sujet du besoin*] is in a relationship that is in some sense immanent
in life; he is entirely coextensive with his participation in life. On the
contrary, the *x* that is called "what the subject wants" refers to the
subject insofar as he constitutes himself by declaring himself to be
and by being in a certain relationship to being.

There is a gap between the purely and simply *interrogative* language of demand, on the one hand, and the language with which
the subject answers the question of what he wants and constitutes
himself in relation to what he is, on the other. It is in this gap that
what is known as desire arises. This is why, in the bipartite nature of
the graph, desire finds its place somewhere in the upper part.

There is some sort of homology between desire and the function
played by the ego.

The ego, which is constituted in a certain imaginary relationship
to the other, the little other, then finds itself caught up in the Other's
discourse, the discourse of the Other with a capital *O*. In effect, to
call on the Other is not merely to aim at the satisfaction of need; the

call loops back on itself [*il se reprend lui-même*] in order to instate itself in what I have sometimes called "full speech." This is committed speech in which the subject constitutes himself in relation to another person by telling the latter, "You are my master" or "You are my wife."

You can follow its trajectory on the graph: the ego [*m* on the graph; see Figure 2.2] is caught up in the Other's discourse [A], which instates it in relation to an object [*i(a)*], before returning here in the form of a message [*s*(A)]. The simple fact that I speak of myself as me [*de moi comme moi*] is based on the capturing of the ego in the Other's discourse. It is a statement that is articulated in a fragmentary way and requires a special type of deciphering in desire.

Where is desire inscribed [on the graph]? With respect to the upper level of discourse – where the subject, through a lifetime of effort, tends to develop fully in something in which his being declares itself – desire, inasmuch as it is a reflection or effect of this effort, situates itself halfway to it. Just as the ego is constituted in a certain relationship to the imaginary other, desire is instituted and fixated in a certain relationship to fantasy.

The subject qua vanishing, the subject insofar as he vanishes in a certain relationship to his elective object, is what I designate for you as fantasy. Fantasy always has this structure. It is not simply an object-relation. It is something that cuts. It implies a certain vanishing or signifying blacking out [*syncope*] of the subject in the presence of an object.

Fantasy involves a certain adjustment [*accommodation*] by the subject to or fixation of the subject on an object that has an elective value.

The elective nature of this value is what I am trying to demonstrate to you this year with the help of a certain number of examples.

The most recent, which I borrowed from Ella Sharpe, requires a demonstration that I must now conclude.

1

In the fantasy that is recounted by Sharpe's patient as a sort of preface or prelude to the dream, the oppositional relationship between the subject and a certain object is implicit.

The patient arrives for his session and begins to speak about his cough, providing a message about a message. His cough is designed to mysteriously warn two people who might be in an amorous embrace in a room, before he enters, warning them that it is time to separate.

Secondly, his associations show us that this cough is closely tied to a fantasy that he immediately recounts. In a past fantasy, he imagined that, being somewhere and not wanting to be found there – because he ought not to be there, wherever that was – he could bark like a dog. And everyone would say to themselves "Oh, it's [just] a dog!" The barking thus turns out to be the signal by which the subject profoundly absents himself from where he is, signaling that he is other than what he is. The cough, for its part, is correlated with the following: the fact that a couple of others, alone together in a room, are doing something pleasurable [*prend du plaisir*].

But a third association shows us that the subject himself is included in this couple. The dog that he pretended to be, barking in order to make himself into something other than he was, emerges in a memory of a real event, one in which a dog began masturbating on his leg. What would have happened if someone had come in and seen *them*?

In short, something structural is sketched out here.

What is at stake in the fantasy of the two, the one across from the other in a certain enclosed space, in the imaginary relationship, is adequately clarified by the memory – which comes back to him right after recounting this fantasy – of the dog, who is, after all, himself imaginary, masturbating on his leg. Masturbation thus shows that he is not absent from the pair of lovers.

As we might have expected, the subject identifies with all parties to the fantasy. The subject is both the one who is outside and announces himself, and the one who is inside and is involved in a couple relationship, with all that the couple relationship brings with it by way of shared imaginary fascination. But that is not what is essential here.

It is the structure that we must bring out. Either the two elements of the imaginary, dyadic couple remain together in a shared fascination with the act – including embracing, coupling, and specular fascination – and the other must not be there; or the other shows himself, the two then separate, and the couple dissolves.

But this structure also distorts the problem.

What does the subject tell us? He tells us that he gave a little cough before entering his analyst's consulting room, whereas it is clear that if he was invited to go up the stairs, it was because no one else was there – she was all alone. Moreover, he says, these are not things that I would allow myself to think about you. Which is precisely the problem.

By coughing, the subject does something whose signification he himself is not aware of, since he wonders what this cough can mean. Let us say that with this cough, as [when he imagines] barking like a dog, he makes himself other than he is. He himself does not know what the message is and yet he announces himself by coughing. What does he imagine in announcing himself by coughing? What does he imagine there is in that room?

He tells us that this cough is, in this case, an impulse or compulsion that escaped him, and it bothers him that it did so. I highlighted in this regard how striking Sharpe's attitude about it is – she feels that she certainly must not talk with him about it because the subject is not conscious of it, and he must not be made conscious of it. In fact, he is so conscious of it that it is he himself who talks to her about it and who underscores the fact that it is a message but that he does not know what the message is.

What does he imagine there is in the room? What object lies behind the door while he is outside, announcing himself, in a way that alienates him, with his little cough, with this message he does not understand? His association that leads from the cough to barking like a dog shows us that he manifests his presence by the cough in order to announce himself as an other – that is, as someone other than himself.

In a vague and ambiguous way, the subject in some sense traces out a first loop here. First he speaks of his cough as a message. Then he has an association, which is the fantasy in which he imagines being a dog. Next comes the memory of something that really happened, his coupling with a dog in a room. He thus goes successively through something that reflects his desire and then incarnates his fantasy. The circle closes on itself there. Then he changes register.

It was on this point that my last class on this patient ended. Sharpe notes that, at this very moment, the subject gives another little cough, as if to punctuate what he just said, and begins recounting the dream that I already read to you.

I want to tell you what our aim is now going to be. We are going to juxtapose the fantasy and the dream – in other words, we will examine which aspect of the relationship between desire and fantasy is manifested in the dream. We will then see, as I already told you, that the dream and the fantasy emphasize things very differently.

In the fantasy, what is emphasized is the subject.

The subject barks like a dog. The barking is both a message or announcement *and* what disguises him. By barking, he announces himself as other than he is. He does not know why he proceeds in this way, but his associations to the cough indicate that the point for him is to put himself in the position of either not being there or, if he is there, of announcing himself as other than he is, in such a way that the couple separates and that what there was to be seen behind the

212

door disappears. What does he imagine was going on in the room before he entered? Therein lies the enigma.

The enigmatic character of what is hidden from him is clearly underscored by the fact that at the moment of entering the analyst's consulting room, he gave this confounded little cough. Why does he want to announce his presence in this way? What can there be behind the door? What can he imagine? What is veiled is the right-hand side of the formula for fantasy [($◊a$)], the object, x. This object is not, I would say, his analyst, but what is found in the room.

Let us now turn to the dream. What is foregrounded there is an object.

This object is an imaginary element, but not just any old which one. As this object figures in a dream, you must expect it to be marked by a certain function, and what I have taught you about dreams would have no meaning if this function were not a signifying function. As we know, what is on the right of the relationship inscribed in the formula for fantasy has a complex function – it is not simply an image, but a signifying element. Nevertheless, this remains veiled and enigmatic to us, and we cannot articulate it as such.

On the other side of the relationship, on the left, there is the subject [$].

All we know about him is that in the fantasy he announced himself as other than he was – in other words, as a subject marked by the signifier, as a barred subject. In the dream, on the other hand, we have an image [of the object, i.e., the woman], and what we do not know is who is on the other side – namely, the subject.

213   What is he in the dream? This is what Sharpe tries to articulate for him in her interpretation.

We will now turn to the associations the subject has to his dream.

2

The narrative of the dream concludes with the patient's remark about the use of the verb "to masturbate."

He employed it transitively in the sentence "she was so disappointed I thought I would masturbate her," whereas it is the intransitive use that is correct. Something different is obviously at stake here – namely, the fact that the patient masturbates. This is clearly what the analyst thinks, for she suggests it to him immediately; he acquiesces and notes that he almost never masturbated anyone else, recalling that he did it but once with another boy. Then he continues:

The dream is in my mind vividly. There was no orgasm. I remember her vagina gripped my finger. I see the front of her genitals, the end of the vulva. Something large and projecting hung downwards like a fold on a hood. Hoodlike it was, and it was this that the woman made use of in maneuvering

– he used the same term, "maneuvering," in his narrative of the dream –

to get my penis. The vagina seemed to close round my finger. The hood seemed strange. [p. 133]

The analyst asks, "What else do you think of – let the look of it be in your mind."

I think of a cave. There is a cave on the hillside where I lived as a child. I often went there with my mother. It is visible from the road along which one walks. Its most remarkable feature is that it has an overhanging top to it which looks very much like a huge lip. [pp. 133–4]

A cave with a part that projects forward is something like the grotto of the Cyclops in Capri, the coast of which is strewn with such caves.
Here he has a remarkable association:

There is some joke about the labia running crosswise and not longitudinally, but I don't remember how the joke was arranged, some comparison between Chinese writing and our own, starting from different sides, or from bottom to top. Of course the labia are side by side, and the vagina walls are back and front, that is, one longitudinal and the other crosswise. I'm still thinking of the hood. [p. 134]

214

The best-known "jokes,"* those that are part of Britain's cultural heritage, usually take the form of limericks.* A limerick* is something that is very important and revealing, I will do no more than indicate this. I looked through a rather large collection of some 3,000 limericks to find the one mentioned by the patient. It surely exists, for some of the ones I saw were quite similar to it.
I do not know why the theme of China comes into it. The inversion of the direction of writing refers back to the similarity, and at the same time to the difference, between the genital slit and the mouth. There is also what is presupposed regarding the transversal

nature of the vagina behind the line of the genital slit. Stated otherwise, all of this is highly ambiguous.

Limerick number 1,381 of a special collection I consulted is the
one that most closely approximates the patient's joke.* It is amusing
owing to the fact that it is not clear why China comes into the
limerick.* It is rather remarkable that one finds in it, as in the one
we are looking for, the essential superimposition of the image of a
mouth and of a genital image.

There was a young lady from China
Who mistook for her mouth her vagina.
Her clitoris huge
She covered with rouge,
And lipsticked her labia minor.

215   [Lacan provides a French translation of it.] It loses a good deal of
its zest in translation.

What am I going to highlight here? This is the kind of thing that
makes analysts immediately slip into thinking in terms of imaginary elements alone – associating, for example, the mouth with
the vagina, or the mother's breast with the earliest sense of being
swallowed up or devoured. One can, indeed, find all sorts of ethnological, folkloric, and psychological evidence that shows that the
earliest relationship between the child and what one might call the
maternal image is a relationship of content and container.

But I ask you, doesn't it seem worth retaining here something
that has much the same inflection as when, a couple of years ago, I
drew your attention to the big giraffe and the small giraffe in Freud's
case of little Hans? What was essential was not that these elements
were the mother and the phallus, but what little Hans did with
them – he could sit on them or crumple them up. I told you at that
time that the giraffes were symbols. One might say – in a way that is
more nuanced, more interrogative, and easier to confirm – that, in
fantasy, they were already things that were transformed into paper.

In order to underscore what is at stake, it is not pointless to introduce here the imaginary element that is so remarkable in the dream,
and that was very precisely depicted as the fold of a hood. This is not
negligible. It is something that already has a certain structure, that
covers, that crowns, and that is also feared. The finger introduced
into this sexual, vaginal element, which seems to "close round"
it, gives us a very precise image. There is no need to drown it in
a general structure of envelopment, devouring, or swallowing up,
especially given the fact that it is explicitly connected in the dream
to the patient's finger.

I would even say that the essential question is, does he or doesn't he put his finger there? It is clear that he does put his finger there and that he does not put anything else there; he specifically does not put his penis there, even though his penis is clearly present in this relationship with what comes to envelop or act like a glove on his hand. This is quite salient and brought center stage as a result of "[considerations of] representability" in the dream, as Freud puts it, in order to designate the third element at work in the *Traumarbeit* – that is, the dream-work.

The question is what we should do with it. Should we immediately reduce it to a series of time-tested [*rédimées*], preformed significations? Should we place behind this image everything we are used to finding there, having put it there ourselves, as if we were pulling it out of a magician's hat? No. We are going to stop and respect it as something that has a specific value.

Assuming you have a little bit more in your head than novelistic notions about what such a fantasy can be, you should realize that such an elaborate image warrants time and attention, and that it is important above all not to submerge it – for example, in the very general notion of being inside the mother's womb, which people talk about so much in relation to fantasies. Moreover, what the dream presents us with here is certainly not the inside of the uterus, since it is "overhanging,"* there being an edge that projects outward.

Sharpe, because she is very astute, underscores a bit further on, in a passage we may turn to later, that we find ourselves presented here with something remarkable – namely, a "projection,"* she says, and she announces immediately thereafter that it "is equivalent to a penis" [p. 144].

That is possible, but why be in such a rush? All the more so in that she also underscores that it is difficult not to consider this projection as related to the presence of the vagina. This is quite seriously emphasized in the dream, and when we consider the very maneuver that the patient engages in – I would say that he substitutes himself for himself by placing his finger and not his penis there – how can we fail to see that this so-to-speak localized thing in this fantasy indeed has, as the patient articulates it, the closest relationship with the front and back wall of the vagina?

In short, to a physician whose profession it is to practice medicine – which was not the case of Sharpe who taught in the humanities, which gave her a fine perspective on psychology – it sounds like vaginal prolapse. It sounds like a prosection or downward displacement of the vaginal walls, the front wall first of all, and then perhaps the back wall, and at a still later stage, it is the extremity of the cervix

216

that appears in the genital orifice. This is extremely common and poses all sorts of problems to surgeons.

This immediately brings into play, of course, the fantasy of the phallic woman. This is so true that I wanted to remind you of an episode from the life of Christina, Queen of Sweden, who was a friend of Descartes' and, like all the women of her time, tough. The women from that marvelous half of the seventeenth century had an influence on history that one cannot overemphasize. I was not able to go back and check the passage, but the fact is well enough known not to be new, I believe, to some of you.

One day, the Queen herself saw appear, there, in the orifice of her vulva, the tip of her uterus which, without us knowing why, turned out, at that particular moment of her life, to hang down. It was a very typical case of uterine prolapse. Seeing this, and lapsing into unbelievable flattery, her doctor fell to his knees before her and said, "It's a miracle! Jupiter has finally given you your true sexual organ." This proves that the fantasy of the phallic woman was not born yesterday in the history of medicine and philosophy.

Now that is not what is going on in the dream in question. It is found neither in the narrative nor in the associations, and, even though the subject must have seen, according to the analyst, his mother's genitals, there is no reason to assume, for example, that the patient's mother had a uterine prolapse. Although you never know.

Whatever the case may be, in Sharpe's articulation of her understanding of what happens, she brings out the following: that certain of the patient's imaginings lead her to think that he likely saw quite a number of things from below. It is in order for her interpretation to be coherent that Sharpe must necessarily assume that he had a certain apprehension of female genitalia, and specifically of his mother's, from under the skirts. Why shouldn't we go in this direction? You will see that *we* are far more justified in doing so than the analyst herself, but we are not at that point just yet.

Before going any further, I will simply indicate to you that, when we refer to body images, and we have them play a role in interpretation, it is important to be precise. One must especially not confuse dread, desire, or fear of the return to the womb with the relationship with the vagina. The latter is not something that the subject is incapable of having some direct or indirect apprehension of, as the case study we are examining clearly shows, after all.

I will highlight now the point on which it is worth dwelling. The patient immediately associates the dream image that is given special emphasis, as I said, with something from an entirely different register, with a ditty. Whether we call it a "joke"* or a "limerick"* makes little difference.

It was not simply to amuse myself that I gave you an example of a limerick*; it was to give you an idea of the style of the thing, which is characterized by extreme literary rigor. It is a defined genre in literary history, a genre that has the strictest of laws, laws that concern writing. We did not find a direct reference to writing in the limerick* that I managed to dig up for you, but the patient asserts that there was a reference to writing in the one he heard. The reference was to the different direction of the lines of writing in our way of writing and the Chinese way. He mentions it at the very moment at which it suddenly comes to his mind that the word "labia" means lips, which creates a connection between the labia majora and the lips of the mouth. It is this same reference to writing that leads him to compare the labia majora to the vaginal walls.

Let us chalk these connections up to the symbolic order, for there is nothing more symbolic than the lines of Chinese characters. This reference is well designed to indicate to us that, in any case, this dream element has a signifying value. It is precisely at this point that some aspect of the relationship between desire and fantasy manifests itself in the dream, insofar as desire must adjust and adapt to it.

Fantasy finds its place on the graph of desire halfway between the signifier of the barred Other, $S(\cancel{A})$, and the signified of the Other, $s(A)$ [see Figure 2.2].

Don't you see that what I am saying here merely expresses in a more articulated way something about our experience when we try to focus in on what the subject's desire is? We are always trying to home in on the subject's position in relation to a certain object that lies midway between a pure and simple signification – that would be owned by him, that would be clear and transparent to him – $s(A)$, on the one hand, and something closed and enigmatic that is not at all a fantasy, or a need, pressure, or "feeling,"* but that is always something akin to a signifier as such, $S(\cancel{A})$, on the other hand.

Between these two poles, there is the object.

The object appears here in the form of an extremely clear and precise visual representation, but at the same time, with his associations, the patient alerts us to the fact that it is signifying.

219

3

What shall I do now? Shall I enter into the way the analyst interprets it? Yes? [The audience acquiesces.] In that case I must make known to you all the material we have at our disposal.

When the patient says "I'm still thinking of the hood," the analyst asks, "Yes, how now?" The patient replies, "A funny man at one of the earliest golf courses I remember." The man ran after him and, the patient adds, "He said he could get me a golf bag cheaply and the material would be 'motor hood cloth'" [p. 134]. That is the fabric people used for the hoods of cars. "It was the accent I remember. I shall never forget it." Here he imitates the man's accent. "Imitating him like that reminds me of a friend who broadcasts impersonations" – "broadcast" is the operative word here –

> which are very clever, but it sounds "swank" to tell you, as swanky as telling you what a marvellous wireless set I have. It picks up all stations with no difficulty.
>
> My friend has a splendid memory. She remembers her childhood too, but mine is so bad below eleven years. I do remember, however, one of the earliest songs we heard at the theatre and she imitated the man afterwards. [p. 134]

It is a tasteful British music-hall song called "Where did you get that hat, where did you get that tile?" The word "tile" especially designates what was known at the time as a "tube," meaning a top hat. It can also mean hat or a man's hat.

The patient continues, "My mind has gone to the hood again and I am remembering the first car I was ever in, but of course they were called motors then when they were new." The patient is undoubtedly somewhat advanced in years. "I remember the hood of it, that's 'motor hood' again you see." Here he describes the remarkable features of the hood. "It was strapped back when not in use. The inside of it was lined with scarlet." And he continues:

> The peak of speed for that car was about sixty [miles per hour], as much as is good for the life of a car. Strange how one speaks of the life of a car as if it were human. I remember I was sick in that car, and that reminds me of the time I had to urinate into a paper bag when I was in a railway train as a child. Still I think of the hood. [p. 135]

We will stop our examination of his associations here, even though they do not go very far yet, because I want to juxtapose what I am bringing you here with the way in which the analyst begins to interpret the material. She says:

> The first thing of importance is to find the cardinal clue to the significance of the dream. We can do that by noting just the moment when it came to the patient's mind. He had been speaking of the incident of a dog masturbating on his leg. The

220

moment before he had been speaking of imitating the dog himself, that is, he identified himself with the dog. Then he gave a cough. Then he remembered the dream, a long and exciting dream from which he awoke hot and perspiring. The deduction concerning the significance of the whole dream is that it is a masturbation phantasy. [p. 138]

I couldn't agree more. "That is of first importance." I concur. "The next thing to notice in connection with this masturbation fantasy is the theme of potency." By this she does not mean sexual potency, but power in the most general sense of the term, "omnipotence," as she puts it later on. "He is travelling around the world. It is the longest dream he has ever had." That is what the patient said:

It would take a whole hour to relate. Correlate with that his deprecation of "wind" regarding his friend's impersonations which are broadcast to the world, and his own wireless set which picks up every station. Note his own imitation of the man whose accent attracted him, a strong colloquial accent, 221 and incidentally he said with regard to this man "he had once been a butcher."
Impersonation here, whether via friend or himself, has the significance of imitating a stronger or better-known person. [pp. 138–9]

Is she mistaken? "This is again a further clue to the meaning of the masturbation phantasy, that is, a phantasy in which he is impersonating another person, one of immense power and potency" [p. 138].
The simple fact that, regarding these impersonations and the possession of a radio, the patient excuses himself for bragging or putting himself forward a bit too much signifies that we have here a fantasy of omnipotence, behind which his masturbation fantasy supposedly lies. Omnipotence has to be of primary importance. This is what the analyst considers to be self-evident. Can we endorse that?
Once again, I ask you to simply note the facts of the case. The least one can say is that there is perhaps some confusion in maintaining that what is at stake here is an omnipotence that is wished for or more or less secretly owned by the subject, whereas, if we stick with a first take on the dream – that is, its manifest content – it seems that, rather than expanding, the subject shrinks. Moreover, the analyst herself underscores this shrunken side of the subject when "hood" reappears in another context.
In fact, the analyst goes much further in her speculations than in the interpretation [she proffers to him]. For she is so influenced

by a certain apprehension of the shrunken nature of the subject's presence in his hood fantasy that she always says that he saw or perceived this or that when he was a "tiny" boy. But what do we in fact see? We see that the subject shrinks in the presence of this vaguely tentacular appendix. He dares at most touch it with a finger, without knowing whether his finger will be covered and protected by it or squeezed, imprisoned, and ripped off by it. In any case, the patient pushes this signifying object away from him and from the exercise of his potency, at least from his sexual potency.

It is perhaps going a bit far to say so, but I see the same confusion here between the omnipotence attributed to the patient, even when it is more or less denied by him, and the omnipotence of speech, which is, on the contrary, altogether clear in this case. Yet there is a world of difference between them. For it is precisely in connection with speech that the patient has difficulty.

222

He is a lawyer and has plenty of talent, but he is plagued by very severe phobias whenever he has to appear in court and speak. We are told at the outset that his father died when he was three years old and that the patient [referred to in the case study as Robert] had a great deal of trouble remembering him. What is the only memory that remains absolutely clear to him? It is when his family told him his father's final words. They were, "Robert must take my place." What did he mean by that? Was the son afraid of his father's death? The dying father spoke; he said, "take my place." But which place? The one I occupy here [in the family] or the one in which I am dying?

The subject's difficulty with respect to speech, the distance which is such that he uses speech in order to be elsewhere, and, conversely, that nothing is more difficult for him than not simply to speak but to say something about his father's speech – this was only very recently accomplished, the analyst tells us, and it was "startling"* to him "when he thought that he must have heard his father speak" [p. 126] – shouldn't all of that incline us to be at least a bit circumspect here? Shouldn't that incline us to highlight in him, more than in others, the division between the Other qua speaking and the other qua imaginary?

The analyst finds confirmation of the patient's omnipotence in the fact that he refers to the dream as "tremendous" [p. 132]. We can only know that it was tremendous from the patient. He is the one who tells us he had a tremendous dream, that there were many scenes before this one, that there was a whole journey around the world, and a hundred thousand adventures that would take forever to recount, but that he will spare the analyst an account of them. But in the end, the mountain turns out to be a molehill: a very short story. We are told that there is a horizon of omnipotence indicated in the narrative, but it is never narrated. Omnipotence is always connected with the Other, with the world of speech as such.

Must we rush, as Sharpe does, to attribute to the patient's structure not simply a fantasy of omnipotence but also the aggressiveness that it implies? The bias that sometimes colors her interpretations is often based on the fact that she overlooks a difference in level, which, when it is sufficiently emphasized in the structure itself, must be respected. It is, moreover, on this condition alone that we know that this difference in level exists.

> The next question that arises from that is why this phantasy of extreme power? The answer is given in the dream. He is going round the world. I would put as commensurate with this idea the actual memory that came to him when he was describing the hood in the dream which was so strange, for it brought out not only the fact that he was describing a projection, a fold of a hood, but that the hood was also overhanging like a lip of a cave. So that we get directly the hood and lips of the vulva compared with the great cave on the hillside to which he went with his mother. Hence the masturbation phantasy is one associated with immense potency because he is dreaming of compassing mother earth, of being adequate to the huge cave beneath the protruding lips. That is the second thing of importance. [p. 139]

When you examine the analyst's train of thought here, you cannot fail to sense that a jump has been made. The fact that there may be a relationship between the childhood memory in which he gets coverage [*subit une couverture*], as they say, and the signifying value of what I will call the fantasy of prolapse need not be ruled out, naturally, there obviously being some relationship owing to the fact of his free association. But to consider on this basis that we are dealing with the classic topic of the Oedipal relation, as it were, the one that rises to the level of embracing one's mother – which here becomes embracing mother earth herself, embracing the entire world – a step has nevertheless been made which seems to me to have perhaps been made a bit too quickly.

It is important not to overlook the fact that, alongside the grandiose schema of the Oedipal hero who proves himself to be at his mother's level, Freud clearly isolated this moment from a phase of development in which the owning of his actual sexual organ is precisely related in the male child to a feeling of inadequacy – which runs counter to what Sharpe says – regarding what he has at his disposal compared to what would be required by an enterprise like conquering or having sex with his mother. This element plays an

224   indisputable role, which is manifested quite insistently, in a very
large number of cases concerning the subject's narcissistic relationship to his penis, insofar as it is considered by him as more or less
insufficient, as too small.

And we must not believe that the only thing that comes into
play in this regard is the relationship with his semblables: his male
rivals. Clinical practice shows us, on the contrary, that the inadequacy of the penis with respect to the female genitalia, assumed to
be altogether enormous compared to the male organ, is much too
important for us to proceed so quickly.

The analyst continues:

> Next I would draw your attention to the associations concern-
> ing lips and labia. The woman who was a stimulus for the
> dream had full red passionate lips. In the dream he had a vivid
> picture of the labia and the hood. The cave had an overhang-
> ing lip. He thinks of things longitudinal like labia and then of
> cross-wise things – where I would now suggest the mouth as
> compared with the vulva. [p. 139]

No comment.

> He thinks, moreover, of the first motor he was in and of its
> hood and of the scarlet lining in that motor. He then thinks
> immediately of the speed of the car, and says "the peak of its
> speed" was so many miles an hour, and then speaks of "the life
> of the car" and notices that he talks of a car as if it were human.
>   From the fact of the dream picture of the vulva and the hood
> . . . [p. 140]

I am going to skip here a little,

> I should deduce that the memory of the actual cave which
> he visited with his mother also acts as a cover memory [i.e.,
> a screen memory]. I would deduce that there is projected on
> to the motor with its scarlet lined hood this same forgotten
> memory and that the peak of speed has the same significance as
> the projection in the genitals in the dream – it is the peak of the
> hood. I infer there is an actual repressed memory of seeing the
> genitals of someone much older than himself; of seeing them
> when he was very tiny and I infer this from both the car and
> the cave and going round the world in conjunction with the
> immense potency required. The peak, the hood, I interpret as
> the clitoris. [p. 140]

I was saying earlier that the mountain made of the dream gives   225
rise to a molehill. We have something analogous here, in what I
would almost call the analyst's droning on and on.

I am willing to admit that this "peak of speed" can be identified
with the peak of the hood, but if it is truly so peaked and enormous,
how can we associate it with a real, lived, childhood memory? There
is something excessive here in concluding so brazenly that we have
here a screen memory related to an actual sight of the female genitalia and especially of the clitoris. This is nevertheless what the analyst
comes to, by highlighting, as a key element, the fact that:

> The patient's sister is eight years older than himself. Considering
> the references made to his woman friend's voice, that is to
> sound, accent, sound of a man's voice, and considering that
> the reference to her is in connection with male impersonation, I
> deduce that at least when very tiny he saw her genitals, noticed
> the clitoris, and heard her urinate. [p. 140]

And right after that she has to mention the following: "But considering all the work in analysis we have done so far I believe in
addition there was some babyhood situation in which he had a quite
definite opportunity of seeing his mother's genitals" [pp. 140–1].

All of these details make the analyst surmise that at such a moment
he would have been "laid on the floor on a blanket" [p. 141].

4

Why am I making all of these critical remarks? I will have to show
my cards here and tell you where I am going with this.

My goal is to teach you how to spell out, as it were, the direction
taken by a certain number of inflections that the analyst imposes on
the comprehension of the material that she presents to us, inflections
that, far from making that material seem all the more limpid to us,
stop us from providing an accurate interpretation of it.

The path her thought process takes leads her to extremely active
and even brutal interpretations. She suggests to the patient that   226
the crux of the matter is the aggressive nature of his own penis.
His penis as an aggressive organ brings into play the harmful and
deleterious nature of the water it releases when he urinates [p. 146].
The analyst thus obtains an effect that should not surprise us much,
which is that an adult patient, who is somewhat advanced in years,
ends up urinating in his sleep the following night [p. 147]. You have
already heard me mention it, but let us leave that to one side.

To get a little bit ahead of myself regarding what I believe I can demonstrate to you by continuing this slow and painful job of analyzing line by line, where does the question arise in what one might call the patient's fundamental fantasy, inasmuch as it is rendered present in the transference? The patient imagines something, we do not know what, about his analyst. I will tell you later how the analyst herself conceptualizes the point they are at in the transference. In any case, at the moment of the session in which he recounts the dream, the transference is of a clearly imaginary type.

The analyst is essentially focused and centered, with regard to the patient, on the dyadic relation, that of one ego to another. The analyst senses very clearly everything rigid, measured, and defensive in the patient's attitude in her presence. This implies that he is in the closest of specular relations with her. But, as opposed to what she says, this is far from indicating that there is no transference – it is a certain type of transference, a type that is fundamentally dyadic and imaginary.

So what is this analyst, who is but a reflection of the patient, doing in her consulting room? This is indisputable: he is clearly warning her with his little cough not to get caught masturbating. That is what he assumes her to be doing.

But how do we know this? We do not know it immediately, and that is very important. How can we know it? We know it from the dream, where it is altogether clear, since it is exactly what the patient says – namely, that someone is masturbating.

The analyst correctly recognizes that the masturbator in question is the patient – that is, the dreamer [p. 138]. Yet the fact that, in the narrative of the dream, the patient manifests his intention to masturbate the woman, while adding that "to masturbate" is an intransitive verb, tips us off. That is to say that the signifying fantasy in question is one of a close connection between a male and a female element, caught up in a sort of envelopment.

Let me explain. I do not mean that the patient is simply caught or contained in the other, but that, inasmuch as he masturbates *her*, he *himself* masturbates, but also does not masturbate. In short, the fundamental image presented in the dream is that of a sort of glove or sheath turned inside out.

Sheath and vagina are, moreover, the same words: *gaine* [sheath] is the same word as *vagin* [vagina]. We have here a linguistic coincidence that is not lacking in signification. There would be a great deal to say, from a linguistic perspective, about sheaths, gloves, and scabbards [*la gaine, le gant, le fourreau*]. And it is extremely important to map an entire chain of images, because they are constantly present, not only in this specific case, but in many others as well.

227

What is involved here is both the imaginary and the signifying character in the dream who is the central image with which the subject in some sense sees that any and all possible expression of his sexuality is enveloped or caught up. It is in relation to this image that he situates his desire. It is there that his desire is in some sense stuck.

I will try to show this to you because I must do a little bit more to justify this notion.

In his series of associations, an idea arises that had flashed through the patient's mind, the analyst tells us, during the preceding associations. The patient "attended a function at which the King and the Queen were to be present" [p. 143]. He was haunted by the idea of his car breaking down in the middle of the road and thereby blocking the way for the royal automobile.

The analyst sees in this yet another manifestation of the patient's omnipotence that he fears will be used against him. She even goes so far as to see in it the fact that the patient must have taken the opportunity to interfere in some primal scene by stopping his parents from having intercourse [p. 145]. We will see all of this in detail next time, but what is quite striking, it seems to me, is the function of the car.

The patient is in a car, he is afraid it will break down, but with this breakdown, if it occurs, he is far from separating anyone at all. He blocks traffic, he undoubtedly blocks others, he blocks everything – this we know because that is what is at stake, that is why he is in analysis – everything stops, he stops the royal, parental couple, who are together in one car, a car that envelops them, like the hood of the car he mentions in his associations as having the same characteristic as the cave's cover.

Sharpe is writing at the time at which Melanie Klein began to come to prominence in English society and began to articulate things of high clinical caliber. Was it truly worth Klein's while to have spoken so much about the "combined parent" – that biparental monster, so to speak – if we cannot recognize here the incredibly specific presence of an ambiguous character related to a certain way of apprehending sexual relations?

Let us say, to take this a step further, that what is at stake in the subject is precisely this: to separate the parents, to separate the male and female principles in them. I would say, in a certain way, that what is proposed here – what is targeted on the horizon by psychoanalytic interpretation – is nothing other than a kind of psychical circumcision. For in the final analysis, what is this protruding, prolapsed vagina?

It is over there, it comes over here, and moreover it presents itself in the form of something that is nowhere, that slips away. I spoke earlier of the magician's hat, but in truth we are familiar with this

228

sort of magic trick; one such trick is called the "egg bag." You turn a specially designed bag inside out and right side in over and over, and first you find nothing in it and then you find in it what you slipped into it with a deft movement.

This sort of perpetual presence and non-presence of the subject has yet another facet, which we find in masturbation as well, inasmuch as masturbation already implies the presence of a certain female element. This is why I speak of a certain circumcision. This protruding element in his dream is also, in certain ways, the foreskin.

Another set of his memories brings out for us the fact that there is a certain relationship between him and the sexual act. There was indisputably one in his childhood. But where was he? He was in his bed and, as you will see, tightly tucked in with pins securing his sheets [p. 141]. There are other elements that also show us the patient strapped into his pram [p. 136]. To the degree to which he himself is bound and blocked, he cannot enjoy his fantasy and participate in it except through a supplemental, derivative, displaced activity: compulsive urination. The sort of supplement or false jouissance he gets from urination is something that we frequently note in patients who have been in close proximity to parental coitus.

What does he become at that moment? He becomes the female partner about whom he tells us that she has such a need for him that he must show her [how to do] everything, and he must do everything, becoming feminized in the process. Insofar as he is impotent, as it were, he is male. And it is clear that this brings him some compensation at the level of his ambition to garner power. But inasmuch as he is liberated, he is feminized.

The problem lies in this duplicitous game of hide and seek or of the non-separation of the two facets of femininity and masculinity in him; it lies in a type of unique fantasized apprehension of genital desire, which is fundamentally masturbatory.

I hope to show next time just how justified I am in orienting my interpretations in this direction, in order to allow the subject to take the next step forward.

January 28, 1959

XI

SACRIFICING THE
TABOO QUEEN

Aphanisis, Jones's term
Where is the phallus?
Cons abound
Chess as a metaphor
Countertransferential pickles

We have now arrived at a point at which we can try to interpret the dream that Ella Sharpe's patient recounted.

This is an enterprise we can only undertake, and for theoretical purposes alone – that is, as an exercise – thanks to the exceptionally detailed discussion of the dream in her book.

According to Sharpe, and I take her word for it, this dream occupied a crucial point in the analysis.

1

Her patient had a "tremendous dream," and it would take him hours to recount it. But he forgot most of it, remembering only the following.

It takes place on a road in Czechoslovakia. He finds himself there, having undertaken a journey around the world with his wife. I even highlighted the fact that he said "a journey with my wife around the world" [p. 132].

On this road, he is prey to the sexual undertakings of a woman who, let me point out, presents herself in a way that is not indicated in the initial dream-text. The patient says, "the woman actually lay on top of me; that has only just come to my mind. She was evidently intending to put my penis in her body." He adds that "the woman [was] maneuvering to get my penis" [pp. 132–3], an expression we will have to come back to later.

Naturally, he adds, "I disagreed with this, but she was so disappointed I thought that I would masturbate her" [p. 133]. He makes
232   a remark here about the fundamentally intransitive nature of the verb "to masturbate" in English [p. 133]. It is already in our interest to realize that what is involved here is, of course, masturbation on the part of the patient himself. Sharpe herself realizes this, although she does not stress as directly as I do the fact that this is based on the grammatical nature of the patient's remark.

Last time, I highlighted the value of an image that appears less in the associations than in the narrative of the dream – namely, the fold, as in the fold of a "hood."* And I showed that resorting to the stock images taken into account by classical psychoanalytic doctrine – even though these manifestly stem from experience – perhaps leads analysts to force things a bit when these images are made to serve as so many separate objects, without very carefully situating their function in relation to the subject. I thus underscored what is paradoxical in the overly hasty interpretation that this odd appendix, this protrusion from the female genitalia, is a sign that what we are dealing with here is the maternal phallus.

Such haste also led Sharpe to take another leap, it being so true that, as opposed to what people say, one imprudent step can only be corrected by another. We learn less from our mistakes than people think, for the only way of saving ourselves from a mistake is to make another one that compensates for it.

I am not saying that Sharpe is completely wrong. I am trying to articulate better ways of proceeding, which might have allowed for greater accuracy. With the caveat, of course, that we can never actually confirm this since we will never have the experience with the patient we would have to have in order to do so.

What is the next leap I mentioned? It concerns the phallus, less that of his imagined partner in the dream than his own. The analyst agrees that the dream has a masturbatory character to it, because everything that comes out in the patient's speech corroborates this. But the patient's phallus is immediately viewed by her to be an instrument of aggression and destruction of an extremely primitive type, such as we find in what we might call psychoanalytic imagery [p. 143].

This is the direction in which Sharpe's thoughts run right from the outset, even though she is far from communicating to him the
233   whole of her interpretation [pp. 144–5]. In the first place, she points out to him elements of what she calls "omnipotence." Secondly, she says that what appears in the dream is masturbation. And thirdly, that this masturbation is omnipotent, in the sense that the patient's phallus is a "biting and boring thing" [p. 146].

We have here a true theoretical extrapolation on the analyst's part! In truth, there are no grounds – either in the dream or the associations – for immediately asserting that the patient's phallus is an aggressive organ here and that the subject is afraid of the possible repercussions of his aggression. When we read such a formulation in Sharpe's case study, we cannot help but realize that it is in no wise justified by the case at hand and that it is motivated instead, without her telling us so, by her theory.

To her credit, she informs us so amply and carefully about her patient – as regards the major issues in his life and what she sees in front of her, which she senses in such detail and with such finesse – that we are justified in saying she is clearly taking a leap. I readily concede that this leap seemed necessary to her. But whether this leap seems necessary to us is another question, and it is here that we will try to re-examine the analysis.

My goal is not to replace the imaginary equivalents she prioritizes with other interpretations, in the sense in which it is ordinarily understood, as in "this bit of data must be understood as follows." The point is not to know what each element of the dream means at one moment or another. On the whole, we can even say that these elements are quite correctly gauged by her, given the tradition of psychoanalytic experience in force at the time at which Sharpe is working, and they are, moreover, perceived with great discernment and finesse.

The point is to see if the problem cannot be clarified by being articulated in a way that better links the interpretation with what I am trying to stress here – namely, the intersubjective topology. This is what I am always trying to construct or reconstruct for you, in various forms, inasmuch as this topology is the very topology of our experience. In psychoanalysis, the places of the subject, the little other, and the Other with a capital O must always be indicated for each phenomenon if we wish to avoid getting bogged down in a sort of tangle, knotted up by a thread that no one knows how to untie, and which forms the daily bread, as it were, of our psychoanalytic explanations.

234

I have already discussed this dream, and in several different ways, enough to be able to begin to articulate something simple and direct, something that is not at all absent from the case study, but that emerges from the reading I have provided of it.

I would say that in reading the preamble that Sharpe provides to her account of the session in which the dream was recounted, where she details the reasons that led the patient to analysis, a word immediately comes to mind – and it is not impossible that it came to her mind, as it is not peculiar to the terminology we use here. To mention it is not to bring in a notion that was beyond her ken, for when she wrote this text, in 1937, the British psychoanalytic scene was dominated by discussions I have spoken to you about regarding the phallic phase and the phallic function in female sexuality, especially the discussions that took place between Ernest Jones and Joan Riviere, whose article "Womanliness as Masquerade" we have explored here [in Seminar V, pp. 254–5].

Jones introduces a term at one point, which he considers necessary if we are to begin to understand what, in psychoanalysis, is truly the most difficult thing to understand, not simply to bring into play – namely, the castration complex. The word Jones introduces is "aphanisis," a word he introduced into psychoanalytic terminology in an interesting way. We cannot consider it to be absent from the British scene, as a great deal was made of it at the time.

Jones understands this term to mean disappearance. We will see further on what he means by that. But I am going to use the word in an entirely different way for the time being – in short, in an impressionistic way – regarding what Sharpe presents us, that is, regarding what is constantly found in the dream material and what surrounds it, as well as in the patient's behavior.

The patient presents himself to her in a way that she describes very prettily – namely, with a sort of profound absence that gives her the sense that there is not a single one of his remarks or gestures which has not been thoroughly thought out or which includes any affect. He keeps his nose completely clean. Moreover, he does not announce his arrival – he simply appears, and as soon as he appears he is even more unfathomable than if he were not there.

235

Let us first consider what he brings up during that day's session prior to recounting the dream.

The patient himself tells us that he is wondering what purpose his little cough might serve [p. 131]. It is designed to make something, which must be there behind the door, disappear. He does not know what it is. He says so himself: regarding the analyst what could there be there that would have to disappear? He recalls in this connection that, in other circumstances, in another context, coughing served as a warning: he coughed to tell a pair of lovers to separate, to move apart, for the situation would otherwise have been embarrassing when he entered, and so on and so forth.

What about the dream itself?

Here, too, we are in the presence of three people, for, above and beyond his sexual partner and himself, there is his wife. She must not be forgotten, even though the subject, after having mentioned her once, says nothing further about her. What exactly does he do with his partner? In a word, he slips away [il se dérobe].

But is it so clear that he slips away? What he enunciates next proves that he is far from being completely absent, since he tells us that he put his finger in this sort of protruding, inside-out, prolapsed vagina that I highlighted. Questions arise here, too, and we are going to raise them. What is at stake? What is the crux of the scene? I am raising the question inasmuch as one can raise such a question about a dream. I am raising it only insofar as all of Freudian theory requires us to raise it.

What come next in his associations are memories connected to the hood constituted by the female genitalia: the cave and Chinese writing. He then recalls someone who, on a golf course, offered him a golf bag.

The patient found him to be quite a character and speaks about him with a kind of amused joy [pp. 134 and 139]. The way he talks about him suggests that the guy was truly the kind about whom one could wonder where he had been knocking about up until then. With a face like that and such a gift of gab, what must he have been? "He had once been a butcher," the patient says in passing [p. 139]. God only knows why he was a butcher! The style and general tenor of the scene, and the fact that the patient immediately begins to imitate the guy's accent, shows that the guy was a conman,* some sort of swindler.

This scene brings up the idea of imitation, which leads the patient to think of his female friend who does such fine imitations of men and who has such talent, talent that she uses in "broadcasting."* Now the first thing that comes to his mind about this is that he is talking too much about knowing such a remarkable person, and that he seems to be bragging or laying it on a bit thick. I checked the word he uses: "swank" is a word that had only recently come into use at that time, and that one might almost consider to be slang.* He uses it to say that he has the impression he is showing off by talking about his friend.

In sum, he does not want to take up too much space on this occasion – he shrinks and disappears. Briefly stated, what we see at every moment and what constantly returns as a theme or leitmotif in the patient's remarks brings to mind the term "aphanisis" – except that its meaning here seems more like "to make disappear" than "to disappear." There is a perpetual game here in which we sense that, in various forms, something that I will call, if you will, the interesting object is never there. The patient is never where we expect him to be, he slips from one point to another in a sort of conman's game. I highlighted this last time. I am going to highlight it again and you will see where this will take us. It will take us to what characterizes what the analyst is confronted with at every level. The patient never

236

puts anything out there without immediately, in some way, taking the essential part of it back.

Here let me comment on the use made by Jones of the term "aphanisis," inasmuch as we find a reversal of perspective in his work that is open to criticism.

Jones studies his patients as they approach the castration complex. What he sees in them at that moment, what he understands or senses, is the fear of aphanisis in the sense of a fear that their desire will disappear. In a sense, he tells us that castration is the symbolization of the loss of desire, although he does not formulate it in this way, since he does not have the theoretical means by which to do so.

It is clear, and I have already emphasized this before, that from any sort of developmental perspective it is very difficult to explain how someone, at a moment of his development at which he is supposed to be at some sort of animal level of subjectivity, begins to see need [*tendance*] detach from itself and become a fear of its own loss. Yet it is here that Jones proposes to make aphanisis into the substance of the fear of castration.

I will point out that this should be broached from the exact opposite direction: it is precisely because there can be castration, it is precisely because the play of signifiers is involved in castration, that a dimension develops in the subject whereby he can become fearful and alarmed at the possible future disappearance of his desire.

Let us begin by observing that it is difficult to conceive how something like desire – if we give it its full meaning, the meaning of need at the level of animal psychology – can be altogether accessible in human experience. Thus, to speak not only of the presence of desire, but of the fear of its absence [*défaut*] as well, constitutes a step that must be explained. In order to explain it, I tell you that the human subject, insofar as he must become inscribed in the signifier, finds a position there on the basis of which he can effectively call his need into question, inasmuch as that need is caught up, modified, and identified in demand. In this context, everything can be quite easily conceptualized.

How do we explain the function of the castration complex? We have to know in what way the assumption by the subject of a position in the signifier implies the loss or sacrifice of one of his signifiers.

I will leave this question to one side for the time being. I will confine myself to saying that, as opposed to what Jones believes, the fear of aphanisis in neurotic subjects must be understood from the perspective of an insufficient articulation or partial foreclosure of the castration complex on their part.

It is because the castration complex does not shelter a subject

237

from the sort of confusion or provoking of anxiety that is manifested in the fear of aphanisis that we effectively see it in neurotics.

We are going to have the opportunity to verify this regarding Sharpe's patient.

2

238

Let us return to the dream-text and to the images we spoke about last time – namely, the representation of the female genitalia in the form of a prolapsed vagina.

This sort of scabbard, sack, or sheath constitutes a rather strange image here, although it is not at all an exceptional or unique case. But we still do not encounter it often and it has not been described in any sort of standardized way in the psychoanalytic literature.

This image is employed here in the signifying articulation of the dream, which means that it takes on its value on the basis of what occurs, on the basis of the reason why it is used. One can raise a question about it: what does it mean to the characters who are present? What we in fact see is that the subject puts his finger in there.

He does not put his penis in there, certainly not, but he puts his finger in there. He turns inside out, re-sheaths, or "reinvaginates" what is "devaginated," and it is almost as if some kind of con [geste d'escamoteur] were taking place. In effect, he puts something in there in the place of what he should put in there, but he also shows that something can be put in there.

Assuming that something can in fact be suggested by the shape of what is presented, namely, the female phallus – this phallus being clearly at stake in the phrase "to get my penis"* – we are justified in wondering what the patient is showing us, since it is as if what were involved here were more an act of exhibitionism than an act of copulation. Let us not forget that this occurs in front of a third party.

I have already mentioned the prestidigitator's move in the trick known as "the egg bag." It involves a wool bag in which the magician alternately makes an egg appear and disappear, making it appear when one does not expect to see it and disappear just when one does.

The showing in question is all the more striking in that the patient's associations have shown us very clearly that he always warns people when he is about to appear, such that nothing of what was there before is seen; or else, as in his fantasy, he has himself taken for a barking dog such that people say, "Oh, it's only a dog."

239

The same sort of conning [*escamotage*] is always going on, in which we do not know what is being hidden [*escamoté*].

It is assuredly and above all the subject himself who is being hidden. But if we seek to locate exactly in the dream what is at stake in this conning, the phrase "to get my penis"* allows us to say that it is certainly the phallus that is at stake. We are, I would say, so habituated and hardened by analytic routine that we almost do not stop and take notice of this particular facet of the dream.

The verb chosen by the subject to designate what the woman here intends to do, "get," has many different uses, all of which go in the sense of obtain, win, grab, grasp, or engage. In general, it concerns something that one obtains. We naturally hear this with the note and echo of *femina penem devoret* [the woman devours the penis], but it is not as simple as all that. Indeed, what is involved in this case is, in the final analysis, far from falling under any such heading. If what is at stake is to get the penis, in any form whatsoever, real or imaginary, the first question we must raise is, "Where is this penis?"

It seems self-evident that it is there, since the patient, according to the account given of the dream, said that the woman was maneuvering "to get [his] penis." We are led to believe from the outset that his penis is situated somewhere in the dream. But if one takes a close look at the text, absolutely nothing indicates this. We cannot conclude that the patient's penis is there just because the partner is trying to get it. This does not in any way suffice to tell us where it is. It is perhaps somewhere else altogether than where our need to complete the scene – in which the subject seems to slip away from the woman's efforts to get his penis – makes us see it. It is not as simple as all that. Where is it? Indeed, we see that therein lies the question.

It is from this starting point that we can realize what is at stake in the odd discordance or strangeness presented by the enigmatic sign that the dream proposes to us – namely, the relationship that indubitably exists between what happens in the dream and masturbation. What does this mean? It is worth looking at the exact passage, for it is highly instructive, even if it is not elucidated or even formulated in the analyst's comments.

What we see is that masturbating the other and the patient masturbating are one and the same thing. Generally speaking, one can even go so far as to say that whatever resembles masturbation here effectively involves a secret narcissistic identification on the patient's part with the other. This involves less a body-to-body identification than an identification of the other's body with the penis. A whole set of stroking [*caresse*] activities bring the phallus into play, inasmuch as, as I have shown you already, it imaginarily emerges in what is beyond the natural partner.

240

I will add that the more the stroking takes on the character of pleasure that is detached, autonomous, and insistent – and even verges on what is called in this case, more or less correctly, a certain sadism – the more obvious this becomes. In effect, the fact that the phallus is involved as a signifier in the relationship between the subject and the other is such that it can be sought out in the realm beyond the embracing of the other where every kind of standard form, that is more or less accentuated in the sense of perversion, begins. It is in this respect that, to the subject, to masturbate the other subject is completely different from allowing his own phallus to be grabbed by the other. This then allows us to posit that, to this patient, masturbating the other is strictly equivalent to engaging in masturbation himself.

I have shown you the meaning of the partner's actions that the subject qualified with the phrase "to get my penis." They are almost tantamount to checking. The point is to ensure that what lies opposite is something terribly important to the subject, something that certainly has the closest connection with the phallus; but these actions show, too, that the phallus is not there, that it is something that flees and slips away, not simply owing to the subject's will, but owing to some structural feature.

This is what is truly in question here, and it colors everything that comes up in his associations to the dream. We find it again both when he is talking about his female friend who behaves so remarkably when she imitates men's voices perfectly, and when discussing this sort of incredible conman [*escamoteur*], this false nice guy whom the subject remembers after all those years. With his unbelievable gift of gab, this character offers him something that is again, oddly enough, one thing instead of another – namely, an envelope in which to wrap up something, but it is a bag made of a material that is designed for some other purpose, it being designed to make a car top ["hood" in the patient's 1930s' vocabulary]. And what is the bag for? To put his golf clubs in.

241

To the patient, things always present themselves in a problematic form. Regardless of what element is involved, it always takes on the same character. Whatever presents itself is never altogether what it seems to be; it is never the real deal.

Let us examine what comes immediately thereafter. Everything that occurs to him is problematic in nature. Childhood memories emerge suddenly. Long ago he had another compulsion, different from the compulsive little cough just before his sessions. Why the devil did he have to "collect leather straps"* and cut up his sister's sandals?

I thought I wanted the strips to make something useful but I expect something quite unnecessary. I dislike thinking it was a compulsion; that's why the cough annoys me. I suppose I cut up my sister's sandals in the same way. I have only the dimmest memory of doing it. I don't know why nor what I wanted the leather for when I had done it. [p. 135]

Here again, we find ourselves faced with a sort of slipping away [*fuite*]. Another one will follow. "I suddenly thought of straps that one sees a child fastened by in a 'pram.'" He curiously and negatively introduces the notion of pram: "immediately I wanted to say there was no 'pram' in our family, and I then thought how silly you are, you must have had a 'pram'" [p. 135]. The analyst notes that there must surely have been one since there were two older children in the family [p. 138]. The same style dominates all of the patient's associations: one thing appears in the form of something else that is missing.

What is the next step that is directly connected to this? "I've suddenly remembered I meant to send off letters admitting two members to the Club. I boasted of being a better secretary than the last and yet here I am forgetting to give people permission to enter the Club" [pp. 135–6]. Immediately thereafter comes a citation – which is put in quotes in Sharpe's text, even though she does not highlight it, as it is well known to the British reader – from the "General Confession," namely one of the prayers found in *The Book of Common Prayer*, which lays out the religious duties of members of the Church of England.

I did not come across *The Book of Common Prayer* for the first time in reading Sharpe's text. I will simply mention here a very pretty object that was created twenty or twenty-five years ago in the surrealist community by my friend Roland Penrose. He showed the inner circle a *Common Book of Prayer* which, when you opened it, had a mirror on each side of the flat inside cover.

This is highly instructive, for the only fault one can find with Sharpe, to whom this text was certainly much more familiar than it is to us, is that she does not mention that the citation given by the patient does not match the text of *The Book of Common Prayer*. He says, "We have undone those things we ought to have done and there is no good thing in us" [p. 136], whereas the original says, "We have *left* undone those things . . ."

A minor detail, you might say. But after that a whole sentence is missing from the "General Confession" which is in some sense the counterpart of the prior one: "And we have done those things which we ought not to have done." The patient feels no need to confess this, and for good reason: in the final analysis, his only concern is with *not doing* things. *Doing* things is not his thing! This is why he says he is altogether incapable of doing anything, for fear of suc- 243 ceeding all too well, as the analyst points out.

This is one point, and not an insignificant one at that. But I want to get to another point. Instead of the missing sentence, the patient adds, "and there is no good thing in us" [p. 136]. This is a total invention on his part. In *The Book of Common Prayer* we find no such thing. We find instead, "there is no health in us." I believe that the "good thing" that he substituted for it is what is truly at work: the good object is not there. This is truly what is involved. He confirms once again for us that what is at stake is the phallus.

It is very important to the subject to say that the good object is not there. We again come across the expression, "it is not there" [i.e., the good thing is not there in us]. It is never where we expect it to be. It is assuredly a "good thing," which is of the utmost importance to him, but it is no less clear that what he tends to show or demonstrate is always one and the same thing – namely, that it is never there. It is never where one could get it or take it. This is what dominates all of the material.

He could not stop himself from cutting the leather straps of his sister's sandals. In light of what I just said, it is possible that the connection with the other compulsion, the cough, now seems less surprising to you. The compulsion to cut has, in effect, a relation with something that, like everyone else, we are only too happy to associate with the theme of castration.

This is a very common psychoanalytic interpretation. If you read Fenichel's work, you will see that boys who cut girls' braids off do so because of their castration complex. But how can we know what exactly is going on without considering each case in great detail? Is it retaliation for castration that involves castrating someone other than oneself? Or is it, on the contrary, the taming of castration by subjecting the other to a castration that is not a true castration and thus does not seem to be as dangerous as all that? Could it be a domestication, as it were, or devaluation of castration, all the more so in that it is always possible that the cut braids will grow back – in other words, reassure you against castration? In short, one could bring to this everything that the sum total of psychoanalytic 244 experience allows us to connect up with this theme.

If we force ourselves not to be hasty, and to maintain things at the level at which we have formulated them heretofore, we will say the following: there is no doubt but that there is some link with castration here. It is obvious that castration is part, as it were, of the context, and that the subject has some relation to castration. But

nothing thus far allows us to postulate that castration is the effect
here of the patient's aggressive intention primitively turned back
against himself; and we would have even less reason to indicate this
to the patient as directly as the analyst did.

Isn't it far more interesting to raise and continually renew the following questions: "Where is the phallus?" "Where must we theorize
it to be?" and "What do we know about it?"

3

The analyst goes out on a limb when she says to the patient that the
phallus is somewhere very far back in you; it is part of an old rivalry
with your father; it is there at the crux of your primordial wishes for
omnipotence; it is there at the source of your fear of retaliation for
your own aggression. Nothing in the text allows us to articulate any
such thing.

Let us try to raise these questions ourselves and perhaps even
answer them a bit more brazenly than we might normally be wont
to.

It seems to me that we cannot react to a case study that was
written up and that we read in the same way as we talk to our students about their cases. If I were dealing with a student, I would
speak much more severely in such an instance. I would say, "What
could have possibly inspired you to say such a thing?" I would
inquire as to where the countertransference came in.

It may seem brazen to raise such concerns about the text of an
author who was, at that point in time, someone we would have
had good reason to lend credence to overall. I smiled to myself
when I wondered about this, because she struck me as a bit over
the top here. Well, one is never wrong, in the final analysis, to be
a bit overly audacious, for it sometimes happens that we find what
we are looking for in that way. And in this case I had to look prior
to finding. I mean that I had read the first few pages of Sharpe's
chapter somewhat distractedly – for, as usual, one never reads very
well – whereas there was something quite lovely there.

You recall the passage about the dead father, the father whom the
analyst cannot manage to bring back to life in the patient's memory.
She says that she had recently gotten things moving a bit such that
the patient marveled at the thought that he must have heard his
father speak when he was little. Right after that she notes that the
patient has the same difficulty with her: "He has no thoughts about
me."

That is something that might already have grabbed our attention.

"He has no thoughts about me. He feels nothing about me. He cannot believe in the theory of transference" [p. 126]. It must be admitted that this is worrisome. But the fact that the patient is not aware of it doesn't mean there isn't any manifestation of transference, for there is, all the same, a kind of obscure gathering of anxiety here and there. This comment escaped me because I had not clearly realized the import of what was to follow.

When you read this you think that it is a general observation of the kind Sharpe sometimes makes.

I think the analysis might be compared to a long-drawn-out game of chess and that it will continue to be so until I cease to be the unconscious avenging father who is bent on cornering him, checkmating him, after which there is no alternative to death. [p. 127]

This curious reference to the game of chess, that nothing seems to hint at in the case study, should give us pause for thought. When I read that page I did not immediately consider its import as regards the transference.

As I was reading this passage, it led me to think, "That's very nice. One should compare the whole unfolding of an analysis to a game of chess." Why? Because what is most beautiful and salient in the game of chess is that each of the pieces is a signifying element. The game involves a series of moves that respond to each other, based on the nature of these signifiers, each having its own characteristic movement based on its position as a signifier; and what occurs is the progressive reduction of the number of signifiers left in the game. One could, after all, describe an analysis in the same way, by saying that what we need to do is eliminate a sufficient number of signifiers for there to remain few enough of them for us to clearly sense where among them the subject's position within the structure lies. Having returned to this notion since then, I believe that it can, in effect, take us quite far.

Regarding Sharpe, everything that I know about her work from other texts or have been able to find out about her indicates that there is in her conception and interpretation of psychoanalytic theory a profound highlighting of the signifying nature of things. She accentuates metaphor in a way that is in no wise discordant with what I teach you. She always knows how to underscore the kind of substitution in symptoms that is, strictly speaking, linguistic in nature, and she employs this in her analyses of literary themes that constitute a considerable part of her work. Similarly, all of the rules regarding technique that she provides are profoundly marked by her experience and apprehension of the play of signifiers as such.

246

One might say that she misrecognizes on this occasion that, at the level of speech, which is of primary importance in this case study, it is her own intentions that are expressed in the term "corner." She herself mentions "cornering him" [p. 127] in the text, before it appears in the patient's discourse when, two sessions after the one in which she provides the interpretation of the dream, he mentions, as I have already indicated, that he finds it impossible in another game, that of tennis, to corner his opponent and deliver the final blow by sending a ball where his opponent cannot reach it. The analyst shows her true colors here.

I am not, for all that, saying that the patient sees them. It is clear that Sharpe is a good analyst.

She tells us in detail how she operates in this analysis. You may have noticed, she says to her students, that it is a case in which I make only the briefest of remarks or else I stay quiet. Why? Because absolutely everything indicates to me that this patient's professed wish to be helped implies the exact opposite – namely, that above all, he wants to remain sheltered, with his little cover or car top [or: hood, *capote*] over him.

To be under the hood* is a thoroughly fundamental position for this patient. Sharpe senses that. Everything related to the effaced memory of the pram revolves around the fact that he was "pinned in bed." He also seems to have very precise notions about what being tied up like that can lead to in a child, even though he can find nothing in his memory that allows him to recall it. Yet he is assuredly wedded to the position of being tied up.

The analyst is, therefore, far from allowing this countertransferential element, which would be too interventionist and aggressive, to appear in the game of chess. But my point is the following: it is precisely because she so clearly senses the aggressive import of the analytic game for this patient that she does not see its exact import. Namely, that what is at stake has the closest relations with signifiers. If we wonder where the phallus is, it is in this direction that we must search for it.

Consider, if you will, the quadrangular schema on which we find the subject, the other, the ego qua other's image, and the Other with a capital *O* [the L schema]. Here the question is where the signifier as such appears. The phallus is never where we expect it to be, but is there all the same. It is there like the purloined letter, where one least expects it and yet where everything points. To put it the way the metaphor of the game of chess allows us to formulate it, I would say that the subject does not want to lose his queen [*dame*].

Let me explain. In his dream, the phallus is not what is present or what the subject is looking at. That is not where the phallus is. The analyst, in her interpretation, perceives this obscurely, as if through a veil – the subject has a certain relation to omnipotence, to potency in short, to power. His power, in this case the phallus, is what he has to preserve at any cost. He must keep the phallus on the sidelines, because otherwise he might lose it in the game.

So this phallus that is kept on the sidelines is, in the dream, represented quite simply by the person who would seem least likely to represent it – namely, his wife. 248

His wife is far from being what she appears to be, a witness to the masturbation scene, for nothing actually indicates that seeing plays an essential role here.

Keep the following in mind, because it is such a clinically obvious fact that it is absolutely unbelievable that it is not common knowledge in psychoanalysis: the female partner qua Other is precisely what represents to this subject, as to many subjects, what is in some sense most taboo in his power and which thus turns out to dominate the entire economy of his desire.

I would say that it is because his wife is his phallus that he made the infinitesimal slip that I mentioned in passing when he spoke about making "a journey with his wife around the world," and not a journey around the world with his wife. Sharpe sees a hint of omnipotence in the phrase "around the world." I believe that the secret of omnipotence in this patient lies in the phrase "with my wife." What is crucial for him is that he not lose her.

This is, in the final analysis, what he must misrecognize, and it is precisely what must be called into question in the analysis. But in order to do so, he would have to realize that his wife is, in this case, the analyst.

The subject does not want to lose his queen, I would say, because he is like those second-rate chess players who believe that to lose their queen is to lose the game, whereas to win at chess is to arrive at what one calls an endgame. In an endgame, your ability to move is the simplest and most reduced, you have a minimum of choices – I mean that your king cannot move to a square that is controlled by your opponent's pieces – and the point is to maneuver in such a way as to get the upper hand. At times, it is advantageous to sacrifice one's queen. This is what the subject absolutely does not want to do.

Why? Because for him the phallic signifier is identical to everything that transpired in his relationship with his mother. The case study clearly hints at the shaky and deficient nature of what the 249 father was able to contribute. We fall back, of course, onto an already known facet of the subject's relation to the parental couple.

What is important, however, is not to go down this particular path, but rather to stress the very hidden, secret relationship between the subject and his partner. This relationship is what must be brought out at the moment at which it appears in the analysis. This moment is the one at which the subject, with his little cough, warns his analyst – if she had, as occurs in the dream, happened to turn her bag inside out, as it were, or showed her cards – to turn it right side in before he arrives; because were he to see that, were he to see that there is nothing but a bag, he might lose everything.

The prudence the patient shows is exactly what keeps him in a relationship to his desire that restrains him like a tightened strap, like the pram-pinned* position of his childhood, and that can only be fantasized. Namely, that he himself must be tied up, in a pram* or elsewhere, truly squeezed and swaddled, so that the signifier or image of his dreamed-of omnipotence can be elsewhere.

This is also how we must understand the whole discussion of automobiles in which omnipotence plays a capital role.

Everyone senses the connection between power and these problematic instruments of our civilization, automobiles – their horsepower, speed, and "peak of speed"* – and everyone obviously considers them to be phallic equivalents, the backup potency of those who are impotent. But at the same time everyone knows that automobiles are coupled with their drivers and that cars are infinitely feminine in nature. It is no accident that in French *automobile* is a feminine noun. And we just so happen to give all kinds of little nicknames to our cars that make them sound like partners of the fairer sex. The patient himself makes problematic remarks on this topic; you recall this one: "Strange how one speaks of the life of a car as if it were human" [p. 135].

This is old hat, of course, but it is no less obvious that there is something quite odd about automobiles – namely, the signifying ambiguity which is such that they are simultaneously what protect him, what strap him in, and what envelop him. In relation to him, they have the exact same position as the protruding hood in the dream – the same word is employed in both cases – this bizarre sexual protuberance in which he happens to place his finger, and which is, moreover, not red-striped but rather lined with red fabric [p. 135]. I had underscored this before but poorly translated it.

Let us turn now to what his analyst tells him.

During the session in which he recounts the dream, she begins to talk to him about his aggression. The next day, we learn that what resulted from this was a curious manifestation on his part, the nature of which she does not completely pick up on, and which one might call psychosomatic: prior to entering the consulting room that day, instead of a cough he experienced a "slight colicky pain" [p. 146]. God only knows if he had to clench his sphincter at that moment. As I said earlier, this is because, at the moment of entering the analyst's consulting room for the next session, he has everything to lose.

Yet it is not that day but the next that Sharpe makes the interpretation that she herself considers to be the most illuminating.

The patient tells her that the night before he had already had "a colicky pain" upon leaving the house. What does he speak about next? He says that "he had been unable to use his car because certain repairs had not been finished." He could not ball his mechanic out, because "[t]he garage man was so very good, so very kind; it was impossible to be angry with him." And Sharpe tells us that he added, no doubt with a note of irritation in his voice: "Not that the car was imperative for him at the moment; it was not a necessity, but he wanted it, he liked it" [p. 146].

The analyst plainly perceives that libido is involved here. "For once," she says, "I was able to deal with the libidinal wishes" [p. 147]. Here we could not agree with her more. If I am critiquing Sharpe's work, it is because I find that she is admirably sensitive at every point in this case study. She understands the importance of the desire present in the patient's life, desire being characterized by its unexplained nature [son caractère non-motivé]. In this case, he has no need for the car. She clearly realizes that this is the first time she has heard something like this from him, the first time he has declared a desire to her, a desire that is explicitly presented by the patient as unreasonable.

She jumps on this – in other words, she underscores it to him. Curiously enough, there is some sort of problem with the projector here, and the image suddenly becomes fuzzy. Whereas Sharpe always very precisely recounts what she said to the patient, even the most audacious or risky things, here we do not know exactly what she said. This is very annoying! What we surmise is that she was, in short, overjoyed and said something like, "You have finally admitted that you desire something," and then compared the mechanic to his father. But we will never know the exact words she uttered. 251

What we *do* know is that she told him something that was similar enough to what she had already told him that, the next day, the patient comes in and reports, half-contentedly, half-wryly, that the night before he wet his bed.

As I already told you, such a transitory symptom – however much it signifies that a nerve has been hit and has certainly reverberated – cannot in and of itself be considered to absolutely confirm that what was said went in the right direction, assuming something was said.

Bed-wetting, assuming we have some notion of what it represents, is certainly an activation of the penis that I would qualify as personal. But it is nevertheless not a genital activation. It is the penis as a real organ that, as clinical work shows us, is very frequently activated in children in response to their parents' sexual activity. It is inasmuch as children, whether male or female, are at a point at which they are profoundly interested in the sexual interactions between their parents that bed-wetting incidents occur that activate the real [i.e., biological] organ as such.

If the activating of the organ as real, not as signifying, shows us that Sharpe's intervention had a certain import, the question is to know whether its import was opportune. This remains to be seen in greater detail.

Yet another reaction follows this intervention. The patient recounts, not without a modicum of self-satisfaction, or so it seems to me, that he was no longer allowing his tennis partners to mock him; he had, in fact, grabbed one of them by the collar and squeezed his throat in the back of the court forcefully enough to stop him from ever mocking him again.

252   It is quite clear that this can in no way be considered to be the type of reaction we should truly wish to obtain. We should not in any case confuse cornering the other during a match and "cornering" him by grabbing his throat [because of his mockery] about the match. These are by no means one and the same thing.

Cornering your opponent after a match and grabbing him by the throat is not a suitable reaction here. It does not even for an instant make you more able to corner him during the game itself – in other words, when relations with the Other occur, the Other as the locus of speech, the locus of the law, the locus of the rules of the game. This is precisely what is missed by this slight drop in the level of Sharpe's analytic intervention.

I think that we have taken things far enough today.

Next class will be the last on what can be gleaned from the analysis of this case in the literature regarding desire and its interpretation. With the help of the graph and related notions, I will try to provide you with several formulas indicating how we should conceptualize the function of what we should very precisely attribute to the phallic signifier in all its generality.

I will also endeavor to show you how you can try to situate the phallic signifier in this schema, in order to help you map this out in your own analytic work.

Furthermore, I will provide you with something that is borrowed from the writings of an author whose work I have already mentioned here, Lewis Carroll. "He thought he saw a Garden-Door" – that famous door to the heavenly garden known as the womb, on

which all psychoanalytic theories are currently centered or by which
they have been swallowed up:

He thought he saw a Garden-Door
That opened with a key:
He looked again, and found it was
A Double Rule of Three.

Next time, I will show you what this "rule of three" is.

February 4, 1959

XII

THE LAUGHTER OF THE IMMORTAL GODS

To be and not to be the phallus
To be not without having it
Being and the One
Critique of Melanie Klein
The other's image and capital *I*

I announced last time that today I would wrap up our study of the dream that we have gone through quite thoroughly as regards its interpretation, but I will be obliged to devote yet one more class to it.

I will begin with a brief reminder.

It was dreamt by a patient who is a lawyer who has serious difficulties in his profession. Ella Sharpe approaches things with circumspection, the patient having every appearance of keeping his nose clean, even though one cannot exactly call his behavior rigid. She does not fail to underscore that everything he recounts is thought out, not felt.

At the point they are at, he has a remarkable dream, which was a turning point in the analysis. The patient boils it down into a few words, even though it was, as he says, "a tremendous dream," so tremendous that, had he remembered it, he would never finish recounting it. Only a fragment of it emerges, and this fragment presents, to a certain degree, characteristics of a recurring dream – I mean, a dream he has already had.

He undertook a journey, as he says, "with his wife around the world" – I highlighted that – and he finds himself in Czechoslovakia. This is the only point on which Sharpe tells us that she obtained insufficient clarification, not having asked the patient what the word Czechoslovakia meant to him, and she regrets having failed to do so. We, however, might have some thoughts about it.

"Sexual play with a woman in front of another woman," his

wife, occurs there [p. 132]. The woman with whom this sexual play occurs adopts a dominant position with respect to him. Moreover, she tries to maneuver in such a way as "to get [his] penis." He does not mention this while recounting the dream, but it comes up in his associations.

I mentioned the very specific nature of the verb "to get" in English. To get is to obtain, but in all sorts of possible ways. "To get" is a verb that is far less limited than *obtenir* [obtain] in French – it is to obtain, catch, grasp, and finish off [*en finir avec*]. And if the woman managed "to get [his] penis," that would mean she had it.

Nevertheless, his penis enters even less into action as the dream ends on the following wish: given how disappointed the woman was, he thought that she should masturbate. As I told you, this is the secret meaning of that moment in the dream, for, in the patient's telling of it, it manifests itself in the following form: the patient thinks that he would be willing to "masturbate her."

There is, in fact, a true exploration of something that is presented to us by the patient as "hoodlike,"* which is interpreted by Sharpe, with a great deal of insistence and care, as being equivalent to a hood. When we look closely, as we have, what should attract our attention is that a female sexual organ is there and not a hood. It is a sort of inside-out or prolapsed vagina, and it is as if the patient's pseudo-masturbation were nothing but an attempt to verify that the phallus is absent.

This is the sense in which I said that the imaginary structure, the manifest articulation, should at least oblige us to limit a bit the extension we give to the register of the signifier. This is in short why I raise the question whether, by using a more prudent method, which might be considered stricter, we cannot arrive at greater precision in the interpretation.

Yet this cannot spare us from taking into account the structural elements with which we have decided to familiarize ourselves. Indeed, we must do so extensively enough that these signifiers allow us to differentiate the meaning of each individual case. In doing so, we see that *the most particular cases are always those whose value is the most universal.*

Nothing included in this case study should be overlooked, because what we want to do is no less than indicate in this case that without which one cannot give the function of the phallus its true position – namely, its character as a signifier.

1

Whereas the function of the phallus is always so important, so immediate, and so much at the crux of things in psychoanalytic interpretation, its handling always leads to impasses.

The most striking among them are those that Melanie Klein's theory translates and betrays [*traduit, trahit*], when, as we know, she makes the phallus into the most important object.

In Klein's theory, and in her interpretation of psychoanalytic experience, how is the phallic object introduced? It is the substitute, she tells us, the first substitute that lies within a child's grasp concerning its own experience, whether we are talking about a little girl or a little boy. It is a sign that is more convenient than others, easier to handle, and more satisfying. This conception is well designed to raise questions about the status and exact role of this entity, about the mechanisms at work, and so on.

Klein describes for us an altogether primordial fantasy in which the subject is in a conflictual and profoundly aggressive relationship with the mother's body, which Klein conceptualizes as the container of good and bad objects, which are there inside of her in a sort of primitive jumble. The subject covets these objects, desires them, and wants to rip them away – these radically different terms are all unfortunately juxtaposed, and this creates difficulties. But Klein does not tell us how to conceptualize the outcome of this conflict, nor does she tell us why such precedence is granted to the phallic object within the mother's body.

Moreover, all of this is conveyed to us with a tone of the greatest authority, and in a startlingly cut-and-dried style. Her statements are so categorical that I would almost say they are not open for discussion. Nevertheless, after having heard them, one cannot fail to recover one's presence of mind and wonder at every moment what she is aiming at. Is it the child who is corroborating the predominance of the phallic object or is it Klein herself? What is it that signals that a specific object takes on the meaning of the phallus? I must say that in many cases we are not enlightened as to how to interpret her remarks.

256

As it turns out, people wonder about my remarks too. I am aware that some of you wonder where the sign of the phallus must be placed among the different elements on the graph on the basis of which we are trying to orient our experience of desire and its interpretation. I have had a few echoes regarding the questions this has given rise to for some of you – for example, what is the relationship between the phallus and the Other with a capital O that we speak about as the locus of speech?

There is, indeed, a relationship between the phallus and the Other with a capital *O*. But it is certainly not a relationship that places the former beyond the latter, in the sense in which the phallus would be the being of the Other with a capital *O* – assuming someone raised the question in these terms. If the phallus has a relationship with something, it is with the *subject's* being.

This is the new and, I believe, important point that I am trying to make about the subject's entry into the dialectical movement that occurs during the unconscious development of various stages of identification, running from the earliest relationship with the mother to the beginnings of the Oedipus complex and of the Law. Although what I have highlighted here is quite palpable in case studies, especially in those concerning the origin of perversions, the relationship between the subject and the phallic signifier nevertheless often remains veiled.

Two years ago, when I began to re-examine the function of the phallus, I took as my point of departure the following: things are very different depending on whether what is involved is for the subject to purely and simply be the phallus in relation to the Other, or whether the relationship to the phallus is already there in the Other, having been established by some pathway, mainspring, or mechanism whose impact on the subject's further development remains to be indicated. In the latter case, as the mother herself already has a certain relationship to the phallus, the subject can only manage to get himself valued in this context by entering into competition with it.

Next, I juxtaposed the two possible forms that can be assumed by the relationship between the subject and the phallic signifier, by introducing an essential distinction: that between being and having. It is essential inasmuch as being and having do not arise at the same stage of identification; the impact is not the same in the one case as in the other. There is a true dividing line between the two: one cannot both be the phallus and have it. In order for the subject, under certain conditions, to come to have it, he must give up on being it.

Nevertheless, things are far less easy to formulate if we try to home in as closely as possible on the dialectic that is at work. When I say that the phallus has a relationship to the subject's being, I am not referring to the pure and simple subject, the so-called subject of knowledge who is a noetic prop for all objects. I am referring to a speaking subject, a subject insofar as he takes on his identity in the field of language. In this regard I would say that the subject both is and is not the phallus. This is why the phallus serves an essentially signifying function.

257

I will ask you to excuse the algebraic tone things will take on today, but we must learn to set ideas out clearly, since, for some of you, questions arise. In my notation, ($\emptyset a$), something presents itself as being a barred subject – namely, a desiring subject [or: subject of desire, *sujet du désir*] – insofar as, in his relationship to the object, he himself is profoundly called into question. This is what constitutes the specificity of his desire. And it is to the degree to which the subject is a barred subject, insofar as he is a speaking subject, that one can say that it is possible, under certain conditions, to designate him with the phallic signifier [*lui donner comme signifiant le phallus*].

The subject both is and is not the phallus. He *is* it, because it is the signifier with which language designates him, and he *is not* it inasmuch as language and the law of language take it away from him.

In fact, these things do not take place at the same level. If the law takes it away from him, it is precisely in order to make things work out; it is because a certain choice is made at that moment. In the final analysis, the law brings a definition, distribution, or change in level into the situation. The law reminds the subject that he has it or does not have it. But what happens in fact occurs entirely in the interval between this signifying identification and this distribution of roles: the subject is the phallus, but the subject, of course, is not the phallus.

258   In the usage of the verb *être* [to be] in French, there is a certain slippage that the very form of the play of negation in speech allows us to grasp in a formulation that I will emphasize, inasmuch as it expresses what happens at the decisive moment, the one around which the assumption [*assomption*] of castration revolves. The formulation is as follows: one can say that the subject both is and is not the phallus, but "he is [also] not without having it."

It is in the inflection of "not being without" – it is around the subjective assumption that is inflected between being and having – that the reality of castration is played out. The central value that the phallus takes on is based on the fact that, in a certain experience, the subject's penis has been weighed in the balance against the object, and has taken on a certain function as an equivalent or standard in the relationship with the object. And one can say that, up to a certain point, it is to the degree to which he gives up his relationship to the phallus that the subject can possess the infinity of objects that characterize the human world.

Note that the formulation, "he is not without having it," whose modulation and stress I beg you to retain, can be found in other forms in all languages – we will come back to this.

Now this is valid only for men. For women, relations to the phallus and to the phallic phase, which has an essential function in the development of female sexuality, must be formulated in the exact opposite manner. This suffices to indicate that, when it comes to sexuality, male subjects and female subjects begin from different points.

A female subject's relation to the phallus can be formulated as follows: "She *is* without having it." This is the only precise formulation that allows us to leave behind the ambiguities, contradictions, and impasses around which we revolve concerning female sexuality. It is this "being without having it" that gives a woman's position its transcendence and that will later allow us to theorize the relationship between a woman and the phallus, a relationship that is highly specific and permanent, whose irreducible nature was insistently underscored by Freud, and that is psychologically translated by him in the form of *Penisneid* [penis envy].

To state things in an extreme manner in order to get them across as clearly as possible, I would say that the penis is restored to a man by a certain action that one can almost say deprives him of it.

This formulation is not exact. I am providing it in order to get you to open up your ears – the second one should not lead those who heard the first one to disparage it – but it nevertheless has its importance because it indicates where the junction occurs between the phallus and what are known as the first relations between the child and the maternal object.

These relations are usually broached developmentally. This is precisely what we must re-examine, and I am going to try to do so with you right now.

259

2

The question for us is to know how to use our algebraic elements to formulate what is involved in these much talked-about relations. Once we have such a formulation, we will be able to conceptualize how these relations are linked to the privileged signifier whose function I am trying to situate here.

If we endorse what psychiatrists claim, the relationship between the child and the mother comes first. Melanie Klein adds to this the notion that the child's first relations are established with the mother's body.

These relations, which are considered to be imaginary, are said to find their ideal locus, as it were, in her body. This is why, as everyone knows, Klein locates the relationship between form and symbol in the earliest experience of the mother's body, even if it is always an imaginary content that she brings out. Nevertheless, when reading her accounts thereof, one has a hard time grasping what the relationship between image and symbol is supposed to be here.

Whatever the case may be, whether it is an image or a symbol, the mother's body is assuredly a sort of One. The opposition between image and symbol almost completely overlaps the philosophical opposition between Being and the One laid out in Plato's famous text, the *Parmenides*. Moreover, the child's relationship with its mother is entirely centered around an apprehension of her unity or totality.

Indeed, according to Klein, the child, as I have told you, apprehends primordial objects as being contained, outside of himself, in the mother's body. The latter presents itself to the child as the universal container of all objects, both good and bad, which reside there, if not in a chaotic state, at least in one of primal disorder. The child's experience progressively teaches him to grasp the plurality of these multiple relations and various fragmented objects in the unity of the privileged object – that is, the maternal object – and this will pave the way for him toward his own unity. What Klein believes is essential to the child's development is this early shift from fragmentation to unity.

How can we formulate this in our algebra? Let us begin by noting that there are obviously not just two terms here, but four. The primordial relationship between the child and the mother's body is the framework in which relations between the child and his own body come to be inscribed.

I have for a long time been trying to explain these relations to you with the notion of specular affect, inasmuch as this term designates the structure of what is known as narcissistic affect. You know that I refer in this context to a very early [*originale*] experience, which occurs at a specific moment of development, and in which the subject recognizes himself both as separate from the image of his own body and as having a special relationship with that image. He accedes to this specular relationship either owing to an experience involving a mirror or in a certain transitive identificatory relationship in the course of games of bearing with the little other – the word "little" indicating here the fact that it involves young comrades.

It is not with just any little others that the subject can have this experience. Age plays a role here that I have stressed when I have written about it. The comrades must be around the same age as the child, indeed quite close to the same age, and their motor development must not go beyond a certain limit. Thus, the mother cannot play this role for the child.

Eros or libido plays a special role here, in the sense that this first relationship holds up only when it is linked to a second one.

260

The couple involving the child and the little other who represents his own image to him [a–a'] becomes juxtaposed to a second relationship in which this couple interferes and under which it becomes subsumed. This second relationship, which is going to come to regulate what happens in the specular couple [a–a'], is the larger and more obscure relationship between the child – whose primitive endeavors are motivated by need-based propensities [or: (pre)disposition, *tendances*] – and the mother's body, insofar as the latter is, in effect, the imaginary object of primal identification.   261

Our point of departure here thus includes two elements: on the one hand, the subject in this primitive, not yet constituted state witnessed by the unconstituted form in which the newborn's cry – his first wailing, or his need-based calling for something – presents itself, and, on the other hand, his mother's body, this universal container which presents itself as a One at the level of the Other. It is the way in which relations between these two elements are established that regulates the relationship of the other two elements [a–a'] right from the outset. These latter elements are, on the one hand, the subject insofar as he constitutes himself specularly – namely, as an ego, and let us not forget that the ego is the other's image – and, on the other hand, a certain other who must be different from the mother: the little other.

The first correspondences between the subject and his own identity do not develop in a simple specular relationship. They develop in a quadripartite relationship. Do not forget that all psychoanalytic authors situate the locus of psychotic or parapsychotic anomalies – which have an impact on the integration, at the borders of the bodily image, of one or another term of the subject's autoerotic relations with himself – in the central relationship between mother and child.

One can easily conceptualize this with the help of the little schema I have used in the past and that I recently recalled to mind, that of the well-known concave mirror [see Figure 7.4]. It involves making appear at the center of a spherical mirror, not the fantasy of a flower, but a real image of a flower inside an actually existing vase. This is achieved only if one looks on from a specific vantage point that is situated in an area determined by lines extending from the mirror's edges. This setup allows us to imagine what is involved in the relationship between mother and child. Just as you must situate yourself in a certain position with respect to the mirror to see the illusion materialize [*se réaliser*], it is inasmuch as the child identifies with a certain position of his being within the mother's powers that he comes into being [*se réalise*].

This is underscored by everything I have said about the importance of the first relations between mother and child. A child must become satisfactorily integrated into the world of insignias that are represented by all his mother's behaviors. If he has situated himself favorably with respect to his mother, then the x that is hidden from him – namely, his tendencies, drives, or desires – can be situated either inside himself, outside himself, or be missing altogether [*manquant à lui*], so to speak. If he has not situated himself favorably, his relationship with his drives will be more or less distorted or deflected right from the outset.

It is not that complicated to imagine this. Recall to mind the manifest, crucial experience described long ago around which my explanation of narcissism revolved. It is the famous example given by St. Augustine in his *Confessions*, that of a child who sees his foster brother being nursed. He writes, "*Vidi ego et expertus sum zelantem parvulum: nondum loquebatur et intuebatur pallidus amaro aspectu conlactaneum suum,*" which I have translated as follows: "I saw with my own eyes and knew very well an infant in the grip of jealousy: he could not yet speak, and already he observed his foster brother, pale and with a bitter look." In Latin, *amaro* is a bit different from the French *amer* [bitter]; one might translate it as *empoisonné* [poisoned or envenomed], but that does not quite satisfy me either.

Once this experience is formalized, its absolutely general scope appears. It involves the relationship of the subject to his own image – that is, to his semblable – but only inasmuch as the subject sees this semblable in a certain relationship with his mother, his mother serving as the earliest [*primitive*] ideal identification here, the first form of the One.

Analysts speak more readily of the mother as a totality than as the One. Ever since they began exploring children's earliest experiences with their mothers, they have been making such a big deal out of totality that they no longer talk about anything else: totality this, realization of totality that. It is as if they were so caught up in this aspect of things that they have forgotten what psychoanalytic experience shows us when it is pursued tenaciously to the outer edge of what we see in the phenomena – which is that it is impossible for human beings to accede to an experience of totality, because they are divided and ripped apart, no analysis being able to restore totality.

The reason for this is that another factor is involved in the dialectic of this experience. If I try to delineate this dialectic as I do, it is because this way of delineating things is literally imposed on us by experience – and, in the first place, by the fact that human beings cannot help but consider themselves to be nothing more than beings who are, in the end, missing something. Whether they are male or female, they are castrated beings. This is why, in our experience of the One, the phallus is essentially related to the dialectic of Being.

Let us come to the moment at which the subject has managed, not without dragging his feet, to overcome fragmentation and assume totality. This is the crucial moment known as the "depressive phase" around which the child's development revolves, according to Klein. This moment arrives when the mother as a totality has finally been perceived by the subject and the subject's first ideal identification occurs.

What happens to the specular couple given this new relationship with the mother? As I told you, the other – the little other or semblable – is in possession of the mother's breast. I add that, owing to this fact, the subject becomes aware of the desired object as such.

I ask you to dwell on this experience, which will be essential to our formalization. It is crucial because it grants the object, which is in this case the mother's breast, the special value of being desired at the same time as it makes the subject conscious of himself as deprived.

According to Ernest Jones – and he says this, naturally, in his discussion of the phallic phase – all deprivation generates a feeling of frustration. Whereas it is exactly the opposite. It is to the degree to which the subject is imaginarily frustrated that his first apprehension of the object, insofar as he is deprived of it, is born.

The subject first has an experience of his semblable, the one who is relating to his mother in a way that should be his, the one who is usurping his role. He feels this imaginary gap as a frustration. He thus experiences himself as deprived. I say that the gap is imaginary because, after all, nothing proves that the subject himself is deprived – some other may be being deprived, he may be taken care of once his turn comes, etc.

With deprivation, a process begins that will allow this object to enter into a new relationship with the subject. Must we put an index on this subject, a little i to show that he is imaginary, given the sort of passionate self-destruction that is absolutely characteristic of the pale, distraught visage depicted to us by the literary brush of he who tells us this story, namely St. Augustine? Or is he a subject whom we can already conceptualize as, strictly speaking, inscribed in the symbolic order? We do not yet know.

264

As for the object, on the other hand, it is clear that it is symbolized and that it has taken on signifying value in this experience. The object involved – namely, the mother's breast – can be conceptualized not only as being there or not being there, but it can also enter into a relationship with something else that takes its place; and, by dint of this fact, it becomes a signifying element. In any case, Klein, without realizing the import of what she is saying at that moment, asserts that there can be something better than the mother's breast – namely, the phallus.

She does not tell us why, however. The point remains mysterious. I say that it all depends on the essential moment that I have pointed to: the moment in child development that involves the birth of metaphor.

Recall what I told you recently about the specific forms of children's activity that disconcert adults and make them react awkwardly, the example I gave you being of a child who – not content to call what you always told him was called "dog" by a signifier he himself picked, "bowwow" – decrees that dogs go meow and that cats go bowwow.

This little tale was designed to illustrate for you the activity of substitution wherein lies the entire mainspring of symbolic progress. This occurs long before the child speaks in an articulated fashion, and there is strictly speaking no articulation without substitution. Nevertheless, if the field of substitutional activity goes far beyond the passionate experience of a child who feels frustrated, the latter is, in any case, included in the former. We can thus formalize this by writing that the other's image $[i(a)]$ is substituted for the subject insofar as he is caught up in his annihilating passion – which is, in this case, jealous passion.

$$\frac{i(a)}{\$}$$

The subject who has been replaced [substitué] in this way finds himself in a certain relationship to the object [a], but only insofar as the latter replaces totality [i.e., the mother as I]. And it is here that we enter into symbolic activity, strictly speaking, the activity that makes human beings into speaking beings and defines all of their future relations with the object.

$$\frac{i(a)}{\$} \; \lozenge \; \frac{a}{I}$$

265   That said, how can these fundamental distinctions help us orient ourselves in Ella Sharpe's case study if we preserve their thoroughly primitive character? We must, on the contrary, use them to create distinctions that will allow us to draw the maximum benefit from facts that are given to us in the dream-experience and in the remarks of the specific patient whose case we are analyzing.

This is what we are going to do now.

3

Ella Sharpe's case can be broached from many different angles. Let us take it up, as far as possible, from the most salient and symptomatic of angles.

We must simultaneously attempt to focus, at every instant, on the relationship known as desire – that is, the relationship between the subject and the object insofar as it is a relationship involving human desire.

Let me remind you that we must always locate therein the relationship of $ across from little a, which is the formula of fantasy, and which implies that the subject verges on being annihilated in his relationship with the object. As the above schema indicates, this formula is itself inscribed in a quadruple relationship, which shows us how the subject manages to give form to what he himself is when he desires – namely, a barred subject who is fundamentally pallid and anguished. He does so by substituting the other's image, $i(a)$ – namely, the successive identifications that will come to constitute the ego – for himself.

What do we find in the different symptomatic elements that can   266
be seen in the material Sharpe's patient presents us?

He tells us that he used to cut the straps of his sister's sandals. This comes up in the course of his associations to the dream, after a certain number of comments are made and questions asked by the analyst, which are quite minimal, but not negligible for all that, which are simply designed to get him to go further, and which lead him little by little, one thing leading to another, to this point. After the hood and the fact that the hood is shaped like the female genitalia, after the hood [or: top] of the car and the straps that serve to hold it down, we arrive at the straps that he would cut off his sister's sandals, without him being able to recall what purpose he intended to use them for at the time, and without him being able to demonstrate that he had any need for them.

These are the exact same terms he uses about his car. In the second session after the one in which he recounted the dream, he tells his analyst that his garage man did not get his car back to him but that he is not thinking of making a scene about it with the nice guy. He has no need for the car, but he would like to have it, even though it is not necessary to him; he says, 'I love it.'

Here, it seems, we have two forms of the object with which the subject has a relationship whose odd character he himself points out by saying that they correspond to no need on his part.

I am not the one who is saying so. I am not saying that "modern man has no need for his car," even though anyone who looks closely at the matter will realize that this is all too obvious. The patient himself says so. He says, in short, "I don't need my car. But I love it, I desire it." And as you know, it is here that Sharpe, with a swift reaction, like that of a hunter who has located her prey – namely, the very object she is seeking – intervenes so energetically, but without telling us, curiously enough, in what terms she did so.

Let us begin to describe what is at stake. And since I want to start with what is simplest, what can be most easily situated in an equation with which you are already long familiar, I would say that the straps are little a. There was even a time at which he collected straps.

I will oblige myself to follow my own formulas to some degree, since if I propose them, they must serve some purpose. The image 267 of a, $i(a)$, here is clearly his sister, about whom we have not spoken much, as we never suspect how complicated it is to bring out the slightest little thing, when it comes to explaining what we are dealing with.

$$\frac{\text{his sister}}{\$} \quad \Diamond \quad \frac{\text{straps}}{X}$$

His sister is eight years older than him. We know this because it is mentioned in the case study. Sharpe does not make much use of this fact, but what is clear is that if she is eight years older than him, she was eleven when he was three, which is the age at which he lost his father.

A certain taste for the signifier has the advantage of making us do a little arithmetic now and then. This is not illicit, for there is no doubt but that, when they are young, children never stop calculating their ages and their differences in age from each other. We, thank God, manage to forget that we are over fifty, and we have reasons for doing so, but children are very concerned with knowing their ages. Having performed this little calculation, one notices something that is very striking: the patient tells us that his memories only begin at age eleven. This is included in the case study even though the author does not make much of it.

This is not simply a random find that I am supplying you with here, because, if you now reread the case study, you will see that it goes much further. Just before telling us that he has virtually no memory of anything that happened before the age of eleven, he tells us about his female friend who is incredibly smart and cool, and who can do impersonations – that is, she can imitate anyone, especially men, in an amazing way, she being called on to do so by the BBC.

It is striking that he speaks about that just before making a remark that seems to stem from a completely different register – namely, that he has no memories of his life prior to age eleven. It seems that this must have some connection with the fact that he is imaginarily alienated in his sister. His sister is clearly *i(a)* for him, and this can explain many things to us, including the fact that he denies that his family ever had a "pram,"* which is a little stroller – a sort of car – for children. At that level, it is in the past, it is his sister's.

All the same, there was a moment at which he caught up with his sister, as it were. He encountered her at the very point at which he had left her regarding a crucial event. Sharpe is right to say that the father's death was crucial. The father's death left the subject confronted with all sorts of elements, except one, which would probably have been very precious in allowing him to overcome the various captivations [*captations*] that arose later. In any case, this is the point that will, of course, be a bit mysterious to us – why straps?

The patient himself emphasizes the fact that he has no idea why. Thank God we are analysts and we can guess that this element is what is there at the level of $ and is located across from it [capital I]. Because we are familiar with other case studies, we must give some idea of what is located at I in this schema.

It is something that is obviously connected with – I will not say castration, for if it were castration that was well assimilated, registered, and assumed by the subject, this little transitory symptom which involved cutting up straps would not have appeared. This symptom obviously revolved around castration, but we have no right to extrapolate for the time being.

In the case at hand, what is capital I, the ego-ideal? We can permit ourselves not to conclude just yet. After all, if someone is in analysis, it is precisely in order to try to understand a little, and to understand what is included in capital I.

I already indicated last time that this patient's ego-ideal identification was extremely peculiar, and that we needed to dwell on it. We can try to specify it now by referring to his relation with his analyst, which has something more developed about it than the I. Well, let us begin by raising questions based on what was going on in the analytic situation at that time.

There are many different ways of broaching this, for one can truly say that all roads lead to Rome in this case. One can begin from the mass of things the subject brings up in reaction to Sharpe's interpretations. In this regard, we agree with him: what are essential are the straps and the car. They are obviously not identical, for something changed in the interval between them.

268

269

Concerning the car, the patient adopted a stance, making some critical remarks that bear traces of a certain irony: "Strange how one speaks of the life of a car as if it were human" [p. 135]. I do not need to stress this, because you can sense, as I already observed, that the obviously symbolic nature of his car has its importance. It is clear that in the course of the patient's existence, his car has been a more satisfying object than the straps were, for the simple reason that he still does not understand anything about the straps, whereas he is able to say that even if the car does not really satisfy a need, he is very attached to it. And, moreover, he has fun with it; he is its master; he is happy when he is in his car.

What is the image of a here? We obviously find different things depending on whether we take things up at the level of fantasy or at the level of the dream. One might also say that there is fantasy on both sides – fantasies in the dream and those in the daydream.

In the daydream, which is also of value, we know what the other's image is. It is something in relation to which the patient adopted very peculiar attitudes. The other's image is the couple of lovers whom – despite the excuse he gives [for coughing], which is that he does not want to disturb them – he never fails, let us note, to disturb in the most concrete way: by ordering them to separate. The other's image is also that other about which everyone will say – recall the rather piquant fantasy that he recalled – 'Oh, there's no need to verify what there is in that room, it's only a dog.'

The other's image is, in short, something that leaves very little room for sexual intercourse. The $i(a)$ requires either separation or, on the contrary, an animal phallus, a phallus that is kept entirely on the sidelines. If there is a phallus, it is a dog's phallus.

270   As you see, the situation seems to have further disintegrated.

If the patient has, for a long time, been someone who has been propped up by his identification with a woman, we observe that his relationship to sex, including embracing and genital satisfaction, presents itself in a way that, in any case, leaves open or gaping the problem of what the phallus has to do with it. It is quite certain, in any case, that the patient is uncomfortable. The question of double or single in the other's image is present – if it is double, it is separated, and if it is single, it is not human. Things do not go smoothly in either case.

As for the subject in the latter case ["it's only a dog"], we need not wonder, as in the former case, what he is or where he is. It is altogether clear: there is no longer anyone there, there is truly οὖτις [no one], a term I mentioned [at the end of Chapter VIII].

What about as regards the dream? A woman does everything possible to get his penis, but nothing happens. One can do whatever one wants with the hand, and even show that there is nothing up one's sleeve, but as for him, there is no one there [*personne*]!

As for his fantasy, it is "What is there in the place where he must not be?" There is in effect no one there. There is no one there because, if there is a phallus, it is that of the dog who masturbated in a room which he would have been very upset if someone had come into. In any case, he is not there.

What do we find at the level of capital I? To be sure, there is Ella Sharpe; she is not without having some relationship to it. With a little cough, he warns her in advance *de ne pas mettre son doigt, elle non plus, entre l'arbre et l'écorce* [not to meddle in other people's affairs either; literally, not to put her finger between the tree and the bark], to invert the usual formulation – in other words, he warns her that if she is in the process of doing something more or less suspect to herself, she must put all that away before he arrives.

Ella Sharpe must, in short, be completely out of reach of the subject's blows. This is what I expressed last time when I referred to the comparison between analysis and a game of chess, with the following words: the subject does not want to lose his queen. He does not want to lose his queen because his queen is undoubtedly the key to all of this, because none of this can hold up unless nothing changes as regards the queen, because omnipotence is connected with the queen.

271

What is strange is that Sharpe sniffs out and sees the idea of omnipotence everywhere – so much so that she says to the patient that he believes himself to be omnipotent because he had "a tremendous dream," for example, even though he is incapable of coughing up any more of it than the little scene that takes place on a road in Czechoslovakia. But it is not the patient who is omnipotent. It is the Other who is omnipotent and this is why the situation is especially frightening to him.

Let us not forget that we are talking about a patient who cannot manage to speak up for a defendant in court [*plaider*]. He cannot, and this is very striking. Why can't he manage to speak up in court? Is it because he must not affect the Other by assuming the place where one always places oneself if one is going to speak up – namely, the Other's place?

In other words, the Other – and in this case, we are talking about women – must absolutely not be castrated. I mean that the Other carries within itself the signifier that takes on all values. And this is indeed how we should consider the phallus.

I am not the only one who does so. Read Chapter 11 of Melanie Klein's book, *The Psychoanalysis of Children*, regarding the development of little girls. Klein clearly says that all the needs a subject has, and of every kind – oral, anal, and urethral – are centered on the phallic signifier. Even before we can speak of genital needs, the phallic signifier takes on all values and especially the drive-related values and aggressive tendencies that the subject has been able to develop.

Incapable of putting the phallic signifier into play, the phallic signifier remaining inherent in the Other as such, this patient finds himself broken down [like a car, *en panne*], as we see him.

But what is altogether striking is that, here, as in every case in which we find ourselves presented with resistance on the patient's part, this resistance is the analyst's resistance. Indeed, if there is something that Sharpe seriously does not allow herself here, it is to speak up [*plaider*]. In this case, where there is a barrier that is there to be crossed, that she could cross, she stops herself from crossing it. Why? She does not know why, but it is clear that she admits she does so. She does not allow herself to cross this barrier because she does not realize why the patient is keeping his nose clean, what he is keeping his nose clean in order to defend against.

It is not, as she thinks, because of some supposed aggression he feels toward his father. The father has been dead and gone for a long time and she has had a terrible time trying to bring him ever so little back to life in the analysis.

Nor is it because of some conflict regarding homosexuality. It is not because he happens to be more or less courageous or aggressive in the presence of people who mock him about his tennis playing because he does not know how to deliver the final "shot."* It is not about inciting the patient to use the phallus as a weapon. None of that is germane here.

The patient is not yet at the point where he must agree to perceive that women are castrated. I am not saying *that women do not have the phallus*, which is what he demonstrates quite ironically in his dream fantasy [*fantasme de rêve*], but rather that the Other as such, owing to the fact that it is included in the Other as language, is subjected to the following: women *are* without having it.

This is precisely what he cannot in any wise accept. To him, women must not be without having it and this is why he cannot let women risk it at any cost. Let us not forget that, in his dream, his wife is on the sidelines. She is there, but apparently plays no role whatsoever. He never even mentions that she is watching. It is there, as it were, that the phallus is tucked away. The patient never has to risk the phallus himself, because it is in play solely in a corner where no one would ever dream of looking for it.

The patient does not go so far as to say that it is located in a woman, yet it is located in a woman – namely, inasmuch as Sharpe is there.

It is not especially inconvenient that his analyst is a woman. It could even be quite convenient if she realized what needed to be said to the patient – namely, that she is there as a woman and that to dare to speak up and plead his case in front of a woman raises questions and difficulties for him, this being precisely what he does not do.

She realizes that he does not do it, and this crucial moment of the analysis revolves around it. She then incites him to use the phallus   273 as a weapon. She says 'Your penis is something that has always been excessively dangerous; don't be afraid of it; that's what it's about; it is boring and biting.' There is nothing in the material that gives us any sort of indication that the patient's phallus is aggressive, and yet this is the way in which Sharpe interprets it.

I do not think that is the best thing to do. Why not? Because of the position the patient has and has apparently kept, and that he will cling to all the more tightly after this intervention, in any case. What position is that? The position that he occupied at a moment in his childhood, the one we are trying to pin down on the basis of the fantasy of the straps that are cut and everything connected to them – namely, identifications with his sister and the absence of a pram. Is there something further? The position that he is sure he must have experienced in his childhood, as you will see if you attentively reread his associations. What experience? Him tied down, him being "pinned"* into his bed.

He was certainly held down and constrained in positions that allow us to suspect some suppression of childhood masturbation or, in any case, of experiences that are not unrelated to his first erotogenic emotions, which everything inclines us to think were traumatic.

Sharpe interprets everything the patient mentions about being tied up in the sense of saying that it is certainly in connection with some primal scene involving parental intercourse. This intercourse, she says, must have been interrupted by him, either by crying or by some sort of intestinal trouble. This is where she comes back to the "colicky pain" that replaces the cough at the moment at which he knocks on her door, and that seems to her to be proof of the accuracy of her interpretation [p. 146].

I wouldn't be so sure. What is a "colicky pain," in reality? It is when the subject releases what is inside his body, either as he did when he was little or later when something by way of a transitory symptom was produced, echoing what was occurring in the analysis. It is a form of incontinence. This does not, however, tell us what its function is.

As you know, this incontinence is then reproduced at the urethral level, but with a different function, no doubt. I already said how important it is to note that every instance of bed-wetting echoes the presence of parents who are having sexual relations. Let us be prudent here. It is important to not always give an unequivocal finality to certain effects. An effect can have its own cause and then later be used secondarily by the subject to intervene as a third party in interparental relations in order to disturb them and even interrupt them.

But quite recently – in other words, at a time not far from that of the dream in question – the patient had a rather unusual fantasy which Sharpe takes to solidly confirm the notion that the patient sought to interrupt his parents while they were having intercourse. He was afraid one day that his car, which is clearly ever more identified with him, would break down, and that it would break down in the middle of a road which was to be taken by the royal couple itself. One might believe that this couple was placed there in order to remind us of the game of chess; but, wherever you find the king, think less of the father than of the subject himself.

Be that as it may, the patient manifests a bit of anxiety. [It is as if he thought,] "Don't let my car break down when I have to go to the function at which the royal couple is expected."

The year is 1934, and the British crown is not being worn by a queen who has a mere consort by her side; we are talking about a real king and queen who might be blocked by the patient's car. Should we thus be satisfied with simply saying [as Sharpe seems to], "Here is something that imaginarily, fantastically renews one of the patient's aggressive attitudes, an attitude of rivalry comparable to that which one can attribute to the fact of wetting his bed"? I am not so sure.

If this fantasy should make us think of something, it is the fact that the royal couple is not in just any old place – it is blocked in a car that is stopped and is thus exposed to the gaze of onlookers. What is involved here seems far more akin to the frantic search for the phallus than a minor instance of bed-wetting.

As regards the subject, the phallus is a sort of slippery, darting animal [furet] which is nowhere, which one must find, and about which it is clear that one will never find it. The subject is in his car, under this hood, under the top, inside the protective shell that has long been constructed around his ego, and this also gives him the possibility of slipping away with a "peak of speed."

On the other hand, at the moment at which the king and queen are going to be blocked under the roof of their car and thus visible to one and all, they are going to find themselves in the same position in which we long ago heard the laughter of the Olympians echo. The subject will be in the position of Vulcan who captures Mars and Venus in one and the same net.

Everyone knows that the laughter of the gods who were assembled on that occasion still resounds in our ears and in Homer's verses.

Where is the phallus? It is always the mainspring of comedy.

Let us not forget, after all, that this fantasy [of blocking the royal couple's car] is above all a fantasy that revolves far more directly around a notion of incongruity than of anything else. It is closely connected with what constitutes the unity of the dream with all that surrounds it – namely, the fundamental situation of aphanisis, not in the sense of the disappearance of desire, but in the strict sense that the word deserves if we make the following noun with it: *aphanisos*. It is less "to disappear" than "to make disappear."

Quite recently, a talented writer by the name of Raymond Queneau used the following words as the epigraph to a lovely novel, *Zazie in the Metro*: ο πλασας ηφανισεν, "He who made it, made it disappear"; he carefully hid its mainsprings.

In the final analysis, this is clearly what is at stake. Aphanisis here is the hiding [*escamotage*] of the object in question – namely, the phallus. If the subject cannot accede to the Other's world, it is inasmuch as the phallus is not included in the game, being preserved, instead, on the sidelines.

As you will see, what makes people most neurotic is not the fear of losing the phallus or the fear of castration.

The thoroughly fundamental mainspring of neurosis is not to want the Other to be castrated.

February 11, 1959

SEVEN CLASSES ON
HAMLET

XIII

IMPOSSIBLE ACTION

Freud on *Hamlet*
A more fundamental framework
Oedipus and Hamlet
The first threads
Ophelia, barometer of desire

I believe that we have taken the structural analysis of the model dream found in Ella Sharpe's book far enough for you to have at least been able to see how important this work is to us, given the path we are trying to follow this year, regarding desire and its interpretation.

Although some of you told me you were unable to figure out in what way I referred to Lewis Carroll in the second-to-last class, I am surprised you did not recall the "double rule of three" I used to organize the two stages of the relationship between the subject and the more or less fetishistic object.

This led in the end to what was expressed as capital I, identification with the Ideal. I intentionally left unanswered what identification boiled down to in the first of the two equations I provided regarding the case, the equation involving his sister's sandals, by writing an x in the place of I.

I do not believe any of you failed to realize that this x was, naturally, the phallus.

$$\frac{\text{his sister}}{\$} \lozenge \frac{\text{straps}}{\text{Phallus}}$$

But what is important here is where the phallus is situated. It is situated precisely in the place of primal identification, I, identification with the mother. This is because the subject did not, in fact,

280   want to deny [*dénier*] his mother the phallus. As psychoanalytic theory has always taught us, subjects want to continue to believe their mothers have a phallus. They refuse the Other's castration.

As I told you, the patient did not want to lose his queen, since it was the game of chess that was at issue. He did not want to put Ella Sharpe into any position but that of the idealized phallus, a position he cautioned her to stay in by giving a "little cough" before entering her consulting room. He instructed her to make certain traces disappear so that he would not in any way have to bring them into play in the analysis.

Regarding the idealized phallus, we will perhaps have the opportunity to return to Lewis Carroll this year. You will see that this is literally what is involved in *Alice's Adventures in Wonderland* and *Through the Looking-Glass*. These two Alice tales are virtually an epic poem of phallic avatars. You can already go ahead and start reading them so that you will be prepared for certain things I may be led to say about them.

Something may have struck you in what I told you and highlighted about the position of Ella Sharpe's patient with respect to the phallus, regarding the opposition between being and having. When I told you that the question that arose for him was that of being, and that he would have had to *be it without having it*, which is how I defined the feminine position, it is impossible that there did not arise in you, regarding this *being and not being the phallus*, an echo that truly forces itself upon us regarding the whole of this particular case study.

It echoes Hamlet's "To be or not to be" which has always been so enigmatic – it has almost become a joke – and which tells a great deal about the style of Hamlet's position.

If we follow this pathway, we will immediately be led to one of the earliest topics of Freud's thought, regarding the way in which the position of desire is organized.

Indeed, it is in the very first edition of the *Traumdeutung* that Freud raised the topic of *Hamlet* to a rank equivalent to that of Oedipus. He had no doubt been thinking about the so-called Oedipus complex for some time by then, as we know from letters he wrote [to Fliess] that were not intended for publication. Oedipus

281   makes his first appearance in print in the *Traumdeutung* in 1900. The footnote regarding *Hamlet* was published at the same time and it was moved into the main body of the text in 1914.

The topic of *Hamlet* was returned to on many occasions after Freud broached it, and I probably will not examine every author who has turned his attention to it. You are aware that Ernest Jones was the first to do so after Freud. Ella Sharpe also formulated a number of things about *Hamlet* that are not devoid of interest, the study of Shakespeare's work having been at the crux of her training. We will perhaps have the opportunity to come back to this.

I believe that taking up the topic of *Hamlet* can serve to bolster our work here on the castration complex, work that aims to indicate how it is concretely articulated as the work of analysis unfolds.

Today we will begin to clear the ground for such an undertaking.

We will begin by asking ourselves what Freud meant by taking up *Hamlet*, and what is demonstrated by what later authors were able to say about it.

1

Here is Freud's comment on *Hamlet*, which is worth reading at the outset of our study of it. I will give it to you in translation.

Freud has just spoken about the Oedipus complex for the first time, and it is worth pointing out that he introduces it regarding "Dreams of the death of persons of whom the dreamer is fond" [Chapter 5, section d]. The dream that served as our point of departure and first guide this year was chosen by me from another chapter of the *Traumdeutung*, because it was one of the simplest having to do with a dead person.

In talking about it, I highlighted something that initially presented itself quite naturally – namely, three signifiers that were pinpointed by Freud – and showed the relationships among them with the help of the two lines of intersubjectivity, one above the other, each of which doubles the other.

The famous words "he did not know" appear in the dream in a form which is incarnated, in some sense, by the father himself, and in a place which is that of the father. It is the precise fact that the father is unaware [or: unconscious, *inconscient*] that is enunciated in the words "he did not know." The image of the father here incarnates the subject's own unconscious, as well as his unconscious wish for his father's death.

The son has another wish regarding his father, one he is aware of, which is why he can want his father not to become aware of it. It is a sort of well-meaning wish, a wish for a relieving or consoling death. We thus see that the subject's lack of awareness regarding his Oedipal death wish is incarnated, in the dream image, in the form of a wish that the father not know that the son had formulated a well-meaning death wish toward him. "He did not know," the dream says absurdly, "that he was dead." This is where the dream-text ends.

282

As for the expression "as he wished," which is not included in the dream and is not known to the subject, even if it is known to the fantasized father, Freud tells us that *this* is the signifier that we must consider to be repressed.

Here now is Freud's footnote on *Hamlet*:

> Another of the great creations of tragic poetry, Shakespeare's *Hamlet*, has its roots in the same soil as *Oedipus Rex*. But the changed treatment of the same material reveals the whole difference in the mental life of these two widely separated epochs of civilization: the secular advance of repression in the emotional life of mankind. [Lacan comments: "the translation of Freud's term *Gemütsleben* by *vie sentimentale* ("emotional life" here) is approximate."] In the *Oedipus* the child's wishful fantasy [*Wunschphantasie*] that underlies it is brought into the open and realized as it would be in a dream. [SE IV, p. 264]

Freud did, in fact, stress that Oedipal dreams are like offshoots of the unconscious desires that are their primary source and that never stop resurfacing. As for Sophocles' *Oedipus* and other versions of the Oedipus tale in Greek tragedy, they are like the development and fabrication of the unconscious desires that always emerge. This is how things are articulated by Freud verbatim, who tells us that in *Hamlet* the child's desire "remains repressed; and – just as in the case of a neurosis – we only learn of its existence from its *Hemmungswirkungen*, its inhibiting consequences."

Strangely enough, the overwhelming effect produced by the more modern tragedy has turned out to be compatible with the fact that people have remained completely in the dark as to the hero's character. The play is built up on Hamlet's hesitations over fulfilling the task of revenge that is assigned to him; but its text offers no reasons or motives for these hesitations and an immense variety of attempts at interpreting them have failed to produce a result. According to the view which was originated by Goethe and is still the prevailing one today, Hamlet represents the type of man whose power of direct action is paralyzed by an excessive development of his intellect [*Gedankentätigkeit: "Von des Gedankens Blässe angekränkelt"*]. (He is "sicklied o'er with the pale cast of thought.") According to another view, the dramatist has tried to portray a pathologically irresolute character which might be classed as neurasthenic. The plot of the drama shows us, however, that Hamlet is far from being represented as a person incapable of taking any action. We

see him doing so on two occasions: first in a sudden outburst
of temper, when he runs his sword through the eavesdropper
behind the arras

– you are aware that this is a reference to Polonius, and that Hamlet
kills him while having a talk with his mother that is far from being
crucial – nothing in the play is ever crucial, except for its lethal
ending, for there, everything that had been put off until then in the
nexus of the action accumulates, in the form of cadavers, in a few
short moments –

and secondly in a premeditated and even crafty fashion,
when, with all the callousness of a Renaissance prince, he
sends the two courtiers [Lacan comments: "Rosencrantz and
Guildenstern, who turn out to be false friends"] to the death
that had been planned for himself. What is it, then, that inhibits
him in fulfilling the task set him by his father's ghost? [SE IV,
pp. 264–5]

You recall that the play opens with the appearance of this ghost on
the platform of Elsinore Castle before two guards who soon afterward alert Hamlet to this.

The answer, once again, is that it is the peculiar nature of the
task. Hamlet is able to do anything – except take vengeance on
the man who did away with his father and took that father's
place with his mother, the man who shows him the repressed
wishes of his own childhood realized. Thus the loathing which
should drive him on to revenge is replaced in him by self-
reproaches, by scruples of conscience, which remind him that
he himself is literally no better than the sinner whom he is to
punish. Here I have translated into conscious terms what was
bound to remain unconscious in Hamlet's mind. [SE IV, p. 265]

Freud's first commentary situates Hamlet's place in such a finely
balanced way that it paves, as it were, the straight and narrow way
we must simply go down in order to follow his lead. This is altogether clear, so much so that everything contributed by later authors
appears to be nothing but so many excursions or embroideries
– and, as you will see, sometimes rather farfetched ones – around   284
Freud's initial sketch. It occasionally happens that the points on
which these later authors focus, as psychoanalytic theory advances,
are valid and confirmed by the play, but it is at the cost of the kind of
rigor with which Freud situated the problem right from the outset.

At the same time, I would say that the whole question lies in what is situated by Freud at the level of "scruples of conscience," which is in short the point in his footnote that has been least exploited and investigated.

Since these scruples of conscience are presented to us as being the way in which we can express at the conscious level what remains unconscious in "the hero's character," it seems legitimate all the same to wonder how this is articulated in the unconscious. Scruples of conscience can only be viewed as a symptomatic development. Now one thing is clear, which is that a symptomatic development is not located in the unconscious; it is located in the conscious, constructed in some way by means of defense. We must thus ask ourselves what in the unconscious corresponds to this conscious structure, and this is precisely the question we are going to try to answer.

Be that as it may, we see that it did not take Freud long to throw a first bridge over the abyss that is *Hamlet*. In truth, it is striking that *Hamlet* remained a total literary enigma until Freud came along. Which does not mean that it is no longer an enigma, but we at least have this first bridge. Other works are similarly enigmatic, like Molière's *Misanthrope*.

Let me read you the remainder of the paragraph:

> The distaste for sexuality expressed by Hamlet in his conversa-
> tion with Ophelia fits in very well with this: the same distaste
> which was destined to take possession of the poet's mind more
> and more during the years that followed, and which reached its
> extreme expression in *Timon of Athens*. [SE IV, p. 265]

I will read you the end of the note too, for in the space of two short sentences, it paves the way for those who have since tried to organize the whole of Shakespeare's work by considering its development as indicative of a personal problem involving repression. One of whom was Ella Sharpe, who did so in her article on *Hamlet* that came out in the *International Journal of Psychoanalysis* and was republished after her death in the volume of her *Collected Papers*. It was certainly imprudent of her to schematize things in this way; in any case her approach can be criticized from a methodological standpoint, which is not to say that she discovered nothing of value.

Here is a bit more of the footnote:

> For it can of course only be the poet's own mind which con-
> fronts us in *Hamlet*. I observe in a book on Shakespeare by
> Georg Brandes (1896) a statement that *Hamlet* was written

285

immediately after the death of Shakespeare's father (in 1601), that is, under the immediate impact of his bereavement and, as we may well assume, while his childhood feelings about his father had been freshly revived. It is known, too, that Shakespeare's own son who died at an early age bore the name of "Hamnet" . . . [SE IV, pp. 265–6]

We can see, in these simple indications, that Freud leaves far behind him what later authors focused on.

I, for one, would like to broach the play on the basis of notions that I have managed to spell out here since the beginning of the year. For I believe they allow us to bring together in a more synthetic and striking way the various mainsprings of what occurs in *Hamlet*.

Thanks to them, we can in some sense simplify the multiplicity of agencies [*instances*] we often find ourselves faced with in current psychoanalytic commentaries, which smack of reduplication, when we see, for example, the same article take up successively the same case, it does not matter which one, in terms of the opposition between the unconscious and defense, then in terms of the opposition between the ego and the id, and, to top it all off, adding everything that can be said when one brings in the superego – these different vantage points never being unified. This tends to give these commentaries a vagueness and excessive weight that makes them of little use to us in our experience.

We try here to develop guides that allow us to resituate the different organs of the mental apparatus, which Freud gave us in the successive stages of his thought, in a way that takes into account the fact that they only partially overlap, semantically speaking.   286

It is not by putting them all together into one big set that we can make them function properly. We can do so, as it were, only by situating them in a framework that we attempt to make more fundamental, in such a way that we know what we are doing with all these references when we work with them.

Let us thus begin to spell out the great tragedy of *Hamlet*.

2

As evocative as Freud's footnote was, I must nevertheless remind you what the play is about.

It begins shortly after the death of a king who was, as his son Hamlet tells us, truly admirable – an ideal king and father – and who died mysteriously.

The story people were told about his death is that he was bitten by a snake in an orchard, an "orchard"* that has been interpreted by psychoanalysts. Very soon after his death, Hamlet's mother married her late husband's brother, Claudius. Claudius is execrated by our hero for reasons that go well beyond the rivalry Hamlet may feel toward him for having taken the throne from Hamlet, including everything he suspects regarding the scandalous goings-on that led his uncle to replace his father.

Moreover, the father then appears as a "ghost"* in order to reveal to Hamlet under what conditions the dramatic betrayal occurred, which, as the ghost tells him, was clearly an assassination. While he was sleeping, a poison, mysteriously named "Hebenon,"* was poured into his ear. This passage has obviously excited the curiosity of psychoanalysts.

"Hebenon" is a made-up sort of word. I am not sure whether it is found in any other text. People have tried to find various equivalents for it, and have come up with a word that is close to it in sound: "henbane." It is quite clear that this assassination through the ear could in no way satisfy a toxicologist, and it has led to plenty of interpretations on the part of analysts.

Let us immediately consider something that stands out for us owing to points we have highlighted. Let us use the keys we have developed here, even if it seems to you that the conditions that led to their emergence are ever so peculiar. The fact that they were created for very specific purposes does not rule out the fact that, in accordance with one of the clearest phases of psychoanalytic experience, what is most particular is what has the most universal value.

It is in this sense that the sentence "He did not know he was dead," which I brought out in the analysis of the dream about the dead father, is of fundamental importance. Indeed, keeping the Other in the dark regarding any specific circumstance is absolutely foundational in one's relation to the Other. You are well aware of this, since you are taught that one of the major turning points in a child's soul is the moment at which the child, after having believed that all his thoughts are known to his parents, realizes that it is nothing of the sort.

We should always have qualms about using expressions like "all his thoughts." We are the ones who call them "thoughts"; as for what the subject experiences, these "thoughts" are all there is. All there is is known to his parents, including even his innermost impulses [*mouvements*].

Hence the importance of the moment at which he realizes that the Other may not know. This "not knowing" in the Other is correlated with the very constitution of the subject's unconscious, and it is indispensable that we take this into account. One is, in some sense, the flip side of the other and perhaps its very foundation. I say "perhaps" because this formulation does not suffice to constitute them as such.

Whatever the case may be, one thing is clear, which serves us as a guide as we broach the tragedy of *Hamlet*. Namely, that we are going to try to refute the historical notion – which is a bit superficial all the same, clearly related to the atmosphere and style of that time – that what we have in *Hamlet* is some sort of modernist tale and that with respect to the incredible stature of Antiquity's writers, Modern writers are but poor degenerates. This is truly a nineteenth-century-type comment, and it is no accident that Freud cites Georg Brandes; we will never know whether Freud was familiar with Nietzsche's work at that time, even if it is probable. But we might find this reference to Modern writers inadequate. Why would Modern writers be more neurotic than those of Antiquity? It is, in any case, a *petitio principii*. What we are trying to articulate should go further than this *petitio principii* or than the simplistic explanation that "things are going to pot because things are going to pot."   288

What we have before us is a work the first threads of which we are going to begin to tease apart.

The first thread in *Hamlet* is that the father quite clearly knows that he is dead as his brother Claudius wished, Claudius having wanted to take his place. The crime is not hidden from him, but from the world, a world that is represented on the stage. This is a crucial point, without which the drama of *Hamlet* could not, of course, even exist.

This point is brought out by Jones, in an article that is easy to lay your hands on, "The Death of Hamlet's Father." Jones mentions there that Shakespeare introduced an essential difference into the original saga in which the king was assassinated in front of everyone, owing to something having to do with his relations with his wife. There, the king was murdered by his brother, but everyone knew it, whereas in *Hamlet* the thing is hidden, but the father knows it. This is what is important. Indeed, it is the father himself who informs us of it.

Horatio comments to Hamlet: "There needs no ghost, my lord, come from the grave / To tell us this" [I, v, 124–5]. Freud cites this several times, it sounding a bit like a proverb. If it is the Oedipal theme that is, in fact, at work here, we already know quite a bit about it. But when *Hamlet* was written, not much was yet known about it. It is significant that the fable is designed in such a way that the father does know.

This is an absolutely essential element, and it constitutes a major difference in thread with respect to the first major tale, the tragedy

of *Oedipus*. Oedipus does not know. But once he does, once he has
discovered everything, the drama moves into high gear, and continues right up to his self-punishment – in other words, his resolving of
things. But the Oedipal crime is committed by Oedipus unwittingly
289   [*dans l'inconscience*]. In *Hamlet*, the Oedipal crime is known, and it
is known to its victim, a victim who emerges in order to bring it to
the subject's awareness [*connaissance*].

You can begin to see the pathway I am following and the method
I am adopting.

It is a classical method that proceeds by comparison, comparison
of different threads of a structure that is taken to be an articulated
whole; and nowhere is there more articulation than in what is
located in the realm of the signifier. I never stop highlighting the
very notion of articulation, and it is, in short, consubstantial with
the signifier. After all, we only speak of articulation in the world
because the signifier gives meaning to this term. Otherwise there is
nothing but continuity and discontinuity, but no articulation.

We will proceed by a sort of comparison of the homologous
threads in the two phases, *Oedipus* and *Hamlet*, just as Freud compares them, and in order to grasp how things cohere. If in one of the
two dramas we come across a note that is the exact opposite of that
found in the other play, we will try to see if, why, how, and to what
degree we find a corresponding modification in it. I assume that
bringing out these correlations will lead us to the junction [*joint*] of
the kind of causality at work in these two tragedies.

The initial idea is thus that what is most instructive to us are these
correlated modifications. Highlighting them and writing them out in
a quasi-algebraic way will allow us to group together the signifying
mainsprings and make them more or less utilizable.

In the dream about the dead father, we placed "he did not know"
on the upper line [of the graph]. In *Hamlet*, we place "he knew he
was dead" there, for the father knows he is dead in accordance with
the murderous wish, his brother's wish, that led him to his grave.

What is the relationship between Claudius and Hamlet like?

In the psychoanalytic tradition, people always go straight for
superimposed identifications. The most convenient concepts being
the least developed ones, God only knows where people will stop
in their use of these identifications. In the final analysis, we are told
that Claudius is a form of Hamlet. What he does is what Hamlet
wants to do. This is to jump the gun.

290   Indeed, in order to situate Hamlet's position with respect to his
desire, we are obliged to bring in the "scruples of conscience." This
gives rise, in the relationship between Hamlet and Claudius, to a
twofold position that is profoundly ambivalent. If Hamlet relates to

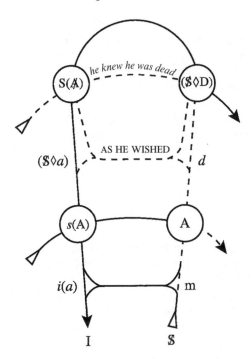

Figure 13.1: The "He knew" in *Hamlet*

Claudius as a rival, we see that this rivalry is quite odd and at one remove, because Claudius is also in reality he who has done what Hamlet would not have dared to do. Because of that, Claudius is surrounded by some sort of mysterious protective shield that we must strive to define.

If Hamlet leaves him unscathed, it is because, we are told, of his scruples of conscience. But how much weight do they carry with respect to what is forced on him once the ghost* has literally ordered him to take revenge on Claudius for him? From the moment of this initial encounter, Hamlet, in order to take action against his father's murderer, who is also the usurper who dispossessed him, is armed with all the necessary feelings – a feeling of having been usurped, of rivalry, and of vengeance – as well as with the explicit order received from a father who is above all admired. Surely, everything in Hamlet is aligned for him to act, and yet he does not act.

291

This is obviously where the problem begins.

To move in the direction of solving it, we must arm ourselves with the greatest simplicity; I mean that we are always led astray when we employ ready-made keys instead of really grappling with the question. Freud tells us that Hamlet's scruples of conscience are the conscious representation of something that is articulated in the unconscious. So what we have to do is find what this unconscious desire means. And we can already say with Freud that, given the way things begin, there is clearly something wrong with Hamlet's desire.

It is here that we are going to select our pathway, which is not easy, as we are not much further along than those who went before us.

What we are going to do is take the tragedy as a whole and consider how Hamlet conducts himself throughout it.

3

Since we have spoken about Hamlet's desire, we must situate his fantasy, inasmuch as fantasy is for us the axis, soul, center, and touchstone of desire.

Analysts have, naturally, looked into this, but they have confined their attention to the relations between Hamlet and the *conscious* object of his desire, about which Shakespeare cannot be said to withhold details from us. But that is not exactly it; that is perhaps not in the same register as fantasy.

In the play, we have a sort of barometer of Hamlet's position with regard to desire. We have it most obviously and clearly in the form of the character Ophelia.

Ophelia is quite obviously one of the most fascinating creations that has ever been offered up to human imagination. It is remarkable to see what we might call the drama of the female object – the drama of desire, such as it appears at the beginning of a civilization in the form of Helen [of Troy] – incarnated in the drama and misfortune of Ophelia, which is perhaps also a culmination. As you know, this drama has been taken up in many forms by artists, whether poets or painters, at least in the pre-Raphaelite era, who went so far as to provide us with polished paintings in which we find the very same terms as those provided by Shakespeare regarding Ophelia floating in her dress down the river into which she, in her madness, allowed herself to slip – for Ophelia's suicide is ambiguous [see Plate 1].

Freud tells us that we see in the play, correlated with what we might strictly speaking call the main drama, a horror of femininity as such, whose terms are articulated, in the strictest sense of the word, by Hamlet himself. For he throws in Ophelia's face all the degrading, fickle, and corrupting possibilities linked to the unfolding of women's lives when they allow themselves to be dragged into all the acts that little by little make them into mothers – in the name of which Hamlet pushes Ophelia away in what seems to be a most sarcastic and cruel way.

There is an essential correlation between the development of Hamlet's position with respect to Ophelia and what determines his overall position with respect to desire.

Let us note in passing that we are presented with an interpretation of this development by a wild, amateur psychoanalyst: Polonius, Ophelia's father. He immediately locates the cause of Hamlet's melancholia. According to Polonius, the problem is that although Hamlet wrote love letters to Ophelia, she responded sharply to them, following instructions that Polonius gave her, he adhering solely to his duty as a father. Stated otherwise, Polonius believes that Hamlet is lovesick. One can always find an easy, external interpretation of events; and Polonius, who is quite a caricature of a character, is there to represent for us the ironic outcome this easy approach deserves.

Although the change in Hamlet's sexual position is profound and altogether crucial, no one doubts but that it is organized somewhat differently. What is involved naturally concerns the relation between Hamlet and what? His action, essentially. Hamlet needs to take action and his entire position as a subject [or: subject position, *position de sujet*] depends upon it.

We see, quite precisely, throughout this play that Hamlet is fundamentally in a position, with respect to action, that the English language designates with a word that is far more often used in English than in French: procrastinating. In French we would say *ajournement* (putting off) or *retardement* (delaying). Indeed, this is what is involved: Hamlet procrastinates, and he does so throughout the play, making it the procrastination play *par excellence.*

We want to know both what it means that whenever he has the opportunity to take the action in question, he puts it off, and what is determinant at the end when he finally takes the plunge. The question that arises is that of the signification of the action he is expected to take. This is the point to be brought out regarding procrastination, at least in this case.

What I have already pointed out to you indicates this adequately: the action Hamlet is expected to take has nothing to do with an Oedipal action – namely, revolt against his father or conflict with his father, in the sense that it is creative in the psyche.

Hamlet's action is not the same as that of Oedipus. Oedipus' action sustained Oedipus' life. It made him into the hero he was prior to his fall, while he knew nothing. It gave the story's conclusion its dramatic character. Hamlet, on the other hand, knows that

293

he is guilty for being. It is unbearable to him to be. Well before the
beginning of the drama, Hamlet knows what it means to have committed the crime of existing. It is on the basis of this beginning that
he finds himself faced with a choice, a choice in which the problem
of existence arises in his own terms – namely, "To be, or not to
be,"* which irremediably involves him in being, as he quite clearly
articulates.

It is precisely because, in *Hamlet*, the Oedipal drama is there at
the beginning and not at the end that a choice is offered to the hero
between *being* and *not being*. The very fact that there is this *either/or*
proves that he is caught up in the signifying chain, in what makes it
such that he is in any case a victim of this choice.

Let me read the passage to you [Lacan reads aloud part of
Letourneur's eighteenth-century translation, which he considers to
be the best translation of *Hamlet* into French]:

> To be, or not to be – that is the question:
> Whether 'tis nobler in the mind to suffer
> The slings and arrows of outrageous fortune
> Or to take arms against a sea of troubles
> And by opposing end them. To die, to sleep –
> No more – and by a sleep to say we end
> The heartache, and the thousand natural shocks
> That flesh is heir to . . .

294

I believe these words are intended to have an impact on us.

> To die, to sleep –
> To sleep – perchance to dream: ay, there's the rub,
> For in that sleep of death what dreams may come
> When we have shuffled off this mortal coil

– "This mortal coil"* is not exactly our envelope, but rather the sort
of twist of something that is wrapped around us –

> Must give us pause. There's the respect
> That makes calamity of so long life.
> For who would bear the whips and scorns of time,
> Th'oppressor's wrong, the proud man's contumely
> The pangs of despised love, the law's delay,
> The insolence of office, and the spurns
> That patient merit of th' unworthy takes,
> When he himself might his quietus make
> With a bare bodkin? [III, i, 56–76]

What does Hamlet find himself faced with when the question "To be, or not to be" arises? He must confront the place occupied by what his father told him. And what his father told him as a ghost is that he was taken by surprise "in the blossoms of [his] sin" [I, v, 76]. The son must deal with the place occupied by the Other's sin, a sin that was not redeemed [*payé*] by the Other.

The one who knows here [the father] is someone who has not paid [*payé*] for the crime of existing, unlike Oedipus who paid for a crime he did not know he had committed. The consequences for the next generation are not inconsequential, moreover, since Oedipus' two sons dream only of killing each other with all the vigor and conviction one might desire. Things are altogether different in Hamlet's case.

Hamlet can neither pay in his father's stead nor leave the debt unpaid. In the final analysis, he must get the debt paid, but, in the conditions in which he finds himself, the blow strikes him. Following a dark plot, which we will discuss at length, it is only after Hamlet has been wounded that he can strike, with the very weapon from which he has received his mortal wound, the criminal who is there within range – namely, Claudius.

The mainspring that constitutes the whole difficulty of the problem Hamlet faces in assuming responsibility for his action [*assumer son acte*], is the fact that both the father and son know – for both of them, their eyes have been opened. We want to figure out by what pathways Hamlet can take action. What are the roundabout pathways that will render possible an action that is in itself impossible, owing to the fact that the Other knows? What are the pathways that will finally allow Hamlet to accomplish what must be accomplished?

These are the pathways that must hold our interest; they are the ones that we will find instructive.

This is the true problem that needed to be introduced today.

I must mention the end of the play, and point out to you how Hamlet finally manages to take action. Let us not forget that, although he manages to do so and although Claudius is struck dead at the end, the job has nevertheless been seriously botched.

Hamlet has had to do nothing less than run through someone whom he certainly cast into the abyss, as you will see – namely, his friend and companion Laertes. Just before that, his mother accidentally poisoned herself with the very goblet that was supposed to have served as a backup murder weapon in case the poisoned tip of the foil did not touch Hamlet. It is only after a number of other victims have fallen, and not before having been dealt a mortal blow himself, that Hamlet can stab Claudius.

Even though he does run him through, even though a sort of rectification of desire occurs *in extremis* that makes it possible for him to act, there is nevertheless something here that raises a question for us. How was the act accomplished? The key, what makes it such that this incredible play has never been replaced by another, better one, bears precisely on this point.

For, in short, what are these great mythical themes that creative poets have been testing their mettle against throughout the ages? This long series of variations for centuries upon centuries is nothing but a sort of long approximation that is such that the myth, whose every possibility has been exploited, ends up by entering, strictly speaking, into our subjectivity and psychology. I maintain, and I will unambiguously maintain – and in doing so, I believe that I am following in Freud's footsteps – that poetic creations generate psychological creations more than they reflect them.

296

The primordial relationship of rivalry between son and father has always had something diffuse about it. As taken up by Shakespeare, this is what gives *Hamlet* its depth and constitutes its veritable crux.

It is precisely because something – namely, castration – is missing in the original, initial situation of the drama of *Hamlet*, insofar as it is distinct from that of Oedipus, that things present themselves in the play in the form of a slow zigzagging progression, following many a detour, a slow birthing of the necessary castration.

It is precisely because something finally becomes equivalent to what was missing, because something finally is realized, that Hamlet takes the final action to which he succumbs. Things having gone so far that he cannot live on, others, like Fortinbras, who are always ready to receive an inheritance, will succeed him.

March 4, 1959

XIV

THE DESIRE TRAP

Myriad commentaries
A bird catcher's net
The unfolding of the play
The "play scene"*
The key point

Last time we began working on *Hamlet*.

Our turning to *Hamlet* was no accident, even if I told you that it came up owing to the formulation "to be or not to be" that forced itself on me as we examined the dream recounted by Ella Sharpe.

I was led to reread some of what has been written about *Hamlet* by psychoanalysts and also by certain authors who wrote about it prior to them. And since these various writers, at least the best among them, never fail to mention those who had written about *Hamlet* well before themselves, I must say that I was led quite far, and even got lost along the way now and then, not without pleasure.

A problem arises here, that of how to bring all this material together in relation to our precise goal, which is to give meaning, or at least new meaning, to the function of desire in psychoanalysis and in analytic interpretation. It should not give us too much trouble, however, because what distinguishes the tragedy of *Hamlet, Prince of Denmark*, as I hope to convince you, is essentially that it is the tragedy of desire.

Hamlet must have been performed for the first time in London during the 1601 winter season, although that is not entirely clear; yet it is what the most rigorous texts suggest. The famous first quarto edition of the text at the time was virtually a "pirate" edition, for it had not been reviewed by the author, but had been borrowed from what were known as "prompt-books,"* booklets used by onstage prompters. This edition – it is quite amusing to know these little tidbits of literary history – remained unknown until 1823 when

298   someone finally got his hands on one of these grimy copies, grimy
             because they were handled a great deal, probably having been used
             during performances. The First Folio edition, the main edition of
             Shakespeare's work, did not start coming out until after his death in
             1623, prior to the still larger edition in which the plays are divided
             into acts; this explains the fact that the division into acts is far less
             decisive and clear in Shakespeare's plays than in those by other
             authors. In fact, it is not thought that Shakespeare ever dreamt of
             dividing his plays into five acts. This is of some importance, because
             we shall see how *Hamlet* is divided up.

             The winter of 1601 was two years before the death of Queen
             Elizabeth, and we can view the turning point that *Hamlet* marks
             between the two periods of Shakespeare's life as approximately
             repeating, as it were, the drama related to the transition between
             two eras in the kingdom, for the tone changes completely when
             James I takes the throne. Something is already announced, as a
             certain author once put it, that breaks the crystalline charm of the
             reign of Elizabeth I, the "Virgin Queen," who had managed to
             procure many long miraculous years of peace following what consti-
             tuted in the history of England, as in many other countries, a period
             of chaos – chaos into which England promptly fell anew, with the
             whole drama of the Puritan revolution.

             In short, 1601 already announces the death of the Queen, which
             obviously could not have been foreseen, with the execution of her
             lover, [Robert Devereux, the second] Earl of Essex; this took place
             the same year as the first performance of the play. These historical
             reference points are not irrelevant, and I am not the only one who
             has tried to situate *Hamlet* in its historical context. But none of what
             I just told you is highlighted by any psychoanalytic writers, even
             though such reference points are quite important.

             In truth, what has been written about *Hamlet* by psychoanalytic
             authors can hardly be qualified as enlightening. But today I will
             not critique what a certain type of analytic interpretation degener-
             ates into when it takes up *Hamlet* line by line. I have been trying to
             find something of interest in it, but, as a matter of fact, one can say
             nothing about it except that the more writers adopt this line-by-line
             approach, the more their understanding of the whole text and of its
             coherence dissipates.

             I must say, too, about our Ella Sharpe, whom I make much of,
299   that in her paper* on *Hamlet* – which was, it is true, unfinished,*
             having been discovered after her death – she greatly disappointed
             me. I will nevertheless discuss her paper because it is indicative. It
             so closely follows the exact same trend that we see dominating psy-
             choanalytic theory, a trend I have been led to explain and critique,

that it is worth highlighting. Nevertheless, we are not going to begin with her paper.

We are going to begin with Jones's article published in 1910, which marks an important date in psychoanalytic history; it is a must-read. It came out in the *American Journal of Psychology* [XXI, 1 (1910): 72–113] and is not easy to get your hands on currently. In a small re-edition he brought out, Jones, I believe, added a few things to his theory of *Hamlet*. The article is entitled "The Oedipus Complex as an Explanation of Hamlet's Mystery: A Study in Motive."

In it, Jones takes up the problem masterfully posed by Freud in the course of the half-page I read you last time, and about which we can say, in the final analysis, that everything is already there, since even distant points on the horizon are already sketched out – namely, the problematic signification of the female object for Shakespeare. This is, I think, absolutely central.

Freud mentioned *Timon of Athens*, which is why Ella Sharpe tried to explore that particular connection. She turned all of Shakespeare's work into a sort of vast cyclothymic oscillation, distinguishing the rising pieces – in other words, the ones we might consider to be optimistic, those in which aggression is directed toward the outside world – from those of the descending phase in which aggression strikes the hero or the poet. This is, according to her, how we can classify Shakespeare's plays and sometimes even date them. I do not believe this is altogether valid.

For the time being, and given where we are at, we will confine our attention to *Hamlet*. I will perhaps make a few points about what follows or precedes it, about *Twelfth Night* or *Troilus and Cressida*, for it is almost impossible, I believe, not to take them into account, given to how great a degree they clarify the problems that we are going to first bring up in connection with *Hamlet* alone.

1

With his grand style of documentation and the solidity that characterizes his writings and highly distinguishes his contributions, Ernest Jones provides a sort of summary of what he quite rightly calls "Hamlet's mystery."

Now either you realize the magnitude of the question or you do not. For those who do not, I am not going to repeat here what we find in Jones's article. Look into it yourselves in one way or another.

I must tell you that the mass of writings on *Hamlet* is unequaled. The abundance of literature on the play is nothing short of incredible. More incredible still is the extraordinary range of interpretations that have been given of it. The most contradictory interpretations have followed one another, having been rolled out in the course of history, posing a problem about the problem – namely, why is everybody trying so hard to understand something in it?

These interpretations provide the most varied, incoherent, and extravagant results, yet we cannot say that they go too far.

Just about everything has been said about *Hamlet*. To give you an extreme example, there is even something called *Popular Science Monthly* – which must be some sort of popularizing publication on more or less medical topics – that published in 1880 an article entitled "The Impediment of Adipose [: A Celebrated Case]." In it we are told that Hamlet is fat and out of breath at the end of the play, and there is a whole discussion of Hamlet's adipose. [By way of a second extreme example,] someone by the name of Vining revealed in 1881 that Hamlet was a woman disguised as a man, whose goal throughout the play was to seduce Horatio, and it was in order to win Horatio's heart that Hamlet did everything he did. It makes for rather nice reading and I cannot even say that it is of absolutely no interest to us, for it is clear that Hamlet's relations with other men are closely related to the problem posed by the play.

Returning to serious matters, let us recall with Jones that critics have tended to go in one of two directions. And when there are two directions in logic, there is always a third [or: middle, *tiers*] one, for, as opposed to what we tend to think, the middle is not as excluded as all that. And it is obviously the middle one that is interesting in this case.

The two different directions have been sustained by some pretty hard hitters.

The first includes those who have explored Hamlet's psychology. They obviously take precedence; they must be given pride of place in our esteem. We find here Goethe, and Coleridge, too, who in his *Lectures on Shakespeare* adopted a highly distinctive stance that I think Jones could have made more of. Jones, curiously enough, primarily provides an extraordinarily in-depth commentary on works on *Hamlet* in German, which proliferated and were even very long-winded. Even though they are not identical, the stances adopted by Goethe and Coleridge are nevertheless closely related, for both of them emphasize Hamlet's intellect.

Schematically put, let us say that, according to Goethe, Hamlet is action paralyzed by thought. As we know, this conception has had many adherents over the centuries. People have pointed out, and not irrelevantly, of course, that Hamlet had lived for a bit too long in Wittenberg; this has led some people to attribute his intellectual problems to too great a familiarity with what is depicted to us, not unjustifiably, as one of the centers where young German students receive a certain kind of education. From this perspective, Hamlet is, in short, a man who sees all the elements of the game of life, all its complexities and motives, and whose ability to take action is, owing to this knowledge, suspended and paralyzed. This is, strictly speaking, a Goethean problematic, and it did not fail to become quite influential, owing especially to the charm and seductiveness of Goethe's style and personality.

Coleridge goes in the same direction. I do not have time to read you a long passage – one that is far less sociological and far more psychological in nature, indeed it is a brilliant bit of psychology – that he devotes to Hamlet's psychasthenic character; to his inability to select a path and, once selected, to truly commit to it; and to his hesitation between multiple motives. What I would like to mention is a comment Coleridge makes in passing, in his easy conversational style, that in my view goes right to the quick: "I have a smack of Hamlet myself, if I may say so."

Coleridge recognizes himself in Hamlet and he is not the only writer to do so. One can find a similar remark in the work of a quasi-contemporary of ours who wrote some incredible things in his *Essays on Shakespeare*. I am referring to Hazlitt, who is not even mentioned by Jones – wrongly so, for he wrote the most remarkable things on the topic at the time.

302

Coleridge goes further still when he says that, in the final analysis, this tragedy has been examined so often that we barely know how to discuss it anymore, no more than we would know how to describe our own faces. He provides another note that goes in the same general direction, and these are lines that I will make much of.

I will only briefly mention the second direction, the one that attributes Hamlet's bind [*embarras*] to an external difficulty – that is, to a problem that comes from the outside.

This conception was developed by a set of German literary critics; the two main critics here, Klein and Werder, were late nineteenth-century Berliners, and Jones rightly groups them together. According to these critics, the task Hamlet undertook was to get his people to recognize Claudius' guilt, Claudius having killed Hamlet's father, married his mother, and usurped the throne of Denmark. This conception does not stand up to scrutiny, however, for the difficulties Hamlet supposedly has in carrying out his task – in either of two ways, either in getting Claudius' guilt recognized before killing him, or in first murdering him and then justifying it afterward – are very easily dissipated just by reading the text, for in it Hamlet never asks himself this sort of question.

His purpose is to take revenge for his father on the person who murdered him and who at the same time seized the throne and the father's wife, whom the father loved more than anything else. These crimes must be atoned for through the most violent action: murder. Not only is this purpose never called into question by Hamlet, but I will read you passages in which he calls himself a coward, while frothing at the mouth onstage, despairing of ever being able to decide to take action. He never doubts this purpose for even a moment. He does not call the validity of this task into question in the slightest.

At the same period, there was a writer named Loening, whom Jones makes much of, who decisively critiqued the theories put forward by Klein and Werder. Let me mention in passing that Jones gives Loening very high praise. He mentions several of Loening's remarks that appear to me to be very insightful indeed.

303   But none of this is terribly important, since this approach is no longer germane from the moment we consider the third direction, the one Jones associates with psychoanalysis. The deliberateness with which I am laying all of this out is necessary, as these earlier views constitute the backdrop against which the mystery of *Hamlet* presents itself to us.

The third conception is as follows: although Hamlet does not doubt even for an instant that he must accomplish this task, for some reason unknown to himself this task disgusts him. In other words, the difficulty resides in the task itself, not in the subject or in what is supposedly happening in the outside world (needless to say, as regards the direction that plays up the outside world, there are versions that are far more subtle than the one I mentioned earlier). It is the task itself that is posited as essentially problematic.

Such is the very solid way in which Jones situates the psychoanalytic perspective on *Hamlet*, and it should serve us as a lesson in method.

Jones shows, moreover, that the notion of an internal contradiction in the task itself was not invented by psychoanalysts; it was already mentioned by Loening, if we are to lend credence to the quotes from his work that Jones provides, and by a certain number of other authors as well. These authors clearly saw that we can grasp the problematic, conflictual nature of the task from certain signs whose clear character no one needed psychoanalysis to notice: namely, the myriad different, self-contradictory, and inconsistent reasons Hamlet gives for deferring the task, for not carrying it out when the opportunity presents itself. Long before psychoanalysis, psychologists had already noticed the superstructural, rationalized, and rationalizing nature of the reasons Hamlet gives, and Jones brings this out very clearly.

Yet the question is to figure out wherein lies the conflict. Those who have written in this vein allow us to glimpse that there is something that presents itself on the surface, and then a sort of underlying difficulty which – although it is not, strictly speaking, articulated as unconscious – is considered to be deeper and partially uncontrolled, not completely elucidated or perceived by the subject. Jones critiques their theories with the considerable know-how we generally find in his articles, which played a considerable role in getting the notion of the unconscious itself accepted by a broad swath of intellectuals.

On the one hand, Jones knows how to powerfully articulate what these authors, some of whom are quite subtle, have argued to be the underlying motives that are blocking Hamlet's action. They have, for example, mentioned a juridical motive – namely, whether or not he has the right to do what he is asked to do. Lord knows that these German authors made no bones about appealing to all sorts of registers, all of this having taken place in a highly Hegelian era. On the other hand, Jones can blithely wax ironic on this score, for he convincingly shows that the unconscious mainspring has nothing to do with motives of a lofty or highly abstract kind, related to morality, the State, or Absolute Knowledge, but that there must be something far more radical and concrete at work.

It was around 1909 that Freud's ideas first began to make it to America, and Jones decided to write and publish an account of Freud's theory of dreams, as we find it in his well-known lectures at Clark University that were first published in English, if memory serves me well.

But what we are concerned with here is Jones's study of *Hamlet* that he publishes in 1910, a study that is designed to lead us to the following conclusion: "We thus reach the apparent paradox that the hero, the poet, and the audience are all profoundly moved by feelings due to a conflict of the source of which they are unaware" ["The Oedipus Complex as an Explanation of Hamlet's Mystery," p. 86]. Even though this does not seem terribly substantial, it should not stop us from realizing that Jones's analysis of *Hamlet* truly goes as far as anyone could have gone at that point in time, I believe, in bringing out what we might call the mythical structure of the Oedipus complex in the unfolding of the drama.

[On the topic of myth,] I must say that we are not all so enlightened as to be able to laugh unconcernedly when we see Hamlet associated with all kinds of people, including Telesphorus, Amphion, Moses, Pharaoh, Zoroaster, Jesus, and Herod, everyone being lumped together in the same package. Around 1900, two authors published an article entitled "Hamlet in Iran" in a well-known journal, in

304

which they relate the myth of *Hamlet* to Iranian myths of the legend of Pyrrhus, about which another writer made a great deal in an unknown, inaccessible journal. It is essential to remark what sort of plunge has been taken at this level, even if I am not saying that it is the only one possible.

Indeed, although a psychological approach to the case of Hamlet preceded the birth of psychoanalysis, as I mentioned, the first psychoanalytic step consisted in transforming the psychological approach, not by referring to some deeper form of psychology but by referring to a mythical structure that is assumed to have the same meaning for all human beings.

Nevertheless, something more is necessary, for *Hamlet* is not, after all, the Pyrrhus saga, stories about Cyrus with Cambyses, or about Perseus and his grandfather Acrisius.

It is something else. And we are going to see what that something is.

305

2

It is not just because there have been myriad commentaries on *Hamlet* that we are talking about it.

The French can, in the end, have no real idea what *Hamlet* is about because, owing to something quite odd, I think I can say, based on my own experience, it cannot be performed in French. I have never seen a good staging of *Hamlet* in French, nor have I ever seen any French actor capable of playing the part of Hamlet or even a French version of the text that was comprehensible.

For those of you who read the text in English, it knocks your socks off, bowls you over, and is altogether unimaginable! There is not a single line or reply in the English text of *Hamlet* that does not hit you with a force and violence that makes the play absolutely stupefying at every moment. One imagines that it must have just been written, that it could not have been written three centuries ago.

In England, where the play is performed in English, a performance of *Hamlet* is always a major event. I would go even further, because, after all, one cannot gauge the audience's psychological tension if not at the box office. I will say what it is like for the actors, which is doubly instructive.

First of all, it is altogether clear that to be cast as Hamlet is, for a British actor, the crowning moment of his career. When it is not the crowning moment, it is nevertheless after having acted in the play that he wishes to retire happily by giving his farewell performance, even if his role was nothing but that of the first gravedigger. There is something important here, and we will have to figure out what it means, for I am not mentioning it at random.

Secondly, there is something curious, which is that, in the end, when a British actor manages to get the part of Hamlet, he plays the role well – indeed, they all play it well. Stranger still is the fact that people talk about this or that actor's Hamlet. There are as many Hamlets as there are great actors. People still talk about Garrick's Hamlet, Kean's Hamlet, and so on. This is also extraordinarily instructive.   306

If there are as many Hamlets as there are great actors, I believe that it is for a reason analogous to the one that makes every performance of the play into a major event and generates such an enormous mass of commentary. It is not the same reason, because it is not same thing to play the role of Hamlet as it is to be interested in it as a spectator or critic. But all this converges on the fact that we can, in the end, believe that if this is the way it is, it is because of the structure of the problem that *Hamlet* itself poses regarding desire.

My thesis here, which I will ask you to consider, is that *Hamlet* brings out the different levels, indeed the very framework that I am trying to present to you here, the framework in which desire is situated. The place of desire is so excellently and exceptionally articulated in *Hamlet* that everybody, I would say, recognizes himself in it. The structure of the play is a type of network or bird catcher's net in which man's desire is caught. And his desire is essentially articulated there in the coordinates that Freud reveals to us – namely, in connection with the Oedipus complex and castration.

This nevertheless assumes that *Hamlet* is not simply another edition or version of the eternal, typical drama or conflict, that of the hero's struggle against the father, the tyrant, the good or bad father. Shakespeare takes things so far that the way in which the fundamental structure of the eternal saga, found over and over since the beginning of time, presents itself is profoundly modified.

Here I am sketching out points that I will fill in later.

The coordinates of this conflict are modified by Shakespeare in such a way as to be able to bring out how, under certain atypical conditions, the problem of desire is played out, in its most essentially problematic nature, inasmuch as man is not simply invested or possessed by it, but must situate or find this desire – and find it at the greatest personal cost and suffering, so much so that he can find it only *in extremis*, namely in an action that can only be completed or realized for him on condition that it be lethal.   307

This incites us to examine the unfolding of the play more closely. I do not want to draw this out interminably, but I must nevertheless bring out the most salient features.

Act I concerns what one might call the presentation of the problem. And here, at the point of intersection, accumulation, and confusion around which the play revolves, we must nevertheless come back to something simple, which is the text. You are going to see that its composition is worth keeping in mind, for it is not something amorphous that wanders off in one direction and then in another.

As you will see, the play begins with a changing of the guard on the platform of Elsinore Castle, and I must say that it is one of the most masterful openings of all of Shakespeare's plays. Not all of them are as masterful from the very moment the curtain rises.

The guard changes at midnight and there are some very cute, striking things in the text. For example, it is the guard who comes to relieve the others who asks "Who's there?" whereas it should be the other way around. Indeed, everything happens abnormally, they are all anxiety-ridden by something they are expecting, and this something only takes forty lines to show up.

Although it is midnight when the changing of the guard occurs, one o'clock sounds from a bell when the ghost appears. And from the moment at which the ghost appears, things move very quickly, but the action is interspersed with rather curious moments of stagnation.

Immediately thereafter, there is a scene in which the king and queen appear, and the king says that it is high time to set aside our mourning; [it is as if he were saying,] "We can cry with one eye but let us laugh with the other" ["With an auspicious and a dropping eye"; I, ii, 11]. Hamlet, who is there, shows how revolted he is by the swiftness of his mother's remarriage and the fact that she married someone who, compared to his father, is totally inferior in character.

At every moment, we see in Hamlet's words an exaltation of his father as a being on whom, as he says later,

every god did seem to set his seal
To give the world assurance of a man. [III, iv, 62–3].

308   It is quite a bit later in the play that this sentence is announced by Hamlet, but he expresses similar sentiments right from this early scene.

Hamlet presents himself as having the sense that he has been betrayed and brought down by his mother's conduct – namely, her hasty remarriage, two months, as we are told, after her husband's death. We find this in the famous dialogue with Horatio:

Thrift, thrift, Horatio. The funeral baked meats
Did coldly furnish forth the marriage tables. [I, ii, 180–1]

I need not remind you of these well-known facts.

In Scene 3, Ophelia and her father Polonius are introduced in connection with a rebuke that Laertes makes to his sister Ophelia, the young girl Hamlet was in love with, as he tells us himself, and whom he is currently repelling sarcastically, given the state he is in. People have rightly wanted to attribute an important role to Laertes with respect to Hamlet in the mythical unfolding of the story, and we will come back to this. Polonius and Laertes successively lecture the unhappy Ophelia about the importance of being prudent and warn her to be wary of Hamlet.

Scenes 4 and 5 bring us the encounter between Hamlet, who has been joined on the platform of Elsinore Castle by Horatio, and his father's ghost. In this encounter Hamlet shows himself to be courageous and impassioned, for he does not hesitate to follow the ghost off to one side and have a rather horrifying conversation with him. Let me underscore the fact that its horrifying nature is articulated by the ghost himself; he cannot reveal to Hamlet the horrible, abominable place where he lives and all that he suffers there, for his son's mortal organs could not bear it. And he gives him an order or command.

It is interesting to immediately note that the command consists of the following: that, however he decides to do it, Hamlet must put an end to the queen's scandalous lust and, moreover, in doing so, he must restrain his own thoughts and feelings – he must not let himself indulge in excessive thoughts about his mother.

Although certain writers have made much of a sort of problematic backdrop in the orders given to Hamlet by the ghost, since the ghost warns the son that he must not trust himself in his relations with his mother, it seems that none of them have pointed out the decisive point – namely that, despite the horrible accusations that are categorically pronounced by the ghost against Claudius, the ghost revealing to Hamlet that he was killed by Claudius, the question to be resolved does not concern the assassin but rather, essentially, already, and immediately, the mother. The order given by the ghost* is not in itself an order. What it enunciates immediately brings to the fore the mother's desire [or: desire for the mother, *le désir de la mère*] as such. This point is absolutely essential and we shall return to it.

Act II is taken up with what we might call the organization of surveillance around Hamlet. We have a sort of prodrome in the guise of the instructions that Polonius, the Lord Chamberlain, gives someone concerning the surveillance of his own son, Laertes, who has left for Paris. It is rather amusing and it shows how the group including Polonius, Laertes, and Ophelia duplicates the one including Claudius, Hamlet, and the queen.

309

Polonius explains to his henchman how he must proceed in informing him about his son. We have here a purple passage on the *eternal truths about police work* that I need not go into [II, i, beginning]. Then we have the arrival, which had been announced in the first act, of Guildenstern and Rosencrantz.

They are not simply the puffed-up characters people think they are. They are former friends of Hamlet's. And Hamlet, who mistrusts them, makes fun of them, rails them, undoes them, and plays an extremely subtle game with them under the cover of madness – we shall see what Hamlet's madness or pseudo-madness means, for it has raised questions – clearly appeals to their former friendship at one moment, with a tone that would be worth highlighting if we had the time.

This tone proves that Hamlet appeals to them without having any confidence in them, and that he does not for even a second drop the ruse or game he is playing with them. Nevertheless, there is a moment at which he is able to speak to them in a certain tone of voice. Rosencrantz and Guildenstern, in coming to sound him out, are working for the king, and Hamlet senses this. He encourages them to admit to him that they were sent to him, asking them what it is they have come to do. And his friends are sufficiently shaken up for one of them to ask the other, "What say you?" [II, ii, 286]. But nothing comes of this, and things unfold in such a way that the wall between them never comes down. That would have unraveled a situation that, from one end to the other, seems to be inextricably knotted up.

At that moment, Rosencrantz and Guildenstern present the actors they have met on their way to see Hamlet and whom Hamlet knows. Hamlet has always been interested in theater and he welcomes these actors in a remarkable way.

Here, too, we must read the first samples they give him of their talent. Hamlet asks them to recite a passage from the tragedy in which Aeneas recounts the end of Troy and the killing of Priam. We have here a lovely scene in English in which we see Pyrrhus hang a dagger over Priam and remain there:

So as a painted tyrant Pyrrhus stood,
And like a neutral to his will and matter
Did nothing. [II, ii, 468–70]

As doing nothing is one of the fundamental themes of the play, it is worth mentioning that it is first presented in this image and by means of actors. This is what is going to give Hamlet the idea of using the actors in the scene that constitutes the body of the third act – this is absolutely essential – a scene that the English have a fixed term for, "the play scene"* or "play-within-the-play scene."* Hamlet concludes:

. . . The play's the thing
Wherein I'll catch the conscience of the king. [II, ii, 590–1]

This rhyme, like the sound of cymbals, puts an end to a long tirade by Hamlet that is entirely written, let me point out, in blank verse.

It is of great introductory value, since this is where the second act ends and the third begins, the one in which the play scene occurs.

The play scene is essential and we are going to examine it now.

3

311

What precedes what I called "the sound of cymbals," namely Hamlet's solitary monologue onstage, shows us the violence both of Hamlet's feelings toward Claudius and of the accusations he levels at himself:

. . . Am I a coward?
Who calls me villain? breaks my pate across?
Plucks off my beard and blows it in my face?
Tweaks me by the nose? gives me the lie i' th' throat
As deep as to the lungs? Who does me this?
Ha! [II, ii, 556–61]

This gives us the general style of the play, which knocks our socks off. And right after that, Hamlet talks about his current stepfather:

'Swounds, I should take it, for it cannot be
But I am pigeon-livered and lack gall
To make oppression bitter, or ere this
I should ha' fatted all the region kites
With this slave's offal. [II, ii, 561–5]

We spoke about "kites"* when we discussed Freud's essay "Leonardo da Vinci and a Memory of His Childhood" [1910]. A kite is a kind of bird. Hamlet is talking about his stepfather as if he were a slave being offered up as a victim to the Muses. And here begins a whole series of insults:

. . . Bloody, bawdy villain!
Remorseless, treacherous, lecherous, kindless villain! [II, ii,
565–6]

The important point here is that these insults are addressed both
to the person designated by the context – namely, Claudius – and to
Hamlet himself. This is the culminating moment of the second act.

Now what constitutes the crux of Hamlet's despair is that he
saw the actor, who was playing the part of Aeneas, crying as he
described the sad fate of Hecuba, before whom her husband Priam
was carved up into little pieces:

When she saw Pyrrhus make malicious sport
In mincing with his sword her husband's limbs. [II, ii, 501–2]

Indeed, after not having budged for a long time, with his dagger
poised above Priam, Pyrrhus takes a malicious pleasure, as the text
tells us, in cutting up Priam's body in front of this woman who is
described quite well, wrapping some sort of blanket around his raw-
boned flanks.

The theme of the passage is that, despite the actor's crying,
paleness, and broken voice in speaking about Hecuba, Hecuba is
nothing to this actor. Thus there are people who can arrive at this
high pitch of emotion for something that in no wise concerns them.
This is what triggers Hamlet's despair, he feeling nothing of the sort.

One cannot overly stress the importance of this passage in presenting what will come afterward – namely, the play scene. Hamlet
has recourse to it because he is in some sense caught up in its mood
and he seems to suddenly perceive what can be achieved with it.
What leads him to it? There is certainly a rational motive here,
which is to suss out the king's conscience. In order to do so, Hamlet
is going to have the play performed in front of the king, with a few
changes introduced by himself, so as to observe the king's emotions
and get him to betray himself.

And this is in fact what happens. At a certain point, the king
can no longer stand it. The way in which he committed the crime is
portrayed so precisely onstage, Hamlet providing a running commentary on it, that the king abruptly cries: "Lights, lights, lights!"
and bolts out noisily. Hamlet says to Horatio that there is no longer
any doubt [as to Claudius' guilt].

313   The play scene is thus essential and I am not the first psychoanalyst to have raised questions as to its function. Otto Rank did
so before me in his article "*Das 'Schauspiel' in* Hamlet," which
came out in *Psychoanalytische Beiträge zur Mythenforschung* in

1919 (Vienna-Leipzig[: Internationaler Psychoanalytischer Verlag], pp. 72–85). The function of the play scene is articulated there in a way that we will return to, but in any case it is clear that this scene raises questions that go beyond its functional role in the unfolding of the play.

We need to know up to what point and how we can interpret the details of the text. Rank confines his attention to listing all the features that show that, in the very structure of the fact of watching a play, there is something that evokes the child's first observations of parental intercourse. This is Rank's view.

I am not saying that it is worthless or even that it is false; I believe it is incomplete. It is worth spelling out [the function of the play scene] in the unfolding of the play as a whole. For in inventing this play scene, what is Hamlet doing? He is trying to create a structure and bring about the disguised dimension of truth that I somewhere called its "fictional structure" – without which he would be unable to reorient himself, beyond the more or less effective nature of the action designed to get Claudius to betray himself.

Rank thus touched on something. There is in Hamlet something that concerns his own orientation with respect to himself. I am merely indicating this to show the interest of the questions that are raised here.

4

Things are not all that simple here, and the third act does not end without the consequences of this articulation appearing in the following form: Hamlet is urgently summoned to his mother's side, she, naturally, being unable to take it any longer. These are the very words she uses: "O Hamlet, speak no more" [III, iv, 90].

As Hamlet is walking toward his mother's apartments, he sees Claudius moving, if not toward an admission of guilt [*résipiscence*], at least toward repentance [*repentir*]. This is the so-called scene of the "prayer of repentance" [III, iii, 76]. This man who has, in some sense, been caught in the very web of what he continues to possess – namely, the fruits of his crime – raises up to God some kind of prayer that he may have the strength to find a way out of it. Hamlet, stumbling upon the king when he is literally on his knees and does not see him, has him at his mercy, revenge being at arm's length. This is where he stops.

If I kill him now, he says to himself, won't he go straight to heaven? Hamlet's father had clearly stressed that he was suffering all the torments of some sort of hell or purgatory. Wouldn't Hamlet

314

be sending Claudius straight to eternal happiness? That is precisely what he must not do, he concludes. It was nevertheless an opportunity to set things right.

I did not bring up the alternative "to be or not to be" the last time for no reason. In my view, it is the very crux of the matter.

Hamlet tells us that his father, owing to the moment at which he died, remains stuck forever "in the blossoms of [his] sin." The line drawn at the bottom of the "audit" [III, iii, 81] or tallying up of his life is such that he remains identical to the sum total of his crimes. It is when faced with this that Hamlet stops, saying, "to be or not to be."

Suicide is not as simple as all that. We are not exactly in the process of imagining, as he did, what happens in the hereafter. What is at stake is simply the following: putting an end to someone's life does not stop a being from remaining identical to all that he did in the course of his life. In this case, there is no "to be or not to be" – whatever the case may be, "to be" is forever.

Hamlet, too, is confronted with this. It is because he is not purely and simply the vehicle of the drama, the one through whom passions transit – as in the case of Eteocles and Polynices who persist in the crime their father [Oedipus] committed by castrating himself – it is because he is concerned with the eternal "to be" of the said Claudius that, at that precise moment, in a way that turns out to be altogether coherent, he does not even draw his sword from its scabbard.

This is essential: what he wants to do is surprise the other in the excess of his pleasures, in other words, in relations with the queen. The key point here is desire for the mother [or: the mother's desire, *désir de la mère*]. And he is going, in effect, to have an emotional scene with his mother that is one of the most extraordinary things ever seen on the stage.

315   In this scene, in which a mirror is held up to the mother so she can see herself as she truly is, there is a dialogue between a son who indisputably loves his mother as she loves him – this we are told – beyond all expression, in which he incites her to break the bonds of what he calls "that monster, custom":

That monster, custom, who all sense doth eat,
Of habits devil, is angel yet in this,
That to the use of actions fair and good
He likewise gives a frock or livery . . . [III, iv, 162–5]

Here he enjoins her to begin to break her habit and not sleep that night with Claudius. It is all put quite crudely, marvelously so. As you will see, he tells her, it will get easier and easier after that.

There are two lines that must, it seems to me, be pointed out, for they echo each other, and everything is going to revolve around them.

At a certain moment, in the course of the play scene, poor Ophelia, about whom I have not yet said much, tells Hamlet that he is doing a fine job playing the part of the chorus – in other words, that he is giving a good running commentary on the play. He responds:

I could interpret between you and your love, if I
could see the puppets dallying. [III, ii, 237–8]

We try to imagine what is happening onstage. In any case, what is at stake is something that is happening between "you" and "your love."

In the scene with the mother now, when the ghost appears – for the ghost appears in it, and at a moment at which Hamlet's entreaties are beginning to flag – it is in order to tell Hamlet:

O, step between her and her fighting soul!
Conceit in weakest bodies strongest works.
Speak to her, Hamlet. [III, iv, 114–6]

The ghost, who appears only to Hamlet here, whereas everyone can usually see it when it appears, has come to tell him to "step between her and her fighting soul." "Conceit" is unequivocal. It is used a lot in this play, precisely in relation to the soul. Conceit is *concetto*, an elaborate literary style, and it is the word that is used to describe the style of the *précieux*. The ghost thus says that conceit works the most powerfully in tired bodies. "Speak to her, Hamlet."

This place between one thing and another where Hamlet is always asked to enter, operate, and intervene shows us the true situation of the drama. This appeal is significant – significant to us, because it is here that we analysts must intervene, "between her and her . . .," that is our job. "Conceit in weakest bodies strongest works" is an appeal addressed to us analysts.

Here, once again, Hamlet caves in. He leaves his mother, telling her to go ahead and allow herself to be caressed after all; Claudius is going to come and give her a big fat kiss on the cheek and caress her neck. He abandons his mother, he literally allows her to go back, to return, as it were, to giving herself over to her desire. This is how Act III ends, except that in the meantime the unfortunate Polonius has had the misfortune of stirring behind the arras and being run through by Hamlet with his sword.

316

5

We arrive now at the fourth act.

It begins rather prettily with a true manhunt, which Hamlet seems to find highly amusing. He hid Polonius's body somewhere and he yells out "Hide fox, and all after" [IV, ii, 29–30]. In the end he tells them not to wear themselves out, for before the end of the month they will begin to smell him – "you shall nose him" – near the stairs [IV, iii, 36], and let no more be said about it.

Shortly before that we have an important comment:

The body is with the king,
but the king is not with the body.
The king is a thing [. . .] of nothing. [IV, ii, 26–9]

This is one of Hamlet's schizophrenic-sounding remarks. It does not fail to give us something that is helpful to us in interpreting the play, as we shall see later on.

Act IV is an act in which many things happen very quickly. Hamlet is, for example, sent off to England and returns before you can say boo. We know why: he uncovered the plot against him – namely, that he was being sent to his death. His return is accompanied by some drama, because Ophelia in the meantime has gone crazy – owing to her father's death, let us say, and probably to something else as well – and Laertes has revolted and has been plotting a minor coup. The king has put a stop to his revolt by telling him that Hamlet is the guilty party, but that no one can be told about it because he is too popular; the thing can be handled quietly by organizing a fixed duel in which he will perish. And this is precisely what happens.

The first scene in Act V is the cemetery scene. I alluded earlier to the first gravedigger. I am sure you all recall the astounding remarks exchanged by the characters who are digging Ophelia's grave and who are tossing around a skull as they speak, one of which is caught by Hamlet who gives a speech about it.

Since I mentioned actors earlier, let me observe that no one has ever seen, as far back as theatre wardrobe assistants can remember, a Hamlet and a first gravedigger who were not ready to kill each other. The first gravedigger has never been able to stand the tone with which Hamlet speaks to him. This detail is worth noting in passing, for it shows us just how powerful the relationships highlighted in this drama can be.

Let us turn to the following, which I will bring more fully to your attention next time.

317

After having been prepared by the long and powerful cemetery scene, the dénouement arrives. We are aware of Hamlet's ever-flagging desire, that exhausted, unfinished, and unfinishable thing that characterizes his position. Why are we suddenly going to see what was impossible become possible? Why are we suddenly going to see Hamlet accept Laertes's challenge under the most unlikely conditions? These conditions are all the more curious as Hamlet is serving as Claudius' champion here.

We see Hamlet best Laertes in all the bouts. He lands him two or three hits, whereas Hamlet himself had been granted a handicap when the bet was placed. And when he is pricked with the poisoned tip, according to plan, a sort of confusion nevertheless ensues in which he winds up wielding the poisoned rapier and wounding Laertes with it. And it is once they are both mortally wounded that the last blow is struck, which is leveled at he who should have been dispatched from the outset – namely, Claudius.

I did not mention Millais's painting of Ophelia floating down the river at random last time. In concluding today, I want to propose another painting. I would like someone to paint a canvas in which we would see the cemetery on the horizon and over here the open grave, with people coming out of it – like those who, at the end of the Oedipus tragedy, disperse and cover their eyes so as not to see what is happening – namely, something like the liquefaction of M. Valdemar.

Something different is at work here. Something has happened to which not enough importance has been attributed. Hamlet, who has just returned unexpectedly, thanks to the pirates who allowed him to foil the plot to assassinate him, happens upon Ophelia's burial. He has not yet heard about her death; he did not know what had happened during his brief absence. We see Laertes clawing at his own chest, and jumping into the grave in order to embrace his sister's cadaver one last time, loudly proclaiming his despair.

Not only can Hamlet not stand this display of grief over the loss of a girl whom he had clearly mistreated up until then, but he throws himself into the grave with Laertes after having truly bellowed, having given a war cry in which he says the most unexpected thing: who is grieving the death of this young girl? And he concludes, "This is I, Hamlet the Dane" [V, i, 244–5].

No one has ever heard him claim that he was Danish. He abhors the Danish! Suddenly, a revolution takes place in him owing to something that is highly significant, I can say, with respect to our schema. It is insofar as $ is there in a certain relationship with little a that he suddenly identifies with something that for the very first time makes him find his desire in its totality.

318

We see Hamlet and Laertes disappear into the hole. They grapple with each other for a while down there. People finally separate them and pull them out. This is what would be depicted in the painting: a hole from which we would see things escaping.

We will see what this might mean next time.

March 11, 1959

XV

THE MOTHER'S DESIRE

From mystery to illusion
Hamlet, a mode of discourse
The prohibition from which the unconscious arises
Hamlet's impure desire
The circuit of desire

Psychoanalytic principles are such that, in order to arrive at a goal, we must not be in a hurry.

Some of you may believe – I think there are not many of you who do – that we have ventured far from clinical work here. This is not at all true, for we are right smack in the middle of it. Given that what we are trying to do is situate the meaning of desire, human desire, the way in which we proceed in order to map it with regard to what has, moreover, been one of the main topics of psychoanalytic thought since the beginning cannot in any way force us to take a detour from what is most urgently required of us.

A great deal has been said about *Hamlet*, and I have tried to show you just how massive the literature on the play is.

Since I spoke to you last time, a document arrived on my doorstep which, in my desire for perfectionism, I had been dying to see – namely, Ernest Jones's *Hamlet and Oedipus* [New York: W. W. Norton & Co., 1949]. In reading it, I perceived that Jones updated his discussion of *Hamlet* so that it takes into account developments in psychoanalysis since 1909. He no longer refers there to Loening as a worthy commentator, but rather to Dover Wilson who wrote a lot about Hamlet and did so very cogently. As I myself had read some of Wilson's work, I believe I have already managed to convey the substance of it to you.

We must now take a step back from all of that.

Jones's speculations are, however, quite penetrating and one might say that, on the whole, they stand apart from everything else that has been written on the subject of *Hamlet* by the analytic community.

Jones points out highly pertinent things, such as the fact that Hamlet is not a real person, which is just plain common sense. What can it then mean to raise the most profound questions about his character? This point is perhaps worth dwelling on a bit more seriously than people ordinarily do.

I am going to begin today by doing so.

1

As always, when we are in a field that concerns psychoanalytic exploration as such, on the one hand, and a specific object, on the other, the pathway that must be followed is twofold.

The path our train of thought follows is based on a certain pre-existing idea we have about the object. It is quite obvious that there are things here whose groundwork should, I would say, be laid immediately.

For example, at the most basic level, in works of art, and especially in dramatic works, there are *characters*, in the sense in which we understand the term in French. A character is someone about whom we assume the author knows everything. The author has created a character, and he is supposed to move us by setting his character traits in motion. In and of itself, this is assumed to introduce us to a supposed reality that is beyond what is given to us in the work of art.

I would say that *Hamlet* has the very important property of making us realize to what degree we must at least suspend judgment regarding this viewpoint – which is widely shared and which we spontaneously adopt whenever we examine a work of art – if not refute it altogether.

In fact, there are two handholds that we can solidly latch onto in every art, they being absolutely solid reference points. We shall see what they are.

Hamlet is a mirror, we are told, in which we all, whether readers or spectators – but let us leave to one side the spectators, who are unfathomable – see ourselves as we want to. Even if this notion is not in the least bit satisfying, the fact remains that if we put together everything that has been proposed and asserted about this play, we cannot fail to realize that, as I think I made sufficiently clear last time, the interpretations by critics contradict each other, they being strictly speaking irreconcilable, which clearly suggests that there is some mystery here. I also mentioned that, for actors, the role of

Hamlet is *the* role *par excellence*, and that people also talk about this person's Hamlet and that person's Hamlet – there are as many Hamlets as there are actors of a certain caliber.

But this goes beyond simply noting a range of Hamlets.

I assume that certain people were a bit put out by all the hubbub there was around Shakespeare's tri-centennial in 1864, there having been a resurgence of Shakespearean themes and a passionate revival of his work on the part of the entire British literary establishment. And in 1917, John Robertson, in his *Mystery of Hamlet*, actually voiced the opinion that *Hamlet* was, strictly speaking, vacuous; that it did not hold water; that there is no key to Hamlet as a character; and that Shakespeare had done what he could to patch up *Hamlet*, which was attributed to an author named Kyd, and had already been performed a dozen years before the autumn of 1601 when we are more or less certain that Shakespeare's *Hamlet* showed for the first time. Philological exploration has, moreover, gone quite far in that direction since 1917.

The Austrian playwright Grillparzer – to whom Freud refers in passing, which is significant, and about whom Jones speaks at the end of the second chapter of his book – goes so far as to articulate in no uncertain terms that the reason for *Hamlet*'s success is its "impenetrability." It is, admittedly, a rather curious opinion; in any case, one cannot deny that it is a strictly anti-Aristotelian opinion, insofar as Aristotle considers the hero's similarity, *omoios*, to us as what accounts for the effect of both comedy and tragedy.

Nevertheless, the fact that such varied things can be said about *Hamlet* is worth pondering.

Let me add that we find here a whole gamut of differing opinions, that present a whole series of nuances. It is not the same thing to say that it is the impenetrability of *Hamlet* that makes for its success as it is to say that *Hamlet* is a failure as a play, as is maintained by no less than T. S. Eliot, who, in a certain milieu, is considered to be more or less the greatest modern English poet. According to Eliot, Shakespeare was not equal to the task of dealing with his hero. If Hamlet is someone who is unequal to the task he is supposed to perform, Shakespeare was just as unequal to the task of articulating Hamlet's role.

These are opinions that one might well consider to be problematic. I am enumerating them for you in order to lead you toward what is at stake. I believe that the most nuanced opinion is the most accurate: there is in the relationship between *Hamlet* and we who apprehend it, whether as readers or spectators, a phenomenon characterized by illusion.

To say *this* is quite different from saying that Hamlet is simply

322

vacuous [*le vide*]. An illusion is not a vacuum [*le vide*]. In order to
produce a ghostlike effect onstage – an effect like the one provided,
if you will, by my little concave mirror with the real image that
emerges and that can be seen only from a certain angle and from
a certain point in space – a good deal of machinery is required. If
Hamlet is an illusion, or the organization of an illusion, we are not
dealing with the same species of illusion as we would be if everyone
were speculating about something vacuous. It is important to make
this distinction; everything seems to confirm that something like this
is involved.

This is the first handhold we can solidly latch onto.

For example, W. F. Trench [*Shakespeare's Hamlet*, London:
1913], who is cited by Jones, writes the following: "We find it hard,
with Shakespeare's help, to understand Hamlet: even Shakespeare,
perhaps, found it hard to understand him: Hamlet himself" – you
can see that the passage is an amusing one, and the author's pen
and thinking is sliding toward the following – "finds it impossible
to understand himself." That is possible. "Better able than other
men to read the hearts and motives of others" – this concerns
neither ourselves nor Shakespeare, but rather Hamlet, who, as
you know, plays all the time at taking apart whatever is said by
his interlocutors, by those who come to interrogate or try to trap
him – "he is yet quite unable to read his own" [Jones, *Hamlet and
Oedipus*, p. 57].

Right after quoting this, Jones tells us what he thinks of these
lines. Although he had begun by indicating his reservations about
considering fictional characters to be real – having said that we must
not allow ourselves to be led to speak of Hamlet like a real person,
and that we have to seek elsewhere when it comes to interpreting
the play (which is the traditional position in psychoanalysis, and
harbors within it, I believe, an error or fallacy to which I would
first like to draw your attention) – Jones himself ends up saying
the following: "I know of no more authentic statement than this in
the whole literature on the Hamlet problem" [p. 57].

In a different text, Jones tells us that, in short, "we reach the
apparent paradox that the hero, the poet, and the audience are
all profoundly moved by feelings due to a conflict of the source of
which they are unaware." This remark makes us realize the strict
equivalence of the first two terms: the hero and the poet are strictly
equivalent to their discourse; they exist only through their discourse.
If one wishes to talk about the communication of what is in their
unconscious, one cannot in any case say that such communication
is embodied in anything other than the articulation of the dramatic
discourse itself.

323

Let us leave the hero to one side. If you follow me in the pathways along which I am trying to lead you, you will see that he is in fact strictly identical to words – above all, when we begin to sense that, in *Hamlet*, what gives our hero his highest dramatic value is that he is a mode of discourse. This is the second handhold that I will ask you to latch onto. This phenomenon is of the same ilk as the aspect that eludes the grasp of everything we can say regarding his consistency. In other words, *Hamlet* proves to be an exemplary work here.

The way in which a work touches us, and most profoundly so – that is, at the unconscious level – has to do with its composition and organization. Although there is no doubt but that we get caught up in it at the level of the unconscious, it is not because of the presence of something in front of us that can really have an unconscious. I mean that, as opposed to what people think, we are not dealing with the poet's unconscious. His unconscious undoubtedly manifests itself in several traces in the work that are not deliberate, such as slips and symbolic elements that went unnoticed by the poet, but this is not what we consider to be of major interest.

One can find a number of such traces in *Hamlet*. This is what Ella Sharpe tried to do, as I told you last time. She tried to root out, here and there, traces of some sort of fixation on feminine or oral metaphors in Hamlet's character. I assure you that, as regards the problem Hamlet poses, this truly seems to be secondary and almost childish, without, of course, being absolutely of no interest whatsoever.

When you go looking in this way, from this perspective, for anything in a work that can tell you something about the author, you are engaging in a biographical investigation about him rather than analyzing the import of the work as such. If *Hamlet* is of major importance to us, it is because its structural value is equivalent to that of *Oedipus*. What interests us and can allow us to structure certain problems is obviously based on the play's deepest plot, the whole of the tragedy, and its articulation as such. This is obviously something other than a fleeting revelation by the author about himself.

This is what I am in the process of emphasizing. The work is of importance to us owing to its organization – that is, owing to the superimposed planes [*plans*] this organization brings with it within which the true dimension of human subjectivity can find its place. If you will allow me to provide a metaphor here, I would say that in order to give its full depth to a play, as one would to a theatre hall or to a set onstage, we need to have multiple superimposed sets [*plans*], side struts [*portants*], and a whole machinery [of pulleys and ropes, for example]. It is within the depth that is thus created that the problem of the articulation of desire can be posed in the fullest way possible.

To spell this out even further: if *Hamlet* has special import to us, if it is truly the greatest drama or one of the greatest dramas of modern tragedy – *Faust* being one of the other greatest dramas – it is not simply because we are dealing with Shakespeare, however marvelous we may assume him to be, and the fact that his life took such and such a turn at a certain moment in time. This is not to deny that *Hamlet* was written at a certain moment in Shakespeare's life, a moment at which something important quite clearly happened.

The only thing we can say for sure is that it involved his father's death. To confine our attention to that would be to content ourselves with very little; people naturally assume that other things related to this event occurred in his life. In any case, *Hamlet* marks an obvious turning point in Shakespeare's production and in the orientation of his work.

Prior to *Hamlet*, he wrote a series of comedies and historical tragedies. These are the two genres that Shakespeare brought to their highest degree of beauty, perfection, and ease. Up until then, one can almost say that he had two great specialties which he practiced masterfully and brilliantly, placing him at the level of the most successful authors of his time.

After *Hamlet*, the picture changes. He writes things that go beyond all limits, that no longer have anything to do with any known literary canon, that are no longer of the same type – consider, for example *King Lear* and many other plays as well, ending with *The Tempest*. These confront us with something else altogether, a human drama that develops and is of an entirely different register. This is the Shakespeare who is the crowning jewel of human history and of the human drama, the Shakespeare who opens up a new dimension in our understanding of mankind.

Thus something truly happened at that moment in his life. But does the fact that we are certain about this allow us to conclude that it was his father's death? Yes, of course, in a sense. But let us observe, nevertheless, that if *Hamlet* is the play that presents itself most as an enigma, it is only too obvious that a play that constitutes a problem is not automatically a good play. An awful play can also pose a problem. And the author's unconscious is probably just as or even *more* present in many a bad play than in many a good one.

If we are moved by a play, it is not because it represents a great deal of effort on the author's part or because of what its author reveals unbeknownst to himself. I repeat that it is because of the space it offers us, owing to the multiple dimensions of its development, in which to lodge what is hidden in *us* – namely, our relationship to our own desire. If this possibility is eminently offered to us by *Hamlet*, it is not because Shakespeare was caught up at that moment in a personal drama. It is because this play furnishes the layering of myriad dimensions and organized levels – and in some ways, the maximum possible number of dimensions and levels – necessary to provide the space for what lies within us to resonate there.

If we take things as far as possible, we believe that we can grasp Shakespeare's personal drama, and yet it eludes us. People have gone so far as to say that it was the drama that furnished the material for the *Sonnets*. You are aware that Shakespeare was doubly deceived, both by his male friend/protector and by his mistress. Yet that particular drama most probably occurred at a different period in Shakespeare's life, a more subdued one. Moreover, we have no certainty about these details; we have but the testimony of the *Sonnets* themselves, a testimony that has itself been elaborately worked over.

I believe that *Hamlet's* seductive power stems from a different source. We can at times try to imagine what might lie behind *Hamlet*. But what is at stake is not what lies behind it but rather the composition of the work itself. What we must dwell on is the high degree of perfection to which the author managed to take it. It is this singular, exceptional articulation that distinguishes Shakespeare's *Hamlet* from all the earlier versions of *Hamlet* that philology has allowed us to discover.

If Shakespeare was able to create such a work, it is probably because of a deepening, which is as much that of his skill as a writer as that of his experience of life as a man, a man who certainly did live and had a happy life. Everything suggests, in effect, that his life involved all kinds of temptations [*solicitations*] and passions. But the fact that Shakespeare's own personal drama may lie behind *Hamlet* is secondary with regard to what constitutes its structure. It is this structure that accounts for the effect *Hamlet* has on us.

This is all the clearer as Hamlet himself, as writers have put it metaphorically, is a character whose depths we cannot fathom, not simply because of our ignorance. Indeed, he is a character who is made up of something: the empty place in which we can situate our ignorance. This is what is important, because a situated ignorance is not purely negative – it renders the unconscious present, no more, no less. This is what gives *Hamlet* its power and its import.

I believe I have succeeded in conveying to you the specifically psychological dimension that is involved in a play like this one, without denying it, without leaving anything aside, and with a plethora of nuances. Certain people say that what I am engaged in is an exercise in what is known as "applied psychoanalysis," whereas it is exactly

327   the opposite. What I am working on here is psychoanalytic theory. Compared to the theoretical question whether psychoanalysis can adequately discuss works of art, any sort of clinical question is one that falls under the heading of applied psychoanalysis.

Some of you who are here listening to me will no doubt want me to say a bit more about this. Ask me questions, should you have any. [Silence.]

If *Hamlet* is truly what I say it is – namely, a composition or structure in which desire can find its place, and be situated in a sufficiently correct and rigorous way for all desires, or, more precisely, all problems raised by the relationship between the subject and desire, to be projected onto it – it should suffice in some sense to read it. I was thus alluding to people who might raise questions about the role of those who act in the play. Where do we situate the role of theatre and performance [*représentation*]?

It is clear that it is not at all the same thing to read *Hamlet* as to see it performed. I do not think this can pose a problem for you for long. In the perspective that I am trying to develop here concerning, in short, the function of the unconscious, the unconscious is defined as the Other's discourse [*le discours de l'Autre*]. Nothing can better illustrate this than the perspective given to us by an experience like that of the audience's relationship to *Hamlet*. It is clear that the unconscious is rendered present here in the form of the Other's discourse, which is a thoroughly written discourse. The hero is present here only through this discourse, as is the poet. Having been dead for a long time, what a poet bequeaths us is, in the final analysis, his discourse.

The dimension that is added by performance – namely, by the actors who perform the play – is strictly analogous to that by which we ourselves are invested in our own unconscious. We are the ones who furnish the material that constitutes our relationship to the unconscious, namely, the signifier – this is what I teach and what I spend my time telling you – with our imaginary, that is, with our relationship to our own body, for that is the imaginary.

People say that I neglect the existence of the body and that I have
328   an incorporeal theory of psychoanalysis. At least that is what you might conclude when you hear about what I say from those who live a bit far from here, for people talk.

Yet what I say is that it is with our own bodily members that we create the alphabet of the discourse that is unconscious – and, of course, we each do so in different ways, for, although we are all caught up in the unconscious, we do not all use the same elements. Analogously, an actor lends his members and presence, not simply like a puppet, but with an unconscious that is truly real – namely, the relationship of his members to his own history.

Plate 1 *Ophelia*, Sir John Everett Millais

Plate 2 *Melancholia*, Albrecht Dürer

If there are good and bad actors, it is to the degree, I believe, to which an actor's unconscious is more or less compatible with this lending of himself as a puppet. Either he lends himself to it or he does not; this is what accounts for the fact that an actor has more or less talent and genius, and even – why not? – that he is more or less suited for certain roles. Even those who have a very wide range can, after all, play certain roles better than others.

Put differently, actors are obviously necessary. It is to the degree to which there is some agreement between what they must perform for us and something that may, indeed, have the closest relationship with their unconscious that they include something in their interpretation of their roles that indisputably adds something – something that is far from constituting the crux of what is communicated, for the crux is the performance of the drama as it was written.

This perspective could open a door for us and take us quite far, I believe, into the psychology of the actor. There are, of course, laws of general compatibility. The relationship between the actor and performance possibilities raises a problem of psychology that is specific to actors. Whether certain psychological makeups are especially well suited for acting is a question that has been broached, notably by someone I saw again recently, and whose article that came out a few years ago on what he called "Hysteria and Theatre" was promising. I will perhaps have the opportunity to speak about it with interest, even if I do not, of course, completely agree with it.

Having addressed this point, let us now return to our main topic.

2   329

What I am trying to get you to understand about the effect of *Hamlet* is essentially the way in which desire can and must find its place in the play as it was written. What, therefore, is this structure in which desire finds its place?

At first glance, it may seem that what I am saying is no different from what is commonly said about *Hamlet* in the psychoanalytic community. Did I make all of these introductory remarks simply in order to end up agreeing with such classic and even banal viewpoints? You will see that it is nothing of the sort.

Let us nevertheless begin with what we are usually told. And don't think that it is all so simple and unequivocal. A certain rectitude is what it is hardest for writers themselves to maintain as they formulate their notions about *Hamlet*, for what constantly occurs is a kind of evasion or oscillation, several examples of which you will see in what I will discuss.

As a first approximation, about which everyone is in agreement, Hamlet is someone who knows not what he wants. When he sees the troops of the young Fortinbras march off and disappear at the far end of the stage, he becomes embittered, suddenly struck by the fact that these people are going to engage in a great action for a trifle, for a little patch of Poland. They are going to sacrifice everything, their lives even, whereas he is there doing nothing even though he has everything he needs to take action: "cause, and will, and strength, and means," as he puts it himself. Hamlet is stuck at the stage of saying, but "'This thing's to do'" [IV, iv, 44–5].

Why doesn't Hamlet take action? This is the question everyone raises. Why is his will* or desire in abeyance? This intersects, as it were, what Sir James Paget, who is cited by Jones, wrote about hysterical paralysis: "Hamlet's advocates say he cannot do his duty, his detractors say he will not, whereas the truth is that he cannot will."

What does the psychoanalytic tradition tell us about this? It says that everything in this case depends on his desire for his mother. Being repressed, this desire makes it such that the hero cannot move forward to take the action he is ordered to take, namely to take revenge on a man who is the current – and oh so illegitimate, because criminal – possessor of the maternal object. And if Hamlet cannot strike he who is designated as the target of his revenge, it is because he himself had in short already committed [in fantasy] the crime for which he was supposed to wreak vengeance.

Inasmuch as the backdrop here – so we are told – is the memory of his childhood desire for his mother and of his Oedipal desire to kill his father, Hamlet thus turns out to be in some sense an accomplice of the current possessor, who is a *beatus possidens* in his eyes. Since he is this man's accomplice, he cannot attack him without attacking himself. But this could also mean – and this mechanism is, nevertheless, the one that is more palpable [*sensible*] in the play – that he cannot attack this possessor without awakening in himself the ancient desire for which he feels guilty.

But must we, after all, remain fascinated by a schema that is surrounded by an aura that gives it an untouchable, non-dialectical, unfathomable character? Can't we also say that all of this can be put the other way around? If Hamlet had immediately attacked his stepfather, people would say that he had taken the opportunity to assuage his own guilt by situating the true guilty party outside himself.

To put it as bluntly as possible, Hamlet does not take action, whereas everything conspires to make him do so.

There is, first of all, the superego commandment, which is in some

330

sense materialized here by a father who returns from the afterlife in the form of a ghost to order Hamlet to wreak vengeance. And this father is provided with all the sacred character of one who returns from beyond the grave, still greater authority stemming from his grandeur, his charm [*séduction*], the fact that he is a victim, and the fact that he was atrociously dispossessed not only of his love object but also of his power, his throne, his very life, his salvation, and his eternal happiness. There is no doubt whatsoever that the father incites Hamlet to take action.

Something else, too, pushes him in the same direction, something one might call, in this case, Hamlet's "natural desire." If, because this desire is repressed, he cannot feel it, and if he is effectively separated from his mother, it is nevertheless indisputable that the fact that his desire is fixated on her affects him; this is what is most certain and apparent in Hamlet's role. I deliberately called this repressed desire "natural" here, for when Jones wrote his article on *Hamlet*, he was still trying to make the case to his readers that the dimension of repression and censorship exists, and every page he writes on this occasion tends to give this censorship a social origin. Curiously enough, he says, "the trends most likely to be 'repressed' are those belonging to what are called the natural instincts."

This truly raises a question. After all, if the dimension of repression and censorship really arises from society, why wasn't society organized in such a way as to satisfy the most natural desires? This question could perhaps take us a bit further.

It is quite palpable, indeed, that the necessities of the life of a group, or sociological necessities – the things we never seem to notice – do not exhaustively explain the sort of prohibition from which the dimension of the unconscious arises in human beings. They explain it so inadequately that, in order to explain the very principles of repression, Freud had to invent a primal myth – a pre-social myth, let us not forget, since it is the one that founds society – that described in *Totem and Taboo*. In Jones's commentary, and because of the date at which it was penned, Jones unfortunately still believes that prohibitions, censorship, and even the Oedipus complex are, at the unconscious level, sociological products, which is a mistake on Jones's part. It may be a deliberate, apologetic mistake, the kind of mistake made by someone who wishes to convince, who wishes to conquer a certain audience of social psychologists. This view is, nevertheless, problematic.

But let us return to our Hamlet.

We see him actuated in the end by two different impulses: an imperative impulse, commanded doubly by his father's authority and by the love Hamlet bears his father, and the impulse to defend

331

his mother and keep her for himself, both of which must drive him in the same direction – to kill Claudius. How could two positive things zero out? It is quite odd.

I realize that this sometimes happens. I encountered a very fine example of this when I broke my leg recently: you shorten one leg, then you shorten the other leg, and in the end there is no more shortening. It is a very fine exercise for us, for we deal with things like this. Yet is that what is involved here?

I do not think so. If we thought it was, we would wind up in an illusory dialectic and content ourselves with a schema that would, after all, only be justified, no doubt, by the fact that there is this character named Hamlet and we feel we have to come up with some explanation for him. The fact remains, all the same, that we have put our finger on something essential here.

There is something that makes Hamlet's action difficult for him, that makes his task repugnant to him, and that thrusts him into a problematic position with respect to his own action; and this something, this x, is his desire. The impure nature of this desire plays an essential role, but it does so unbeknownst to Hamlet. In some sense, it is inasmuch as his action is not disinterested, not motivated in some Kantian way, that Hamlet cannot carry it out.

I believe that this is something we can in fact assert. Let us not, however, forget that it was pretty much known prior to psychoanalytic investigation. We have traces of this – and this is partly why Jones's bibliography is of interest, for it shows us this – in the works of certain authors who glimpsed this in writings around 1880 or 1890, long before Freud began to articulate the *Ödipuskomplex*. Nevertheless, I believe that we can analytically formulate something more accurate than these authors did, and go further than what the theories psychoanalysts have provided on this topic boil down to. In order to do so, we need but carefully read the text of the play.

When we do so, we cannot fail to realize that what Hamlet is constantly dealing or grappling with is a desire which is far from being his own. As it is situated in the play, it is the desire, not *for* his mother, but *of* his mother – that is, it is his mother's desire. That alone is what is at work.

The pivotal point is his encounter with his mother after the "play scene."* I would have to read the whole scene with you.

Hamlet has had a play performed that has had an effect on the king's conscience. As everyone grows more and more anxious about Hamlet's intentions, it is decided that he will be asked to have a talk with his mother. This is exactly what he wants. He is going to take the opportunity, he says, to twist the knife in the wound – he explicitly mentions daggers [III, ii, 381] – in his mother's heart. Then we have a long scene, which is a theatrical climax, the closet scene about which I said last time that it is virtually unbearable to read, in which he pathetically implores his mother to sit up and take notice of what she is doing.

I am sorry I cannot read the whole scene with you here, but please do so yourselves, pen in hand, as one does in school. Hamlet says to her, 'What the heck kind of life are you leading? You're no spring chicken anymore, you should calm down a bit!' These are the sorts of things he says to her in his admirable language. They are things we cannot believe anyone would ever say, and that could not be said in any more penetrating a manner; they are things that could not correspond any better to what, in effect, Hamlet has rushed to say to his mother – things that are designed to break her heart and that she experiences as such, as she herself says to him: "O Hamlet, thou hast cleft my heart in twain" [III, iv, 157]. And she literally groans under the pressure.

The mother is at least forty-five years old at this point. We are more or less certain that Hamlet is thirty. This is debatable, but in the graveyard scene there is an indication from which it can be deduced, for Hamlet remembers poor Yorick who died about thirty years ago and who kissed him on the lips. It is important to keep in mind that Hamlet is not some naive young man.

Back, now, to the closet scene. Hamlet compares his father to Hyperion –

A combination and a form indeed,
Where every god did seem to set his seal

– and next to him we have this piece of rubbish, "A king of shreds and patches" [III, iv, 103], a conman or pimp with whom you are up to your ears in mud. This is what his speech is about, and it is worth articulating. You will see further on what is at stake. But, whatever the case may be, it is about his mother's desire, and about a plea on Hamlet's part, which is a demand of the following sort: get hold of yourself, get control of yourself, follow – as I told you last time – the pathway of good manners, begin by no longer sleeping with my uncle. He says it that directly. And everyone knows, he says, that appetite comes with eating, and that this devil, habit, which ties us to the worst possible things, can also work in the opposite way: once you start behaving better, it will get easier and easier.

What do we see here if not the articulation of a demand which is manifestly made by Hamlet in the name of something that is at the level, not simply of the law, but of dignity, and which is expressed

334

with force, vigor, and even cruelty – the least one can say about it is
that it leads to discomfort.

The point they arrive at is one where the mother is literally
panting, so much so that people have wondered if the ghost that
reappears in the closet is not there in order to say to Hamlet
'Tallyho, tallyho! Go on!' But in a certain respect the ghost also
calls Hamlet to order; he protects the mother against some sort of
overflowing aggression on the son's part, before which she herself
momentarily trembles: "What wilt thou do? Thou wilt not murder
me?" [III, iv, 22]. How far will you go? His father reminds him to
"step between her and her fighting soul!" [III, iv, 114].

At the climax of the scene Hamlet suddenly backs down and says
to her, now that I have said all that, do as you like and go recount
all of that to Uncle Claudius. You're going to allow him to give you
a little kiss on the cheek, a little tickle on the neck, a little scratch on
the stomach, and all will end as usual in a complete shambles. This
is exactly what Hamlet says.

We are following the oscillating motion we see in Hamlet here. He
storms, he insults, he implores, and then his discourse collapses – he
gives up. We see in his very words a disappearance or vanishing of
his appeal when he consents to his mother's desire, laying down his
arms before something that seems ineluctable.

His mother's desire here takes on anew for him the value of something that can in no way be dominated, moved, or eliminated.

3

I have proceeded even more slowly than I had imagined I would. I
will thus be forced to stop at a point which, as you see, will require
us to spend perhaps two more of our meetings deciphering *Hamlet*.

335   Today, in concluding, I will try to show you the relationship
between what I am in the process of articulating and the graph of
desire.

Where do I want to lead you with *Hamlet*? I will tell you very
precisely, by reminding you first what the graph tells us about the
location of desire.

This is the upper level of the graph. On the lower line, $s(A) \rightarrow A$,
you have the elementary discourse of demand, the one that subjects
the subject's need to the consent, caprice, and arbitrary will of the
Other as such. The Other's discourse thus has the power to structure
human tension and intention in the fragmentation brought on by
the signifier. This is the first stage, the first relationship to the Other.

What is at stake for the subject within the Other's discourse that

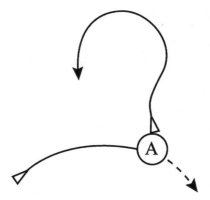

Figure 15.1: The interrogative hook

shapes him – that is, within this already structured world? He must orient himself therein, locate himself therein. The Other's demand having necessarily fragmented and fractured him, if he is to be able to locate himself, he must go through a fundamental stage in which what becomes *his* discourse is taken beyond the Other. It is there that the subject questions himself about what is known as his "will,"* his own will – namely, about what is the most problematic for him, as we analysts know – that is, what he truly desires. The subject must go beyond the necessities of demand inasmuch as he seeks to find anew [*retrouver*] his desire in its ingenuous nature.

How can desire be refound? This is a problem we always have to deal with. In other words, what happens beyond the Other, at the upper level of the graph?

We find there the interrogative hook that I have drawn here,

336

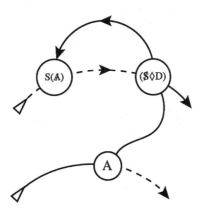

Figure 15.2: The unconscious signifying chain

whose uninterrupted line represents the subject's questioning about what he wants, but that is not all we find there. Psychoanalysis tells us that we also find what allows the subject to orient himself there [*s'y retrouver*] – namely, a signifying chain that I draw with a dotted line. It is homologous to the signifying chain at the lower level, but here it is strictly speaking called the unconscious, and it provides the signifying basis by which the subject can get his bearings there.

On the right, you see ($\lozenge$D), which is the subject's relation to his own demand. Indeed, a register is established here, thanks to which the subject can perceive not, as people say, that his demand is oral, anal, or this or that, but that, qua subject, he has a special relationship with capital D – in other words, with a certain form of demand. And this is why I inscribed this abbreviation on the upper level in the place where the code is found [on the lower level, namely: A].

The hooked line that goes beyond the Other, the one that represents the subject's questioning, is drawn here with an uninterrupted line. Why? Because it is conscious. In effect, before there were psychoanalysts, human beings asked themselves the question – and constantly asked themselves the question, believe you me, as they still do in our time, and as they have done since Freud's time – where their true will lies. This line thus belongs to the personality system as

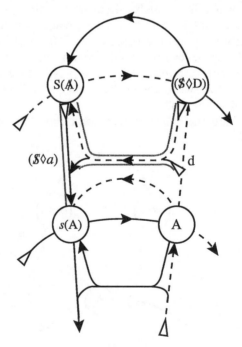

Figure 15.3: The line of desire

such. Call it conscious or preconscious – for the time being I will not
go into any further details about it.

But what does the graph tell us about desire? Desire is an x, and
that x is situated somewhere on the line that returns from the unconscious code [$D] – in the opposite direction from the intentional
line which is across from it – namely, the return segment: ($D)→d.
Desire [d] is there, floating somewhere in what lies beyond the Other
[A].

Yet we also know that desire is subjected to a certain regulation.
The latter is represented for us here by the height at which it is fixated
[*hauteur de fixation*], as it were, at the level of a determinate point of
the line which, returning from the unconscious message, S(A), goes
in the direction of s(A), the Other's message at the imaginary level.
This line stops midway at ($a), for it is fantasy that regulates the
height at which desire is fixated and determines its location.

You will note in passing that the relationship between desire and
fantasy is homologous to the relationship between the ego [*m* for
moi] and the image of the other [*i(a)*; see Figure 1.4].

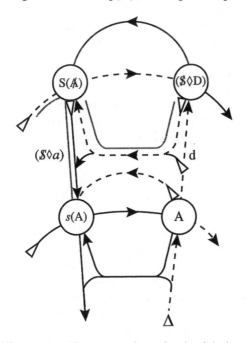

Figure 15.4: The unconscious circuit of desire

Let us now follow the whole of the circuit indicated by the dotted
line, that is, the unconscious circuit.

It begins on the right, at the extremity of the unconscious vector, provisionally denoted Δ. It rises to the level of the message, S(A), continues over to the code ($◊D), drops back down to the level of desire, d, and from there heads toward fantasy ($◊a). This is the circuit of the formation of desire at the level of the unconscious, and these are the stages it goes through and the directions in which it goes through them. If you are attentive to the way the graph is constructed, you will notice that the line d→($◊a) is a return pathway with respect to the unconscious, but that it itself has no return path toward the unconscious.

Now this circuit is going to help us follow the very movement of Hamlet's desire, assuming we stick to the scene in the closet in which the son confronts his mother.

What can we say about this, if not, in the first place, that there is no moment at which the formulation "man's desire is the Other's desire" is more tangible or manifest, no moment at which it is more completely realized, no way in which it could more thoroughly cancel out the subject?

In other words, the subject does not address the Other with his own will, but rather with a will of which he is at that moment the medium and representative – namely, his father's will, as well as the will of the social order, and of modesty and decency, too. I am not giving all of these terms to make things sound sophisticated, for I have already discussed the demon of shame [*Écrits*, p. 584 n] and you will see the role it plays in what follows. At the first stage, the subject articulates a discourse to his mother that goes beyond her qua Other, but only to back down and return to the strict level of the Other before whom he can but bow.

The movement of this scene can be depicted more or less as follows.

The subject's plea goes beyond the Other, trying to join up with the level of the code or law ($◊D), and then drops backs down. Except that the subject's drop does not stop at the level of the line d→($◊a), where he would meet up with his own desire, for he no longer has any desire – Ophelia has been rejected, and we shall see next time what role she plays here. Schematically put, let us say that it is as if the subject, in dropping back down along the return pathway, returned purely and simply to the Other's message – as if he could receive no other message from the Other's articulation than the Other's signified, s(A) – namely, his mother's response.

And what is this message? 'I am what I am. In my case there's nothing to be done, I'm a true genital personality' – I'm referring here to the way in which this term is used in volume 1 of *La Psychanalyse d'aujourd'hui* – 'I know nothing of mourning.' "The funeral baked meats / Did coldly furnish forth the marriage tables"

339

[I, ii, 180–1]. "Thrift, thrift!" is Hamlet's comment on this. She is simply a gaping cunt. When one leaves, another enters. That is what is being said here.

If *Hamlet* is the drama of desire, what is the drama of desire? We have seen it throughout this scene, it is the drama that there may be a worthy object and an unworthy object. 'Madam, I beg you to show some propriety here. There is a huge difference between that god and this piece of garbage!' That is what is involved here.

It is quite odd that we use a word like "object" all the time, but that the first time we encounter it [in the play] we do not recognize it, even though there is talk of nothing else from one end of *Hamlet* to the other. No one has ever discussed "object relations" regarding Hamlet. People remain confused about this and yet it is the only thing that is at stake. The discourse I alluded to earlier concerning the true genital personality, whether female or male, is a coherent discourse, for it tells us that one of the characteristics of the true genital personality is that it mourns only lightly. This can be found in the first volume of *La Psychanalyse d'aujourd'hui.* It is a marvelous commentary on the dialectic of *Hamlet.*

340

Now, we cannot but be struck by the fact that it is by means of mourning that we see the object come into view. I will go a bit quickly here because I must give you a glimpse of the horizons I am heading toward; but we can already say that *Hamlet* will perhaps allow us to add something to what Freud provides in *Trauer und Melancholie* ["Mourning and Melancholia"]. Freud tells us there that when mourning takes place, it is owing to introjection of the lost object. But in order for it to be introjected, there is perhaps a prior condition – namely, that it be constituted as an object. And its constitution as an object is perhaps not purely and simply related to the co-instinctual stages that are usually mentioned.

Something else already gives us an indication that, with the question of mourning and the object, we have arrived at the heart of the problem. This is where I ended last time, and our next few classes will follow up on this. It is the key point, the decisive point starting from which Hamlet takes the bit between his teeth, as it were.

For, as has been clearly noted, after having long dallied, Hamlet has a sudden burst of energy. He dives headfirst into an improbable situation that presents itself.

He must kill his stepfather. He is asked to win a sort of wager for this stepfather. The wager consists in fencing with someone about whom the least one can say is that, given the moment in time at which this is occurring, he knows this man is not favorably disposed toward him. For it is neither more nor less than the brother of the unhappy Ophelia, who has just put an end to her life, and she has done so owing to problems in which Hamlet played an important part. Hamlet knows, in any case, that this man holds it against him. Hamlet likes this man a lot, as he tells him, and nevertheless it is with him that he is going to cross swords to win a bet for the very person whom he must, in theory, slaughter.

341   He suddenly proves to be a true, absolutely unprecedented killer, and does not allow Laertes to hit him even once [at first]. It is quite clear that we have here a headlong rush forward on Hamlet's part. What is the decisive point that leads Hamlet to take the bit between his teeth?

It is the point on which I ended last time, with my little map of the graveyard and of the two guys grappling with each other at the bottom of the grave, which is an odd scene, all the same, and truly Shakespearean, for there is no trace of it in the earlier versions of *Hamlet*.

What happens? Why did Hamlet decide to jump in? Because he could not bear to see someone other than himself showing everyone what? Overflowing grief.

I would have to support what I am telling you here with a reading of *Hamlet*, but it would take me too long to do so. There is not a single word I am using here that is not based on something found in the text. Hamlet says it himself: 'I couldn't bear for Laertes to make such a big deal of or place such emphasis* on his mourning' [see V, i, 264–71]. He explains this afterward in order to excuse himself for having been so violent: the ostentatious display of the other's pain,

> The bravery of his grief did put me
> Into a tow'ring passion [V, ii, 78–9].

Hamlet sees Laertes jump into the grave in order to embrace his sister, and he jumps in after him to do the same. I must say that we might well form curious ideas about what must be happening in the grave, and I suggested this to you last time with my little imaginary painting. Stated otherwise, Hamlet proceeds by the pathway of mourning, but it is a type of mourning that is adopted in the narcissistic relationship that obtains between *m*, the ego, and the image of the other, *i(a)*.

The backdrop is this scene in which Hamlet suddenly sees the passionate relationship of a subject with an object, this relationship being manifested by someone else [Laertes]. This scene grabs him and offers him a prop by which his own relationship as a subject, $, with Ophelia – little object *a*, which had been rejected owing to the confusion or compounding of objects – is suddenly re-established.

And it is this suddenly re-established level that is momentarily going to make a man of him. It is, in other words, going to make him into someone capable – for only a brief moment, no doubt, but a moment that suffices for the play to end – of fighting and killing.

I am not, of course, saying that Shakespeare said all of these pretty things to himself. The fact remains that he included, in the play's articulation, an odd character like Laertes in order to have him serve – at the crucial moment of the play, at its climax – the role of an example and prop. Hamlet furiously wrestles him to the ground, and gets him into a hold from which he literally leaves other than before, with the cry I mentioned last time: "This is I, Hamlet the Dane" [V, i, 245].

I will invite you to read the commentaries that have been written about this cry, as they corroborate what I am telling you – namely, that this is the moment at which something happens that allows Hamlet to take hold of his desire anew. This proves to you that we are clearly at the heart of the economy of what is involved.

Of course, this almost has but a limited interest, after all, which is that of showing us on which point all the avenues of the play's articulation converge. Our interest is constantly focused on these avenues, and it is owing to the meanders of the action that we participate in the drama. The interest of getting to the graveyard scene has to do with the fact that prior to it there were four acts in which other things happened, things that we are now going to re-examine by reversing course.

In the foreground, there is the role of the play scene. What is this performance [représentation]? What does it mean? Why did Shakespeare find it to be indispensable? It has more than one motive, more than one raison d'être, but we will try to see its most profound raison d'être.

I believe that I have adequately indicated to you today why we are studying Hamlet, and sketched out what it means to us. The stakes for us are psychoanalytic experience and the articulation of its structure. Once we have completed this study, what will we be able to keep that will be useful and schematic to us in mapping desire?

I will tell you. I will show you what Hamlet's desire is. It is the neurotic's desire at every moment of its impact [incidence].

People have said that Hamlet's desire is an hysteric's desire. This is perhaps quite true. Other people have said that it is an obsessive's desire. That, too, might be argued, for it is a fact that he is full of psychasthenic symptoms, even severe ones. But that is not the point. In truth, Hamlet is both. He is purely and simply the place of desire. Hamlet is not a clinical case. Hamlet, of course – this is all too obvious, and there is no need to recall it to mind – is not a real being. Hamlet is, if you will, a sort of hub where a desire is situated, and we can find all the features of desire in him.

We can interpret and orient his desire in the same way as we work with an hysteric's desire in a dream – namely, his desire is there unbeknownst to the subject, and he is thus forced to construct it. It is in this respect that I will say that Hamlet's problem is closer to the hysteric's desire, for his problem is to find anew the place of his desire. Moreover, what Hamlet does closely resembles what an hysteric is capable of doing – in other words, creating an unsatisfied desire for himself.

But it is equally true that Hamlet's is an obsessive desire, inasmuch as he attempts to prop himself up on the basis of an impossible desire. This is not quite the same thing.

Both are true. You will see that we will go as much in one direction as in the other when we interpret Hamlet's remarks and actions. What you must manage to grasp is something that is more radical than this or that type of person's desire, than the desire with which you pinpoint hysterics versus obsessives.

When our colleague N* mentions the hysteric's character, it is in order to say that everyone knows that an hysteric is incapable of loving. When I read things like that, I always want to ask the author, "And what about you? Are you capable of loving?" He says that hysterics are detached from reality – what about him?

Doctors always talk as if they themselves were perfectly well ensconced in their boots, the boots of love, desire, will, and all that follows therefrom. Yet this is a very odd position, and we should have long since realized that it is a dangerous position. It is the kind of position that makes people adopt countertransferential stances owing to which they understand nothing about the patients with whom they work.

This is the realm in which we operate, which is why it is essential to articulate where desire is situated.

March 18, 1959

XVI

THERE IS NO OTHER OF
THE OTHER

A father who knew the truth
The meaning of the symbol S(Ⱥ)
The big secret of psychoanalysis
The object, a cursor of the level of desire
The "fading"* of the subject

'Give me my desire!' This is the meaning I told you *Hamlet* has for all those – whether critics, actors, or spectators – who take it up.

This is so, as I also said, because of the exceptional and brilliant structural rigor the Hamlet theme reaches in this play, after an obscure development that began in the twelfth and thirteenth centuries with Saxo Grammaticus, continued on in the novelistic version by Belleforest, and then, no doubt, in a sketch by Kyd. There was another sketch by Shakespeare himself, it seems, before it arrived at the form in which we have it today.

This form is characterized, in my view, using the method we employ here, by something that I call structure.

I am trying to give you a key to this structure that allows you to orient yourselves with complete confidence – namely, the topological shape that I call the graph and that we might call a gramma [or: writing, letter, or element with which terms are formed, *gramme*].

1

Let us return to our *Hamlet*.

Given that I have been speaking to you about the play for three classes already, I imagine you have all read it at least once. Let me try to summarize its movement, which is simple and yet profoundly marked by the detours that have allowed for so many different interpretations.

346   If it can be simultaneously so simple and yet endless, it is not very
difficult to know why: *the tragedy of Hamlet is the encounter with
death.*

Others, to whom I alluded in our preceding classes, have emphasized the first scene, which so prodigiously foreshadows what is to
come. It takes place on the platform of Elsinore Castle. The ghost
that the sentinels have already seen twice, returns in its hellish form
[*forme d'En-bas*], and no one yet knows, at this point in time, what
this form is, what it is bringing with it, or what it means.

On this point, I mentioned a comment by Coleridge. I am mentioning him again today because I perhaps gave you the impression
two classes back that I was criticizing him. In telling you that he did
no better than to see himself in Hamlet, the character, I seemed to be
minimizing the import of his commentary, whereas he was the first
to have sounded the depths of *Hamlet* – and of many other things as
well. He underscores in his notes on the play, which are so fine – and
easily accessible, as they are included in his *Lectures on Shakespeare*
– that owing to Shakespeare's art, even Hume, who was otherwise
so opposed to ghosts, "could not but have had faith in this Ghost
dramatically," says Coleridge, "let his anti-ghostism have been as
strong as Sampson against other ghosts less powerfully raised."

Here Sampson lies prostrate [*terrassé*], and this is indubitably
because Shakespeare came very close to something that was not a
"ghost"* but rather an actual encounter, not with a dead man [*le
mort*], but with death itself [*la mort*]. The encounter with death is,
in short, at the crux of the play. *Hamlet's venturing out to meet with
death* is the point from which we must set out in order to conceptualize what we are promised from the very first time the ghost appears,
at the precise moment at which the clock strikes one o'clock, "The
bell then beating one" [I, i, 39].

We find this "one"* again at the end of the play. It is the moment
at which, after many detours, Hamlet finds himself on the verge of
taking the action that will simultaneously seal his fate. Advancing
almost with his eyes closed toward the man he must kill, he ends up
telling Horatio – and this is not at just any old moment – that "a
man's life's no more than to say 'one'" [V, ii, 74].

Obviously, in order to approach this moment, he takes side
streets; he takes the long way around [*l'école buissonnière*], as they
347   say. This exact expression can be found in the text. I am borrowing
it from Horatio, a paragon of modesty and kindness, at the moment
at which he comes to assist Hamlet. He says at that point that he has
"a truant disposition," which means that he moseys along [I, ii, 168].
No one says that about Hamlet, yet that is what has always struck

critics. Why doesn't Hamlet go straight for it? Instead, he tarries. In short, what we are trying to fathom here is why he does so.

Don't think that, on this point, we are taking the long way around or a side street. The route we are following is no doubt different from that followed by the critics who have preceded us, but it differs from theirs only in the following respect, that it situates the question in a slightly different place. What they have said does not lose its import for all that. The proof thereof is that what they sensed was immediately foregrounded by Freud.

What are we told first? We are told that the action in question, the action of putting someone to death – an action that is so pressing and that in the final analysis takes such a short time to execute, we not knowing why it takes the hero so long – encounters an obstacle in Hamlet, that of desire.

This discovery is both a reason and a paradox. For, as I showed you, Hamlet's enigma remains unsolved, and we are forced to contemplate the following: the desire in question, since it is the desire discovered by Freud – that is, desire for the mother, desire insofar as it incites rivalry with he who possesses her – this desire should, good Lord, go in the same direction as the action. What, then, can it mean if desire serves to obstruct action here?

Let us begin to decipher it. This will lead us, in the end, to the mythical function of Hamlet that makes him Oedipus' equal.

Claudius must be killed. He must be murdered by Hamlet – indeed, Hamlet wants to commit the murder – and it will be a just murder. As opposed to what certain authors have suggested, as I told you, Hamlet is not conflicted over rights or orders – that is, the grounds for the serving of justice. There is no ambiguity in his mind between public order, the execution of the law, and private tasks. He has no doubt but that this murder is exactly what the law commands. But what we immediately see when we read the text is *the close link between this murder*, whose necessity he does call into question, *and his own death*.

This murder is not committed until Hamlet has already been given a fatal blow, in the short space of time remaining to him between the deathblow and the moment at which he will be no more. We must take this rendezvous with death, to which we can give its full meaning, as our point of departure.

This last of all rendezvous, onto which Hamlet's action is projected and by which he orients himself at the end, has no meaning except in relation to the subject as we attempt to define and articulate him here: a subject that has not yet come to light because his advent was delayed by strictly philosophical articulations; the subject as Freud tells us he is constructed; a subject who is distinguished from

348

the subject Western philosophy has been talking about since there
has been a theory of knowledge; a subject who is in no wise the universal prop of objects, but who is in some sense the negative of that
subject and his ubiquitous prop; a subject insofar as he speaks, and
insofar as he is structured in a complex relationship with the signifier, the very relationship we are trying to formulate here with the
help of the graph.

To trace it out once again, the intersection of demand's intention
and the signifying chain occurs for the first time at point A, which
we have defined as the Other with a capital *O*, qua locus of truth.

This is the locus in which speech is situated. Taking up its place
there, speech establishes the order of truth, an order that is evoked
and invoked whenever the subject articulates something, whenever
he speaks. Indeed, speech does something that is different from all
the immanent forms of captivation of one [person] with respect to
another, since it establishes a third element – namely, the locus of
the Other in which speech is inscribed as truth even when it lies.
Nothing in the imaginary register can be equated with that.

This discourse for the Other, or reference to the Other, extends
beyond the Other, inasmuch as it is taken up by the subject on the
basis of the Other in order to constitute the question, "What do I
want?" Better stated, the question is addressed to the subject here,
and in an already inverted form: "What do *you* want?"

Beyond alienated demand – in the system of discourse that is
located at A, residing in the locus of the Other – the subject, pro-
pelling himself, wonders what he is as a subject. What must he
encounter beyond the locus of truth? Beyond the locus of truth, he
must encounter what the very genius, not of language, but of the
extreme metaphor that tends to be formulated when we are faced
with certain significant spectacles, calls by a name that we will recognize here in passing: the *moment* [literally: hour, *heure*] of truth.

In an era in which all of philosophy has taken the path of articulating what links time [*temps*] with being, let us not forget that past,
present, and future, the constitutive times [or: tenses, *temps*] of temporality, are those of grammar. The notion that time is mapped only
with respect to the act of speaking is quite elementary. The present
is the moment at which I am speaking, and nothing else. It is strictly
impossible for us to conceptualize a temporality in the animal
dimension – in other words, in the dimension of appetite. Even the
ABCs of temporality require the structure of language.

In going beyond the Other – in this discourse which is no longer
a discourse for the Other, but the Other's discourse, strictly speaking, in which the dotted [or: discontinuous or broken, *brisée*] line
of unconscious signifiers is constituted, in this Other in which the

349

subject advances owing to his question – what the subject aims at
is, in the final analysis, the moment [*heure*] of the encounter with
himself, with his will, with something that we are going to try to
formulate. We cannot immediately enumerate its elements, even if
certain signs here nevertheless represent them for us, signs that serve
us as a map or prefiguration of the tiering [or: layering or different
levels, *étagement*] of what awaits us in what one might call the stages
or necessary steps of the question.

Let us nevertheless note what Hamlet demonstrates to us on this
score.

Hamlet, as I told you, is not this or that, is neither an obsessive
nor an hysteric. Why? Because he is first and foremost a poetic creation. Hamlet does not have a neurosis; he demonstrates neurosis to
us, which is something altogether different than to be neurotic.
Nevertheless, when we look at Hamlet in a certain mirrored
lighting, specific sentences make him appear to have something
bordering on obsessive structure. This has to do with the element
that reveals structure in the obsessive, the element that is highlighted
maximally by obsessive neurosis – namely, that the major function
of desire consists here in keeping at bay and awaiting the hour of the
desired encounter.

Here I am using a term that Freud provides us in *Inhibitions,*   350
Symptoms and Anxiety – namely, *Erwartung*, which he explicitly
distinguishes from *abwarten*, meaning to brace oneself [*tendre le
dos*]. *Erwartung* means to await (or expect) it, in the active sense,
and also to make it wait. Playing a game with respect to the moment
of the encounter essentially dominates the obsessive's relation to his
desire. Hamlet certainly shows us a whole dialectic, a whole range
of other ways of playing with the object as well, but this is the most
obvious one; it is the one that appears on the surface, strikes us,
provides the style of the play, and has always constituted its enigma.

Let us now try to discern the coordinates that the play gives us in
other elements.

What, in short, distinguishes Hamlet's position from that of
Oedipus? What makes it such a striking variation on the latter?
Oedipus did not beat around the bush like Hamlet did, as Freud
nicely remarks in his explanatory footnote.

When people throw in the towel, they resort to the following sort
of rot: "Good Lord, everything is going to pot, we modern folk are in
a period of decadence, we go back and forth 600 times before doing
what other people – the good, courageous, people of yore – did right
off the bat." This is not an explanation, and we should be suspicious
of any reference to the idea of decadence. If it is true that our contemporaries have arrived at such a pass, we must, at least if we are

psychoanalysts, consider that it is for some other reason than the supposed fact that their nerves are not as solid as their fathers' were.

We can examine what is involved from other angles. I believe we must situate the question elsewhere. I have already drawn your attention to an essential element that is constitutive of the structure of the Oedipus myth: Oedipus did not have to go back and forth dozens of times before taking action; he did so even before thinking about it and without even knowing he was doing it.

Recall now what I began our Seminar with this year. From what angle did I present the gramma to you as the key to the problem posed by desire? It is no accident that I chose a very simple dream from "Formulations on the Two Principles of Mental Functioning," the one in which the dead father appears. Recall that I wrote on the upper line [of the graph], the line of enunciation in the dream, "he did not know." This is where I situate the blissful ignorance of those who are submerged in the necessary drama that follows from the fact that the subject who speaks is subjected to the signifier. Let me note in passing that no one explains why this is so.

For if the father, who had fallen asleep in the garden, was laid low by having this delicate juice, hebenon, poured into his ear (*oneille*, as Jarry writes it, instead of *oreille*), he should not have been aware of it. We are never told that he woke up from his sleep to observe what was happening, and the scurf patches that covered his body were never seen by any but those who discovered his corpse. We must then assume that people in the hereafter are very well informed about how they got there. Although this might, in theory, be possible, it is nevertheless not something that we must immediately consider to be true. I am saying all of this to underscore the arbitrary nature of the father's initial revelation, the revelation that gives the entire plot of *Hamlet* its impetus.

The fact that the father reveals the truth about his death is an essential coordinate in *Hamlet*, which distinguishes the play from what occurs in the myth of Oedipus. A veil is lifted, the one that weighs on the articulation of the unconscious line. This is the veil that we analysts try to lift in our clinical practice and, as you know, we certainly have our work cut out for us.

Analysts' interventions aim to re-establish the coherence of the signifying chain at the level of the unconscious. If these interventions present so many difficulties and are met with so much opposition on the subject's part – so many refusals, everything we refer to as "resistance," which is the pivotal point of the whole history of psychoanalysis – we can but assume that this veil must serve an essential function in preserving the safety, I would say, of the subject insofar as he speaks.

351

In *Hamlet*, the question is resolved – the father knew. And because he knew, Hamlet also knows. In other words, he has the answer. He has the answer, and there can be only one answer.

This answer cannot necessarily be formulated in psychological terms. I mean, it is not an answer that is necessarily comprehensible, and still less one that hits you in the gut. But it is a fatal type of answer, all the same.

Let us try to see what this answer is.

2

I already symbolized this answer for you because I was forced to, owing to which I asked you to lend me credence. It is, in short, the message [S(A̶)] at the point at which it is constituted on the upper line, that of the unconscious.

But it is easier and more honest to ask someone to lend you credence regarding something which at the outset has no meaning whatsoever, for that does not tie your hands in any way, except that it perhaps requires you to seek out this meaning, which nevertheless leaves you free to create it by yourself.

I began to articulate this answer in the following form. First of all, we have capital S, which stands for "signifier." This already distinguishes the answer at the level of the upper line from the answer at the level of the lower line, which is written with a lowercase *s*, standing for "signified."

In effect, at the level of simple discourse, the meaning of what we meant is shaped by the speech that unfolds at the level of the Other. The answer is thus always, with respect to this speech, the Other's signified, *s*(A̶). But there is something beyond simple discourse where the subject asks himself the question, "Who is speaking?" "Who meant this or that at the level of the Other?" "What have I, in the final analysis, become in all of that?" At this level, the answer is, as I told you, the signifier of the Other with a bar through it: S(A̶).

There are a thousand ways to begin to discuss what this symbol includes, but since we are talking about *Hamlet*, we will choose the clear, obvious, emotional, and dramatic pathway today. It is furnished to us by *Hamlet*, and the value of the play is that it allows us to accede to the meaning of S(A̶).

The meaning of what Hamlet learns from his father is right in front of our noses and very clear indeed. It is the irremediable, absolute, unfathomable betrayal of love – of the purest love, the love this king had. Like all men, this king may, of course, have been a serious rascal, but with his wife, in any case, he went so far as to shield her face from "the winds of heaven" [I, ii, 141] – at least if we are to take Hamlet's word for it. The meaning of what Hamlet learns from his father is the absolute duplicity of what had seemed to Hamlet to be the very epitome and essence of beauty and truth.

The answer lies there. Hamlet's truth is a hopeless truth. There is no trace in the whole play of an ascension toward something that might lie beyond this, some sort of redemption. We are told that the first encounter [was with what] came from hell. *Hamlet* is, in effect, situated in the infernal relationship to the Acheron, which Freud chose to move, since he was unable to bend the higher powers to his will.

Nothing is more clear, simple, or obvious, and it is nevertheless quite curious to see that certain writers barely highlight this regarding *Hamlet*, out of some sort of sense of propriety – one must not alarm sensitive souls, no doubt.

But however painful this answer may be, I am only giving it to you as a single step forward in the realm of what is sensed or felt. For any conclusion or verdict, as radically as it may take on the guise of what is known as pessimism, is nevertheless designed to cast a veil over what is at stake.

We must be able to formulate this answer in a way that homes in more closely on what led me to choose this abbreviation, S(Ⱥ). This abbreviation does not imply that whatever happens at the level of A is of no value whatsoever – otherwise stated, that all truth is fallacious. This is the kind of comment that can make people laugh in those amusing postwar periods, when people come up, for example, with things like the philosophy of the absurd, which is appreciated above all in underground nightclubs [*caves*]. Let us try to articulate something more serious, or lighter in tone.

I believe that the moment has come to deliver up to you what, in essence, this abbreviation means, even though you are likely to think I am coming at it from a rather peculiar angle. Still, I do not believe it to be a contingent one.

Barred A means the following. At A – which is not a being, but rather the locus of speech, the locus where the whole system of signifiers, that is, a whole language, resides in a developed or enveloped form – something is missing. What is missing can only be a signifier, hence the S. The formulation that gives S(Ⱥ) its most radical value is as follows: the signifier that is missing at the level of the Other.

This is the big secret of psychoanalysis, if I may say so myself. The big secret is that there is no Other of the Other.

Indeed, psychoanalytic experience reveals to us that the subject who speaks is necessarily structured in a way that distinguishes him from the perennial subject, even if the latter has been revamped in

353

354

the course of developments in philosophy in a sense that might well strike us, after all – from a certain perspective, looking at things retrospectively – as delusional. It may be a "fecund delusion," but that does not stop it from being delusional. In traditional philosophy, the subject subjectifies himself indefinitely. If I am because I think, I am because I think that I am, and so on and so forth – there is no reason for that to ever stop. People have long since perceived that it is not so clear that I am because I think, and that we can only be sure of one thing, which is that I am because I think that I am. That is surely true. Yet, what psychoanalysis teaches us is something else altogether. It is that I am precisely *not* the one who is in the process of thinking that I am, for the simple reason that, owing to the fact that I think that I am, I am thinking in the locus of the Other. The upshot being that I am something other than he who thinks "I am."

Now, the problem is that I have absolutely no guarantee that this Other, owing to what he has in his system, can give me back, if I may express myself thus, what I gave him – namely, his being and his essence as truth. As I told you, there is no Other of the Other. There is no signifier in the Other that can, in this case, answer for [*répondre de*] what I am. And to state things differently, the hopeless truth I mentioned earlier, the one we encounter at the level of the unconscious, is a faceless, closed truth, a truth that can be bent in any direction one likes. As we know only too well, it is truth without truth.

This is what constitutes the biggest obstacle to those who try to broach our work from the outside – that is, from other fields. As they do not participate with us in *work in which interpretations are designed to have an effect*, which can only be conceptualized as metaphorical, and inasmuch as our interpretations always play and resonate between the two lines of the graph, they cannot understand what is involved in psychoanalytic interpretation.

If we can speak of a signifier that the Other does not have at its disposal, it is because this signifier is nevertheless somewhere. With this little gramma, I am telling you where it is so that you do not lose your bearings. If I have done so as carefully as I could, it was   355 certainly not in order to make things more confusing for you.

You can recognize the signifier of the barred Other wherever you find the bar on the Other. The hidden signifier, the one that is not at the Other's disposal, is precisely the one that concerns us. It is the very signifier that we bring into play, insofar as we mere simpletons have been caught up in this damned thing known as *logos* ever since we were born. It is the part of us that is sacrificed therein.

It is not purely and simply sacrificed, physically sacrificed, as they

say, or really sacrificed, but symbolically sacrificed. Now this part
of you that has taken on a signifying function is not nothing. Which
is why there is only one and not dozens of them. We are talking
very precisely here about the enigmatic function of what we call the
phallus.

The phallus is something that is sacrificed from the organism,
from life, from the vital pressure [*poussée vitale*], and that ends up
symbolized. "Vital pressure" is, as you know, an expression that I
do not believe we should use in just any old which way, but which
– once clearly delineated and symbolized, and put in its place,
especially where it serves a function, where it is in fact caught up,
namely in the unconscious – takes on meaning. Vital turgidity – this
enigmatic, universal thing that is more male than female, but which
the female can nevertheless become a symbol of – is what is involved
in the phallus. Although it is the very symbol of the life that the
subject makes signifying, the phallus is not available in the Other
and cannot in any way guarantee the signification of the Other's
discourse. In other words, regardless of how much he may have
sacrificed his life, it is not given back to him by the Other. The Other
replies: S(Ⱥ).

Hamlet's point of departure is the answer given by the Other, and
it is because he has received a radical revelation [from the ghost]
that he is led to follow the whole trajectory that the play traces out,
which leads him to his rendezvous with fate.

In order to reach it with him, we are now going to return to what
happens in the play.

3

Without returning for the time being to the questions I mentioned
last time that are raised by the play scene, the scene in which we
see the traveling actors, today I would like to bring up an essential
element.

It concerns what we are approaching, after having established the
function of the two lines of the graph – namely, what lies in the gap
between them. The distance the subject can maintain between the
two lines is where he breathes freely, as it were, as long as he lives,
and this is what we call desire.

Now I have already told you what pressure, abolition, and
destruction this desire undergoes because it meets up with [*se ren-
contre avec*] a certain something from the real Other – the mother
as she is, this mother like so many others – who is less desire than
gluttony and even engulfment, albeit structured.

Well, this something was obviously, for Shakespeare – at this point in his life, we do not know why, but after all, what difference does it make? – a revelation. The problem posed by women was certainly always present in Shakespeare's work, and there had been man-eaters [*luronnes*] before *Hamlet*, but there were never any as abyssal, ferocious, or sad before *Hamlet*.

See *Troilus and Cressida*, for example. The play was performed the year after *Hamlet*, and perhaps allows us to go more deeply into what Shakespeare thought about women at that time. It is a true marvel, one of the most sublime creations, I believe, one can find in the whole of dramatic literature, and its value has certainly not been fully appreciated.

What is the climax of the play in *Hamlet*? It is undoubtedly the dialogue between Hamlet and his mother, the main lines of which I discussed last time. He implores his mother in more or less the following terms: 'Don't destroy beauty, the world order, don't confuse Hyperion himself' – it is his father whom he designates thusly – 'with the most abject of beings.' And then we see him back down, give up his plea before what he knows to be the fatal necessity of a sort of desire that brooks nothing and withholds nothing.

There are myriad passages I could cite to illustrate Shakespeare's thinking about women. I will confine myself to one that I came across while on vacation, in an entirely different context. It is from *Twelfth Night*.

357

It concerns someone – The Duke, as they call him – who is quite in love, but who is also, it must be said, rather nutty, even if he is a good man. In order to win his heart, a girl who loves him approaches him – even though nothing in his behavior calls his interest in women into question, since he is in love with a woman – disguised as a boy, which is, all the same, an odd way to get oneself appreciated as a girl. I am not giving you these details at random, but because of what they contribute to the creation of a character whom I am going to introduce to you, Ophelia.

This disguised girl, Viola, is a creation that predates Ophelia. *Twelfth Night* precedes the writing of *Hamlet* by about two years. We have here an example of the way in which the women Shakespeare created come in succession and are transformed, their truly immortally poetic nature manifesting a whole facet of his genius. They are, as you know, among the most fascinating, attractive, captivating, and simultaneously equivocal women in literature. The boy-girl or girl-boy is quite a typical creation here, and a feature appears in it that is going to introduce us to our topic today, introduce us to the next step we are going to take – namely, the role of the object in desire.

After having taken this opportunity to contextualize for you our question about Ophelia, let me return to *Twelfth Night*.

Consider what Duke Orsino – without knowing that the person before him is a girl, much less that she loves him – replies to her fallacious questions. He is in deep despair, and the girl says to him, "How can you complain?"

> Say that some lady, as perhaps there is,
> Hath for your love as great a pang of heart
> As you have for Olivia. You cannot love her. [II, iv, 88–90]

This is, indeed, the case; this is what he suffers from.

> You tell her so. Must she not then be answered? [II, iv, 91]

'You must not, thus, hold against others what you yourself would certainly do.' The Duke, who is blind and stuck in the enigma, addresses a whole speech to her about the difference between woman's desire and man's desire:

> There is no woman's sides
> Can bide the beating of so strong a passion
> As love doth give my heart; no woman's heart
> So big to hold so much; they lack retention. [II, iv, 92–5]

And everything he goes on to say shows desire to be, in essence, the distance found in the specific relationship the subject as barred has with the object expressed in the symbol little a – in other words, in the relationship ($\$ \lozenge a$), which I place on the graph on the line that returns from the x of unconscious will, and which is, as it were, the cursor of the level at which desire in the subject, strictly speaking, is situated.

I would like now to introduce Ophelia as a character by taking advantage of what philological, textual research has contributed about her antecedents, so to speak. As the play we are studying was written by Shakespeare, we should pay attention to how he transformed the open weave canvas [or: framework, *canevas*] he received from his predecessors. This canvas had already evolved quite a bit, but we are led to believe that it offered still more, and this was undoubtedly enough for it to be accepted. Whatever the case may be, this evolution shows us quite a vista and the vast amount of ground that Shakespeare covered.

Some cretin whose work I read mentioned how happy he was the day he realized – something he should have long since noticed, but

358

that it took him forever to see – that there is someone who plays the role of Ophelia in Belleforest's tale. In Belleforest's text we are just as perplexed by what happens to Hamlet – namely, that he plainly seems to be crazy. We are not very reassured, for it is clear that this madman nevertheless knows rather well what he wants, and what he wants is what we do not know – it is many things. What he wants is a question for all the other characters.

He is sent a prostitute who, drawing him into the deepest depths of the woods, is supposed to get him to reveal his innermost thoughts while someone else eavesdrops, someone who will then know a bit more about what he wants. The strategy fails, as it should, thanks, I believe, to the girl's love for him. What is clear is that the cretin in question was thrilled to come across this sort of arche-Ophelia, believing that she accounted for the ambiguities in Ophelia's character.

I will obviously not examine with you all of Ophelia's lines here, but you are aware that this incredibly emotional, overwhelming character – whom we might call one of the great figures of humanity – is presented in an extremely ambiguous light. No one has ever yet been able to say if Ophelia is innocence itself that is speaking and that alludes to the most carnal impulses with the simplicity of purity that knows no shame, or whether she is, on the contrary, a slut who is ready for anything. Her lines are tantamount to smoke and mirrors, and they allow for every possible sort of interpretation. Above all, they exude a great deal of charm, something we sense quite palpably in the madness scene, for example.

In truth, it is surprising that our biases concerning the character, nature, signification, and, in a word, mores of women are still so deeply ingrained in us that people can continue to raise such questions about Ophelia. The thing is, in fact, altogether clear. If, on the one hand, Hamlet behaves toward Ophelia with quite exceptional cruelty – cruelty that troubles us, that smarts, as they say, and that gives us the impression that the young woman is a victim – we sense, on the other hand, that she is not, and far from it, the disembodied or disincarnate creature she was made out to be in the pre-Raphaelite painting I mentioned. She is something else altogether.

It seems that Ophelia is quite simply what every girl is, whether or not she has gone beyond the taboo against deflowering – after all, we know nothing about it, and the question seems not to be raised regarding Ophelia. What we want to know is why Shakespeare brought in this character who seems to represent a type of extreme point on a curved line running from his first heroines, who are boy-girls, to something that later returns to the same formula, but transformed, in another guise.

359

Ophelia seems to be Shakespeare's consummate female character, she being a bud about to blossom – a bud that is threatened by
an insect eating away at its heart – offering us a view of life that is
ready to blossom and of life that bears all lives within itself. This
is, moreover, how Hamlet qualifies her when he pushes her away:
you will be "a breeder of sinners" [III, i, 121–2]. In short, Ophelia
presents us with the image of someone who is bursting with life and
who, more than any other female character, I believe, illustrates for
us an equation I have highlighted in my classes, the equation girl =
phallus. This is something we can very easily recognize in her.

I will not dwell on things that seem to me to owe, in fact, but to an
odd coincidence. I was curious to see where the name Ophelia came
from, and I found references to it in an article in Boisacq's etymo-
logical dictionary of Greek. Shakespeare undoubtedly did not have
at his disposal the dictionaries we use today, but one occasionally
comes across, in writings of his time, alongside unbelievable ignorance, such stupefying and penetrating things that coincide with the
findings of the most modern criticism, that I can in this case bring
out something that is in notes I forgot to bring with me today.

It is in Homer's work, if I recall correctly, that we find *ophelio*,
meaning "to make swell or enlarge." The word is used for molting
or the fermentation of living things, more or less in the sense of
"allowing something to change" or "to thicken." The funniest thing
– I cannot help but mention it – is that in the same article, Boisacq,
who was an author who paid close attention to the way in which he
strung together his signifying chains, felt it necessary to explicitly
refer to the verbal form of the word: *ophallos*.

We don't need Boisacq's commentary to see the connection
between Ophelia and *phallos*. We see it in the structure. The point
is not to indicate now in what respect Ophelia can be the phallus;
since she truly *is* the phallus, as we say, it is worth examining how
Shakespeare has her fill this role.

What is important here is the fact that Shakespeare takes to a new
level what he finds in Belleforest's work. In the legend, as it is related
by Belleforest, the courtesan is the bait designed to rip Hamlet's
secret away from him – that is, the dark designs he is mulling over
– and the goal is to get him to confess them within earshot of those
around him who are not too sure how far he might go. Shakespeare
transposes this to the upper level where the true question resides:
Ophelia, too, is asked to investigate a secret, but, as I will show you
next time, it is the secret of desire.

The relations between Hamlet and Ophelia are punctuated in the
course of the play by a series of stages [*temps*] that we will examine,
for what is articulated there will allow us to grasp in an especially

lively way the relationship between the subject insofar as he speaks
– that is to say, insofar as he is subjected to his rendezvous with
fate – and the object. But this term must take on another meaning,
the meaning it has in psychoanalysis and owing to psychoanalysis.
It is no accident that the term "object" has become so prevalent and
that it is now so much more widespread and omnipresent than it was
in Freud's work, to the point that certain people talk about a shift
that has made it change meaning; for libido, which was previously
defined as pleasure-seeking, is now defined as object-seeking.

As I have told you, psychoanalysis has taken the wrong road. It
formulates and defines this object in a way that misses its goal, in a
way that does not undergird what is truly involved in the relationship with the object as such, such as it is inscribed in the formula
($\lozenge a$). The castrated subject, $, is subjected there to something that
I will teach you to decipher next time with the name I give it, "the
fading* of the subject," as opposed to the notion of the "splitting"*
of the object.

What is the object of desire? On a certain occasion, which was no
other, I think, than our second class this year, I quoted something
the author of which I hope someone here has since identified. She
said that what the miser misses when he loses his treasure would,
if we knew what it was, teach us a lot about human desire. It was
Simone Weil who said that.

This is what we are going to try to home in on as we examine
the thread that runs throughout the tragedy between Ophelia and
Hamlet.

April 8, 1959

XVII

OPHELIA, THE OBJECT

The paradoxes of fantasy
When fantasy emphasizes object (*a*)
. . . and when it emphasizes the barred subject
Hamlet is forever on other people's time
The pathology of fantasized vacillation

It was essentially in order to bait you that I announced that I would talk today about Ophelia as bait. But I suspect I will keep my word, for this object, topic, or character fits nicely into the series of remarks I have made at our last four meetings, which is designed to point out the tragedy of desire in *Hamlet*.

If this play can be characterized as the tragedy of desire, it is to the degree to which desire as such – human desire, the desire we deal with in psychoanalysis, the desire that we are in a position to inflect, depending on our aim with regard to it, but that we sometimes confuse with other things – can only be conceptualized and situated with respect to the fixed coordinates of subjectivity whose function Freud demonstrated.

These coordinates install the subject and the signifier at a certain distance from each other. They situate the subject as dependent on the signifier in a specific way. This means, for example, that we cannot account for psychoanalytic experience by basing it on the idea that the signifier is but a pure and simple reflection, product, or even instrument of what people sometimes call interpersonal relations. The signifier is, on the contrary, one of the essential, initial components of a topology without which all psychoanalytic phenomena would be reduced or flattened out, which would then render us unable to account for what one might call the presuppositions of our experience.

If, in following this path [regarding desire], I have selected *Hamlet* as an example, it is because it offers us a very lively dramatic sense of the coordinates of this topology. I attribute its exceptional power to captivate us to this. It is also what makes me say that, if critics have such a preference for this play and if it never fails to seduce those who go see it, this is because the poet has in some way incorporated insights from his own experience into it. Everything indicates this, in fact, at the sort of turning point that *Hamlet* represents in Shakespeare's opus. One can also say that his experience as a poet, in the technical sense of the term, little by little showed him the way forward here.

It is essential to grasp the import, in his creation, of certain twists and turns that I believe we can interpret with the help of the landmarks articulated in our gramma. A certain twist is employed differently in *Hamlet* than in the plays by Shakespeare that preceded it, than in the earlier tales by Saxo Grammaticus and Belleforest, and than in the plays of which we have but a few fragmentary details. The character involved in this twist is Ophelia, a character who is present in the story right from the beginning.

As I told you, Ophelia is a trap.

Right from the outset of the *Hamlet* legend, Saxo Grammaticus' Ophelia is a trap into which Hamlet does not fall, first of all because he is forewarned, and secondly because the bait itself – namely, the character – does not lend herself to it, even though she has been in love with Prince Hamlet for a long time, as Belleforest's text tells us.

Shakespeare did something completely different with Ophelia. Perhaps he merely deepened the role that the plot assigns to Ophelia in the legend, destined as she is to find out and appropriate Hamlet's secret. Nevertheless, in Shakespeare's *Hamlet*, she becomes one of Hamlet's innermost elements, Hamlet having lost the pathway of his desire.

Ophelia is an essential element in the progression that makes Hamlet move toward what, last time, I called the moment [*heure*] of his fatal rendezvous, his rendezvous with the action he carries out in spite of himself in some sense.

We are going to see still more clearly to what degree Hamlet is the image of the level of the subject at which his fate is articulated in terms of pure signifiers, one might say, the subject being in some sense but the flipside of a message that is not even his own.

365

1

The first step we took along this pathway was thus to articulate to what degree the play is the drama of desire insofar as desire is related to the Other's desire.

I showed you to what degree this play is dominated by the Other whose desire we are talking about here. She is unambiguously the mother – that is to say, the primordial subject to whom demands are addressed. This subject [the mother, not the child] is, as I showed you, the true all-powerful subject that we always talk about in psychoanalysis. Women are not in themselves omnipotent – they do not have within themselves the dimension of the so-called omnipotence of thought; what is at issue here is the presumed omnipotence of the subject to whom one's first demands are addressed; as I told you in our first discussions on the topic, omnipotence is always attributed [by the child] to that subject.

What we find at the level of the Other's desire primarily presents itself to Prince Hamlet – that is, to the main character – as a tragedy, as the drama of a subjectivity, Hamlet's, a subjectivity that is always present and, as we may say, far more than in any other drama. The drama always presents itself in a twofold manner, its elements being both inter- and intra-subjective.

Thus, from the subject's perspective, from that of Prince Hamlet, the Other's desire – that is, his mother's desire – essentially presents itself as a desire that cannot tell the difference between an eminent, idealized, and exalted object, Hamlet's father, and a disparaged object worthy only of scorn, Claudius, the criminal and adulterous brother. If the mother cannot distinguish between them, it is because of something in her that is akin to an instinctual voracity. Let us say that the sacrosanct "genital object" that we find in recent psychoanalytic terminology presents itself in her as no other than the object of a jouissance that is truly the direct satisfaction of a need.

This dimension is essential, and it forms one of the poles between which Hamlet's plea to his mother vacillates. I showed this to you in the scene in which, when face to face with her, Hamlet calls on her to become abstinent, in the crudest and cruelest terms, moreover, at the moment at which he communicates to her the essential message that the ghost, his father, charged him with transmitting. Suddenly this plea collapses, and Hamlet sends his mother back to Claudius' bed, back to the caresses of a man who will not fail to make her yield yet again.

In the sort of collapsing or caving in that manifests itself at the end of Hamlet's plea, we find the very model that allows us to conceptualize in what respect there is a waning [*retombée*] of his own desire, of his impulse toward the action he is dying to take, the whole world becoming a living reproach to him that he is not equal to his own will. If this action founders [*retombe*] in the same way as his plea to his mother does, it is essentially because of the dependence of the subject's desire on the Other subject. This is the major accent, the very accent of the drama of *Hamlet*, what one might call its constant dimension.

What we need to do now is see in a more articulated way – entering into psychological detail that would remain, I must say, fundamentally enigmatic if it were not enlisted in the overall aim that constitutes the meaning of *Hamlet* as a tragedy – how this reverberates in the very heart of Hamlet's will, which, on my graph, is the hook or question mark constituted by the "*Che vuoi?*" of the subjectivity that is constituted in the Other and articulated in the Other [see Figure 1.3].

This is the thrust of what I have to say today. It concerns what one might call the imaginary setting [or: regulating, *réglage*] that is brought about by what constitutes desire's prop.

Here, at the beginning of the curve that represents the assumption by the subject of his essential will, we have an indeterminate, variable point [d]. This point is determined [*réglé*] on the basis of something that lies somewhere across from it, and as we can immediately say, at the level of the unconscious subject [see, for example, Figure 15.4]. I designate the endpoint of what constitutes the subject's question as S barred in the presence of little *a* ($\$ \lozenge a$), and call it fantasy. In the psychical economy, it represents something you are familiar with; this something is ambiguous because, when we broach it from a certain phase, it is in fact a final term in the conscious, the endpoint of all human passion insofar as it is marked by some of the traits that we refer to as "traits of perversion."

The mystery of fantasy, insofar as it is in some sense the final   367
term of a desire, is based on the fact that it always presents itself in a more or less paradoxical guise. This explains why the Ancient Greeks rejected the dimension of fantasy as absurd. The essential step in interpreting it was only made in the modern era, by psychoanalysis. In effect, it could only be conceptualized by being related to an unconscious economy that underpins it qua perverse. If fantasy appears as the endpoint of desire, as its final term and enigma, it can only be understood in terms of an unconscious circuit that is articulated through a signifying chain that is profoundly different from the one that the subject commands, $s(A) \rightarrow A$, which initially lies at the level of demand.

In the lower chain, fantasy both intervenes and does not intervene. Some aspect of fantasy does not normally arrive there by the pathway ($\$ \lozenge a) \rightarrow s(A)$; it does not usually reach $s(A)$. If it *does* reach $s(A)$, we find ourselves in an atypical situation. Fantasy usually remains unconscious; it is separate, it does not arrive at the message, at the Other's signified [$s(A)$], which is the module or sum total of all the significations acquired by the subject in interpersonal exchange and all of discourse. Nevertheless, at certain phases, which are more or less pathological, it goes beyond this.

Later on, I will give names to the moments at which it goes beyond this, the latter occurring only in a single direction, as the schema indicates. I am pointing out this essential articulation because we are, in short, here in order to make headway in using the device I call the gramma; but for the time being we are simply going to see how something in Shakespeare's tragedy functions – namely, what I have called the moment at which Hamlet's desire founders, inasmuch as it makes sense to relate it to this imaginary setting [*réglage*].

In this mapping, Ophelia is situated at the level of the letter *a*. This letter is inscribed in our symbolization of fantasy, fantasy being the imaginary prop or substrate of desire insofar as desire is different from demand and also from need. This *a* corresponds to something toward which all of psychoanalysis is currently heading when it seeks to define the object and object relations.

There is something right-minded in the current direction of analysis. As object relations theory usually articulates it, the object clearly plays a decisive role: it fundamentally structures the subject's way of apprehending the world. However, in the majority of the recent works that attribute a more or less major role to object relations – whether it be the volume that came out in our neck of the woods, the one to which I have already alluded as the most caricatural example, or others that are more elaborate, those by Federn, for example, and certain others – the explanations we ordinarily find are marked by an error and a confusion based on the theorization of the object as a so-called pre-genital object. Moreover, the genital object itself is situated by their authors within the various forms of the pre-genital object: the oral object, the anal object, and so on.

The confusion in question can be seen on our schema [the graph of desire]. It involves mistaking the dialectic of the object for the dialectic of demand. This confusion is understandable because in both cases the subject finds himself in the same position in his relationship with the signifier: he is eclipsed there.

Consider two points on our gramma. Over here we have the code at the level of the unconscious, ($\lozenge$D) – in other words, the series of relationships that the subject has with a certain apparatus of demand. Over there we have the imaginary relationship ($\lozenge$a) that preferentially constitutes him in a certain position, which is also defined by his relationship to the signifier, wherein he is faced with an object *a*. The subject is eclipsed at both of these points.

I began to articulate this eclipsed status last time with the term "fading."* I selected this term for all sorts of philological reasons, and also because it has become quite familiar to us in the context

368

of the communication devices we use. Fading* is precisely what happens in a communication device designed to transmit sound when someone's voice disappears, or breaks up, only to reappear owing to some variation in transmission quality. I will naturally provide real examples to fill out what is merely a metaphor here.

It is thus insofar as the subject is in one and the same moment of oscillation – the one that characterizes fading* when faced with demand and when faced with the object – that the confusion can occur.

What are known as object relations are, in fact, always relations between the subject and, not objects, as people say, but rather signifiers of demand; and these relations arise especially at the specific moment called "the fading* of the subject." Inasmuch as demand remains fixed, one can articulate the various modes of the signifying apparatus that correspond to the different types of demand – oral, anal, and so on – in a way that clinically corresponds, in effect, to the relationship to the object. The fact remains that it is highly problematic to confuse the relationship to the signifier with the relationship to the object.

369

For the object, qua object of desire, has a different meaning. All kinds of things make it necessary not to overlook this, even when we would like to give, as people do, their full, determinant, primitive value to the signifiers of demand, insofar as they are oral or anal signifiers, in order to make them correspond to all the subdivisions and different orientations or polarizations the object itself can take on in relationship to the subject. The correlation between the object and the subject as marked by the bar is, let me point out, the very thing that is overlooked by object relations theory as it is currently formulated.

Even when we consider the subject at the most primitive stages of the oral period – as it has been articulated, for example, by Melanie Klein in a way that is experience-near, rigorous, and precise – we find ourselves faced with certain paradoxes that are visible in Klein's texts. These paradoxes cannot be inscribed in a straightforward theorization of the subject as faced with an object that corresponds to a need, the breast in this case, if only because the subject is faced specifically with the nipple [*mamelon*].

A paradox arises here because, right from the outset, another enigmatic signifier presents itself at the horizon of this relationship. This fact is clearly brought out by Klein. Her only claim to fame in this context is that she does not hesitate to run headlong toward something, which is to ratify what she encounters in her clinical experience. Lacking an adequate theory, she clearly contents herself with rather poor explanations; yet she plainly attests to the fact that the phallus is already there, as such, [in the relationship between the child and the breast] and as, strictly speaking, destructive with regard to the subject. Right from the outset, she makes the phallus into a primordial object that is both the best and the worst, and around which all the avatars of the paranoid phase and the depressive phase revolve.

370

I am doing no more here, of course, than mentioning this and recalling it to mind. If S barred is of interest to us today, it is not, in fact, insofar as it is connected up with demand but with the element that we are going to try to home in on as closely as possible this year: little *a*.

Little *a* is the essential object around which the dialectic of desire revolves. The subject experiences himself here as faced with an element that is alterity at the imaginary level, as I have already formulated and defined it many times. It is an image, and it is pathos.

The other, which the object of desire is, serves a function that defines desire with twofold coordinates such that it does not aim at an object that satisfies a need, not in the slightest, but rather at an already-relativized object – I mean an object that has some relation to the subject, and specifically the subject who is present in fantasy. This is phenomenologically obvious and I shall return to it later on.

The subject is present in fantasy, and the object – which is the object of desire solely insofar as it is one of the terms in fantasy – takes the place, I would say, of what the subject is deprived of symbolically. This may appear a bit abstract to those here who have not followed the whole of my preceding path with me. For them, let me say that, in the articulation of fantasy, the object takes the place of what the subject is deprived of – namely, the phallus. It is owing to this that the object assumes the function it has in fantasy, and that desire is constituted with fantasy as its prop. It is difficult, I think, to go any further regarding what I mean about desire and its relationship with fantasy.

The object in fantasy is the alterity – image and pathos – by which an other takes the place of what the subject is deprived of symbolically. This formulation indicates the direction that allows us to conceptualize in what respect this imaginary object finds itself in a position in which what one might call the virtues or the dimension of being converge on it; it goes so far as to become the true decoy [or: lure, *leurre*] of being that the object of human desire is. This is what Simone Weil realized when she pointed to the thickest, most opaque relation that can be presented to us regarding man and the object of his desire – namely, the relationship between the miser and his treasure. The fetishistic character of the object of human desire is most blatant there. All of desire's objects are fetishistic in character.

371

It is quite comical to hear, as I did recently, some guy try to explain the relationship between the theory of signification and Marxism by saying that we cannot broach the theory of signification without taking interpersonal relations as our point of departure. He went rather far, since, after three minutes, he claimed that the signifier is the instrument thanks to which men transmit their private thoughts to their fellow men. These are the exact words of someone who supposedly based his ideas on Marx's work. If we do not take interpersonal relations as our foundation, we fall, according to him, into the trap of fetishizing what is involved in the realm of language.

I assuredly agree that we encounter something fetishistic, but I wonder if what is known as a fetish is not one of the very dimensions of the human world, and precisely the dimension *we* must account for. If we locate interpersonal relations at the root of everything, we end up relating the fetishization of human objects to some sort of interpersonal misunderstanding, which in turn means relating it to significations. Similarly, the private thoughts in question – in a developmental perspective, I think – must make us laugh, for if they are already there, why bother to look any further?

In short, it is rather surprising that a thesis that considers human subjectivity to precede human praxis can be defended by someone who considers himself to be a Marxist. It seems to me, on the contrary, that it suffices to open the first volume of *Capital* to realize that the very first step of Marx's analysis of the fetishistic nature of commodities consists precisely in broaching the problem from the level of the signifier, even if the term is not used there. The relations between values are defined as signifying relations, and all subjectivity, and possibly even that of fetishization, comes to be inscribed within this signifying dialectic. This is true beyond a shadow of a doubt.

This is but a simple tangent – a reflection of the occasional indignation and boredom I feel when I have wasted my time – that I am pouring into your ears.   372

2

Let us now try to use this relationship, $ in the presence of little a, which to us is the fantasized prop of desire. We must articulate it clearly. What does a, this imaginary other, mean?

It means that something more encompassing than a person can be included therein – a whole chain or scenario. I have no need to return here to what I brought out last year in my analysis of Jean Genet's *The Balcony*. To explain what I mean in this context, I need but refer to what we might call the diffuse brothel, inasmuch as it becomes the cause of what analysts think of as the sacrosanct genital stage.

What is important in the structural element of imaginary fantasy that is situated at the level of a?

First of all, its opaque character, which specifies it in the most accentuated forms as the pole of perverse desire – stated otherwise, it is the structural element of the perversions. Perversion is characterized by the fact that in perverse fantasy, the entire emphasis is placed on the side of the strictly imaginary correlative. In other words, it is placed on the other, little a, or the parenthesis $(a + b + c$, etc.), in which the most elaborate objects can be found together and combined depending on the trajectory, consequences, and residues in which the function of a fantasy in a perverse desire crystallizes.

Nevertheless, what is essential is the phenomenological element that I alluded to earlier. As strange or bizarre as fantasy in perverse desire may appear to be, desire is always in some way involved – involved in a relationship that is always linked to pathos, to the pain of existing as such, of existing purely and simply, or existing as a sexual term. If a sadistic fantasy subsists, it is quite obviously because he who is subjected to the abuse in the fantasy interests the subject, insofar as the subject himself might be exposed to the same sort of abuse. We can but be surprised that people thought even for a single instant that they could avoid this dimension by relating sadistic tendencies to primal aggression, pure and simple.

But I am already saying too much here. If I am doing so, it is merely in order to emphasize the direction in which we must now articulate the true opposition between perversion and neurosis. Perversion is situated at exactly the same level, as you will see, as neurosis; it is something that is, of course, articulated, interpretable, and analyzable. Nevertheless, in perversion, something concerning the essential relationship between the subject and his being becomes fixated on imaginary elements, as people have always said, in an essentially localized form, whereas neurosis is distinguished by the fact that the emphasis is placed there on the other term of fantasy – in other words, the barred subject.

I told you that fantasy as such is situated at the extreme point of subjective questioning – at its tip, endpoint, or reflection – inasmuch as, beyond demand, the subject attempts to get his bearings anew [*se resaisir*] in the dimension of the Other's discourse in which he must refind what was lost owing to the fact of his entrance into discourse. As I told you, what is involved is, in the final analysis, not the level of truth but the moment of truth.

This allows us to designate what most profoundly distinguishes neurotic fantasy from perverse fantasy. Perverse fantasy, as I told you, can be called upon [*appelé*], it is located in space, it suspends some sort of essential relationship to time – it is not strictly speaking atemporal, but lies outside of time. In neurosis, on the other hand, the subject's relationship to time is all too infrequently talked about, whereas it is the very basis of the subject's relations to his object at the level of fantasy.

In neurosis, the object takes on a signification that must be sought out in what I call "the moment [*heure*] of truth." The object there is always an hour ahead of schedule or an hour behind. Hysteria is characterized by the function of a desire qua unsatisfied, and obsession by the function of an impossible desire; but beyond those two terms, there is a phenomenon that has a twofold and inverse relationship to them. This phenomenon constantly arises and manifests itself in the obsessive's procrastination, which is moreover founded on the fact that he always prepares himself for things when it is too late [*anticipe trop tard*]. Similarly, the hysteric always repeats what initially occurred in her trauma – namely, something that came too soon, a fundamental unreadiness [*immaturation*].

The subject always seeks to find his moment [*heure*] in his object. One might even say that he learns how to tell time from it. This is the foundation of neurotic behavior, in its most general form. It is here that we once again intersect Hamlet.

Hamlet has been assigned every form of neurotic behavior, no matter how extreme – depending on which analyst was interpreting him – even character neurosis, for a legitimate reason that runs throughout the plot and that truly constitutes one of the common factors of Hamlet's structure. The first factor is his dependence on the Other's desire – that is, on his mother's desire. The second common factor, which I will ask you to look for when you read or reread the play, is that Hamlet is always tributary to the other's time [*suspendu à l'heure de l'autre*], and this is true right up until the end of the play.

Do you recall one of the first turning points we discussed as we began to decipher the text of *Hamlet*, the one that is situated after the play scene, the scene involving the traveling actors? The king gets upset about what is happening onstage, and visibly betrays his own crime in front of everyone, proving that he cannot bear the sight of it. Hamlet triumphs, exults, and scorns the man who has thus given himself away. Then he goes to the rendezvous with his mother that he had scheduled before the play scene, a rendezvous that everyone was pressing him to have as soon as possible. The major scene that I have already so often emphasized takes place with her.

On the way to the rendezvous, Hamlet comes across the king, who

374

is praying. Shaken to his very foundations by the scene that has just shown him the visage of his own actions, his own scenario, Claudius prays. Hamlet stands there before the king, and everything seems to suggest that the latter is not only disinclined to defend himself, but that he does not even perceive the threat that hangs over him. Hamlet stops at that point because it is not the right time [*heure*].

It is not the other's time [*heure*]. It is not the right moment [*heure*] for him to account for himself to God. To kill him now would be too good for him and too bad for Hamlet's father. It would not sufficiently revenge the latter's death because, owing to Claudius' repentance in his prayer, salvation might be open to him. Be that as it may, one thing is clear, which is that, having just caught the king's conscience as he had hoped – "The play's the thing / Wherein I'll catch the conscience of the king" [II, ii, 590–1] – Hamlet stops. Not for a single instant does he think this is the right time. Whatever may happen afterward, this is not the other's time, and he refrains from acting. Similarly, whatever Hamlet does, it is only and always on the other's time that he does it. He puts up with anything and everything.

Let us not forget, all the same, that at the outset of the play – disgusted as he was already, even before his encounter with the ghost* and the unveiling of the crime, by his mother's remarriage – he was thinking of one thing and one thing alone: leaving for Wittenberg. Someone recently underscored this by commenting on a certain practical style that is tending to become established in contemporary mores; he noted that Hamlet was the finest example of the fact that one can avoid many dramas by issuing people passports, allowing them to leave town, in time. If Hamlet had been granted his passport to leave for Wittenberg, there would have been no drama.

It is owing to his parents' agenda [*heure*] that he stays put. It is in accordance with the other's schedule [*heure*] that he puts his crime on hold. It is owing to his stepfather's plans [*heure*] that he departs for England. It is owing to Rosencrantz and Guildenstern's mission [*heure*] that he is led to send them to their deaths, thanks to the rather prettily executed trick that so impressed Freud. And it is all the same owing to Ophelia's time, the time at which she commits suicide, that the tragedy finds its terminus at a moment at which Hamlet – who has just, it seems, perceived that it is not so difficult to kill someone, the time "to say 'one'" – will not even have time to say "Phew!"

People propose that he do something that in no way resembles an opportunity to kill Claudius – namely, fight in a very pretty fencing contest. All the details of the contest have been minutely worked

375

out. The stakes involve what we will call a series of objects, in the collector's [*collectionniste*] sense of the term, for they are all precious objects, collector's objects. We would have to re-examine the text, for even here there are subtleties and we enter into the realm of collections – they involve "rapiers" and "their assigns" [V, ii, 145], things that have value only as luxury objects. Hamlet is in fact provoked to engage in a sort of jousting, it being asserted that he is the inferior fencer and must be granted a handicap in the challenge.* In short it is a complicated ceremony.

376

We, of course, realize that it is a trap concocted by his stepfather and his friend Laertes. But let us not forget that for him it is tantamount to accepting once again to take the long way around [*l'école buissonnière*]. They are going to have a lot of fun.

He nevertheless feels a little warning in his heart; something stirs him up. The dialectic of presentiment on the hero's part gives emphasis to the drama for a moment. But it is still essentially on the other's time, and far more ridiculously, in order to win the other's bet for him – recall that it is not Hamlet's possessions that are wagered – that he agrees to fight this battle for his stepfather's benefit and as his advocate. In theory, the battle will be courteously fought, yet Hamlet will be facing off against someone who is presumed to be a more accomplished fencer than him and who, as such, will arouse feelings of rivalry and honor in him, a trap in which they are sure they will catch him.

And he runs straight into the trap. The only thing that is new at this point is, I would say, the heat and heart with which he runs. Right up till the end – right up until the final hour [*heure*], an hour that is so determinate that it will be his own hour, for he will be mortally wounded before he can strike his enemy – it is always by the other's watch [*heure*] that the plot of the tragedy proceeds and is brought to an end. This is an absolutely essential framework if we are to conceptualize what is involved.

If Hamlet, the character, and the drama of *Hamlet* metaphysically resonate with the problematic of the modern hero, it is inasmuch as something has, in effect, changed for heroes in relation to their destiny. As I told you, what distinguishes Hamlet from Oedipus is that Hamlet knows. Led to this critical point, we are now in a position to explain what I have called superficial features, such as Hamlet's madness.

In the tragedies of Antiquity we encounter heroes who *are* crazy, but to the best of my knowledge there are none who – in tragedy, as I said, I am not talking about legends – *act* crazy. Does everything in Hamlet's madness come down to pretending to be crazy? Let us consider this.

377   Why is he acting crazy? Undoubtedly because he knows that he is
the weaker party. As superficial as this feature may be, I am pointing it out, not because it corroborates my perspective [but simply
because it is secondary]. Nevertheless, if we consider it carefully, it
is not secondary if we wish to understand what Shakespeare meant
to convey to us with *Hamlet*. Pretending to be crazy is, in fact, an
essential feature of the original legend, as we find it in the versions
written by Saxo Grammaticus and Belleforest.

Shakespeare selected the theme of a hero who is forced to act
crazy in order to continue down the path that leads him to accomplish his task. This is a strictly modern dimension. He who knows
is intrinsically in such a dangerous position, is so doomed to failure
and sacrifice, that his path must be, as Pascal says somewhere, one
in which he is crazy like everyone else.

Pretending to be crazy is one of the dimensions of what I might
call the politics of the modern hero. It should not be overlooked,
for it is what Shakespeare latched onto when he decided to write
the tragedy of *Hamlet*. This is essentially what the prior authors
bequeathed him. And the whole point is to figure out what the
madman is thinking.

The fact that Shakespeare selected his subject within this problematic is altogether essential.

We have now arrived at the point at which Ophelia must play her
part.

3

If the play truly has in its structure everything that I have just laid
out, why bother to bring in Ophelia?

Some of you reproach me for having only timidly made headway.
I do not think that I have shown exceptional timidity. I would not
like to encourage you to proffer the sort of twaddle with which psychoanalytic texts abound; I simply was astonished that no one had
mentioned that Ophelia is *omphalos*, given that one finds so many
other wild and crazy things, things that do not pull any punches,
merely by opening up Ella Sharpe's "Unfinished Paper on *Hamlet*,"
378   which was perhaps regrettably uncompleted at her death and that
maybe should never have been published.

Ophelia is obviously essential. She will forever be linked to the
figure of Hamlet, for centuries to come. Since it is too late for me to
be able to complete my discussion of Ophelia today, I simply want
to punctuate for you what happens in the course of the play.

We first hear her spoken about as the cause of Hamlet's sorry state. This is Polonius's psychoanalytic-style wisdom: "Hamlet is sad because he is not happy, and if he is not happy it is because of my daughter. You don't know her? She is a rare flower – and I, her father, will naturally not tolerate this."

We see her do something that immediately shows her to be someone quite remarkable – namely, she makes clinical observations. She is, in fact, fortunate enough to be the first person Hamlet runs into after encountering the ghost.* Right after this encounter, which shook him up rather badly, he meets Ophelia, and the way he behaves with her is, I believe, worth repeating here. [As she tells her father:]

> My lord, as I was sewing in my closet,
> Lord Hamlet, with his doublet all unbraced,
> No hat upon his head, his stockings fouled,
> Ungartered, and down-gyved to his ancle,
> Pale as his shirt, his knees knocking each other,
> And with a look so piteous in purport
> As if he had been loosed out of hell
> To speak of horrors – he comes before me.
> [. . .]
> He took me by the wrist and held me hard.
> Then goes he to the length of all his arm,
> And with his other hand thus o'er his brow
> He falls to such perusal of my face
> As 'a would draw it. Long stayed he so.
> At last, a little shaking of mine arm
> And thrice his head thus waving up and down,
> He raised a sigh so piteous and profound
> As it did seem to shatter all his bulk
> And end his being. That done, he lets me go,
> And with his head over his shoulder turned
> He seemed to find his way without his eyes,
> For out o' doors he went without their helps
> And to the last bended their light on me. [II, i, 77–100]

379

Polonius immediately cries, "Mad for thy love?" [85] Yet, in my view, Hamlet's obvious scrutiny of Ophelia shows us Hamlet questioning the object, taking some distance with respect to the object as if to endeavor to identify it, something that has now become difficult for him, and vacillating in the presence of what had hitherto been a supremely exalted object to him. This gives us the first stage [temps] of the relation to the object, which involves, as it were, estrangement.*

We cannot say any more about that. Nevertheless, it would not be much of a stretch to designate this moment, at which Hamlet is so sartorially disheveled, as strictly pathological. We can consider it to be akin to those periods in which some sort of subjective disorganization irrupts. Such a phenomenon takes place inasmuch as something vacillates in someone's fantasy and brings out its components, which are registered in what is known as an experience of depersonalization. This is what is manifested in his symptoms. The imaginary limits between the subject and the object manage to be transformed and pass over into the realm of what is known as the fantastical, in the strict sense of the term.

This is exactly what happens when something in the imaginary structure of fantasy, ($\Diamond a$), establishes a communication pathway with what far more easily reaches the level of the message, $s(A)$ – namely, the other's image, $i(a)$, insofar as it is my own ego [m], which is situated below the message. Authors like Federn indicate with a great deal of finesse the necessary correlations between the feeling of one's own body and the strangeness of what happens to the subject in certain crises, breaks, or attacks [*atteinte*] of the object at the level specified by ($\Diamond a$).

If I have perhaps forced things a little bit here in my design to get you interested, it was to show you in what respect this drama is related to certain specific experiences in our clinical work. We will no doubt return to this, but keep in mind, at any rate, that if we do not refer to this pathological schema, it is impossible to clearly situate what Freud situated for the first time at the analytic level: *das Unheimliche* [the uncanny]. The phenomenon is not linked, as certain people thought, to irruptions of the unconscious, but to a sort of imbalance that occurs in fantasy when, going beyond the limits initially assigned to it, it breaks down and meets back up with the other's image. This is actually but one facet of it.

In Hamlet's case, it seems that after this episode Ophelia has completely ceased to exist for him as a love object. "I did love you once," says Hamlet [III, i, 115]. His cruel aggression, along with his highly sarcastic remarks, make these scenes with Ophelia among the strangest in classical literature. Certain writers have struck the same cord in rather extreme plays, but it is quite unusual to see a scene like the one that takes place between Hamlet and Ophelia be given such a central role, to see it right smack in the middle of a tragic play.

In Hamlet's attitude toward Ophelia, we find a trace of the imbalance in the fantasized relationship that I mentioned earlier – the fantasy tilts toward the object, toward perversion. This is one of the features of their relationship. Another is that the object in question is no longer treated as she had been before – that is, as a woman.

380

To Hamlet, Ophelia becomes a bearer of children and of sins of all ilks. She is doomed to engender sinners and to then have to succumb to all sorts of calumny. She becomes the pure and simple medium for a form of life that is, in its essence, now condemned. In short, what happens at this moment is the destruction or loss of the object, which is reintegrated into its narcissistic frame.

To the subject, the object appears outside, as it were. The formulation that I provided earlier indicates to you what this object is equivalent to, what it takes the place of, and what cannot be given to the subject except at the moment at which he literally sacrifices himself, at which he is no longer it himself, at which he rejects it with his whole being. This object is clearly no other than the phallus.

Yes, Ophelia is at that moment the phallus, the phallus qua signifying symbol of life, the phallus that the subject externalizes and rejects as such. This is the second stage of the relationship to the object.

We do not have much time left and so I hesitate to give you all the coordinates here. I will return to this. But the fact that this is what is involved – namely, a transformation of the formula [($\emptyset a$) into] ($\emptyset\phi$) in the guise of rejection [*rejet*] – is demonstrated, once you realize it, by something that has nothing to do with the etymology of Ophelia's name.   381

First of all, the only thing at issue here is fecundity. "Conception is a blessing," Hamlet says to Polonius, "but as your daughter may conceive, friend, look to 't" [II, ii, 184–6]. The entire dialogue with Ophelia shows that woman is conceptualized here only as carrying the vital turgescence that must be cursed and stopped up. As semantic usage shows, "nunnery" could also at that time designate a brothel.

Secondly, the relationship between the phallus and the object is also designated by Hamlet's attitude toward Ophelia during the play scene. When his mother, who is also there, asks him to sit by her, he replies, "No, good mother. Here's metal more attractive" [III, ii, 105], and puts his head between Ophelia's legs, asking her explicitly, "Lady, shall I lie in your lap?" [107]. The phallic quality of the object of desire [*Le rapport phallique de l'objet du désir*] is clearly indicated here.

I do not believe that it is superfluous to indicate, furthermore, since the iconography [devoted to *Hamlet*] has highlighted this so emphatically, that among the flowers surrounding Ophelia as she drowns, there are "dead men's fingers" [IV, vii, 170], and explicit mention is made of the fact that they are called by a cruder name by common folk. The plant in question is *orchis mascula*, and it bears some relation to mandragora [or mandrake] and thus to the phallic element. I looked up dead men's fingers in the *New English Dictionary*, but I was highly disappointed to find that, even though the name is cited in reference to the term "finger," no mention is made there of what Shakespeare was alluding to with this term.

I have already led you to the third stage of the relation to the object several times, and I am going to end with it again today. It is the stage of the cemetery scene. We should highlight here a connection between what presents itself as a reintegration of *a* and Hamlet's possibility of finishing things off [or: coming full circle, *boucler la boucle*] – in other words, of finally running headlong toward his destiny.

The cemetery scene, which may seem completely gratuitous, is of absolutely capital importance. It is specifically designed so that something occurs, something that Shakespeare found in none of the earlier versions: a furious battle at the bottom of a grave. I have already emphasized this.

In this scene, the highest function of the object is in some sense traced out. The object is reconquered here only at the price of mourning and death. It is on this point that I believe I will be able to complete our discussion of *Hamlet* next time.

April 15, 1959

382

XVIII

MOURNING AND DESIRE

Procrastination and precipitation
A mathematical metaphor of the phallus
Hamlet and his double
Why and how Hamlet acts crazy
On what is foreclosed in the real

Hamlet, as I have been telling you, cannot stand to have to keep an appointment. For him, the appointment [*rendez-vous*] always comes too soon and so he postpones it.

The commentaries that I have become more and more familiar with in the course of our study of *Hamlet* would like to dismiss the element of procrastination. But we cannot in any way agree to do so. To my way of thinking, procrastination remains one of the essential dimensions of the tragedy.

Yet, when Hamlet takes action it is always with precipitation. He takes action when it suddenly seems to him that an opportunity is presenting itself, when an event beyond his control, resolution, and decision seems to call out to him and offer him some sort of ambiguous opening, which is, strictly speaking, what introduced the perspective that we analysts call flight into the dimension of achievement [*accomplicement*].

This is never clearer than at the moment at which he runs headlong at something that is stirring behind the arras and kills Polonius. There are other such moments as well. For example, when he awakens at night on the boat during the storm, you see the almost mysterious way in which he, while virtually in an altered state, breaks the seals of the message Guildenstern and Rosencrantz are carrying. Consider, too, the almost automatic way in which he substitutes one message for another and, thanks to his ring, re-creates the royal seal, before availing himself of the prodigious opportunity offered when the pirate ship attacks, he taking advantage of the occasion to escape from his guardians, who then unsuspectingly proceed toward their own execution [IV, vi].

We have here a true phenomenology of the life of the neurotic, since we must call a spade a spade. Its tenor is easily recognizable and almost well known to us from our practice, and from our theory as well. But beyond these tangible characteristics, there is the structural reference that runs throughout the play which I highlighted last time: Hamlet is always operating on the Other's time [*à l'heure de l'Autre*].

This is merely a mirage, of course. There is no Other of the Other, as I explained before by giving you what I called the final answer, in the form of the signifier of the barred Other [S(A̶)]. In the signifier, there is no guarantor of the dimension of truth that is founded by the signifier. For Hamlet, the only time [*heure*] is his own time and there is also but one time: the moment [*heure*] of his downfall. The entire tragedy consists in showing us Hamlet's implacable progress toward that hour.

Nevertheless, the appointment with his downfall is not solely related to the common lot, and thus applicable to all human destiny. If Hamlet's fate did not have a specific sign, it would not have the eminent value that it has for us. What is it, then, that specifies his destiny, that gives it its highly problematic value?

This is the point we have arrived at. This is where we ended last time.

1

What is Hamlet missing?

To what extent does the general outline of the tragedy of *Hamlet*, as Shakespeare composed it, allow us to locate a lack that goes beyond the approximations with which we always make do? Such approximations make for the confusion inherent not only in the language we use, but also in the way we act with our patients, and even – it must be admitted – in the suggestions we make to them.

Let us nevertheless begin with an approximate formulation of what is at stake. What Hamlet is always missing is, as we might put it in everyday language, that he does not set his sights on any goal, his action having no object(ive), the latter always involving what we call arbitrariness. As we have seen, and we have even begun to explore why, Hamlet is someone who, as womenfolk are wont to say, does not know what he wants.

This first dimension is in some sense made clear in the lines Shakespeare has him proffer at a certain turning point that is quite significant, which is his eclipse in the tragedy, I mean the brief moment at which he is not present. This is when he is at sea, having embarked only to return exceedingly quickly, having barely left port.

Ever obedient, Hamlet leaves for England in compliance with the king's orders. He encounters Fortinbras's troops at the Danish border, Fortinbras being someone who forms part of the backdrop of the tragedy; he is mentioned right from the beginning and cleans house at the end of the play, collecting the dead and putting the pieces back together. Consider how our Hamlet speaks of Fortinbras. He is struck when he sees the valiant troops that are going to conquer a few acres of Poland in the name of a more or less futile *casus belli*, and it gives him the opportunity to reflect on his own conduct.

> How all occasions do inform against me
> And spur my dull revenge! What is a man,
> If his chief good and market of his time
> Be but to sleep and feed? A beast, no more.
> Sure he that made us with such large discourse,
> Looking before and after, gave us not
> That capability and godlike reason
> To fust in us unused . . . [IV, iv, 32–9]

"Reason" in this context is grand or fundamental discourse, what I will call "actual [or: concrete, *concret*] discourse" here.

> . . . Now whether it be
> Bestial oblivion

– this is one of the key words of the dimension of his being in the tragedy –

> Bestial oblivion, or some craven scruple
> Of thinking too precisely on th' event –
> A thought which, quartered, hath but one part wisdom
> And ever three parts coward – I do not know
> Why yet I live to say, "This thing's to do,"
> Sith I have cause, and will, and strength, and means
> To do 't. Examples gross as earth exhort me.
> Witness this army of such mass and charge,
> Led by a delicate and tender prince,
> Whose spirit, with divine ambition puffed
> Makes mouths at the invisible event,

386

Exposing what is mortal and unsure
To all that fortune, death, and danger dare,
Even for an eggshell. Rightly to be great
Is not to stir without great argument,
But greatly to find quarrel in a straw
When honour's at the stake. How stand I then,
That have a father killed, a mother stained,
Excitements of my reason and my blood,
And let all sleep, while to my shame I see
The imminent death of twenty thousand men
That for a fantasy and trick of fame
Go to their graves like beds, fight for a plot
Whereon the numbers cannot try the cause,
Which is not tomb enough and continent
To hide the slain? O, from this time forth,
My thoughts be bloody, or be nothing worth! [IV, iv, 40–66]

Such are Hamlet's meditations on what I will call the object(ive) of human action. This object(ive) leaves the door open to all sorts of specifications on which we ordinarily dwell. For example, the shedding of blood for a noble cause, for the sake of honor, honor also being designated by the fact of having given one's word – we will call that a gift or oblativity.

It is clear that, as analysts, we cannot fail to encounter instances of such concrete resolve or be struck by their weight, whether in flesh or commitments. Nevertheless, when I write the formula ($\lozenge a$) for you, it is not in order to try to provide the usual form – that is, the lowest common denominator – of such resolve. It is not an articulation that could be characterized as a mere formalism.

Indeed, this formula is inscribed at the end of the question that the subject raises in the Other, when seeking a final answer, by asking the Other: "What do you want?" "*Che vuoi?*" But the subject has no chance of receiving an answer; there is nothing there that is in fact open to investigation, except under special conditions that we call analytic – except, in other words, with the assistance the subject receives from exploring the unconscious signifying chain that was discovered by Freud's practice. On the graph, this chain is represented by the upper circuit.

387

What we are dealing with here is the imaginary short circuit that lies halfway between the upper and the lower circuits, where desire connects up with what lies across from it: fantasy. What I express in the formula ($\lozenge a$) is the general structure of fantasy. The subject designated by the barred S is the subject insofar as he is irreducibly affected by the signifier, with all the consequences that stem therefrom, in particular the fact of placing him in a certain, specific relationship with an imaginary conjunction in its essence, a – not the object *of* desire, but the object *in* desire.

The function of the object in desire is what we need to broach, and it is because the tragedy of *Hamlet* allows us to broach it and spell it out in an exemplary manner that I am examining the structure of this text with such unflagging interest.

Let us look more closely. The formula ($\$ \lozenge a$) signifies the following: a specific object becomes an object of desire insofar as the subject is deprived of something of himself that has taken on the value of the very signifier of his alienation – and this something is the phallus – deprived of something that is related to his very life because it has taken on the value of what links him to the signifier.

To be an object of desire is quintessentially different from being an object of any specific need. The temporal subsistence of the object in desire is related to the following: it takes the place of what remains masked to the subject, owing to its nature – namely, that part of himself that he sacrifices, the pound of flesh involved in his relationship to the signifier. It is because something takes its place that this something becomes an object in desire.

What is involved here is profoundly enigmatic, because it is fundamentally a relationship to something that is hidden or occulted. If this is the way it is – please allow me a formulation that came to me while I was jotting down some notes and that has just come back to me, but don't take it as a doctrinal formulation, take it at most as something designed to give you an image – it is insofar as human life can be defined as a form of arithmetic in which zero would be an irrational number.

This formulation is a mere mathematical metaphor. In speaking of the irrational, I am not referring to some sort of unfathomable affective realm, but to something that we encounter in mathematics in the form of what is known as an imaginary number, which is $\sqrt{-1}$. In effect, if there is something that does not correspond to anything that can be intuited and whose entire function must nevertheless be maintained, it is clearly the relationship between the object and the hidden element – which is the subject's living prop – inasmuch as, taking on the function of the signifier, it cannot be subjectified as such.

388

The square root of minus one cannot in itself correspond to anything real, in the mathematical sense of the term. The same is true of the object. This is why we cannot grasp its true function except by running through the whole series of its possible relations with barred S – in other words, the S that, at the precise point at which a takes on its maximal value, can only be occulted.

Does the tragedy of *Hamlet* allow us to run through *all* of the functions of the object? That would be saying a lot, but it allows us in any case to go much further in this direction than people have ever gone by any other pathway.

Let us begin from the end, from the encounter, the time of the rendezvous or final action into which Hamlet at last throws the entire weight of his life, which is what carrying out his action costs him.

2

The final action deserves to be called an action that Hamlet activates and that he undergoes, for everything surrounding this action is colored by a mort-like tone [*un air d'hallali*].

At the moment at which he takes action, Hamlet is also Diana's hunted-down stag. The plot against him is closing in on him, with incredible cynicism and malice – I am not sure you realize this – on the parts of Claudius and Laertes, whatever their different motives may be. A tarantula-like being is probably also involved in the plot: the ridiculous courtesan [Osric] who comes to propose that Hamlet participate in the contest in which the conspiracy against him is hidden.

Such is the structure. It is quite clear. I have already emphasized several of its features.

389 The contest that is proposed to him thrusts him into the position of being another's champion, since Hamlet is the one who is to uphold the bet or wager made by his uncle and stepfather, Claudius. The stakes are objects *a*, with all their brilliance. Like all objects and stakes in the world of human desire, they are essentially characterized by what the religious tradition, in exemplary images, teaches us to call *vanitas*, which refers to petit point tapestries in which we see a proliferation of pricey objects weighed in the balance against death.

The king has wagered "six Barbary horses," against which Laertes has wagered "six French rapiers and poniards" – namely, all the gear required by duelists – and their "assigns," such as the girdles and hangers they are hung from (their scabbards, I believe). Three of them have what the text calls "carriages," an especially precious word that designates a kind of hoop in which one hangs one's sword [V, ii, 143–8]. This collector's term also means the carriage of a cannon, and the double meaning gives rise to a whole exchange between Hamlet and Osric who informs Hamlet about the conditions of the contest. In a rather long dialogue, the quality, number, and panoply of these objects is designed to dazzle us, giving a lively tone to a trial whose paradoxical and even absurd nature I have already mentioned.

Hamlet seems once again to show interest, as though nothing in him could get in the way of his being fundamentally open to whatever comes along. His answer here is very significant:

> Sir, I will walk here in the hall. If it please his
> majesty, it is the breathing time of day with me. Let the
> foils be brought, the gentleman willing, and the king
> hold his purpose, I will win for him an I can; if not, I
> will gain nothing but my shame and the odd hits. [V, ii, 167–71]

It is in this regard that the final action shows us the very structure of fantasy. The hero is finally at his maximal resolve. Yet, as always, just before his resolve, we see him literally rent himself out to someone else, and for nothing whatsoever, as gratuitously as possible, this other person being his enemy and the very man he must strike down. He places what he must accomplish in the balance with the things of this world that interest him the least, for these collector's objects are not at that moment his major concern, and, what is more, he is going to strive to win them for someone else. 390

There is, of course, this $i(a)$ at the lower level of the graph with which the others believe they can captivate him. It is not altogether foreign to him, naturally, though not in the way the others think. But he is nevertheless intrigued at the level at which the others situate him. In being pitted against a rival who is, as it turns out, admired, his honor is at stake – in other words, he is intrigued at the level that Hegel calls the fight to the death of pure prestige.

We cannot fail to dwell for a moment on the sureness of the connection established by Shakespeare, for you recognize in it an element that has long been part of our discourse and dialogue here – namely, the mirror stage. It is expressly stated in the text that Laertes is, at this level, a semblable for Hamlet. He is indirectly Hamlet's semblable – at least within a parody.

I am referring to the response he makes to Osric, the overly narrow-minded courtesan. Coming to Hamlet to propose that he participate in a duel, Osric highlights the outstanding skill of the adversary to whom Hamlet will have to prove his mettle. Hamlet cuts him off and ups the ante:

> Sir, his definement suffers no perdition in you,
> though, I know, to divide him inventorially would dozy
> th' arithmetic of memory, and yet but yaw neither, in
> respect of his quick sail. [V, ii, 112–15]

And he gives an extremely precious, complicated speech that in some sense parodies the style of his interlocutor, before concluding,

I take him to be a soul of
great article, and his infusion of
such dearth and rareness, as, to make true diction of him,
his semblable is his mirror, and who else would trace
him, his umbrage, nothing more. [V, ii, 115–19]

In short, regarding Laertes' qualities, Hamlet refers to the other's image as something that cannot fail to be completely absorbing to he who contemplates it. All of this is puffed up in a highly Gongoresque manner, in the fullest sense of the word *concetto*, and it is with this same attitude and on the same ground that Hamlet meets Laertes prior to the duel. It is quite significant that the playwright situates the manifest point of aggressiveness at the height of imaginary absorption, formally articulated as a specular, mirror relationship.

391

The person we most admire is the one we are battling. He who is my ideal ego is also he who must be killed, according to Hegel's formulation regarding the impossibility of our coexisting. Hamlet only kills him in a way that we might call disinterested, in the midst of a contest. He only enters into it [*s'y engage*] in a way that one might qualify as merely formal, or even fictional. Thus it is without foreknowledge that he nevertheless begins to play the most serious of games.

What does this mean? It means that he does not enter the game with, let us say, his phallus. It means that what presents itself in this aggressive relationship is a decoy or mirage; that it is in spite of himself that he is going to lose his life in it; and that it is unbeknownst to him that he is going, at that precise moment, to both carry out his action and meet with his own death. The two occur almost simultaneously.

To say that he does not enter the game with his phallus is a way of expressing what we are in the process of seeking – namely, where the lack lies, where the specificity of Hamlet's position as a subject in the drama resides. He plays the game all the same, for the foils merely appear to be buttoned. In reality, there is at least one that is not buttoned, one that, at the moment at which the swords are distributed, has already been carefully marked in advance as the one to be given to Laertes. That sword has a true "unbated" point and it is, moreover, "envenomed" [V, ii, 306].

It is striking that the scriptwriter's gall meets up here with what one might call the playwright's formidable intuition. During the fight, the poisoned weapon changes hands, God only knows how. This must be one of the difficulties of the staging, and the script-writer does not work terribly hard to explain it to us. After Laertes has dealt Hamlet the blow from which he cannot recover, from which he must perish, there is a sort of scuffle in which they are grap-pling with each other, and a few moments later the poisoned rapier is in Hamlet's hand. No one gives much thought to explaining how such an astonishing switch can occur.

No one need, moreover, give it any thought, for what is at stake is to show that the instrument of death, the instrument that kills – which is in this case the most veiled instrument of the drama, one which Hamlet can only receive from the other – lies elsewhere than in what can be represented materially here. For the accom-plishment of Hamlet's desire does not take place at the level of the skill displayed [or: parrying, *parade*] in the contest, at the level of the rivalry with he who is his semblable, albeit more handsome than him, the rivalry with the *himself* [*moi-même*] that he can love. The drama is played out beyond that. And the phallus is what lies beyond that.

In the end, Hamlet identifies with the fatal signifier in the course of his encounter with the other. Curiously enough, this is found in the text itself, where we come across the word "foil."

The King mentions foils when they are handed out: "Give them the foils, young Osric" [V, ii, 248]. Before that, Hamlet had said, "Give us the foils." But, in between these two occurrences of the word, Hamlet makes a pun:

I'll be your foil, Laertes. In mine ignorance
Your skill shall, like a star i' th' darkest night,
Stick fiery off indeed. [V, ii, 244–6]

[Lacan comments on how French translators have tried to render this.] "Foil" cannot mean rapier [alone] here. It had another perfectly well-known meaning at the time, which was even rather frequently used: "foil," which is the same word as *feuille* in old French, is used preciously to designate the foil leaf in which some-thing precious is carried – that is, a case or setting [*écrin*].

In short, Hamlet says, in fighting with you, Laertes, I will be your setting, I will merely highlight "your star-like brightness in the dark sky." These are, moreover, the very conditions on which the duel was accepted. Hamlet, who is thought to have no chance of winning, will be proclaimed the winner if, in the course of twelve passes, his opponent does not hit him three times more than he hits his oppo-nent. Given the way the wager is structured, if Laertes obtains only

392

seven hits to Hamlet's five, Laertes will have lost. Hamlet is thus given a handicap.

One of Hamlet's functions is to constantly play on words, proffer double entendres, and equivocate. The pun involving "foil" is not included here by accident, and it is justifiable to explore what is included in its depths. When he says to Laertes "I'll be your foil," Hamlet uses a word that also means rapier. The subject thus identifies with the mortal phallus itself here. "I'll be your foil," he says to Laertes, "to showcase your skill," but a moment later Laertes' sword strikes, the sword that fatally wounds Hamlet before he himself has it in hand and completes his trajectory by killing both his opponent and he who is the final object of his mission – namely, the king.

Let me repeat that it is no accident that this word is used in the text. It is altogether justifiable to highlight it. The play of signifiers belongs to the very texture of *Hamlet*. A whole discussion should be devoted to this specific dimension.

You are aware of the essential role played by the clowns known as court jesters [*fous*]. With their no-holds-barred way of speaking, they can allow themselves to reveal people's most hidden motives and character traits that politeness prohibits people from mentioning directly. It is not just cynicism that is involved, nor is it just a more or less insulting, playful way of speaking. These characters operate primarily by equivocating, speaking metaphorically, punning, concocting *concetti*, speaking preciously, and replacing one signifier with another, the essential function of all of which I emphasize here.

This way of proceeding gives Shakespeare's theatre as a whole a tenor that is absolutely characteristic of his style and creates its psychological dimension. The fact that Hamlet is such an anxiety-provoking character must not hide from us the fact that, in a certain way, this tragedy raises someone who is, strictly speaking, a fool, clown, or jokester, to the rank of a hero. As someone once pointed out, to remove the jests from *Hamlet* would be to cut out four-fifths of the play.

Indeed, one of the dimensions in which the play's dramatic tension unfolds is constant equivocation. The latter is in some sense dissimulated, as it were, by the masked aspect of things – what gets played out between Claudius, the tyrant and usurper, and his killer, Hamlet, is the unmasking of the latter's intentions. Namely, why is he pretending to be mad [or: playing the fool, *faire le fou*]? We must not, for all that, forget the way in which he pretends to be mad, which gives his discourse an almost manic quality.

Hamlet never stops latching onto ideas and chances to equivocate

on the fly, and these ideas allow him to momentarily blind his   394
adversaries with a sort of flash of meaning. The latter do not see
discordant speech in them. They find them strange, in that they are
especially relevant, and they are struck by them so much that they
themselves sometimes become inventive and even tell tall tales. It is
thus not simply a hiding game [*jeu*] that is being played, but a mind
game [or: play of wit, *jeu d'esprit*] that is being played out at the level
of signifiers and in the dimension of meaning. Therein lies what one
might call the very spirit [or: wit, *esprit*] of the play.

This ambiguous disposition makes all of Hamlet's remarks – as
well, thus, as the reaction of those around him – into a problem in
which the spectator himself gets lost in ceaseless wondering. It is at
this level that the play takes on its full import. I am only recalling
this to mind here in order to emphasize that there is nothing excessive or arbitrary about giving its full weight to this last pun on the
word "foil."

Such is the nature of the constellation within which Hamlet's final
action unfolds during his duel with Laertes.

For Hamlet, Laertes is a sort of semblable or double who is more
handsome than Hamlet himself. As I have already said, this element
is located at the lower level of our graph, at *i(a)*. Hamlet, for whom
men and women are no longer anything but insubstantial and putrid
shadows, finds a worthy rival in this remodeled semblable, whose
presence allows him, at least for a moment, to uphold the human
wager [*soutenir la gageure humaine*] that he, too, is a man.

The remodeling here is but a consequence, not a point of departure. I mean that it is the consequence of what is manifested in the
situation – namely, the subject's position in the presence of the other
qua object of desire. The presence of the phallus is immanent in this
object. The phallus cannot assume its formal function except with
the disappearance of the subject himself.

What makes it possible for the subject to succumb even before
taking in hand the foil* with which he himself becomes a killer?

This brings us back to that very odd crossroads whose essential
character I have already indicated – namely, the cemetery scene and
what occurs in the vault.

3   395

We will now broach a topic that should interest one of our colleagues who, as it turns out, has done especially fine work on both
jealousy and mourning. The jealousy involved in mourning is, in
effect, one of the most salient aspects of this tragedy.

Reread the end of the act in which we find the cemetery scene, which I have now commented on three times in the course of this Seminar. There Hamlet articulates exactly what he finds unbearable in Laertes' attitude, bearing, and ostentation at the moment at which Ophelia is being buried. His partner's ostentatious mourning has the effect of ripping him away from himself; he is overwhelmed and shaken to his very foundations, to the point of not being able to handle it.

This first manifestation of Hamlet's rivalry with Laertes is far more authentic than the second. Hamlet approaches the duel with all the ceremony of courtly manners and with a buttoned foil, whereas in the cemetery scene he goes straight for Laertes' throat, jumping into the hole in which Ophelia's body has just been lowered. And he hurls:

'Swounds, show me what thou't do:
Woo't weep? woo't fight? woo't fast? [. . .]
I'll do't. Dost thou come here to whine?
To outface me with leaping in her grave?
Be buried quick with her, and so will I.
And, if thou prate of mountains, let them throw
Millions of acres on us, till our ground,
Singeing his pate against the burning zone,
Make Ossa like a wart! Nay, an thou'lt mouth,
I'll rant as well as thou. [V, i, 261–70]

At that, everyone is appalled and hurries to separate these warring brothers who are choking each other.

Hamlet then adds the following:

Hear you, sir.
What is the reason that you use me thus?
I loved you ever. But it is no matter.
Let Hercules himself do what he may,
The cat will mew, and dog will have his day. [V, i, 275–9]

I will leave some of you the task of bringing out the full value of this proverbial element, as I cannot dwell on it now. Hamlet later explains to Horatio what is essential here: he could not bear to see "the bravery of [Laertes'] grief" [V, ii, 79].

This brings us to the very heart of the dimension of mourning, which is going to open up an entire problematic for us. What relationship is there between what I have formulated in the form of ($◊a$), concerning the constitution of the object in desire, and

396

mourning? Let us broach what presents itself to us via its most manifest characteristics, which can also seem to be furthest from the heart of what we are seeking here.

We have seen Hamlet behave quite scornfully and cruelly toward Ophelia. I highlighted the degrading, humiliating aggression to which he constantly subjected her, she who suddenly became for him the very symbol of the rejection of his desire. We cannot fail to be struck when this object suddenly reassumes its full value to him. Consider in what terms the challenge he addresses to Laertes begins:

I loved Ophelia. Forty thousand brothers
Could not with all their quantity of love
Make up my sum. What wilt thou do for her? [V, i, 56–8]

In short, it is to the extent to which Ophelia has become an impossible object that she once again becomes the object of his desire. This feature completes in another guise what I said about the structure of Hamlet's desire. We believe we find ourselves here on a familiar path, where we can recognize one of the characteristics of the obsessive's desire, but let us not too quickly stop at such overly obvious appearances.

What characterizes the obsessive is not so much that the object of his desire is impossible, for there is always a note of impossibility in the object of desire, which has to do with the very structure and foundations of desire. The fact that the object of desire is impossible is just one of the especially manifest forms of an aspect of human desire. What specifically characterizes the obsessive is that he emphasizes the encounter with this impossibility. In other words, he orchestrates things in such a way that the object of his desire takes on the essential value of signifying this impossibility.

Something more profound is in store for us, however, which concerns mourning.

Our theory, our tradition, and Freud's formulations have already taught us to formulate mourning in terms of object relations. There have long been psychologists who think, yet Freud was the first – isn't it striking? – to highlight the object that is mourned. It is in a certain identificatory relationship that this object takes on its import, and that its manifestations come together and become organized.

With the vocabulary we have learned to use here, can't we try to rearticulate more precisely the [kind of] identification involved in mourning, which Freud tried to define most precisely by designating it as an incorporation? Exploring the question with the help of my symbolic devices [*appareils*], we will see that only they bring

397

out consequences that I believe are new and eminently suggestive regarding the function of mourning. I mean that they open up for us effective and fruitful insights we cannot reach by any other pathway.

The nature of identification must be clarified by the categories that I have been developing here with you for years – namely, those of the symbolic, the imaginary, and the real.

What is meant by incorporation of the lost object? What does the work of mourning consist of? Not being suitably articulated, the topic remains bogged down in obscurity, which explains why we have made so little progress down the path that Freud paved for us concerning mourning and melancholia.

Let us confine our attention to the first, most obvious aspects of the experience of mourning. The subject succumbs to the vertigo of pain, and finds himself in a certain relationship to the missing object that is, in some sense, illustrated for us by what occurs in the cemetery scene. Laertes jumps into the grave and, out of his mind, embraces the object whose disappearance is causing him pain. It is clear that the object here has an existence that is all the more absolute because it no longer corresponds to anything that exists.

In other words, mourning, which involves a veritable, intolerable loss to human beings, gives rise in them to a hole in reality [*réel*]. The relationship in question is the converse of the one that I proposed with the term *Verwerfung* [foreclosure] when I told you that what is rejected in the symbolic reappears in reality. This formulation, like its converse, should be taken literally.

The truly intolerable dimension of human experience that comes with mourning is not the experience of your own death, which no one has, but that of the death of another person, when that other person is essential to you. Such a loss constitutes a *Verwerfung*, a hole, [not in the symbolic] but in reality. Owing to the same correspondence as the one I articulate regarding *Verwerfung*, this hole turns out to provide a place onto which the missing signifier is projected.

398 What we have here is the signifier that is essential to the structure of the Other, the signifier whose absence renders the Other unable to give you your answer. You can only redeem [or: pay for, *payer*] this signifier with your flesh and blood. It is essentially the phallus behind the veil.

This signifier finds its place here. And at the same time it cannot find its place because this signifier cannot be articulated at the level of the Other. Owing to this, and as in psychosis, all the images that have to do with the phenomena of mourning proliferate in its place. Mourning is akin to psychosis in this regard.

Among these phenomena we should include those by which is

manifested, not some specific form of madness, but one of the most essential forms of collective madness in the human world. If some rite has not been performed for the departed, for the person who has just disappeared, strange things begin to happen. This is what explains, for example, the appearance, at the most basic level in the tragedy of *Hamlet*, of an image that can affect the soul of each and every one of us – namely, the ghost.*

What, in the final analysis, are funeral rites designed to do? To propitiate [*satisfaire à*] what we call the memory of the departed. And what do these rites involve if not the total, massive intervention, from hell to heaven, of the entire symbolic system [*jeu symbolique*].

I would love to have the time to devote several classes to the subject of funeral rites through an ethnological investigation. I recall having spent some time, many years ago, reading a book which admirably does so and which is exemplary in that it is from a civilization that is distant enough from our own for the function of such rites to be strikingly brought out in it. It is [Confucius' *Book of Rites:*] *Liji*, a sacred Chinese book.

Funeral rites have a macrocosmic nature, since there is nothing that can fill the hole in the real with signifiers unless it is the totality of the signifier itself. The work of mourning is carried out at the level of logos – I am saying this so as not to say at the level of the group or community, even though the group and the community as culturally organized naturally support this. The work of mourning presents itself first of all as a palliative for [*satisfaction donnée à*] the chaos that ensues owing to the inability of all signifying elements to deal with the hole in existence that has been created by someone's death. The entire signifying system is brought to bear on even the slightest case of mourning.

This is what explains the fact that all folk beliefs establish the closest relationship between two facts: if something is overlooked, elided, or refused in the propitiation [*satisfaction*] owed to the departed, all kinds of phenomena occur that stem from the coming into play and operating of the power of ghosts and worms [*larves*] in the place left unfilled by the missing signifying rite.

We see here a new dimension of the tragedy of *Hamlet*.

I told you at the outset that *Hamlet* is a tragedy of the underworld. The ghost* appears owing to an unatonable offense. In this perspective, Ophelia appears to be neutral, as nothing other than a victim offered up to [propitiate] the primordial offense. Polonius's death; the extraordinary scene of his cadaver being ridiculously dragged by the foot and hidden in defiance of the sensibility and concern of all and sundry; Hamlet who is suddenly and literally out of control [*déchaîné*], who makes fun of everyone who asks where the cadaver

399

is and who enjoys coming up with a whole series of enigmas in very bad taste which culminates in the formulation, "Hide fox, and all after" [IV, ii, 29], which refers to a kind of hide-and-go-seek game – all of that derides what is at stake, which is a mourning that has not been completed [*satisfait*].

I have not yet been able to give you the last word today, but you can already catch a glimpse here of the paradoxical relationship between fantasy, ($\$\lozenge a$), and the object-relation, which seems to be only distantly related to it, but on which mourning allows us to shed light.

Next time we will go into detail, once again taking up the twists and turns in *Hamlet*, inasmuch as the play allows us to better grasp the economy, which is tightly linked here, of the real, the imaginary, and the symbolic.

In the course of our exploration, many of your preconceived ideas will perhaps break down and even, I hope, be shattered. Nevertheless, I think that you will be prepared for it by my commentary on this tragedy in which we are spared no cadavers. This purely ideational damage will no doubt seem insignificant to you next to the damage Hamlet leaves in his wake.

400

In short, you can find consolation for the perchance difficult path I am taking you down with this Hamletesque formulation: you can't make a Hamlet without breaking eggs.

April 22, 1959

XIX

PHALLOPHANIES

Hamlet and *Oedipus*
Mourning the loss of the phallus
. . . and its transformation into a signifier
Forms of the subject's disappearance
A real and rotten phallus

If the tragedy of *Hamlet* is the tragedy of desire, it is time to notice what one always notices last – namely, what is most obvious.

Indeed, I do not believe that any author has ever dwelt on the fact that people talk about nothing but mourning from one end of *Hamlet* to the other, a fact that is difficult to overlook once it is formulated. This is where we left off last time.

The first remark Hamlet makes in the play concerns the scandalous nature of his mother's remarriage so soon after her husband's death. The mother herself, in her anxiety to know what is tormenting her beloved son, calls it "our o'erhasty marriage":

I doubt it is no other but the main,
His father's death and our o'erhasty marriage. [II, ii, 56–7]

No need to remind you of Hamlet's words about the leftovers of the funeral meal being served at the wedding feast: "Thrift [*Économie*], thrift, Horatio!" [I, ii, 180]. The word he uses nicely alerts us to what is overlooked when we explore the world of objects on the basis of the modern conceptual framework involving use value and exchange value, not to mention all the related notions that have been generated around them. Perhaps Marxist economic analysis, which dominates the thinking of our era, neglects something whose power and amplitude we deal with all the time: ritual values.

Even though we constantly pinpoint these latter in our practice, it might be worth our while to isolate and articulate them as essential.

I mentioned the function of rituals in mourning last time. Rituals serve a mediating function with regard to the gap opened up by [the loss of a loved one, leading to] mourning. More accurately speaking, mourning coincides with an essential gap, the major symbolic gap, the symbolic lack – in short, the point *x*, of which the dream's navel, which Freud mentions somewhere, is perhaps but a psychological correlate.

Thus we cannot fail to be struck by the fact that, in all the major instances of mourning that are called into question in *Hamlet*, what we always find is that the rituals have been abbreviated or carried out clandestinely. Polonius is buried secretly, quickly, and unceremoniously for political reasons. And you remember what happens with regard to Ophelia's burial.

Whereas she probably died having wanted to die, having deliberately drowned herself – that, at least, is the people's opinion – she was nevertheless buried on Christian ground and granted some modicum of Christian rites. The gravediggers are sure that, had she not been a gentlewoman, she would have been treated otherwise – which is the way the preacher says it should have been, for he believed she should have been denied funeral honors – she would have been thrown into "ground unsanctified," and "Shards, flints, and pebbles [would have been] thrown on her" [V, i, 216–8]. Here, too, the preacher only agreed to limited rites ["maimed rites"].

All of this is clearly emphasized at the end of the cemetery scene. We cannot but take all of these elements into account, especially when we add plenty of others to them. The father's shade [*ombre*] has an unatonable grievance, for he was, we are told, forever offended, having been surprised "in the blossoms of [his] sin" [I, v, 76]. This is not the least of the mysteries we encounter when we try to decipher the meaning of this tragedy. Before his death, the father did not have time to prepare himself to appear at the Last Judgment.

We have here traces, "clues"* as they say in English, eminently significant ones, which converge too obviously for us not to consider them. We are obliged to wonder, as we began to do last time, about the relationship between the drama of desire and what is involved in mourning and its exigencies.

This is the point I would like to focus on today in order to try to explore the nature of the object with you.

1

We broach the object in psychoanalysis in various forms. We broach it here in the sense of the object of desire. There is, it seems, a simple relationship between the object and desire. But can the rendezvous between desire and its object be articulated as if it were a mere appointment*? Perhaps it is something else.

We broach the question from a different angle when we speak of the object with which the subject identifies in mourning, and which he can, so people say, reintegrate into his ego.* What do we have here? Aren't there in fact two phases, which are not articulated and synchronized in psychoanalysis? Isn't this a problem that requires us to try to make headway here?

What I have just said about mourning in *Hamlet* must not hide from us the fact that, in both *Hamlet* and *Oedipus*, mourning is premised on a crime. Up to a certain point, all the instances of mourning that come cascading down on us are the aftermath and consequences of the crime that sets the drama in motion. It is in this respect that *Hamlet* is, I am saying, an Oedipal drama, a drama that I consider to be *Oedipus'* equal, and that I rank at the same functional level in the genealogy of tragedy.

It is the role played by crime in *Hamlet* that put Freud, and his disciples after him, on the scent of the importance this play takes on for us as analysts. In the psychoanalytic tradition, Hamlet is situated at the heart of speculation about origins, since we are in the habit of recognizing in Oedipus's crime the most essential plot [*trame*] involving the subject and what we call the Other here – namely, the locus in which the law is inscribed. Connecting these things should give us the opportunity to return to the way in which relations between the subject and what one might call the original crime have been articulated up until now and to recall a few essential terms.

Instead of doing what people always do, leaving things vague in a way that does nothing to facilitate speculation, we are going to introduce a clear distinction. We are presented with two stages.

First, there is Freud's myth, which deserves to be called one. *Totem and Taboo* lays out what we can, strictly speaking, call a myth. I already touched on this point when I told you that Freud's construction is perhaps the only example of a myth that has been concocted in our own time.

This myth indicates to us the early, essential, and altogether necessary link that is such that we cannot conceptualize the law, as an order, except on the basis of a still earlier fact that presents itself as a crime. This is the meaning of Freud's myth. The crime is the primal killing of the father. In Freud's view, it forms, let us note, the horizon or endpoint of the problem of origins in all psychoanalytic matters, for Freud finds it everywhere and no topic seems to him to have been exhausted if it has not yet been connected up with it. It is all too obvious that this primal killing of the father has a mythical

404

necessity for him, whether he situates it at the origin of the primal horde or at the origin of the Judaic tradition.

The relationship between the primal law and the primal crime is one thing; the drama that shapes the Oedipus complex is another. By this, I mean what happens when the tragic hero – who is Oedipus, but who is also, virtually, each of us at some point of our being when we reproduce the Oedipal drama – kills his father and sleeps with his mother, accomplishing at the tragic level, in a sort of lustral bath, the rebirth of the law.

Oedipus corresponds perfectly to the definition I just gave of ritual reproduction of the myth. Oedipus is, in short, completely innocent and unconscious. He repeats – unbeknownst to himself, in the sort of dream his life consists of, "Life is a dream" – actions that run from the crime to the restoring of order and the punishment he administers to himself, which makes him seem castrated to us at the end.

This castration is the essential element to take into account, and it remains veiled when one confines oneself to the level at which we see the genesis of the primal murder. In the final analysis, the meaning that shines through is that this punishment, sanction, or castration contains its result – namely, the humanization of man's sexuality – within itself, under lock and key. It is a key that we, owing to our practice, are in the habit of using in order to account for all the incidents that arise in the course of the unfolding of desire.

It is worth bringing out here the various dissymmetries between the tragedy of *Oedipus* and that of *Hamlet*, even if to spell them out in detail would be almost too clever [*brillante*].

In *Oedipus*, the crime occurs during the hero's generation. In *Hamlet*, it occurs in the prior generation. In *Oedipus*, the crime is committed when the hero does not know what he is doing and is in some sense guided by *fatum* [fate]. In *Hamlet*, the crime is committed in a deliberate manner, since it is committed through treachery.

In *Hamlet*, the crime catches its victim, Hamlet's father, while he is sleeping. There is something about this sleep that absolutely does not fit in [or: does not make sense, *pas intégré*]. Whereas in *Oedipus* the hero plays out the drama the way each of us repeats it in his dreams, in *Hamlet* the father has truly been taken by surprise in a way that is completely foreign to his train of thought at the time. As he puts it, he was "Cut off even in the blossoms of [his] sin" [I, v, 76]. A blow strikes him, coming from a quarter from which he did not expect it; it is a true intrusion from the real, a true breaking of the thread of destiny. He dies on a bed of flowers, as Shakespeare's text tells us, and during the play scene the actors even go so far as to reproduce this bed of flowers for us in their sort of preliminary pantomime. There is undoubtedly some sort of mystery here.

Furthermore, this exceedingly odd fact – namely, the irruption of a criminal act that is so foreign to the subject – appears in some sense to be counterbalanced by the fact that in this case the subject knows. I mean that Hamlet is informed by his father, who knows what happened. This paradoxical contrast, which I pointed out to you from the outset, is certainly not one of the least enigmatic elements of the play.

The drama of *Hamlet*, as opposed to that of *Oedipus*, does not begin from questions like "What is happening?" "What crime was committed?" and "Who is the guilty party?" It begins from the revelation of the crime, whispered into the subject's ear, and it is on the basis of this revelation that the drama unfolds. This revelation – and we see all of its ambiguity and its contrast with *Oedipus* – can thus be written in the way I notate messages from the unconscious: namely, as the signifier of barred A, S(Ⱥ).

406

In the, as it were, "normal" form of the Oedipus complex, this signifier manages to get incarnated in the figure of the father. The sanction given by the locus of the Other, the truth about truth [*la vérité de la vérité*], is expected from the father and is called for from him, insofar as he should be the author of the law. Nevertheless, he is never anything more than someone who is subject to the law; he cannot guarantee it, no more than anyone else can, for he, too, has to submit to the bar, which makes him a castrated father inasmuch as he is a real father.

Things are quite different – even if they can be symbolized in the same way – not at the end of *Hamlet*, but at its outset. In the father's message, with which the drama begins, we see the Other present himself in the most signifying form as a barred A. He has been wiped away not only from the surface of the living, but from the recompense that should have been his. The crime sent him into the bowels of hell – in other words, he has a debt that he has been unable to pay, an unatonable debt, as he puts it. To his son, this is the most horrible and anxiety-provoking meaning of the father's revelation.

Returning to the case of Oedipus, we see that he himself paid. He presents himself as someone who shoulders the burden of the discharged debt in his destiny as a hero. What Hamlet's father shall complain of for all eternity is that the thread of his destiny was interrupted and broken, such that he will never be able to answer for it. As you see, our investigation, as it progresses, is leading us to what is involved in retribution, punishment, and castration, and is heading toward the relationship to the phallic signifier, since it is in this sense that we have begun to articulate castration.

We see an ambiguity here in relation to what Freud formulated, in a way that was a bit *fin de siècle* – namely, that we are doomed to no longer experience the Oedipus complex except in a somewhat distorted form. This assertion is assuredly echoed in *Hamlet*. Consider one of his first cries at the end of the first act:

The time is out of joint. O cursed spite
That ever I was born to set it right! [I, v, 188–9]

There is no way to translate the word "spite," which is found throughout Shakespeare's *Sonnets*, into French except with the word "*dépit*." *Dépit* has, however, taken on a subjective meaning for us. The first step I would have to take in order to help you understand the Elizabethans would be to make a certain number of words double-jointed again. *Dépit* must be situated somewhere between objective and subjective spite.

407

We seem to have lost this reference point. We no longer know how to articulate words that can lie between objective and subjective, that can operate both at the heart of the subject's lived experience and at the level of the world order. What Hamlet is designating when he says "O cursed spite" is what he is bitterly disappointed about: the way in which time is unjust to him, or what he can designate as injustice in the world. Perhaps you recognize here in passing the mistake made by the beautiful soul, which we have not left behind, far from it, despite all our efforts, but that Shakespeare's vocabulary transcends, and it is no accident that I so blithely mentioned his *Sonnets*.

In the lines, "The time is out of joint. O cursed spite / That ever I was born to set it right!" something is justified but also deepened that may appear to us to illustrate in *Hamlet* a decadent form, a sort of incomplete *Untergang* [fall or dissolution] of the Oedipus complex.

This contrasts with what Freud describes in each individual's life in his 1924 paper entitled *Das Untergang des Ödipuskomplexes* ["The Dissolution of the Oedipus Complex"].

I would now like to draw your attention to this short text, which you can find in volume XIII of Freud's *Gesammelte Werke* [pp. 395–402].

2

What, in the final analysis, is the enigma of the Oedipus complex? Freud highlights that it is not simply the fact that the subject wants to kill his father and rape his mother, but that this [desire] comes to dwell in the unconscious.

And it so clearly dwells in the unconscious that, in the course of the so-called latency period – which is, in human beings, the source of the building blocks [*points de construction*] of their entire objective world – subjects are no longer thinking about this. This goes so far, as you know, that Freud suggests – at least when he first provides this theoretical formulation – that the ideal case would be that no longer being concerned with it becomes definitive, happily so.

Let us consider what Freud says. Afterward we will see in what respect this can help us in our current undertaking. The Oedipus complex begins its *Untergang* – its decline or dissolution, which is decisive for the whole of the subject's later development – after what?

Freud tells us that the subject must have tried out and experienced both vertices of the Oedipal triangle. Inasmuch as a boy, as his father's rival, wants to take his father's place, he becomes the target of a concrete threat, which is no other than that of castration: he will be castrated. If, instead, he takes his mother's place, he will lose the phallus anyway – Freud says this literally – since at the point at which the Oedipus complex comes to fruition, the boy has also fully realized that women are castrated.

At the level of the relationship to the thing known as the phallus, the subject thus finds himself in a bind that leaves him no way out. This situation, in which the phallus is the key, constitutes the essential drama of the Oedipus complex insofar as it marks, I would say, the juncture and turning point that conveys the subject from the level of demand to that of desire.

I said "thing" [known as the phallus], not "object," inasmuch as what is involved is something real, something that is not yet symbolized but that may, in some sense, become symbolized. In short, it is what we can call a signifier, vaguely speaking.

Freud thus presents the phallus to us as the key to the *Untergang* of the Oedipus complex. The Oedipus complex begins to dissolve when the subject enters into a relationship, we might say, of lassitude – this is what we find in Freud's text – with regard to gratification. This is when the subject realizes that no gratification can be expected in this context; he knows that the articulated emergence of the *thing* will not occur; and he gives up trying to be equal to the task. Freud articulates it for the boy and still more for the girl, for he places her in a position about which I will not say that it is not dissymmetrical, but it is *not so very* dissymmetrical.

In short, the subject must mourn the loss of the phallus. This comes across very clearly – the *Untergang* of the Oedipus complex is

played out around mourning. How can we not but relate this to the
general problematic of mourning?

Let me underscore that the moment at which the dissolution of
the Oedipus complex occurs plays a decisive role in what follows,
not only because the fragments and detritus it leaves in its wake,
which are more or less incompletely repressed, will come out at
puberty in the form of neurotic symptoms, but above all because,
as the shared experience of psychoanalysts attests, the subject's normalization at the genital level depends on this moment – not in the
subject's unconscious economy alone but in the subject's imaginary
economy as well. Which is to say that there is no happy outcome
as regards genital maturity except by going through the entirety of
the Oedipus complex, insofar as its consequence, in both men and
women, is the scar [or: mark, *stigmate*] of the castration complex.
Synthesizing this with the mechanism of mourning, as it is described
to us by Freud, will perhaps allow us to clarify the mechanism of
mourning the loss of the phallus, which is no doubt peculiar since
the phallus is an object like no other.

But, I ask you, what defines the scope and limits of the set of
objects that we may be led to mourn? This, too, has never before
been articulated. We suspect, of course, that the phallus is different
from the other objects that we may be led to mourn. Here as everywhere else, it must have its own separate place; but this is precisely
what must be specified. And, as in many cases, to specify something
is to indicate its place against a backdrop. It is in pinpointing it
against this backdrop that the place of the backdrop also manages
to get retroactively specified.

What I am calling the place of the object in desire is completely
new territory. Our analysis of *Hamlet* is designed, in the end, to
help us make headway in this realm. I am tilling this ground here
by plowing a series of concentric rows. I am conveying it to you in a
way that is at times emphatic, at times resonant. And I hope to make
it more and more precise as we go on.

What does Freud tell us about mourning the loss of the phallus?
He presents the subject's narcissistic demand [*exigence*] as one of its
fundamental mainsprings, insofar as this demand is what gives the
phallus its value, which is precisely what we are seeking. He brings
in this factor without the slightest precaution, as he always does. I
mean that he shakes us up, as is his wont, and thank God he did it
his whole life long; if not, he would never have gotten to the end of
what he needed to sketch out in his field.

The subject thus gets to the point at which he is in the presence of
the final exit from his Oedipal demands; he is at the critical moment
at which he realizes that he will be castrated and deprived of the

phallus in either case. Well, Freud tells us, rather than abandon the phallus, he prefers to abandon, as it were, a whole part of himself, which will henceforth and forever be prohibited to him. This part is what is transmitted by the dotted signifying chain found at the top of the graph of desire [see Figure 15.4].

Stated otherwise, the subject lets go of what was most important to him – namely, the love relationship as it presented itself to him in the parental dialectic into which he had to enter one way or another – because, Freud tells us, of his narcissistic relationship with a term that was introduced right from the outset and that has enigmatically and yet clearly run throughout his experience: the phallus.

What can this mean to us, in our vocabulary? This vocabulary can shed light on what is at stake in what Freud designates as a narcissistic demand, and which he had to leave to one side, as I was just saying, because he did not have the time to dwell at length on his premises, and because he needed to go right to the quick, to the core of the subject. Which is, moreover, how every action is grounded, still more every true action, as is, or should be, the action we are concerned with here – namely, psychoanalytic action.

Let us thus translate this into our own terms and reference points: to say that the demand in question is narcissistic implies that it is situated at the imaginary level. On the other hand, the subject's demand for love has begun to express itself in the field organized by the symbolic, what we call the locus of the Other. The critical moment arrives once the subject has run the gamut of all possible relations there and has reached the end. The upshot is the loss of the phallus, experienced as a radical loss that no satisfaction can plug up.

I have already indicated that what happens then is akin to a psychotic mechanism: the subject can only respond to this mourning with his imaginary texture. What Freud presents us, in a veiled form, as the narcissistic link between the subject and the phallus, allows us to identify the phallus with something that represents lack as such in the subject at the imaginary level. This lack places something in reserve – in the form of nihilation [or: obliteration or "nothingizing," *sous une forme néantisée*], as it were – something that will serve as a mold in which the subject's assumption of his position in the genital function will later be recast.

But isn't this to conclude too quickly about what is involved?   411
Doesn't this lead us to believe, as we ordinarily do, that the relationship to the genital object is a relationship that changes from positive to negative? As you will see, it is nothing of the sort. Our notation is superior because it allows us to articulate how the problem really presents itself. Let me specifically remind you of what I already laid

out when I distinguished among the functions of castration, frustration, and deprivation [see Seminar IV].

If you recall, I wrote the following: *castration* is a symbolic action, *frustration* is an imaginary term, and *deprivation* is a real term. I also indicated their relations to objects: I told you that castration is related to the imaginary phallic object; that frustration, which is imaginary in nature, is always related to a real possession [*bien*] or term; and that deprivation, which is real, is related to a symbolic term. I added at that time that there is no sort of gap or crack in the real. Lack always involves something that is missing from its [usual] place; the fact of being missing from its place is [what is known as] a symbolic lack [*Tout manque est manque à sa place, mais le manque à sa place est manque symbolique*].

Table 19.1: Table of lacking objects

AGENT	LACK	OBJECT
	Castration S	i
Symbolic mother	Frustration I	r
	Deprivation R	s

The column on the left [Table 19.1] concerns the agent of these actions. I only discussed one of the agents: the agent of frustration – namely, the mother. I showed you that, qua locus of the demand for love, she is at first symbolized in the twofold register of presence and absence, and that she thereby finds herself to be in the position of setting the generative [or: developmental, *génétique*] dialectic in motion, inasmuch as, qua real mother, she turns what the subject is really deprived of – the breast, for example – into a symbol of her love.

I stopped there, leaving blank the boxes corresponding to the term "agent" in the other two relationships. As for its place, the term "agent" is related to the subject. I could not at that time clearly articulate the different stages of the subject. It is only now that I can indicate what is involved.

At the level of frustration, where I had placed the mother's actual locus, I am inscribing the term by which everything that happens owing to her takes on its value – in other words, the A of the Other insofar as it is there that demand is articulated.

At the level of castration, we have a subject qua real, but in the form in which we have learned to formulate and discover it since – in other words, as the speaking or actual subject. He is marked by the sign of speech. We write this, of course, as barred S.

It seems to me that this is what philosophers have been trying to articulate for some time concerning the peculiar nature of human action. It is impossible to broach this topic without realizing that there is something fishy in the illusory idea of turning some sort of absolute beginning into a final term with which to pinpoint the notion of the agent. People have tried, over time, to present this something fishy to us in the form of varied speculations about a type of freedom that is supposedly at the same time necessity. This is the terminus at which philosophers have arrived in articulating the following: that there is no other true action than to align yourself in some sense with God's will.

What I am contributing here can at least claim to stem from a completely different register owing to the specific quality of its articulation. I say that the subject, qua real, stands in a specific relation to speech, and that this relation gives rise in him to an eclipse or fundamental lack that structures him at the symbolic level in relation to castration. I am not saying that this is a pot of gold or a skeleton key that opens all doors. It is no more than the beginning of an articulation, but it is something that has never been said before, and this is perhaps worth emphasizing.

What then appears at the level of deprivation? What does the subject who has been symbolically castrated become at this level? 413 Note that he has been symbolically castrated at the level of his position as a speaking subject, and not at the level of his being. What is involved becomes far clearer and easier to indicate once we formulate the problem in terms of mourning. The being in question must mourn something that he must offer up as a sacrifice or holocaust, in order to raise it to the level of its function as a missing signifier.

At the imaginary level, the subject is identical to the biological images that guide him and that trace out the wake prepared for his behavior,* for what is going to attract him, by all the pathways of voracity and coupling. It is at the imaginary level that something is caught up, marked, and subtracted. The upshot is a really deprived subject. Our conceptual framework and knowledge do not allow us to locate or situate this deprivation anywhere in the real, because the real as such is defined as always full.

We encounter here again, but in a different and otherwise highlighted form, something that has been remarked by what is rightly or wrongly known as existentialist thought – namely, that it is the living, human subject who introduces a "nihilation" [*néantisation*] into reality. That is what *they* call it; we give it a different name.

This nihilation, which comforts philosophers, and even grants them pleasant weekends – see Raymond Queneau's novel [*Le Dimanche de la vie, The Sunday of Life*] – is inadequate for us and does not satisfy us, given the more than artificial uses to which it is put in modern dialectical prestidigitation.

We call it minus phi ($-\varphi$). It is what Freud pinpointed as essential in the mark left on man by his relation to logos – that is, castration, which is, in effect, assumed [*assumée*] here at the imaginary level. This notation will allow us to define desire's object *a* as it appears in our formulation of fantasy, and we will situate it in relation to the categories, chapter headings, and registers we are used to working with in psychoanalysis.

Desire's object *a* is the object that sustains the relationship between the subject and what he is not – up to that point, we go more or less as far, although a bit further, than what traditional and existentialist philosophy formulated as the negativity or nihilation of the existing subject – but we add: it sustains the relationship between the subject and what he is not *insofar as he is not the phallus*. Object *a* sustains the subject in the privileged position he is led to occupy in certain situations, which is strictly speaking the following: that he is not the phallus.

It has now become essential for us to provide an apt definition of object *a*. At the very least, the time has come for us to try to see how what we have rightly or wrongly begun to articulate as being the object, up until now in our field, is organized and at the same time differentiated.

We are going to have to raise the question: with this object, insofar as it is *a*, are we defining the genital object? Does this mean that pre-genital objects are not objects? I am not answering this question; I am simply saying that it arises as soon as we formulate the problem in this way.

It is clear that the answer cannot be altogether simple. Nevertheless, our way of formulating the question has at least one advantage, which is to allow us to see the distinction, angle, or cleavage plane that arises between the phallic phase (or stage) – or what has been called that up until now (I am closely following the generally accepted vocabulary here) – and the genital phase (or stage), the one in which the formation and maturation of the object occurs. In [the psychoanalytic literature that has come out in] recent years, it has, indeed, been quite impossible to grasp the relationship between the two.

At the level of deprivation, in which the subject is a desiring subject, his position is always veiled. His position can only be glimpsed in "phanies" [appearances or manifestations], lightning-fast appearances of its reflection at the level of the object, in the form of having it or not having it. But, as such, the subject's radical position is that of *not* being the phallus – he himself being a negative object, as it were. You see how far I am taking this.

The three forms in which the subject appears at the level of the three terms, castration, frustration, and deprivation, may well be called alienated, on the condition of giving this alienation a tangibly different, varied articulation in each case. At the level of castration, the subject appears in a blacking out [*syncope*] of the signifier [S]. Things are quite different when he appears at the level of frustration, as subjected to the law that applies to everyone, the Other's law [A]. They are different again when, at the level of deprivation, he himself must situate himself in desire.

This latter form of the subject's disappearance thus appears to us to have an odd originality with respect to the other two, which incites us to go further into it.   415

This is in fact what occurs in our practice, and what the unfolding of the tragedy of *Hamlet* leads us toward.

3

The "something . . . rotten" [I, iv, 90] that poor Hamlet needs to set right is closely related to his position as a subject with respect to the phallus.

Throughout the play, we sense that the phallus is present everywhere in the obvious mess [*désordre*] that is Hamlet's whenever he approaches the hotspots, as it were, of his action. Today I can only quickly indicate to you the points that allow us to follow him step by step.

There is something very strange in the way Hamlet speaks about his dead father; he does so with an idealizing exaltation that more or less boils down to the following: his voice fails him when he tries to say what he has to say about him. In truth, he chokes, only to conclude with one of the specific forms of the signifier known as "pregnant"* in English [II, ii, 206–7] – in other words, an expression that has meaning beyond its meaning – he finds nothing other to say about his father than that he was "a man" like any other. What he means to say is obviously the exact opposite. This is the first trace of what is involved.

There are many other traces as well. The rejection, abuse, and scorn he heaps on Claudius smacks mightily of negation [*dénégation*]. He generates a slew of insults about him, especially in front of his mother, culminating in an expression that cannot fail to indicate to us that here, too, there is something problematic: "A king of shreds and patches" [III, iv, 103].

We cannot fail to connect this up with an obvious fact in the tragedy of *Hamlet*, and one that distinguishes it from the Oedipal tragedy: after the father has been killed, the phallus is still there. It is quite plainly there, for it is Claudius who is given the task of embodying it. What is constantly at stake is Claudius' real phallus.

In short, Hamlet has nothing else to reproach his mother for than to have gotten herself filled up by it the minute his father disappeared. And he ends up sending her back, with discouraged arm and speech, to this fatal and fateful object which is quite real here. The whole drama seems to revolve around this.

We are obliged to think that there is something very powerful attaching his mother to her partner, given the human feelings she displays in other contexts; indeed, she does not appear to us to be a woman who, by nature, is so very different from other women. It seems that Hamlet's action revolves and hesitates around this point. Here his "daunted genius" trembles, as it were, before something completely unexpected.

For the phallus is in an entirely ectopic position here with respect to the Oedipal position as it is articulated by psychoanalysis. The phallus is clearly real here; it is in this respect that it is important to strike it, and Hamlet always balks at doing so. His uncertainty and hesitation before the object that must be struck is manifest at the moment at which he finds our Claudius praying and says to himself that he could obviously kill him: "Now might I do it pat" [III, iii, 73]. The precise mainspring of what constantly deflects Hamlet's arm is the very narcissistic link that Freud tells us about in "The Dissolution of the Oedipus Complex." One cannot strike the phallus because, even if it is clearly real, it is but a shadow [*ombre*].

I will ask you to contemplate this in connection with all sorts of very strange, paradoxical things, and especially in connection with how very much we were all stirred up at the time when we wondered why, after all, no one had assassinated Hitler. He perfectly incarnated the object whose function Freud outlines in his *Massenpsychologie* where he spells out how a mass of people becomes homogenized by way of identification with an object on the horizon, an object *x*, which is unlike any other. Doesn't that link up with what we are talking about here?

What is involved is the altogether enigmatic manifestation of the signifier of power as such. When it presents itself in a particularly striking form in reality [*réel*], as occurs in *Hamlet* – that of a criminal who becomes instated as the usurper – Oedipus deflects Hamlet's arm, not because Hamlet is afraid of this man whom he scorns, but because he knows that what he must strike is something other than what is there. This is so true that, two minutes after stumbling upon Claudius praying, when he arrives in his mother's closet and begins to shake her up bigtime, he hears a sound behind the curtain and runs headlong at it without even looking.

Some astute commentator has pointed out that Hamlet cannot possibly believe it is Claudius behind the tapestry, for he just left Claudius in the next room. Nevertheless, after he has eviscerated poor Polonius, he reflects,

Thou wretched, rash, intruding fool, farewell!
I took thee for thy better. [III, iv, 32–3]

Everyone believes that he wanted to kill Claudius, but he stopped short of killing him because he wanted to have a better one – in other words, to catch Claudius himself "in the blossoms of [his] sin" [I, v, 76]. Given how he presented himself there, he was not the right one.

It is the phallus that is at stake here. Which is why Hamlet can never reach it until the moment at which he has sacrificed – in spite of himself, moreover – his entire narcissistic attachment. It is only when he is fatally wounded, and knows that he is, that he can perform the action that lays Claudius low.

This is odd, obvious, and also inscribed, I would say, in all sorts of little enigmas of Hamlet's style.

Consider the moment at which he shoves Polonius – who for him is merely a "calf," a "capital . . . calf" [III, ii, 101–2], that he has in some sense offered up as a sacrifice to his father's manes and whose assassination barely affects him – into a closet under the stairs. Everybody asks him what is going on and he comes out with a few of his little jokes that are always so disconcerting to his enemies.

Everyone wonders if this is truly the whole story, whether what he says is what he means, for what he says tickles everybody's funny bone, but in order for him to say what he says he must know so much that they cannot believe it, and so on and so forth. This should sound rather familiar to us, given how subjects often reveal things to us.

Hamlet thus says the following things, which have remained up until now quite perplexing to commentators. "The body is with the king" – please note that he does not use the word "corpse," he says "body" – "but the king is not with the body" [IV, ii, 26–7]. I would ask you to simply replace the word "king" with the word "phallus" to realize that it is the phallus that is involved here. For the body is tightly bound up in this business of the phallus, but on the other

418

hand the phallus is bound to nothing and always slips between your fingers.

Immediately thereafter, he adds, "The king is a thing –" "A thing, my lord?" his interlocutors ask [IV, ii, 27–8], completely shocked as they are whenever he comes out with one of his aphorisms, and Hamlet replies, "Of nothing" [29]. At which point commentators tend to calm down, thinking that it must be a quotation from the *Psalms* in which it is said that "Man is like a thing of nought." I think that in order to shed light on this it is better to rely on Shakespeare's own work.

An attentive reading of the *Sonnets* inclines me to believe that, in his own life, Shakespeare was imbued with a rather extreme and peculiar desire. Somewhere, in one of the sonnets, whose audacity we can hardly imagine – I am astonished that people can talk about them as though they were ambiguous – he speaks to his love object who, as everyone knows, was of the same sex as him, quite a charming young man, it seems, who appears to have been the Earl of Essex. Your looks leave nothing to be desired, he says to this young man; you look like a woman in every regard; there is but "one thing" that nature wanted to give you, God only knows why, and I unfortunately could not care less about this little thing: it is "to my purpose nothing." Too bad it delights women. And Shakespeare adds, oh well, as long as "Mine be thy love, and thy love's use their treasure."

The terms "thing" and "nothing" are used in their strict sense here, and they are indubitably part of Shakespeare's standard vocabulary. Yet this vocabulary is of but secondary importance here, after all. The question is whether we can fathom Shakespeare's creative position.

At the sexual level, his position can undoubtedly be called inverted, but it is perhaps not all that perverted at the level of love.

To enter into the path of the *Sonnets* will allow us to indicate a little more precisely the dialectic of the subject with the object of his desire. In particular, we shall see what happens at moments when the object – disappearing and vanishing step by step by some pathway, the major one being the pathway of mourning – exposes the true nature of what corresponds to it in the subject for a while, a while that can last no more than an instant: what I will call appearances of the phallus, "phallophanies."

I will leave it at that today.

April 29, 1959

THE DIALECTIC
OF DESIRE

XX

THE FUNDAMENTAL FANTASY

No pre-established harmony between desire and the world
Synchrony's privilege
Desire and reality in Glover's work and in Hartmann's
Our experience with homosexuality
The dialectic grasped in its synchronic structure

We are thus talking about desire. The path I have been following this year, like any path, sometimes obliges me to take long detours. This is why I tried, during the break over the last two weeks, to re-center things in order to conceptualize anew the origin and aim of our work here.

This led me to come up with a clarification of the topic, which is also, I believe, designed for you, and which will be but yet another way for us to focus our attention in order to make headway in our research.

At the point we are at, let us try to articulate that with which *we* have a rendezvous. It is not simply the rendezvous of this Seminar, nor the rendezvous of our daily work as analysts. It is above all the rendezvous we have with our function as analysts and with the meaning of analysis.

If psychoanalysis were merely a therapeutic enterprise – like others that have appeared in the course of history – which is more or less founded and successful, we could not fail to be surprised by its longevity. There is no prior example of any theory or psychical orthopedics that has lasted for more than half a century.

What has allowed for the longevity of psychoanalysis, and of the role it plays beyond its use by physicians, that no one, in the end, dreams of disputing? We cannot fail to sense that it is the fact that psychoanalysis brings something with it that concerns man in a way that is simultaneously new, serious, and authentic – new in what it contributes, serious in its import, and authenticated by what?

Surely by something other than its often debatable and sometimes precarious results.

What is most characteristic here is, I think, the feeling people have that the thing I once called "the Freudian thing" is something that is being talked about for the first time. I would go further still, to the point of saying, regarding the authenticity of the thing, that its clearest manifestation, what attests to it every day, is the bountiful verbiage that surrounds it.

Indeed, what is striking, when you consider the massive production of psychoanalytic literature, is that its authors always strive to articulate the principle that guides their actions in analysis, without ever arriving, in the end, at anything that is closed, finished, or satisfying. This perpetual dialectical slippage, which constitutes the very movement and life of analytic research, attests to the specificity of the problem with which our research is connected.

Everything that our research includes that is clumsy, confused, or not terribly well founded, even in its principles, everything our practice contains that is equivocal – in which we always encounter what we intended to avoid, namely suggestion, persuasion, construction, and even initiation into mysteries – all of these contradictions in the psychoanalytic movement do no more than point out the specificity of the Freudian thing.

1

The Freudian thing is desire. That is how I am envisioning it this year at least, as an hypothesis, but one which is supported by the concentric progress of my previous work.

Nevertheless, in saying that the Freudian thing is desire, we perceive a sort of contradiction, insofar as the whole thrust of analysts' attempts at theorization seems to go in the direction of making desire lose the accent it originally had – and that it still has, as we cannot fail to note when we deal with it in our experience.

We cannot in any way view desire as functioning in a reduced or normalized way, in conformity with the requirements of some sort of preformed organic system that supposedly leads it down pathways traced out in advance, and along which we would have to redirect it when it goes off course. On the contrary, ever since Freud began to develop psychoanalysis, desire has presented itself with the characteristic designated by the English word "lust,"* which means both covetousness [or: longing, *convoitise*] and lasciviousness [*luxure*]. The same word is included in the German term *Lustprinzip* [known in English as the pleasure principle], and

425

you are aware that it is ambiguous insofar as it oscillates between pleasure and desire.

In psychoanalytic experience, desire presents itself at first as a problem [*trouble*]. It disturbs [*trouble*] our perception of the object. We see this in poets' and moralists' curses: desire denigrates, disorganizes, debases, and in any case undermines the object, going so far at times as to even dissolve he who perceives it – namely, the subject.

We find the very same perspective at the heart of Freud's position. Nevertheless, *Lust*, as it is brought to the fore by Freud, is formulated in a radically different way from everything that could have been said up until then about desire. The *Lustprinzip* is presented to us as being, at its very core, opposed to the reality principle. The original experience of desire seems to run counter to the construction of reality. The seeking [*recherche*] involved in it is blind in nature. In short, desire presents itself as a torment to man.

Now all those who had tried before Freud to spell out the meaning of the pathways taken by man in his quest had always adopted the principle that man seeks his own good. Over the centuries, philosophers never formulated a single moral theory in which the pleasure principle, whatever it may be, was not immediately defined as hedonistic. This means that man, whether he knows it or not, fundamentally seeks his own good, such that the errors and aberrations of his desire in practice can only be viewed as accidents.

Freud, on the other hand, proffers for the first time a theory of human nature whose principle fundamentally contradicts the hedonistic principle. An entirely different emphasis is given to pleasure, inasmuch as, in Freud's work, the very signifier is contaminated by the specific accent with which *Lust*, "lust"* – covetousness and desire – presents itself.

As opposed to what a harmonious and optimistic idea of human development might, after all, lead us to believe, there is no preestablished harmony between desire and the way the world works. Desire is not organized or put together in that way, psychoanalytic experience teaching us that things go in an entirely different direction. As I have indicated here, psychoanalysis leads us down a path of experience whose very development makes us give up the emphasis on primordial instincts, invalidating it for us.

This means that the history of desire is organized in the form of a discourse that unfolds in the realm of the nonsensical [*l'insensé*]. This is the unconscious. The displacements and condensations in its discourse are undoubtedly the same as the displacements and condensations in discourse in general – in other words, metonymies and metaphors. But in this case they are metaphors that generate

426

no meaning, and displacements that bring no being with them and in which the subject does not recognize anything that is displaced.

Psychoanalytic experience has advanced by devoting itself to the exploration of the discourse of the unconscious. The core dimension involved there is diachrony. Yet it is synchrony that constitutes the essence of the work we are engaged in here this year. I am attempting to reconceptualize the status of desire in order to situate it in the synchronic dimension.

Whenever we broach our experience – whether by reading the major account of it, the textbook* of the earliest experience of psychoanalysis, namely, *The Interpretation of Dreams*, or by considering a series of interpretations in any given analytic session – we realize that every interpretation involves a deferral [*renvoi*] from one wish to another in which the movement of the subject is inscribed, as well as the distance at which he finds himself from his own wishes. Although this mechanism of endless deferral never presents us with desire in anything but an articulated form, it nevertheless presupposes something that necessitates it at its core.

It is here that our strictly linguistic reference to structure comes into play. It reminds us that there can be no use of symbolism without there being primordially – that is, prior to any and all use of speech, which is known as discourse – a synchronism, that is, a language structure qua synchronic system. It seems to me that it is thus legitimate to hope that we will also manage to locate the function of desire in synchrony.

427   What we call man is therefore an x, a barred subject, insofar as he is the subject of logos and insofar as he constitutes himself as a subject in the signifier.

Where is desire situated in the synchronic relationship between the subject and the signifier?

It is enough to see what pathways psychoanalytic research, in its neglect of structural organization, is following today to sense just how necessary it is to re-elaborate or revamp the concept of desire, as we are doing, on this basis.

2

When, a few minutes ago, I mentioned the theoretical distinction made by Freud between the pleasure principle and the reality principle, did you realize that we had reached the precise point at which writers try to theorize analysis in the very terms that I said should be avoided because desire does not square with them?

It squares with them only to the degree to which these authors feel a need to believe that desire coincides with what everyone else thinks it is. They do everything possible to deduce their idea of optimal, or at least desirable, development from the notion that experience supposedly converges on maturation.

At the same time, if these writers could in fact formulate psychoanalytic theory in such terms and be content with the idea that the subject ontologically adapts to his experience of the world, this would mean they had abandoned all contact with their practice as analysts. The further they try to take this project, the more they make revealing mistakes – mistakes that reveal that they need to formulate things differently – and the more they arrive at paradoxes.

I will give an example, which I will take from one of the best analytic authors around, one who pays the most attention to formulating things correctly, not only regarding our practice but also regarding the sum total of our practice's initial data, and who also deserves credit for having striven to survey the notions and concepts we employ. I am talking about Edward Glover.

His work should be read because of the vast number of cases that it summarizes. It is among the most useful to anyone who wishes to know what he is doing, which is still more indispensable in analysis than elsewhere. I will take up one of his many articles, one you must read, which came out in the *International Journal of Psychoanalysis* in October 1933, volume 14, number 4 [pp. 486–504]. It is entitled "The Relation of Perversion-Formation to the Development of Reality-Sense."

428

Many things in this article are worth discussing, if only the initial terms Glover provides in view of correctly broaching what he intends to show us. Specifically:

1 He defines "reality-sense" as "a faculty the existence of which we infer by examining the processes of reality-testing" [p. 486]. It is sometimes of great interest that things be formulated clearly.
2 He defines "efficient reality-testing" as the capacity, "for any subject who has passed the age of puberty, [. . .] to retain psychic contact with the objects that promote gratification of instinct, including here both modified and residual infantile impulse" [p. 486].
3 He defines "objectivity" as "the capacity to assess correctly the relation of instinctual impulse to instinctual object, whether or not the aims of the impulse are, can be or will be gratified" [p. 486].

These are his very important premises. You cannot fail to be struck by the fact that the author defines the term "objectivity" in a way in which it is not usually defined. This reminds us that not everything Freud said has been completely forgotten, because this definition of objectivity overthrows what hitherto seemed to us to be a category necessitated by our worldview.

On this basis, Glover undertakes a study of what is meant by perversion formations, understood most broadly, in relation to reality-sense. What is, in the end, the spirit of the article? It is to conceptualize perversion as a means by which a subject can deal with everything that does not fit for him into a coherent reality, including rips and things that flop.* Perversion is very precisely articulated by Glover as the "means of salvation for the subject to assure continuous existence to this reality."

This is quite an original viewpoint, since the upshot is that perversion becomes ubiquitous. Glover then tries to trace out a developmental chronology, establishing a timeline on which psychotic disturbances are the earliest occurrences and neurotic disturbances come later. Between the two he situates drug addiction, which thus corresponds in his view to an intermediate stage. The point for him is, in short, to determine the chronological turning points or historically important developmental moments that give rise to different problems.

This point of view is open to criticism, as is every such attempt to provide a simple developmental timeline of analyzable complaints. As we cannot enter here into a detailed critique of the article, I will select a single paragraph that highlights the paradox that arises whenever people attempt to reduce the desire function or desire principle we deal with, to a preliminary, preparatory, not-yet-informed stage which involves adaptation to reality – whenever, that is, people attempt to reduce it to the first form of our relationship to reality. The principle that serves as Glover's point of departure, here as elsewhere, in developing his theory is, in effect, to classify perversion with respect to reality-sense.

I will simply indicate to you the consequences this principle brings with it by citing a short passage from his article, which differs from thousands of others in his writings only by the colorful, literary, paradoxical, and truly expressive form in which it is presented. Let me make it clear that this article was written during what one might call Glover's Kleinian phase, his work here having a great deal in common with Klein's system – in spite of the struggle against Klein he felt he had to engage in at the theoretical level.

In this passage, Glover is discussing the moment at which, he tells us, the subject's so-called paranoid phase gives way to the "reality system" that he calls "oral-anal." Glover describes the external world, in which children supposedly live, as something that "represent[s] a combination of a butcher's shop, a public lavatory under shell-fire, and a post-mortem room" – and Glover explains to us here that the point at that moment is to transform this world, which is rather tumultuous and catastrophic, "into a more reassuring and fascinating chemist's shop," one in which there is nevertheless a little problem: "the poison cupboard is left unlocked" [p. 492]. 430

This is quite cute and picturesque. But however implicit, profound, and buried children's experience may be, or we may assume it to be, there is nevertheless a problem in theorizing that children actually broach reality in the form of a butcher's shop, a public lavatory under shell-fire, or a morgue.

It is not because this formulation is initially shocking that we can rule it out, but at the same time we would be justified in doubting its accuracy. It obviously cannot coincide with the usual form of child development, especially when one views this development as characterized by the ways in which the subject adapts to reality.

At the very least, such a formulation necessarily implies the hypothesis of a twofold reality. In one form of reality we could locate behaviorism, but there would be another reality on whose eruptions in the subject's behavior we would then have to keep an eye. Otherwise stated, we are immediately obliged to restore the autonomy and originality of another dimension which is not primitive reality, but which is, right from the outset, something that goes beyond the subject's lived experience.

Once it is articulated, this contradiction becomes so obvious that I may need to apologize for having discussed it at such length. Nevertheless, it is so well disguised in certain people's work that it gives rise to a serious equivocation in the use of the term "reality." When we assume that reality undergoes a development parallel to that of the instincts – and this is the most widespread belief – we arrive at strange paradoxes that inevitably have repercussions on analytic practice.

If we assume that desire is already there – in other words, that it exists in reality – it becomes necessary to talk about it, not in a disguised form, but in its earliest form: instinct. The latter is supposedly involved in both evolution and in psychoanalytic experience. To say that desire is inscribed in a realm that is homogeneous with reality, that it is part and parcel of the same realm as reality, and that it can be thoroughly explained and taken up in terms of reality – these being formulations that we find nowadays in virtually all of psychoanalytic theory – implies the following paradox: what allows the world to achieve its full objectivity is the maturing of desire. This proposition is part and parcel of the basic belief system of a certain form of analysis. 431

Here I would like to raise a question about what this means concretely. What is a world, to we living beings? What is reality in Hartmann's version of psychoanalysis, for example?

Hartmann gives full credit to the structuring elements that ego organization brings with it. This ego, he says, has adapted in such a way as to move about efficiently within constituted reality. Well I, too, would like to provide an image that conveys to you what we are talking about. To give you a concrete image of the most typical and developed form of world we are talking about, adult reality, I will liken it to the world of American lawyers.

For the world of American lawyers is not simply an important field in our universe, but is, it seems to me, currently the most elaborate world that we can define when it comes to our relationship with reality – or at least with what we call such. For we find there the complete gamut running from a certain violence – whose presence is essential, fundamental, and can always be required so that one cannot say that reality is in any way elided there – to subtleties of legal procedure that allow one to introduce into this world all sorts of paradoxical novelties, novelties that are defined by a relationship to the law that is essentially constituted by the detours required to obtain the most perfect violation of that very law.

Such is the world of reality. Now, what relationship can there be between this world and what one might call a "mature desire," in the sense of genital maturity?

The question can assuredly be answered in several ways, one of which is that of experience – namely, the sexual behavior of American lawyers. Now, nothing so far seems to confirm that there is an exact correlation between the optimal development of a world, all of whose activities are so well managed, and a perfect harmony in relations with the other, inasmuch as these relations involve some success or concord at the level of love. Nothing proves it, and almost no one would even dream of maintaining it.

432

I am merely sketching out for you where the question arises. The question is based on the fact that there is a confusion here regarding the term "object."

There are, on the one hand, objects that are supposedly situated in reality, in the sense that I have just articulated it; and there are, on the other hand, objects that are inscribed in the relationship between the subject and the object, a relationship that at least latently implies knowledge. When people claim that the object matures as desire matures, what object are they talking about?

It is an object that is quite different from the one that we can actually situate in the place where an objective mapping allows us to characterize reality-based relations. We have long been familiar with the object we are talking about; it goes by the name of the object of knowledge, even if it is altogether veiled there.

This object has been the goal, aim, and endpoint of research for millennia. Such research is still there, behind the fruits it yielded when it became what we call "science," after having had to follow the pathways of the subject's rootedness in the world for a long time. It was undeniably on the basis of this rootedness, I mean at the philosophical level, that science was able to find its point of departure at a certain moment, even if science – like a child who becomes independent after having been nourished for many years – has now taken its distance from this form of reflection. We see traces of this original rootedness in the guise of the theory of knowledge.

In this realm, people came as close as they could to a profound identification between the two terms in the subject/object relationship. For them, knowing is related to a co-naturalness, and any attempt to grasp the object manifests something related to a harmony that has to exist.

Let us not forget that this is certainly but the result of a specialized practice, one that stands out in a history that gave rise to several branches. I will confine my attention here to our branch, that of Greek philosophy.

The attempt to pinpoint and promote what is known as the object involves a theoretical attitude which we would be completely wrong to think that, now that results have been obtained, we can eliminate, as if this theoretical stance had no impact on its effect.

433

What did this attempt to know imply about the status of desire? We analysts are certainly able to raise this question, but it was not unnoticed by religious thinkers, and we can, here as elsewhere, merely follow in their wake. Inasmuch as religious practice has other aims than psychoanalysis, it has specified this desire as the desire to know, *cupido sciendi*. We merely add our own two cents' worth to this when we indicate that it has a more fundamental basis: some ambivalent drive like scopophilia or even oral incorporativeness.

Be that as it may, one thing is clear, which is that the development of knowledge, including the implicit notions about the object it brings with it, results from a choice. The establishment of every philosophical position has, throughout the ages, necessarily involved being recognized as a stance that involves sacrificing something. The entrance of the subject into the realm of what is known as pure research [*recherche désinteressée*], the fruit of which is objectivity – after all, attaining objectivity has never been defined in any other way than as grasping a certain reality from an unbiased [*désinteressée*] perspective – entails the exclusion, at least in theory, of a certain form of desire.

This is the perspective from which the concept of the object was developed. It is not pointless for us to reintroduce it here. After all, we know what we are doing, because this perspective is implicit in the presupposition of a virtual and latent correspondence – which must always be found anew or obtained – between the investigation of desire and the object that this investigation explores.

We have reason to distinguish, on the contrary, between the object that satisfies the desire for knowledge – the philosophical notion of which has been the fruit of centuries of elaboration – and the object of a desire.

It is owing to a confusion between these two notions that analysts have been so easily led to posit a correspondence between a certain constituting of the object and a certain maturing of the drive.

Taking a stand against this, I have tried to provide you with a different formulation of the relationship between desire and its object, which I claim to be closer to our experience.

We are now going to turn to the true articulation, which I call synchronic.

434

3

The symbolic formula ($\$\Diamond a$) gives form to what I call the fundamental fantasy.

This is the true form of the supposed "object-relation," not the form in which it has been articulated up until now.

To say that we are talking here about the fundamental fantasy means nothing more than that, from a synchronic perspective, it gives desire its minimal supporting structure.

It contains two terms and their twofold relationship to each other constitutes fantasy. Their relationship is still more complex insofar as the subject is constituted qua desire in a tertiary relation to fantasy.

Today I will take up this tertiary perspective. Moreover, I will show that the subject's assumption [*assomption*] involves *a*. This is just as legitimate as to show that it involves the barred subject, given that desire is sustained in a confrontational relationship to ($\$\Diamond a$).

I believe that I have already taken things far enough here that it will not shock you, throw you off, or surprise you if I claim that object *a* is defined first of all as the prop that the subject gives himself inasmuch as he falters [*défaille*] . . . – I will interrupt myself here for a moment and begin by saying something approximate that may have some impact on you – . . . *inasmuch as he falters in his certainty as a subject*. Now I will give you the exact term, but it is not very intuitive, which is why I did not want to give it to you right away: *inasmuch as he falters in his designation as a subject.*

What is at stake here is based entirely on what happens in the Other, inasmuch as the Other is the locus of the subject's desire. Now, in the Other, in the Other's discourse which the unconscious is, the subject is missing something [or: something is not available to the subject, *quelque chose fait défaut au sujet*]. We will come back to this later, we will come back to it as often as necessary, and we will come back to it right up to the end.

Owing to the very structure that establishes the relationship between the subject and the Other qua locus of speech, something is missing [*fait défaut*] at the level of the Other. What is missing there is precisely that which would allow the subject to identify himself as the subject of his own discourse. Insofar as this discourse is the discourse of the unconscious, the subject instead disappears in it.

In order to designate himself, the subject must consequently employ something that is taken at his own expense. Not at his expense as a subject constituted in speech, but at his expense as a real, live subject, at the expense of something which, taken by itself, is not a subject at all. The subject who pays the price necessary to be able to locate himself as faltering is thus brought into the dimension that is always present whenever desire is involved: having to pay for castration.

Stated otherwise, something real, which he has a hold on in an imaginary relationship, is raised to the pure and simple function of a signifier. This is the final and most profound meaning of castration as such.

Freud's essential discovery is the fact, which had been overlooked hitherto, that castration is involved as soon as desire manifests itself clearly as such. This fact opened up for us all sorts of historical perspectives, which people have translated in various mythical fashions, and which people then tried to reduce to developmental terms. This developmental approach – involving the diachronic dimension – was undoubtedly fruitful, but it cannot spare us the trouble of exploring the other dimension, the synchronic dimension, to see what the essential relationship involved *there* is.

The latter is the relationship between the subject and the signifying system [*le signifiant*], inasmuch as the subject cannot designate himself in it, or name himself as a subject in it. He must make up for this inability [*défaut*] through personal sacrifice [*payer de sa personne*], as it were. I am trying to be as evocative as I can be here, and thus am not always employing the most rigorous terms.

We can find an analogue of what happens next in the function of certain symbols that linguists distinguish in the lexical system, which go by the name "shifter symbols."* I have already mentioned the personal pronoun "I," which designates the person who is speaking. At the unconscious level, the same is true for little *a*. This *a*, which is not a symbol but rather one of the subject's real elements, is what intervenes to support the moment, in the synchronic sense, at which the subject falters in attempting to designate himself [or: because he designates himself, *défaille pour se désigner*] at the level of the instance of desire.

I realize that mental gymnastics of this kind can be tiring to you. Which is why, in order to give you a break, I will illustrate this with terms from our concrete practice. I have said that *a* is the effect of castration. I did not say that it was the object of castration. The object of castration is what we call the phallus. What is the phallus?

We see it appear in what, last time, I called the artificial phallophanies of analysis. Here too, psychoanalysis shows itself to be an original, absolutely unique form of practice, for before it there was no form of alchemy, whether therapeutic or not, in which the phallus appeared. In the work of Hieronymus Bosch, there are all sorts of detached members. And there is the anything but fragrant *flatus* [gas] that Ernest Jones took as the prototype for the Holy Ghost. We have very clear images of all this, but you can note that we do not see the phallus very often. Yet we ourselves see it, and we also realize that it is not very easy to pinpoint exactly. This is but a tangent.

Our experience with homosexuality only became defined once we began to analyze homosexuals. At first, people did not analyze them. In 1905, Professor Freud could not go any further, as he tells us in *The Three Essays on the Theory of Sexuality*, than the notion that male homosexuality is based on the subject's narcissistic requirement that his object have a phallus, it being considered essential by the subject.

Then we began analyzing homosexuals. Have a look at the truly exemplary work done by Felix Boehm, who was one of the first to have taken an interest in this. His work begins in the 1920s and continues up until 1933 and beyond that as well. I mentioned a number of other works on homosexuality when I spoke to you about the importance of the articles by [text missing here].

Such analytic work showed that homosexuality is far from being a primordial, instinctual requirement, and that it cannot be identified with a pure and simple fixation or deviation of instinct. People also realized that the phallus that plays a role, of one kind or another, in the mechanism of homosexuality is far from having the same status as other objects, and they identified it, perhaps too hastily, with the father's phallus. The latter was supposed to have its home in the woman's vagina, and to be feared because of that, which supposedly explains why the subject finds himself forced into an extreme position, that of homosexuality. We see there, in any case, a phallus of an entirely different import, with a thoroughly different function, and situated in an altogether different place than what had been mentioned earlier.

That's not all. After being overjoyed, as it were, that we now had the bull by the horns, we continued to analyze homosexuals and realized that the image of the phallus as an appendix that the subject at first believes women have, inasmuch as they are not yet castrated, is not the last word regarding this matter.

Indeed, in being looked at more closely, this image – which at a later date was brought into play in the psychoanalytic theorization of homosexuality – turned out to be what one might call an evagination, that is, the turning inside out of the vagina. In this fantasy – that we already encountered in the dream of the hat turned inside out whose analysis I went through with you at such length – the phallic appendix seems to be made from the externalization of the insides. Thus, in analysis, when one presents a homosexual the everyday dialectic of his desire, in a certain investigatory perspective, this turns out to be the final imaginary term with which he finds himself confronted.

The homosexual in question here is one of those who was analyzed by Boehm, and on this point I am relying heavily on his work, which is especially illustrative and confirmed by a great deal of experience.   438

What can we say about this fantasy if not that the phallus presents itself here in a radical form, inasmuch as its function, in the end, is to show on the outside what is in the subject's imaginary inside?

We should almost not be surprised that a certain convergence is established here between the imaginary and symbolic.

What is found in the imaginary in an inside-out, extirpated, almost detached, but not yet detached position with respect to the inside of the body can be raised quite naturally to the function of a symbol, without for all that being detached from its radical insertion, which is such that it is felt to be a threat to the integrity of one's self-image.

4

I do not want to end today on the point I just made.

For it is not what will provide us with the meaning and function of little *a* as an object, most generally speaking.

Inasmuch as the subject is desire, he is always imminently threatened with castration. What props his position up is, as I told you, the object in fantasy, which is the most complete form of the object. I would now like to show you in what sort of synchrony this relationship can be articulated.

Let me underscore the word *synchrony*, for the necessity of discourse will force me to give you a formulation of it that is diachronic. The upshot being that you will be prone to confusing it with some sort of genesis. Yet it is nothing of the sort.

The relations between the letters that I am now going to write on the blackboard [see Table 20.1] are designed to allow you to situate little *a* in its proper place. It is insofar as the subject is in the presence of imminent castration that he is related to this object. I will provisionally designate this relation to the object as the price that must be paid [*rançon*] for the subject's position, because I must also emphasize what I mean by talking about this relation as desire's prop.

439   Table 20.1 Synchronic schema of the dialectic of desire

A	D
rS	$\cancel{D}$
$\cancel{A}$	S
a	$\cancel{S}$
A'	
A''	
A'''	

How is the synchronic relationship generated? We begin from the earliest subjective position, that of demand. You see it indicated on the top line, on the right, by capital D. It is the manifestation, illustration, or example in the individual's behavior that allows us to grasp essentially how the subject is constituted insofar as he enters into the signifier.

The synchronic relationship in question is established according to a very simple algorithm, which is that of division. It is indicated by the vertical line. A horizontal line separating the levels is provided here, too, but there is nothing essential about it since it can be repeated at each level.

The subject's most primordial relationship is that involving demand addressed to the Other qua locus of speech. The Other figures here in the form of the letter capital A. It is on the basis of the relationship A divided by D that the dialectic begins whose remainder will give us the position of *a*, the object.

At the beginning of this process, the subject's need is primordially articulated in terms of a signifying alternative, and everything is established that later structures the subject's relationship to himself known as desire. The Other, who is someone real here, a real subject, rS, finds himself in a position – owing to the fact that he is called upon by demand – to transform demand, whatever it may be for, into something else, which is a demand for love, insofar as the latter purely and simply refers to the presence/absence alternative. This is why, in the second row, I place a bar on capital D.

440

Let me point out in passing that I could not fail to be surprised, touched, and even moved when I found in Shakespeare's *Sonnets* the literal term "present-absent," complete with a hyphen, at the point at which he was describing love relationships.

We thus see the subject constituted here insofar as the Other is a real person, the one through whom demand itself becomes laden with signification, the one through whom the subject's demand becomes something other than what it explicitly asks for, which is the satisfaction of a need.

There is no subject except to another subject – this is a principle we must maintain as having forever been true. Owing to the fact that the Other is primordially posited as he who, in the presence of demand, can play a certain game or not, the Other is already established as a subject and as a term in the tragedy that is going to be played out. In other words, the introduction of the subject or individual into the signifier takes on the function of subjectifying the Other, which is what leads me to write the letter capital S preceded by a lower case r below the letter capital A.

It is insofar as the Other himself is a subject that our subject is instated, and that he can establish himself as a subject in a new relationship to the Other – one in which he must get himself recognized as a subject by this Other, no longer as demand, nor as love, but as a subject.

Am I in the process of attributing here to some sort of larva all the dimensions of self-consciousness concocted by philosophical reflection? This is not what is involved. Or, better stated, this is involved but in a form that is truly concrete and real, instead of being hidden or veiled as it is in philosophy.

What guarantee can he find for the Other's function and functioning in reality, as responding to his demand? What can attest to the truth of the Other's behavior, whatever it may be? What is at the concrete foundation of the notions of truth and of intersubjectivity? What gives its full meaning to the term "truth"* in English, which simply expresses Truth with a capital T? Everything depends on what we call in French, in a breaking down of language that turns

441   out to be a product of the linguistic system, *foi en la parole*, "faith in speech." In other words, in what respect can we count on the Other?

This is what is at issue when I tell you that "there is no Other of the Other." What does this mean if it is not that no signifier exists that can guarantee any concrete, serial manifestation of signifiers. It is here that the term A barred comes in.

Under the pressure of the subject's demand for a guarantor, what happens at the level of the Other is primordially something related to a lack [Ⱥ] in relation to which the subject must situate himself. Let us note that this lack is produced at the level of the Other qua locus of speech and not at the level of the Other qua real. Nothing real on the Other's side [of the table] can make up for this, except by a series of additions, A', A'', A''', that will never be exhausted.

The Other will manifest himself to the subject, over the course of his entire existence, through gifts or refusals. But that will never be situated anywhere other than in the margins of the fundamental lack that is itself found at the level of the signifier. The subject will be historically invested in all sorts of experiences with the Other, the maternal Other in this case, but none of that will be able to exhaust the lack that exists at the level of the signifier as such, which is the level at which the subject must situate himself in order to constitute himself as a subject and get himself recognized by the Other.

The subject himself is marked by this failure [*défaillance*] or non-guarantee at the level of the truth about the Other [or: level of the Other's truth, *niveau de la vérité de l'Autre*]. And this is why he will have to institute what I already tried to broach earlier in the form of his genesis – namely, little *a*. These two terms, S barred and little *a*, face each other in the fourth row of the table.

Little *a* is that something that turns out to be subjected to the condition of expressing the subject's final tension, the tension that is the remainder or residue, the tension that lies in the margins of all of these demands [or: latent within all of these demands, *en marge de toutes ces demandes*], and that none of these demands can exhaust. This something is destined to represent a lack and to represent it with a real tension on the subject's part.

This is the hitch [*os*], so to speak, in the object's function in desire. This is the price that has to be paid for the fact that the subject cannot situate himself in desire without castrating himself – in other words, without losing what is most essential about his life. Simone

442   Weil's remark, "To ascertain exactly what the miser whose treasure was stolen lost: thus we should learn much," already pinpointed what this form is situated around, it being one of the most exemplary forms of desire.

It is, naturally, in order to save his life that the miser keeps little *a*, the object of his desire, locked up in an enclosure – which, let us note, is an essential dimension. But owing to this very fact, this object turns out to be a mortified object. What is placed in a treasure chest is removed from the circuit of life, being subtracted therefrom, in order to be preserved as the shadow of nothing, and this is what makes it the miser's object.

Thus the French expression *Qui veut garder sa vie, la perd*, "he who wishes to save his life will lose it," is corroborated. Does this imply that he who consents to lose his life finds it anew as directly as all that? Not so fast. We will try to see next time where he finds it anew.

Our trajectory today shows us – and this is not the least contribution it makes – that the path the subject goes down to find his life anew will in any case present him with what he consents to lose: the phallus.

If the subject has mourned the loss of the phallus – which, as I have indicated, is a necessary stage – from then on he can only aim at the phallus as a hidden object.

Little *a* is an obscure, opaque term, part and parcel of a nothing to which it is reduced. It is beyond this nothing that the subject will seek out the shadow of that life of his which he at first lost.

The table on the blackboard gives you the contours of the functioning of desire. It shows you that the lost object, the object to be found anew, is not the one that the developmental perspective has proposed as the primal object of a primordial impression. It is part and parcel of desire's very nature to constitute the object in accordance with this dialectic.

We will pick it up there next time.

May 13, 1959

XXI

IN THE FORM OF A CUT

The subject's "*Est-ce?*"
Real versus knowledge
On the subject's real
Three examples of object *a*
Breathing and the voice

We are going to pick up today where we left off last time. I had formalized a sort of operation for you in the form of a subjective division involving [or: in, *dans*] demand. We shall return to it, and this will lead us next to examine the formula for fantasy, inasmuch as it props up the pivotal relationship that I am trying to lay out this year in the functioning of psychoanalysis.

1

You may recall that I put the letters A/D on the board in order to designate demand's imposition or proposition [or: proposal, *proposition*] in the Other's locus, which I presented to you as the earliest ideal stage [see Table 20.1].

This is no more than a reconstruction, naturally. And yet nothing is more concrete or real. It is to the degree to which a child's demand begins to be articulated that the process begins – or at least I intend to show that it begins – by which the *Spaltung* [splitting] brought on by [*du*] discourse, that is expressed in the effects the unconscious has, forms.

Now I am going to write rA/S on the board. To the right, we have the subject's first position, grasped in the act of the first articulation of demand. Its necessary counterweight is the position of the real Other, rA, insofar as it is all-powerful in responding to this demand. This stage is essential if we are to understand the foundation of the

first relationship to the Other, who is the mother here, where we find
the first form of omnipotence.

Nevertheless, as I said, it is not by examining the Other, but rather by considering what occurs at the level of demand that we are going to extend the process of logical generation. I had expressed it to you last time with the letters rS/Ð. On the left, I introduced the Other as a real subject, whereas demand, which is initially demand for the satisfaction of a need, turns out to take on a different import as it becomes demand for love, and this is what is designated by the D shown here with a bar through it.

I no longer recall if it was in this form that I wrote it on the board. [The audience says yes.] Fine. It does not matter much, anyway, since this is designed to generate the entire palette of the subject's real experiences, which will be inscribed in a certain number of responses, whether gratifying or frustrating. Even though they are, of course, highly essential, inasmuch as a certain modulation of the subject's history is inscribed in them, they do not affect the formal, synchronic analysis that I am currently conducting here.

If we begin from an initial stage at which the Other is the real Other who responds to demand, we see that at the next stage, the subject questions the Other as a subject, our subject appearing to himself to be a subject inasmuch as he is viewed as a subject by this Other. The relationship, designated by Å/S, is the first stage of the actual constitution of the subject.

This means that the subject is constituted in relation to another subject, one who speaks. He must get his bearings in the fundamental strategy that arises with the appearance of the dimension of language, and that begins with this dimension alone. Owing to the fact that the Other has become structured in language, she becomes the possible subject of a strategy, with respect to which the subject himself can be constituted as a subject recognized in the Other, as a subject to another subject.

On the one hand, there can be no subject who is not a subject to another subject; on the other hand, it is only as a speaking subject, as a subject of speech, that the first subject can be established as such. And since the Other is herself marked by the necessities of language, she is no longer a real Other; rather, she is established as the locus of the articulation of speech [or: locus in which speech is articulated]. The first possible position for a subject as such – a subject who can grasp himself as a subject, who can grasp himself as a subject in the Other, insofar as this Other thinks of him as a
subject – is created in that locus.

As I mentioned last time, there is nothing more concrete than this. It is in no wise a stage in philosophical thinking; it is something primitive that is established in a trusting relationship. To what degree and up to what point can I count on the Other? What portion of the Other's behavior is reliable? What consequences can I expect from what she has already promised?

These are the questions around which one of the earliest conflicts in the relationship between the child and the Other revolves, even what is undoubtedly the earliest conflict, from the vantage point that interests us. This – and not pure and simple frustration or gratification – is the basis on which the principles of the child's history are built; this is the mainspring of what is repeated at the deepest level of his destiny; this is what commands his behavior's unconscious modulation. Psychoanalysis, and even our daily experience of psychoanalysis, teaches us that the question whether the subject can or cannot rely on some Other is what determines what we find to be most crucial in the patient's unconscious modulation, whether he be neurotic or not.

At this stage, the Other is a subject of speech [or: a speaking subject or one of speech's subjects, *sujet de la parole*], insofar as speech is primordially articulated. It is in relation to the Other thus defined that the subject himself is constituted as a subject who speaks, and not as some sort of primitive knowing subject – that is, not as the subject talked about by philosophers. The subject at stake here is posited as being observed by the Other and as being able to respond to him in the name of a shared strategy. He is the one who can interpret everything the Other articulates about her most profound intention and about her good or bad faith.

At this level – at which the subject is in abeyance – S is truly posited, if you will allow me a play on words, not only as the S written with a letter, but also as the *Es* of Freud's topography of the subject. This S is the id [*Ça*], and in an interrogative form. If you add a question mark, S is in fact articulated as *Est-ce?* ["Is it?" or "Is this?"] This is all the subject thus far formulates about himself at this level. He is here *in statu nascendi*, in the presence of the Other's speech [*articulation*], inasmuch as that speech responds to him.

In this speech, the Other responds to the subject beyond what the latter formulated in his demand. If the subject wants to get his bearings [or: get ahold of himself, *se saisir*] in the beyond that speech brings with it [*dans cet au-delà de la parole*], he will thus have to take a step that brings him to the following stage: *a/$* [see Table 20.1].

This subject is marked with a bar that primordially divides him from himself qua subject of speech. It is thus as a barred subject that he can, must, and intends to find the answer. But he does not find

446

it, for at this level he encounters in the Other the hollow or empty space that I formulated by telling you that "there is no Other of the Other"; that no possible signifier can guarantee the authenticity of the series of signifiers; that there is nothing, at the level of the signifier, that guarantees or authenticates the signifying chain or speech in any way. This is why the subject depends so essentially on the Other's goodwill.

It is at this point that the subject brings in from elsewhere – namely, from the imaginary register – a part of himself that is involved in the imaginary relationship to the other. This is little *a*. It arises at the very place where S wonders what he truly is and what he truly wants.

What we call object *a* is undoubtedly the object of desire, but on condition that we make it clear that it does not, for all that, adapt to desire. It comes into play in a complex that we will call fantasy. The subject manages to prop himself up with this object at the moment at which he vanishes when faced with the signifier's failure [or: inability, *carence*] to answer for his place as a subject at the level of the Other.

At the level at which the subject attempts to reconstruct himself, to meet back up with himself in the demand he makes to the Other, and to authenticate himself as a subject of speech, the operation of division stops. For the quotient that the subject is seeking to reach remains in abeyance [or: suspended] in the presence of the appearance, at the level of the Other, of the remainder [object *a*] owing to which the subject himself pays the ransom for, and comes to make up for [*suppléer*] the deficiency [or: absence, *carence*] of the signifier that responds to him at the level of the Other. This quotient [$] and this remainder [*a*] remain in each other's presence here and prop each other up, as it were. Fantasy is nothing but the perpetual confrontation between barred S and little *a*.

The barred subject marks the moment of the subject's fading* in which the subject finds nothing in the Other that can clearly guarantee the subject, that authenticates him, that allows him to situate and name himself at the level of the Other's discourse – in other words, qua subject of the unconscious. It is in response to this moment that an imaginary element, the correlative term of fantasy's structure, arises to make up for [or: to stand in for, *comme suppléant du*] the missing signifier. I designate this element in its most general form as S's prop at the moment at which S tries to designate himself [*s'indiquer*] as the subject of unconscious discourse.

It seems to me that I need say nothing further on this point. I am going to say a bit more anyway to indicate what this means in Freud's discourse. Let us reconsider, for example, Freud's claim,

447

Wo Es war, soll Ich werden, translated as follows: *Là où C'était, là Je dois devenir* [Where it (or id) was, I must come into being].

This is very precise. What is involved here is *Ich* [that is, the personal pronoun I], which is not *das Ich*, the ego. *Ich* is used here as the subject of the sentence. *Là où C'était* means where It/id [*Ça*] speaks – in other words, where just a moment before, there was something: unconscious desire.

It is there [where unconscious desire was] that *I* must designate myself, that *I* must be. This *I* is the goal, end, and terminus of analysis before it names itself, forms, and is articulated – assuming it ever does or is, because the *soll Ich werden* in Freud's formulation must be understood as *dois-Je devenir* [I must become]. The I is the subject of a becoming, of a duty [*devoir*] that is proposed to us.

Freud tells us in this sentence that we must reconquer the lost field of the subject's being. And he illustrates it with a lovely comparison to Holland and its peaceful draining of the Zuider Zee, of the submerged lands. What is at stake here is the field of the unconscious that we must win back in the course of the Great Work of psychoanalysis.

But a question arises: before this is done, what designates to us the place, *là où Ça était* [where It/id was], the place of the *I* that must come to light? The index of desire, precisely speaking. I mean of desire qua function and terminus of what is at stake in the unconscious, desire sustained by the coexistence and opposition of two terms, $ and little *a*.

At this edge where the unconscious begins, the subject loses himself. We are not just talking here about the absence of something that one might call consciousness. Another dimension begins here where it is no longer possible for the subject to know either who he is or where he is. Any and all possibility of naming himself ends here.

But at this terminus we also find the index [of desire]. The object right in front of the subject indubitably fascinates him. But this is not its major function. Appearances to the contrary notwithstanding, this object is also what stops the subject from blacking out, from having his pure and simple existence wiped out.

This is what constitutes the structure of what I call fantasy. We are now going to see just how broadly the formula for fantasy can be applied. We are thus going to consider fantasy's synchronic function.

What does that mean?

What is involved is the place occupied by fantasy in the subject's self-references, his references to what he is at the level of the unconscious – not when he wonders about what he is, but when he

448

is, in short, borne along [*porté*] by the question about what he is, *which is the very definition of neurosis.*

2

What is targeted at the moment of desire is, as I say, a naming of the subject that proves to be deficient [*défaillante*].

In fantasy, the subject is on the verge of this naming, and this is what defines fantasy's structural role.

This is a culminating point at which the subject undergoes – maximally, as it were – what one might call the virulence of logos, at which he registers the full alienating effect of his involvement in logos.

The fact that man is caught in the grips of logos – that is, in the fundamental combinatory that is its essential characteristic – undoubtedly raises a question: what does it mean for man to be necessary to the action of logos in the world? But it is for others to answer that question. What we must examine here is what the upshot of this is for man and how man deals with it. The first formulation that might come to mind is that he must really bear [*soutenir*] it, he must sustain it [*soutienne*] with his real, with himself as real – which is also what always remains most mysterious to him.

A digression would not be amiss here, in order to try to grasp what the term "real" – a term that I employ, contrasting it with the symbolic and the imaginary – can, in the final analysis, actually mean, which is something that a number of you have been wondering about for a long time.   449

On this point, it is certainly worth noting that our era, which has witnessed the invention of psychoanalysis, is also an era in which something has been forced on us, despite our ever-so-great resistance to it: a crisis in the theory of knowledge, or a crisis of knowledge itself.

I already endeavored to draw your attention to what the scientific venture signifies last time. Science was created and grafted onto a longstanding culture that involved adopting a stance that was biased [*partiale*] enough for us to call it partial [*partielle*]. Indeed, it involved a certain retreat – on the part of man, for whom the world was present – from stances that were initially contemplative.

As I have pointed out, we can assuredly specify these stances as constituting a discipline, ascesis, or choice. They did not entail a desiring stance as such, but rather the election of a certain form of desire – namely, as I said, the desire to know. What resulted from this is, as we know, science, our modern science, which is distinguished from others by the exceptional grip [*prise*] it has on the world – a grip that reassures us, in a way, when we speak of reality.

We know that we have at least some handle [*prise*] on the real. But what sort of handle is it, after all? Is it a cognitive handle? Do we take cognizance of the real? I can provide only a partial answer here.

If we consider what results from the scientific process at the point we are at today, and especially at the point at which the development of physics has arrived – which is the form of this process in which the grip of our symbolic chains on something that we call experiments [or: experience, *l'expérience*], which are constructed experiments, has gone the furthest and has encountered the greatest success – doesn't it seem to you immediately, at first glance, that we have less than ever the feeling that we have reached the ideal that the earliest philosophy set for itself?

From a Greek, Aristotelian, perspective, the goal of knowing – what rewarded the efforts of the philosopher or sage – was identification with the being that was known. At the end of the process, the subject – or rather he who was thinking, he who was seeking knowledge, for he was not called a subject at the time – was supposed to identify with the object of his contemplation. What do we identify with at the end of the process of modern science? I do not believe that there is a single branch of science that proposes anything of the sort, whether it be the branch in which we have arrived at the most perfect and most advanced results [physics], or even the branch in which science is still taking its first step, trying to sketch out its foundations – I am referring to the form of psychology known as behaviorism.

The latter is still but a science in its infancy. It seems to want to imitate the little angel in Dürer's *Melencolia I*, the one who, alongside the adult Melencolia, is just beginning to spread its wings [see Plate 2]. Behaviorism can, nevertheless, be instructive to us. It shows us that when people found a psychology that claims to be scientific, they begin by positing that they are going to do simple behaviorism – in other words, they are going to confine themselves to looking at what is right in front of them and will above all refuse any sort of aim involving identification [with the object of study]. Above and beyond the method at stake, there is at the very crux of science a refusal to believe that one can, in the end, arrive at what Antiquity's ideal of knowledge entailed.

What is truly exemplary in behaviorism is such as to make us contemplate what we are told by another form of psychology – which we do not formulate as a science, of course, but which is nevertheless considered to be paradoxical with respect to the method thus far defined for a scientific approach – Freudian psychology.

450

The latter states, in effect, that a subject's real must not be conceptualized as correlated with some sort of knowledge. From the outset, the real, as a real in which a subject is involved, is not situated with respect to a knowing subject, since something in the subject is articulated that is beyond any possible knowledge he may have. Yet he is already a subject.

Furthermore, the subject recognizes himself in the fact that he is a subject of a chain that is articulated like a discourse is. Now, a discourse cannot be sustained without some sort of prop, and it would not be going too far to qualify this prop with the term "being." After all, if the term "being" means anything, if we give it its minimal definition, it is the real inasmuch as the real is inscribed in the symbolic.

A real is involved in this chain, and Freud tells us that it is coherent and commands the subject's behavior, beyond all the motives that are accessible to the play of consciousness [or: cognition or   451
knowledge, *connaissance*]. It is a real that is articulated in the symbolic, that has come to occupy a place in the symbolic, and that has come to occupy it beyond the knowing [or: conscious] subject. This is truly something that deserves to be designated as along the lines of being, in the full sense of the word.

We arrive here at the end of the digression I began earlier.

It is at the very moment at which the branch of the tree of knowledge known as science – and which has given us results that undoubtedly go much further than any sort of effect expected from knowledge – proved to disappoint knowledge's hope of attaining identification with the object, that Freud pointed (in an experience of subjectivity as it is established in the confidential disclosing of things that goes on in analysis) to a chain in which things are articulated in a way that is structured just like any other symbolic chain, just like what we know as discourse, but which is not accessible to the subject. For, as opposed to what occurs in contemplation, the subject cannot rely on that chain as though it were an object in which he can recognize himself. On the contrary, he fundamentally misrecognizes itself in it.

The harder he tries to broach this chain and to name or locate himself there, the less he can do so.

He is only ever there in gaps and cuts. Every time he tries to get his bearings there, he is only ever in a gap.

This is why the imaginary object of fantasy with which he then tries to prop himself up is structured as it is.

There are many other things to demonstrate about the formalization ($\$\Diamond a$), but I would now like to show you how little a is constructed.

3

Let us first consider the formal properties of object *a* in the structure of fantasy, such as analytic experience allows us to recognize them.

As I just mentioned, the subject encounters himself as a cut or gap at the endpoint of his questioning. Moreover, it is essentially in the guise of a cut that *a* shows us its form, in all its generality. I am simply going to list here a certain number of shared properties of the different forms of this object that are already known to you.

For those of you who are analysts, I can proceed quickly, with the proviso that I will have to go into detail and comment on this again later. What, for example, is going to allow us to recognize that the object in fantasy takes the form of a cut? Frankly, I believe that, at the level of the result, you will be a step ahead of me, at least I dare to hope so.

The subject, at the point at which he wonders about himself as a barred subject, finds nothing to prop himself up with but a series of terms that we call *a* insofar as they are objects in fantasy. As a first approximation, we can provide three examples of this. This does not imply that there are only three, but almost.

This list is not altogether exhaustive, inasmuch as taking things up at the level of what I will call the result – in other words, at the level of *a* qua constituted – is not a terribly legitimate approach. If I am adopting it, it is simply in order to start from already familiar terrain, in order to make it easier for you to cover the ground we need to cover. It is not the most rigorous pathway, as you will see when we follow the pathway of structure, which begins with the barred subject, insofar as it is the latter who necessitates the term "object." I am beginning with the object because it will allow you to get your bearings more easily.

There are three types of little *a* that have heretofore been identified and located in analytic experience: *a*, φ, and d.

The first type is the one that, rightly or wrongly, we usually call the pregenital object.

The second type is the sort of object that is involved in what is known as the castration complex, and you are aware that, in its most general form, it is the phallus.

The third type introduces the only term that will perhaps surprise you as new – but, actually, I think that those of you who have taken a close look at what I have written about the psychoses will not be terribly puzzled here. The third type of object [d] – which fulfills the exact same function with respect to the subject at his breaking point and fading* – is neither more nor less than what is commonly called a "delusion." This is why Freud wrote, very early on in his practice, in his first reflections, "they love their delusions as they love themselves," "*Sie lieben also den Wahn wie sich selbst*" [SE I, p. 212].

We are going to take up these three forms of the object one by one in order to grasp what in their form allows them to serve the function of becoming signifiers that the subject draws from his own substance in order to be able to bear [*soutenir*] [something right] in front of him: the hole or absence of the signifier at the level of the unconscious chain.

As a pregenital object, what does little *a* mean?

A formulation comes to mind here, which summarizes, for more than one materialist thinker, what is, after all, the functioning of an organism, even if it is human, at the level of material exchanges: namely, and I am not the one who invented this, that an animal is nothing more than a tube with two orifices, one that things go into and another that things come out of. Well, this is how the so-called pregenital object is constituted, inasmuch as it comes to serve its signifying function in fantasy.

What nourishes the subject is cut off from him at a certain moment, not to mention the fact that, at times, things are reversed – this is the oral-sadistic stage – he himself cuts it off, or at least endeavors to bite it off. There is thus, on the one hand, the object qua object involved in weaning, which means, strictly speaking, the object involved in the cut [or: object cut off, *objet de coupure*], and there is, on the other hand, at the other end of the tube, the object he ejects and that is cut from him. All training in rituals and forms of toilet training thus consists of teaching the subject to cut from himself what he himself ejects.

In everyday analytic practice, what we make into the fundamental form of the object of the so-called oral and anal stages is tantamount to cutting [*la coupure*]. At the oral level, the object is the nipple, that part of the breast that the subject can hold in his buccal orifice, which is also what he is separated from. The object is also excrement, which at a different moment becomes the most significant form of the subject's relationship to objects, too.

These objects are very precisely selected insofar as they manifest in their form, in an exemplary manner, the structure of cutting [*coupure*]. Owing to this, they serve as props at the level of the signifier where the subject turns out to be situated as structured by a cut [*coupure*]. This explains why these objects are chosen over others.   454

People could not fail to ask why, if it were simply a question of the subject eroticizing one or another of his vital functions, there would not also be a more primitive and fundamental stage in which he would be attached to a function that is just as vital as that of nourishment – the latter starting at the mouth and ending with excretion from the intestinal orifice – namely, breathing.

Yet breathing does not in any way involve the element of cutting. Breathing does not cut itself off, and if it is cut off, it is in a way that does not fail to generate some drama. Nothing is inscribed in a cutting off of breathing except in an exceptional manner. Breathing is rhythm, pulsation, and vital alternation; there is nothing about it that allows us to symbolize, at the imaginary level, precisely what is at stake – namely, a gap or cut.

This is not to say, however, that nothing that goes through the respiratory orifice can, as such, be subjected to scansion, since it is through this very same orifice that the voice passes. Now, vocal production is something that is cut and scanned [*se scande*]. This is why later today we will come back to the voice when we turn to delusions.

When cutting or scansion is not imposed on this production, and it is simply *pneuma* or *flatus* [breath or wind], then, at the deepest level of our experience of it in the unconscious, it is not specified as being of a respiratory order, but is related to anal *flatus*. Furthermore, the latter paradoxically turns out to symbolize most profoundly what is at issue whenever the subject is symbolized by the phallus at the level of the unconscious. This is one of those unpleasant surprises that psychoanalysis has sprung on us.

It is to Jones's credit that he glimpsed this, and I recommend you read his studies on the topic.

455   Let us turn now to the second level.

I call it second merely for the artificial purposes of exposition, for there is neither a first nor a second level. All objects *a* have the same function. At the point we are at along our path, we simply want to know why they take one form or another. When we describe their form synchronically, however, we try to bring out their common characteristics.

When we turn to the castration complex, we find another form of little *a*, which is mutilation.

In effect, if what is at issue is cutting, it is necessary and sufficient that the subject separate himself from some part of himself, that he be able to mutilate himself. At first glance, this does not seem to introduce anything terribly new, as analytic writers have clearly seen, they reminding us what we have learned about mutilation from history and ethnography. Which is that – among all the initiation rites by which man seeks to define his access to his own reality, to a higher level of self-realization, and to the consecration of his full-fledged manhood – there are a certain number of forms of marking [*stigmatisation*] that I do not need to list for you here. Mutilation is one of them, and it plays an especially eminent role.

I will simply remind you now, taking the opportunity to put our finger on it, that what is involved here again, in another form, is something that we can clearly call a cut – truly so inasmuch as the cut inaugurates the shift to a signifying function here. What remains of this mutilation is a mark. Owing to this fact, a subject – who has undergone the mutilation as a particular individual in the flock – henceforth bears the mark of a signifier that extracts him from an initial state in order to convey him toward and identify him with the power to be different and better. This is the meaning of every type of initiatory practice.

This signification is found again at the level of the castration complex. Which is not to say that we have exhausted the question of what is at stake at this level. You must have noticed the ambiguities that revolve around the function of the phallus since I first began trying to broach it with you.

In a certain way, at the level of the castration complex, it is the phallus that is marked and raised to the function of a signifier. Nevertheless, castration is not altogether implied by the ceremonies that lead to one or another type of deformity or circumcision. We must not confuse the mark that is brought to bear in this way on the phallus with the specific function of negativization that is ascribed to the phallus in the castration complex and that constitutes a type of extirpation.

We cannot grasp the latter at this stage in my exposition. We will return to it next time, I think, when we will have to explain a problem that arises for us, now that we are broaching these things anew and are inventorying them. I am simply indicating this to you today.

Why was Freud able to do something so outrageous at the outset, which involved tying the castration complex to something that inspection shows is not all that closely related to it – namely, a dominating, cruel, tyrannical function, that of a sort of absolute father? This is assuredly a myth. And like everything Freud bequeathed us – and this is quite miraculous – it is a myth that holds up. I will try to explain why.

Let us return to initiation rites, and the forms of marking and mutilation they entail. They are designed, by those who practice them, to transform the subject. This is why the angle from which we are broaching them today clearly shows that, in their fundamental function, they play the role of little *a*.

Initiation rites in primitive societies are designed to change the meaning of the subject's natural desires, which are allowed to run

456

free and remain inchoate at the pre-initiation stage. The point is to give those desires a function with which the subject's being can identify and by which it can be designated as such, he becoming thereby, as it were, a full-fledged man. There are rites for becoming a woman, too. Mutilation serves to orient desire here, to have it function as the kind of index I spoke about earlier.

As an index of what? Of something that is actualized but that cannot be expressed except in a symbolic beyond. Today I have called this beyond "being." Let us thus say that mutilation indexes the actualization of the subject's being here.

457

A few tangential remarks are in order here.

It is of course no accident if what receives a signifying mark in initiation rites is whatever sticks out. The phallic appendage is not the only one, as you know, that is employed for this purpose, even if there is no doubt but that the relationship of the subject to himself that makes him most apprehensive – namely, that of tumescence – naturally designates the phallus as the object that is most often offered up to the cutting function, and in a way that is more assuredly feared and scabrous than when it comes to any other object.

The same is true of the function of narcissism as the imaginary relationship of the subject to himself, which must be taken as the main structural support in which the formation of the significant object is inscribed. In our experience of the mirror stage, the subject turns out to be able to place his own tension or erection in the image of himself that comes to him from the other – namely, from beyond himself.

This is what allows us to perceive what may be legitimate in how the tradition of philosopher/psychologists had already broached the function of the ego. I am alluding here to what Maine de Biran contributed in his subtle analysis of the feeling of effort. Effort is a pressure [or: push or thrust, *poussée*] apprehended by the subject from both sides at once, inasmuch as he is the author of the pressure, but also the one who contains it, inasmuch as he feels [*éprouve*] the pressure he exerts within himself. Nevertheless, although he perceives himself [*s'éprouve*], he is never able to grasp himself, since there is, strictly speaking, no possible cut or mark here.

This allows us to notice the link that must be located between the experience of tumescence and that of fatigue – I mean what is known, at the level of erotic practice, as the neurotic's fatigue, whose mirage-like character and unobjectifiable nature you are aware of, since it has nothing to do with any muscular fatigue we can factually measure. If the effort cannot in any way serve the subject, nothing allowing us to stamp it with a signifying cut, this fatigue, which is

symptomatic and paradoxical, seems conversely to be the aftermath [458]
or trace in the subject of an effort on his part to "turn (or make) into
signifiers" [*signifiantiser*], as I will call it.

It is here that we might be able to find, in its most general form,
what – at the level of the subject's tumescence or pressure – shows
us the limits at which possible consecration in the signifying mark
vanishes. I felt it was important to mention this in passing.

We come now to the third form of little *a*, inasmuch as it can serve
as an object.

Here I would really like it if people would try not to get this
wrong, even though I do not have enough time today to go into
all the details about what I will emphasize. Without undertaking a
close rereading, which I will ask you to do, of what I wrote in "On
a Question Preliminary to Any Possible Treatment of Psychosis" [in
Écrits] – in which I laid out what allows us to formulate, in such an
advanced and developed way, Judge Schreber's delusion – what I
think is most likely to show you what is at stake and how I mean it
is to try here to spell out the voice's function in delusions.

We will not be able to understand the phenomenological characteristics of the voice in delusions unless we have first been able to
grasp in what respect it corresponds quite specifically to the formal
requirements of little *a*, insofar as it can be raised to the signifying
function of a cut or gap as such.

In the usual case, a subject produces a voice. I would go even
further and say that the function of the voice always brings into
discourse the subject's weight, his real weight. A raised voice [*La
grosse voix*], for example, must be included in the formation of the
superego as an agency, in which it represents the agency of an Other
manifesting himself as real.

Is this the voice that is heard by someone who is delusional? Is
it what Jean Cocteau tried to pinpoint the dramatic function of in
his work entitled *La Voix humaine* [*The Human Voice*]? It suffices to
consider the everyday experience we in fact have of the voice in an
isolated form – in the very form in which Cocteau, with a great deal
of relevance and flair, showed us its pure impact – namely, on the
telephone.

What does the voice itself teach us, beyond what it says on the
telephone? There is certainly no reason to lay out here the whole [459]
range of experiences of it that one may have. It should suffice to
mention the times you try to place an order, or make any other sort
of request, at a shop, and lo and behold you end up with one of
those voices, at the other end of the line, whose indifference immediately informs you of the ill-will of the person you are dealing with,

his well-established will to elude what may be pressing or personal in your request. This sort of voice instantly indicates that you can expect nothing from the person with whom you are speaking. I will call this type of voice, using a term that has been beautifully crafted by the genius of the French language, *une voix de* "contremaître" [the voice of a foreman, supervisor, or overseer] – it is not that this guy is against [*contre*] the master [*maître*], but he is truly the contrary of the master. It is in this way that certain voices can some-times convey vanity, irrelevance, and bureaucratic emptiness.

Is that what I mean when I speak of the voice functioning at the level of *a*? No, absolutely not.

In delusions, the voice presents itself as pure articulation, and this is what renders paradoxical what a person having a delusion tells us when we question him about the nature of the voices he hears. What he has to communicate always seems to slip away in the oddest way, whereas there is nothing more solid to him than the consistency and existence of the voice as such. Of course, it is precisely because the voice is reduced in his experience to its most cutting and purest form that the subject can but take it to be forcing itself on him.

This is why I emphasized, when we analyzed Judge Schreber's delusion, the (characteristic of) cutting that is altogether obvious there, since the voices heard by Schreber articulate only the begin-nings of sentences, such as, *Sie sollen werden.* . . . The sentences are interrupted before the significant words are uttered, allowing a call for signification to arise after the sentence is cut short. The subject is indeed concerned by this [or: caught up in this, *y est intéressé*], but solely insofar as he himself disappears, succumbs, and is swallowed up whole in a signification that targets him only very generally.

460   Before closing, I will summarize for you what I have tried to home in on today with the words *il l'intéresse* [it interests him, concerns him, he is caught up in it].

I agree that today's class has perhaps been one of the most difficult of all those I have ever given here. You will, I hope, be rewarded next time, when we will proceed by less austere pathways.

I have asked you today to hold onto the notion of interest [*intérêt*]. He who is concerned [*intéressé*] is the subject inasmuch as he resides in the gap constituted by unconscious discourse [*l'intervalle du discours de l'inconscient*]. The subject is, strictly speaking, the metonymy of the being who expresses himself in the unconscious chain.

If the voices and senseless sentences get the subject especially interested in the delusion, it is for the same reason as for all the other forms of the object that I have enumerated for you today. It is at the level of the cut or gap that he becomes fascinated and fixated in order to sustain himself [or: thereby sustaining himself] – at the instant at which he targets himself and questions himself – as a being, as the being of his unconscious.

I do not want to close, however, without conveying – at least to those who have come here for the first time today – the import of the little link this lecture constitutes between others I have given lately.

It is important for us to see what we must do about fantasy, whose most radical and simple forms I have shown you, forms in which, as we know, it constitutes the preferred objects of the subject's unconscious desire. But fantasy is mobile. If we upset it, we must not believe that it can, just like that, jettison one of its members. I know of no examples of fantasies which, when suitably attacked, do not react by reiterating their fantasy form.

We are aware how complicated fantasy can become. In its so-called perverse form, it insists, it preserves and complexifies its structure, and it strives to ever more closely serve its function.

"Interpret fantasy," people say.

Is it purely and simply a question of bringing the subject back to actuality as we see it, to the actuality of reality that we can define as men of science, or as men who imagine that everything can be cognized, known? It seems that a major trend in analytic technique is inclined to reduce the subject to reality functions – reality, for certain analysts, seeming not to have to be articulated otherwise than as the world of American lawyers, as I called it last time. Isn't this enterprise indubitably beyond the scope of the means employed by those with a certain modicum of conviction?

461

Doesn't the place occupied by fantasy require us to take another dimension into account? This dimension is that of what one might call the subject's true exigencies. This dimension cannot be confused with reality; it cannot be reduced to the everyday world; it is a dimension of being.

In this dimension, the subject bears within himself something that is, good Lord, perhaps as hard to bear as Hamlet's message, and which may doom him to a fatal destiny.

The main question is to know what value we analysts grant the experience of desire. Is it to us but a simple bump in the road, something rather bothersome, something that will go away if we wait long enough, when old age sets in, allowing the subject to quite naturally return to the pathways of peace and wisdom? Or does desire designate something else to us?

How should we operate with this something else?

What is our mission? What, in the final analysis, is our duty? These are the questions I am raising when I speak about the interpretation of desire.

May 20, 1959

XXII

CUT AND FANTASY

Choice, drive, and repetition
The creative cut
Details in works of art
Is the ghost* a liar?
Hamlet's fantasy

Today we will continue our study of the place where fantasy as a function is situated. Fantasy includes the part of the subject that is marked by speech's effects, in relation to an object *a* that we tried to define last time.

1

You know where fantasy as a function is situated on what I call the graph.

It is, in short, very simple. The intersecting of the two signifying chains, the upper and lower chains [left-to-right arrows], by a loop which is that of subjective intention, defines four points. I have referred to those on the right, A, and above it, ($◊D), as the points at which we find the code, whereas the other two are points at which we find the message, S(A̶), and below it *s*(A), owing to the retroactive effect of the signifying chain as regards signification.

These are thus the four points that we have learned to give the following significations. The two points on the lower chain are loci where the subject's intention encounters the concrete fact that there is language. Today we are going to examine the other two signs – namely, the barred subject in the presence of D and the signifier of the barred Other.

I have long since elucidated what the two signifying chains represent.

The lower chain is that of the subject's actual discourse. As a first sketch, let us say that it is accessible to consciousness. That said, it is because it is based on illusions, as psychoanalysis has taught us, that we assert it to be completely transparent to consciousness.

If it were not, why would I have spent several years emphasizing what is illusory in this transparency effect, and used every means to convince you of this? I tried to show you, using a fable that you perhaps recall, that it is theoretically possible to imagine that a specular image can subsist independently of any subjective prop; it can persist long after the subject has ceased to exist; and it can even produce effects owing to a mechanism that persists in the subjective nothingness realized by the destruction of all life. I showed you this not for the simple pleasure of constructing such an apparatus, but to illustrate the fact that a montage structured like the montage of the signifying chain can be assumed to last far longer than any of the subjects who prop it up.

Our practice, which constantly brings us into contact with the subject's systematic misrecognition [*méconnaissance*], teaches us that consciousness – insofar as it gives us the feeling of being "me" [*moi*] in discourse – is not an immediately given fact, but is, rather, first experienced in an image, that of one's semblable. This experience throws an appearance of consciousness over what is implied by the subject's relations to the earliest, naive signifying chain, by his relations to innocent demand and actual discourse. I am talking about the type of discourse that flies from one mouth to the next, that gets repeated by one person after another, that organizes what there is by way of discourse in history itself – this actual, shared, everyday speech [*discours universel*] that envelops everything that in fact occurs at a greater or lesser distance from it, that envelops all real, social activity of human groups.

The other signifying chain [i.e., the upper chain] is the one that is clearly shown in psychoanalytic experience to be inaccessible to consciousness. That said, given that we doubt whether the first chain is altogether conscious, to characterize the second chain as inaccessible to consciousness raises many questions about the meaning of this inaccessibility. We must thus indicate what we mean by it.

Must we assume that the chain that is inaccessible to consciousness is constructed like a signifying chain? I will return to this later. Let us consider it first as it presents itself to us.

We have here the line $S(A)\rightarrow(\$\lozenge D)$, which is drawn as a dotted line in order to indicate that the subject does not articulate it as a discourse. What he currently articulates is something different, something that is situated in the intentional loop $(\$\lozenge D)\rightarrow S(A)$. In effect, it is inasmuch as the subject situates himself as operating within the play of speech while alienated by signifierness [*en tant qu'agissant dans l'aliénation de la signifiance avec le jeu de la parole*] that he articulates himself very precisely as a question or an enigma.

This is tangible in human development when, beyond the first demand, with all the consequences it already has, the child seeks to ratify [*sanctionner*] things in the realm established by signifierness – he says "What?" and he says "Why?" This constitutes an explicit reference to discourse and transforms the subject's first intention, that involving demand, into a second intention, that involving discourse itself. Here, discourse itself is questioned, things are questioned in relation to it, in relation to how they are situated in discourse. We are no longer dealing here with exclamations, interpellations, or cries based on need, but rather with naming.

I show the subject's second intention beginning from the locus A. Indeed, it is because the subject is thoroughly alienated by spoken articulation [i.e., speech] and signifierness that a question arises, the one I expressed last time in the guise of *Est-ce?* with a question mark. I expressed it thus not to indulge in equivocation, but because this guise corresponds to the current stage of my formulation of the topic here. In effect, once the subject has been instituted *in* speech, he tries to situate himself as the subject *of* speech [or speaking subject, *sujet de la parole*]. This is why he asks "Is it?" "What?" "Why?" "Who is speaking?" and "Where is it speaking?" What we see here is questioning that is internal to discourse, to the established locus of speech.

This question in effect constitutes the subject as a subject of speech. But the fact remains that, at this level, what is articulated at the level of the signifying chain is not articulable. The existence of the unconscious stems from that.

Some of you may worry that I am presenting the relationship between the unconscious chain and the subject's questioning as identical to the relationship between the earliest discourse involving demand and the intention that arises out of need, as if this were an arbitrary construction. 466

Let me simply remind you that if the unconscious has a meaning, this meaning has all the characteristics of the signifying chain as a function. And I will complete this brief reminder by alluding to a little story that most of my audience here has already heard me tell when I spoke about the signifying chain. Those who do not recall it can have a look at the published version of it.

I am alluding to the fable of the white disks and the black disks [pinned to three prisoners' backs]. This fable illustrates something structural in subject-to-subject relationships, inasmuch as there are three subjects involved. In this fable, a pair of differential signs, white and black, allows us to discern the relationship between one subject and two others. Each subject situates himself with respect to the reasoning process engaged in by the other two subjects, which is based on the color of the disks that they see him and one of the others wearing. The three go through a succession of synchronous oscillations that lead them to conclusively make what I will call a *Wahl*, a choice, a fundamental choice, by which each of them decides what color disk he is wearing, white or black, and shows himself ready to declare it, which is what the fable was constructed for in the first place.

Now, isn't that something we are familiar with from the structure of the drive?

In this fable, we find identification relative to others, negation, refusal to articulate, and defense, which are as consistent with the drive as are two sides of the same coin. The matter is concluded with a decision that marks for the subject the fact that he indeed always makes the same choice in the same situations. We refer to this power of repetition, depending on whom we are dealing with, as we can – as a masochistic tendency, a penchant for failure, the return of the repressed, or a fundamental evoking of the primal scene – but we are dealing with one and the same thing: repetition in the subject of a type of sanction [*sanction*] whose forms go well beyond the characteristics of the content.

In essence, the unconscious always presents itself to us as an indefinitely repeated articulation. If it is legitimate to situate it on the graph in the form of a dotted line, it is, as I have said, because the subject does not accede to it. At this level, the subject is, in the end, he who bears the mark or stigmata of a repetition that remains not only ambiguous, but strictly speaking inaccessible to him, until psychoanalytic experience – which puts a stop to it – allows him to name, situate, and designate himself in it as the medium [*support*] of the sanction.

467

He cannot say "I" at this level. Things present themselves, on the contrary, as "coming from the outside" [*Ça arrive du dehors*]. To say that a thing is coming is already a lot, for he can only read it as "it is speaking" [*Ça parle*]. There is such a great gap here that it is not clear that the subject can, in any way, bridge it and attain the goal that Freud enjoins us to aim at with the commandment *Wo Es war, soll Ich werden*.

Let us now turn to ($0D). What is signified by this so-called code point, symbolized here by the confrontation between the barred subject and demand, capital D?

Let me emphasize first that this point only takes on its import when the deciphering of the coherence of the upper chain begins in the course of psychoanalysis. It is the precise point at which the chain of the subject's speech – insofar as he wonders about himself in what lies beyond actual discourse – encounters demand.

The subject in question here is the one that we retroactively assume to be the medium of the articulation of the unconscious [*l'articulation de l'inconscient*], inasmuch as he sees it, hears it, and reads it. He is the subject qua subject of the unconscious. What role does demand play here? It is assigned its truly symbolic form, and this is what is meant by the lozenge, ◊, between $ and D.

Demand comes in at this level inasmuch as, beyond what it insists on by way of need satisfaction, it presents itself as a demand for love that establishes the Other to whom it is addressed as someone who can be present or absent. It is in this respect that demand, whether it be oral or anal, takes on a metaphorical function here, and comes to symbolize a relationship with the Other. The subjective relationship to demand plays a code function here, inasmuch as it allows us to constitute the subject as being situated, for example, at the level of what, in our vocabulary, we call the oral or anal stage.

With the code, the subject can receive as a message a question that connotes, in what lies beyond the Other, the first taking up of the subject in the signifying chain. It is a question that comes from the Other – on this [curved upper] line, which is also dotted – in the form "*Che vuoi?*": "What do you want?" It is also a question that the subject, again in what lies beyond the Other, asks himself in the form *Est-ce?*

The answer is symbolized on the schema by the Other's signifierness [*signifiance*] qua S(Ⱥ).

I grant this signifierness a broader meaning at this level, into which the adventure of the actual subject – that is, his subjective history – is going to flow. In its most general form, this meaning can be enunciated as follows: there is nothing in the Other or signifierness that can suffice at this level of signifying articulation; there is nothing in signifierness that can guarantee truth; there is no other guarantee of truth than the Other's good faith; and this good faith always presents itself to the subject in a problematic form. Everything that the realm of speech brings into existence for the subject continues to depend on utter and complete faith in the Other.

Does this mean that the subject is done with his question here? This is precisely where we come to fantasy.

I already showed you last time that fantasy is the point we concretely butt up against by which we approach the shores of the unconscious. At the precise point at which the subject finds nothing that can articulate him qua subject of his unconscious discourse, fantasy plays for him the role of an imaginary prop.

468

This is what we are returning to today, for we must more closely examine what this phenomenon is about.

2

As you see on the graph, I locate fantasy across from the [vertical] line A→($◊D) where the subject situates himself in order to accede to the level of the unconscious chain.

Let me remind you of what I said last time. Everything transpires as if, in fantasy, the object plays the same role qua mirage as the image of the specular other, $i(a)$, plays with respect to the ego, m, at the lower level. Except that in fantasy, the object is the imaginary prop of a relationship involving cutting with which the subject must prop himself up at this level. This leads us to a phenomenology of cutting.

469

We have seen the object at three levels: the pregenital object, castrating mutilation, and hallucinatory voices. Let me point out in passing that, as the third object here involves an incarnated voice, it is less an interrupted discourse than a voice that is cut from the text of the subject's internal monologue.

Let us see today if there is not a good deal more to say about this, assuming we return to the meaning of what I already discussed last time, concerning the difference between the vantage point of the real and the vantage point of knowledge.

The point is to know what level we are at here regarding the subject, when we introduce him as barred S. Is this *Est-ce?* [pronounced exactly like S] anything other than an equivocation, which can be given whatever meaning we like? Are we going to dwell on the fact that it is a conjugation of *Esse*, the verb "to be" in Latin?

I already commented on this a bit last time when I talked about reality. Indeed, the subject does not simply refer to discourse, but also to some facet of reality. If there is something that we can coherently call reality, I mean the reality we make a point of mentioning in analytic discourse, I would situate it on the graph in the field that is below actual discourse.

In fact, actual discourse envelops the field of reality and encloses it within itself; it constitutes a reserve of knowledge that can be extended to everything that speaks to man. I mean that man is not obliged to constantly recognize every aspect of his reality and history that he has already included in his discourse. It is here, for example, that alienation, as it is presented in Marxist dialectic, can be coherently articulated.

I would go further still: let us not forget the cut. It is already at work in the first type of fantasy object, the pregenital object. What are fantasy objects here if not real objects? As separated as they may be from the subject, they are nevertheless closely related to his life drives.

In short, it is only too obvious that reality is not a compact continuum; it is made up of cuts, including and going far beyond the cuts made by language.   470

Plato long ago compared the philosopher to a good cook, one who knows how to place his knife in the right place, and cut through the joints [of an animal carcass] without crushing them. Up to a point, the relationship between real cuts and linguistic cuts thus seems to agree with what the philosophical tradition has always assumed – namely, that what is involved is merely the overlapping of one system of cuts with another. Yet if I say that Freud's question comes in here, it is inasmuch as the distance that science has now covered allows us to formulate that the scientific venture goes far beyond the notion that natural cuts are overlaid by cuts made by discourse, made by any discourse whatsoever.

Efforts – that essentially involved eliminating the mythological elements from all scientific explanation – have led us to the point we are at right now, which seems to me to be adequately characterized, without being overly dramatic, by the term "disintegration of matter." This term is well designed to suggest to us that it is not pure and simple knowledge that is at work in the scientific venture.

Situating ourselves at the level of the real, or, if you will, of what I will provisionally call "the great All" – with all the necessary irony, for I am certainly not inclined to call it that – science and its venture do not in any way show us the real lining up with its own cuts [*se renvoyant à lui-même ses propres coupures*], but rather cuts which are elements that create something new that has the virtue of proliferating.

As human beings, we certainly cannot deny that a question arises here: that of knowing whether the consequences of what manifests itself in this way do not go somewhat beyond us in our mediating function. This remark, which I am deliberately keeping sober and limited in scope, nevertheless takes on a current and dramatic accent which I assume has not escaped you. In short, it is only too clear that man enters into this game at his own expense.

There is perhaps no reason for us to go further here. Indeed, if I have referred to the scientific venture, it was not in order to mention all the dramatic effects it has had on human history. It was in order   471 to home in on the relationship between the subject and the sort of cut constituted by the fact that he *is* not in a certain unconscious discourse, and that he does not know what he is in it.

The subject as real insofar as he enters into the cut, the advent of the subject at the level of the cut, his relationship to something that we must call the real, but which is symbolized by nothing: this is what is at stake. I designate the specific point of the subject's relationship to what we might call his "pure being as a subject" – and this will perhaps seem to you to be going too far – at the level of the cut, which I have called a pure manifestation of this being.

Desire's fantasy [*le fantasme du désir*] thus takes on the function of designating this point. This is why, at another point in time, I defined the function fulfilled by fantasy as a metonymy of being, and identified desire itself at this level.

It should be clear that the question remains entirely open at this level whether we can call what is indicated in this way "man." Indeed, what can we call "man," if not what has already been actually symbolized and which, whenever people talk about it, turns out to be laden with all sorts of historical admissions [*reconnaissances*]? The word "humanism" generally designates nothing here, even if there is, of course, something real in it, which is necessary, and which suffices to assure, in psychoanalytic practice itself, the dimension – which we usually, and rather improperly, I believe, call a depth, so let us instead say a beyond – which is such that being can be identified with none of the roles (to employ the term currently used) that it takes on.

To my mind, the dignity, so to speak, of this being has nothing to do with the fact that he is cut – if I may express myself thus, with the whole backdrop, and especially the castrating references, you may attribute to this – nor with the fact that he is *un coupable* [a guilty party, but also someone who is cuttable], to allow myself a play on words. His dignity is based on the cut itself.

The cut is, in the end, the final structural characteristic of the symbolic order. It is in this direction – and I am saying so in passing – that I have already taught you to seek the meaning of what Freud called the death instinct, that by which the death instinct may turn out to converge with being.

472   As all of this may be a bit problematic to you, I would now like to try to fill it out by referring to a work of art, and to works of art in general, in order to illustrate what is involved here.

3

I will begin with a very interesting article, that does not go too far: Kurt Eissler's "The Function of Details in the Interpretation of Works of Literature," which came out in *The Psychoanalytic Quarterly*.

Eissler begins his discourse, and ends it, too, with a remark that one may qualify in various ways, depending on whether one considers it to be confused or simply unexplained. The term "detail" seems to him to be particularly apposite when it comes to the work of a specific author [Ferdinand Raimund] who is completely unknown outside of Austrian circles, an "actor-poet" who Eissler considers to be a sort of unrecognized Shakespeare. I am taking up his article here because I am going to return to Hamlet later today.

Regarding this quasi-Shakespeare who lived in nineteenth-century Vienna, Eissler tells us one of those pretty little stories that are quite typical of what is known as "applied psychoanalysis." In other words, like others before him, he finds in the life of this author a certain number of indicative and paradoxical elements that allow him to raise questions that must forever remain unanswered. We thus learn that Raimund was especially affected, five years before writing one of his chefs-d'oeuvre, by the death of someone who was a sort of model for him, but a model who was so thoroughly embraced that all kinds of questions about paternal, maternal, and sexual identifications arise, as well as any other identifications you might like to add to the mix. The question in itself leaves me rather cold. It is one of those gratuitous papers which, in this genre, appear again and again with an annoying note of conviction. But that is not what is at issue.

Eissler emphasizes the function of what in English he calls the "relevant detail,"* the one that does not fit in with the rest and attracts attention [p. 19]. Eissler's ears perk up when, in a rather well-constructed play by Raimund, something comes out of the blue, as it were, something that nothing has prepared us for. One thing leads to another and Eissler manages to find a certain number of biographical facts of obvious interest. What is at stake is thus the value of relevant details as a guide.

Eissler contrasts what happens in clinical work to what often happens in the so-called applied psychoanalysis of a literary work. He repeats this contrast twice, and if I had time I would read the passages to you to convey their curious opacity [pp. 3 and 19].

In short, he says that a symptom and a relevant detail play more or less the same role, with the following proviso: in analysis, we begin from a symptom that is taken to be relevant by the subject, and it is by interpreting it that we move toward a solution. In the case of a literary work, on the other hand, it is the detail that introduces us to the problem. It is when we find something in a text – he does not even go so far as to define what a text is – that is not especially well motivated, a discordant element, that a path opens up that can lead us to the author's personality.

473

When we look more closely, this does not amount to much of a contrast. Moreover, if there is a contrast to be made, there is also a parallel to be made. Eissler's remark should lead him to realize that discordance in the symbolic – in the symbolic as such, in a written work, and at least in this one – plays a functional role that can be thoroughly identified with a real symptom, in any case from the standpoint of the progress of an analysis, if this progress is to be considered to involve progress in knowledge of the subject.

Be that as it may, this comparison of two things is of genuine interest. But the question arises whether only typographical errors are going to turn out to be of significance to us in literary works. And why not, after all? It is clear that, in the analysis of literary works, typographical errors – you understand what I mean by that, what presents itself to us as a discontinuity – can tip us off as to where to seek, in its unconscious import, one or another incident of the author's life that might shed major light on it, and this is in fact what happens in this article.

In any case, doesn't this shed light for us on the dimension of works of art? Owing to this sole fact – but as we shall see, it also goes well beyond this fact – we can no longer consider a work of art to be a transposition or sublimation, call it as you will, of reality. One can no longer say that it involves imitation or amounts to mimesis, for it always constitutes a profound reworking of the said reality. But I believe that we have already gone well beyond this point, and it is not to this that I wish to draw your attention.

I will say, confining my attention here to written works of art, that artworks, far from transfiguring reality in any way whatsoever, no matter how broadly viewed, bring the advent of cutting [*la coupure*] into their very structure, because a subject's real is manifested therein, insofar as, beyond what he says, he is an unconscious subject.

The subject is certainly prohibited from acceding to his relation to the advent of cutting, since his unconscious lies there. On the other hand, this access is not prohibited to him insofar as he is familiar with fantasy – namely, insofar as he is actuated by the relationship known as desire. Now, fantasy is intimately woven into literary works. Hence it becomes possible for a literary work to express the dimension of a subject's reality, which is the advent of being beyond all possible subjective realization, as I called it earlier.

The form of the work of art – of the work of art that succeeds as well as of the one that fails – has the virtue of involving this dimension. If I may use, in this regard, the topology of my graph to convey this, this dimension is not parallel to the field of reality created in reality [*réel*] by human symbolization, but cuts across

474

it, inasmuch as man's most intimate relationship to the cut goes beyond all natural cuts. For there is the essential cut constituted by his existence – namely, the fact that he is here and that he must be situated in the very advent of the cut.

This is what is involved in works of art, and especially in the one we have broached most recently because it is, in this regard, the most problematic work – namely, *Hamlet*.

4   475

There are all sorts of relevant things in *Hamlet*, too, in the sense of details that do not fit or make sense.

I would even say that it is owing to them that we made headway, but in a completely enigmatic way, for we were unable to ever do otherwise than wonder about what such relevance* means. One thing is clear, which is that we can never rule out the possibility that Shakespeare wanted it this way.

Kurt Eissler may find it bizarre – rightly or wrongly, it does not matter – that Ferdinand Raimund mentions, at a certain moment in his play, a period of five years that no character had ever mentioned before, and claim this is a relevant* detail that puts him on the scent of something. I did not proceed in the same way at all regarding *Hamlet*. For I was sure that the fabric of relevant details could not in any case be purely and simply resolved by saying that Shakespeare allowed himself to be led here by some sort of divine inspiration [*bon génie*]. I had the impression that Shakespeare himself had contributed to it.

But had he contributed to it nothing other than the manifestation of his deepest unconscious, it is in any case the architecture of these relevant details that shows us that he managed to make the major assertion that I described earlier. Namely, that he brought out the most profound facet of the subject as a speaking subject – in other words, his true relationship to the cut.

This is what the architecture of *Hamlet* shows us, inasmuch as the tragedy is founded on the subject's relationship to truth.

In contrast to the dream with which we began our exploration this year – that in which the dead father appears before his son, a son who is suffering greatly – in *Hamlet* the father knows he is dead and tells his son how he died, they then being the only two who know this. Shakespeare's text differs on this point from the Hamlet story as it is found in the prior literature where the murder took place publicly; in prior accounts, everyone knew that there was a crime and Hamlet acted crazy in order to dissimulate his intentions.

In Shakespeare's version, there are only two who know, one of
whom is a ghost.* The ghost* makes his appearance right from the
beginning of *Hamlet*, and other commentators have demonstrated
the function served by the fact that it is foregrounded in this way.
Now, what is a ghost* if not a representation of the kind of paradox
that only works of art can pose? Shakespeare makes his altogether
believable to us.

What does his ghost* say? He says very strange things and I am
astonished that no one – I am not saying has attempted to psycho-
analyze the ghost* – but has wondered much about what he says.
What he says is that the betrayal was absolute, there having been
nothing greater or more perfect than his loyalty to his wife, the
queen; there is no more complete betrayal imaginable than the one
that laid him low. Everything that falls under the heading of good
faith, loyalty, and vows is thus presented to Hamlet as not merely
being revocable, but as having actually been revoked.

This absolute revocation unfolds at the level of the signifying
chain, but it is quite different from the fact I spoke to you about that
there is no signifier that could constitute a guarantee [*la carence du
signifiant de la garantie*]; for something is clearly guaranteed here,
which is an untruth. This sort of revelation, as it were, of a lie – a
theme that would be worth exploring in its own right – leads to
the sort of stupor with which Hamlet is overcome after his father's
revelations. It is translated in Shakespeare's text in a remarkable
manner, for when Hamlet is asked what the ghost* told him, he does
not want to say, and for good reason, yet he expresses it in a very
specific way:

There's never a villain dwelling in all Denmark
But he's an arrant knave. [I, v, 23–4]

In other words, he expresses himself in the register of tautology.

But let us leave that aside, for these are mere details and anec-
dotes. The question lies elsewhere. It is the following: how did we
make such a mistake?

For it is generally agreed that dead men don't tell lies. Why is
that? For the same reason, perhaps, which makes it such that all of
our science still maintains the internal postulate that Einstein – who
occasionally said things that were not altogether superficial, philo-
sophically speaking – highlighted in his own terms by saying, "God
may be subtle, but he is assuredly honest." Can we say as much
about a father who categorically claims that he is being subjected
to all of hell's torments owing to absolutely odious crimes? There
is some discordance here that cannot fail to make our ears perk up.

Can't we discern the effect on Hamlet of his father's assertion that he is eternally damned? We can conceptualize that Hamlet remains trapped within this claim [*parole*] and that this dooms him to see truth forever escape him. Mustn't we wonder what this claim means, at least functionally, with respect to the genesis and unfolding of the entire drama?

Many other things could be connected up with this, including something that is said by the ghost:*

But virtue, as it never will be moved,
Though lewdness court it in a shape of heaven,
So lust, though to a radiant angel linked,
Will sate itself in a celestial bed
And prey on garbage. [I, v, 53–7]

Which radiant angel are we talking about here? It is the angel who introduced lewdness into this broken love relationship. The entire responsibility for the sin falls on the angel. But is it really possible that, here more than anywhere else, he who bears witness in this case to the harm that has forever been done him bore no responsibility whatsoever? This is, of course, the key that can never be turned, the secret that can never be found out.

Yet doesn't a clue put us on the scent here of the word that will tip us off as to what is at stake? This word, here as elsewhere, is fantasy. And the clue? However primitive we may assume the brains of Shakespeare's contemporaries to have been, and rightly so, it was quite a curious choice, all the same, on the playwright's part to cast a never-to-be-resolved enigma in the form of a vial of poison poured into someone's ear. Let us not forget that the ear in question is that of Hamlet, Hamlet the father, for both he and his son are named Hamlet.

Psychoanalysts have only glancingly touched on this point. A few have indicated that some symbolic element must perhaps be recognized here. Yet it is something that can, in any case, be situated using our method: it is the father's revelation, whose paradoxical nature I just highlighted, that lives on in its consequences.

His revelation is presented to us in the form of the wall that it forms, the hole that it digs, and the impenetrable enigma that it constitutes. We have here a structure that is not merely fanta-sized, but that fits in perfectly well with what takes place – for, if there is anyone who gets poisoned through the ear, it is Hamlet himself. And what plays the role of poison in his case is his father's speech.

Shakespeare's intention is somewhat clarified thereby. First he

478

shows us the relationship between desire and this revelation. Hamlet remains devastated by this revelation for two full months. How does he little by little reclaim the use of his members? Through a work of art. The actors come just at the right time for him to bench test "the conscience of the king," as the text tells us [II, ii, 591].

It is clearly by means of this test that he is able to enter back into action, back into a circuit that necessarily unfolds starting from the first of the consequences of his father's revelation. This character who, from the moment of his father's revelation, wished only for his own dissolution –

O that this too too sullied flesh would melt,
Thaw, and resolve itself into a dew [I, ii, 129–30]

– is overtaken at the end of the [actors'] play by a kind of drunkenness that has a very precise name, which is that of *artifex*. He is overjoyed at having managed to corroborate the ghost's horrific story, he can no longer be held back, and Horatio just barely manages to contain Hamlet's exuberance by grabbing onto his coattails.

When Hamlet asks Horatio, couldn't I now "get me a fellow-ship in a cry of players, sir?" the latter replies, "Half a share" [III, ii, 267–9]. He knows what is going on. Things are far from having been settled for Hamlet by means of this play; it is not because he is *artifex* [ingenious, crafty, or artful] that he has now found his role. But it is enough for us to know that he is *artifex* to understand that he will accept the first role he finds. He will, in the final analysis, do whatever he is ordered to do – I will read you the passage in the text another time.

A certain poison, once ingested by a rat – and you realize that rats are never far from all such goings-on, especially in *Hamlet* – gives the rat a thirst from which it will die, for thirst completely dissolves this mortal poison in him. Well, this is the sort of thing Hamlet was immediately inspired to do.

Something can be added to what I just told you, which allows me to emphasize this more forcefully. An author by the name of Walter Wilson Greg was astonished by something that every spectator should have long since noticed – namely, that Claudius shows himself to be completely impervious to what precedes the scene in which Hamlet has the unfolding of his crime acted out before him. There is, in fact, by way of a prologue, a long pantomimed scene in which we see the queen of comedy proclaim her loyalty to and love for the king of comedy; this precedes the scene in which the king, who has fallen asleep in the very same garden, has poison poured into his ear by a third character. Claudius displays no reaction

479

whatsoever to the prologue. Walter Wilson Greg concludes that the ghost was lying, perish the thought!

Whole careers have been wagered on this point! John Dover Wilson wrote an extremely long book explaining how it is possible that Claudius, who is so obviously guilty, did not recognize himself in the scene, and constructed all sorts of minute logical arguments to demonstrate that he did not recognize himself in it because he was looking elsewhere at the time. This is not indicated in the staging. Perhaps this is not worth the work of a lifetime, after all.

Can't we suggest that Claudius was assuredly in on these dark dealings, since he admits it himself and proclaims it to heaven? He has destroyed not only the conjugal balance of Hamlet the father, but a great deal else, and his own life to boot. It is quite true that his crime, as he says, smells bad: "O, my offense is rank, it smells to heaven" [III, iii, 36].

Claudius clearly realizes that there is a smell of sulfur in the air. He even asks Hamlet, "Is there no offense in 't?" To which Hamlet replies, "no offense i' th' world" [III, ii, 224–7]. But when the actor playing Lucianus, the king's nephew, comes on stage and pours poison into the sleeping man's ear, and Hamlet tells Claudius that the assassin is now going to win the love of the king's spouse, Claudius feels that things have gone a bit too far and, cut to the quick, he jumps to his feet.

In truth, things remain totally ambiguous. From that time on, everyone is appalled, the entire court considers Hamlet to be impossible, and the courtesans are all on the king's side. This is because they have not recognized Claudius' crime, for no one knows anything about how Claudius exterminated Hamlet the father, and, apart from Hamlet and his confidant, no one ever knows anything about it until the very end.

The function of fantasy thus seems to be truly different here from that of "the means employed" [*moyen*], as it is put in detective novels.

This becomes much clearer if we assume, and I believe I am making this assumption plausible to you, that Shakespeare was one of those beings who went the furthest in exploring subjective oscillations, to the point that his work describes for us a sort of cartography of all possible human relations, but includes the scar known as desire as a contact point, which irreducibly designates his being. This is what makes it such that his work, each part of which corroborates the rest, displays a miraculous unity.

Isn't it absolutely marvelous that he himself undoubtedly experienced the adventure described in the sonnet* that allows us to precisely corroborate the fundamental positions of desire? I will come back to this later.

480

This astonishing man lived through the era of Elizabethan England without going unnoticed, of course, having written almost forty plays, and we no doubt have some traces of him, I mean some first-hand accounts. Yet you need but read one good book that summarizes more or less everything that has been found out about Shakespeare to see that, apart from the fact that he surely existed, we truly cannot say anything about him, his attachments, his milieu, his loves, or his friendships. Everything has disappeared without a trace.

Our author presents himself to us analysts as the enigma we can point to in our history that has the most radically and forever vanished, dissolved, and disappeared.

May 27, 1959

XXIII

THE FUNCTION OF THE SUBJECTIVE SLIT IN PERVERSE FANTASIES

*Not on*e
The Last Judgment
An artificial perversion
Voyeurism and exhibitionism
When little *a* is the Other's desire

I am continuing my attempt to articulate what must guide our actions in psychoanalysis insofar as we deal therein with a subject's unconscious.

I know that this is not easy to do. Which is why I do not allow myself just any old thing in the kind of formulation to which I would like to lead you. My tangents are related to the sense I have that I need to convey to you the importance of the approach I am taking. This does not mean that I always succeed in speaking in such a way that you do not lose your bearings along the way. I nevertheless ask you to follow and trust me.

And to begin from where we left off last time, I will articulate more simply what I formulated – not without precautions, not without making an effort to avoid ambiguities – when I foregrounded the term "being."

1

I am going to take some pretty gigantic steps here by asking that, however risky this may appear to you, we reintegrate into our everyday thinking terms that are so massive [*gros*] that for several centuries now no one has dared go near them without respectfully trembling. I am speaking about Being and the One.

It is only by using them that we can test their coherence. Let us say that what I call being – and what I went so far last time as to call "pure being" at a certain level of its emergence – must be situated in relation to terms by which we orient ourselves here, namely the real and the symbolic.

We are not idealists, as it is put in books of philosophy; we are not among those who think that being precedes thought. But in order to orient ourselves in our work as analysts, we need to refer to being – no less than that! I am sorry to have to invoke the firmament of philosophy for you; I am only doing so because I feel forced to do so and, after all, because I cannot find anything better with which to make headway.

I will thus say that being truly is the real insofar as it manifests itself in the symbolic. This means that being is at the level of the symbolic. In any case, we need not consider to lie elsewhere than in the symbolic the simple fact that we add something to a thing when we say that it *is* this or that, this comment targeting the real, because it is in the symbolic that the real is affirmed or rejected or denied.

Being lies nowhere else – let this be quite clear – than in gaps, where it is the least signifying of signifiers – namely, the cut [*la coupure*]. Being is the same thing as cutting [*la coupure*]. Cutting renders being present in the symbolic.

What about the "pure being" that we are also talking about? I will put it more directly, since it seems – and I am quite willing to admit this – that certain formulations that I proposed last time struck some of you as circumlocutory, not to say confused. The pure being in question is the same being whose general definition I just gave, and this is so because a signifying chain, going by the name of the unconscious, subsists in accordance with a formulation that you will be so kind as to allow me to propose: every subject is *not one* [*tout sujet est* pas un].

Here I must request that you be so indulgent as to go along with me. This simply means that you will not imagine that I am proposing what I am proposing with fewer precautions than I proposed being. I am asking you to credit me for having already perceived what I am now going to propose before coming to speak to you about it today: namely, that the One [*l'Un*] is not an *un*equivocal notion.

Encyclopedias of philosophy remind us that there are different uses of this term. The One that is the All is not to be confused, in its various guises, with the One as a number, 1, the latter presupposing the whole system and series of numbers, the one that can actually be isolated. It appears that, if things are correctly deduced, the first One [the All] is secondary to the institution of numbers themselves.

In any case, empirical approaches leave no doubt about this. It is not at random that I will refer here to what purports to be the most basic approach, that of English psychology, when it attempts to

483

reconstruct the ways in which numbers became part of our experience. Moreover, I have already pointed out that it is impossible to structure human experience, I mean the most common actual experience, without beginning from the fact that human beings count and count themselves [or: are counted, *se compte*].

I will say, in an abbreviated way – for I cannot go any further without assuming that you have by now digested what I have already said, owing to the time you have had to reflect – that desire is closely related to what happens owing to the fact that human beings must express themselves in the signifier; and that, qua being, it is in the gaps of the signifying chain that a human being appears as a barred subject. I shall try to articulate the level at which the subject is a barred subject further on with the help of a notion that I will deliberately begin by making more ambiguous than that of the One as I have just introduced it, because I do not think that people have yet realized how ambiguous this notion is. It is the notion of the *not one*. It is insofar as the barred subject appears here as *not one* that we will deal with him today.

Let us nevertheless take things up again at the level of experience, I mean at the level of desire here.

If desire serves the subject as an index at the point at which he cannot designate himself without vanishing, I will say – to play on words and their ambiguities – that at the level of desire the subject *counts himself* [or: is counted, *se compte*]. This is what I want to draw your attention to first. Given our usual inclination to forget what we are dealing with in the experience of those that we have the audacity to take on, our patients, I will ask you to consider your own experience here – in desire we count ourselves (as) counting [*nous nous comptons comptant*].

It is in desire and not in the computus [*comput*] that the subject appears as counting, where we say he has to come to terms with what, in the final analysis, makes him who he is. Must analysts be reminded that nothing more definitively constitutes proof of the subject's presence than desire? The fact that, from that point on, the counting begins to change by giving itself over to all sorts of transactions that dissolve it into variously fiduciary equivalents – this is obviously a whole separate problem. But a moment inevitably comes at which one must pay cash [*payer comptant*].

When people come to see us for analysis, it is usually because things do not work out for them when it comes time to pay the piper [*payer comptant*], regardless of what is involved, whether it be sexual desire or action, in the simplest sense of the term. The question of the object arises here. It is clear that if the object were simple, it not only would not be difficult for the subject to deal directly [*comptant*]

484

with his feelings, but, if you will allow me this play on words, he would be more often content [*content*, another homonym] with the object, whereas, instead, he has to content himself with it [*s'en contente*], which is a horse of a different color.

This is obviously related to the fact that, when it comes to desire, the object that is able to satisfy us is not, to say the least, easily accessed. I would even say that it is not easy to find it, and this is true for structural reasons which we are now going to try to examine. I do not seem to be making headway quickly here, but it is because it is difficult, even if, let me repeat, we are talking about everyday experience.

If the object of desire were the most mature and "adult" of objects, as people put it in the sort of blithering drunkenness in which they exalt "genital desire," we would not constantly be dealing with the division that regularly enters into the register of the object, and that forces us to distinguish between the level at which the object is an object of love or, as people put it, of tenderness – whereby we give another person the gift of our uniqueness – and the level at which this same other person is considered to be an instrument of our desire.

Since the supposition that subjects can be very conciliatory and can harmonize these two levels seems to be more or less problematic, people rely on the other's love [or: love for the other, *l'amour de l'autre*] to resolve everything. But in doing so, they go beyond the limits of our model, because they rely in the final analysis not on our own dispositions, but on the other's, on his affection [*tendresse*]. We expect that the other – and undoubtedly at the cost of a certain decentering of himself – will live up to the most exacting standards of what desire requires by way of an object.

In the end, it seems that people quite simply bring back in here old religious distinctions, in a more or less disguised fashion – for example, the distinction between loving affection, in the concrete (or, as it is put, "passionate" or "carnal") sense of the term, and charitable love [or: Christian love, *amour de charité*]. If this is truly what is involved, why not send our patients to pastors who will preach it to them better than we can?

Thus one cannot say that we do not receive a warning from our patients, who are very good at anticipating slippage in our terminology. They tell us now and then that if we are going to preach fine moral principles, they can go and get them elsewhere. Curiously enough, it sometimes happens that this gets on their nerves so much that they do not want to hear any more about it. I am being flippantly ironic here. Nevertheless, it is not pure and simple irony.

I would go further still. I would say that, in the final analysis, the only theory of desire in which we can recognize – assuming we dot the i's and cross the t's – a sketch of the numbers that will serve me in articulating this to you, is the theory that is oriented by religious dogma. It is no accident that desire is clearly inscribed in religious discourse – in protected corners of it, naturally, whose access is reserved, not open to ordinary mortals or the faithful – in corners that are referred to as mystical. As such, the satisfaction of desire is tied to an entire divine organization which, to ordinary mortals, presents itself in the form of the mysteries – to others too, probably, whom I have no need to name. We need but consider what terms that are quite vibrant, like those of "incarnation" and "redemption," represent to believers with sensitive souls.

But I will go still further. We would be quite wrong not to see that the most profound of all dogmas, which is known as the Trinity, is not unrelated to the number three, which we deal with constantly, inasmuch as we perceive that there is no possible balanced access to so-called normal desire without an experience that involves a certain subjective triad. Why not say these things, since we find them in an extremely simple form here?

As for me, I will say that not only do I not balk at such references, I like them just as much as the somewhat vague apprehensions of primitive ceremonies – whether totemic or others – in which the best elements are not very different from these structural elements. Of course, it is precisely because we try to broach things in a way which, even if it is not exhaustive, does not involve the angle of mystery, that I believe there is some interest in our following this pathway. 486

Similarly, it is not superfluous to recall to mind here certain questions with a moral or even, I would say, a social horizon. It seems clear in contemporary experience that there cannot be satisfaction of one person without the satisfaction of all [*tous*]. This is at the core of a movement which, even if we are not very involved with others in it, impinges on us from every direction, and certainly enough to be ready to disrupt many of our creature comforts.

Let us not forget, however, that the satisfaction in question is such that we must ask whether it concerns solely the satisfaction of needs. The people I am talking about – let us put them under the heading of the movement that considers itself to be Marxist in perspective, and whose main principle is the one I just expressed – would not dare to claim this, since the precise goal of this movement, with the revolutions that it brings with it, is in the end to have "everyone" [*tous*] accede to freedom – a freedom that is no doubt far off, and posited as having to be post-revolutionary. Yet what other content can we give this freedom than the notion that each person has his own desire at his disposal?

Now, in this perspective, the satisfaction of desire is a post-revolutionary matter, which is something we perceive every day, and which does not make things easy. We cannot, in effect, defer the desire we deal with to a post-revolutionary stage.

You realize, of course, that I am not criticizing one lifestyle or another, whether it lies shy of or beyond a certain border. The question of desire remains at the forefront of the preoccupations of the powers that be, by which I mean that there has to be some social and collective way of managing* desire. This is no easier to do on one side of a certain curtain than on the other. The point is always to temper a certain discontent, the discontent in civilization, as Freud called it. There is no other discontent in civilization than the discontent of desire.

To hammer this home for you, I would ask each of you – not as analysts, for analysts are overly inclined, less here than elsewhere, to believe they are destined to rule over other people's desires – what the expression "to realize your desire" means to you at the heart of your existence. What does it mean to realize your desire?

Desires do get realized, after all! Things happen. Things get deflected a bit to the right, a bit to the left, twisted, confused, and become a greater or lesser pain in the neck, but there are nevertheless things that at a certain moment we can summarize by saying, "This went in the direction of realizing my desire." Nevertheless, if I ask you to articulate what it means to realize your desire, I am wagering that you will not be able to express it very easily.

If I may highlight a formidable bit of black humor that the religion I referred to a moment ago, the one that is alive and well around us, the Christian religion, proposed that goes by the name of the Last Judgment, I will simply ask you if I shouldn't project the following question onto this most suitable locus.

On the day of the Last Judgment, won't what we will be able to say about what we have done, in our unique existence, to realize our desire weigh as heavily as what we will have done along the lines – which does not refute it in the slightest, which does not counterbalance it in any way – of doing what is known as the good?

We are now going to return to the topic of the structure of desire.

2

It is no longer simply a question of the function of the object as I tried to formulate it two years ago, nor is it the function of the subject, which, as I have tried to show you this year, is distinguished, at the key point of desire, by a vanishing of the subject insofar as he

must name himself. What interests us is the correlation between the   488
two.

The correlation is such that the object has the precise function of signifying the point at which the subject cannot name himself. It is in this respect that modesty [*pudeur*] is, I would say, the royal form of what shows up in symptoms in the guise of shame and disgust.

Nevertheless, before going into this, I will ask for a moment of your attention to make a remark that I am obliged to leave here as a marker, without being able to explore it as I would like.

Comedy, as opposed to what stupid people think, is what gives us the most profound access to the workings of the [theatrical] stage insofar as it grants human beings a spectral decomposition of their situation in the world. Comedy goes beyond modesty, whereas tragedy ends with the name of the hero and with total identification of the hero. Hamlet is Hamlet, he is [the person who goes by] that specific name. And this is even so because his father before him was already Hamlet. In the final analysis, everything resolves there: Hamlet is definitively abolished in his desire. I think I have now said enough about Hamlet.

But comedy is a very curious sort of desire trap. Whenever a desire trap functions, we are in the realm of comedy. It is desire insofar as it appears where we were not expecting it. The ridiculous father, the hypocritical pious person, the virtuous man in the throes of adultery – that's the stuff of comedy. There has to be an element which is such that desire is not owned. It is masked and unmasked, it is buffeted about, and it is occasionally punished, but only for appearances' sake. For in true comedies, punishment never even grazes the raven's wing of desire, the latter getting off absolutely scot-free. Tartuffe is exactly the same when the exempt taps him on the shoulder as he was before. Arnolphe goes "whew" – in other words, he is still Arnolphe, and there is no reason why he would not start up again with another Agnes. Harpagon is not cured by the more or less artificial conclusion of Molière's comedy. In comedies, desire is unmasked, not refuted.

I have given you but a quick sketch here. What I would like to go into with you now is how we must situate ourselves in analysis with regard to desire. Thus I am going to present something to you that   489
will serve this purpose.

As one of our great poets – even though he was a still greater painter [Picasso] – put it, desire can be caught "by the tail," in other words, in fantasy. The subject, insofar as he desires, does not know where he is at with regard to unconscious articulation, that is, with regard to the sign or scansion he repeats qua unconscious. Where is the subject himself? Is he where he desires? The aim of my class today is to show you that the subject is not where he desires, but that he is somewhere in fantasy, and that the way we interpret depends on that.

Some time back I discussed a fine case study that came out in Belgium in a little bulletin, which concerns the appearance of a transitory perversion during a psychoanalytic treatment.

The patient was incorrectly diagnosed as suffering from a form of phobia, whereas something else was clearly involved. The case study is very conscientious, and is useful to us owing to questions that the author – that is, the woman who directed the treatment [Ruth Lebovici] – herself raises. Had she been better guided herself, she would no doubt have had all the qualities necessary to see much more clearly and to go much further. In the name of certain principles, in the name of the so-called reality principle in this case, the analyst was wrong to allow herself to meddle with the subject's desire as if she were dealing with something that had to be put back in its place [or: put away, *remis en place*].

The patient thus begins to fantasize that the treatment will not be over until he has had sexual intercourse with the analyst. It is obviously no accident if something as crude as this comes to the fore during analytic treatment. It is undoubtedly a result of the general orientation of the treatment.

The crucial point was the interpretation of a fantasy. The fantasy involved, quite magnificently, I will not say a man in a suit of armor, but a suit of armor advancing behind the subject and armed with a syringe full of bug spray – the funniest and most stereotypical representation of the destructive phallus one can imagine. In retrospect, the author was embarrassed to realize that it was her interpretation that set off the subsequent artificial perversion.

In effect, she interpreted his fantasy in terms of reality, as reflecting a real experience he had had of the phallic mother. Yet a close examination of the case – starting from any point at which one cares to take it up – clearly shows that the subject brought out here the necessary, yet missing, image of a father, inasmuch as a father is required to stabilize the subject's desire. Nothing could be more satisfying than to see this missing character appear in the form of a montage, which gives us the living image of the subject as reconstructed with the help of cuts or joints in the suit of armor, which are truly pure articulations [*jointures*].

It is in this direction that one could concretely rethink the type of intervention that would have been necessary. The "cure" in this case could perhaps have been obtained more easily than by creating a transitory perversion that was played out in reality; this indisputably shows us in what respect the reference to reality, in a

490

certain form of practice, represents a regression when it comes to treatment.

I am now going to indicate what I would like to convey to you regarding the relations between $ and *a*, by first providing a model of them, which is no more than a model: *fort-da*.

I have no need to comment on it otherwise than to remind you that we can theoretically consider it to be the first moment of the subject's entry into the symbolic order. *Fort-da* resides in the alternation of a signifying pair with regard to a small object, whatever it may be. The element in question may be a ball, or just as easily a bit of string, or a worn-out edge of bedding, as long as it holds fast and can be thrown away and reeled back in. This moment is situated just before the one in which we see the appearance of $ – in other words, before the moment at which the subject wonders about the Other as present or absent.

This is thus the locus or level at which the subject enters into the symbolic order. This entrance immediately brings out something that Winnicott designated with the term "transitional object," which he invented. In his thought, which revolves altogether around the earliest experiences of frustration, the transitional object is necessary to all of human development. The transitional object is the little ball involved in the *fort-da* game.

491

When can we consider this game to be given its function in desire? From the moment at which it becomes a fantasy. For that, the subject must no longer enter into the game, he must short-circuit it, in order to bring himself forward [*s'anticiper*] and include himself altogether in the fantasy, where he catches hold of himself [or: gets his bearings, *se saisit*] in his very disappearance. He does so with a certain amount of difficulty, of course, but for what I call fantasy, qua prop of desire, it is necessary that the subject be represented therein at the very moment of his disappearance.

I am not saying anything extraordinary here. I am simply articulating the idea Ernest Jones dwelt on when he attempted to give concrete meaning to the term "castration complex." He identified the castration complex with the fear of the disappearance of desire, and that is exactly what I am saying to you in a different form.

Why did Jones go there and not elsewhere? For reasons based on the requirements of his personal understanding: this is how things were phenomenologically understandable to him. People are clearly impeded by the limits of understanding when they try to understand at any cost. And these are the limits that I am trying to get you to go a bit beyond by inviting you to stop trying to understand. It is in this regard that I am not a phenomenologist.

Since the subject fears that his desire may disappear, this must clearly signify that in some way he wants to desire [*il se désire désir-ant*]. This is the structure of the neurotic's – pay attention here – the neurotic's desire.

I will not take up neurosis right away because that would strike you as involving an overly simple doubling of the type "I desire to desire" [*je me désire désirant*] and "I want to desire and to be desired" [*je me désire désirant désiré*], etc. That is not what is involved here at all.

To show this to you, it is worth once again spelling out perverse fantasy.

3

Today I will examine one of the most accessible perverse fantasies, which is, moreover, closely related to the one I mentioned earlier in the case study [by Ruth Lebovici].

It is the fantasy of the exhibitionist, that of the voyeur too, for it is perhaps fitting not to confine ourselves to the way the structure in question is usually portrayed.

People generally tell us: "The perverse fantasy involving the scop-tophilic drive is very simple and very pretty. People naturally like to look, and people naturally like to be looked at." These are among the "charming life drives," as Paul Éluard puts it somewhere. We have here, in short, something that is known as the drive, and that enjoys "putting on a show" [*donner à voir*], to borrow the lovely title of Éluard's book of poetry. It is a manifestation of the [human] form offering itself of its own accord to the other.

Let me point out that this is not insignificant, for it already implies a certain subjectivity.

At our society's scientific meeting last night, we were talking about the implicit subjectivity there may be in the life of an animal. It is hardly possible to conceptualize this "putting on of a show" [*donner à voir*] itself without hearing the word *donner* [to give] in the full sense of the virtues of the gift [*don*], which implies a reference – undoubtedly innocent, not intentional – of this form to its own richness. We know of many concrete indications of the extravagant lengths to which animals go in their captivating display, and espe-cially in sexual display.

I am not going to trot out the stickleback again here – I think I have spoken about it often enough for what I am saying today to make sense to you. I will simply say that, however instinctual we assume it to be, a certain behavior can include in its trajectory a little backward motion, and simultaneously an anticipatory motion, that the graph shows you in the trajectory of speech. In the drive's exuberance to show itself – the drive such as we find it in nature – a temporal projection is tangible.

As a side note, I will recommend that the person who spoke last night about this topic take note of the following: in certain circumstances, we undoubtedly observe a temporal anticipation or expectation on the part of animals. But what can justify you in characterizing the disappointment of this expectation as a "deception" [*tromperie*]? There is reason to temper this, and in my view, until someone convinces me of the contrary, I will say that the medium [of deception] seems to me to be constituted by a promise. In order to be able to talk about deception, instead of disappointment of an expectation, we have to assume that the animal promises itself to succeed with one or another of its behaviors, and therein lies the whole question.

Let us return now to our exhibitionist.

Is he inscribed in the dialectic of "showing"? In no way, shape, or form. Yet, showing is connected here to the pathways of the Other. In effect, in the exhibitionist's relationship to the Other – the terms I am going to employ somewhat awkwardly in order to convey something to you are certainly not the best, or the most literary – it is necessary that this Other be, as far as desire is concerned, complicit (and Lord knows that she is truly complicit at times) in what is happening in front of her and which takes on the value of a break.

Note that this break is not just any old break. It is essential that it be a desire trap. It is perceived by the Other to whom it is addressed, insofar as it goes unnoticed to, let us say, most people. Everyone thus knows that there is no true exhibitionist in private life – apart from some supplemental subtlety, of course. In order for there to be pleasure, the exhibition must take place in a public space.

So here we show up in our big clodhoppers and we tell the exhibitionist: "My little friend, you expose yourself from so far away because you are afraid of getting close to your object. Move closer, move closer." What a load of malarkey! Do you think exhibitionists don't fuck? Clinical experience shows us this is not the case. They are at times very good husbands with their wives. But their desire lies elsewhere and their satisfaction requires other conditions. These are conditions on which we must dwell here.

The satisfaction of so-called exhibitionist desire requires that a specific kind of communication occur with the Other. It is necessary that the exhibition, as a manifestation of being and the real, be inscribed in the symbolic frame as such. This is precisely what necessitates a public space, in order that one be quite sure that one is within the symbolic frame.

493

494   Stated differently, whereas people reproach exhibitionists for not
daring to get close to their objects, for giving into some sort of fear, I
am saying that the satisfaction of their desire depends on the condition that there be maximal danger. On this point, the same people,
without worrying about the contradiction between this and their
preceding remark, say that exhibitionists seek out danger.

This is not impossible, but before going that far let us observe
what sometimes happens for what figures here as the object, namely
the interested party or parties, one or more little girls – over whom
let us shed a tear in passing like kind souls. Little girls, especially if
there are several of them, are sometimes highly amused by this. This
may even be part of the exhibitionist's pleasure, as a variant. An
essential element of the situation is thus the Other's desire, insofar
as she is surprised, is involved beyond all modesty, or is complicit
here – all such variations are possible.

What about the exhibitionist himself? There is what he shows,
you will tell me. Indeed, this is what I pointed out the structure of
to you and just indicated again. Nevertheless, I would say that in
this case what he shows – which is rather variable, and more or less
glorious – is in fact redundant, hiding rather than revealing what is
at stake.

Don't kid yourself here – what he shows, the erection that attests
to his desire, is distinct from the apparatus of that desire. The apparatus that instates what is glimpsed in a certain relationship to what
is not glimpsed is what I quite crudely call a pair of pants that opens
and shuts. It is essentially constituted by what we might call the slit
in desire. There is no erection, however successful one may suppose
it to be, that can take the place of the essential element in the
structure of the situation here – namely, the slit itself. The subject
designates himself in the slit; and he designates himself, strictly
speaking, as what must be filled by the object.

We will come back to this later, because I want to corroborate
this with the correlative phenomenology of the voyeur. Here I think
I can proceed more quickly. Nevertheless, as going too quickly
always allows one to dissimulate what is at stake, I will broach the
voyeur with the same circumspection.

495   Regarding the scoptophilic drive, people always omit what is
essential, which is the slit. For a voyeur, the slit is an absolutely
indispensable structural element. And the terms of the relationship
between what is glimpsed and what is not glimpsed, even though
they are distributed differently here than for exhibitionists, are nevertheless quite distinct.

Let me go into this in detail. Since the satisfaction here, which is
voyeuristic, is based on an object – in other words, on an other – it is

important that the person who is seen be involved in the scene. This is part of the fantasy.

There is no doubt but that the object seen is very often seen unbeknownst to her. The, let us say, female object – since it seems that it is no accident that the object spied on is female – undoubtedly does not know that she is being seen. But the voyeur's satisfaction, I mean what props up his desire, involves the following element. As innocently, as it were, as she presents herself, something in her lends itself to the function of a spectacle. The object is out in the open; she is potentially participating in the dimension of indiscretion. The voyeur's jouissance reaches its true height when something in the gestures of the woman he is spying on allows him to suspect that, in some way, she is capable of offering herself up to his jouissance.

The secretly observed creature is all the more "eroticizable," I would say, when something in her gestures reveals her to be offering herself up to what I will call the "invisible hosts of the air." It is no accident that I am alluding here to the angels of Christianity that Anatole France had the gall to invoke in this context. Read his *Revolt of the Angels*, and at the very least you will see a precise link between the dialectic of desire and the virtual nature of an eye that can never be grasped but that can always be imagined. In his book, *La Rôtisserie de la reine Pédauque*, the aim of which is very focused, Anatole France knows what he is doing when he refers to the *Comte de Gabalis* regarding the mystical wedding of men with sylphs and undines.

The voyeur's pleasure is thus at its height when he catches the creature in an activity in which she appears in a secret relationship to herself, in gestures that betray the permanence of an unavowed witness.

Isn't it obvious to you that, in both cases, the subject is reduced to the artifice of the slit? This artifice occupies the place of the subject, and shows him to be truly reduced to the miserable function that is his. Insofar as he is in his fantasy, the subject is the slit.

496

The form that corresponds to it in the place of a woman's sexual organ is, according to our field, what is symbolically the most unbearable. What relationship is there between the subjective slit and the female slit? This is a separate question that I will leave for future discussion.

Let us now reconsider the whole. Let us begin with the famous poetic metaphor from *La Jeune Parque*, "*Je me voyais me voir*" [I saw myself seeing myself]. It is clear that no desire realizes this dream of perfect closure or complete self-sufficiency, if not the poetic virgin's superhuman desire.

What justifies the voyeur's and the exhibitionist's entry into the situation? The fact that they put themselves in the place of *Je me voyais* [I was looking at myself]. But the Other does not see her *Je me voyais*; her jouissance is unconscious; she is in some sense decapitated by the third party. The Other does not know that she may potentially be seen by a voyeur. When faced with an exhibitionist, she does not know what is represented by the fact that she is shaken by what she sees – in other words, by the unusual object that is presented to her. This object has an effect on the Other only inasmuch as she is in fact the object of the exhibitionist's desire, but without her knowing it, without her recognizing it at that precise moment.

We are thus faced with twofold ignorance here. The Other does not realize what is supposed to be realized in the mind of someone who exhibits herself or is seen, not knowing that she is a possible manifestation of desire. Inversely, the exhibitionist or the voyeur is not aware of the function of the cut in his desire; he does not realize that the cut abolishes him in a clandestine automatism, that it crushes him in a moment whose spontaneity he absolutely does not recognize. What is actually communicated by the act – which is unknown although present, yet in abeyance – is then at its acme, and that is what is designated by the cut, whereas the subject is aware only of an oblique maneuver like that of a shameful animal that exposes itself to blows.

Regardless of the form in which the slit presents itself – whether as part of a shutter, telescope, or any sort of screen – it is what allows the perverse subject to enter into the Other's desire. This slit is the symbolic slit of a more profound mystery that we must elucidate. Namely, where in the unconscious is it fitting to situate the pervert? What is his relationship to the structure of desire itself? For what he aims at is the Other's desire, reproducing the structure of his own.

The perverse solution to the problem of the subject's situation in fantasy is the following: target the Other's desire and believe one sees an object therein.

It is late enough that I could stop here.

That, too, would be a cut. But it would have the disadvantage of being arbitrary, and of stopping me from showing you the originality of this solution when compared to the neurotic solution. At the very least, you should realize that it is of interest to compare them.

I will show you the function played by the neurotic subject in his fantasy on the basis of the pervert's fundamental fantasy. I fortunately already indicated this function to you earlier – he wants to desire, as I put it. Now why can't he desire? Why is it so necessary that he desire? Everyone knows what is involved here – the phallus, strictly speaking. You have seen that, up until now, I have left to one side the role played in this economy by the phallus, the good old phallus of yesteryear.

Twice – once in our re-examination of the Oedipus complex last year, and once in my article on the psychoses – I showed you that the phallus is linked to the paternal metaphor – namely, insofar as it gives the subject a signified. But it was impossible to bring it back into the dialectic at issue today without first introducing a structural element into the constitution of fantasy, an element whose symbolism I will ask you to accept – in a last effort before we part today.

I have written on the blackboard all the different types of cuts, including those that reflect the subject as a cut [*la coupure du sujet* (this schema is missing)].

This is how we will henceforth notate the barred subject in fantasy. Remember that I asked you to accept the notion of the "not one." You see that I allow myself to be so ridiculous here as to even refer to the notation of the square root of minus one, $\sqrt{-1}$, concerning imaginary numbers.

When I told you about the vanishing of the subject, I left you on the verge of this "not one." I will begin with it next time and even with the *comme pas un* [like no one else], which brings up the subject's uniqueness. If I am asking you to notate it in this way, it is precisely in order that you not see in it the most general form, and therefore the vaguest form, of negation.

498

If it is so difficult to speak of negation, it is because no one knows what it is. Yet at the beginning of this year I pointed out the difference between foreclosure and discordance. For the time being, it is in this closed – but for that reason decisive – symbolic form that I am pointing out another form of negation, one that situates the subject on another scale altogether.

As for little *a*, with which the subject is confronted in fantasy, you realize that I showed you today that it was more complicated than the three forms I had given you as a first sketch, since, in the cases that I presented to you, little *a* is the Other's desire.

June 3, 1959

XXIV

THE DIALECTIC OF DESIRE
IN NEUROSIS

The traumatic Other
The hysteric and his double
The obsessive's hiding place
To be the phallus or to be no one
When jouissance crushes desire

In our last class, I laid out the structure of fantasy insofar as it props up, as I put it, the subject's desire.

Where it is possible to grasp fantasy in a structure that is sufficiently complete, it can in some sense serve as a hub for what we are led to relate to it as regards different, let us say, nosological structures, those we encounter in our practice – in other words, the relationship between the subject's desire and what I have long designated, from a psychoanalytic perspective, as not simply its reference point but its essence: the Other's desire.

As announced, today I will try to situate the position of desire for you in the different clinical structures, and to begin with, in neurotic structure.

1

Last time I discussed perverse fantasies to help you locate in them what corresponds to the function of the subject and what corresponds to the function of the object.

Fantasy is the prop and index of a certain position of the subject in desire. At the outset, it is the other's image that serves to prop up the subject, at least at the point at which he qualifies as desire. Later comes the more complex structure known as fantasy.

For profound reasons, I decided to take up a specific, especially exemplary form of perverse fantasy last time, the one that is found among exhibitionists and voyeurs. I showed you that – as opposed to what is all too often said when people jump the gun – they are not reciprocal positions that complete each other: "the one who shows" and "the one who sees." On the contrary, these two positions are strictly parallel, paradoxically enough.

In both cases the subject turns out to be indicated in the fantasy by what I called the slit or gap, something that is both a hole and a flash in the real, inasmuch as the voyeur spies from behind his shutter and the exhibitionist opens his screen just slightly, leaving it ajar. The subject is indicated here in his place in the activity. He is nothing but the flash of the object people speak of, and which is experienced and perceived by the subject as the opening up of a gap that situates him as open. Open to what? To a desire other than his own, his own desire being profoundly impacted, struck, and shaken by what is perceived during the flash.

In one case, [what is perceived is] the Other's emotion that goes beyond her modesty; in the other case, [what is perceived is] the opening up of the Other, the Other's virtual expectation, inasmuch as this Other does not sense that she is seen and yet is perceived as offering herself up to be seen – this is what characterizes the object's position in the structure. The latter is so fundamental that it was noted from the very moment psychoanalysis first investigated the causes and stigmata that generate the neurotic position. I mean that there is, at the starting point of neurosis, a perceived scene, the so-called primal scene.

If the primal scene is part and parcel of this structure, it is undoubtedly insofar as it reverses it. This reversal is such that the subject sees something open up, suddenly perceives a gap whose traumatic value is related to the Other's desire, which is truly glimpsed and perceived. The Other's desire remains like an enigmatic nucleus until later, when, after the fact, the subject can reintegrate that lived moment in the chain, which will not necessarily be the right chain, but which will in any case be a chain that constitutes a whole unconscious modulation – a chain that thus constitutes the nucleus of neurosis.

Let us now turn our attention to the structure of fantasy.

As I stress, what makes for its value as an index is a suspended or stopped time, an interruption [*temps d'arrêt*] that corresponds to a moment of action at which the subject can only establish himself in a certain way, x – which is precisely what we are trying to pinpoint in the function of desire – on condition that he lose all sense [*sens*] of his position, which is marked by the fact that the fantasy is opaque to him. *We* can designate his place in fantasy, and he can perhaps glimpse it himself; but the meaning [*sens*] of the position, the reason

501

why he is there, and what comes to light regarding his being – that he cannot say.

This is the essential point – aphanisis occurs. The term is no doubt a felicitous one. In any case, it serves us, even if – as opposed to the function given to it by Jones in his interpretation of the castration complex – its form remains enigmatic to us.

Indeed, if the word "aphanisis" – disappearance or "fading,"* as I put it – can serve us regarding fantasy, it is not as the aphanisis of desire; it is insofar as an aphanisis of the subject occurs at the height of desire. Where *it speaks* in the unconscious chain, the subject cannot situate himself in his place, or articulate himself as *I*. He can only indicate himself qua disappearing from his position as a subject.

As I have defined it, this is the extreme, imaginary point where the subject's being resides, as it were, in its greatest density. This is merely an image that I am providing so that you can have a metaphor to latch onto. The subject's being must be articulated and named in the unconscious, but in the end, it cannot be. It is solely indicated at the level of fantasy by what turns out to be a slit, a structure based on a cut [*structure de coupure*].

In each and every domain, it is legitimate to situate an imaginary point if we can spell out its structure by what begins from there. Here the imaginary point will allow us to situate what actually occurs in the different forms of the subject.

These different forms need not be homogeneous – a form that is comprehensible to a subject situated on one side is not necessarily comprehensible to a subject situated on the other side. We know only too well what can lead us astray in understanding a psychosis. When we try to reconstruct and lay out a structure, as is the case here, we must be careful not to understand.

Let me remind you that we find a trace of the notion of the disappearance of the subject in Freud's work when he talks about the dream's navel as the point at which all the dreamer's associations converge only to disappear. At that point, they can only be related to what he calls the *Unerkannt*. This is what is at issue here.

What does the subject see opening up [*s'ouvrir*] across from him at the moment at which he disappears? Nothing but another gap. This may go so far as to engender an infinite reflection of one desire in another desire. But the concrete thing that experience shows us in the voyeur's and the exhibitionist's fantasy – even if it is not very easy to grasp – is that the subject turns out to be dependent on the Other's desire, indeed, at its mercy.

This is precisely what is involved in little Hans's neurosis, which I spoke to you about at length two years ago.

I highlighted the crisis that little Hans encountered at a certain moment of his development. This crisis went much further than his rivalry, which was nevertheless critical, with the new person on the scene, his little sister; and it was much more serious than the first stirrings of sexual maturation that made him capable of having erections, and even – the question remains an open one according to specialists – orgasms. As I stressed, spelled out, and even hammered home, the crisis in question did not arise at the interpsychological level, strictly speaking, or at the level of the integration of a new drive [*tendance*]. There was a crisis because, at that specific moment in time, and owing to the effect of a certain closing down [*fermeture*], the subject found himself confronted with his mother's actual desire, and he had no recourse in the presence of this desire.

In his 1917 article entitled "The Unconscious," Freud calls the fact of having no recourse *Hilflosigkeit*. *Hilflosigkeit* comes before anything else – before anxiety, for example, which already involves a first sketch of an organization inasmuch as it involves expectation, *Erwartung*, even if one does not know what one is expecting, and even if one does not articulate it immediately. Prior to anxiety there is *Hilflosigkeit*, the fact of having "no recourse."

Having "no recourse" in the face of what? This can only be defined as the Other's desire. The relation between the subject's desire and the Other's desire is dramatic, inasmuch as the subject's desire must be situated in relation to the Other's desire, but the latter literally absorbs his and leaves him no recourse. An essential structure – not only neurosis, but every analytically defined structure – is constituted by this drama.

We will begin here with neurosis. Nevertheless, since we started   503
with something rather different, perversion, you can glimpse in what way perversion is related to the same drama. I will nevertheless point out that I only brought in perversion regarding the instantaneous moment of fantasy – fantasy that in perversion is the only thing that reveals the *passage à l'acte* [acting out].

In the case of little Hans, what is related to the structure that I am formulating for you here is the fertile moment of neurosis known as a phobia. It is the simplest form of neurosis. We can put our finger on what characterizes the solution that it brings with it, and I have already discussed this with you at length: it is the coming into play of the phobic object insofar as it is an all-purpose signifier [*signifiant à toutes fins*].

The phobic object is situated between the subject's desire and the Other's desire, and it fulfills a function of protection or defense there. There is no ambiguity whatsoever regarding Freud's formulation here. What is fear of the phobic object designed to protect the subject from? Freud tells us that it protects him from desire's approach [*l'approche de son désir*]. If we look more closely, we see that his desire is at stake insofar as Hans is defenseless in relation to what emerges [*s'ouvre*] for him in the Other – the mother in this case – as the sign of his absolute dependence on her.

She will take him to the ends of the earth; she will take him further still; she will take him with her as often as she herself disappears, slips away. At that moment she no longer appears to him only as someone who can satisfy all of his demands; she appears to him with the supplemental mystery of being herself prey [*ouverte*] to a lack whose meaning appears to Hans to be in a certain relationship to the phallus – a phallus that he does not have.

It is at the level of the mother's want-to-be [*manque-à-être*] that for Hans a drama begins [*s'ouvre*] that he cannot resolve without forging the phobic signifier whose polyvalent function I showed you. This signifier is a kind of skeleton key, a key that opens all doors, allowing him to protect himself against the emergence of an anxiety that is far more dreadful than the fear that is localized by the phobia.

All experienced analysts have perceived this, and in an unequivocal way. But what is worth examining is the following: how – at this moment, which involves a relationship based on desire – can the subject (the subject who in the structure of fantasy is juxtaposed as $ to a) find something that lightens his load [or: improves his situation, *allège sa part*], find something that sustains his presence, find something to latch onto? This is, in short, where a symptom is going to be produced, inasmuch as, in neurosis at its most profound level, it concerns the subject's position most generally.

504

I will proceed as follows, if you will be so kind as to allow me to. First, we are going to unpack this, then we are going to inquire whether the structure of fantasy is as fatal as all that. At the onset of the whirlwind of fantasy, on the verge of the point of loss or disappearance indicated in the structure of fantasy, there is something that holds or stands firm – how is this something possible?

The neurotic accedes to fantasy. He accedes to it at certain specific moments at which his desire is satisfied. But as we all know, this is merely a functional use of fantasy. On the other hand, his relation to his whole world, and to the real others in it, is profoundly marked by what? By a repressed drive, as people have always said.

It is this repressed drive that we are trying to explain a bit better, a bit more precisely, and in a way that is more clinically obvious.

We are going to begin by indicating how it presents itself.

2

Let us consider obsessives, if you will, and hysterics. Let us consider them together inasmuch as they shed light on a certain number of each other's features.

Given that the object in fantasy is connected to the Other's desire, the goal is not to approach it. There are obviously several ways of reaching this goal.

One way, as we have seen, is by creating a phobic object, a pro-hibited object. What must be prohibited? In the final analysis, a jouissance that is dangerous because it exposes the true abyss of desire to the subject.

I already sketched out two other ways to you in the paper I gave at Royaumont. The subject can sustain his desire when faced with the Other's desire in two manners: as an unsatisfied desire – that is the case in hysteria – or as an impossible desire, which is the case in obsession.

Let me remind you of the example of the butcher's wife, in which the structure of unsatisfied desire appears most clearly [SE IV, pp. 146–51; *Écrits*, pp. 522–3]. In her associations to the dream she had, the hysteric's operation is in some sense avowed: the butcher's wife wants to eat caviar, but she does not want her husband to buy it for her, because her desire for it must remain unsatisfied. This is one of the little maneuvers with which the fabric, text, and everyday life of the hysteric is woven. But the structure thus illustrated in fact goes much further.

This little tale reveals the function that the hysteric grants herself: she herself is the obstacle, she is the one who does not want. Stated otherwise, in her fantasy she comes to occupy the tertiary posi-tion between the subject and the object which was occupied by the phobic signifier in our earlier example. Here, she is the one who is the obstacle. She derives jouissance from blocking desire. This is one of the fundamental functions of hysterical subjects in the situa-tions they fabricate: stopping desire from being satisfied so that they themselves can remain what is at stake in desire.

The place the hysteric takes on in such situations is that of what we might call, using an English word, a "puppet,"* something like a dummy but with the more extended meaning of pretense. The hys-teric in effect brings in a shadow, who is her double, in the guise of another woman; the hysteric's desire manages to slip in by means of this other woman, but in a hidden way, for she must not see it. This position is so common that it is truly recognizable in case studies, assuming we have this key at our disposal.

505

Although the hysteric presents herself in this case as the main-spring of the machine on which these sorts of marionettes depend, even in relation to each other, in a redoubled relationship which is that of the subject in relation to the object, ($\lozenge a$), she nevertheless plays her part in the game in the form of she who is at stake, in the final analysis. The obsessive, on the other hand, has a rather differ-ent position. He stays outside the game.

Trust in these formulations when you are dealing with sub-jects who can be clinically qualified as obsessive. The obsessive is someone who is truly never where something that could be called his desire is at stake. He is not where he apparently runs a risk. He makes $ – the disappearance of the subject at the point of desire's approach – into his weapon and his hiding place. He has learned how to use $ in order to be elsewhere.

He can only do so by putting off or deferring until later his com-mitment to a true relationship involving desire. Whereas the relation to desire in hysteria has an instantaneous structure, the obsessive always puts off until tomorrow committing his true desire. This does not mean that he commits to nothing while awaiting that day, far from it – [in the meantime,] he proves himself. Moreover, he may go so far as to consider what he does as a means of acquiring merit. What does he think he merits? The Other's deference to his desires [Des mérites à quoi ? – à la révérence de l'Autre à l'endroit de ses désirs].

You will clearly observe this mechanism, which shows up every-where, even when the obsessive does not recognize it. But it is important that you are able to recognize and designate it. It would be inopportune, indeed, if you were led to crush this mechanism in the analysis under the weight of all the intersubjective relations it brings in its wake, and which can only be conceptualized as organ-ized with respect to the fundamental relation or relations that I am trying to spell out for you.

What shows its face in this neurotic position is a call for help by the subject, for help sustaining his desire, for help sustaining it in the presence of the Other's desire, for help constituting himself as desiring.

As I said last time, the only thing he does not know is that his approach is profoundly marked by the danger constituted for him by desire's drift. In constituting himself as desiring and in the very constitution of his desire, he defends against something. His very desire is a defense and can be nothing else. This is what the subject does not perceive.

Yet in order to sustain his desire he must always call on something that presents itself in a tertiary position for help in dealing with the Other's desire. This is where he situates himself in order for the

506

wannabe [*aspirante*], vanishing relation of $ when faced with *a* to be tenable.

The role of this thing is to allow the subject to symbolize his situation in relation to the real Other – in other words, to keep a situation in which he can be recognized and satisfied as a subject going. When in analysis he is able to get some perspective on his situation, he is shocked to perceive that the subject who is sustained in this situation is prey to all sorts of contorted and paradoxical attitudes. This allows him to realize that he is a neurotic prey to symptoms.

And it is here that the element that psychoanalytic experience has taught us to consider a key point of signifying functions – the phallus – comes in.

507

3

If the phallus plays a key role here, it is obviously insofar as it is a signifier.

This signifier is linked to something that Freud – who absolutely did not hide its place in the economy of the unconscious – called the law.

It is fruitless to try to reduce the phallus to the status of something that is balanced by and juxtaposed with some other functional correspondent in the opposite sex. Although this conception has generative [or: developmental, *génétique*] value, as it were, from the vantage point of the subject's interrelations, it neglects what is essential in valuing the phallus – namely, that it is not purely and simply an organ.

At the level at which it is an organ, it is the instrument of a jouissance, and it is not integrated into the mechanism of desire, for the latter is situated at another level. To understand what the mechanism of desire is, we must define it as seen from the other side, in other words once cultural relations have been instituted – whether it be on the basis of the myth of the killing [of the primal father] or not.

Desire is distinguished from all demands by the fact that it is a demand that is subject to the law. This formulation is almost painfully obvious, but we must nevertheless realize that this is what is involved when Freud distinguishes demands that correspond to the so-called needs related to the survival of the species or of the individual from demands that are situated at another level.

Why tell us that the demands that are situated at this other level are different from the first demands in that they can be deferred? After all, to say that sexual desire in men can be deferred in its effects – that is, in its execution [*passage à l'acte*] – is not unambiguous. Why can it be deferred more easily in men than in animals,

508

where such deferral is not terribly well tolerated? It is undoubtedly owing to genetic flexibility, but it owes [still more] essentially to the fact that the primal order of exchanges is built on sexual desire, the primal order that founds the law by which the realm of numbers comes alive in human interpsychology – namely, the so-called law of marriage and kinship.

Nothing is articulated in psychoanalysis if not at this level. And it is at this level that we see the fundamental signification of the phallus appear. Fundamentally speaking, the phallus is the subject qua object of sexual desire, this object being subjected to what I will call the law of fertility.

It is in the guise of a fertility symbol that the phallus plays a role in initiation ceremonies, when it is unveiled at the end of those ceremonies to the people who participate in them. As for the father, who, for a subject, is the "author of his days," as they say in French [figuratively, "my revered father"], he is merely the signifier of what I am calling the law of fertility here, inasmuch as this signifier regulates desire by tying it to a law.

This is where the whole dialectic of desire comes in.

In the law of exchanges – defined by the fundamental relations that regulate desire's interreactions in culture, real bonds, relations with real others, and the real creation of a line of descent – the subject presents himself qua phallus. But desire comes in along the trajectory of the functionalization of the subject qua phallus. In effect, the subject's being – at the point of its loss – is expressed in desire because, as we have seen, the subject can no longer get his bearings [se saisir] in desire starting at a certain moment: he is no longer, he fails to be [il manque à être]. It is this lack [manque] that encounters the phallic function. And the balance [or: tipping] point – the one we dwelt on at the end of the dream recounted by Ella Sharpe's patient – is produced by this encounter.

I also connected this up with my humungous digression on *Hamlet*, inasmuch as, in this patient's dream, he presented us, in the purest form, the alternative "to be or not . . ."* that I highlighted so extensively.

We are considering here the moment at which the subject gets close to his desire, at which he just barely puts his finger on it, at which he must choose to be completely taken up in the devouring desire of a woman or to be no one. It is immediately thereafter that he is summoned to be or not to be. It must be noted that the second "to be"* in this formulation does not have the same meaning as the first one. In the second one, what comes to light is the "not to be" of desire's primordial structure. In the first one, the point for Hamlet is to be what he can be as a subject – in other words, "to be the

509

phallus." But to be the phallus that is marked as the Other's exposes him to the threat "not to have it."

If you will allow me to use a so-called logical sign, the V which is used to designate the "either/or" of disjunction, I would say that the subject sees here that there is a choice to be made. Either "not to be it," not to be the phallus, and disappear, fail to be. Or, if he is it, in other words, if he is the phallus for the Other in the intersubjective dialectic, "not to have it." This is the game that is at work. And it is in this game that the neurotic senses that getting close to or integrating his [or: her, *son*] desire threatens him with loss.

The "not one," by which the barred subject in desire's fundamental structure designates himself, is transformed into a "one too many" or "something that is too much." Or it is transformed into "something missing" for men who are threatened by castration, and for women for whom the phallus is experienced as an absence.

This is why not everything is resolved at the end of the psychoanalytic demystification of the neurotic's position. At least this is what Freud tells us based on his own experience: there is something that takes the form of a remainder, and which in all cases is such that the subject remains in an inadequate position, that of peril as regards the phallus in men, and that of absence of the phallus in women.

This is perhaps owing to the approach that was initially adopted to solve the neurotic's problem. This approach leads us to neglect the transverse dimension – namely, that by which the subject, when it comes to desire, is dealing with the manifestation of his being as such, with himself as the possible author of the cut.

In other words, analysts tend to try to shrink the neurotic's desiring position, whereas they should strive to free up desire's true position and release it from being bogged down in the specific dialectic which is that of the neurotic.

4

How can I go back over these points in order to better convey to you how they are linked? For I have assuredly led you along the purest path already.

It is clear that this brings with it not only all the subject's anecdotal history, but also other elements of his past, which are structural and which I brought out years ago. I am talking about the narcissistic drama, the subject's relation to his own image, and his narcissistic relation to the other's image.

As Freud often stressed in his own terms, it is here, of course, that, in the final analysis, the fear of losing the phallus, or the feeling of not having [or: missing or lacking] a phallus, comes in for the subject.

In other words, the ego is involved. It can intervene at the level of the complex dialectic in which the subject is afraid of losing what constitutes his privilege in relation to the other. But let us note that, if it intervenes, it is certainly not because of something that we could call its weakness, for in every case in which we observe a weakness of the ego, we witness, on the contrary, a diffusing or even a blockage of the situation.

I need but refer here to a case that you are all familiar with. It is a notorious case of Melanie Klein's, the case of Dick ["The Importance of Symbol-Formation in the Development of the Ego," *IJP* 11 (1930): 24–39]. Klein describes a child who, assuming he had truly been brought into the relationship between desire and the signifier, found himself completely dependent on the imaginary level in relation to the other, on the possible relation with the other at the gestural, communicative, and life-sustaining level.

As we do not know everything about this case, we can merely say that it is a remarkable one, inasmuch as this child, who does not speak, is already so open to and touched by Klein's spoken interventions that for us, in our register, his behavior is truly striking. In effect, right from his first moments with Klein it is clear that the only structures in the world that are accessible and available to him are those that bear within themselves the characteristics of the signifying chain.

He plays, for example, with a train, which is a little chain – that is, a series constituted by elements that are attached to each other. We have a door that opens or closes, which is tantamount to the simplest form of the alternative "yes or no" that conditions the signifier as such. "A gate must be open or closed," as I reminded you here when I tried to show you how we can put cybernetic schemas to use with our symbols.

The child's behavior is limited to that; and yet, simply by grazing it with words that are nevertheless sentences, something essentially verbal, what do Klein's interventions immediately do? The child's first reaction is, in my view, almost unbelievable in its exemplary character: he runs into the dark "space between the outer and inner doors of the [consulting] room" [p. 31]. We are surprised that Klein – who, in certain ways, so clearly saw the structural elements of introjection and expulsion, namely, the limit of the outer world of what one might call the inner shadows with regard to a subject – did not see the import of this intermediary zone, which is nothing less than the one where, to our way of thinking, desire is situated.

This zone is neither outside nor inside, and however small it may be in this subject, it is articulated and constructed. We find in certain primitive village structures these sorts of empty spaces between the village and pure, unadulterated nature. Let us say that it is in this sort of "no man's land"* that the little subject's desire broke down.

It is here that the ego might possibly intervene. Naturally, as I have repeated dozens of times, it is to the degree to which this ego is not weak, but strong, that the subject's resistances are organized, they being the very forms of his neurotic construction's coherence. This is how the subject organizes himself in order to subsist as desire, in order not to be the place of this desire, in order to be sheltered from the Other's desire as such. It is the distance that is maintained between his most profound manifestation as desire and the Other's desire; it is the means [alibi] by which he constitutes himself as phobic, hysteric, or obsessive respectively.

I must return here to the elaborate example Freud provides us of a fantasy, "A child is being beaten." It is worth returning to it after having taken this detour. In it, we can perceive the stages at which we find anew the structural relationship that I am trying to formulate today.

What do we have here? An obsessive fantasy. Girls and boys use this fantasy to arrive at what? Masturbatory jouissance. The relationship to desire is clear. What is the function of this jouissance? Its function here is that of any and every satisfaction of need in relation to that which lies beyond it, which is determined by human language. Which is to say that masturbatory jouissance is not the solution to desire here; it represents, instead, the crushing of desire – just as a child at the breast crushes his demand for love from his mother with the satisfaction of nursing.

This is virtually countersigned by the testimony of history.

I alluded at the time [I discussed Freud's paper, "A Child is Being Beaten"] to the hedonist perspective and its inability to truly characterize human desire. Let us not forget one of its paradoxical points, which has an exemplary character for us – even though it was obviously left in the shadows by those who have gone down in history as sages. Their discipline had as its aim – qualified as philosophical, and for reasons that were after all, valid, since they were methodological – the choice of a stance with respect to desire, consisting at the outset of excluding it and rendering it null and void.

Every perspective that is, strictly speaking, hedonistic shares in this exclusionary stance, as is demonstrated by the paradoxical example that I will remind you of here, the stance of the cynics. Tradition has, as we know from Chrysippus, if I recall correctly, passed this down to us. Diogenes the Cynic claimed that the solution to the problem of sexual desire was, as it were, at hand's reach

512

for each of us, and, through an act that was not one of exhibitionism but of demonstration, he proved it brilliantly by masturbating
in public.

The obsessive's fantasy bears a relation to jouissance, and this
relation can even become one of its conditions. But it also has a
structure whose value as an index, as I call it, Freud demonstrated
to us, inasmuch as this fantasy indicates nothing other than a feature
of the subject's history, a feature that is inscribed in his diachrony.
Namely, that the subject, in a forgotten past, saw, Freud's text tells
us, a rival – whether of the same sex or of the opposite, it does not
matter – being subjected to punishment by the beloved being, the
father in this case, and was overjoyed by this early situation.

513   In what way does the fantasized instant perpetuate, as it were, this
favorite instant of happiness? It is here that the intermediary stage
that Freud designates takes on its demonstrative value. This stage,
he tells us, [is never remembered; it] can only be reconstructed.

Freud sometimes tells us that certain unconscious stages are
altogether inaccessible. Whether he is right or wrong in this precise
case is not germane. Thus he is not wrong, but that is not what is of
importance here; what is important is that he designates this intermediate stage as something that can only be reconstructed.

At the first stage of the fantasy's construction, we find the
memory of a moment of triumph on the subject's part, a memory
that is merely repressed, at worst, and can thus be brought to light:
a memory of the other, the rival brother, falling prey to the anger
of the beloved object [the father here] and to the punishment that
the beloved object is meting out to him. At the third stage, the
fantasized instant plays the role of an index inasmuch as it immor-
talizes, as it were, this stage by making it into a point that something
entirely different is attached to – namely, the subject's desire. But the
process involves an intermediary stage which is, I will say, strictly
speaking metaphorical.

What is at work in the second stage, which is, as Freud tells us,
essential to understanding the functioning of this fantasy? The
subject puts himself in his rival's shoes: it is the subject himself who
is punished. What is the subject seeking in this metaphor or transference? We find ourselves faced here with an utter and complete
enigma.

How strange it is to proceed, after the moment of his triumph, to
a scene in which he himself suffers the other's humiliating defeat!
Freud does not hide the fact that we find ourselves faced here with
the ultimate enigma of what in psychoanalysis we call masochism.
A conjunction presents itself here in a pure form, a conjunction
by which something in the subject perpetuates the happiness of

the initial situation in a hidden, latent, unconscious situation of unhappiness.

In this hypothetical second stage, what is involved is, in short, the oscillation, ambivalence, or, more precisely, ambiguity of the act being engaged in by the authority, the father here, inasmuch as the punishment is also a form of recognition. The subject slides here from a short-lived incident in his life history to a structure in which he appears as an actual being. The decisive step of his jouissance lies – insofar as it leads to the fantasized instant, "a child is being beaten" [*On bat un enfant*, literally "someone is beating a child"] where he himself is no longer anything but *On* ["someone"] – in the fact of alienating himself, in other words, in taking the other's place as a victim.

514

On the one hand, the subject is *On bat* ["someone is beating"], the instrument of alienation insofar as it devalues [the one who is beaten]. This is why I told you that, up to a certain point, he purely and simply becomes the phallic instrument, insofar as it is the instrument here of his cancellation.

On the other hand, he is confronted with what? With "a child," a faceless, sexless child, a child who is no longer the child originally involved in the first stage, nor even the child the subject himself was at the second stage. A close examination of the succession of fantasies laid out by Freud shows that the subject is confronted here with what one might call an extract of the object.

We nevertheless see traces, in the recounting of the fantasy, of what constitutes the subject's favorite instant of jouissance. I will juxtapose the neurotic's jouissance next time with something very unusual, whose common factor does not seem to have been found up until now. It is not perversion in general – which plays a pivotal role in the structure we are exploring – that is at work, but rather homosexuality.

To confine our attention today to neurosis, I will tell you what its most common, fundamental structure is, in the final analysis.

If the neurotic wants to desire, what does he desire? He desires what allows him to sustain his desire in its very precariousness, without knowing that all of his phantasmagoria is designed for this purpose and that his symptoms, which in themselves provide so little satisfaction, are the very locus where he finds jouissance.

The subject thus does not present himself as a "pure being" [*être pur*] – which is what I began from in order to indicate to you what is meant by the subject's relation to the real – but a "being for" [*être pour*].

The ambiguity of the neurotic's position lies precisely in this metonymy, which is such that it is in this *être pour* that all of his *pour être* [in order to be] lies.

June 10, 1959

XXV

THE EITHER/OR
CONCERNING THE OBJECT

Perverse fantasy and perversion
Fantasy and the construction of reality
The paradox of the bad internal object
The radical nature of female jealousy
The function of substitutes in neurosis

There is something instructive, I will not say "even in," but "above all in" mistakes [*erreurs*] – or instances of going astray [*errances*], if you will.

This is why you have noticed that I rather constantly refer to the hesitations and impasses that manifest themselves in psychoanalytic theory, and use them as being in and of themselves revealing as concerns the structure of the reality we deal with.

In this regard, there is something interesting, noteworthy, and significant to us in a paper that is not very old, since it came out in 1956 in the July–October issue of the *International Journal of Psychoanalysis*. It was written by several of our Parisian colleagues, whose names I will not mention, since I am not targeting their position insofar as it may be personal.

They endeavored to closely define the meaning of perversion. Curiously enough, the article's conclusions are as reserved as they could possibly be. The only formally articulated conclusion included is, however, rather striking: "Thus there is no specific unconscious content in the sexual perversions, since we find the same content in cases of neurosis and psychosis."

The entire article illustrates this, but in a way that is not altogether convincing. Even without taking a bird's eye view, we realize that the article is based on a constantly maintained confusion between perverse fantasy and perversion. The authors note that there are conscious and unconscious fantasies in the neuroses and the perversions that seem to overlap, and to our astonishment they facilely conclude therefrom that there is no fundamental difference, from the vantage point of the unconscious, between neurosis and perversion.

We find in this article reflections that are presented without taking any precautions or manifesting any regard for the psychoanalytic tradition, and that proceed toward a sort of overturning of the values and principles of that tradition. The authors stop only once they have concluded that perversion is, in short, an abnormal relation that is eroticized. It thus does not involve the relationship to an object, but rather the eroticization of a relation for economic reasons. To anyone who undertakes an even slightly sensible examination of the matter, this eroticized relation to the object can be only of "soporific value."

I myself am now led, after having begun last time to broach the relationship between fantasy and neurosis in order to indicate their most general terms, to discuss the relationship between fantasy and perversion.

1

First a word about what has happened in the course of the history of psychoanalysis, which can be laid out more rigorously in light of our progress here.

Very shortly after having spelled out the functions of the unconscious, especially in hysteria, the neuroses, and dreams, Freud was led to posit the presence in the unconscious of what he called *polymorph perverse Anlage*: a "polymorphously perverse disposition" [GW V, p. 91; SE VII, p. 191].

For a time, one that has long since passed, naturally, things remained at that point. Nevertheless, what people failed to realize, it seems, is that in formulating the notion of a polymorphously perverse disposition in the unconscious, Freud discovered nothing less than the very structure of unconscious fantasies. He observed that their structure resembles the relational mode that blossoms, comes fully to the light of day, and is demonstrated in the perversions.

In effect, the form taken by unconscious fantasies overlaps what occupies the imaginative field of the pervert's desire.

What perverts stage in their fantasies presents itself in a way that is obvious in clinical work. It presents itself as a movie* sequence, by which I mean a sequence that is isolated [*coupée*] from the development of the drama – is that what is called a "rush"*? I'm not sure of the term – like trailers that are designed to whet our appetite to come back next week to see the film from which the images we are

517

watching were extracted. What is seductive about them is that they are removed [*désinsérées*] from the chain and disconnected from the plot.

Something like that is involved in perverts' fantasies. Naturally, psychoanalysis has taught us to recontextualize them, link them back up with the fuller plot, and reattach them to the subjects' histories. To varying degrees, and even at the cost of several modifications, some touching up, and reversals, they reassume their place and meaning. Nevertheless, the extraction [*désinsertion*] by which they present themselves confirms what I have formulated regarding the position of desire – namely, that desire is situated in what is beyond what is nameable, in what is beyond the subject.

I will add in passing, and as a reminder, that this is what retrospectively explains the characteristic quality that fantasies, whether those of a pervert or not, take on when they are avowed. Namely, the state of being ill at ease that we should give a name to when it is at its height, and which often stops patients from revealing their fantasies for a long time. This ridiculous facet can only be explained by the relations that we have already been able to perceive between the position of desire and the realm of comedy.

A question thus immediately arose [in the analytic literature] as to the real nature of perverse fantasy. Is it absolutely crucial, natural, and definitive, or should it be viewed instead as something as complex, elaborate, and in short, significant as a neurotic symptom?

This question gave rise to a whole way of thinking that became integrated into the problem of perversion, and that plays an essential role in the elaboration of what is known as object relations theory.

It was at this point in time that people gave object relations a developmental definition. People did not simply turn the steps regulating the subject's development into specific stages [*momentalités*] of his Eros – that is, erogenous phases – but into modes of his relation to the world. I need not remind you here of the initiators – Abraham, Ferenczi, and others – of the so-called tables of correlated stages, which made the so-called dispositional reservoirs [or: reservoirs of the tendencies, needs, or drives] correspond to specific libidinal forms of the ego.* A particular ego* structure, specifying a certain type of relation to reality, was supposed to correspond to every form of libido.

You are aware of what this theory has brought with it by way of clarity and even enrichment, and also what it has posed by way of problems. Writers have tried to show us the aforementioned correspondences in concrete cases, but it suffices to read their works to realize that these correspondences are always established in a somewhat theoretical way, and that their own texts suggest that

518

an accurate assessment of things is lacking. Right from the very first discussions, an opposition between "partial object" and "total object" is made, for example, but in a way that is unsustainable in my view.

In more recent works, we find, for example, the notorious notion, which I have often mentioned, of "distance from the object," which so thoroughly dominates articles dealing with rules of technique. A certain French author believes that the notion of distance is decisive in obsessive neurosis, whereas it is in certain perversions that it plays a decisive role – for example, the distance of an object [from oneself] is obviously far more manifest in the phenomenology of fetishism. Many other forms [of perversion] can be articulated in much the same way.

The first truth we will have to bring out here is that the notion of distance is so essential that it is perhaps, after all, truly unelimina-ble from desire itself, by which I mean that it is necessary in order to maintain, sustain, and even preserve the dimension of desire. It would be hard, indeed, to conceptualize how desire could sustain itself were the myth of a relationship to the object without any dis-tance from it to be realized.

We have here – in a truly mythical form, I am saying – the idea of a sort of harmony [*accord*] between subject and object. This harmony has two facets, two faces, or two mirages: animal on the one side and mystical on the other. Needless to say, this idea in no way coincides with the facts of experience or with psychoanalytic theory, which views the object as a remainder [or: leftover, *reste*].

519

Thus the supposed "bad distance at which the obsessive stays from the object" is also thought to be corrected and rectified, over-come in the *hic et nunc* [here and now] of the analytic relationship. And this is supposed to happen owing to an ideal and even ideal-izing identification with the analyst, who is considered in this case not as an object but as the prototype of a satisfying object-relation. What exactly can such an ideal correspond to when one tries to realize it in analysis? I have already broached this question, but we will have to return to it later to formulate it differently.

The problems raised by object relations have been broached far more assiduously and seriously in other contexts by other groups. As you know, I place Edward Glover's work at the top of the list; I have already mentioned his article entitled "The Relation of Perversion-Formation to the Development of Reality-Sense" which came out in the *International Journal of Psychoanalysis* in 1933.

In his concern to construct a developmental theory of the rela-tions between the subject and the world – that is, the reality around him – Glover demands that development be examined as closely as possible: through reconstruction in the analyses of adults, and through the direct observation of behavior in children. He proposes to situate the perversions on a timeline that includes, as it were, the times in life at which the different psychical anomalies we deal with in analysis arise. He lays out a whole series of them, and the order in which they appear on his timeline is, as usual, open to criticism. Without going into it in detail, I will point out that he highlights the extremely early nature of psychotic disturbances – paranoid disturbances in particular – and situates after them the different forms of neurosis in order from the earliest to the latest.

The earliest is obsessive neurosis, which is thus located right at the border with paranoid forms of psychosis. Glover felt that he had rather precisely situated the relations between paranoia and the neuroses in an article on "drug addictions"* written the year before this one. In it he tried to situate the perversions in terms of the stage at which they arise, the time in life at which they begin, and the mode of the subject's relationship to the real to which they correspond.

In his view, the standard paranoid stage, which is considered to arise very early on in life, is characterized by a highly specific mode of object-relation, linked to primitive mechanisms of projection and introjection. This is where he situates drug addictions.* He clearly indicates that, on this point, he endorses Klein's theory, whereas, as you know, he went on to very publicly critique her.

This is the context in which the instructive passage I read you a few classes ago appears, where, in a brilliant, metaphorical way, Glover does not hesitate to compare the child's earliest world to "a combination of a butcher's shop, a public lavatory under shell-fire, and a post-mortem room" [*IJP* 14, no. 4 (1933): 492]. The stage that follows this inaugural spectacle of life brings with it what is assuredly a far more benign organization, that of a pharmacy with its store of objects, some beneficial, some poisonous. This passage shows us in what direction Glover and Klein – for there is no difference between them here – seek to define fantasy as functioning in such a way as to organize the construction of reality by the subject.

In her article "The Importance of Symbol-Formation in the Development of the Ego" [*IJP* 11 (1930): 24–39], Klein clearly articulates the way in which objects are successively mastered by the child. At the outset, owing to frustrations the child undergoes, objects are sources of anxiety to him, which is why his fundamental relations with those around him are colored by aggression and sadism. The subject's interest next shifts to more benign objects, objects that are further removed from his needs; these objects become, in turn, imbued with the same anxiety. The progressive extension of the child's world is understood to proceed in this manner.

Note that we have here a mechanism that we might call "contra-phobic" – phobic objects are replaced by contraphobic objects, even if the latter become phobic in turn. It is thus in a contraphobic dialectic that the progressive extension of the world of objects – in other words, the conquest of reality – supposedly comes about.

To determine whether this conception corresponds to clinical work or not is not my direct interest here. In clinical work, many things run counter to it. I believe that it attests to a unilateral viewpoint, inasmuch as such a mechanism, even if it plays a role in the conquest of reality, does not strictly speaking constitute reality.

521

But my goal here is not to critique Klein's theory. I am after something else altogether – namely, to shed light on the nature of a function, that of desire. We immediately see the consequences of her theory, for Glover arrives at a paradox, which should certainly be more instructive to him than it is to us, for there is nothing in it for us to be surprised by.

What he concretely tries to do is to situate the various perversions with respect to a dialectic or mechanism that he hopes to integrate into the notion of steady ego* development, ego development that supposedly parallels changes in the libido. The upshot is that the subject's entire fate and structuring turn out to be theorized as a purely individual experience of the conquest of reality. That is the whole story.

This is what makes for the difference, for example, between the theory I provide you with of the phobias, and that proposed by certain recent French authors.

The latter seek to reconstruct the development of a phobia on the basis of structural forms of childhood experience – the way, for example, in which the child negotiates his relations with those around him, or deals with the passage from light to darkness. Development is understood here as something that is purely experimental, the possibility of phobia being deduced from and generated by a concrete experience of fear.

What I teach you here, on the other hand, is that there can be no accurate theory of phobia that does not include the true function of the signifier. This function presupposes the existence of a dimension which is not that of the relation of the subject to those around him, or to any reality, if it is not the reality and dimension of language. The fact that the subject must situate himself in discourse and manifest himself there as a being is where it all starts.

It is striking to see how greatly someone as perspicacious as Glover can misjudge the phobias. In his attempt to explain the development and stabilization of a phobia, he declares the following: "It is more advantageous to suffer from a tiger-phobia in London than in an

522   Indian jungle." One could retort that this is not the register in which the problem arises. One could even reverse his claim and say that a tiger-phobia would be quite advantageous in helping an Indian child adapt to his real situation, whereas it is quite cumbersome to suffer from a tiger-phobia if one lives in London, whether one is a child or further along in one's development. For in London, the behavior of a subject who is prey to such a phobia would surely be quite constricted and would bear no relation whatsoever to reality.

Glover then finds himself faced with the following problem: how can one situate perversion in a developmental perspective when it includes the widest variety of distortions of reality? He can only do so by isolating different types of perversion and inserting them into every supposed or presupposed stage of development. He is thus obliged to accept the existence of very archaic perversions, ones that are more or less contemporary with the paranoid or even the depressive phase, alongside other perversions that are situated at very advanced stages of development – not simply phallic, but Oedipal and even genital, strictly speaking.

Breaking perversion down into different types does not seem to Glover to constitute an objection to his conceptualization, and here is why. The perspective from which he begins forces him, when all is said and done, to define perversion as one of the various forms of reality testing.* When reality testing fails in some way or location, perversion comes to cover over the hole* through a specific mode of apprehending reality – which is, in this case, a psychical reality, a projected and indeed introjected reality.

Perversion thus serves the function of safeguarding reality for the subject, for otherwise the equilibrium of the whole of reality would be threatened by some overload [*décharge*] or moment of instability. Perversion serves to repair [*reprise*] – in the sense in which one speaks in French of a fabric that is darned [*reprisé*] – reality and, moreover, serves as reality's keystone. In short, perversion is unambiguously conceptualized by Glover as a form of salvation when compared with the supposed threat of psychosis.

That is one way of looking at it. Perhaps certain case studies do,
523   in fact, include elements that seem to corroborate this, but many others would have us look elsewhere.

Nevertheless, it seems quite paradoxical to grant perversion an economic role that is contradicted by many elements – not to mention the fact that it is certainly not the precarious nature of the pervert's edifice that strikes us, at least at first glance, either clinically or in psychoanalytic experience.

Before moving on, I will point out here in what regard Klein picks up on and takes a first stab at the question I am raising here.

2

Klein postulates two stages, the paranoid phase and the depressive phase that follows it.

In the second phase, the subject relates to his major, prevalent object, his mother, as a whole [person]. Prior to that, he deals only with separate elements that a split divides into good and bad objects, giving rise thereby to the operations of projection and introjection. All of this characterizes the paranoid barrier.

What is going on in this initial process, situated at the outset of the subject's life, if we reformulate it from our own vantage point?

What Klein shows us is, in short, that reality, as based on the child's first apprehensions of the object, comes from the fact that the object – whether it is good or bad, beneficial or frustrating – is first and foremost meaningful [*significatif*]. The strict opposition between good and bad, without any nuances or intermediary states [*transitions*] – without taking into account in the slightest degree the fact that it is the same object, the mother, who can be good or bad at different times – makes it clear that what is involved here are not a child's actual experiences, with everything such experiences usually bring with them that is transitional, but rather a shift in the function of the object itself to that of a signifying opposition.

This is what is at the crux of the whole of Klein's theory.

People rarely notice, it seems to me, that, as well-founded as it may be, it is diametrically opposed to what I have brought out in our practice – namely, that the lively communication that takes place in the course of mothering plays an essential role in the child's development. It belongs to a different register, one that is contemporary with hers, but cannot be confused with hers.

What Klein proposes is a sort of primitive algebra that we can say connects up perfectly with what I am trying to bring out here under the following heading: "function of the signifier." What Klein rightly or wrongly describes to us, and we need but register this, are the earliest forms of the functioning of the signifier, whether the signifier is in fact present at that early moment in time or simply a *Rückphantasie*, a fantasy that is constructed retrospectively.

What value does the frontier between her two phases thus take on? I am referring to the stage between the paranoid phase – with its division between good objects that are "internalized"* by the child and bad ones that are rejected – and the depressive phase where the notion of the subject as a whole comes into view. Let us note that it is, in fact, only from the moment at which the subject considers himself to be a whole [entity] that there can be an inside and

524

an outside. It is only then that it is conceivable that the process of "internalization"* and "externalization,"* of introjection and projection – which is decisive in Klein's eyes in structuring the primitive animal – can occur.

The conceptual landmarks we use here allow us to grasp what is at issue in the move from one phase to the next. What Klein calls the primitive division of objects into good and bad is transferred, she says, into another register, which is that of the subject's inside and outside. Now we can relate this register – without, I believe, going too far out on a limb – to what I call the mirror stage. It is the other's image that gives the subject the notion [forme] of the other's unity, on the basis of which the division between inside and outside can be established, and with regard to which good and bad objects are then redeployed.

The good objects must come inside, and the bad ones must remain outside. What Klein manages to define here in the clearest possible way, because it is forced on us by experience, can be formulated in our own terms: the discourse that really organizes the world of objects in accordance with the subject's being goes, I would say, beyond the discourse in which the subject recognizes himself in the ordeal constituted by the mirror stage, [where] it is in the relationship of narcissistic identification of one image with another that he recognizes himself as mastery and as a unique ego – as mastery of an ego.

525   In order to understand what is at stake in what Klein describes, we must accept the non-overlapping nature of two experiences (note that I myself am not saying that the whole of development is necessarily organized in this way):

1 the experience that defines the subject as an object of the first identification with the mother, and in particular with her insignias; this experience continues to have an assimilating value to the subject, going beyond what he will be able to place inside himself;
2 the register of experience that defines this inside and in which the subject is $i(a)$ – in other words, typically and ideally, the image of his young semblable, with whom we most clearly see him have his first experiences of mastery and bearing.

Between the two there is a field, x, where $i(a)$ is both part of the subject and not part of the subject. What is it? It is what Klein calls the bad internal object.

People do not seem surprised by the paradox that it constitutes with respect to the premises we began from, whereas it presents itself immediately in Klein's dialectic, and in the most manifest way possible, as a problematic object.

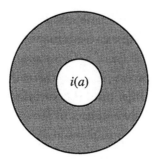

Figure 25.1: The bad internal object

Indeed, if we look at it from the outside, as it were, where the subject is not a subject but where we must take him to be a real being, we can wonder whether the subject is not, in fact, the bad object with which he supposedly identifies. Conversely, if we look at it from the inside – from the point of view of *crasia* or mastery, from the point of view of the subject's first attempt to stand up, assert himself, and contain himself – a question arises. Does the subject have the bad object – which will play an absolutely decisive role thereafter – or doesn't he?

526

According to Klein, as we have seen, the division of objects into good and bad determines the subject's structuring process. The child internalizes good objects, making them part of himself right from the outset, whereas he rejects the bad objects as being not him. The paradox of the bad internalized object thus comes to the fore: the subject internalizes it, making it his own, and at the same time he in a sense disavows [*dénie*] it for being virtually bad.

The bad object never stops presenting itself, with regard to the subject's being, in the form of a permanent, anxiety-producing enigma. What will put an end to it is clearly the later function of prohibition. Prohibition puts an end to it by introducing an essential delineation into the bad object: if the subject is the bad object, he does not have it; insofar as he *is* [*est*] identified with it, he is forbidden to *have* [*ait*] it – we should take advantage of the similarity in pronunciation in French between the subjunctive of the verb *avoir,* to have, and the present tense of the verb *être,* to be. Otherwise stated, insofar as he is it, he does not have it, and insofar as he has it, he is not it.

Stated in still other terms, it is at the level of the bad object that the subject experiences the slavery of his mastery, if I may put it thus. The true master – everyone knows that he has no face, that he is somewhere in language, although he may even be nowhere in it – allows the subject limited use of the bad object itself, insofar as it is an object that is not situated with respect to demand, an object that cannot be demanded. It is on this basis that what we encounter in our practice takes on its import.

We can see this in a striking way in the precise cases that Klein presents.

The incredibly inhibited child [Dick] whom she presents in "The Importance of Symbol-Formation in the Development of the Ego" has manifestly arrived at an impasse, which is constituted by the field of what truly cannot be demanded. As soon as she begins to speak to him, what she immediately achieves crystallizes in a panicked question: "Nurse coming?"* Immediately thereafter, Klein indicates, as an astonishing, decisive fact, that the child allows himself to enter into contact with objects, from which he initially appeared to be oddly separate.

He does so, as you recall, by making a little cut or tear with the help of a pair of scissors. The child can hardly be called inept, for he is able to handle all sorts of things, like door-handles [p. 29], but he has never been able to hold scissors before. Here, however, he manages to hold them, use them, and detach a tiny lump of coal from something that is not devoid of signification, since it is part of the train set [*chaîne du train*] with which people have managed to get him to play.

What is involved here is a "tender."* I won't go here into all the curious plays on words that could be made around this English word. It is not the *Carte du Tendre* we are used to, but the Carte du Tender.

In truth, the child isolates himself, defines himself, and situates himself in this little piece that is detached from the signifying chain – in this remainder, this minuscule lump, this sketch of an object, appearing here only in the form of a little bit, a very little bit. A similar little bit suddenly gives rise to both panic and sympathy on his part when he sees pencil shavings on Klein's lap [p. 33].

At that point, showing some emotion for the first time in the presence of this other person, he cries out, "Poor Mrs. Klein!"

3

Thus desire is not demand. This first intuition, which we experience at every moment and which brings us back to the earliest conditions, must not stop us from looking further.

Someone comes to see us for an analysis. Why? What is he asking for? In theory, satisfaction and well-being – except that satisfaction does not always bring him well-being, far from it. How do analysts usually respond to him? They set about organizing his history as a subject, as one might organize the history of psychoanalysis or the history of technique, in order to respond to his demand for satisfaction. By what pathway? By attempting to obtain a reduction of his desires to his needs.   528

Isn't it paradoxical to do so? For all of our work is, we can say, sustained in the dimension of desire. This is, moreover, as obvious to the subject as it is to us: to us, because everything that we have formulated will come down to what I will say; and to the subject, because in the final analysis, he knows this full well when he comes to see us.

I was just informed that someone is in the process of writing an important thesis on the social signification of psychoanalysis, and this led me to believe that it will include elements that are extremely rich in experience and especially well thought out. I think that the social representation of psychoanalysis is in fact much less distorted in society as a whole than we tend to think. Owing to that, I dare to hope that something – which is frankly at the very basis and core of what is implied by the fact that a person comes to see us – will come out of this thesis in the clearest way possible: the fact that at the root of his demand we find that he does not trust (in) his desire [or: he does not have faith in (or rely on) his desire, *il ne se fie pas à son désir*]. What all of the subjects who contact us have in common is that they do not trust (in) their desire.

The fact that, owing to our artifices, their desire can, following our lead, be reduced to need – or even be led toward sublimation along the elevated pathways of love – does not alter the fact that what characterizes their desire at the outset is that there is something that cannot actually be demanded, and regarding which a question arises. This is the dimension of desire, strictly speaking.

In order to introduce the dialectic of desire, do you recall what I did at a very precise moment, namely two and a half years ago? I began from what Freud says regarding the Oedipus complex in women [Seminar IV, Chapters 6–8]. Isn't what I have just said legible in the fact that there is good reason to pinpoint – in psychoanalytic practice, in our work with the unconscious – what women demand at the outset, which is that by which, Freud tells us, they enter into the Oedipus complex? They do not demand satisfaction; they demand to have what they do not have. What is involved is, as you know, the phallus.

This is the source of the myriad problems that arise when one tries to reduce the unfolding of the dialectic of desire in women to a   529
natural process.

Whether we manage to reduce it to a natural process or not, we must deal with something that emerges at a critical moment, that Freud highlights, in the development of little girls. Whether it is a primary or a secondary process does not matter much to us, after all; it is a salient and irreducible process, in any case. It is the following: what little girls demand – namely, to have the phallus – they demand to have in the place where they would have had it if they were men. This is what is involved and there are no two ways about it.

They will no doubt manage to have it – to have this phallus which is a signifier, a signifier, I repeat – to really have it in a man. This is even what makes it such that women are in a highly privileged position and that their affective problems are relatively simple compared to those experienced by men, but this relative simplicity must not blind us. The fact remains that at the outset, the real phallus that women can have enters into their dialectic and its unfolding as a signifier. Owing to which, they will always have it, at a certain level of their experience, *en moins* (as an absence, as something missing).

Naturally, I always reserve for women the marginal possibility [*possibilité-limite*] of perfect union with a being – namely, that in a sexual embrace there could be a complete fusion for a woman between her beloved and his organ. The fact remains, however, that in everyday experience, the difficulties that present themselves regarding sex revolve precisely around the following point: the ideal moment – which is in some sense poetic and even apocalyptic – of perfect sexual union is only situated in the margins [*limite*], whereas in fact, in the everyday test of experience, women, even when they fully realize their femininity, always deal with the phallic object qua separate. It is precisely because they deal with the phallus as such and in this register that their actions and impact can be perceived by men as castrating.

Moreover, they remain unconscious of this, until they go into analysis, just as they remain unconscious of the fact that symbolically they *are* the very phallus they do not *have* inasmuch as they are the object of the Other's desire. They do not know either of these things.

This specific position lasts as long as they remain unconscious of it, which means as long as it exists solely for the Other [*en tant qu'elle ne vaut que pour l'Autre*], the partner. Nevertheless, the extremely odd and paradoxical formulation by which women's relations to the phallus are resolved is that, in the unconscious, they both are it and have it.

The peculiar position of the phallus alongside the ideal woman, alongside this woman in her fantasized world, is one of the oddest effects of our relationship to discourse. In the unconscious, she is it and she has it, in the best of cases – except that she can only know it

530

via her desire. Consequently, there is an odd similarity between her as it were trans-subjective formulation – that is, between her unconscious formulation – and that of the pervert.

What have we discovered about women's unconscious economy if not that they manage to find phallic equivalences for all the objects that can be separated from them, including, and first on the list, the most natural object that separates from them – namely, the children to whom they give birth? I am merely reciting the ABCs of psychoanalytic doctrine here. Owing to this fact, the objects from which they separate end up taking on for them, as naturally as can be, if you will, the function of objects of desire. And this is what explains, I believe, the lower frequency of perversion in women. Insofar as their satisfactions are inscribed in a cultural context – and it is out of the question that they not be – they manage to be situated in the dialectic of separation, which is the dialectic of desire's signifying objects.

More than one analytic author has already clearly expressed what I have just said – and in a way that will undoubtedly appear far more concrete to you – by saying that, if there are fewer perversions among women than among men, it is because they generally manage to satisfy their perverse tendencies in their relations with their children. This is not why "your daughter is mute," but it is why there are a number of children who need our help. As you see, we come back here to first truths; but it is not pointless to return to them, assuming we do so by the proper pathway.

I will take advantage of the point we are at here to also give you an indication designed to temper what the male portion of my audience might experience by way of surprise and even impatience when faced with one of the odd features of their relations with their partners of the opposite sex. I mean what is commonly referred to as jealousy.

Psychoanalysts, who have brought us so much clarity, have naturally brought us just as much obscurity. As Nestroy, whom Freud greatly appreciated, said, "every step forward is only half as big as it looks at first." This is why the problem of female jealousy has been conflated in psychoanalysis with the very different problem of male jealousy. Assuming the two sexes have very different ways of loving, female jealousy is something that, I believe, can truly be situated only at the most radical point.

Consider my little illustration of demand, if you recall it [Table 20.1]. The subject questions his relationship to the Other and then strikes the Other with signifying death, as it were, as Ⱥ, only to himself appear as fallen, $, in the presence of this little a which is, in the final analysis, the remainder of the division: an irreducible and undemandable something that is the object of desire. Well, insofar as the subject, the woman here, makes herself into an object of love, she views this remainder as what is most essential to her. Which is why she attributes so much importance to manifestations of her partner's desire.

For in the end, it is obvious that in real life, love and desire are two different things. We should speak clearly and say that we can love someone a great deal and desire someone else.

To the degree to which women occupy the specific position that I mentioned, they know the value of desire full well. They know that, beyond all of love's sublimations, desire has a relationship to being, even in its most limited, restricted, fetishistic, and, in short, its stupidest form – that is, even in the marginal form in which in fantasy the subject, qua blinded, is literally nothing more than a prop and a sign, the sign of little *a* as the signifying remainder of relations with the Other. Nevertheless, in the final analysis, women view little *a* as ultimate proof that the Other is verily and truly addressing them.

A man can truly love a woman with all the affection and devotion we can imagine, but the fact remains that if he desires another woman – even if the first woman knows that what he desires in this other woman is her shoe, the hem of her dress, or the makeup she wears on her face – his homage to being thus goes to the other woman.

It is necessary to remind people of first truths from time to time, which is why I think you will excuse the possibly forced tone of this digression.

Let us now consider the exact nature of the zone of the object in which this ambiguity is established. What is the true function of the phallus? You cannot fail to feel it has already been singularly sketched out by what I told you earlier today about the bad internal object.

One could say that, in the guise of the phallus, the paternal metaphor, as I have called it, institutes a split in the object that precisely overlaps, as we should have expected, what I consider to be the general form of prohibition – namely, either the subject is not it or the subject does not have it.

If the subject is the phallus – something that can be immediately illustrated when the subject is the object of his mother's desire – then he does not have it, in other words he has no right to use it; this is the basic meaning of the law prohibiting incest. On the other hand, if he has it, in other words if he has identified with his father, then he clearly is not the phallus.

This is what is signified, at the symbolic level that I will call radical, by the introduction of the Oedipus complex as a dimension.

And everything that will ever be said on this topic will always boil down to the "either/or" that introduces the realm of an object that one cannot demand.

How is the neurotic characterized? He of course makes use of this alternative [either/or], and since he fully situates himself in the Oedipus complex, in its signifying structuring, he makes use of it in a way that I will call metonymic. I would even say that this metonymy is regressive to the degree to which "he is not it" presents itself there as prior to "she does not have it."

Allow me to explain this. The neurotic uses the fundamental alternative in a metonymic form in that, for him, "not to have it" is the form in which he disguisedly asserts himself "to be it." He "does not have" the phallus "in order to be" the phallus in a hidden, unconscious way. It is on this somewhat enigmatic "in order to be" [pour être] that I ended last time.

Note that "it is an other who has it," whereas "he is it" unconsciously. In his desiring function, the subject elects a substitute. This is the crux of neurosis. Consider what actually happens at the end of the obsessive's complicated maneuvers – he is not the one who enjoys. Similarly for the hysteric: she is not the one who is enjoyed.

The imaginary substitution that is at work here is a substitution of the ego for the subject – that is, for the $ that is involved at the level of desire. It is because the ego takes the place of the subject that he brings demand into desire's question. Someone who is not the subject, but who is his image [i.e., the ego], is substituted for him in the dialectic of desire.

This is why the neurotic can only demand substitutes, in the final analysis. What is characteristic about his experience, and he may even sense this, is that he demands everything that he demands for something else [or: for some other reason, autre chose]. This is the other consequence of the role that the imaginary comes to play and what I called the neurotic's regressive metonymy, for in this realm he cannot be stopped – once the subject has been replaced at the level of his desire, he can only demand replacements while believing he is demanding what he desires.

To take this a step further, experience shows that the ego, owing to its very form – that is, insofar as it is the reflection of a reflection, and is the other's form – also takes the place of the person from whom [dont] the subject demands something. Nowhere more easily than in the neurotic does this separate ego come to take the place of the separate object that I designate as the earliest form of the object of desire.

The neurotic's altruism is, as opposed to what people say, permanent. To obtain the satisfactions he seeks, nothing is more common

533

than to see him take a pathway about which we can say that it consists in *devoting himself to satisfying* – as much as he can here – all
of the other's demands, even though he knows that those demands
constitute a perpetual obstacle to his own desire. In other words,
in his devotion to the other, he blinds himself to his own lack of
satisfaction.

These are things that are not, I think, comprehensible outside of the
perspective that I am trying to articulate for you here.

For the neurotic, the barred S of the formula ($\lozenge a$) transforms
– I am saying this summarily and with caveats – into something
in which identification of his unconscious being with the phallus is
inscribed. For this reason, I will give it the same sign as the subject:
just as there is a "barred subject," I will write "barred phallus." This
barred phallus finds itself in the presence of an object that I will
write in the most general form of an object of desire – namely, in
the form of the imaginary other in which the subject situates himself
and finds himself anew: $\Phi \lozenge i(a)$.

We must now turn to perversion, but as it is late, I will defer this
till next time. I cannot advance any more quickly here. See nothing
in this but an effect of the difficult ground we must cover.

June 17, 1959

XXVI

THE FUNCTION OF
SPLITTING* IN PERVERSION

The locus of perverse desire in *Lolita*
A feature of masochistic jouissance
The machine in schizophrenia
The idolized woman in homosexuality
Desire on the horizon or desire at the heart of . . .

The difficulty we are facing is not a new one; it is one of those about which the entire ethical tradition has speculated. Need I echo here from long, long ago the bitterness of the sages or pseudo-sages regarding the disappointing nature of human desire?

The question takes on an explicit form in psychoanalysis, where the partial nature of the drives appears right from the outset, as does the fact that our connection with the object depends on the complex, complicated, and incredibly risky arrangement of those drives. All access to the object, insofar as it depends on a combination of partial drives, is fundamentally problematic in character.

If there is a theory here, it runs counter to the notion of instinct, as counter to that notion as one can possibly imagine. However flexibly one may posit its hypothesis of finality, the whole theory of instinct is, as it were, based on the centering of the object. In other words, the natural process of the living organism is such that an object is progressively fixated in a certain field and caught there in a certain behavior. The process presents itself in the guise of a progressive concentration of the field.

The process and dialectic that psychoanalysis shows us is altogether different. Here, we progress on the contrary through the addition and combination of partial drives. It is only after taking the trouble to synthesize all sorts of interchangeable and variable drives, and at the endpoint of highly diverse combinations, that we manage to conceptualize the advent of a satisfying object, one that corresponds to the two poles of masculinity and femininity.

536   This might lead you to think that ($◊a$) – situated on the graph we use here to map the position of desire in a speaking subject – is a very simple notation. In line with this, we might say the following: in desire, something is required, which is the relationship between the subject and the object; little *a* is the object, barred S is the subject, and that's it. What is most original in this notation is still the little bar on S, which reminds us that, at the culminating point at which desire is rendered present to mind, the subject is himself marked by speech. But this amounts, after all, to nothing more than a reminder that the drives are fragmented.

It is worth pointing out here that this notation is broader in scope.

It does not designate a relationship between the subject and the object; it designates fantasy, insofar as fantasy sustains the subject as desiring – in other words, at a point beyond his discourse. This notation signifies that the subject is present in fantasy as the subject of unconscious discourse. He is present in fantasy insofar as he is represented there by the function of cutting, that is, by the essential function that is his in discourse – and not in just any old discourse; it is a discourse that escapes him [or: slips out, *lui échappe*], the discourse of the unconscious.

If you follow the thread of this notation, you will not fail to be struck by the fact that it brings out dimensions that are always overlooked when it comes to perverse fantasies.

1

I already indicated to you last time how prudently we must broach such fantasies.

Perverse fantasies are not perversion proper.

The biggest mistake we – such as we are, in other words, insofar as we are more or less neurotic around the edges – can make is to imagine that we understand perversion because we have access to perverse fantasies. For the comprehensive access that we have to perverse fantasies does not give us access to perversion as a structure, even if those fantasies call, as it were, for a reconceptualization of perversion.

537   If you will allow me to take a little liberty in my discourse today in order to give myself over to a little gambol outside it, I will discuss with you a book marked by the seal of our times, which is entitled *Lolita*.

I am no more asking you to read this book than a whole series of others that could indicate a certain constellation of interest around the mainspring of desire. There are things that are better constructed than *Lolita* at a theoretical level, so to speak, but it is a rather exemplary product all the same.

For those who open the book, nothing will seem obscure as to the function that is reserved for *i(a)* in it. This function is manifested in it in a way that is all the less ambiguous as, curiously enough, the author expresses a frank opposition to what he calls "Freudian voodooism." He nevertheless clearly attests, several times and in a way that he truly does not perceive, to the symbolic function of the image *i(a)*. For example, the hero, shortly before approaching Lolita decisively, has a dream in which she appears in the form of "a small hairy hermaphrodite."

But that is not what is of the essence. What is of the essence lies in the structure of the work, emphasizing, as it does, the brilliant contrast between the first and the second part, between the sparkling nature of desire as long as it is contemplated by the subject for some thirty years of his life, then its prodigious decline into an embroiled reality in the course of the miserable voyage of this couple across America the beautiful, during which the subject finds himself without any means whatsoever to get through to his partner. This is why *Lolita* presents all the characteristics of the subject's relation to a fantasy that is strictly speaking neurotic.

What is exemplary here is the way in which, owing to the very coherence of the construction, perverse desire shows itself. This desire does not appear in the hero, but in someone else [*un autre*] who is both more and something quite other than his double, for he is literally his persecutor. He appears in the margins of the story, as if the desire at stake in the subject could only live in another person, where it is literally impenetrable and altogether unknown. This substitution is clearly avowed in the novel.

The character who takes the hero's place at a certain moment in the plot is a pervert, strictly speaking. He really accedes to the object. The key to this character is only given to us by his final groans when he is shot by the hero with a revolver. The relation to the object relies, in effect, on a sort of negative of the hero. This configuration has something exemplary about it, which can serve us as a schema for understanding that it is only by extrapolating that we can grasp perverse structure.

538

The structure of desire in neurosis is of a very different nature from the structure of desire in perversion, but we can nevertheless say that the two structures are opposites.

What will serve us here as a pole in broaching perversion is the most radical of the perverse positions of desire, the one that is placed by analytic theory at the basis of development, as its earliest

point, and also at the endpoint of the most extreme regressions –
namely, masochism.

Why not begin by highlighting something obvious that fantasy
brings the subject, in order to underscore the degree to which certain
levels are neglected when analysts rush to provide collapsed formulations of the nature of masochism?

People tend, as we know, to reduce masochism in its various
forms to the subject's most basic relation to his own life. They
invoke certain valid and precious indications given by Freud on this
topic in order to justify their conflation of masochism with the death
instinct and to maintain that something that runs counter to the
organization of the instincts makes itself immediately felt at the very
level of the drive, viewed as an organic impulse. There is undoubtedly some sort of target here on which it may be of interest to set our
sights in order to raise certain questions.

If we return to our schema – the one that situates desire in a relationship in which the subject's relation to discourse takes the form
of a long division [Table 20.1] – a singular feature that we would be
wrong to neglect shines forth from within the fantasy world [*la fan-
tasmatique*] of what people call masochism.

While conceptualizing masochism as the result of one of the
most central instincts, analysts are undoubtedly in agreement that
masochistic jouissance essentially requires one not to go beyond a
certain point when it comes to physical abuse. Now certain features
of this jouissance, when they are highlighted, are, I believe, such as
to enlighten us as regards at least a middle register [*médium*] of this
jouissance, in which we can recognize the relationship between the
subject and the Other's discourse.

Indeed, it suffices to have had a masochist confide in you – or to
have read any of the numerous writings that are devoted to masochism, some decent ones having come out again just recently – to
recognize that an essential dimension of masochistic jouissance lies
in the specific sort of passivity experienced by the subject: he enjoys
thinking that his fate is being decided in some upper echelon, by
a certain number of people who are around him and who debate
his fate in his presence as if he were not there. Isn't this one of the
most salient and perceptible dimensions of the masochist's jouissance? The subject himself emphasizes this as one of the constituent
features of masochistic relationships.

In short, nothing allows us to better grasp the fact that the subject
is constituted as a subject in discourse than this fantasy in which
discourse itself is lit up, explicit, and revealed. The possibility that
this discourse may view the subject as nil [*néant*] is taken to extremes
here.

539

We find here one of the first steps – a step, good Lord, that is rather important, since it is starting from it that a certain number of symptomatic manifestations will develop – a step from which we can see the following relationship sketch itself out on the horizon: the relationship there may be between the death instinct, considered to be one of the most central instances, and what in discourse gives us a prop without which we cannot accede to the death instinct – namely, the cut – a prop of nonbeing, the latter being one of the earliest, constitutive, and implicit dimensions which is at the root of all symbolization.

For a whole year, the one I devoted to Freud's *Beyond the Pleasure Principle* [Seminar II], I explained that the true function of symbolization must be located in the foundation of the cut. A cut is that by which the current of an early tension, whatever it may be, is taken up into a series of alternatives that inaugurate what one might call the most basic machine. This machine is precisely what we rediscover in a detached and isolated form at the core of schizophrenia. In schizophrenia, the subject identifies with the very discordance between this machine and his life-sustaining [*vital*] current.

540

We are putting our finger here – I am pointing this out in passing – in an exemplary way, which is both radical and altogether accessible, on one of the most eminent forms of the function of *Verwerfung* [foreclosure]. Assuming that the cut is both constitutive of discourse and irremediably external to it, one can say that the subject is *verworfen* [foreclosed] insofar as he identifies with the cut. It is because of this that he apprehends himself and perceives himself to be real.

Here I am merely indicating to you another form of Descartes' "I am thinking, therefore I am," a form that is, naturally, articulated and explored quite differently than in Descartes' work, but that I do not view as fundamentally distinct from his. What we have in addition to the Cartesian dimension is that the discourse in which the subject participates escapes him [*lui échappe*], and he is [divided in] two unbeknownst to himself. Insofar as he is the cut in this discourse, the subject is at the pinnacle of an "I am" whose singular property is to get its bearings [*se saisir*] in a reality that is truly the last reality in which a subject can get his bearings – namely, in the possibility of cutting the discourse somewhere, of providing punctuation.

The subject's essential being lies in this property. For the only real intrusion that he radically brings to the world as a subject nevertheless excludes him from it.

The upshot being that it will require, on the basis of all of his other life-sustaining relations, every detour that we analysts are aware of in order for the *I* to become reintegrated into the world.

2

Last time I spoke briefly about the way things work for neurotics.

As I said, for neurotics, the problem involves the paternal metaphor – that is, the fiction, whether real or not, of he who enjoys the object in peace. At what cost? At the cost of something perverse.

I also said that the paternal metaphor actually masks a metonymy. Behind the metaphor of the father as a subject of the law [or: law-abiding subject, *sujet de la loi*], as a peaceful possessor of jouissance, the metonymy of castration is hidden.

If you examine it closely, you will see that the son's castration is but the consequence or equivalent of the father's castration here. All the primitive myths that underpin Freud's myth of the [primal] father indicate this sufficiently: prior to the establishment of the heavenly monarchy, Cronos castrates Uranus, and Zeus castrates Cronos.

The metonymy in question is based, in the final analysis, on the fact that there is never just one phallus in the game. And this is precisely what must not be seen in neurotic structure. The neurotic can only be the phallus in the name of the Other [or: on the Other's behalf, *au nom de l'Autre*]. He does not have it – this is, as everyone knows, what we call the castration complex. There is thus someone who has the phallus, someone upon whom the neurotic's being depends. But if no one has the phallus, the neurotic has it still less, naturally.

What is the neurotic's desire?

As the entire development of Freud's work indicates, the neurotic is altogether dependent on the signifier's good faith. The neurotic latches on to this mythical guarantee in order to live in something other than a permanent state of vertigo. Moreover, as everyone knows, there is a close, historical relationship between Freud's anatomy of this desire and the characteristics of the era in which we live and about which we cannot know to what form of human – vaguely predicted by prophets of various ilks – it will lead or stumble.

This allows us to arrive at a condensed formulation, which in a certain way summarizes what I would like to convey to you: the neurotic's desire is, I would say, what is born when there is no God.

This is tangible in our practice as long as we do not hesitate to articulate it. But don't put words in my mouth; don't say that I am saying the situation is simpler when there is a God. I am saying that the suspension of the supreme Guarantor is what the neurotic hides within himself, and that it is at this level that the neurotic's desire is situated, stops, and is in abeyance.

The neurotic's desire is a desire only on the horizon of all of his behaviors. Indeed, if I can relay to you one of those formulations that allow you to recognize the style of a behavior, I would say that, with regard to the desire in which he situates himself, the neurotic is always on his own horizon and preparing his own advent.   542

If you will allow me an expression that is modeled on all sorts of things we see in everyday life, the neurotic is always busy packing his bags or examining his conscience – it's the same thing – or organizing his labyrinth – that's the same thing, too. He gathers his bags, he forgets some of them or he checks them at the baggage checkroom, but they amount to nothing more than luggage for a trip he will never take.

This is an absolutely essential point to consider if we wish to realize that – notwithstanding what lazy thinking proposes, thinking that inches along the edge of the phenomenon like a snail, without ever trying to get a bird's eye view of it – there is a very distinct contrast to be made between the structure of the neurotic's desire and the structure of the pervert's desire.

There is a gap for the pervert too, of course. He, too, represents his being in the cut, since this is the fundamental subjective relationship. The only question is thus to know how this cut is experienced and borne by the pervert.

Here we can assuredly take into account work done by analysts over the years, insofar as their experience with perverse patients has allowed them to articulate theories which, although they sometimes contradict each other or fit together badly, are nevertheless suggestive of the type of difficulty they deal with. We can speak of it as material that, in and of itself, betrays certain structural necessities, necessities which are precisely those that we are trying to formulate here. I will thus say that the attempt we are making here to establish the real function of desire can include everything up to and including the discrete delusion, and even the well-organized delusion, to which certain analysts have been led who have broached the topic from the angle of behavior.

I will give you an example. I think that, overall, no one currently has more to say about perversion than a man who is very discreet and funny – I am talking about William H. Gillespie. To those who   543
read English, I recommend they peruse the following articles, all of which came out in the *International Journal of Psychoanalysis*, and from which they will learn a great deal: Gillespie's first paper on the topic, "A Contribution to the Study of Fetishism" (1940); then his "Notes on the Analysis of Sexual Perversions" (1952); and finally his most recent article, "The General Theory of Sexual Perversion" (1956).

One gets the impression that the author is a free spirit who gauges rather well the different directions from which people have attempted to broach perversion. Perversion is, naturally, far more complex than one might imagine when one confines one's attention to the summary view that it is the drive nakedly showing itself, and that's it. Which is not, for all that, to lend credence to the approach that tends to lump perversion and neurosis together.

I will go straight to what must be expressed, and which will henceforth serve us as a landmark for examining perversion in certain ways.

The notion of splitting* [in French, *refente*] is essential to Gillespie's conception of perversion. We could applaud him for this – but don't believe that I am going to rush to do so – believing that his conception overlaps the function in which I teach you to recognize the subjective component of fantasy: the subject's identification with the slit [*fente*] or cut provided by discourse. It just so happens that the type of precipitation implied by this recognition has already led certain writers who have studied perversion to insights of which they were a bit ashamed.

In order to corroborate this, I need but refer to the third case Gillespie discusses in the second of his articles. I will briefly depict the patient for you. He is a thirty-year-old fetishist. In the course of his analysis, it comes out that his fantasy is to be split in two by his mother's teeth while he penetrates her, she suddenly changing "into a hairy gorilla-like creature." The creature's cutting edge, as it were, is represented by the fact that "she bites off his female nipples," which he turns out to have; and [in another fantasy] she kicks him, her shoe "splitting up his anus and rectum" [p. 75].

In short, there is a whole decomposition/recomposition that goes on here, Gillespie relating it to what he calls castration anxiety, including his mother's demand [that he be a girl] or regret [that he wasn't], and identification with the female genitalia as split. This identification, which grows out of one of Melanie Klein's theories, is not, I must say, demonstrated in this case; it is simply assumed by the analyst at the end of the analysis.

Gillespie concludes with a sort of insight or intuition that is only half-owned, it remaining a question for him. This is, in my view, indicative of the extremes to which he – someone who attentively followed the way the explanation, that only analysis was able to give, of the deepest recesses of perverse structure has developed over the course of time – was led. Gillespie writes, "The configuration of the material at this point led me to a speculation about the phantasy associated with the split ego" [p. 75].

As I believe you know, Freud died before he could complete his article *Die Ichspaltung*, "The Splitting of the Ego." The article was found after his death and it led Gillespie to speculate about the connection between the split ego and the split object.

Gillespie asks:

> Is not the female genital the split object *par excellence*, and cannot the phantasy of a split ego arise from an identification with this split genital? I am aware that when we speak of splitting of the ego and of the object we are referring to mental mechanisms which we assume to underlie the phenomena,

– he is essentially telling us that we are doing science here and are working with scientific concepts –

and that phantasies pertain to a different level of discourse. [p. 75]

Here the type of question that Gillespie raises becomes interesting:

> [N]evertheless, phantasies, our own no less than our patients', must always play a part in the way we conceptualise these underlying processes. It seems to me, therefore, that the phantasy of being oneself split in pieces just as the vulva is split may well be very relevant to the mental mechanism of splitting of the object and introjection of the split object, leading to splitting of the ego. It is implicit, of course, in such a phantasy of the vulva as a split object that it was once intact, and that the splitting is the result of a sadistic attack, whether by the father or by oneself. [p. 75]

545

We cannot fail to be struck by such considerations, coming as they do from someone as prudent and measured as Gillespie. It is clear that he allows himself to go as far as his thought can take him when he reduces the explanation he gives of the subject's personality structure to a sort of primordial identificatory schema, that of splitting. His whole article is devoted to this, not just this one particular case.

Splittings,* which are what are often today called "divisions in the personality," are in effect tangible and come apart in the transference with perverts. Nevertheless, to model the division of the pervert's personality on the two flaps of an organ from which fantasy life originates strikes me as laughable if not disconcerting.

What we find here under the heading of splitting,* and which must be grasped, in extremely different forms, at every level of the pervert's personality formation, is something I have already indicated – for example, in the article I devoted to the case of André Gide, a writer who was so remarkably studied by Jean Delay.

3

In the case of André Gide, splitting* presents itself in the form of an opposition between two identificatory sections, one of which is specifically linked to his narcissistic image of himself, $i(a)$, and the other to his mother.

This illustrious patient tells us this in a thousand different ways in his work, and we must undoubtedly take the importance of his literary work into account, for it adds something to the subject's stability.

But it is not about this topic that I would like to fully elaborate what I am indicating to you. As the time left to us this year is almost gone, I must prime the pump a bit and propose a few little things designed to show you what our work here this year now allows us to broach.

In the very title of my article on Gide, I foregrounded a relationship that is especially salient in his case, the one that the schema of fantasy spells out between desire and the letter. What does this mean? It means that we must situate the process of sublimation, assuming we wish to give the term "sublimation" a suitable meaning, in the reconversion of desire into a production involving symbols – which is not the supra-reality people think it is. It is, on the contrary, essentially made up of shards of reality, of the latter's decomposition into signifying parts. Sublimation, I am saying, lies in the reconversion of desire's impasse into signifying materiality.

There is no doubt but that Gide deserves to be situated in the category of subjects who raise the problem of homosexuality for us. And what do we see in his case, if not the twofold relationship between the subject and a divided object?

On the one hand, the object is narcissistic, the reflection of this ungracious – or even "disgraced," as a certain writer put it – boy that Gide was early on. In his furtive relations with narcissistic objects, the presence of the phallus is essential. It is in this regard that Gide is homosexual.

Nevertheless, and it is to Jean Delay's credit to have shown this to us in his biography of Gide, it is altogether impossible to focus on one of the sexual anomalies of Gide as a subject without juxtaposing it with what Gide himself attested to with the following formulation:

"No one can imagine the love of an Uranist." What is at issue here is his hyper-idealized love for his wife.

Its origins are very clearly spelled out by Delay, and I had no trouble at all bringing them together and highlighting everything that connects this love to his relationship with his mother. It is not solely a question of the real mother as we know her, but of the mother insofar as she harbors within herself a structure whose true nature we will try to detect. I will immediately say that the presence – I would go even further and say the topography – of the bad object is essential to that structure.

I cannot dwell here on each point of Gide's history, such as his work, at its different stages, lays it out. I will confine my attention to citing the following passages: 547

> But to show how greatly a child's instinct may go astray, I will mention more particularly two of the themes that gave me physical enjoyment [*jouissance*]: one was furnished me very innocently by George Sand in her charming story of *Gribouille*. Gribouille throws himself into the water one day that it is raining very hard, not to avoid the rain, as his wicked brothers say, but to avoid his brothers, who are laughing at him. For some time, he struggles in the water and tries to swim; then he lets himself go; and as soon as he lets himself go, he floats; then he feels himself becoming tiny, light, odd, vegetable; leaves sprout out of him all over his body; and soon Gribouille turns into a slender, graceful sprig of oak, which the water gently deposits on the bank of the stream. Absurd! But that is my very reason for telling it; I say what is true and not what I think may redound to my credit. No doubt "the grandmother of Nohant" had not the slightest intention of writing anything demoralising; but I bear witness that no schoolboy was ever troubled by any page of *Aphrodite* so much as I – ignorant little boy that I was – by the metamorphosis of Gribouille. [pp. 50–1]

Before returning to this passage, whose importance we must not overlook, I will add the second example that Gide gives us of a fantasy that gave rise to his earliest jouissances:

> There was also a stupid little play of Madame de Ségur's called *Les Dîners de Mademoiselle Justine*. There is a passage in it where the servants take advantage of their masters' absence to have a bout of gormandising; they ransack the cupboards; they gorge themselves with food; then suddenly, as Justine is stooping to lift a pile of plates out of the cupboard, the coachman

steals up behind her and puts his arm around her waist; Justine is ticklish and drops the pile. Crash! The whole of the crockery is smashed to pieces. This disaster made me swoon with delight. [p. 51]

Could we need anything further to realize in what respect this second fantasy illustrates something that is altogether primordial, which we must articulate in the relationship between the subject and the cut? In such subjects, it is very common that one of the fundamental fantasies of their first masturbatory experiences is also a fantasy involving a verbal revelation. I might mention, for example, a subject whose fantasy revolved around an actual sexual initiation.

In the first of Gide's fantasies, the relationship that is revealed of the subject to something detached, which progressively blossoms, presents us with the realm of the subject's identification with the phallus, inasmuch as the phallus emerges from his fantasizing about an object inside his mother. This is a structure that is commonly encountered and demonstrated by a hundred different psychoanalytic case studies, such that no analyst could refuse to recognize it. But it is not enough to see that an identification, representing one of the subject's first erotic experiences, is caught up in the fantasy and propped up by it. We must figure out what sort of identification we are talking about here.

In the neurotic's metonymy, the subject is, as I have said, the phallus – ultimately, in other words, at a point he can only reach in the receding perspective of his symptoms – only insofar as he does not have it. This is what must not be revealed. The upshot is that as the analysis proceeds, his castration anxiety grows.

In perversion, on the other hand, there is something that we might call a reversal of the proof process. What must be proven by the neurotic – namely, the continued existence of his desire – becomes the basis of the proof in perversion. The latter in some sense restores to its place of honor what is known in analysis as a *reductio ad absurdum*.

For the pervert, in effect, a conjunction is made that unites "he is it" and "he has it" into a single term. For this it is enough that there be a slight opening that allows for a very specific identification with the Other – namely, that "he has it" be in this case "she has it." This "she" is the object with whom he first identified. He will have the phallus – whether this object has transformed into a fetish, in one case, or into an idol, in the other. We have here the wide range of forms taken by homosexual love, from the fetishistic form to the idolatrous form illustrated by Gide.

A bond is established, if I may put it thus, in the natural medium [or: prop, *support*]. Perversion presents itself as a sort of natural simulation of the cut. It is here that Gillespie's intuition serves us as a sort of index. What the subject does not have, he has through [or: in, *dans*] the object. What the subject is not, his ideal object is. In short, a certain natural relationship is taken up as material for the subjective split which, in perversion as in neurosis, must be symbolized. The subject is the phallus qua object within the mother, and he has it in [or: possesses it via] the object of his desire.

549

This is more or less what we see in male homosexuals. What about female homosexuals? Recall the case of the so-called young homosexual woman, which we analyzed here in comparing it to the case of Dora. What happens at the turning point at which Freud's young patient runs headlong toward homosexual idealization? She is clearly the phallus, but in what respect?

What is at stake there is also the phallus as an object within the mother. This can be seen very clearly when, at the climax of the crisis, she throws herself over the guardrail onto the railroad tracks below. Freud sees an identification with this maternal attribute in this *niederkommen* [to deliver or give birth]. In falling like an object, she makes herself into the phallus. Her suicide attempt constitutes a supreme effort to give the phallus to her idol. More precisely, by giving what she does not have – namely, the phallus that is the object of her adoration – to the odd character who is the object of her homosexual love, she raises this person to new heights of idealization.

I am proposing this as a structure. You will find it in every case, if you take the trouble to study it – not only in perversion in general, but especially in homosexuality.

It is of course relevant to object that this form is extremely polymorphous, all the more so in that the ordinary use of the term "homosexuality" leads us to subsume under it I don't know how many varied forms that experience presents us with. It is certainly legitimate to include all sorts of peripheral, intermediary forms between perversion and psychosis, let us say, such as drug addiction or other forms in our nosographic field. But wouldn't it be of interest, after all, to situate something that could constitute the crux of homosexuality in terms of perversion?

Let us take our bearings, for example, from what I tried to formulate last time as the point on which the neurotic's desire for desire is based. I said that it is thanks to the relationship between the ego and the image of the other that a whole game of substitutions can be established in which the neurotic never has to put what is at stake – namely, that he is the phallus, that is, clearly $\Phi \lozenge i(a)$ – to the test. Well, in homosexuality I will say that what we are dealing with is

550

the relationship between the primal, symbolic identification, I, and narcissistic, specular identification, $i(a)$.

In homosexuals, there is already a schism in the subject that is traced out between I – his first identificatory, symbolic accession to the primordial relationship with his mother – and his first *Verwerfungen* [foreclosures]. This is connected to the subject's second identification, his imaginary identification with his specular form, $i(a)$. And this is what the subject uses to symbolize the term in which he inscribes himself insofar as he intervenes in the fantasized relationship, the term that, following Gillespie, I call "split."

In neurotics, the Other's desire frightens the subject, the subject feeling that he is the one who runs all the risks. In homosexuals, on the other hand, the Other's desire finds its symbol, having emerged from the mother, in the phallus, which is the essential signifying element here, the center around which the whole of the pervert's construction gets organized. Which means that, in his case, the Other's desire is what is the farthest removed and hardest to access. This is what makes for the depth and difficulty of the analyses of childhood experience that have allowed us to proffer constructions and speculations related especially to the subject's earliest object identifications.

Had Gide offered himself up at his own expense to psychoanalytic exploration, nothing says that it could have been taken far enough. In any case, he did not do so. His analysis occurred only in a so-called sublimated dimension. But, as superficial as it was, it nevertheless gives us strange hints about his relationship to the object. There is one in particular with which I will close today.

It concerns something that appears to be a little behavioral quirk. To the best of my knowledge, no one has given it much consideration, whereas its symptomatic accent is almost a dead giveaway as to what is at issue – namely, what lies beyond the mother figure, or, more precisely, her inside, her very heart. For what lies at the heart of the earliest identification is found anew at the foundation of the perverse subject's very structure.

Desire is on the horizon of all of the neurotic's demands, which are deployed at length and are literally interminable. By way of contrast, desire "is at the heart" of all of the pervert's demands and, in reading that desire as it unfolds, it indisputably appears tied to aesthetic requirements. But what is most striking is the modulation of the successive themes around which it unfolds.

551

How can we fail to feel transported to the furthest reaches of fragmenting experience when – right from the first lines of the volume [*If It Die . . .*], and on the first six or seven pages – Gide's fragmented, kaleidoscopic vision appears? But there is more. At a certain moment, Gide has a certain perception that he articulates in the notion that, no doubt, "there is reality and there are dreams," but "there is *another* reality as well" [p. 20]. Further on, he recounts the so-called story of the knot in a wooden door. This is what I would like to get at. It is the tiniest of hints, but for us, as everyone knows, these are the most important ones.

In a wooden door somewhere in the town of Uzès, there is a hole because a knot was removed from it. And the young Gide is told that at the bottom of the hole is a little marble that his father slipped in there when he was Gide's age. Gide then tells us, to the admiration of those interested in character, that he spent the whole of the next year letting the nail on his pinky grow so it would be long enough to extract the little marble from the hole in the wood.

When he managed to do so, he found that he had in hand nothing more than a grayish object that he would be ashamed to show anyone [pp. 46–7]. This led him to put it back in its place, cut his fingernail, and not talk about it to anyone – except to us, posterity, who have immortalized this story.

It would, I think, be difficult to find a better introduction to the notion of the object, an object that is, in the final analysis, rejected through a magnificent *Sublimierung* [sublimation]. It is clearly the form in which the perverse subject's relationship to the internal object presents itself. For the object that he tracks down with perseverance is an object at the heart of the Other.

The imaginary dimension of the Other's desire – his mother's desire in this case – which is primordial in nature, plays the central, decisive, symbolizing role here; this allows us to postulate that at the level of desire, the pervert identifies with the imaginary form of the phallus.

It is on this topic that next week I will give the last class of the year.

June 24, 1959

CONCLUSION AND OVERTURE

XXVII

TOWARD SUBLIMATION

Critique of so-called reality
Defending the dimension of desire
The inexorability of the real
Reducing drives to signifiers
Perversion's value as a protest

We have now arrived at the end of a year that I have devoted, at my risk as much as yours, to desire and its interpretation.

The question that preoccupied me, and that I have continued to work on without deviating from it, was, as you may have noticed, that of the place of desire in the economy of psychoanalytic experience. I believe, in fact, that the specific interpretation of any desire must begin from there.

It has not been easy to pinpoint the place of desire. Today, by way of conclusion, I would simply like to mention the cardinal points that can help us situate the function of desire, such as I have spelled it out this year, in a way that I hope conveyed its importance to you.

1

At the point in analytic history at which we find ourselves, and which began already about twenty years ago, the case studies that people enjoy publishing concern cases that, compared to the typical neuroses found in the older psychoanalytic literature, involve "neurotic character" [*caractères névrotiques*] – that is, cases that are situated at the very edge of neurosis.

We find this constantly, and it can be seen in almost any modern psychoanalytic text you care to open.

I read a number of them recently, in order to be up to speed, and the question I would raise concerns how the subjects we meet with in

analysis are broached. Where is psychoanalytic thinking at concerning what constitutes the crux of the progress implied by experience?
Well, in short, one might say that with a surprising consistency, and
almost regardless of which school an analyst gets his watchwords
from, psychoanalysis is currently dominated by object relations.
Everything is converging on object relations.

Among the organizing poles of psychoanalytic thought that
structure research today, object relations is most closely connected
to Melanie Klein's work. It is true that the inclusion of her notions
in such articles seems symptomatic, rather than reflecting the cir-
culation of a theory that has been particularly well thought out.
Nevertheless, none of the other contemporary poles of psychoanalytic thought has strayed far from this one, object relations having
come to dominate our entire conception of analytic progress.

If this observation is not the least striking of those we could
make here, the following is more striking still. When one concretely
follows the unfolding of a case study written in order to illustrate
any structure whatsoever in our nosological field, one realizes that
the analysis seems to be carried out, for at least a certain period of
time, along lines that one might well qualify as those of moralizing
normalization.

I am not saying that analysts' interventions go directly in this
direction – that depends on the case – but this perspective gives
analysts their bearings. This can be seen in the very way in which
analysts articulate the particularities of a subject's position with
respect to those around him, with respect to the object he deals
with. The subject is always situated with respect to a supposedly
normal way of approaching other people, and it is in comparison
with this normal way that analysts gauge the deficiencies of their
patients' apprehension of the object. Analysts' minds dwell essentially on deterioration in the dimension of the other, an other who
is always mapped as being forever neglected, forgotten, ousted from
his position as an independent, autonomous subject, and stripped
of his status as a pure, absolute other. And that's it. In every case,
analysts' attention is entirely focused on the patient's ability (or lack
thereof) to appreciate other people in all their depth and autonomy.

What is most striking is not so much this mapping, with all the
cultural presuppositions it entails, for it is no worse than any other,
after all. It is the implicit rallying of analysts to what one might call
a system of values, which, although it is implicit, is nevertheless
present.

At the beginning of an analysis, we see the analyst talk at length
with the subject about the inadequacies of his affective apprehension of other people. Next we see some sort of turning point in the

concrete analysis, unless it simply reflects haste on the analyst's part to summarize what seems to him to be the final key to the analysis. In any case, we generally see the essentially moralizing discussion of the case suddenly slip into the background, and note that the final explanation of the patient's problems involves a series of extremely early identifications, which, regardless of what they are called, are always more or less directly linked to the notion of good and bad objects, internalized or interjected objects, or externalized,* projected objects.

To have recourse to such early identifications always betrays a certain Kleinian penchant on the analyst's part. It sometimes happens that this penchant is masked by the highlighting of the sources of the patient's fixations, which are designated using older terms, borrowed from drive theory – people say, for example, that in such and such a case, oral sadism profoundly impacted the Oedipal relationship. But in order to explain this particularity of the Oedipal drama, analysts always end up referring to something in the realm of early identifications. The entire development of the subjective drama of a neurosis is, after all is said and done, attributed to those identifications, as is the entire development of a perversion.

Now these identifications leave the very notion of subjectivity extremely ambiguous. In such accounts, the subject essentially appears to be an identification with something that he may consider to derive more or less from himself. Therapeutic progress is presented as entailing a rearrangement of these identifications in the course of an experience that appeals to reality as its guiding principle.

Things thus take on an extremely random appearance, because in the final analysis, *the* reality referred to is nothing more than *a* reality, the reality presumed to exist by the analyst. This reality implies – in a form that is still more implicit this time, still more masked, and which can be altogether scabrous – an ideal of normality [*normativité*] that turns the analyst's ideals into the final standard that the patient, in concluding, in an identificatory conclusion, is encouraged to rally around: "I am, in the end, what I recognize to be good in myself. I aspire to conform to an ideal of normality which, although hidden and implicit, is nevertheless the one I recognize, after so many detours, as having been designated for me." The analysis proceeds here by what is tantamount to a subtle set of suggestions; they may be more subtle than other suggestions, but in the end they are still suggestions.

The form of practice that has become organized in this way, through a sort of progressive departure from Freud's recommendations, masks ever more completely the essential question that lies at

558

its heart, and without which there cannot be, I believe, any accurate assessment of psychoanalytic action – namely, the question of the place of desire. My theorization of desire is designed to foreground – in a way that is not ambiguous, but truly crucial – the notion that what we are dealing with is a subjectivity.

Is desire [the same thing as] subjectivity? This question did not have to await the arrival on the historical stage of psychoanalysis to be raised. It has always been there, since the origin of what one might call "ethical practice." Desire is both subjectivity – it is what is at the very heart of our subjectivity, what is most essentially subjective – and at the same time its opposite, for it opposes subjectivity like a resistance, a paradox, or a rejected, refutable nucleus.

It is on this basis, as I have said several times, that ethics developed in a tradition at the end of which we find Spinoza's enigmatic formulation: "desire, *cupiditas*, is the very essence of man." This formulation is enigmatic inasmuch as it leaves a question unanswered: is what we desire the same as what is desirable?

Even in psychoanalysis, we observe a distance between what is desired and what is desirable. Psychoanalytic practice has been established and formulated on this very basis. Desire is not simply exiled, or pushed away when it comes to action and to the crux of our servitude, as it had been prior to analysis. It is questioned as being the key or the mainspring in us of a whole series of actions and behaviors that are understood to represent what is most profoundly true about us. This is the ideal aim from which analytic practice constantly tends to deviate.

559

Does this mean that the desire in question is a pure and simple vital impulse, as people thought for a long time? Not at all, since, as soon as we spell out our practice, we find that the more we examine this desire, the less it resembles a pure and simple impulse. Rather, it disintegrates, falls apart, and deviates ever more from anything that might be characterized as a harmonious relationship. In the progressive regression involved in psychoanalytic experience, no desire ever fails to present itself as problematic, dispersed, polymorphous, contradictory, and, in short, far from any oriented coaptation.

We need to set our sights on experience involving desire [*expérience du désir*], which is absolutely original and irreducible. We cannot leave it without exploring it, without producing some theory that gives us a fix on its meaning – whereas, as I have said, everything in the way in which psychoanalytic experience is currently formulated is designed to veil the meaning of desire and to make us turn away from it.

Transference is the only way the pathways toward the object can be cleared in psychoanalysis. But to define transference as an experience of repetition obtained through regression, which itself depends on frustration, is merely to point to the negative, for it leaves aside the fundamental relationship between frustration and demand. It is only my way of formulating things that allows us to see that, if demand regresses in analysis, it is because – presenting itself there as a developed demand – it remains unanswered.

Analysts today profess to answer it themselves, in a roundabout way, in order to guide their patients toward the object. This gives rise to all kinds of incredible ideas, including that of the "adjustment of the distance" from the object, which I have already critiqued. Although this notion plays a role in the French context above all, it shows clearly enough, all by itself, what sort of contradictory impasse analysis has gotten into by focusing so narrowly on object relations; for every relationship – regardless of what you may say about it, regardless of what it may be, regardless of the normal state it should supposedly conform to – clearly presumes the maintenance of a certain distance. As a matter of fact, we can recognize in this notion an abbreviated and backwards application of several of my considerations on the mirror stage and the narcissistic relationship; they were part of the theoretical baggage of the authors who brought so-called "analytic action" to the fore at a time when they could not situate its place with more encompassing references.

560

In fact, everything that is organized in such terms – relating psychoanalytic experience to something that is supposedly based, in the end, on reality, and takes this reality as the standard of what must be eliminated in the transferential relationship, correlating this eliminating action with the more or less thought-out notion of "ego distortion" [distorsion du moi] with reference to what supposedly subsists in the ego that might possibly function as an ally in the endeavor to reduce analysis to a specific reality – does no more than restore the separation between doctor and patient on which the entire classical nosography is based.

In and of itself, this does not constitute an objection; but the ineffectiveness of a subjective therapeutics that is in no way distinguished from pre-analytic psychotherapy does. The patient's experience is delivered over here to the omnipotent norm constituted by the physician's judgment. Although the patient is assuredly taken to be a man like oneself [semblable], he is viewed as following the wrong path, with everything that this brings with it as concerns distance and uneliminable misrecognition. The intersubjective structuring that analysis establishes is strictly distinguished from the one that came before, in that, as far from our norms as the patient may be – possibly even verging on psychosis and madness – we assume him to be our fellow man, to whom we are linked by the bonds of kindness [*charité*] and respect for [those made in] our image.

Such a relationship undoubtedly constituted historical progress in our way of behaving with mental patients. But the decisive step established by psychoanalysis was to consider the patient essentially, owing to his nature, as a speaking subject who, regardless of his position, is caught up – just like we are – in the consequences and risks speech entails.

This perspective suffices to thoroughly change our relations with this passive subject. Indeed, it implies that desire, far from being equatable with the feeling of an obscure and radical pressure [*poussée*], is situated beyond it.

This drive, call, or pressure is only of interest, exists, is defined, and is theorized by Freud inasmuch as it is caught up in the unusual temporal sequence that we call the signifying chain. This chain has a marked impact on everything we deal with, such as pressure. The signifying chain disconnects pressure from everything that defines it and situates it as life-sustaining, rendering it separable from everything that assures its living consistency. The signifying chain makes it possible – as Freud proposes right from the beginning – for the [drive's] pressure to be separated from its source, object, and tendency [or: (pre)disposition, *tendance*], as it were. It is even separated from itself, since it is recognizable in an inverted form in the tendency. This pressure is primitively and primordially decomposable and decomposed, and in short, in a state of signifying decomposition.

Desire is not this sequence. It is a mapping of the subject with respect to this sequence, whereby he is reflected in the dimension of the Other's desire.

Let us take an example. Let us consider the earliest form of it that we find in psychoanalytic experience – namely, the child's relationship to a newborn who enters the family constellation.

What people call in this case an "attack" is not an attack, it is a death wish. As unconscious as we assume it to be, it is something that is expressed as follows: "Would that he die!" [*Qu'il meure !*] And this can only be conceptualized in the register of articulation – in other words, where signifiers exist. The rival semblable is attacked in articulated signifying terms, however primitive we assume them to be, whereas an animal, when he attacks his little semblables, bites them, pushes them, and even shoves them out of the nest in which they are fed. The fact that this early rivalry becomes unconscious [in human beings] is related to the existence of an articulation, as rudimentary as we may assume it to be, whose nature is not essentially different from that of the spoken articulation "Would that he die!"

It is because signifiers are involved here that "Would that he die!" can remain hidden behind "Oh, he's so cute!" or "I love him," which is the later discourse that is superimposed on the earlier one. The desire we deal with is situated in the gap between these two discourses.

We might hypothesize that Melanie Klein's bad object is constituted in this gap. We see now how the rejected drive and the introjected object can converge here in such an ambiguous manner.

But how is their relationship in the gap structured? What form does the imaginary function take on here insofar as it is attached to and reaches the two chains of discourse, the repressed chain and the patent, manifest chain?

In order to know exactly at what level desire is situated, we must now go into this in detail.

2

You may at some point have gotten the impression, or suggested, that my conception of desire here is phallocentric.

It is quite obvious that the phallus plays an essential role in this dialectic. But how can we truly understand its function without the help of the ontological landmarks that I am attempting to introduce?

Let us first see how we can conceptualize Klein's use of the phallus, when she deals with a child's earliest experience.

At a point in time at which a child is caught up in certain developmental difficulties that can, at times, be severe, Klein will immediately interpret the little toy he is holding – with which he touches something else in the course of the play with which the analysis begins – by saying: "That is daddy's penis."

Someone who is not part of her group recounted these experiences to me very faithfully. No one outside her group can fail to be somewhat shocked by the incredibly brutal brazenness of such an interpretation – but still more by the fact that, in the end, it takes. In certain cases the child may resist the interpretation; but if he does, it is assuredly, and Klein does not doubt this, because something is at stake there which must not make us despair that it will not be comprehended later on. And Lord knows that Klein allows herself to repeat her interpretations again and again.

It is clear that the phallic symbol enters into the child's play at this very early stage, as if the subject were merely awaiting it. Klein at times justifies her interpretive use of the phallus by saying that it is simply a nipple that is easier to handle and more convenient, but this is tantamount to begging the question. What justifies such an interpretation in our register can only be expressed in the following

562

563

terms: in most cases, the child has only the most indirect experience of this object and accepts it only as a signifier. It is as a signifier that the impact of the phallus is justified most clearly.

We are perhaps doomed to never know whether a child, at his age, takes the phallus to be a signifier or an element of reality. But what is clear is that whenever Klein refers to the phallus, it is because, whether she knows it or not, she has no better signifier of desire at her disposal.

If there is something that the phallus qua signifier signifies, it is desire for the Other's desire [*désir du désir de l'Autre*], and this is why it plays its specific role at the level of the object. Nevertheless, I am far from remaining in the phallocentric position that is attributed to me by those who look only at the outer appearance of what I am in the process of formulating. The true problem lies elsewhere. The true problem is that the object we are dealing with from the outset when it comes to desire is in no wise an object that is predestined to satisfy the instincts, in no wise an object destined to satisfy the subject by serving as his instinctual complement; the object of desire is the signifier of desire for desire [*signifiant du désir du désir*].

The object of desire – in other words, object *a* on the graph, if you will – is actually the Other's desire insofar as it comes to the attention [or: knowledge or consciousness, *connaissance*] – assuming the word has a meaning – of an unconscious subject. Which is to say that the object is in a contradictory position with respect to the unconscious subject; this is indicated by the formulation "consciousness of an unconscious subject." The latter is not at all unthinkable; it remains an open question, which means that, if the object comes to [the attention of] the unconscious subject, it comes there insofar as the object is itself the wish to recognize it, being a signifier of its recognition [*reconnaissance*]. In short, desire has no other object than the signifier of its recognition.

The character of the object qua object of desire must thus be sought out where human experience shows it to us in its most paradoxical form – that of fetishes, as we commonly call them.

Fetishes are always more or less implicit in everything that generally constitutes objects of exchange among people; but they are of course masked there by the regular or regulated nature of these exchanges. People have spoken about commodity fetishism, and it is not simply a homophony, for the two uses of the word "fetish" definitely share a meaning. Nevertheless, when we talk about the object of desire, we must first and foremost emphasize the fact that it is borrowed from signifying material.

"I saw the devil the other night," Paul-Jean Toulet says somewhere, "and when you look under his fur . . ." The poem ends with

"The fruits of Science do not all fall, you see!" Well, let this be the case for us here, too, that they do not all fall – so that we will perceive that it is less the hidden fruits than the mirage, or fur, present in desire that counts. A fetish is in fact the fur, edge, fringe, or frill, the thing that hides, and nothing is better designated to serve the function of signifier of the Other's desire.

Let us start again from the child's relationship to the demanding subject [or: the subject to whom he addresses his demands, *sujet de la demande*]. In this relationship, the child first deals with the mother's desire – in other words, with what the demanding subject truly is apart from demand. Now, the child cannot decipher this desire, if not in the most virtual way, by means of a signifier – a signifier that we analysts, regardless of what we do in our discourse, relate to the phallus as a yardstick [*commune mesure*], a central point of the signifying game here.

The phallus is nothing other than the signifier of the desire for desire. Desire has no other object than the signifier of its recognition. This is what allows us to no longer be dupes of the exchange that occurs at the level of desire, when we realize that the subject has shifted to the other side of the subject/object relationship – namely, that he has become *a*. We must conceptualize the fact that in this position, the subject is no longer anything but the signifier of the recognition of desire, no longer anything but the signifier of desire for desire.

Yet it is important to maintain an opposition, that of $ across from *a*, on the basis of which this exchange occurs. As for the barred subject, he is a subject here who is undoubtedly imaginary, but in the most radical sense, in the sense that he is the pure subject of disconnection or of spoken cuts [*de la coupure parlée*], insofar as such cuts constitute the essential scansions on which speech is built. This subject is grouped here with a signifier that is nothing other than the signifier of the being with whom the subject is confronted, insofar as this being is himself marked by the signifier. As for little *a*, the object of desire, it is a residue or remainder by nature – namely, the residue left by the being with whom the speaking subject is confronted, the remainder of any and every possible demand.

565

It is in this way that the object meets up with the real; it is in this way that the object shares in it. I am saying "the real" here, not "reality," because reality is constituted by all the halters that human symbolism, more or less perspicaciously, throws around the neck of the real insofar as it fabricates the objects of its experience with it. Let us note that what characterizes objects of experience is precisely that they leave aside – as La Palice would say – everything in the object that is not encompassed by this experience.

This is why, as opposed to what people believe, experience, so-called experience, is a double-edged sword. If, for example, you find yourself in a historical predicament, in resolving it your chances of making mistakes, even serious ones, are just as great if you trust to experience as if you neglect it, for the very simple reason that, by definition, trusting to experience involves overlooking what is new in the present situation.

The object at stake, insofar as it meets up with the real, shares in it in the sense that the real here presents itself as what resists demand, as what I will call the inexorable. The object of desire is what is truly inexorable. If it meets up with the real – the real that I discussed when I analyzed the case of Schreber – it is because it is in the form of the real that it best incarnates this inexorability. The form of the real that is called inexorable is found in the fact that the real always returns to the same place.

This is why, curiously enough, we see the prototype of the real in the heavens. How else can we explain man's interest, at the origin of cultural experience, in an object that is truly the least interesting for any purpose that is vital to him – namely, the stars?

If culture and the subject's position in the realm of desire – inasmuch as his desire is established – are fundamentally instituted in this symbolic structure as such, our interest in the stars is explained by the fact that they are what is the most purely real in all of reality.

Their mapping requires a single condition. With respect to what does the shepherd, in his solitude – the first to begin to observe that which has no other interest than the fact that it always returns to the same place – map it if not to that with which he establishes himself as an object – namely, with respect to a kind of slit?

However primitive you may presume them to be, slits are what allow us to map the real when it returns to the same place.

3

This is what we thus arrive at by positing that the object of desire must be fundamentally defined as the signifier of a relationship that is itself a relationship, and that is thus in some sense endlessly reflected.

If desire is desire for the Other's desire, it begins with the enigma of what the Other's desire actually is. The Other's desire is fundamentally articulated and structured in the subject's relation to speech – in other words, in disconnecting from everything that has to do with mere survival.

This desire is the central, pivotal point of the entire economy we deal with in analysis. If we fail to locate its function, we are necessarily led to find our bearings only in what is in fact symbolized by the terms "reality," "existing reality," and "social context." When we stick to that dimension, we are led, it seems, to overlook another dimension, the dimension of desire that Freud especially reintegrated into human experience as something that is absolutely essential.

Here certain facts that I have often relied on take on their value, facts that show what analysts' interventions lead to when they attempt to reduce transferential experiences to the current reality – this oh so simple reality, as people say, as if it were not artifice itself – of the analytic session. We must obviously take up whatever the subject experiences, as naturally as can be – and for good reason, because that is what we expect from him – but we must certainly not reduce it to any immediate reality.

567

I have often emphasized, in different ways, the common characteristic of phenomena that occur whenever analysts' interventions – in an overly insistent and even brutal manner – aim to prove that one of the patient's typical object relations is being repeated in the reality of the analysis. Whereas myriad case studies attest to the regular occurrence of these phenomena, it does not seem that analysts have always identified them.

Whatever the case may be, I will refer once again to the notorious case study that appeared in the *Bulletin des analystes belges* which I have already critiqued once, because it strikingly intersects the article in which Glover attempts to situate the function of perversion in relation to the system of the subject's reality.

In the first case study, the female analyst, when her patient tells her about his fantasy of sleeping with her, literally tells him the following: "You are scaring yourself about something that you know will never happen." This speaks volumes about the style of her analytic interventions. I will not discuss the analyst's personal motives that can be glimpsed here. I will confine my attention to what orients her in her actions, inasmuch as she was being supervised by someone whom I already alluded to today when I spoke about the topic of distance [from the object].

Whatever role panic may have played in this comment on the analyst's part, people will try to justify it as an accurate assessment of the said reality – namely, the relationship between objects in each other's presence. It is clear that this relationship is decisive, because right after the analyst makes this comment, something occurs that is the very topic of the paper: the brutal emergence in the subject of shame that has haunted him, that related to being too tall. Moreover, we find here a whole series of themes akin to those of depersonalization, which must not be underestimated.

This patient was probably not very well diagnosed – he is said to have a phobia, whereas the case definitely suggests traces of paranoid illusions. But what is clear is that what occurs is a neo-formation. The explicit topic of the article is, moreover, what the author refers to as the subject's "transitory perversion" – I am not the one who is saying he had one. For he runs, at a certain point, to a geographic place – a movie theater – where things were arranged in such a way that it was easy for him to observe females urinating, there being a slit in the partition wall between cubicles. This had played absolutely no role in his symptomatology prior to that time.

Now, a similar phenomenon is noted on page 494 of the *International Journal of Psychoanalysis* (XIV, 4 [October 1933]) in Glover's article, "The Relation of Perversion-formation to the Development of Reality-sense." Glover's case is quite similar to the preceding one, in the sense that Glover suggests a diagnosis of para-noia, whereas I would, on the other hand, willingly propose phobia. Interventions on Glover's part – that were undoubtedly similar to those made by the abovementioned analyst – produce an analogous staging of a transitory and occasional perverse explosion. There is no essential difference between the two cases.

This should also be related to an example I emphasized in my paper, "Function and Field of Speech and Language" – namely, Ernst Kris's interpretation of a phobic fear of plagiarizing that a patient of his felt. Kris told him that he was not a plagiarist at all, the patient promptly rushing out of the consulting room and into a restaurant where he asked for a dish of "fresh brains" – to the great joy of his analyst who saw in it a truly significant reaction to his interpretation.

Let us say that this is, in an attenuated form, how the subject's characteristic dimension reacts whenever an analyst's intervention attempts to collapse it, or to compress it into a pure and simple reduction to facts that people refer to as objective, whereas they are merely coherent with the analyst's own biases.

4

If you will be so kind as to allow me to, I will end today with a remark that introduces the place where we analysts must situate ourselves with respect to desire.

This cannot, in fact, work if we do not know how to coherently conceptualize our function with respect to social norms.

If there is a practice that should teach us how problematic social norms are – how much they must be questioned, and how much they are designed to do something other than adapt [people to reality] – it is clearly psychoanalysis.

In our work with the logical subject, a dimension is revealed to us that is always latent, but also always present, in intersubjective relationships. This dimension, which is that of desire, is found in a relation of interaction and exchange with everything that crystallizes on that basis in social structure. If we know how to take this dimension into account, we should arrive at more or less the following conception.

What I designate by the word "culture" – a word I am not very attached to, not at all, when you come right down to it – is a certain history of the subject in relation to logos. This relation to logos was assuredly able to remain masked over the course of time, and in our era it is difficult not to see what sort of gap it represents and at what distance it is situated with respect to a certain social inertia. This is why Freudianism exists in our time.

Some facet of what we call culture passes over into society. We can provisionally define the relationship between culture and society as a relationship of entropy, inasmuch as what passes over from culture into society always includes a disintegrating function.

What presents itself in society as culture – and which has thus entered, in various guises, into a certain number of stable conditions, which are also latent, that determine the circuits of exchanges within the flock – establishes a movement or dialectic in society that leaves open there the same gap as the one in which we situate the function of desire. It is in this sense that we can posit that the perversion that is produced reflects, at the level of the logical subject, a protest against what the subject undergoes at the level of identification, insofar as identification is the relationship that establishes and organizes the norms of social stabilization of the different functions.

Here we cannot fail to see what relates any structure that is similar to perversion to what Freud enunciates in his article "Neurosis and Psychosis" in the following terms: "It will be possible for the ego to avoid a rupture in any direction by deforming itself, by submitting to encroachments on its own unity and even perhaps by effecting a cleavage or division of itself" [SE XIX, pp. 152–3]. Here Freud provides one of those insights that always make his texts especially illuminating, compared to the more ordinary analytic literature we generally read. "In this way the inconsistencies, eccentricities and follies of men (*Inkonsequenzen, Verschrobenheiten und Narrheiten der Menschen*) would appear in a similar light to their sexual perversions, through the acceptance of which they spare themselves repressions" [p. 153].

Freud is targeting here, in the clearest fashion possible, what

570

presents itself in our social context as paradoxes, inconsistencies, confusional states, and madness. *Narr* means "court jester" in the fabric of the most common and ordinary social life.

We could say, in short, that something like a circuit is established that alternates between, on the one hand, the conformism, or socially conformist forms, of so-called cultural activity – the term "cultural" truly outdoes itself here, defining everything about culture that is capitalized on and becomes alienated in society – and perversion, on the other hand, inasmuch as perversion represents, at the level of the logical subject, and through a series of gradations, a protest that, with regard to conforming, arises in the dimension of desire, insofar as desire is the subject's relation to his being.

Here we encounter "sublimation," a notorious notion that we will perhaps begin to discuss next year. In truth, nothing better justifies what I am in the process of endeavoring to propose than Freud's notion of sublimation.

What exactly is sublimation? What can it be, if we define it, as Freud does, as "a sexual activity insofar as it is desexualized"? How can we even conceptualize such a thing, when what is involved no longer includes a source, a direction of the tendency, or an object, involving instead the very nature of what is called, in this case, the energy invested.

In order to grasp to what degree this notion is problematic, I think it suffices to read an article by Glover in the *International Journal of Psychoanalysis* in which he broaches the topic of sublimation, with the critical concerns that are uniquely his. This notion remains problematic, unless we define it as the very form into which desire flows. What Freud in fact indicates is that this form can be emptied of the sexual drive; or, more precisely stated, that the drive, far from being equatable with the substance of sexual relations, is this very form. Put differently, the drive can ultimately be reduced to the pure play of the signifier. Which is how we can define sublimation as well.

Sublimation, as I wrote somewhere, is that by which desire and the letter can be equated. Here – at a point as paradoxical as perversion is, perversion being understood in its most general form as what in human beings resists all normalization – we can see a discourse being produced, a process apparently starting from nothing [*élaboration à vide*] that we call sublimation, and which is, in both its nature and its products, distinct from the social value it will later be granted. The difficulties we find in attaching the notion of social value to the term "sublimation" are especially well brought out in the article by Glover that I mentioned.

Sublimation is thus truly placed at the level of the logical subject, where everything that is, strictly speaking, creative work in the

571

realm of logos is established and unfolds. On that basis, cultural activities – with all the impacts and risks they involve, up to and including the revamping of formally established conformisms and even their explosion – come more or less to be inserted into society, finding their place at the social level.

To situate at its proper and organizing level what is at stake in desire, we could, at least provisionally, point to the closed circuit constituted by the four terms on the graph: d, ($0a$), S(A), and ($0D$).

The problem we arrive at here is the same one I left you with last year in the paper I gave at the Royaumont Congress, "Direction of the Treatment."

The subject's desire, qua desire for desire, opens out onto the cut or pure being, manifested in A in the form of lack. In the end, what desire does the subject confront in analysis if it is not the analyst's desire? It is precisely for this reason that it is so necessary that we remain mindful of this dimension regarding the function of desire.

Psychoanalysis is not a simple reconstruction of the past, nor is it a reduction to pre-established norms; analysis is neither an epos nor an ethos. If I had to compare it to something, it would be to a narrative that would itself be the locus of the encounter at stake in the narrative.

The problem of analysis resides in the paradoxical situation in which we find the Other's desire that the subject must encounter – that is, our desire, which is only too present in what the subject assumes we are asking from him. Indeed, the Other's desire, which for us is the subject's desire, must not be guided toward our desire but toward an other. We help ripen the subject's desire for someone other than ourselves. We find ourselves in the paradoxical position of being desire's matchmakers, or its midwives – those who preside over its advent.

How can we occupy such a position? It can only be occupied by maintaining an artifice which is that of the whole of the fundamental rule of psychoanalysis. But what is the final mainspring of this artifice? As always, it is both the most trivial and yet the most hidden truth.

Psychoanalysis is undoubtedly a situation in which the analyst agrees to let all demands be addressed to him without responding to any of them. But is the mainspring of our presence found solely in the fact that we do not respond (it being clear that our not responding is far from absolute)? Must we not leave room for an element that is immanent in the situation and recurs at the end of each session? I mean the empty space [*vide*] to which our desire must be confined, the place that we leave for desire so that it can situate itself there – in short, the cut.

The cut is undoubtedly the most effective mode of psychoanalytic

572

interpretation. Many analysts would like to make it mechanical and subject it to a preordained length of time. Well, I not only cut sessions altogether differently, but I add that it is one of the most effective methods of intervening. Let us emphasize this and develop it.

That said, let us not forget the presence, in this cut, of what we have learned to identify as the phallic object, which is latent in every relationship involving demand as the signifier of desire.

573   In closing today, and to remind you of something that will be a sort of pre-announcement of what I will talk about in class next year, I would like to conclude with a sentence that I will propose to you as an enigma. We shall see if you are any better at deciphering spoonerisms than the myriad visitors I have tested.

In a journal entitled *Phantômas* that came out in Brussels around 1953–4, the poet Désiré Viardot proposed a little hermetic enigma, and we shall see if someone in the audience can immediately find the key: "Women have a mark of fancy on their skin" [*La femme a dans la peau un grain de fantaisie*].

This mark [or: touch] of fancy is assuredly what is at stake, in the final analysis, in what modulates and models the relations of the subject on the person to whom he addresses his demands, whoever that may be. And it undoubtedly plays a role in the fact that we discovered the horizon of the subject who contains everything in the form of the universal Mother.

This is what makes it such that we can at times be mistaken about the subject's relation to the All, believing that it will be delivered up to us by analytic archetypes, whereas it is something else altogether that is involved – namely, the gap that opens out onto something radically new that is introduced by any and every cut based on speech.

Here it is not from women alone that we must wish for this touch of fancy – or this "touch of poetry" [*grain de poésie*] – it is from psychoanalysis itself.

July 1, 1959

APPENDIX

MARGINALIA ON THE SEMINAR ON DESIRE

Some useful references,
along with associations that came to mind
by Jacques-Alain Miller.

I   Constructing the Graph

4. Fairbairn

Nowadays, when you come across a name like Fairbairn that you do not know, you look it up on Wikipedia and you find a solid article which, even to someone like me who knew him, is informative. There is a photo of him in uniform, but my impression is that it must be of someone who has the same name as him, the Lieut. Col. William E. Fairbairn [the photo has since been taken down]. In this case, I will simply provide the Wikipedia article [Miller provides the article found at https://fr.wikipedia.org/wiki/William_Ronald_Dodds_Fairbairn; the English-language Wikipedia site is far more extensive.]

After the entry, references are provided. His *Psychoanalytic Studies of the Personality* was published in 1952 by Tavistock and republished in paperback* in 1994 (under the Routledge imprint in the United States and Canada).

6. Roses and lilies [*Les roses et les lys*]

Do a Google search for these words and you find a Wikipedia article about a song written in honor of Henry IV. The song is entitled *Vive Henri IV!* and is said to have been "long popular in France." In the second stanza, added in 1770, one finds the following simplistic verses:

Comme nos pères
Chantons en vrais amis

Au choc des verres
Les roses et les lys.

[Let us sing – as true friends, just like our fathers did, clinking our glasses – to roses and lilies.]
What sorts of examples can we find of what Lacan calls "figurative poetry"? The simplest are the *Blasons du corps féminin*.

6. John Donne
Your turn to look up Donne. I could write at length about the man and his work. At Janson-de-Silly high school, I had an excellent English teacher by the name of Kerst, who wrote some fine textbooks. He had no compunction about making us read, translate, and comment on a poem by Donne entitled *The Flea*, one of the funniest and most erotic poems I have ever read. That gave me a taste for Donne and he remains my favorite English poet. When I met Lacan, I was happy that he knew and liked Donne's work. The fact that Lacan's theory accounts for what I had always experienced – namely, the strong libidinal content of signifying subtleties – played an important role in rallying me to his ideas. I very much admired Jean Fuzier's translation of Donne's poems into French.

577   6. The physical theory of love as opposed to the ecstatic theory of love
Here Lacan follows the work of Pierre Rousselot, *Pour l'Histoire du problème de l'amour au Moyen Age* [*The Problem of Love in the Middle Ages: A Historical Contribution* (Milwaukee WI: Marquette University Press, 2002)], Rousselot having invented this distinction. Those who believe in the physical – that is, natural – conception of love base love on "the natural propensity beings have to seek their own good." Those who believe in the ecstatic conception of love juxtapose love for others with selfish inclinations; to their way of thinking, the more love places the subject "outside of himself," the more closely it corresponds to its concept.
Rousselot was a Jesuit and was Henri de Lubac's teacher. I heard about Rousselot's work through Lacan, but I already knew Lubac from his *Drame de l'humanisme athée* ["Drama (or Tragedy) of Atheistic Humanism"]. François Regnault had me read his treatise on the four meanings of the Scriptures, and gave me Lubac's *La Postérité spirituelle de Joachim de Fiore* [Paris: Editions du Cerf, 2014 (1979–81)] for my birthday. Such admirable scholars! The tragedy of my own atheistic humanism is that I do not appeal to Jesuits. They flocked to Lacan but have deserted me, holding me responsible for Lacan's drift toward logic. Gentlemen, this is a false

and absurd notion, rotten to the core, but as André Maurois, who is quoted in the *Robert* dictionary under the heading *faux* [false], once said, "nothing is more difficult to refute than what is completely false."

7–8. Aristotle on brutishness [or: beastiality]; Spinoza and desire; Lalande's *Vocabulaire technique et critique de la philosophie* [a dictionary]

Look them up yourselves! "Charming Lalande" suggests that Lacan knew him. I know nothing about it. And in my day, people did not read his dictionary.

9. Rauh and Revault d'Allonnes
Check them out yourself.

11. The stimulus-response cycle
People spent a lot of time thinking about this back then. Someone could write a book on its history, and perhaps has already done so. There is, in any case, a well-known book by Canguilhem, *La Formation du concept de reflexe aux XVIIe et XVIIIe siècles* (Paris: PUF, 1955; it was republished by Vrin in Paris in 1994). Regarding the reflex arc in Lacan's work, one should at least be familiar with (1) *Der Aufbau des Organismus*, by Kurt Goldstein [The Hague: Martinus Nijhoff, 1934; *The Organism: A Holistic Approach to Biology Derived from Pathological Data in Man* (New York: Zone Books, 1995)], and (2) Merleau-Ponty's second thesis, *The Structure of Behavior*, which was first published by PUF in 1942 [Boston: Beacon Press, 1963]. Lacan never stopped reformulating his notions about this.

578

11. Three is the minimum number of terms
Lacan is thinking of the schema found in *The Meaning of Meaning*, by I. A. Richards and C. K. Ogden (New York: Harcourt, Brace, 1945 [1923]).

12. The graph
In Lacan's earlier work, see Seminar V where Lacan introduces the first stage of the graph; in his later work, see the article in which he finalizes his conception four years later: "The Subversion of the Subject and the Dialectic of Desire in the Freudian Unconscious," *Écrits*, pp. 671–702. As Lacan himself indicates, this article, which summarized the remarks he made in 1960 at the famous colloquium in Royaumont which was in theory designed to make his ideas known outside of the circle of his students, was not published as

planned, and was not made known to the public or to myself until 1966 with the publication of *Écrits*.

15. Jacques Cazotte's *The Devil in Love*
The Wikipedia.fr article on Cazotte, who died by the guillotine, is excellent. Nevertheless, it fails to mention the following: the very fine text by Nerval on Cazotte in *Les Illuminés*, which one must read; the preface by Nodier on Cazotte in his edition of the *Contes* [Tales]; Breton's preface to the 1954 edition of *Melmoth ou l'Homme errant* (published by Pauvert); Bastien's 1816–17 edition of the *Oeuvres badines et morals, historiques et philosophiques*, which was the first complete edition of the work with the exception of two brochures written on the occasion of the *Querelle des Bouffons*. I was familiar with Cazotte's work, and had read *The Devil in Love*, before meeting Lacan, through Nerval, Nodier, and Breton, and through a book that became very well known by Max Milner, *Le Diable dans la littérature française, de Cazotte à Baudelaire, 1772–1861*, which I purchased at Corti's bookshop which I would stop by at after school at Louis-le-Grand. A textbook published by Hatier in 1984 continued the study from Cazotte to Gracq. Pierre Castex, in his *Anthologie du conte fantastique français* (Paris: Corti, 1963), considers Cazotte to be "the true inventor of modern fantastical literature." Borges wrote a preface for the edition of *The Devil in Love* that came out in *La Bibliothèque de Babel*; it is intelligently discussed by Ricardo Romero Rozas in *Jorge Luis Borges et la littérature française* (Paris: L'Harmattan, 2011), which I have in the form of an e-book. Many different editions of *The Devil in Love* are available today.

16. The "bar"
See *Écrits*, pp. 414–17.

17. *Hilflosigkeit*
On this topic, see Freud's *Inhibitions, Symptoms, and Anxiety*, and Lacan's Seminar X.

18. *Urbild*
This term is repeatedly found in Lacan's earliest texts and Seminars devoted to the imaginary in its relations with the symbolic. The same is true of references to mirror schemas.

19. Man thinks with his soul
This is one of Lacan's favorite sentences. We find this use of the word "with" in the title of "Kant with Sade." By highlighting the instrumental nature of the soul, Lacan is fully aligned with

Aristotle's *De anima* [On the Soul]. According to Aristotle, the soul is analogous to the hand (432a1).

20. Darwin

Lacan is mistaken in thinking that he read this anecdote in Darwin's book, *The Expression of the Emotions in Man and Animals*. It is found in *The Life and Letters of Charles Darwin, Including an Autobiographical Chapter*, which was edited by his son, Francis Darwin (London: John Murray, 1887); here is the relevant passage from volume 1, page 75:

> Of other great literary men, I once met Sydney Smith at Dean Milman's house. There was something inexplicably amusing in every word which he uttered. Perhaps this was partly due to the expectation of being amused. He was talking about Lady Cork, who was then extremely old. This was the lady who, as he said, was once so much affected by one of his charity sermons, that she borrowed a guinea from a friend to put in the plate. He now said "It is generally believed that my dear old friend Lady Cork has been overlooked," and he said this in such a manner that no one could for a moment doubt that he meant that his dear old friend had been overlooked by the devil. How he managed to express this I know not.

Who was Sydney Smith? "An English wit, writer and Anglican cleric," according to Wikipedia.org, which provides a fine article on him. We learn there that he may have been the model for Henry Tilney, the hero of *Northanger Abbey*, which is perhaps Jane Austen's most beautiful novel.

22. *Volpone*

This is a reference to the play by Ben Jonson, *Volpone, or the Fox*, a fox hated by Christine Angot who only liked hedgehogs.

The entire text has been made available online by Project Gutenberg, and includes the following introduction:

> The greatest of English dramatists except Shakespeare, the first literary dictator and poet-laureate, a writer of verse, prose, satire, and criticism who most potently of all the men of his time affected the subsequent course of English letters: such was Ben Jonson.

I first discovered the play through the film by Maurice Tourneur made in 1941, starring Harry Baur (as Volpone), Louis Jouvet, and

Charles Dullin. I liked the film because the minor role of Voltore was played by Jean Témerson, the younger brother of Louis Témerson (known as Bébé), who was a neighbor of mine and had been wounded in the First World War; he and his wife Juliette (often called Yéyette) would look after my brother and me when my parents went out. Bébé's wisdom had a profound influence on me. He was a serious *marcheur* [womanizer], as people put it at the time, and he strongly advised me not to defer experiencing the pleasures the opposite sex could offer me. It is to him that I owe having understood already at ten years of age the meaning of the expression, rarely used today, "half-virgin" [*demi-vierge*]. The Témersons were Jewish, and acting in a film in 1941 must have been rather complicated for them. When I read the stenography of this Seminar for the first time, I was enchanted to see that Lacan knew the play.

The article provided by Wikipedia.org is solid. I would like to have read everything listed under the heading "further readings," but the truth is that I have read none of the works included there.

23. The absolute master
This is an allusion to Hegel's master/slave dialectic.

23. "The tribe's words"
This is a reference to Mallarmé's verse "*donner un sens plus pur aux mots de la tribu*," found in *Le Tombeau d'Edgar Poe*. [In English, see "The Tomb of Edgar Poe," translated by Peter Manson (Miami, FL: Miami University Press, 2013):

They, like an upstart hydra hearing the angel once
purify the meaning of tribal words
proclaimed out loud the prophecy drunk
without honour in the tide of some black mixture.]

24. Ear, skin, even the phallus
The pointy leaves of red Romaine lettuce are known in France as *oreilles du diable*, "devil's ears." The sea, when it is whipped up by a choppy swell, is described as *la peau du diable*, "the devil's skin." The devil's tail [or: dick, *queue*] figures in the French expression, *tirer le diable par la queue* [literally, to pull the devil by the tail; figuratively, to live from hand to mouth].

II   Further Explanation

Here and there in the chapter: Glover, Sartre, Judge Schreber, Abelard and Heloise, and Freud I'll let you look them up yourselves.

III   The Dream about the Dead Father

50. Marjorie Brierley   582
Brierley was a Kleinian analyst (1893–1984) whose contributions were collected in *Trends in Psycho-Analysis* (London: Hogarth, 1951). Her article "Affects in Theory and Practice" [*IJP* 18 (1937): 256–68] had a significant impact.

55. Believe we believe, as Prévert puts it
A reference to Jacques Prévert's famous "*Tentative de déscription d'un dîner de têtes à Paris-France*" (in *Paroles* [Paris: Gallimard, 1949], p. 7).

56. Psychologists from what is known as the Marburg School; Brentano
Brentano is a crossroads where Freud, Husserl, and Heidegger all meet up. Freud was especially interested in his *Psychologie vom empirischen Standpunkt* (Leipzig: Duncker & Humblot, 1874) [*Psychology from an Empirical Standpoint* (London and New York: Routledge, 1973)], from which Husserl drew the notion of intentionality, and Heidegger was especially interested in his book on Aristotle, *Von der mannigfachen Bedeutung des Seienden nach Aristoteles* [Hildesheim, Zurich, and New York: Georg Olms, 1984 (1862); *On the Several Senses of Being in Aristotle* (Berkeley, CA: University of California Press, 1975)]. Freud and Husserl both came from Moravia. Judith and I made a pilgrimage to Prague when Czechoslovakia still existed. We visited the Spielberg in memory of Fabrice del Dongo; Freiberg (Pfibor) in memory of Freud; Prostejov in memory of Husserl; and the Kromeriz Castle to contemplate Titian's *The Flaying of Marsyas* for a full hour. Ernst Mach was also born in Moravia, as was Gödel, not to mention Mendel, Mucha, Schumpeter, Zatopeck, or Alfred Brendel. Or Janacek or Kundera. It is a place where the Spirit has passed.

The Austro-Hungarian Empire was a prison for certain peoples, but it also allowed kids born in the boonies like Freud and Husserl to have fine careers, one in Vienna, and the other in Germany.

Lacan was fond of empires, and at the age of twenty he thought of moving to the French colonies, partly in order to spread Charles Maurras's ideas.

Brentano was the nephew of Bettina von Arnim, a strange bird. Wikipedia has a suggestive article on her.

IV   Little Anna's Dream

71. Binet

This example has become famous since the publication of Seminar XI, *The Four Fundamental Concepts of Psychoanalysis*, in which Lacan referred to it. It comes from Alfred Binet and Théodore Simon, *La Mesure de développement de l'intelligence chez les jeunes enfants* (1905), in the chapter entitled "critique of absurd sentences," which can now be found in the form of an e-book published by L'Harmattan. I'd like to publish e-books from now on. I want to, I just don't know how to.

Binet was born Alfredo Binetti and was from Nice. He was Babinski's protégé. "He married the daughter of the embryologist, Édouard-Gérard Balbiani, and began studying natural science at the Sorbonne under his father-in-law's supervision." Isn't that unbelievable! He studied under the supervision of his wife's father! Isn't that against the law? And such a one claims to measure intelligence!

V   The Dream about the Dead Father (II)

86. *Être une belle fille* ["To be a beautiful blonde"]

The poetess in question is Lise Deharme (1898–1980), who was one of Surrealism's muses. André Breton, whom she is said to have "fascinated," turned her into the character Lise Meyer in his novel *Nadja*. She was a brunette and somber. She established a literary salon in Neuilly and, in 1933, created an ephemeral journal, *Le Phare de Neuilly*, to which Lacan contributed his well-known sonnet, *Hiatus irrationalis*. That same year, she brought out a small collection of poetry, *Cahier de curieuse personne* (Paris: Cahiers Libres, 1933), in which we find the poem entitled *Voeux secrets* (p. 27). The text of the poem is preceded by an epigraph from Louis Aragon's work: "Des chansons sortaient de la bouche des égouts" [Songs came out of the mouth of sewers (or manholes)], which comes from his poem, *Transfiguration de Paris* (found in *La Grande Gaîté* [Paris: Gallimard, 1929]).

VII   Desire's Phallic Mediation

115. Trotsky's dream
See *Trotsky's Diary in Exile, 1935* (Cambridge, MA, and London: Harvard University Press, 1976). Trotsky was better than the Trotskyites, just as Lacan was better than the Lacanians. For Jesus and his followers, that is obvious. Have masters always been better than their disciples? No. Consider, for example, Aristotle and Alexander the Great. Or Raymond Aron and Kissinger. In science, the disciple is there to go further than the master. But a problem arises when the scientific spirit disappears. Yet in science, too, it is something of a knife fight.

123. A recent novel
The novel in question was *Histoire d'O*, which was overly kitsch. I never liked the story. It's shoddy. It was clear that it was "Made in Gallimard," just as Robbe-Grillet's eroticism was "Made in Minuit." I read it shortly after beginning my studies at l'École normale supérieure. The only funny moment comes right at the beginning, when he asks O to take off her panties in the taxi. Nothing to write home about. Sade's *Juliette* and *Justine* are solid gold ingots. No comparison.

VIII   The Little Cough as a Message

142. Ella Sharpe
See Ella Freeman Sharpe, *Dream Analysis* (London: The Hogarth Press and the Institute of Psycho-Analysis, 1937). A new edition came out in 1978 with a preface by Masud Khan.

IX   The Fantasy about the Barking Dog

166. Darwin
Darwin granted his young disciple George John Romanes access to his notes. The anecdote is recounted in a book written by Romanes, *Mental Evolution in Man: Origin of Human Faculty* [London: Kegan Paul, Trench & Co., 1888], in Chapter 13 entitled "Roots of Language," p. 283. Psychologists who specialize in language acquisition consider the following passage to be the first observation of the phenomenon that is known today as "overextension":

For instance, the late Mr. Darwin gave me the following particulars with regard to a grandchild of his own, who was then living in his house. I quote the account from notes taken at the time.

"The child, who was just beginning to speak, called a duck 'quack'; and, by special association, it also called water 'quack.' By an appreciation of the resemblance of qualities, it next extended the term 'quack' to denote all birds and insects on the one hand, and all fluid substances on the other. Lastly, by a still more delicate appreciation of resemblance, the child eventually called all coins 'quack,' because on the back of a French sou it had once seen the representation of an eagle. Hence, to the child, the sign 'quack,' from having originally had a very specialized meaning, became more and more extended in its signification, until it now serves to designate such apparently different objects as 'fly,' 'wine,' and 'coin.'"

X   The Image of the Inside-Out Glove

178. Limericks
I am inclined to think that the collection Lacan consulted was the one that was, at the time, the most complete: *The Limerick: 1700 Examples with Notes, Variants, and Index* by Gershon Legman, published in English in Paris by the *École des Haute Études* in 1953. The author, who was an American persecuted for obscenity by the U.S. Postal Service, was forced to go into exile. He later brought out *The New Limerick: 2750 Unpublished Examples, American and British* (New York: Crown Publishers, 1977). The article about him on Wikipedia.org depicts him as a rather colorful nonconformist.

Just for the heck of it, I will provide here a few other vaginal limericks:

There was a fat lady of China
Who'd a really enormous vagina,
And when she was dead
They painted it red,
And used it for docking a liner.

There once was a lady from China
Who went for a cruise on a liner
She slipped on the deck
And twisted her neck
And now she can see right behind her.

586

The was a young lady from Cue
Who filled her vagina with glue.
She said with a grin,
"If they pay to get in,
They'll pay to get out of it too . . ."

180. Christina, Queen of Sweden
The flattering physician was French: the abbot Bourdelot. I assume
that Lacan had read the anecdote in René-Jean Denichou's doctoral
dissertation in medicine entitled *Un Médecin du Grand Siècle: l'abbé
Bourdelot* (Paris: Louis Arnette, 1928). Dr. Bertrand Lahutte tried
to find the book for me at the *Bibliothèque interuniversitaire de santé*,
but it was not there.

XI Sacrificing the Taboo Queen   587

198. *Femina penem devoret*
The stenography reads "*femina curam et penem devoret,*" which
is obviously erroneous. No matter how I varied the terms or put
them together, I was unable to find any corresponding literary
or medical expression using Google. Nor was I able to find any
enlightenment in [Krafft-Ebing's] *Psychopathia Sexualis*, in James
Noel Adam's *Latin Sexual Vocabulary* (Baltimore: Johns Hopkins
University Press, 1982), or in several other collections of maxims.
Nevertheless, Google provided one and only one occurrence of two
of the words together: *penem devoret*. It occurs in a passage of the
German edition of the *Kamasutra* (II, 9, 19) regarding the "mouth
congress," *auparishtaka*, in the ultimate form known as *sangara* (in
Latin, *devoratio*), in which the partner puts the entire penis in his or
her mouth in order to stimulate it to ejaculation.
     In any case, longstanding medical tradition has generally pre-
ferred to employ Latin when sexual, salacious, and scabrous matters
are being discussed. In this case, the formulation chosen by Lacan
undoubtedly refers to fellatio, which he figuratively associated with
the words "to get my penis" before rejecting this reading. It is possible that we are not dealing here with a true citation, but merely an
approximate allusion.
     I have opted to provide in the text a reading which, although
incomplete, is correct; it signifies that "the woman eats up" or
"swallows the penis."

200. Roland Penrose

Lacan may have known him when the two associated with Picasso. Penrose brought surrealism to England and became the main British surrealist artist. The date Lacan provides here suggests that the work in question might have been presented in Paris in 1947 at the famous Surrealist exhibition in Aimé Maeght's gallery. I have never seen a reproduction of it, nor do I know where it is today.

209. Lewis Carroll

The verses cited come from *The Mad Gardener's Song*, which is found in *Sylvie and Bruno*:

> He thought he saw a Garden-Door
> That opened with a key:
> He looked again, and found it was
> A Double Rule of Three:
> "And all its mystery," he said,
> "Is clear as day to me!"

XII   The Laughter of the Immortal Gods

218. St. Augustine

This passage, which is often mentioned by Lacan, is found in Chapter 7 of Book I of Augustine's *Confessions*.

229. The laughter of the gods

This episode is narrated in the *Odyssey*, Book 8, lines 266–369. It has often been represented in art, but people generally leave out the gods who have been summoned by Vulcan. You can find them in the painting by Maarten van Heemskerck, *Vulcan, Venus, and Mars* ([a.k.a. *Mars and Venus Trapped in Vulcan's Net*] c. 1540), which is displayed at the Kunsthistorisches Museum in Vienna.

XIII   Impossible Action

234. These two Alice tales are virtually an epic poem of phallic avatars

Lacan commented on this in a charming little paper that I published in the journal *Ornicar?* [50 (2002): 9–12], entitling it "Hommage rendu à Lewis Carroll."

239. Spell out the great tragedy of Hamlet   589
I have relied here on the text of *Hamlet* provided in 2006 by Ann
Thompson and Neil Taylor in *The Arden Shakespeare*, which is now
in its third edition since 1899. The text has a reputation for being the
best, and the notes it provides help resolve various difficulties.

240. A poison, mysteriously named Hebenon
The reader can find a very complete discussion of the "cursed
hebona" (*Hamlet*, I, i) and the many hypotheses about it put
forward over the centuries in the excellent study by Anatoly
Lieberman entitled *An Analytic Dictionary of English Etymology:
An Introduction* (Minneapolis, MN: University of Minnesota Press,
2008), pp. 110–11. Lieberman concludes that "hebona" undoubtedly stands for "henbane," but that it is impossible to know why
Shakespeare, and Marlowe before him (who speaks of the "juice
of Hebon" in *The Jew of Malta*, 1589) did not use its real name: "It
remains a mystery."

It seems to me that the two poets might well have balked at the
triviality of the word "henbane," which literally signifies "chicken
poison." In French, the plant in question, *Hyoscyamus niger*, is also
known as "pigs' beans."

It is of some interest to know the pharmacological profile and
historical fate of this toxic plant. Like *belladonna* [or deadly night-
shade] and *daturas* [or devil's trumpets], it has an impact on the
central nervous system. It has anesthetic effects, can induce drunkenness, sleep, and/or visual hallucinations, and gives the subject
the feeling he is flying. It was part and parcel of the pharmacopeia
of black magic. Its use as a hallucinogen was already mentioned
in the Sumerian clay tablets; it was used as an aphrodisiac in the
Middle Ages, where it was called "*l'herbe au somme*" (the sleeping
herb or grass); it was used in making a cream that sorcerers were
said, in the sixteenth and seventeenth centuries, to smear on their
bodies before flying off to their witching-hour ceremonies. See,
among others: Anthony John Carter, "Narcosis and Nightshade,"
British Medical Journal, 313 (1996): 1630–2; Anthony John Carter,
"Myths and Mandrakes," *Journal of the Royal Society of Medicine*
96 (2003): 144–7; Claude Myers, "Mythologies, histoires, actualités   590
des drogues" (Paris: L'Harmattan, 2007); and the well-documented
Wikipedia.fr article on *jusquiame noire.*

The infamous Dr. Crippen supposedly poisoned his wife in 1910
with a poisonous alkaloid extracted from henbane, scopolamine.

244. Ophelia floating in her dress
I initially imagined that I would put Millais's *Ophelia* on the cover of Seminar VI. But at the last moment I balked. To illustrate desire, one can do better. I preferred the sinuous, luminous body of Bronzino's *Venus*, surrounded by enigmatic figures whose meaning has never been completely discovered. Lacan liked this canvas.

246. Letourneur
Pierre-Prime-Félicien Letourneur, *libraire du Roy* (the King's book-seller), was the first person to bring Shakespeare to France. He translated all of Shakespeare's work, including *Hamlet* in 1779. This was the translation that Raymond Queneau included in his collection, *Écrivains célèbres* (Paris: Mazenod, 1971).

XIV   The Desire Trap

252. The Impediment of Adipose
The article in question, entitled "The Impediment of Adipose: A Celebrated Case," was published in *Popular Science Monthly* 17 (1880). Its author was Euphemia Vale Blake. It can be found on Wikisource.

252. Someone by the name of Vining
Edward Payson Vining, *The Mystery of Hamlet: An Attempt to Solve an Old Problem* (Philadelphia: J. B. Lippincott & Co., 1881). "For Vining, Hamlet was not only a 'womanly man,' but 'in very deed a woman, desperately striving to fill a place for which she was by nature unfitted . . .'"

252. Goethe
See Wolfgang Höllrigl's *Wenn Shakespeare und Goethe Bridge gespielt hätten. Ein heiterer Versuch, Dichtern und Schriftstellern, die über Bridge nichts geschrieben haben, zu untersteen, sie hätten das getan!* (Munich: Idea Verlag, 1999).

253. Coleridge
Samuel Taylor Coleridge, *Lectures and Notes on Shakespeare and Other English Poets* (London: G. Bell, 1883).

253. Hazlitt
William Haziett, *Lectures on the Literature of the Age of Elizabeth, and Characters of Shakespeare's Plays* (London: R. Hunter, 1817).

267. M. Valdemar
Valdemar is a character invented by Edgar Allan Poe in his 1845 story, "The Facts in the Case of M. Valdemar," which was separately republished as *Mesmerism in Articulo Mortis*, and later as "The Last Days of M. Valdemar." Like "The Purloined Letter," it was included in a collection prepared by Baudelaire, *Histoires extraordinaires* (1856). Lacan refers to it on page 486 of *Écrits*: he compares the IPA to M. Valdemar, and tells us that his own "return to Freud" amounts to giving a decent burial to an organization that has outlived its purpose.

XV The Mother's Desire   592

269. Dover Wilson
John Dover Wilson, *What Happens in* Hamlet (Cambridge, UK: Cambridge University Press, 1951 [1935]).

271. Kyd
It seems that the source of Shakespeare's *Hamlet* was a play by Thomas Kyd that has now been lost, and that scholars designate as the *Ur-Hamlet*.

271. T. S. Eliot
See Eliot's "Hamlet and His Problems," an essay written in 1919, which came out in 1920 in the collection *The Sacred Wood: Essays on Poetry and Criticism*. It was subsequently included in Eliot's *Selected Essays, 1917–1932* (London: Faber and Faber, 1932).

277. An article that came out a few years ago
The article in question is "Hystérie et théâtre" by P. C. Racamier. It came out in the journal *L'Évolution psychiatrique*, 2 (1952): 257–89.

XVI There is No Other of the Other

292. A comment by Coleridge
Coleridge's comment can be found in the annotations he made to his specially bound edition of Shakespeare, specifically those annotations made in preparation for the lecture he gave on January 7, 1819: "Hume himself could not but have faith in this Ghost dramatically, let his anti-ghostism be as strong as Sampson against

ghosts less powerfully raised." The passage is included in *Coleridge's Criticism of Shakespeare: A Selection*, edited by R. A. Foakes (Detroit, MI: Wayne State University Press, 1989), p. 81.

593

This is a supposition on Coleridge's part, for Hume nowhere mentions the ghost in *Hamlet*. Hume's well-known critique of ghosts can be found in his *Enquiry concerning Human Understanding* (London: A. Millar, 1748), Section 10 entitled "Of Miracles."

296. "Oneille," as Jarry writes it
The word is found for the first time in *Ubu roi*: "Un soldat dit: Seigneur Ubu, voilà le ciseau à oneille qui tombe" (Act III, scene 8). It is found anew in Act IV, scene 5: "*Père Ubu : Eh ! sire Cotice, votre oneille, comment va-t-elle? – Cotice : Aussi bien, Monsieuye, qu'elle peut aller tout en allant très mal.*" And so on.

In addition, *L'Almanach du Père Ubu* (1899) includes a calendar in which September 29 is the day of St. Oneille. *L'Almanach de 1901* provides a "pataphysical calendar" on which April 25 becomes Flunky 6, the saints day of hussy Oneille. I did not look any further.

A recent volume devoted to *Ubu enchaîné* [Ubu Bound] says the following about the word "*oneille*": "The *r* in *oreille* (which emigrated to '*merdre*' [a condensation of *mère*, mother, and *merde*, shit]) is replaced by an *n* in order to create a new Ubu-like neologism. '*L'oneille*' is a part of the body that is subjected to Ubu's punishments: the *oneilles* are rubbed, pulled, twisted, ripped off, or plugged up by the *gidouille* [another made-up word meaning something like belly]. Such phonetic distortions roll off Ubu's tongue whenever he loses his cool (and one finds this also in vowels, such as '*ji ti . . .*')." This passage is from the "Dossier pédagogique édité par la délégation à l'action culturelle de l'Académie de Caen," directed by Nicole Cellier and Ivan Perrot, 2012.

According to Carey Taylor, in "Le vocabulaire d'Alfred Jarry," *Cahiers de l'Association international des études françaises*, 11 (1959): 307–22, the word was probably a slang term used by Jarry's fellow students at his high school in Rennes.

Lastly, the Collège de patapsychique published in 1947, through Les Films Arquevit, a brochure entitled *Zoneilles*. It is a film script written by Michel Arnaud, Raymond Queneau, and Boris Vian.

594   **XVIII   Mourning and Desire**

331. The way the wager was structured
The 2006 Arden edition considers the precise terms of the wager to constitute "an insoluble problem" (p. 444), and indicates that a

debate on the topic in the *Times Literary Supplement* on February 6, 2004, was unable to clarify the matter.

XIX   Phallophanies

348. The functions of castration, frustration, and deprivation
Lacan maintains here, in Seminar VI, that prior to this he had left empty the squares corresponding to castration and deprivation in the "agent of frustration" column. However, in Seminar IV, two years earlier, we find on page 59 a table of the three functions, which was completed on page 215; in those two boxes we find "the imaginary father" and "the real father," the explanation for which is found on pages 219–21. Lacan had apparently forgotten he had already completed the table.

350. See Raymond Queneau's novel
Lacan often mentioned the novel by Queneau entitled *Le Dimanche de la vie* (Paris: Gallimard, 1952) [*The Sunday of Life* (Surrey, UK: Alma Books, 2013)], seeing in it an illustration of what awaits man when he arrives at "absolute knowledge" (*das absolute Wissen*), assuming it exists, this being the final stage of the trajectory proposed in Hegel's *Phenomenology of Spirit* (1807).

There is no doubt but that Queneau's novel is full of indications and allusions to Hegel's work, whose presence is constant in Lacan's teaching – especially in the form of the famous master/slave dialectic that Kojève took to be its fundamental matrix. It is well known that Lacan and Queneau both attended the Seminar that Kojève devoted to Hegel's *Phenomenology* from 1933 to 1936. Queneau published a write-up of the Seminar in a book entitled *Introduction à la lecture de Hegel: Leçons sur la Phénoménologie de l'Esprit professées de 1933 à 1939 à l'École des Hautes Études* (Paris: Gallimard, 1947) [abridged and translated into English as *Introduction to the Reading of Hegel: Lectures on the Phenomenology of Spirit* (New York: Basic Books, 1969)]. As for Lacan, who did not often give such praise, he referred to Kojève as "*mon maître*" (my master or teacher) in Seminar VIII, *Transference*. In fact, the only other person that he honored in this way was de Clérambault, whom he called "my only master in psychiatry" (*Écrits*, p. 51).

According to Lacan, Queneau's novel derides men who have attained absolute knowledge. Lacan mentions in this regard "the advent of the lazy bumpkin and of the good for nothing, demonstrating the knowledge that can satisfy animals in the form of absolute laziness" [*Autres Écrits* (Paris, Seuil: 2001), p. 331] as well as "the satiated rest of a sort of colossal seventh day on this Sunday of life on which the human animal can finally shove its muzzle in the grass, the great machine being henceforth calibrated down to the last carat of the materialized nothingness provided by this conception of knowledge" [Seminar IX, class given on November 22, 1961].

Lacan's interpretation here is not original. It stems directly from Kojève's work. According to Kojève, the attaining of absolute knowledge and the concomitant appearance of the "Sage" imply the disappearance of what he calls "Man," the end of history, and a return to our animal nature. To his way of thinking, the novel by his student Queneau described this "post-historical" state of humanity, and he said so in an article written shortly after the novel came out, "Les Romans de la sagesse" [*Critique*, LX (1952)]. This article had quite an impact.

Now, this doctrine of absolute knowledge is completely Kojèvian in inspiration. Hegel did not in any way intend to close his *Phenomenology of Spirit* on this Ubu-like "end of history" that inspired a bestseller by someone who was a neo-conservative at the time, *The End of History and the Last Man* (New York: The Free Press, 1992). Inspired by the fall of the Berlin Wall and the disappearance of the Soviet Union, Francis Fukuyama prophesied "the universalization of Western liberal democracy as the final form of human government."

At the end of Hegel's *Phenomenology*, as a science of consciousness, "pure knowledge distills out, as the final and absolute truth of this consciousness," which "is liberated from its immediacy and its concreteness," as Hegel wrote in his *Science of Logic*. As Gwendolyn Jarczyk and Pierre-Jean Labarrière, whose fine analysis I am following here, indicate, absolute knowledge is, rather, a "level of intelligibility" in which consciousness overcomes its dualism, allowing contingency to find its place in the element of the concept; see *De Kojève à Hegel* (Paris: Alvin Michel, 1996), p. 221, and the entirety of their conclusion.

596   Note, furthermore, that while Queneau's *Sunday of Life* refers to Hegel's *Phenomenology of Spirit*, the expression "the Sunday of life" is found in Hegel's *Aesthetics*, at the end of the chapter devoted to painting, from which the novel's epigraph is borrowed: "it is the Sunday of life which equalizes everything and removes all evil; people who are so wholeheartedly cheerful cannot be altogether evil and base" [G. W. F. Hegel, *Aesthetics: Lectures on Fine Art*, vol. 2, trans. T. M. Knox (Oxford: Clarendon Press, 1975), p. 877].

This passage stems from Hegel's solid praise of the Dutch Protestants, who "had overcome the Spanish despotism of church and crown" [p. 885]. According to him, the Dutch are heroic, prudent, and modest, and rose up "without any fear of exposing themselves to all sorts of danger in face of the tremendous repute of the Spanish domination of half the world" [p. 885]. Through painting, this population "wishes now in painting too to delight in this existence which is as powerful as just, satisfying, and comfortable" [p. 886]. The expression "the Sunday of life" is also found in the introduction to Hegel's *Lectures on the History of Philosophy*: it is the day of the Lord, that allows us to "devote ourselves to what is True, and to bring it to consciousness" (as cited in the Pléiade edition of his complete works, volume 3 [Paris: Gallimard, 2006], p. 1678).

Hegel's sympathy for the institution of the Sunday of life and for the Dutch bourgeoisie, which was industrious and courageous, without being prideful, is thus quite clear, as is Queneau's for these characters, "little people, who are not imbeciles," as he put it in an interview (cited in the above-mentioned edition, p. 1674). In *L'Oeil écoute*, Claudel also spoke about Dutch painting in positive terms, and Roland Barthes saw in Dutch painting "all history reach[ing] the grandeur of its own mystery" (in *Essais Critiques* [Paris: Seuil, 1964], p. 28 [*A Barthes Reader* (New York: Macmillan, 1983), p. 72]).

These positive appraisals contrast with the scorn with which Kojève and Lacan greet the characters in Queneau's *The Sunday of Life*. Must we see in this an aristocratic reaction to the "everyday folk" Queneau included in his novels and about whom he speaks tenderly? It is more complicated than that, and the three pals must be distinguished here.

Kojève could not identify with the rebellious people described by Hegel in his *Aesthetics*. He was, as it were, an Imperial. The admiration he had for Stalin is well documented, and he dreamt of a Latin Empire for France. The ambitions of the Habsburgs certainly did not seem monstrous to either Kojève or Hegel.

To the best of my knowledge, it was Queneau, not Kojève, who mischievously fused the Sunday of life with absolute knowledge, and the chapter on painting in Hegel's *Aesthetics* with Chapter 8 of Hegel's *Phenomenology*. In this way he inscribed the everyday folk in his novels in the sweeping gesture of his sardonic master, who became a member of the Common Market's upper administration.

As for Lacan, the notion of wisdom – promoted by Kojève in "Les Romans de la sagesse" as a state of "perfect satisfaction [. . .] accompanied by a fullness of self-consciousness" – could not but repulse him. To praise the absence of division, whether in the subject, knowledge, or satisfaction, was contrary to his most consistently expressed views. The present Seminar clearly attests to this:

597

Hamlet, a king's son who pretends to be crazy, is the opposite of Valentin Brû [in Queneau's *The Sunday of Life*]. Valentin "devotes his vast leisure time," says Kojève jokingly, "to identifying the nothingness of his subjective certainty with the Annihilation of temporal Being-in-itself." Hamlet's bustling activity, which his uncertainty brings on, is deployed in the dimension of language; and time, with which he is grappling, is not "in itself," but "for others," calibrated to other people's time, as Lacan says. With Hamlet, Shakespeare reinvents the tragic hero, whereas Queneau incarnated the Kojevian Sage in the soldier Brû.

In homage to the master? Or to deride him? The question has long been raised whether Kojève, who published little, rushed to bless Queneau's novel. But this Sage was already a deriding of Hegel by his commentator.

Lacan spoke again about *The Sunday of Life* in his seminar later on. But I have said enough here.

353. A "capital . . . calf"
See *Hamlet*, III, ii, 101–2. Polonius indicates that he once acted the part of Julius Caesar, killed by Brutus, in a play. Hamlet qualifies Caesar as "so capital a calf." The Arden edition suggests that the adjective "capital" may imply a pun on "capitol," and indicates that "calf" also means fool.

XX   The Fundamental Fantasy

361. "The Relation of Perversion-Formation to the Development of Reality-Sense."
I published a French translation, by Jean-Louis Henrion and Sophie Poloczanska, of this article in the journal *Ornicar?*, 43 (1987): 17–37.

368: Anything but fragrant *flatus*
See Ernest Jones's 1922 article, "A Study of the Holy Ghost Concept," found in *Essays in Applied Psychoanalysis*, Vol. 2 (London: Hogarth, 1951), pp. 358–73.

XXI   In the Form of a Cut

375. The process of logical generation
In notes taken by those present at the Seminar, we find the following schema, which appears to represent a reworking by Lacan of the schema he had provided the week before, modified in order to

show in what respect "it is not by examining the Other, but rather by considering what occurs at the level of demand that we are going to extend the process of logical generation":

Table A.1: The Process of Logical Generation

A	$D \rightarrow S(\cancel{A})$
rA	S
a	$\cancel{S}$

To my mind, we have here a quick sketch that was designed to show a specific point in passing. I did not want to include it in the main body of the text since, in the remainder of class XXI, Lacan goes back to commenting on the fuller schema he had provided in class XX.

378. Let us reconsider, for example, Freud's claim, *Wo Es war, soll Ich werden*

599

This is the penultimate sentence in Lecture 31 of Freud's *New Introductory Lectures on Psychoanalysis*, entitled "The Dissection of the Psychical Personality." The last sentence is "It is a work of culture – not unlike the draining of the Zuider Zee" [SE XXII, p. 80].

383. *Sie lieben also den Wahn wie sich selbst*
This sentence is found in a letter to Wilhelm Fliess. See *Briefe an Wilhelm Fliess* (Frankfurt: S. Fischer, 1986), p. 110 [SE I, p. 212].

384. Breathing
Lacan mentions a breathing stage here, comparable to the oral or anal stage, in order to suggest that there is no such thing. Jean-Louis Tristani tried to demonstrate just the opposite in his book *Le Stade du respir* (Paris: Minuit, 1978).

386 and 387. Maine de Biran and Cocteau
I no longer have time to take up the *Mémoire sur la decomposition de la pensée* or *La voix humaine*.

XXII   Cut and Fantasy

392. Imagine that a specular image can subsist independently of any subjective prop
Lacan is alluding here to *The Invention of Morel*, a novel by Adolfo Bioy Casares (who was a friend of Borges's) that Lacan commented

on in Seminar II. The novel came out in 1940 and bears some affinity to H. G. Wells's novel, *The Island of Doctor Moreau*.

600   393. The fable of the white disks and the black disks
Lacan is referring his audience to his paper, "Logical Time and the Assertion of Anticipated Certainty," which came out in the journal *Cahiers d'art*, 1940–4, and was republished in *Écrits*, pp. 161–75. A whole book was devoted to the study of this paper: Erik Porge, *Se Compter trois. Le temps logique de Lacan* (Paris: Erès, 1990). I did a detailed examination of the article in my course, *L'Orientation lacanienne* (forthcoming).

397. Plato long ago compared the philosopher to a good cook
Lacan is alluding here to Plato's *Phaedrus*, 265e. A dialectician must be able to divide things "into species according to the natural formation, where the joint is, not breaking any part as a bad carver might."

398. A very interesting article by Kurt Eissler, that does not go too far
The reference here is to Kurt Eissler's "The Function of Details in the Interpretation of Works of Literature," which came out in *PQ* 28 (1959): 1–20.

404. Walter Wilson Greg
Greg was a major Shakespearean scholar of the last century; Dover Wilson's *What Happens in* Hamlet, which came out in 1935, was dedicated to him. The book's "epistle dedicatory" is a bravura passage. Greg had published an article entitled "Hamlet's Hallucination" in *The Modern Language Review* in October 1917; in that article he made the point about Claudius mentioned by Lacan. Dover Wilson had a revelation when he read Greg's article a month later: "From the first, I realized that I had been born to answer it." He, in effect, dedicated his whole life to *Hamlet*. This extraordinary episode was the inspiration for Pierre Bayard's *Enquête sur Hamlet. Le dialogue de sourds* (Paris: Minuit, 2002).

601   **XXIII   The Function of the Subjective Slit in Perverse Fantasies**

407. I am speaking about Being and the One
I would note here that Lacan was familiar with the work of Étienne Gilson. He very much appreciated his type of erudition.

408. English psychology
I balk at the thought of saying anything here about John Stuart Mill, whose work I studied in the past.

411. There cannot be satisfaction of one person without the satisfaction of all
This is Lacan's version of communism, as inspired by Kojève. He first formulated it, or something like it, in the "Rome Report," if memory serves.

413. *Tartuffe*
Lacan is alluding here to the famous scene in Act V. It was in Lacan's company that I recall seeing the best production of *Tartuffe* I have ever seen, which was directed by Planchon. When I knew Lacan, he almost never went to performances anymore, except those of Fellini, Molière, and Mozart.

413. Arnolphe
Lacan commented on Molière's *L'École des femmes* in his Seminar. Arnolphe's "*Ouf!*" comes in Act V, Scene 9, line 1765. In the latest edition of Corneille's theatrical works published by Gallimard in the Pléiade edition, one finds a note by Georges Couton regarding "*ouf*."

413. Desire can be caught "by the tail"
Lacan is alluding here to the play by Picasso, *Le Désir attrapé par la queue* (Desire Caught by the Tail). The famous group photo by Man Ray was taken at a private performance of the play.

414. A fine case study that came out in Belgium in a little bulletin   602
Lacan is referring here to Ruth Lebovici's case study; see *Écrits*, p. 540.

415. The subject fears that his desire may disappear
This is the well-known "aphanisis" that captured Lacan's attention and that he returned to several times. He ends up saying the following on the topic: "there is no subject without aphanisis (disappearance) of the subject somewhere, and it is in this alienation, in this fundamental division, that the dialectic of the subject is established" (Seminar XI, p. 221). The whole of Chapter 17 [in Seminar XI] is worth reading, as is the paper he comments on there, "Position of the Unconscious" (*Écrits*, pp. 703–21).

416. Paul Éluard
The collection entitled *Donner à voir* [Paris: Gallimard, 1978]
was first published in 1939; it can now be found in volume one of
Éluard's complete works published by Gallimard in the Pléiade
edition. I was unable to find the phrase "*charmantes pulsions vitales*"
[charming life drives].

419. Anatole France [. . .] refers to the *Comte de Gabalis*
The stenography gives the name as Cabanis. The context shows
that Lacan was not talking about the seventeenth-century physi-
ologist, but was referring to a famous book by the abbot Henri de
Montfaucon de Villars, *Le Comte de Gabalis, ou Entretiens sur les
sciences secrètes.*

See the excellent edition of this work edited by Didier Kahn and
published by Honoré Champion in 2010; it includes an adaptation by Blaise de Vignenère of the *Liber de Nymphis* by Paracelsus
(1583). Be sure to read the fascinating introduction. Montfaucon de
Villars's style is borrowed from Pascal's in his *Provinciales*, and his
ideas are borrowed from Descartes. He wishes to "destroy belief in
the Devil's actions."

Lacan liked Anatole France's work. In *La Rôtisserie de la reine
Pédauque,* France includes "editorial notes" referring to cabalists
and their beliefs in sylphs, salamanders, and so on, especially in the
Comte de Gabalis, the 1700 edition of which he recommends.

Coming after Lacan's borrowing of the question "*Che vuoi?*"
from Jacques Cazotte, this allusion to *Le Comte de Gabalis*
demonstrates Lacan's interest in literature *noir*, and also in the
period that saw the decline of magic and the rise of scientific
discourse.

XXIV   The Dialectic of Desire in Neurosis

424. *Unerkannt*
The German term means less what is unknown than what is unrecognized. Lefebvre translated it into French as the *non connu* (not
known). The word can be found in *The Interpretation of Dreams*,
VI, D, regarding the dream's navel: "This [tangle] is the dream's
navel, the spot where it reaches down into the unknown" [this is
Strachey's translation in SE V, p. 525].

424. Little Hans's neurosis
Lacan devoted half of Seminar IV to a commentary on little Hans.
Hans having no recourse when faced with his mother's desire:

Hilflosigkeit. Freud uses the term in his 1917 metapsychological paper, "The Unconscious" [SE XIV, pp. 166–215].

427. The paper I gave at the Royaumont Congress
A reference to "Direction of the Treatment," *Écrits*, pp. 489–542.

430. The so-called law of marriage and kinship   604
Lacan is obviously thinking here of Lévi-Strauss's thesis, *The Elementary Structures of Kinship*.

432. Melanie Klein
The case of little Dick is related by Klein in her article, "The Importance of Symbol-Formation in the Development of the Ego" [*IJP* 11 (1930): 24–39].

432. Cybernetic schemas
See Seminar II, the chapter entitled "Psychoanalysis and Cybernetics" [and *Écrits*, pp. 33–46].

433. A child is being beaten
Freud's article came out for the first time in *Int. Z. Psychoanal.*, 5 (1919): 151–72 [SE XVII, pp. 179–204]. Lacan commented on it in Seminar V, the year before this one, and often referred to it. *La Psychanalyse*, the journal of the Société française de psychanalyse, of which Lacan was one of the editors, published a translation of it.

433. Diogenes the Cynic
Diogenes Laertius, in Book VI, 69, of *Lives and Opinions of Eminent Philosophers*, relates the following about Diogenes of Sinope, also known as the dog: "It was his habit to do everything in public, the works of Demeter and of Aphrodite alike. [. . .] Behaving indecently in public, he wished 'it were as easy to banish hunger by rubbing the belly.'"

XXV   The Either/Or Concerning the Object   605

436. Our Parisian colleagues
Lacan is referring to the article by S. Nacht, R. Diatkine, and J. Favreau, "The Ego in Perverse Relationships," which came out in *IJP* [37 (1956): 404–13] and in the journal of the Société parisienne de psychanalyse the same year [*"Le moi dans la relation perverse,"* *RFP* 20 (1956): 457–78].

437. Polymorphously perverse disposition
Polymorphously perverse tendencies or inclinations were brought
out by Freud in his *Three Essays on the Theory of Sexuality*. This is
common knowledge.

438. So-called tables of correlated stages
See Karl Abraham's 1916 paper, "The First Pregenital Stage of the
Libido," which, according to Ferenczi, earned the author the Freud
prize [in 1918]; see, also, his 1924 "Short Study of the Development
of the Libido, Viewed in the Light of Mental Disorders." Both
articles can be found in his *Selected Papers on Psycho-Analysis*
(London: Hogarth Press, 1927). See Sandor Ferenczi's *A Theory of
Genitality* (London: Karnac, 1989).

439. The supposed "bad distance at which the obsessive stays from
the object"
The reference here is to Maurice Bouvet's notion that Lacan often
takes aim at in the years that followed the 1953 split. See Bouvet's
1958 article, "Les variations de la technique (distance et variations)"
[Variations in Technique (Distance and Variations)] in volume one
of his *Oeuvres psychanalytiques* (Paris: Payot, 1967), pp. 251–93.

440. An article on "drug addictions"* written the year before
The reference here is to Edward Glover's article "On the Aetiology
of Drug-Addiction," *IJP* 13 (1932): 298–328.

440. Melanie Klein
Lacan is commenting here on her 1930 article, "The Importance of
Symbol-Formation in the Development of the Ego" [*IJP* 11 (1930):
24–39].

447. An important thesis on the social signification of
psychoanalysis
Lacan is undoubtedly referring here to Serge Moscovici's thesis,
which was published as *La Psychanalyse, son image, son public*
(Paris: PUF, 1961).

449. "Your daughter is mute"
The expression is from Molière. It is spoken by Sganarelle, speak-
ing about Lucinde, Géronte's daughter, in *The Doctor in Spite of
Himself*, Act II, Scene 4. Here is the passage:

> Which is caused by the acridity of the humors engendered in
> the concavity of the diaphragm, it happens that these vapors

. . . Ossabandus, anorexia, mausoleum, amo, amas, amamus, candida albicians, tyranasaurus rex, potarium, invertabratum, quipsa milus. This is precisely what has rendered your daughter mute.

449. Nestroy
The sentence can be found in "The Question of Lay Analysis," which came out in 1926, regarding psychoanalysis as practiced by those who are not medical doctors [SE XX, pp. 183–258]. This was a crucial episode: Freud argued against the attempt that was being made by doctors to monopolize psychoanalysis. Here is the relevant passage:

If I seem to be aggressive, that is only a way of defending myself. And when I think of all the mischief some analysts have done with the interpretation of dreams I might lose heart and echo the pessimistic pronouncement of our great satirist Nestroy when he says that every step forward is only half as big as it looks at first. (p. 193)

Johann Nestroy (1801–62) was, starting in 1833, a shining light in Austrian culture. He was a satirist. He used irony, insinuation, and Viennese dialect to convey his criticism of the old regime that Metternich devoted himself to defending in Austria and in the part of Europe that was involved in the Holy Alliance. He wrote more than eighty plays from 1840 to 1850. He had a deep influence on Karl Kraus, and was cited several times by Freud, who appreciated his work.

607

XXVI The Function of Splitting in Perversion

454. *Lolita*
Lolita needs no introduction. The book, and then the film by Stanley Kubrick, have been discussed by numerous literary critics. Lacan's clinical commentary here stands in stark contrast to everything else I have read. Nabokov had nothing but scorn for psychoanalysis.

457. *Beyond the Pleasure Principle*
The year that Lacan devoted to Freud's *Beyond the Pleasure Principle* was that in which he gave Seminar II.

457. "I am thinking, therefore I am"

Lacan very often commented on and varied Descartes' formulation of the cogito. See, in particular, "The Instance of the Letter" (*Écrits*, p. 429) and "Subversion of the Subject" (*Écrits*, p. 694); in the latter Lacan identified the signified of the proper name with the square root of negative one, namely, "what the subject is missing in thinking he is exhaustively accounted for by his cogito – he is missing what is unthinkable about him." Later on, Lacan revamped this significantly in Seminar XII and in the summary of that Seminar which he wrote for the *Annuaire de l'École des Hautes Études*.

459. Gillespie

Here are the exact references to the articles by W. H. Gillespie that are cited by Lacan: "A Contribution to the Study of Fetishism," *IJP* 21 (1940): 401–15; "Notes on the Analysis of Sexual Perversions," *IJP* 33 (1952): 397–402; "The General Theory of Sexual Perversion," *IJP* 37 (1956): 396–403.

461. "*Die Ichspaltung*"

Freud stopped writing mid-sentence, as it were, while he was working on his article "*Die Ichspaltung* [The Splitting of the Ego] im Abwehrvorgang [in the Defensive Process]" [SE XXIII, pp. 275–8] and he left it unfinished. Lacan refers to it in the last sentence of his paper on "The Direction of the Treatment" (*Écrits*, p. 537).

462. The article I devoted to the case of André Gide

Lacan is referring here to his paper entitled "The Youth of Gide, or the Letter and Desire" (*Écrits*, pp. 623–44). It originally came out in the journal *Critique* [131 (April 1958): 291–315], and discusses Jean Delay's book, *The Youth of Gide*, and Jean Schlumberger's book, *Madeleine et André Gide*.

462. Ungracious – or even "disgraced," as a certain writer put it – boy

Lacan is referring here to Mauriac, who is cited by Jean Delay in *La Jeunesse de Gide* (*The Youth of Gide*), vol. I, p. 225 n.1.

463. Gide's history

The passages cited by Lacan come from *Si le grain ne meurt*. In the Pléiade edition of Gide's *Journal, 1939–1949* [Paris: Gallimard, 1954], see pp. 386 and 387.

608

XXVII   Toward Sublimation

474. Desire, *cupiditas*
The sentence is from Spinoza's *Ethics*. It opens the appendix to
Book III entitled "General Definition of Emotions," and reads as
follows: "Desire [*cupiditas*] is man's very essence, insofar as it is
conceived to be determined, from any given affection of it, to do
something."

477. Phallocentric conception
In his paper "On a Question Prior to Any Possible Treatment of
Psychosis," Lacan makes the "problem of the perversions" revolve
around a child's identification with the imaginary object of his
mother's desire, insofar as she symbolizes it in the phallus. And he
adds: "The phallocentrism produced by this dialectic is all that need
concern us here" (*Écrits*, p. 463).

478. Paul-Jean Toulet
As a young man, Lacan had a special predilection for this poet.
He cites here a poem from the collection entitled *Les Contrerimes*
(1921), found in *Œuvres complètes*, published in 1986 by Robert
Laffont. Here is the complete text of the poem in question, *J'ai vu le
Diable, l'autre nuit*.

J'ai vu le Diable, l'autre nuit;
Et, dessous sa pelure,
Il n'est pas aisé de conclure
S'il faut dire: Elle, ou: Lui.

Sa gorge, – avait l'air sous la faille,
De trembler de désir:
Tel, aux mains près de le saisir,
Un bel oiseau défaille.

Telle, à la soif, dans Blidah bleu,
S'offre la pomme douce;
Ou bien l'orange, sous la mousse,
Lorsque tout bas il pleut.

"Ah !" dit Satan, et le silence
Frémissait à sa voix,
"Ils ne tombent pas tous, tu vois,
Les fruits de la Science."

482. Ernst Kris's interpretation
Lacan is referring here to Kris's paper, "Ego Psychology and Interpretation in Psychoanalytic Therapy," which was presented in New York in December 1948, and published in *PQ*, 20, no. 1 (1951): 15–30. Lacan had mentioned it in "Function and Field of Speech and Language," but above all in his response to Hyppolite on pages 327–32 of *Écrits*. He often returned to it. I published a French translation of it by Jacques Adam in *Ornicar?* 46 (1988): 5–20.

483. "Neurosis and Psychosis"
This text by Freud can be found in SE XIX, pp. 149–53, and the passage in question is from pages 152–3. Lacan returned to sublimation at some length the next year in Seminar VII.

486. A mark of fancy
The journal *Phantômas* was the main organ of surrealism in Belgium. The first issue was printed on December 15, 1953. Désiré Viardot was one of the three members of the editorial board. Philippe Hellebois was willing to help me find the exact location of the spoonerism cited by Lacan. He found it in Désiré Viardot's *Ripopée*, Brussels (1956), p. 7, in the following form: "Like all women, I have a mark of fancy on my skin." This fifteen-page brochure is presented as the first work in the "collection of experimental literature" by *Phantômas* publishers.

Index

affects
  positional affects related to being
    141
  unconscious 51–2
anal symbolism 106
animal dreams 62–3, 68, 69
animal psychology 105–6, 196
animal subjectivity 416–17
anxiety 3
  as "distress" 17–18, 19–20
"aphanisis" 100–1, 103, 195–6, 229,
    424
  see also "fading of the subject"
Aristotle 7, 19, 139
associationism 45–8
  dreams 168, 173–4, 176–81, 189,
    197–8, 199, 427
  "free association" 46, 138–9
Augustine, St. 218, 219

bad object 444–6, 463, 477
barking dog fantasy 161–7, 174–6,
    197, 220
bed-wetting 154, 207–8, 228
behaviorism 368, 380–1
Being and the One 216, 218–19,
    407–9
Belleforest, François de 291, 303,
    304, 307, 318
Binet, Alfred 71, 72, 79
Boehm, Felix 368, 369
The Book of Common Prayer 200–1
Brandes, Georg 238–9, 241

breast/nipple 121, 219–20, 311, 383
breathing and voice 384
Brierley, Marjorie 50
Brosse, Jacques 105–6
Buffon, Comte de 105–6

"caprice" 102
car (dream image) 182, 186–7, 189,
    206, 207, 221–2, 223–4, 228–9
Carroll, Lewis 167, 208–9, 233, 234
castration 35, 96, 100–1, 103, 117,
    214, 367, 368, 396
  complex 196–7, 201–2, 382, 385,
    415, 458
  frustration and deprivation 348–51
  Hamlet 257
  Other 229, 234
  see also Oedipus complex
cave image in dream interpretation
    177, 185, 186, 189, 195
Cazotte, Jacques 15
censorship 73–4, 79, 279
chess game metaphor 203, 204–6, 225
child case studies
  Dick 432–3, 446
  little Anna 62, 67–71, 72–7, 78
  little Hans 104, 178, 424–6
child development
  graph 13–15, 19
  phallus 121, 219–20, 477–8, 479
  see also object relations theory
"child is being beaten" 109–10,
    121–5, 433–5

child–family relationship 476–7
child–mother relationship *see* mother
childhood dreams 78–9, 136
    little Anna 62, 67–71, 72–7, 78
childhood fantasies/memories 149,
        150, 190, 199–200
    parents' sexual activity/primal
        scene 189, 190, 208, 227, 228,
        423
    pram 190, 200, 204, 206, 223, 227
childhood game (*fort-da*) 415
childhood language 163–7, 220
choice, drive and repetition 394
Christian religion 410, 411, 412, 419
Claudius (*Hamlet*) 240, 241, 242–3,
        247–8, 253, 259, 261, 262–5,
        267, 293, 308, 316–17, 328,
        351–3, 404–5
Cocteau, Jean 387
Coleridge, Samuel Taylor 252, 253,
        292
"colicky pain" 206–7, 227–8
comedy
    as desire trap 413
    see also jokes
conman's game 195–6, 199
consciousness and signifying chain
        392
contiguity in word association
        46–8
continuity and fragmentation
        29–30
contraphobic object 441
countertransference 202, 204
culture and society, perversion as
        protest against 482–5
cut/cutting 381, 382, 383–7, 388,
        396–7, 398, 408, 421, 457, 459,
        485–6
    in literary works of art 400–1

Damourette, Jacques 95
Darwin, Charles
    and the Devil 20–4
    and duck's quack 166–7
death *see* father's death
death instinct 456, 457

defense
    against distress 19–20
    neurosis as 3, 4
Delay, Jean 462–4
"delusion" 382–3, 387–9
demand 17, 27, 28–30, 34, 43–4
    call and wish 118
    and fantasy 391–6
    made to the Other 374–7
    for phallus, women 447–9
    for satisfaction 446–52
"depressive phase" 219, 443
Descartes, René 457
"desire"
    definitions 4–5, 8–9
    and interpretation (overview)
        10–24
developmental theory *see* child
        development; object relations
        theory
dialectic of Being 218–19
dialectic of desire 430–2, 447–9, 451
dialectic with the Other 83–4
Diogenes the Cynic 433–4
disappearance of desire *see*
        "aphanisis"; "fading of the
        subject"
discordance and foreclosure 81–3, 95,
        421, 457
discourse/speech 26–36, 70–7, 88–94,
        370–2, 374–7
    childhood 163–7, 220
    Hamlet 273–7
    poetic 5–6, 16, 85–7
    unconscious 359–60, 367, 454
    see also under Other
displaced desire 105
"distance from the object" 439
    psychoanalysis as adjustment of
        475
"distress" 17–18, 19–20
dog
    barking 161–7, 174–6, 197, 220
    masturbating 167–70, 174, 182–3,
        225
    phallus 224
Donne, John 6

dream interpretation 133–41
  Freud 37–8, 43–5, 52–9, 60–70,
    71–3, 77, 78–9, 86–7, 88–94,
    96–8, 102–3, 112–16, 134–8,
    139–40, 144, 179, 235–6, 255,
    360, 424
  graph of desire 89, 133–4, 136–8,
    158–9, 168, 172–3, 181
  Sharpe 142–51, 152–70, 171–90,
    191–209, 210–11, 220, 221–9,
    233–4, 430
drives 49, 394, 453, 476
drug addiction 440
Dürer, Albrecht: *Melencolia I* 380

ego
  development 440–1, 446
  in discourse 36
  ego-ideal 18–19, 169
  id and superego 40, 239
  in neurosis 451–2
  and Other 116, 172–3, 204,
    432–3
  pressure function 386
  splitting 460–1
  structuring elements of 364
"ego distortion" 475
Einstein, Albert 402
Eissler, Kurt 398–400, 401
either/or of object 451
Eliot, T. S. 106
elision 56, 58
erogenous phases 438
exhibitionism 416, 417–18, 419–20,
    422–3, 424
expectation (*Erwartung*) 125, 295,
    425
"externalization" 443–4

"fading of the subject" 305, 310–11,
    377, 382–3, 424
  see also "aphanisis"
Fairbairn, William Ronald Dodds
    4
fantasy 389, 396–8, 422–4
  constructed retrospectively 443
  construction stages 434–5

and dream, link between 173–6,
    179, 185, 224
  graph of desire 391–6
  object *a* in 382–5
  paradoxes of 309–10, 311–13
  and the subject of unconscious
    discourse 454
  synchronistic function 378–9
  see also neurosis; perverse
    fantasies
father, identification with 108–9
father's death (dream interpretation)
  Freud 53–9, 71–2, 77, 88–94, 96–8,
    112–16, 144, 235–6
  Sharpe 144, 146, 184, 203–4,
    222–3, 226
father's death and ghost (*Hamlet*)
  235–6, 239–44, 247, 253–4,
    258, 259, 264, 265, 274, 278–9,
    296–7, 401–5
  see also Oedipus complex,
    Hamlet
fear of the object 109
female genitals (dream and fantasy)
  176–81, 185–7, 188–9, 195,
    197, 211
feminine and masculine, non-
    separation of 190
Ferenczi, Sandor 62, 438
fetishism/fetishization 312–13, 439,
    478–9
Fliess, Wilhelm 66, 234
foreclosure
  and discordance 81–3, 95, 421,
    457
  and negation 58, 76–7, 81–3, 95
fort-da game 415
fragmentation
  and continuity 29–30
  in dreams 137, 138, 139–40
  of signifier 129, 137
  symbolic and imaginary 128–9
France, Anatole 419
"free association" 46, 138–9
Freud, Sigmund 3, 4, 5, 7–8, 481
  anal symbolism 106
  and behaviorism 380–1

Freud, Sigmund (*cont.*)
  case studies
    Dora 465
    little Hans 104, 178, 424–6
    see also little Anna's dream
  castration 367, 385
  "child is being beaten" 109–10,
    121–5, 433–5
  delusions 383
  discontent in civilization 412
  dreams *see under* dream
    interpretation
  drive 476
  expectation (*Erwartung*) 125, 295,
    425
  and graph of desire 17–18, 26, 34,
    35, 37–8, 39, 40
  homosexuality 368
  I and unconscious desire 377–8
  "kites" 261
  law 429
  masochism 456
  minus phi 350
  mirror illusion 128
  mourning 287, 335–6, 345–7
  neurosis 458
  Oedipus complex 344–8, 447
    see also Oedipus complex,
    Hamlet
  penis envy 125–6, 215
  phallic phase 117–18
  phallus, fear of losing 431–2
  "polymorphously perverse
    disposition" 437
  repression 279
  social context and sublimation
    483–4
  unconscious 48–52
  the uncanny 320
  women's purpose 107–8
"Freudian thing," desire as 358–60
fundamental fantasy *see* ($\$\lozenge a$)
funeral rites 337, 340

garden metaphor of womb 208–9
"genital desire" 4, 410
genital maturity 364

genitals *see* female genitals (dream
    and fantasy); phallus
Gide, André 462–4
Gillespie, W. H. 459–62
Glover, Edward 30–1, 50, 361–3,
    439–40, 441–2, 481, 482, 484
Goethe, J. W. von 236, 252–3
good and bad objects 443–6, 463, 477
Granoff, Wladimir 63
graph of desire
  first stage 11–13, 23
  second stage 13–17, 23
  third stage 17–20, 23
  two levels and four trajectories
    26–36
  two topographies, relationship
    between 39–40
graph of desire (illustrations/
    applications)
  childhood language 165–6
  Darwin and the Devil 20–4
  dream interpretation 89, 133–4,
    136–8, 158–9, 168, 172–3, 181
  fantasy 391–6
  Freud 36–40
  Hamlet 282–90, 297–300, 309–10
  problem of psychoanalysis 485
  see also S(A); ($\$\lozenge a$)
Greg, Walter Wilson 404–5

half-dead, instance of 58–9
hallucinations 52, 63–5, 396
Hamlet 234–48, 413
  Act I 258–9
  Act II 259–63
  Act III 263–5
  Act IV 266
  Act V 266–8
  desire 277–82, 289–90, 291
    graph 282–90, 297–300, 309–10
  encounter with death 292–7
  English performances 256–7
  father *see* father's death and ghost;
    Oedipus complex
  history of commentaries 250–6
  history of 249–50
  as mirror 270–2

mode of discourse 273–7
mother 264, 265, 280–2, 308–9,
  321, 339, 352
mourning and crime 341–4
mourning and desire
  cemetery scene 333–8, 340
  having no object(ive) and
    fantasy of object of/in desire
    (*$◊a*) 324–8
  procrastination and
    precipitation 323–4
  taking action and equivocation
    328–33
  no Other of the Other 324
  "play scene" 280–2
  and Shakespearean women
    characters 300–5
  truth and fantasy 401–6
  see also Ophelia *and main*
    characters
harmony 364, 365
Hartmann, Heinz 364
hidden signifier 159, 299–300
hippopotamus, behavior of 106
Homer 229, 304
homological relationship 36
homosexuality 368–9, 462–7
hood (dream image) 177, 178, 181–2,
  183–4, 186–7, 192, 199, 206,
  211, 221
Horatio (*Hamlet*) 259, 262, 292, 404
hysteria
  lived experience 51
  obsession and neurosis 289–90,
    295, 427–9

I (the symbol)
  as ego-ideal 223
  identification with mother/phallus
    233–4
  integration with reality 457
  Other's image and 220
  statement and enunciation 71–2,
    74–6, 78–9, 82–3, 88–94, 139
  subject of becoming 378
  two levels of 31–3
idea (*Vorstellung*) 51–2, 63, 64, 67

and representation
  (*Vorstellungsrepräsentanz*) 49,
    50–1, 52, 55
identification
  early 473
  with father 108–9
  and mourning 335–6
  with the Other 30–1, 126
  stages 213, 214
imaginary and symbolic 19–20,
  128–9
indestructible desire 86–7
initiation rites, mutilation in 384–6
inscription (*Niederschriften*) 66, 68
instinct 65, 66, 453
"internalization"
  of bad object 444–6
  and introjection 443–4

jealousy 220
  and mourning 333–8
  women 449–50
jokes
  limerick 177–8, 180–1
  and unconscious 60–1
Jones, Ernest 97, 100–1, 107, 108,
  117, 120–1, 126, 194, 196, 219,
  384, 415, 424
  Hamlet 234, 241, 251–6, 269–70,
    278, 279
jouissance
  blocking desire 427
  false 190
  fantasies 463–4
  legal term 105
  masochistic 456
  masturbatory 433–4
  phallus as instrument of 429
  of voyeur 419–20
  see also satisfaction of desire

Klein, Melanie 189, 212, 215–16,
  219–20, 225–6, 311–12, 362,
  432, 440–1, 443–6, 472,
  477–8
knowledge 365, 379–80, 381, 397
Kris, Ernst 482

L schema, the Other in 116–17, 204
Laertes (*Hamlet*) 247, 259, 266, 267,
        268, 288–9, 317, 329–32, 333,
        334, 336
Lalande, André 8, 9, 10
Last Judgment 412
"latent dream-thoughts" 134, 138
law 105, 429–30
Lear, Edward 167
Lebovici, Ruth 414, 416
Lévi-Strauss, Claude 107
libido 4–5, 6–7, 216–17, 305, 438, 441
limerick (young lady from China)
        177–8, 180–1
literary works of art 398–401
        see also Hamlet
little *a* 312, 313–14, 368, 372–3, 377,
        378, 415, 449–50, 478, 479
    and capital A 370–1, 372
    construction and types 382–5,
        387–8
    dream analysis 105, 109, 109–10
    as the Other's desire 421
little Anna's dream 62, 67–71, 72–7,
        78
"little cough" 148–50, 156–9, 169–70,
        173–6, 194, 206, 224, 225
little Hans 104, 178, 424–6
Loening, Richard 254
Lolita 455
love 4–5, 6, 129, 410, 450
Lustprinzip see pleasure principle

Maine de Biran 386
Marburg School 56
Marx, Karl/Marxism 106–7, 313, 396
masochism 123, 455–6
masturbation 144–5, 149, 150–1,
        155–6, 176–7, 185, 188, 190,
        192, 198, 211
    dog 167–70, 174, 182–3, 225
masturbatory jouissance 433–4
mathematical metaphor of phallus
        327
"mature desire" 364
metaphors
    cherries as lips 47–8

dreams as 56–7
garden as womb 208–9
of phallus 327, 420–1
psychoanalysis as chess game 203,
        204–6, 225
metonymy 23, 46, 458, 464
Mill, John Stuart 107
Millais,John Everett 267
mirror, *Hamlet* as 270–2
mirror illusion 18–19, 126–8, 217
mirror stage 386, 444
Molière 413
mother 31
    body in object relations theory
        212, 215–20, 311–12, 383,
        443–4
    Hamlet 264, 265, 280–2, 308–9,
        321, 339, 352
    I as identification with 233–4
    phallic mother fantasy 414
mourning *see under Hamlet*
mouth and vagina 177–9, 181, 185,
        186
mutilation in initiation rites 384–6

narcissism 104, 109, 216, 218, 386
negation (*Verneinung*) 79–80, 81–3,
        95, 214, 421
    and foreclosure 58, 76–7, 81–2,
        95
neurosis
    as defense 3, 4
    essence and characterization 120,
        451–2, 458–9
    Hamlet 324
    historical and modern
        psychoanalysis 471–2
    hysteria, obsession and 289–90,
        295, 427–9
    as not to want the Other to be
        castrated 229
    and paranoid forms of psychosis
        440
    phallus, loss of/absent 431
    structure of fantasy 423–6
    see also little Hans; perverse
        fantasies; perversion

Niederschriften see inscription
"no recourse" when faced with the
    Other's desire 425
"not one" 421, 431

object
    and desire 409–10
    either/or of 451
    function of 412–13
    and signifier 478
    split 460
    and subject 84–5, 98–101, 102–5
object relations theory 438–42,
    443–6, 481
    mourning 335–6
    Other's desire and 307–13
"object-seeking" 4, 6–7, 305
"objectivity" 361–2, 365
obsession, hysteria and neurosis
    289–90, 295, 427–9
obsessive fantasy 433–4
obsessive neurosis 440
Oedipus complex 185–6, 213, 344–8,
    421, 450–1
    dream interpretation 91, 93, 96–7,
        103–4
    girls/women 125–6, 447–9
    Hamlet 278–9, 295–7, 317,
        351–4
        Freud 235–7, 241–2, 245–7, 248,
            251, 255, 257, 293–4, 341–2,
            344
        mourning and crime 341–4
    and phallus 345–7, 351–4
omnipotence 183, 184–5, 189, 192,
    225
One and the Other 217
Ophelia (*Hamlet*) 238, 244–5, 259,
    265, 267, 302–5, 306–7
    cemetery scene 333–8, 340
    as desire trap 307
optimal genital development 120
"oral-anal" phase 118, 362–3,
    383–4
oral-sadistic stage 383
Other
    castration 229, 234

demand made to 374–7
dialectic with 83–4
discourse/speech 367, 375–7, 456
    Hamlet 276, 282–7, 294–5
    and signifier 158–9, 168, 172–3
and ego 116, 172–3, 204
and exhibitionist/voyeur 417–18,
    420, 423, 424
and hysterics/obsessives 427, 428–9
identification with 30–1, 126
image and I 220
L schema 116–17, 204
and no Other of the Other 324, 372
"not knowing" 240–1
One and 217
and phallus 212–13, 225, 300
and phobic object 425–6
real (rA) relationship 374–5, 429
relationship with 13, 14–15, 16–17,
    18–19, 23, 34
and S(Ⱥ) 297–300, 324, 395,
    449–50
signifier 158–9, 168, 172–3, 395
    and mourning 336–7
in synchronic relationship 370–2
see also little *a*
Other's desire 476, 478, 479, 480–1,
    485
    in neurosis 466
    object relations theory 307–13

pain
    "colicky pain" 206–7, 227–8
    and death of father 90–3, 96, 113,
        115–16
paranoid phase 362–3, 440, 443
parents' sexual activity/primal scene
    189, 190, 208, 227, 228, 423
Pascal, Blaise 318
paternal metaphor, phallus as 421
penis *see* phallus
penis envy 125–6, 215
Penrose, Roger 200
perverse fantasies 416, 420–1, 422–3,
    437–42
    and neurotic fantasy, distinction
        314–15

perverse fantasies (*cont.*)
and perversion, distinction 436–7,
454–5
subjective slit in 418, 419, 420, 424
perversion 362, 459–62
as brutishness 7
function of 442
function of splitting in 460–7
and perverse fantasies, distinction
436–7, 454–5
as protest 482–5
transitory, during psychoanalysis
414–15, 482
see also women/girls
phallic mother fantasy 414
phallic phase 117, 120–1, 219, 350
in women/girls 125–6, 194, 214–15
phallic woman fantasy 180
phallus 429–31, 464, 465–6
artificial phallophanies of analysis
368
barred 452
"big enough" 99–100
in child development 121, 219–20,
477–8, 479
and dialectic of Being 218–19
dog 224
in dream 144, 187, 191, 197–8, 199,
208, 211, 224–5
Hamlet 330, 331, 333, 345–7, 351–4
in initiation rites 385, 386
loss of/absent 345–7, 373, 431–2
see also castration
mathematical metaphor of 327
and object of desire 321
in Oedipus complex 345–7, 351–4,
450–1
and the Other 212–13, 225, 300
as paternal metaphor 420–1
in psychoanalytic experience 212
as signifier 23–4, 101, 104, 120,
128–9, 204–6, 211, 213, 214,
225–6, 385, 429, 448, 478,
479, 486
and subject 213, 214
tumescence/pressure 386–7
see also women/girls

phobias 425–6, 441–2, 482
Piaget, Jean 71, 72
Picasso, Pablo 123–4, 413
Pichon, Edouard 81–2, 95
Plato 47, 216, 397
pleasure principle
and idea (*Vorstellung*) 63, 64, 67
and reality principle 52, 65–6, 67,
112, 358–9, 360–1
"pleasure-seeking" 4, 6–7, 305
poetic discourse/poetry 5–6, 16,
85–7
Polonius (*Hamlet*) 232, 237, 245,
259–60, 265, 266, 319, 321,
337–8, 353
"polymorphously perverse
disposition" 437
pram in childhood memories 190,
200, 204, 206, 223, 227
pregenital object 382, 383, 396–7
primal scene/parents' sexual
activity 189, 190, 208, 227,
228, 423
primary process 52, 63–7
primary masochism 123
prisoners' fable 393–4
projection 443–4
Proudhon, Pierre-Joseph 106–7
psychoanalytic theory 3–4, 9–10
and reality 436–7
see also object relations theory;
specific theorists
psychoanalytic experience 357–60,
446–7, 471–7, 481, 482–6
chess game metaphor 203, 204–6,
225
phallus in 212
subject and object 84–5, 98–101,
102–5
symptoms 111–12
unconscious vocabulary 119

Queen of Sweden 180
Queneau, Raymond 229, 350

Raimund, Ferdinand 399, 401
Rank, Otto 262–3

real and object 479–80
reality 379–81, 396–8
  and desire 361–6
  developmental construction of
    439–42
  and fantasy "cure" 414–15
  presumed by analyst 473
  and psychoanalytic theory 436–7
  of subject 381
  and symbolic 408
reality principle and pleasure
    principle 52, 65–6, 67, 112,
    358–9, 360–1
reality testing 442
realization of desire 412
religion 410, 411, 412, 419
Renoir, Jean 85
representation
    (*Vorstellungsrepräsentanz*) 49,
    50–1, 52, 55
repressed representation 49, 50–1,
    55
repressed signifiers 140
repression
  censorship 73–4, 79, 279
  and elision 56, 58
  topology of 69–70, 73–4, 75–7
  and unconscious 39–40
Riviere, Joan 194
Rosencrantz and Guildenstern
    (*Hamlet*) 237, 260, 316, 323
The Rules of the Game (film) 85

($◊a$) 19, 366–7
  in dream analysis 94, 96, 98, 105,
    109–10, 168, 214
  Hamlet 286, 302, 305, 309–10, 320,
    326–8
  in neurosis 428, 452
  perverse fantasies 454
  phallic mediation 116–17, 119, 120,
    126
  see also little *a*
S($Å$) and the Other 297–300, 324,
    395, 449–50
Sand, George 463
Sartre, Jean-Paul 32, 43

satisfaction of desire 44–5, 101–2,
    411–12
  demand for 446–52
  see also jouissance
Saxo Grammaticus 291, 307, 318
Schreber, Judge 387, 388, 480
scientific knowledge 365, 379–80,
    381, 397
sensory experience 10–11
sexual activity, parents'/primal scene
    189, 190, 208, 227, 228, 423
sexual dreams 37–8
  see also dream interpretation,
    Sharpe
sexual fantasies concerning analyst
    160–1, 169, 414, 481
sexual perversion *see* perverse
    fantasies; perversion
Shakespeare, William 238–9, 251, 271
  First Folio 250
  Raimund 399, 401
  Sonnets 275, 344, 354, 371
  women characters 300–5
  see also Hamlet
Sharpe, Ella
  Dream Analysis 142ff.
  Hamlet 234–5, 238, 249, 250–1,
    273, 318
  see also dream interpretation,
    Sharpe
"shifter symbols" 367–8
signification
  effect 138
  and fetishization 313
signifying systems 67, 70
signifier(s) 5, 11, 48, 49
  in dreams 55, 56, 57–8, 77, 159,
    162–3
  in fantasy 163–70
  function of 443
  and object 478
  phallus *see under* phallus
  primary process 52, 66–7
  and signified 16–17
  and subject 44, 360, 367–8
  topology of 66–7
  and trace 80

signifying chain(s) 10, 11–13, 16–17,
        45, 57–8, 172, 408
    child case study (Dick) 432–3, 446
    child–family relationship 476–7
    facets 138–40, 391–5
    fantasy 391–6
    Hamlet 246, 294, 309–10
signifying order 409
similarity of signifier, principle of
        16–17
sister's sandal straps (dream image)
        199–200, 201, 221, 222, 223,
        233
Smith, Sydney 20–4
Sonnets (Shakespeare) 354
Sophocles 236
speech *see* discourse/speech
Spinoza, Baruch 7–8, 125, 474
splitting function in perversion 460–7
statement and enunciation 71–2,
        74–6, 78–9, 82–3, 88–94,
        113–14, 135–8, 139, 139–40
subject
    hidden 198
    metonym of being 23
    and object 84–5, 98–101, 102–5
    and the Other *see* Other
    and phallus 213, 214
    and signifier 44, 360, 367–8
    speaking 26–7, 32–4, 38, 40
    unconscious 23, 478
    wishing (*Wunsch*) 44–5
subjective slit in perverse fantasies
        418, 419, 420, 424
subjectivity and desire 474
sublimation 484–5
substitution
    in neurosis 451, 455, 465–6
    principle of 16
subtraction 55
suicide (*Hamlet*)
    Ophelia 244, 316
    "to be or not to be" 234, 246–7,
        249, 264, 430–1
superego 40, 239
symbolic and imaginary 19–20, 128–9
symbolic and real 408

symptoms 111–12
synchrony 270–3, 366–9
    and diachrony 360
    function of fantasy 378–9

Toulet, P.-J. 478–9
transference 188, 203, 474–5, 481
    countertransference 202, 204
"transitional object" 415
transitory perversion during
        psychoanalysis 414–15, 482
Troilus and Cressida (Shakespeare)
        301
Trotsky, Leon 115
Twelfth Night (Shakespeare) 301–2

unconscious 23, 48–52, 393–4, 395
    "free association" 46, 138–9
    Hamlet 273, 276, 277, 297, 299,
        300
    and jokes 60–1
    and repression 39–40
    scruples of conscience 237–8,
        242–4
    women and phallus 448–9
    see also dream interpretation;
        fantasy
unconscious articulations 34, 394
unconscious desire 378–9
unconscious discourse 359–60, 367,
        454
unconscious fantasies, structure of
        437
unconscious incestuous position 121
unconscious signifiers 35–6
unconscious subject 23, 478
"understanding" 25–6
use value and exchange value 106–7

vagina *see* female genitals
Verneinung see negation
Viardot, Désiré 486
voice(s) 387–9
    breathing and 384
    hallucinatory 396
Vorstellung see idea
voyeurism 314, 418–20, 422–3, 424

Weil, Simon 312, 372
Wilson, John Dover 269, 405
Winnicott, Donald 415
wish for father's death 53–6, 235–6, 240, 242
wishing (*Wunsch*) subject 44–5
women/girls
 genitals (dream and fantasy) 176–81, 185–7, 188–9, 195, 197, 211
 homosexuality 465

jealousy 449–50
Oedipus complex 125–6, 447–9
phallic phase 125–6, 194, 214–15
phallic woman fantasy 180
phallus
 demand for 447–9
 without 226–7
 purpose 107–8
 Shakespearean characters 300–5
 see also mother
word association 46–8